Networking
Essentials

UNLEASHED

Networking Essentials

Essentials

Mark A. Sportack

SAMS
PUBLISHING

201 West 103rd Street
Indianapolis, IN 46290

UNLEASHED

To my precious wife, Karen. I recognize the tremendous sacrifices you make in support of my authoring. If I were more articulate, perhaps I could adequately convey my appreciation. I love you. To my son Adam, you truly are my best little boy. To my daughter Jennifer, you remind me of your mother. —Mark

Copyright © 1998 by Sams Publishing

International Standard Book Number: 0-672-31210-7

Library of Congress Catalog Card Number: 97-61927

2000   99   98   3   2   1

Interpretation of the printing code: the rightmost double-digit number is the year of the book's printing; the rightmost single-digit, the number of the book's printing. For example, a printing code of 98-1 shows that the first printing of the book occurred in 1998.

Composed in AGaramond and MCPdigital by Macmillan Computer Publishing

Printed in the United States of America

Trademarks

President	*Richard K. Swadley*
Publisher	*David Dwyer*
Executive Editor	*Laurie Petrycki*
Managing Editor	*Sarah Kearns*

Acquisitions Editors
Sean Angus
Cari Skaggs

Development Editors
Jeff Koch
Kezia Endsley

Project Editor
Margo Catts

Cover Designer
Jason Grisham

Book Designer
Gary Adair

Production Manager
Laurie Casey

Indexer
Craig Small

Production Team Supervisor
Andrew Stone

Production
Betsy Deeter
Cyndi Davis-Hubler
Chris Livengood
Brad Lenser
Donna Martin
Shawn Ring
Becky Stutzman

Contents

Acknowledgments

I would like to extend my deepest gratitude to my boss, Portia Johnson, for her continued support of my authoring, as well as to my Corporate Sponsor Mike Parfett. I would also like to thank my new management team at AT&T, Steve Clayton and Rich Bennett, for so readily accepting me despite my part-time job. :)

I would also like to recognize the contributions made by my friends and co-workers Stan Griff and Dave Kurtiak. I appreciate having the privilege of your company (not to mention your collective knowledge base and technical reference libraries!). Thanks also to Art Cooper for coming to the rescue. Wish you could have done more!

Finally, I'd like to thank Sean Angus, Cari Skaggs, Margo Catts, Kezia Endsley, and everyone else at Macmillan who worked on this book. Thank you for continuing to believe in me. Karen thanks you too, for keeping me away from the microwave!

-Mark A. Sportack

About the Authors

Mark A. Sportack

Mark A. Sportack is an experienced Information Technology (IT) professional with over 15 years experience in progressive levels of responsibility and in many facets of IT. He has an MBA in Management of Technology, and his experience includes project management, forecasting and managing multi-million-dollar capital budgets, short- and long-range IT infrastructure planning, systems and applications design/development, direction of implementation teams, and management of both technology and technical personnel. He is currently employed by AT&T and is an Information Technology Architect for AT&T's CIO organization.

Richard Peete

Richard Peete has worked in the computer industry for almost two decades. From humble beginnings working as a Computer Operator for the U.S. Army Corps of Engineers, to managing a 15-member software engineering team which developed a large-scale, client/server, cross-platform database management application for the educational marketplace, Richard has spent his career pushing the envelope of technology to implement software systems for both commercial and government customers. Richard has extensive experience with networks, having been responsible for local area networks running under Novell NetWare, Microsoft Windows NT, and UNIX.

James F. Causey

James F. Causey, MCSE, MCP-IT, works for Indiana University Information Technology Services as Intel Systems Specialist. He performs software development and third-tier NT server and network support for Indiana University departmental computing professionals. He is also a freelance writer for Macmillan Publishing, having worked as lead author on *Windows NT Installation, Configuration, and Customization* and *Teach Yourself MCSE TCP/IP in 14 Days*, and has contributed to *High Performance Networking Unleashed* and *Teach Yourself MCSE NT Server*, as well as the upcoming *Teach Yourself MCSE Internet Information Server 4.0 in 14 Days*. James also writes reviews for an online magazine for audiophiles. He's occasionally been known to have some non-technical hobbies, when he actually has free time. James came be reached at jcausey@bluemarble.net.

Arthur Cooper

Arthur Cooper has over 20 years of telecommunications networking experience. Currently he is a Project Manager for MCI Telecommunications, Inc. He is managing MCI's Year-2000 project on the MCI Internal Data Network (IDN) Backbone. Mr. Cooper is also an Associate

Professor at Regis University where he teaches LAN and WAN network courses. Mr. Cooper has an AA in Computer Science, an AAS in Electronic Systems Technology, a BS in Organizational Management, and an MA in Curriculum and Instruction. His wife Linda and his two sons Zachary and Ryan join him in loving life in beautiful Colorado Springs, Colorado. He can be reached via e-mail at `arthur.cooper@mci.com`.

Theresa Hadden

Theresa Hadden, MCSE, MCT, has over 10 years of System Administration experience using Novell, Unix, and Windows NT. She is presently teaching in the MCSE program at a local college where she teaches Windows NT 4.0, Networking Essentials, TCP/IP, and Internet-related products, both in the classroom and on a one-on-one basis. She is actively involved in the design and implementation of online courses that include instructor access utilizing audio conferencing via the Internet. She is the mother of two sons and presently living in New Mexico.

James M. Spann

James (Jay) M. Spann is a corporate trainer who has spent the last several years teaching classes with the firm of Spann & Associates, Inc. Jay is a Microsoft Certified Professional and has been working with computers almost all his life. Although Jay spends most of the year traveling around the world to teach classes on computers, networks, communications, and related subjects, he still finds time to spend with his family. Anyone interested in more information from Jay about his chapters or classes can contact him at `jay@surfsol.com`.

David P. Welk

David P. Welk has been working in the networking industry for over ten years with extensive telecommunications and LAN/WAN experience. Many years spent administering Novell networks enabled Dave to complete the set of 7 CNE tests within an 18-day time period in March of 1994. Today, he routinely assists in analyzing and designing networks that include thousands of computers and rooms full of servers. Dave has a bachelor's degree in management and recently completed his Master of Project Management degree. He has been certified by just about every major manufacturer of networking products including Bay Networks, 3COM, Fore Systems, and Network General.

Tony Northrup

Tony Northrup is both a Microsoft Certified Systems Engineer and a Compaq Accredited Systems Engineer. Travelling as a consultant, he has had the opportunity to work at many of the most prestigious companies throughout the United States. His focus in recent years has been integrating Windows NT and BackOffice into the Internet. He and his wife currently live outside of Boston, where he is employed by GTE Internetworking, providing systems and network engineering for many of the largest sites on the Internet.

Tell Us What You Think!

As a reader, you are the most important critic and commentator of our books. We value your opinion and want to know what we're doing right, what we could do better, what areas you'd like to see us publish in, and any other words of wisdom you're willing to pass our way. You can help us make strong books that meet your needs and give you the computer guidance you require.

Do you have access to the World Wide Web? Then check out our site at http://www.mcp.com.

> **NOTE**
>
> If you have a technical question about this book, call the technical support line at 317-581-3833 or send email to support@mcp.com.

As the team leader of the group that created this book, I welcome your comments. You can fax, e-mail, or write me directly to let me know what you did or didn't like about this book—as well as what we can do to make our books stronger. Here's the information:

Fax: 317-581-4669

Mail: Laurie Petrycki
        Sams Publishing
        201 W. 103rd Street
        Indianapolis, IN 46290

Introduction

by Mark A. Sportack

In this age of highly distributed computing, networks have become an essential component of Information Technology infrastructures. Unfortunately, the degree to which they are understood has not increased commensurate with their architectural prominence. If anything, networks have become less understood due to the proliferation of graphical user interfaces (GUIs). This creates a potentially dangerous situation for any organization that uses distributed computing.

Networking Essentials Unleashed is designed to reverse this trend. This book consists of 5 parts:

- Network Fundamentals
- Building Local Area Networks
- Building Wide Area Networks
- Operating Networks
- A Technical Glossary of Terms

These sections are designed to impart a deep and lasting appreciation for the mechanics of networking. This is a quantum leap beyond merely preparing you for a certification test. It helps you prepare for any test on the essentials of networking. More importantly, however, this book prepares you for thinking your way through the myriad challenges that await Information Technology professionals in the real world in this age of distributed computing.

IN THIS PART

PART

I

Network Fundamentals

A Networking Primer

by Mark A. Sportack

IN THIS CHAPTER

CHAPTER 1

In this age of distributed computing, networks have become a ubiquitous fixture in virtually all work environments. A network is the mechanism that enables distributed computers, and the carbon-based life forms that infest them (also known as "users"), to communicate and share resources. Despite their widespread use, networks remain the most mysterious and unfamiliar of the information technologies.

This chapter presents the basics of networking, identifies the different types of networks, and demonstrates how their evolution created the need for industry standards.

Networking standards are set by several different standards bodies. These various standards bodies, their standards, and any interrelationships between them are also presented. One of the more significant of these is the *Open Systems Interconnect (OSI) Reference Model*. In this model, each layer supports a distinct functionality set. This model serves as a marvelous tool for understanding networks by dissecting them into their various functional components. These components are stratified into *layers*. The OSI Reference Model is also presented and explained in this chapter.

Evolution of Networks

Networks originally were highly proprietary connectivity solutions that were an integral part of an equally proprietary bundled computing solution. Companies that automated their data processing or accounting functions during the primitive days before personal computers had to commit to a single vendor for a turnkey solution.

Typical configurations included dumb terminals that were hard-wired to device controllers. The device controllers provided a communal, or multiplexed, access to the communications facilities that provided connectivity to the mainframes. These communications facilities were aggregated in a Front End Processor (FEP) at the mainframe side. The FEP allowed many communications facilities to share a single channel to the mainframe. Given the speed differences between input/output and the mainframe's processors, this represented the most cost-effective solution. This is illustrated in Figure 1.1.

Otherwise, a low-bandwidth leased line was used to span the geographic distance to the mainframe. At that location, the leased line was linked to the mainframe's I/O channel. This is illustrated in Figure 1.2.

In these depicted environments, the application software executed only in an environment supported by a single operating system. The operating system could execute only within the safety of the same vendor's hardware products. Even the users' terminal equipment and connectivity to the computer were part of the same, one-vendor integrated solution.

During the reign of the single-vendor integrated solutions, two different technological developments occurred that changed the future course of computing. First, the primitive ancestors of today's PCs began to appear. These devices were innovative in that they placed computational power right at the desktop.

1

A NETWORKING
PRIMER

FIGURE 1.1.
Hard-wired access to mainframes.

FIGURE 1.2.
Leased-line access to mainframes.

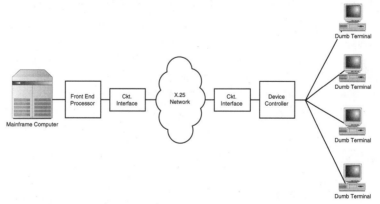

Second, the scientists at Xerox's Palo Alto Research Center (PARC) began wrestling with ways to improve their own productivity. Specifically, they looked for a way to improve the sharing of files and data between their intelligent workstations. The existing method of sharing floppy disks was time consuming and problematic.

Their solution was the original Local Area Network (LAN). They called it "ethernet." It was a crude and simple LAN that relied upon higher-layer internetworking protocols for much of its definition and behavior. The market potential of this technology was quickly realized. The original ethernet, now known as PARC Ethernet, or Ethernet I, was superseded by a slightly better-behaved version. This version, developed by Xerox, Digital, and Intel, became known as DIX Ethernet or Ethernet II. Digital, Intel, and Xerox, in combination, set the "standards" for Ethernet II, and produced its component technologies.

Together, intelligent user devices and Local Area Networks would spawn a new paradigm: open, distributed computing.

Standards Organizations

The success of Ethernets I and II demonstrated that the marketplace was tired of the proprietary approach to bundled networking and computing. Customers began demanding a more open environment that would enable them to build applications from mixed and matched products from different vendors. Interoperability would also, as evidenced by Ethernet, foster competition through technological innovation. Thus, the interrelated goals of openness were

- Lower costs
- Greater capabilities
- Cross-vendor interoperability

Cross-vendor interoperability required the different platforms to recognize each other, and to know how to communicate and share data. This necessitated the development of unbiased, industry-wide standards for every aspect of networked computing.

The need for standardization precipitated a flurry of standardization efforts. Today, many different standards bodies are responsible for defining national and/or international standards for different aspects of information technologies, including data communications and networking. Frequently, these standards bodies either collaborate or cooperate to ensure as universal a set of standards as possible. This can lead to some confusion, although the overwhelming effect is positive. The more pertinent standards bodies are presented here, and their interrelationships are described.

ANSI

The American National Standards Institute (ANSI) is a private, non-profit organization. Its charter is to facilitate the development, coordination, and publication of voluntary national standards. ANSI standards are voluntary in that ANSI does not actively police or enforce its standards. Rather, through participation in global standards bodies like the IOS, IEC, and so forth, non-compliance with its standards results in non-compliance with global standards. Such non-compliance is self-punishing in the age of open computing.

IEEE

The Institute of Electrical and Electronic Engineers (IEEE) is responsible for defining and publishing telecommunications and data communications standards. Its most significant effort to date has been the definition of the standards for Local and Metropolitan Area Networks (LANs and MANs). These standards, embodied in a large and complex series of technical standards, is generically referred to as Project 802, or the 802 series of standards.

The intent of the IEEE is to develop standards that will be accepted by the American National Standards Institute (ANSI). This acceptance will result in a broader audience for the IEEE standards, because ANSI participates on global standards bodies.

The ISO

The International Organization for Standardization was founded in 1946, and is headquartered in Geneva, Switzerland. Certain reference sources identify this organization with the acronym *IOS*. Although, technically, this is the correct acronym, that organization eschews it in favor of a mnemonic abbreviation: *ISO*. This mnemonic derives from the Greek word *isos*, which means equal or standard. This is the appropriate way to identify the International Organization for Standardization, provided, of course, you don't want to use its full name. It is a voluntary, non-treaty organization that is chartered by the United Nations to define international standards. Its charter includes literally all fields, except for anything electrical or electronic.

Currently, the ISO membership consists of over 90 different standards bodies from around the world. Perhaps the single most important standard developed by the ISO was its Open Systems Interconnection (OSI) Reference Model. This model is described in much more detail later in this chapter, in the section entitled, "The OSI Reference Model."

The IEC

The International Electrotechnical Commission (IEC), also headquartered in Geneva, was founded in 1909. The IEC sets international standards for anything electrical and electronic. Its current membership includes committees from over 40 countries. The American National Standards Institute (ANSI) is the USA's representative on both the IEC and ISO.

The IEC and ISO recognized that information technologies were an important area of potential overlap. They formed the Joint Technical Committee (JTC1) specifically to define standards for information technologies.

IAB

The Internet Architecture Board, formerly known as the Internet Activities Board, governs the technical development of the Internet. It contains two working committees, the Internet Engineering Task Force (IETF) and the Internet Research Task Force (IRTF). As their names imply, they are functionally separate. The IRTF researches new technologies that may be of value to, or have an impact upon, the Internet. The IETF is the recipient of the IRTF's research. The IETF is responsible for setting the technical standards for the Internet, as well as the definition of new standards for Internet technologies including the Internet Protocol (IP).

> **NOTE**
>
> IP is a Layer 3, or Network Layer, protocol. As such, it is inherently connectionless. It is also incapable of identifying packets that need to be retransmitted, or performing any resequencing of packets that may have arrived in a different order than that in which they were sent. To make IP—or any Layer 3 protocol—more usable requires a Layer 4 (Transport Layer) protocol. Examples of Layer 4 protocols that use IP are TCP, UDP, and even the experimental TTCP. A "/" is used to separate the layer 3 and 4 protocol names whenever they are used together. For example, TCP/IP or UDP/IP. This has the unfortunate effect of confusing the distinctions between Layer 3 and 4. Consequently, it is not uncommon to find technically proficient people using the term TCP/IP when, in fact, they really mean only IP.
>
> For more information on protocols that operate at Layers 3 and 4 of the OSI Reference Model, please refer to Chapter 12, "Network Protocols."

The OSI Reference Model

ISO developed the Open Systems Interconnection (OSI) Reference Model to facilitate the open interconnection of computer systems. An open interconnection is one that can be supported in a multi-vendor environment. This model established the global standard for defining the functional layers required to support such a connection between computers.

When the OSI Reference Model was developed almost twenty years ago, it was viewed as radical. Computer manufacturers, at that time, locked customers into proprietary, single-vendor architectures. Open communication was viewed as an invitation to competition. From the manufacturer's perspective, competition was undesirable. Consequently, all functions were integrated as tightly as possible. The notion of functional modularity, or layering, seemed antithetical to any manufacturer's mission.

It is important to note that the model has been so successful at achieving its original goals as to almost render the model moot. The previous proprietary, integrated approach has disappeared. Open communications today are requisite. Curiously, very few products are fully OSI compliant. Instead, its basic layered framework is frequently adapted to new standards. Nevertheless, the OSI Reference Model remains a viable mechanism for demonstrating the functional mechanics of a network.

Despite its successes, numerous misperceptions about the OSI Reference Model persist. Consequently, it is necessary to provide yet another overview of this model in this section. The overview identifies and corrects these misperceptions.

The first misperception is that the OSI Reference Model was developed by the Paris-based International Standards Organization (ISO). It was not. The OSI Reference Model was developed by the International Organization for Standardization.

CAUTION

The International Standards Organization is frequently, but incorrectly, credited with the development of the OSI Reference Model. The model was developed by the International Organization for Standardization.

For the purposes of any certification exam that might be lurking in your future, International Standards Organization is the "correct" answer. It is inaccurate, but expected on the examinations.

The OSI model categorizes the various processes that are needed in a communications session into seven distinct functional layers. The layers are organized based on the natural sequence of events that occurs during a communications session.

Figure 1.3 illustrates the OSI Reference Model. Layers 1–3 provide network access, while Layers 4–7 are dedicated to the logistics of supporting end-to-end communications.

FIGURE 1.3.
The OSI Reference Model.

OSI Reference Model Layer Description	Layer Number
Application	7
Presentation	6
Session	5
Transport	4
Network	3
Data Link	2
Physical	1

Layer 1: The Physical Layer

The bottom layer is called the *Physical Layer*. This layer is responsible for the transmission of the bit stream. It accepts frames of data from Layer 2, the Data Link Layer, and transmits their structure and content serially, one bit at a time.

It is also responsible for the reception of incoming streams of data, one bit at a time. These streams are then passed on to the Data Link Layer for reframing.

This layer, quite literally, sees only 1s and 0s. It has no mechanism for determining the significance of the bits it transmits or receives. It is solely concerned with the physical characteristics of electrical and/or optical signaling techniques. This includes the voltage of the electrical current used to transport the signal, the media type and impedance characteristics, and even the physical shape of the connector that is used to terminate the media.

> **NOTE**
>
> A common misperception is that OSI's Layer 1 includes anything that either generates or carries the data communications signals. This is not true. It is a *functional* model only.
>
> Layer 1, the Physical Layer, is limited to just the processes and mechanisms needed to place signals onto the transmission media, and to receive signals from that media. Its lower boundary is the physical connector that attaches to the transmission media. *It does not include the transmission media!*
>
> Transmission media include any means of actually transporting signals generated by the OSI's Layer 1 mechanisms. Some examples of transmission media are coaxial cabling, fiber optic cabling, and twisted pair wiring. The confusion seems to stem from the fact that the Physical Layer does provide specifications for the media's performance. These are the performance characteristics that are required, and assumed to exist, by the processes and mechanisms defined in the Physical Layer.
>
> Consequently, transmission media remain outside the scope of the Physical Layer and are sometimes referred to as *Layer 0*.

Layer 2: The Data Link Layer

The second layer of the OSI Reference Model is called the Data Link Layer. As all the layers do, it has two sets of responsibilities: transmit and receive. It is responsible for providing end-to-end validity of the data being transmitted.

On the transmit side, the Data Link Layer is responsible for packing instructions, data, and so forth, into frames. A *frame* is a structure indigenous to the Data Link Layer that contains enough information to make sure that the data can be successfully sent across a Local Area Network to its destination.

Successful delivery means that the frame reaches its intended destination intact. Thus, the frame must also contain a mechanism to verify the integrity of its contents upon delivery.

Two things must happen for guaranteed delivery to occur:

■ The originating node must receive an acknowledgment of each frame received intact by the destination node.

■ The destination node, prior to acknowledging receipt of a frame, must verify the integrity of that frame's contents.

Numerous situations can result in transmitted frames either not reaching the destination or becoming damaged and unusable during transit. The Data Link Layer is responsible for detecting and correcting any and all such errors.

The Data Link Layer is also responsible for reassembling any binary streams that are received from the Physical Layer back into frames. Given that both the structure and content of a frame are transmitted, however, the Data Link Layer isn't really rebuilding a frame. Rather, it is buffering the incoming bits until it has a complete frame.

Layers 1 and 2 are required for each and every type of communication, regardless of whether the network is a LAN or WAN.

Layer 3: The Network Layer

The Network Layer is responsible for establishing the route to be used between the originating and destination computers. This layer lacks any native transmission error detection/correction mechanisms and, consequently, is forced to rely upon the end-to-end reliable transmission service of the Data Link Layer.

The Network Layer is used to establish communications with computer systems that lie beyond the local LAN segment. It can do so because it has its own routing addressing architecture, which is separate and distinct from the Layer 2 machine addressing.

Routable protocols include

- IP
- IPX
- AppleTalk

The use of the Network Layer is optional. It is required only if the computer systems reside on different network segments that are separated by a router.

Layer 4: The Transport Layer

The Transport Layer provides a similar service to the Data Link Layer, in that it is responsible for the end-to-end integrity of transmissions. Unlike the Data Link Layer, the Transport Layer is capable of providing this function beyond the local LAN segment. It can detect packets that are discarded by routers and automatically generate a retransmit request.

Another significant function of the Transport Layer is the resequencing of packets that may have arrived out of order. This can happen for a variety of reasons. The packets may have taken different paths through the network, for example, or some may have been damaged in transit. In any case, the Transport Layer is capable of identifying the original sequence of packets, and must put them back into that sequence before passing their contents up to the Session Layer.

Layer 5: The Session Layer

The fifth layer of the OSI Model is the Session Layer. This layer is relatively disused; many protocols bundle this layer's functionality into their transport layers.

The function of the OSI Session Layer is to manage the flow of communications during a connection between two computer systems. This flow of communications is known as a *session*. It determines whether communications can be mono- or bi-directional. It also ensures that one request is completed before a new one is accepted.

Layer 6: The Presentation Layer

The Presentation Layer is responsible for managing the way that data is encoded. Not every computer system uses the same data encoding scheme, and the Presentation Layer is responsible for providing the translation between otherwise incompatible data-encoding schemes, like American Standard Code for Information Interchange (ASCII) and Extended Binary Coded Decimal Interchange Code (EBCDIC).

The Presentation Layer can be used to mediate differences in floating point formats, as well as to provide encryption and decryption services.

Layer 7: The Application Layer

The top layer in the OSI Reference Model is the Application Layer. Despite its name, this layer does not include user applications. Rather, it provides the interface between those applications and the network's services.

This layer can be thought of as the reason for initiating the communications session. For example, an e-mail client might generate a request to retrieve new messages from the e-mail server. This client application automatically generates a request to the appropriate Layer 7 protocol(s) and launches a communications session to get the needed files.

The Model's Usage

The vertical orientation of the stack is an acknowledgment of the functional flow of processes and data. Each layer has interfaces to its adjacent layers. In order to communicate, two systems must pass data, instructions, addresses, and so forth, between the layers. The differences between the logical flow of communications and the actual flow of the session are illustrated in Figure 1.4.

NOTE

Although the Reference Model includes seven layers, not all layers are required for any given communications session. For example, communications across a single LAN segment can operate strictly at Layers 1 and 2 of the model, without requiring the other two communications layers.

FIGURE 1.4.
Actual versus logical flow of layered communications.

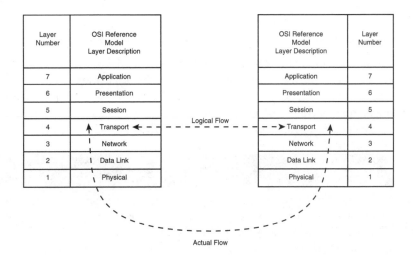

Although communications flow vertically through the stack, each layer perceives itself to be capable of directly communicating with its counterpart layers on remote computers. To create this logical adjacency of layers, each layer of the originating machine's protocol stack adds a header. This header can be recognized and used by only that layer or its counterparts on other machines. The receiving machine's protocol stack removes the headers, one layer at a time, as the data is passed up to its application. This process is illustrated in Figure 1.5.

FIGURE 1.5.
Use of layered headers to support logical adjacency.

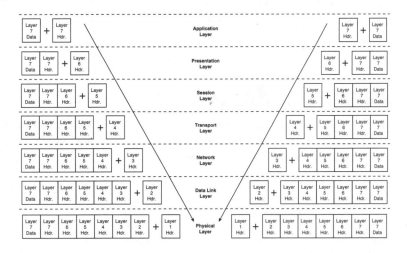

For example, segments of data are packaged by Layer 4 of an origination machine for presentation to Layer 3. Layer 3 bundles data received from Layer 4 into packets (that is, Layer 3 *packetizes* the segments), addresses them, and sends them to the destination machine's Layer 3 protocol by way of its own Layer 2. Layer 2 encases the packets with frames, complete with addressing that is recognized by the LAN. These frames are presented to Layer 1 for conversion into a stream of binary digits (bits) that are transmitted to the destination machine's Layer 1.

The destination machine reverses this flow of handoffs, with each layer stripping off the headers that were added by their counterparts on the origination machine. By the time the data reaches the destination machine's Layer 4, the data is back in the same form into which the originating machine's Layer 4 put it. Consequently, the two Layer 4 protocols appear to be physically adjacent and communicating directly.

> **NOTE**
>
> Please note that most of today's networking protocols use their own layered models. These models vary in the degree to which they adhere to the separation of functions demonstrated by the OSI Reference Model. It is quite common for these models to collapse the seven OSI layers into five or fewer layers. It is also common for higher layers to not correspond perfectly to their OSI-equivalent layers.

In fact, each Layer 3 passes the data down to Layer 2 which, in turn, converts the frames to a bit stream. After the bit stream is received by the destination computer's Layer 1 device, it is passed up to the Data Link Layer for reassembly into a frame. After the frame's receipt is successfully completed, the framing is stripped off and the packet that was embedded in it is passed up to the recipient's Layer 3. It arrives in exactly the same form as that in which it was sent. To the Layer 3s, communications between them were virtually direct.

The fact that communication can appear to occur between adjacent layers (from the perspective of those layers) is a tribute to the success of the model.

Networking Basics

A network, at its simplest, is anything that enables two or more computers to communicate with each other and/or other devices. This enables users to use computers and networks to share information, collaborate on a work item, print, and even communicate directly through individually addressed messages.

Networks consist of many components, including both hardware and software. Some components can even be completely intangible.

Before delving too far into the basic network components, it is important to note that networks have evolved into two distinct categories: Local Area Networks (LANs) and Wide Area Networks (WANs). The distinction between them is fairly simple. LANs are used to interconnect devices that are in relatively close proximity. WANs are necessary to interconnect LANs across geographic distances.

NOTE

A third category of network is the *Metropolitan Area Network*, or MAN. Although defined through the IEEE's Project 802, the same initiative that standardized LANs, MANs are more closely related to WANs than LANs. They remain relatively obscure and are seldom used.

There are, of course, many exceptions to these two simple definitions. They are presented solely as a starting point; their definitions become increasingly precise throughout this book.

Hardware Components

The basic hardware components of a network include three types of devices:

- Transmission facilities
- Access devices
- Devices that repeat transmitted signals

These components are basic in that all networks must either contain them or, at a minimum, work around them. The remainder of this section describes these components, as they support LANs and WANs. Further details on these topics are described in much more detail throughout this entire book.

Transmission Facilities

Transmission facilities are the media used to transport a network's signals to their destination. Media types can include coaxial cables, twisted pair, and even fiber optic cabling. The more common LAN transmission media are presented in further detail in Chapter 3, "The Physical Layer."

LAN media types can also be intangible. They can be light, radio, or even microwave signals that are transmitted through open air. Though the atmosphere, itself, is the actual media used to support these various forms of transmission, describing it as a media type is rather pointless. It is more useful to describe the mechanisms that generate the transmissions than it is to describe the air that carries the transmissions. These are presented in Chapter 4, "The 'Not-so-Physical' Physical Layer."

The WAN, too, has its own transmission facilities. Such facilities are often thought of in terms of their clock rate and frame structure, rather than simple transmission media (a 1.544Mbps Frame Relay leased line, for example). Their physical media are inconsequential to their actual performance. These transmission facilities are discussed in more detail in Chapter 14, "Leased Lines," Chapter 15, "Circuit Switched Transmission Facilities," and Chapter 16, "Packet Switched Transmission Facilities."

Access Devices

An access device is responsible for the following:

- Properly formatting data so that it can be accepted in the network
- Placing it on the network
- Accepting transmitted data that is addressed to it

In a Local Area Network, the access device is known as a Network Interface Card (NIC). The NIC is a circuit board that is installed in a computer and occupies an I/O slot on its motherboard. The network is then cabled to the port provided by this board. The NIC frames data that the computer's applications need to transmit, puts that data onto the network in binary form, and accepts inbound frames that are addressed to that computer. The process of framing data and placing it onto the network is described in Chapter 5, "The Data Link Layer."

In a Wide Area Network (WAN), the access device is a router. Routers operate at Layer 3 of the OSI Reference model, and include two types of protocols: routing and routable. Routable protocols, like IP, are used to transport data beyond the boundary of Layer 2 domains. These protocols are addressed in much more detail in Chapter 12.

Routing protocols provide all the functions necessary to

- Determine optimal paths through a WAN, for any given destination address
- Accept and forward packets through those paths to their destinations.

A WAN is used to interconnect two or more LANs. More information on this topic is presented in Chapter 13, "Wide Area Networking."

Repeaters

A *repeater* is a device that accepts transmitted signals, amplifies them, and puts them back on the network. In a LAN, a repeater—more popularly referred to as a *hub*—enables multiple devices to be networked together by providing multiple ingress points to the network. This function is so critical to today's LANs that its real purpose—signal regeneration—is often forgotten.

The hub's capability to regenerate signals is every bit as crucial to the success of a LAN as its capability to provide ingress points. The inescapable reality is that transmitted signals are affected by the media that transports them. Electronic signals placed on a wire inevitably deteriorate. This deterioration can take one of two possible forms: attenuation and distortion.

Attenuation is a decrease in the strength of the signal. *Distortion* is the unwanted modification of signals in transit. Each of these forms of deterioration must be addressed and rectified separately.

Attenuation can be compensated for by keeping wire lengths short enough to guarantee that the signal is strong enough to reach all destinations on the wire. If the wire must be relatively lengthy, however, a repeater can be installed in the line.

Distortion is a more severe problem for signal transmission. This is different from attenuation. Distorted signals corrupt whatever data was being transported. Repeaters are incapable of differentiating legitimate signals from distorted ones; they repeat signals indiscriminately. There are, however, several other ways to combat distortion.

- Adhere rigidly to any installation guidelines that may have been provided with your transmission media. More information on transmission media is presented in Chapter 3, "The Physical Layer."

- Identify the cause(s) of the distortion. Next, try to route cabling away from those sources. Also, it may be beneficial to use network transmission technologies, such as fiber optic cabling, that can resist that distortion. These technologies are discussed throughout this book.

- Use network protocols that are capable of detecting and automatically correcting any transmission errors that may occur. These protocols are discussed in Chapter 5, and in Chapter 12.

Software Components

The software components required in a network include

- Protocols that define and regulate the way two or more devices communicate
- Hardware-level software, known as *microcode* or *drivers*, that guide the functionality of individual devices like the Network Interface Card (NIC)
- Communications software

Protocols

Providing the physical connectivity for a network is the easy part. The real challenge lies in developing standard ways for computers, and even other network-attached devices, to communicate. These ways are more formally known as *protocols*. The simplest example of a protocol can be found in the way that most people communicate over a telephone. In most of the world, the first thing that is said in any phone conversation is "Hello" (or its regional equivalent).

This simple greeting universally conveys that the calling party has successfully established a communications session with someone else. The next step is for the caller to respond so that the recipient of the phone call can tell that the communications link works in both directions.

If both parties are familiar with each other, this simple two-word exchange is usually sufficient to predicate even the most intimate of conversations. If, however, both parties are unknown to each other, additional protocols are needed to establish each other's identity. After this is established, the conversation can move on to the purpose for the call.

This simple example has become so ingrained that violations of this protocol are often interpreted as a lack of manners or even deliberate rudeness.

Computers are no different. Merely having a network to connect them is only one part of what is needed to support meaningful communications and resource sharing. Direct communications between two computers enables them, and their users, to share resources. Given that precious few people actually work in isolation, enabling computers to share information and other resources was a revolutionary step toward an information technology infrastructure that more closely approximated the way groups of people actually work.

Protocols for LANs are frequently called *LAN architectures*, as they are embodied in the NIC. They predetermine much of the shape, size, and mechanics of the LAN. These are described in Part 2 (Chapters 7 through 12) of this book, "Building Local Area Networks."

Protocols for WANs usually come in bundles, and are responsible for a great variety of services. These protocols are further described in Chapter 12.

Device Drivers

A device driver is a hardware-level program that controls a specific device. A device driver can best be thought of as a miniature operating system for a single piece of hardware. Each driver contains all the logic and data that is needed to ensure the proper functioning of its particular device. In the case of a NIC, this includes providing an interface for its host's operating system.

The device driver frequently resides in firmware inside the device it operates.

Communications Software

All the previously described hardware and software components of a network stop shy of enabling a user to actually *use* a network. They simply provide the infrastructure and mechanisms that permit its use. The task of actually using the network falls to the specialized application software that controls communications.

The dawn of drag-and-drop computing has made communications software so simple to use that it is not uncommon for a user to be running a communications program and not even know it. Some examples include linking to drives or share areas in Windows NT. Others are a bit more obvious, like the World Wide Web's (WWW) Hypertext Transport Protocol (HTTP), telnet, tn3270, file transfer programs, and even electronic mail.

Regardless of the application's type or sophistication, communications application software is the mechanism that makes the available network bandwidth actually usable.

Making Networks from Components

The hardware and software components—and their functions—still don't make a network. They must be integrated. The following examples of networks demonstrate some of the ways that the hardware components can be integrated to form very simple networks. This should also demonstrate some of the flexibility that one enjoys when building networks.

1

A NETWORKING PRIMER

Repeaterless LAN

Two stations, equipped with compatible NICs, can communicate directly with each other, without a repeater (also known as a *hub*). This assumes, of course, that the two stations are in close enough proximity. This relationship is illustrated in Figure 1.6.

FIGURE 1.6.
Two stations communicating directly without a hub.

Cross-over cable

Laser printer

PC   PC

NOTE

The example presented in Figure 1.6 assumes that the wiring provides for the cross-over of their transmit and receive paths. This is an issue only with twisted pair wiring. Coaxial cable uses the same physical path for both transmits and receives. Twisted pair wiring uses two or more pairs of wire. A two-pair wire scheme would use one pair for transmit and one pair for receive. Each pair dedicates one wire for positive and one for negative voltages. Given that such interfaces are standardized, a 4-pair twisted pair cable strung between two PCs would result in both PCs attempting to transmit on the same pair of wires. They would also be listening on the same pair of wires for inbound frames. In other words, they would not be able to communicate. A cross-over cable inverts the transmit and receive pairs so that the pair on which one device transmits becomes the pair to which the other device listens for inbound transmissions.

Bus-Based LAN

The simplest form of LAN is based on a bus. A *bus* is a network that relies upon the interface card to drive communications across the network. Some LAN technologies use a bus topology as a native part of their protocol specification. Alternatively, LAN architectures designed to be used in a hub-based LAN can sometimes be wired together without the hub to form a bus-based LAN.

A bus-based LAN consists of the following components:

- Transmission media (the bus)
- Physical interface, or transceiver, for each device to be connected
- Transmission and communications protocols
- Application software that enables the users to communicate and share resources

As evidenced by this list, as well as Figure 1.7, a bus-based LAN doesn't use a signal repeater. This automatically limits both the distances over which the networked devices can communicate and the number of devices that can be networked together.

FIGURE 1.7
Bus LAN.

The significant limitations imposed by a bus LAN, in conjunction with the relatively low cost of hubs, makes this an all-but-forgotten network type. Nevertheless, it must be acknowledged as a legitimate network topology, and serves to illustrate the functionality of the basic network components.

Hub-Based LAN

The hub is the device that, as its name implies, is the center of the network. A simple, hub-based LAN is illustrated in Figure 1.8. A hub has two advantages over a bus-based LAN. First, the hub repeats signals, thereby enabling the LAN to stretch over greater distances than can be served by a bus. Second, the hub can also connect to one or more other hubs, thereby increasing the number of devices that can be attached to the LAN. Chaining hubs also serves to further increase the distances that can be spanned by the LAN.

> **NOTE**
>
> Not all hubs are repeaters. Some hubs are non-repeating station aggregators. They are used only to provide a star topology to a LAN, and to interconnect other hubs. This enables more users to be interconnected to the LAN, but does not provide the signal regeneration that would be needed to expand the LAN in terms of its linear dimensions.
>
> Hubs (or repeaters) have been successfully adapted to bus-based LAN architectures to create a new topology: the star bus.

Figure 1.8.
Hub-based LAN.

A hub-based LAN requires all the basic components required by the bus-based LAN, in addition to the hub or repeater. These components were listed in the previous section, titled "Bus-Based LAN."

WAN

A Wide Area Network, or WAN, interconnects LANs with a device known as a *router*. This enables each LAN to offer its users access to resources stored on other interconnected LANs without compromising its own identity. In other words, a router interconnects them, without condensing them into just one big LAN. Two LANs are interconnected, using a router, to form a WAN in Figure 1.9.

The WAN depicted in Figure 1.9 could span any geographic distance. The LANs could be co-located in the same building or on different continents. Repeaters, of course, are needed to support the extension of WAN facilities across great geographic distances.

FIGURE 1.9.
Wide Area Network (WAN).

> **NOTE**
>
> The repeater, a Layer 1 device, takes on different forms for LANs and WANs. LAN repeaters are commonly called hubs. WAN repeaters are seldom, if ever, seen by the users and administrators of the WAN. They are integral to the commercial infrastructure that provides the WAN connectivity, and remain invisible.

Summary

The basic network components presented in this chapter, their functions, and even their uses, are just the beginning. They are the proverbial building blocks that are explored in much greater detail throughout the remainder of this book. They have been presented to give you an appreciation for their historical development and for some of the fundamental terms and concepts that are indigenous to networking.

These basics are discussed in the context of the various industry standards that dominate networking today. The OSI Reference Model, in particular, is used throughout this book to help you understand the mechanics of these basic networking concepts by presenting a common frame of reference for the different standards.

LAN Types and Topologies

by Mark A. Sportack

IN THIS CHAPTER

Local Area Networks (LANs) have become ubiquitous in today's business environment. Despite their familiarity, they remain little more than a mystery to most people. It is easy to point to the hubs and/or switches and declare them to be "the network," but they are just pieces of one type of network.

As was explained in Chapter 1, "A Networking Primer," LANs are easiest to understand when they are dissected into their physical components. Often, these components are stratified into *layers*, as defined by the Open Systems Interconnect (OSI) Reference Model. This model was presented in detail in Chapter 1. Each layer supports a distinct functionality set.

A necessary prerequisite to this layered dissection of a LAN is an exploration of two other attributes: resource access methodology and topology. A LAN's resource access methodology describes the manner in which network-attached resources are shared. Frequently, this aspect of a network is referred to as its "type." The two prevailing types are peer-to-peer and client/server.

A LAN's topology refers to its physical arrangement of hubs and wiring. The basic topologies include bus, star, ring, and switched.

Together, these attributes help form the context for your detailed exploration of a LAN's functional layers. This chapter explores all the possible permutations of both LAN types and topologies. Their benefits, limitations, and possible uses are also presented.

LAN-Attached Devices

Before you delve into LAN types and topologies, it is beneficial to first examine some of the basic resources that can be found on a LAN. The three most common primary devices are clients, servers, and printers. A primary device is one that can either directly access other devices, or be accessed by other devices.

A *server* is any LAN-attached computer that hosts resources that are shared by other LAN-attached devices. A *client* is any computer that accesses resources stored on servers, via the LAN. Printers, of course, are output devices that produce hard-copies of files. Numerous other devices, like CD-ROM drives and tape archives, can also be accessed via a LAN, but they tend to be secondary resources. That is, they are connected to a primary device. Subordination of a device to another device, like a CD-ROM drive to a server, is known as *slaving*. Printers, too, can be slaved off a primary device, or they can be primary devices that are directly connected to the network. Figure 2.1 illustrates the primary resources found in a LAN, as well as the relationship of secondary resources to those primaries.

Types of Servers

"Server" is a word that is frequently used generically to describe all multi-user computers. It is important to note, however, that servers are a rather heterogeneous group. They are frequently specialized by function, and described with an adjective. For example, there are file servers, print servers, and application servers.

FIGURE 2.1.
Primary and secondary LAN resources.

File Servers

One of the most basic and familiar of the specialized servers is the file server. The file server is a centralized storage mechanism for files that are needed by a user group. Placing these files in one centralized location, rather than scattered across numerous client-level machines, imparts several benefits. These benefits include:

- Centralized location—All users enjoy a single, constant repository for shared files. This provides a dual benefit. Users don't have to search multiple potential storage locations to find a file; files are stored in one place. Users also are relieved of the burden of maintaining separate logon credentials to multiple machines. One logon provides them with access to all the files they require.

- Electric power conditioning—The use of a centralized server for file storage also enables the introduction of many techniques that can provide protection for data from inconsistencies in electric power. Fluctuations in the frequency of electricity, or even the sudden loss of power, can damage both a computer's data and hardware. Power filtration and battery backup through an Uninterruptible Power Supply (UPS) is cost-effective on a single server. Similar protection in a peer-to-peer network might be cost-prohibitive because of the numbers of computers that would need protection.

- Consistent data archiving—Storing all shared files in a common, centralized location greatly facilitates backups, as only a single output device and routine are required. Decentralized storage of data (at every desktop, for example) means that every desktop's data must be backed up separately. Backups are an essential protection against lost or damaged files. Suitable devices for backups include tape drives, writeable optical drives, and even hard drives. Multiple hard drives can also be used in a technique known as *striping*. Striping involves multiple, simultaneous writes to different hard drives. Although this is primarily done to provide faster reading of data, it can also be used to create redundancy with every write operation.

■ Speed—The typical server is a more robust and fully configured platform than the typical client computer. This directly translates into a demonstrable performance gain relative to retrieving files in a peer-to-peer network.

> **NOTE**
>
> The use of a file server does not always yield an increase in speed. You can always access files that are stored locally more quickly than files that are stored on a remote computer and retrieved over a LAN. The speed increase discussed here is relative to the speed with which files can be retrieved from other client-level machines in a peer-to-peer network, not the speed with which files can be retrieved from a local hard drive.

Not all files are good candidates for storage on a file server. Files that are sensitive, proprietary, or not suitable for access by the user community are best left on a local hard drive. Storing them on a file server still imparts some of the benefits of a file server (like automated back-ups) but may pose an unnecessary risk.

Print Servers

Servers can also be used to share printers among the users of a LAN. Although the costs of printers, especially laser printers, have decreased considerably since their introduction, most organizations would be hard-pressed to justify one for every desktop. Instead, servers are used to share one or more printers among the user population.

A print server's only function is to accept print requests from all networked devices, put them in a queue, and "spool" (send) them to the appropriate printer. This arrangement is illustrated in Figure 2.2.

FIGURE 2.2.

Simple print server arrangement.

2

> **NOTE**
>
> Although the word *spool* has become a verb that is synonymous with printing, it is an acronym. SPOOL originally meant Simultaneous Peripheral Operations On Line. It is the temporary storage of programs and/or data in the form of output streams on a magnetic media for later output or execution.

Each printer connected to a print server has its own queue, or waiting list. These queues represent the pecking order of all requests that are temporarily stored and awaiting their turns to print. Requests are generally processed in the order that they are received. Microsoft's client operating systems Windows 95 and NT Workstation both enable a printer to be shared.

An alternative to using a print server is to directly attach the printer to the LAN. Many printers can be configured with a *network interface card* (NIC) that enables them to be directly LAN-attached. This enables the printers to become print queue servers. Connecting printers directly to the LAN will work well for all but the most print-intensive operations.

Application Servers

Servers are also frequently used as a central repository of application software. Application servers, although superficially similar to file servers, are unique creatures. An *application server* hosts executable application software. To run that application software, a client must establish a connection across a network to that server. The application runs on that server. Servers that enable clients to download copies of an application for execution on their desktop computers are *file servers*. Their files are actually application software files, but they are functioning as file servers.

Application servers can enable an organization to reduce its overall cost of application software. Purchase prices and maintenance of a single, multi-user copy of an application are usually much less than the costs of acquiring and maintaining separate copies for each desktop.

> **NOTE**
>
> Installing a commercially purchased single-user application software package on an application or file server might violate the terms and conditions set forth in its Copyright Agreement. In much the same way as an individual user might pass around the original install media of an application, a server makes a single copy of a program available to any and all network users. *This constitutes software piracy.* Always ensure that any software package that you install on a server has been purchased through some form of multi-user agreement.

Although it is usually desirable to separate application software from its data files by using separate servers (for example, an application server and a file server), there is one important exception to this rule. Some applications build and maintain large relational databases. These applications and their databases should co-reside on the application server.

The reason for this is simple: the mechanics of retrieving data from a database is very different from simply pulling down a Word or Excel file. The relational database application only releases the data that was requested, and keeps everything else in its database. Office automation applications, like Word and Excel, store information in standalone files that, typically, are not interdependent with other data in a complex structure. The relational database application is directly responsible for the integrity of the database and its indices. Managing the database across a network increases the risk of corrupting the indices and disabling the application.

Network Type

The network's type describes the manner in which attached resources can be accessed. Resources can be clients, servers, or any devices, files, and so on, that reside on a client or server. These resources can be accessed in one of two ways: peer-to-peer and server-based.

Peer-to-Peer Networks

A peer-to-peer network supports unstructured access to network-attached resources. Each device in a peer-to-peer network can be a client and a server simultaneously. All devices in the network are capable of accessing data, software, and other network resources directly. In other words, each networked computer is a *peer* of every other networked computer; there is no hierarchy.

Figure 2.3 illustrates a peer-to-peer network.

FIGURE 2.3.

A peer-to-peer network.

Benefits

There are four main benefits to having a peer-to-peer network.

■ Peer-to-peer networks are relatively easy to implement and operate. They are little more than a collection of client computers that have a network operating system that permits peer-to-peer resource sharing. Thus, establishing a peer-to-peer network requires only the procurement and installation of a LAN hub or hubs, the computers, wiring, and an operating system that permits this resource-access methodology.

■ Peer-to-peer networks are also inexpensive to operate. They lack expensive, sophisticated, dedicated servers that require special administrative care and climate conditioning. The lack of dedicated servers also eliminates the attendant expenses of a staffing and training, as well as the additional real estate costs for developing a climate-controlled room just for the servers. Each machine resides, at least in theory, on a desktop and is cared for by its primary user.

■ A peer-to-peer network can be established with familiar operating systems like Windows95, Windows NT, and Windows for Workgroups.

■ Their lack of a hierarchical dependence makes peer-to-peer networks much more fault-tolerant than server-based networks. In theory, a server in a client/server network is a single point of failure. Single points of failure are a vulnerability that can impact the entire network. In a peer-to-peer network, the failure of any given machine results in the unavailability of only a subset of the network's attached resources.

Limitations

Peer-to-peer networking is not without its risks or faults. Some of the more serious of these limitations are in the areas of security, performance, and administration.

The peer-to-peer network suffers from numerous security weaknesses:

■ Users must maintain multiple passwords, typically one for each machine that they need to access.

■ The lack of a central repository for shared resources imposes the burden of finding information squarely on each user. This difficulty can be overcome with methods and procedures, provided each member of the workgroup complies. Users tend to devise very creative means of coping with an excess of passwords. Most of these ways directly compromise the security of every machine in the peer-to-peer network.

■ Like the network-attached resources, security is distributed evenly throughout the peer-to-peer network. Security in this form of network usually consists of user authentication via an ID and password, coupled with specific access permissions for specific resources. It is up to the "administrator" of each networked computer to define these permission structures for all other users in the network.

> **NOTE**
>
> Although each machine's user, in a peer-to-peer network, can be considered that machine's administrator, it is rare for these users to have the knowledge and skill sets to be proficient at their administrative duties. It is even rarer for the administrative skill levels to be consistent across even a small workgroup. This is one of the pitfalls of peer-to-peer networking.

■ Unfortunately, technical proficiency is usually not homogeneously distributed. Consequently, the security of the entire network is predicated upon the skills and abilities of the least technically proficient member! One of the better metaphors used to describe this scenario is that of a chain. A chain is only as strong as its weakest link. Security, in a peer-to-peer network, is only as strong as its weakest peer.

Although the administrative burden is less in a peer-to-peer network than in a client/server network, this burden is spread across users. This creates some logistical issues. The two gravest are:

■ Uncoordinated—and probably highly inconsistent—backups of data and software. Each user is responsible for his own machine, so it is possible, and even likely, that each is going to perform backups at his own leisure.

■ Decentralized responsibility for enforcing file-naming conventions and storage locations. Given that there is no central repository for stored information, or any other logic by which LAN-attached resources are organized, keeping current with what information is stored where can be quite challenging. As with everything else in a peer-to-peer network, the effectiveness of the whole is directly dependent upon the degree to which methods and procedures are adhered to by all participants.

Lastly, performance also suffers. An integral aspect of a peer-to-peer network is that each machine is a multi-user machine. The typical machine is better suited for use as a single-user client-only computer than it is for multi-user support. Consequently, the performance of any given machine suffers noticeably, as perceived by its primary user, whenever remote users logon and share its resources.

The availability of files, and any other resources that a given peer may host, are only as available as that host. In other words, if a machine's primary user is out of the office and left the computer powered down, its resources are unavailable to the rest of the networked computers. This can be circumvented by leaving all machines powered on all the time, but doing so raises questions about other issues, like security.

Another, more subtle aspect of performance is scalability. The peer-to-peer methodology is inherently non-scalable. The more peers are networked together, the more unmanageable the network becomes.

Uses

Peer-to-peer networking has two primary uses. First, it is ideally suited for small organizations with a limited budget for information technologies, and limited need for information sharing. Alternatively, workgroups within larger organizations can also use this methodology for a tighter sharing of information within that group.

Server-Based Networks

Server-based networks introduce a hierarchy that is designed to improve the manageability of a network's various supported functions as the size of the network scales upward. Often, server-based networks are referred to as client/server networks. Figure 2.4 illustrates this hierarchy of clients and servers.

FIGURE 2.4.
A client/server network.

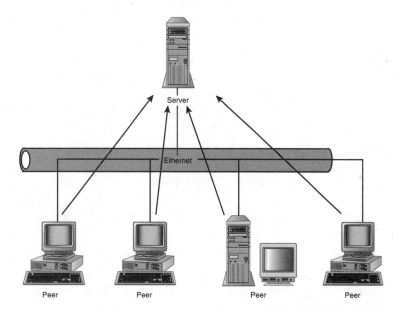

In a server-based network, frequently shared resources are consolidated onto a separate tier of computers, known as servers. Servers, typically, do not have a primary user. Rather, they are multi-user machines that regulate the sharing of their resources across the base of clients. In this type of network, clients are relieved of the burden of functioning as servers to other clients.

Benefits

There are many benefits inherent in the server-based approach to accessing network resources. These benefits directly correspond to the limitations of a peer-to-peer network. The areas of benefit are security, performance, and administration.

Server-based networks can be made, and kept, much more secure than peer-to-peer networks. Multiple factors contribute to this. First, security is managed centrally. Networked resources are no longer subjected to the "weakest link in the chain" theory that is an integral part of a peer-to-peer network.

Instead, all user accounts (also known as "IDs")and passwords are centrally managed and verified before any user is granted access to requested resources. Coincidentally, this also makes the lives of the users better, by diminishing the need for multiple passwords.

Another benefit of this centralization of resources is that administrative tasks, like backups, can be done consistently and reliably.

Server-based networks offer improved performance for networked computers in several ways. First, each client is relieved of the burden of processing requests from other clients for its stores. Each client in a server-based network need only keep up with the requests generated by its primary (and only!) user.

More significantly, this processing is offloaded onto a server whose configuration is optimized for that service. Typically, a server contains more processing power, more memory, and larger, faster disk drives than are found in a client computer. The net effect is that users' client computers are able to better satisfy their own requests, and requests for resources centralized on a server are fulfilled much more effectively.

Users, too, are spared the effort that would otherwise be required to learn which resources are stored where in a network. In a server-based network, the possible "hiding places" are reduced to just the number of servers on the network. In a Microsoft Windows NT server environment, server-based resources can be linked to as a logical drive. After the network drive linkage is established, remote resources stored on the server can be accessed as easily as any that are locally resident on a user's PC.

A server-based network is also very scalable. Regardless of how many clients are connected to the network, the resources are always centrally located. In addition, these resources are always centrally managed and secured. Consequently, the performance of the aggregate network isn't compromised by increases in scale.

Limitations

The server-based network has one limitation: it costs much more to implement and operate than a peer-to-peer network. There are many facets of this significant cost difference.

First, the hardware and software costs are significantly increased because of the need for a separate networked computer that services the clients. Servers can be fairly sophisticated—which translates into "expensive"—machines.

The costs of operating a server-based network are also much higher. This is due to the need to have a trained professional administer the network and its servers. In a peer-to-peer network, each user is responsible for the maintenance of his or her own machine; no individual needs to be dedicated to this function.

The last aspect of cost is the potential cost of downtime. In a peer-to-peer network, the loss of any given peer translates into an only modest decrement in the available resources on the LAN. In a server-based LAN, the loss of a server can directly, and significantly, impact virtually all the users of the network. This increases the potential business risks of a server-based network. Numerous approaches, including clustering servers for redundancy, can be used to combat this risk. Unfortunately, every one of these approaches only further drives up the cost of a server-based network.

Uses

Server-based networks are extremely useful in large organizations. They can also be useful in any circumstances that warrant tighter security, or more consistent management of network-attached resources. The added cost of server-based networks, however, might place them beyond the reach of very small organizations.

Combination Networks

The distinctions between peer-to-peer and server-based networking aren't quite so clear as the preceding sections might suggest. They were presented as distinct types intentionally, and for academic purposes. In reality, the distinctions between them have been blurred through the capabilities of numerous operating systems, like Microsoft's Windows for Workgroups, Windows 95, and Windows NT.

The norm today is a combination of peer-to-peer and server-based resource access in a single network. An example of this is a network with a server-based architecture that centralizes resources that are universally needed. Within this context, local workgroups can optionally provide peer-based access among themselves.

LAN Topologies

Local area network topologies can be described using either a physical or a logical perspective. A physical topology describes the geometric arrangement of components that make up the LAN. The topology is not a map of the network. It is a theoretical construct that graphically conveys the shape and structure of the LAN.

A logical topology describes the possible connections between pairs of networked endpoints that can communicate. This is useful in describing which endpoints can communicate with which other endpoints, and whether or not those pairs capable of communicating have a direct physical connection to each other. This chapter focuses only on physical topological descriptions.

Until recently, there have been three basic physical topologies: bus, ring, and star. Each basic topology is dictated by the physical LAN technology selected. For example, Token Ring networks, by definition, have historically used ring topologies. However, MSAUs (Token Ring's hubs, known more properly as *Multi-Station Access Units*), blurred the distinction between a ring and star topology for Token Ring networks. The result is known as a *star ring*. Similarly, the introduction of LAN switching is, again, changing the perception of topology. Switched

LANs, regardless of frame type or access method, are topologically similar. The ring that used to exist at the electronics level within Token Ring's MSAUs no longer interconnects all the devices connected to that hub. Instead, each enjoys its own mini-ring that is populated with just two devices: the station device and the switch port. Consequently, "switched" should now be added to the long-standing triad of basic LAN topologies as a distinct fourth topology.

> **NOTE**
>
> Switches implement a star topology, without regard for which Data Link Layer protocol they are designed. Given that the word "switch" has become readily understood (thanks to the tireless marketing campaigns of switch manufacturers!), "switch" has become more descriptive and readily understood than "star bus" or "star ring." Consequently, switching can be regarded as a topology unto itself. For the purposes of any MCSE exam that might be lurking in your not-too-distant future, however, you might want to remember the words "star bus" or "star ring."

Switching has decoupled this historic coupling of topology and LAN technology: literally all LAN technologies can be purchased in a switched implementation. This has significant ramifications on network access and, consequently, overall network performance. These ramifications are explored in more detail in the section of this chapter titled "Switched Topology."

> **NOTE**
>
> Even though switches can be purchased to support any LAN type, including Ethernet, Token Ring, FDDI, and so forth, they are *not* translating bridges. That is, they are incapable of switching frames between dissimilar LAN architectures.

Bus Topology

A bus topology features all networked nodes interconnected peer to peer using a single, open-ended cable. This cable can support only a single channel. The cable is called the *bus*. Some bus-based technologies use more than a single cable. Consequently, they can support more than one channel, although each cable remains limited to just one transmission channel.

Both ends of the bus must be terminated with a resistive load, known as a "terminating resistor." These resistors serve to prevent *signal bounce*. Whenever a station transmits, the signal that it puts on the wire automatically propagates in both directions. If a terminating resistor is not encountered, the signal reaches the end of the bus and reverses direction. Consequently, a single transmission can completely usurp all available bandwidth and prevent any other stations from transmitting. An example of bus topology is illustrated in Figure 2.5.

Figure 2.5.

Typical bus topology.

The typical bus topology features a single cable, supported by no external electronics, that interconnects all networked nodes in a peer-to-peer fashion. All connected devices listen to the bussed transmissions and accept those packets addressed to them. The lack of any external electronics, like repeaters, makes bus LANs simple and inexpensive. The downside is that it also imposes severe limitations on distances, functionality, and scalability.

This topology is impractical for all but the smallest of LANs. Consequently, today's commercially available LAN products that use a bus topology are inexpensive peer-to-peer networks that provide basic connectivity. These products are targeted at home and small office environments.

One exception to this was the IEEE's 802.4 Token Bus LAN specification. This technology was fairly robust, deterministic, and bore many similarities to a Token Ring LAN. Deterministic LANs offer the administrator a high degree of control in determining the maximum amount of time that a frame of data can be in transmission. The primary difference, obviously, was that Token Bus was implemented on a bus topology.

Token Bus found extremely limited market support. Its implementation tended to be limited to factory production lines. Bus topologies, in general, prospered in myriad other forms. Two early forms of Ethernet, 10Base2 and 10Base5, used a bus topology and coaxial cabling. Buses also became a critical technology for interconnecting system-level components and peripheral devices within the internal architectures of computers.

Ring Topology

The ring topology started out as a simple peer-to-peer LAN topology. Each networked workstation had two connections: one to each of its nearest neighbors (see Figure 2.6). The interconnection had to form a physical loop, or ring. Data was transmitted unidirectionally around the ring. Each workstation acted as a repeater, accepting and responding to packets addressed to it, and forwarding on the other packets to the next workstation on the ring.

The original LAN ring topology featured peer-to-peer connections between workstations. These connections had to be closed; that is, they had to form a ring. The benefit of such LANs was that response time was fairly predictable. The more devices there were in the ring, the longer the network delays. The drawback was that early ring networks could be completely disabled if one of the workstations failed.

FIGURE 2.6.

Peer-to-peer ring topology.

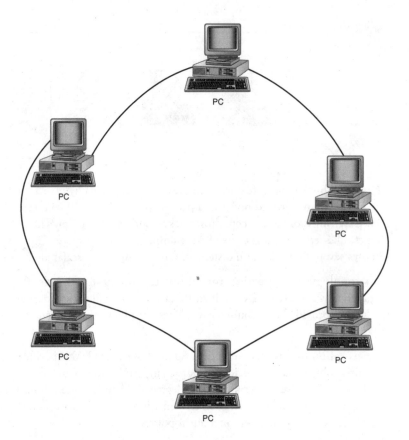

These primitive rings were made obsolete by IBM's Token Ring, which was later standardized by the IEEE's 802.5 specification. Token Ring departed from the peer-to-peer interconnection in favor of a repeating hub. This eliminated ring networks' vulnerability to workstation failure by eliminating the peer-to-peer ring construction. Token Ring networks, despite their name, are implemented with a star topology and a circular access method, as shown in Figure 2.7.

LANs can be implemented in a star topology, yet retain a circular access method. The Token Ring network illustrated in Figure 2.7 demonstrates the virtual ring that is formed by the round-robin access method. The solid lines represent physical connections and the dashed line represents the logical flow of regulated media access.

Functionally, the access token passes in a circular sequence, round-robin fashion, among the networked endpoints, even though they are all interconnected to a common hub. Thus, many people succumb to the temptation of describing Token Ring networks as having a "logical" ring topology, even though they are physically shaped like a star. Evidence of this is found in Microsoft's Networking Essentials course and exam. They regard Token Ring as having a ring, not a star topology. In fact, the Token Ring hub, known more properly as a *Multi-Station Access Unit* (MSAU), provides a physical ring internally, at the electronics level.

FIGURE 2.7.
Star-shaped ring topology.

Star Topology

Star topology LANs have connections to networked devices that "radiate" out from a common point, that is, the *hub*, as shown in Figure 2.8. Unlike ring topologies—physical or virtual—each networked device in a star topology can access the media independently. These devices have to share the hub's available bandwidth. An example of a LAN with a star topology is 10BaseT Ethernet.

FIGURE 2.8.
Star topology.

A small LAN with a star topology features connections that radiate out from a common point. Each connected device can initiate media access independent of the other connected devices.

Star topologies have become the dominant topology type in contemporary LANs. They are flexible, scalable, and relatively inexpensive compared to more sophisticated LANs with strictly regulated access methods. Stars have all but made buses and rings obsolete in LAN topologies and have formed the basis for the final LAN topology: switched.

Switched Topology

A switch is a multiport, Data Link Layer (OSI Reference Model Layer 2) device. A switch "learns" Media Access Control (MAC) addresses and stores them in an internal lookup table. Temporary, switched paths are created between the frame's originator and its intended recipient, and the frames are forwarded along that temporary path.

The typical LAN with a switched topology is illustrated in Figure 2.9. It features multiple connections to a switching hub. Each port, and the device to which it connects, has its own dedicated bandwidth. Although originally switches forwarded frames based upon the frames' MAC addresses, technological advances are rapidly changing this. Switches are available that can process cells, frames, and even packets that use a Layer 3 address like IP.

> **NOTE**
>
> A frame is a variable-length structure that contains data, source, and destination addresses, and other data fields required for its carriage and forwarding in Layer 2 of the OSI Reference Model. Cells are very similar to frames, except that they feature a fixed, not variable, length. Packets are a construct of protocols that operate at Layer 3 of the OSI Reference Model. IP and IPX are two examples of Layer 3 protocols that use packets to encapsulate data for transport to foreign domains.

FIGURE 2.9.

Switched topology.

Switches can improve the performance of a LAN in two important ways. First, they increase the aggregate bandwidth available throughout that network. For example, a switched Ethernet hub with 8 ports contains 8 separate collision domains of 10Mbps each, for an aggregate of 80Mbps of bandwidth.

The second way that switches improve LAN performance is by reducing the number of devices that are forced to share each segment of bandwidth. Each switch-delineated collision domain is inhabited by only two devices: the networked device and the port on the switching hub to which it connects. These are the only two devices that can compete for the 10Mbps of bandwidth on their segment. In networks that do not utilize a media access method that is based on competition for bandwidth—like Token Ring or FDDI—the tokens circulate among a much smaller number of networked machines than are typically supported in competition-based networks.

One area for concern with large switched implementations is that switches do not isolate broadcasts. They bolster performance solely by segmenting collision, not broadcast, domains. Excessive broadcast traffic can significantly and adversely impact LAN performance.

Complex Topologies

Complex topologies are extensions and/or combinations of basic physical topologies. Basic topologies, by themselves, are adequate for only very small LANs. The scalability of the basic topologies is extremely limited. Complex topologies are formed from these building blocks to achieve a custom-fitted, scalable topology.

Daisy Chains

The simplest of the complex topologies is developed by serially interconnecting all the hubs of a network, as shown in Figure 2.10. This is known as *daisy-chaining*. This simple approach uses ports on existing hubs for interconnecting the hubs. Thus, no incremental cost is incurred during the development of such a backbone.

FIGURE 2.10.
Daisy-chaining hubs.

Small LANs can be scaled upward by daisy-chaining hubs together. Daisy chains are easily built and don't require any special administrator skills. Daisy chains were, historically, the interconnection method of choice for emerging, first-generation LANs.

The limits of daisy-chaining can be discovered in a number of ways. LAN technology specifications, like 802.3 Ethernet, dictate the maximum size of the LAN in terms of the number of hubs and/or repeaters that may be strung together in sequence. The distance limitations imposed by the Physical Layer, multiplied by the number of devices, dictate the maximum size of a LAN. This size is referred to as a *maximum network diameter*. Scaling beyond this diameter adversely affects the normal functioning of that LAN. Maximum network diameters frequently limit the number of hubs that can be interconnected in this fashion. This is particularly true of contemporary high-performance LANs, like Fast Ethernet, that place strict limitations on network diameter and the number of repeaters that can be strung together.

> **NOTE**
>
> A repeater is a device that accepts an incoming signal, amplifies it back to its original volume, and places it back on the network. Typically, signal amplification and repetition functions are incorporated into hubs. Consequently, the two terms (repeaters and hubs) can be used synonymously.

Daisy-chaining networks that use a contention-based media access method can become problematic long before network diameter is compromised, however. Daisy-chaining increases the number of connections—and therefore the number of devices—on a LAN. It does not increase aggregate bandwidth or segment collision domains. Daisy-chaining simply increases the number of machines sharing the network's available bandwidth. Too many devices competing for the same amount of bandwidth can create collisions and quickly incapacitate a LAN.

This topology is best left to LANs with less than a handful of hubs and little, if any, wide area networking.

Hierarchies

Hierarchical topologies consist of more than one layer of hubs. Each layer serves a different network function. The bottom tier would be reserved for user station and server connectivity. Higher-level tiers provide aggregation of the user-level tier. In much simpler terms, many user-level hubs are interconnected via a lesser number of higher-level hubs. The hubs, themselves, can be identical devices; their only distinction lies in their application. A hierarchical arrangement is best suited for medium to large-sized LANs that must be concerned with scalability of the network and with traffic aggregation.

Hierarchical Rings

Ring networks can be scaled up by interconnecting multiple rings in a hierarchical fashion, as shown in Figure 2.11. User station and server connectivity can be provided by as many limited size rings as are necessary to provide the required level of performance. A second tier ring, either Token Ring or FDDI, can be used to interconnect all the user-level rings and to provide aggregated access to the Wide Area Network (WAN).

FIGURE 2.11.

Hierarchical ring topology.

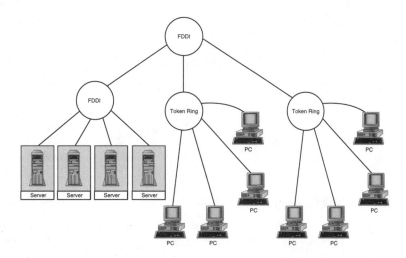

Small ring LANs can be scaled by interconnecting multiple rings hierarchically. In Figure 2.11, two distinct 16 Mbps Token Rings (shown logically as loops) are used to interconnect the user stations, and separate FDDI loops are used for the servers and backbone tier.

Hierarchical Stars

Star topologies, too, can be implemented in hierarchical arrangements of multiple stars, as shown in Figure 2.12. Hierarchical stars can be implemented as a single collision domain, or segmented into multiple collision domains using switches, routers, or bridges.

> **NOTE**
>
> A collision domain consists of all the devices that compete for the right to transmit on a shared media. Switches, bridges, and routers all segment the collision domain. That is, they create multiple, smaller collision domains.

A hierarchical star topology uses one tier for user and server connectivity and the second tier as a backbone.

FIGURE 2.12.

*Hierarchical star
topology.*

Hierarchical Combinations

Overall network performance can be enhanced by not force-fitting all the functional requirements of the LAN into a single solution. Today's high-end switching hubs enable you to mix
multiple technologies. New topologies can be introduced by simply inserting the appropriate
circuit board into the multi-slot chassis of the switching hub. A hierarchical topology lends
itself to combinations of topologies, as shown in Figure 2.13.

FIGURE 2.13.

*Hierarchical
combination topology.*

In this example of a hierarchical combination topology, an Asynchronous Transfer Mode (ATM) backbone is used to interconnect the user-level hubs. FDDI interconnects the server farm; Ethernet interconnects the user stations. This approach differentiates the LAN into functional components (station0-connect, server-connect, and backbone) and enables the ideal technology for each function to be used. These functional areas are addressed further in the next section, "LAN Functional Areas."

LAN Functional Areas

Topological variation can be an important way to optimize network performance for each of the various functional areas of a LAN. LANs contain four distinct functional areas, including station connectivity, server connectivity, WAN connectivity, and backbone. Each may be best served by a different basic or complex topology.

Station Connectivity

The primary function of most LANs is station connectivity. Station connectivity, as its name implies, is the portion of the LAN that is used to connect the user stations to the network. This functional area tends to have the least stringent performance requirements of the LAN's functional areas. There are obvious exceptions to this, like CAD/CAM workstations, desktop videoconferencing, and so on. In general, though, compromises in the cost and performance of this part of a LAN's technology and topology are less likely to adversely affect the network's performance.

Providing connectivity to machines that have divergent network performance requirements may require the use of multiple LAN technologies, as shown in Figure 2.14. Fortunately, many of today's hub manufacturers can support multiple technologies from the same hub chassis.

FIGURE 2.14.

Station connectivity LAN.

LANs provide basic connectivity to user stations and the peripherals that inhabit them. Differences in the network performance requirements of user station equipment can necessitate a mixed topology/technology solution.

Server Connectivity

Servers tend to be much more robust than user workstations. Servers tend to be a point of traffic aggregation and must serve many clients and/or other servers. In the case of high-volume servers, this aggregation must be designed into a LAN's topology; otherwise, clients and servers suffer degraded network performance. Network connectivity to servers, typically, should also be more robust than station connectivity in terms of available bandwidth and robustness of access method.

LAN topologies can also be manipulated to accommodate the robust network performance requirements of servers and server clusters. In Figure 2.15, for example, a hierarchical combination topology is employed. The server farm is interconnected with a small FDDI loop; the less robust user stations are interconnected with Ethernet.

FIGURE 2.15.

Server connectivity LAN.

WAN Connectivity

A frequently overlooked aspect of a LAN's topology is its connection to the Wide Area Network (WAN). In many cases, WAN connectivity is provided by a single connection from the backbone to a router, as shown in Figure 2.16.

FIGURE 2.16.
*WAN connectivity
LAN.*

2

LAN TYPES AND
TOPOLOGIES

The LAN's connection to the router that provides WAN connectivity is a crucial link in a building's overall LAN topology. Improper technology selection at this critical point can result in unacceptably deteriorated levels of performance for all traffic entering or exiting the building's LAN. LAN technologies that use a contention-based access method are highly inappropriate for this function.

Networks that support a large quantity of WAN-to-LAN and LAN-to-WAN traffic benefit greatly from having the most robust connection possible in this aspect of their overall topology. The technology selected should be robust in terms of its nominal transmission rate and its access method. Contention-based technologies should be avoided at all costs. The use of a contention-based media, even on a dedicated switched port, may become problematic in high-usage networks. This is the bottleneck for all traffic coming into, and trying to get out of, the building's LAN.

Backbone Connectivity

A LAN's *backbone* is the portion of its facilities used to interconnect all the hubs. A backbone can be implemented in several topologies and with several different network components, as shown in Figure 2.17.

FIGURE 2.17.
LAN backbone.

FIGURE 2.17.
LAN backbone.

The LAN's backbone provides a critical function. It interconnects all the locally networked resources and, if applicable, the WAN. The logical depiction of a backbone shown in Figure 2.17 can be implemented in a wide variety of ways.

Determining which backbone topology is correct for your LAN is not easy. Some options are easier to implement, very affordable, and easy to manage. Others can be more costly to acquire and operate. Another important difference lies in the scalability of the various backbone topologies. Some are easy to scale, up to a point, and then require reinvestment to maintain acceptable levels of performance. Each option must be examined individually, relative to your particular situation and requirements.

Serial Backbone

A serial backbone, shown in Figure 2.18, is nothing more than a series of hubs daisy-chained together. As described in the preceding section, this topology is inappropriate for all but the smallest of networks.

FIGURE 2.18.
Serial backbone, also known as "daisy chain."

Distributed Backbone

A distributed backbone is a form of hierarchical topology that can be built by installing a backbone hub in a central location. A building's PBX room usually serves as the center of its wiring topology. Consequently, it is the ideal location for a distributed backbone hub. Connections from this hub are distributed to other hubs throughout the building, as shown in Figure 2.19.

FIGURE 2.19.
Distributed backbone.

2

LAN TYPES AND
TOPOLOGIES

A distributed backbone can be developed by centrally locating the backbone hub. Connections are distributed from this hub to other hubs throughout the building. Unlike the serial backbone, this topology enables LANs to span large buildings without compromising maximum network diameters.

If you consider a distributed backbone, make sure you understand the building's wire topology and the distance limitations of the various LAN media choices. In medium to large locations, the only viable option for implementing a distributed backbone is probably fiber-optic cabling.

Collapsed Backbone

A collapsed backbone topology features a centralized router that interconnects all the LAN segments in a given building. The router effectively creates multiple collision and broadcast domains, thereby increasing the performance of each of the LAN segments.

Routers operate at Layer 3 of the OSI Reference Model. They are incapable of operating as quickly as hubs. Consequently, they can limit effective throughputs for any LAN traffic that originates on one LAN segment, but terminates on another.

Collapsed backbones, like the one shown in Figure 2.20, also introduce a single point of failure in the LAN. This is not a fatal flaw. In fact, many of the other topologies also introduce a single point of failure into the LAN. Nevertheless, that weakness must be considered when planning a network topology.

FIGURE 2.20.

Collapsed backbone.

An important consideration in collapsed backbone topologies is that user communities are seldom conveniently distributed throughout a building. Instead, users are scattered far and wide. This means that there is a good chance that they will be found on both sides of the LAN's collapsed backbone router. Subsequently, simple network tasks among the members of a workgroup are likely to traverse the router. Care should be taken when designing collapsed backbone LANs to absolutely minimize the amount of traffic that must cross the router. Use it as a traffic aggregator for LAN-level resources, like WAN facilities, and not indiscriminately as a bridge.

Parallel Backbone

In some of the cases where collapsed backbones are an untenable solution, a modified version may prove ideal. This modification is known as the *parallel backbone*. The reasons for installing a parallel backbone are many. User communities may be widely dispersed throughout a building. Some groups and/or applications may have stringent network security requirements. High network availability may be required. Regardless of the reason, running parallel connections from a building's collapsed backbone router to the same telephone closet enables supporting multiple segments to be run from each closet, as shown in Figure 2.21.

FIGURE 2.21.

Parallel backbone topology.

The parallel backbone topology is a modification of the collapsed backbone. Multiple segments can be supported in the same telephone closet or equipment room. This marginally increases the cost of the network, but can increase the performance of each segment, and satisfy additional network criteria, such as security.

Careful understanding of the performance requirements imposed by customers, stratified by LAN functional areas, is the key to developing the ideal topology for any set of user requirements. The potential combinations are limited only by one's imagination. Continued technological innovation will only increase the topological variety available to network designers.

> **CAUTION**
>
> Many of the complex topologies presented in this chapter are for your edification only. They are of more practical use on the job than they are during your MCSE exam. In fact, vendors frequently refer to many of these complex topologies by different names. Rather than get caught up in names, try to grasp their concepts, strengths, and weaknesses.

Summary

An important aspect of a LAN is the manner in which it supports resource access. Although this is more a function of the network operating systems than it is LAN hardware, it directly impacts the traffic flows and performance of the LAN.

LAN topology, too, is directly related to the efficacy of your LAN. The four basic topologies can be mixed and matched, stacked or linked, in an almost infinite variety. Understanding the benefits and limitations of the basic topologies, and using them wisely, is critical to the selection of one that best satisfies the expected demands.

The topics presented in this chapter should reinforce the fact that there's more to networks than just their hardware and wiring. The way that the physical components are arranged, and the manner with which attached resources are accessed, are equally important to technology selection.

The Physical Layer

by Mark A. Sportack

IN THIS CHAPTER

CHAPTER 3

The previous chapter, Chapter 2, "LAN Types and Topologies," described the various shapes and resource access methods that can be used in a Local Area Network. The shapes, in particular, were presented in an abstract way that did not delve into the intricacies of the Physical Layer.

The Physical Layer, as defined by the OSI Reference Model, includes all the processes, mechanisms, electronics, and protocols that are needed for a computing device to transmit and receive binary data streams. Included in the Physical Layer specification of LAN technologies are the expectations for the performance of the transmission media that interconnects two communicating devices. The model, however, does not extend to the media themselves.

This chapter describes the role and significance of the Physical Layer in LANs, and then goes beyond the limitations of that Layer in its examination of Physical Layer phenomena. This chapter, in addition to describing the functionality of the Physical Layer, also includes detailed examinations of fiber optics, coaxial cabling, and the myriad grades of twisted pair wiring. Included in this description are the performance characteristics and limitations of each media type.

Layer 1: The Physical Layer

The foundation upon which the OSI Reference Model is built is the Physical Layer. It defines everything that is required to support the transmission and reception of signals. The Physical Layer has four functional areas:

- Mechanical
- Electrical
- Functional
- Procedural

Together, these areas encompass all the mechanisms that are needed to support the electrical and/or optical transmission of data. Included within these areas are signaling techniques, the voltage of the electrical current used to transport the signal, the media types and their respective impedance characteristics, the electronic components on the Network Interface Card (NIC), and even the physical shape of the connector that is used to terminate the media.

A very common misperception held about the Physical Layer concerns its scope. It is commonly believed that the OSI model's Physical Layer includes anything that either generates or carries the signals. This is not true. Remember, it is the bottom layer of a protocol stack. The stack must reside on a device. Thus, the bottom layer is limited to the description and/or specification of the processes and mechanisms needed by that communicating device to support communications with other compatible devices. *The Physical Layer does not include anything that is not contained within the host.* Specific examples of mechanisms that are needed to support data communications but are outside the scope of the Physical Layer include:

- Physical media
- Hubs
- Routers
- Switches

These articles are necessary to effectively transport signals between the communicating devices but are outside the scope of the Physical Layer.

The lower boundary of this layer is the physical connector port of the communicating device that attaches to the transmission media. Rather than try to define the specifications for the entire network and its subcomponents, the model simply establishes the performance characteristics that it expects of the network and stops there. The model does not include anything else that exists between the physical connectors of the two communicating devices. Consequently, transmission media remain outside the scope of the Physical Layer, and are sometimes referred to as "Layer 0." The confusion over the scope of the Physical Layer seems to stem from the fact that the Physical Layer does provide specifications for the media's performance. In other words, the Physical Layer describes the expected performance of the physical plant, but does not define that physical plant.

Physical Layer Functions

The Physical Layer performs the transmission and reception of signals on behalf of the rest of its protocol stack, and applications that use that stack. This support requires the Physical Layer to perform several critical functions. For transmission, the Physical Layer must:

- Convert framed data from the Data Link Layer to a binary stream
- Implement the Media Access Method dictated by the Data Link Layer's media access method
- Transmit framed data serially (that is, one bit at a time), as a binary stream

For reception, the Physical Layer must:

- Listen for inbound transmissions that are addressed to its host device
- Accept appropriately addressed streams
- Pass the binary stream up to the Data Link Layer for reassembly into frames

Conspicuously absent from this list is any means of verifying the integrity of received data. This layer transmits and receives only 1s and 0s. It has no mechanism for determining the significance of the bits it transmits or receives. Consequently, it is unable to make an independent determination as to the validity of any given bit or stream of bits. The onus for this is passed on to higher layer protocols.

Encoding Signals

The Physical Layer is responsible for encoding data into a form that can propagate through a transmission media. These forms must, necessarily, vary with the transmission media, because each media has its own physical characteristics. There are many different techniques for physically encoding data, but all use electromagnetic waves to encode and transport the data.

An electromagnetic wave is the physical form of the energy described by the Electromagnetic Spectrum. This spectrum starts at zero oscillations, rises through the range of frequencies that can be perceived by the human ear (up to 25,000 oscillations per second), through the various forms of light, and finally into the range of ridiculously large numbers inhabited by X-rays and gamma rays.

> **NOTE**
>
> This spectrum is defined, and described, in much more detail in Chapter 4, "The 'Not-so-Physical' Physical Layer."

The electromagnetic wave continuously oscillates in a somewhat symmetrical pattern, from positive to negative, as it travels. The rate at which this oscillation occurs is called *frequency*. It is measured in *Hertz* (Hz). One cycle, or Hertz, represents a 360° change in one second.

> **NOTE**
>
> Thousands of Hertz per second is abbreviated to KHz, millions of Hertz per second is MHz, and billions of Hertz is abbreviated to GHz.

Another metric used to measure the intensity of electromagnetic energy is a *wavelength*. A wavelength is the distance from the top of one wave's crest to the top of the next wave's crest. Besides this difference in how they measure, the more important difference between Hz and wavelength lies in their application. Hz is used to describe lower frequency bands, whereas wavelength is reserved for the higher-frequency phenomena, like light, X-rays, and gamma rays. The length of a wave can be billionths of a meter or several meters. Other than these two differentiating points, one should remember that they are more alike than different; they are two different ways of measuring the same thing!

Figure 3.1 illustrates one Hz and one wavelength.

Regardless of whether Hz or wavelengths are used to describe frequency, it is important to note that the physical characteristics of the wave, and its propagation, change with movement along the spectrum. Generally speaking, as frequency increases, the capability to encode data increases. Quite simply, there are more state changes per second in higher frequencies than in lower frequencies. State changes are used to encode data.

FIGURE 3.1.

One Hz versus one wavelength.

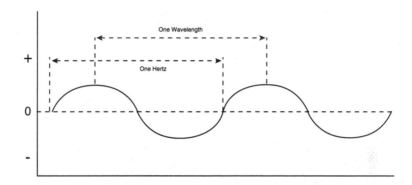

Another important change is the persistence of the signal. Lower frequencies tend to be remarkably durable and can penetrate almost anything without attenuating completely. Toward the portion of the spectrum inhabited by light, however, frequencies and their signals can be completely and instantly attenuated by even the least significant or dense of opaque materials. Of course, proceeding into the frequencies beyond light—into the range of X-rays—this statement becomes invalid. For the purposes of encoding and transporting data in LANs, however, that generalization remains valid.

The last change to note is the inverse relationship between wavelengths and frequencies. The longer the wavelength, the lower the frequency. Quite simply, a wavelength of one meter per second oscillates slowly between positive and negative states. In contrast, a wavelength of 850 millionths of a meter (or nanometers, abbreviated as "nm"), has a relatively fast oscillation rate. As was indicated previously, the lower the frequency, the lower the potential for carrying data.

Regardless of the wave's intensity, the transmission media serves two purposes:

■ Guide the wavelength's transmission

■ Protect the wavelength, to the extent that it is capable, during transmission

Whenever electrical vibrations are used to transport data—whether analog or digital—the series of vibrations is known as a *signal*. Signals can occur at any frequency, although it is generally acknowledged that anything below 300,000 Hz does not offer enough bandwidth to be practical for use by electrical devices.

The curvature of the wave presented in Figure 3.2 is distinctly analog in its shape. Digital signals feature flattened plateaus and valleys, with crisp phase changes as opposed to gradual, organic, changes. The shape of a digital signal, as compared to an analog signal, is presented in Figure 3.2.

FIGURE 3.2.

Digital versus analog signals.

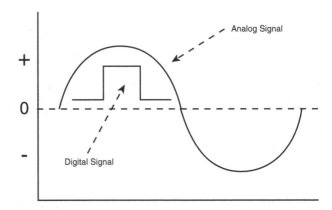

The Physical Layer, as implemented on a Network Interface Card, expects a specific transmission media type. Given this media type, it knows what frequency to use, how to encode data on it, and what bandwidth can be supported over a pre-determined maximum cable length.

Bandwidth

Bandwidth is the *width* of a communications channel, measured in Hz. This limits the quantity of data that can be encoded by the Physical Layer electronics, for any given set of frequencies. It is the difference between the upper and lower frequency boundaries of a communications channel. For example, the 902-928 *Megahertz* (MHz—millions of Hertz) band yields 26MHz of bandwidth. This bandwidth provides the basic limiting factor in the signaling and data transmission rates of any data communications technology that would use this band.

WARNING

The yield of a band should not be misconstrued as a frequency! In the given example, the band is 26MHz in width. There is also a valid spectral frequency of 26MHz. To get a yield of 26MHz from that frequency would require a band of at least the same width—for example, from 26MHz to 52MHz. Unfortunately, this frequency is so low that it cannot accommodate the inefficiencies of physical signal encoding as well as higher frequency bands. Consequently, you'd be extremely hard-pressed to try and get 26MHz worth of bandwidth from a 26MHz band in that low of a frequency.

To further illustrate this point, the 902-928MHz band was not selected at random. It is the range at which many pagers and other low bandwidth, spread spectrum radio frequency devices operate. The inefficiencies of this band can be demonstrated by examining any of the wireless LAN products that operate at this range. They are able to eke out only 2Mbps from the 26MHz band.

The overuse, and increasing generalization, of the term "bandwidth" creates the potential for confusion with other concepts, like data rate and even transmission frequency. Older concepts, too, like baud rate, add to the complexity of describing the robustness of data transmissions. *Baud* is the number of discrete signaling elements that are transmitted in one second. Baud is an artifact from the early days of communications, when 300 baud modems were replacing 110 baud acoustic couplers. These modems were capable of transmitting 300bps. At higher signaling speeds, multiple bits can be encoded per baud. Consequently, 2400bps modems actually ran at 1200 baud by placing two bits per baud.

In LAN environments, the actual transmission frequency is all but ignored. The potential bandwidth of a data communications frequency, and the physical media that supports its transmission, can be measured more precisely using the number of *bits per second* (bps) that can actually be transmitted, rather than Hz. Hz (the number of cycles per second) is usually used only to describe extremely low frequencies, like those used for voice communications. At these low frequencies, Hz and bps are usually synonymous.

> **NOTE**
>
> At the higher frequencies, the relationship between Hz and bits per second becomes obscured. For example, the potential bandwidth of fiber optic cabling is rated in wavelengths. For example, 62.5 micron fiber optic cabling can be rated at 850 nanometers (nm). This reflects the maximum wavelength that can be supported over a specific distance, usually 100 meters.

The communications devices that use the higher frequencies tend to be more sophisticated. Implicit with this increased sophistication are more advanced data encoding techniques. These techniques can support the encoding of more than one bit per Hz, or can be used to manipulate one's perception about the robustness of a technology. A good example of an intentional manipulation of perception by misusing communications rate metrics is Gigabit Ethernet. Gigabit Ethernet (which is examined in more detail in Chapter 8, "Faster Ethernets") was cobbled together using the IEEE's 802.3 Data Link Layer and Fibre Channel's Physical Layer. Despite its marketing nomenclature, it uses a maximum signaling speed described as 1024 Megabaud, or 1 Gigabaud. The frequencies used vary, based on the selection of physical media.

Gigabit Ethernet uses an encoding scheme known as 4B/5B. Simply put, the Physical Layer of this architecture creates a 5-bit pattern for every 4-bit string that must be transmitted. This 20% overhead at the Physical Layer automatically reduces the maximum bandwidth to 800Mbps. Filtering out the overheads of the Gigabit Ethernet's framing and protocol, the IP packet structure and protocols, and the overheads of any other protocols that exist at Layers 4 through 7, further reduces the effective throughput. Its gross bandwidth is 800Mbps, but actual, sustainable, and demonstrable data rates are lower. Unfortunately, even giving them the benefit of the doubt and calling it "800Mbps Ethernet" lacks the market appeal of "Gigabit Ethernet." And so, for the sake of marketing, technical accuracy is compromised.

Given this, it becomes clear that *bandwidth* is the maximum amount of data that can be carried over a specific transmission media.

Distance Implications

The potential bandwidth of any given media type is limited by both the frequency that it can support and the distance over which the media must support it. Distance is a critical factor for several reasons. First, the greater the distance, the longer a signal takes to reach its destination. Also, the greater the distance, the more the signal disperses (radiates). This results in the slow, but steady, deterioration in the volume of the signal. Ultimately, the signal reaches a minimum threshold, below which it is unintelligible to the recipient. This form of signal degradation is known as *attenuation*.

Long cable distances also directly increase the exposure of the cable and its signals to interference from sources of electromagnetic noise, like the ballast of fluorescent lamps, AC electrical cables, and so forth. This form of deterioration is known as *distortion*.

Attenuation

Passing an electrical current, which is the form that a transmitted signal takes, results in the slow but steady degradation of the signal's strength. In addition to its continuous radiation of energy, the signal also consumes energy to move along its wire path. Remember, the signal is an electromagnetic wave: like all electrical currents, it consumes its own energy to overcome the resistance inherent in its conductive media as it moves through it. The result is a continuous decrease in the magnitude of the signal, without altering its shape.

> **NOTE**
>
> All signals, even optical ones, are inherently electromagnetic. A common misperception is that electrical current is viable for transmission only over conductive materials, like copper. Fiber optic cabling uses light-based transmissions. Light is still an electromagnetic phenomenon; it just has a much higher frequency than the waves that can pass through metallic conductors. Consequently, even light-based signals are prone to attenuation.
>
> The glass media through which light-based transmissions travel tend to have very little electrical resistance. Instead, attenuation of an optical signal is caused by one or both of the following:
>
> - Radial dispersion of signal away from the center axis of the fiber
> - Collision with impurities in the fiber
>
> Remember, light is an extremely frangible beam. It attenuates completely whenever it impacts an opaque solid.

Figure 3.3 illustrates a signal that is attenuating.

FIGURE 3.3.

Attenuation of a signal.

The longer a cable is, the more resistance the signal encounters. Left unchecked, normal attenuation can result in a signal deteriorating to the point that its data is no longer discernible by the recipient. Consequently, the Physical Layer dictates a series of specifications to guarantee that this does not happen—at least, not in networks that comply with the specification.

Attenuation can be compensated for by keeping wire lengths short enough to guarantee that the signal is strong enough to reach all destinations on the wire. Alternatively, if the wire must be relatively lengthy, a repeater can be installed in the line. A *repeater* is any device that takes an incoming signal, amplifies its strength, and puts it back on the wire. See Figure 3.4 for a functional depiction of a repeater.

FIGURE 3.4.

Regeneration of attenuating signal using a repeater.

This basic and primary function of a repeater is often lost on the users and administrators of a LAN. To them, the repeater is a hub, and the hub provides only ports for interconnecting multiple devices. For all their successes, repeaters are not without limitation. They are incapable of discerning legitimate data and frame structures from damaged ones. Any errors or distortions received are repeated at a stronger signal level.

Distortion

Distortion is a severe problem for signal transmission. Distortion is the unwanted modification of signals in transit. After data or framing has been distorted, it is useless. The recipient, if it can still determine that it is the intended recipient, passes the binary stream up to its Data Link Layer protocols. These protocols recognize the distortion and notify the frame's originator of the need to retransmit that frame. This is a decidedly reactive approach to combating distortion. Figure 3.5 illustrates a distorted signal.

3

THE PHYSICAL LAYER

FIGURE 3.5.

Distorted signal.

There are, however, several proactive ways to obviate distortion:

- Adhere rigidly to any installation guidelines that may have been provided with your transmission media. Use the correct grade of wire, make sure its installation and terminations are in compliance with manufacturer recommendations, and keep the wire path within acceptable distances. Forcing data to travel over wire paths longer than the recommended maximum is a good way to institutionalize retransmissions.

- Recognize potential causes of distortion, and route cabling away from those sources.

- Use network protocols that are capable of detecting, and automatically correcting, any transmission errors that may occur. These protocols are discussed in Chapter 5, "The Data Link Layer," and in Chapter 12, "Network Protocols."

> **WARNING**
>
> One form of signal distortion is known as *crosstalk*. Crosstalk is a phenomenon of twisted pair wiring. Twisted pair uses different wires within the same sheath for different functions—for example, one wire for transmit and another for receive. Crosstalk is the induction of unwanted signals from one wire to another within the same sheath. This form of distortion is also sometimes referenced as NEXT or Near-End Cross-Talk. Crosstalk can be avoided by making sure that your twisted pair wiring is installed and terminated properly.

Minor signal distortion can be cleaned up through the use of a device that actually regenerates the received signal, rather than simply amplifying it. For example, in a LAN, a hub is a simple repeater. It simply amplifies and repeats any distorted signals that it receives.

A router, on the other hand, is an intelligent device that can apply logic to its processing of each packet. Packets are received and buffered while it determines what to do with them. If the packet's header structure has been damaged in transit, the router is unable to forward it. For lack of an appropriate route for the damaged packet, the router discards it, leaving the originating host's transmission control protocol to detect the loss and retransmit.

Packets that are received intact, and have a destination address that the router recognizes, are routed. This process involves looking up the destination address in the routing table to determine both the next hop and, more importantly, out of which interface the packet should be sent. Then the packet is sent. Implicit in this description is the fact that routers regenerate packets; they do not simply amplify them and send them on their way as repeaters do.

> **NOTE**
>
> Routers operate at Layer 3 of the OSI Reference Model. As such, they receive and transmit packets, not frames. Frames are indigenous to Layer 2, the Data Link Layer.

Physical Transmission Media

In order to reliably and consistently perform its transmit and receive functions, the Physical Layer must make certain assumptions about the world between the media interfaces of the two communicating devices. For example, the Physical Layer protocols must assume certain levels of performance for the media types that they support. The Physical Layer expects the actual performance of the media to be in compliance, regardless of what must be done to maintain that compliance.

Transmission media include any means of actually transporting signals generated by the OSI's Layer 1 mechanisms. Given this definition, transmission media can be either tangible or intangible. The intangible media are described in Chapter 4, "The 'Not-so-Physical' Physical Layer."

Tangible transmission media types include:

- Coaxial cable
- Twisted pair wire
- Fiber optic cabling

These media types, and their strengths, limitations, and LAN uses, are described throughout the remainder of this chapter.

Coaxial Cable

Coaxial cable, almost always referred to as "co-ax," has two concentric conductors. It is, quite literally, coaxial in that both conductors share a common axis. The most common version of this cable type consists of a single conducting copper wire insulated by a dielectric material. This dielectric material is then wrapped in another cylindrical conductor. This cylindrical conductor can be either a solid or braided wire. It is then wrapped in another layer of insulation and the whole assembly is covered with a protective outer jacket of either polyvinyl chloride (PVC) or Teflon. A sectional view is presented in Figure 3.6.

FIGURE 3.6.

Sectional view of a typical coaxial cable.

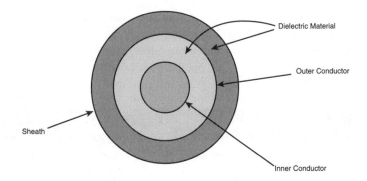

A side perspective of coaxial cable is rendered in Figure 3.7, with the layers peeled back to reveal its anatomy. Although coaxial cables may look the same, they have many different grades of impedance. They are rated by a *Radio Grade* (RG) scale. For example, the 10Base-2 Ethernet variant uses RG-58, which offers a 50 ohm impedance in a wire that's 3/8 of an inch thick. In the 10Base-2 Physical Layer specification, this translates into a 10Mbps signaling speed for up to 185 meters.

FIGURE 3.7.

Side perspective of coaxial cable.

Other, more highly specialized types of coaxial cabling exist, like fused-disk coaxial cabling, but these are distinctly outside the scope of LANs.

The advantage of co-ax cable is that it can support high bandwidth communications over relatively long, repeater-less runs. Co-ax was the original transmission media specified for Ethernet.

Since then, it has been completely supplanted by the various twisted pair-based Ethernet Physical Layer specifications.

The reasons for this functional obsolescence are simple. Co-ax is a relatively fragile cable assembly. Co-ax does not suffer kinks, severe bends, or even crushing pressure gracefully. Any of these can permanently damage the cable structure and directly inhibit signal transmission.

Additional disincentives to use co-ax are its cost and its size. Coaxial cabling is more expensive than twisted pair, due to its more complex construction. Each cable is also 3/8 inch or more in diameter. Thus, co-ax consumes a tremendous amount of space in cable ducts, raceways, and so forth. Even a modest concentration of co-ax devices quickly consumes any available space for cable runs.

Today, co-ax is limited to delivery of broadband Cable Television (CATV) signals to cable subscribers.

Twisted Pair Wire

Twisted Pair wiring, long used to support voice communications, has become the de facto standard wiring technology for LANs. A twisted pair consists of two relatively thin wires, 18 to 24 American Wire Gauge (AWG)—or 0.016 to 0.035 inches in diameter. These wires are coated with a thin layer of polyvinyl chloride (PVC), and spiraled around each other. This twist is highly functional: it helps cancel out any electromagnetic interference (EMI) that would otherwise be inducted into the copper by providing a balanced radiation of energy between the two wires.

The gauge, or thickness, of the wire is directly related to its performance capabilities. Thicker wires translate into a wider potential communications band (in other words, greater bandwidth) and longer potential wire runs. Unfortunately, as the bandwidth increases with wire gauge, so does attenuation. Consequently, a balance must be struck between bandwidth and distance for each gauge of wire. Striking this balance is one of the key features of a Physical Layer specification. It does not describe the wire path, but does specify gauge, terminator types, maximum distances, and bandwidth.

> **NOTE**
>
> Straight, untwisted copper wire of this gauge is known as an antenna! It is more adept at picking up ambient electromagnetic radiation than it is at retaining it. As will be seen later in this chapter, twisted pair wiring is twisted for a reason; it enables cancellation of signal distortion. Without the twist, this cancellation mechanism is defeated. Remember this the next time you are tempted to install flat wire under the carpets rather than twisted pair.

Twisted pair wiring comes in a wide variety of shapes and sizes that range from a single pair of voice-grade wiring all the way up to 600-pair trunk cables. Some of these varieties, like the number of pairs bundled together, are intended to improve capacity. Others improve throughput. Several techniques can be used to improve throughput:

- Increase the thickness of the conductor.
- Increase the twist rate.
- Use several different twist rates in bundles of multiple pairs.
- Shield the pairs with a metallic barrier.

For LANs, four pairs of twisted pair wires are usually bundled together within a common sheathing. The sheathing can be either another layer of PVC or Teflon. Teflon is much more expensive and rigid than PVC, but it does not emit toxic fumes when combusting. Consequently, it must be used for cable runs through any ducts or plenums that supply air to the occupants of a building.

The two main varieties of twisted four-pair are *shielded* and *unshielded*.

Shielded Twisted Pair

Shielded twisted pair (STP) features an extra layer of either foil or braided metallic wire that envelops the twisted pairs. This shielding lies directly below the surface of the jacketing. The intent of its design was to enable the twisted pairs to operate in environments prone to Electromagnetic Interference (EMI) and/or Radio Frequency Interference (RFI). In practice, it actually impeded the normal functioning of the twisted pairs. Electromagnetic radiation normally emanates from the signals transmitted over a copper wire. This radiation is illustrated in Figure 3.8, and establishes a point of reference for understanding the implications of using shielded twisted pair.

FIGURE 3.8.

Normal electromagnetic radiation.

Shielding the wire with a metallic barrier protects the signal from ambient radiation that may be inducted. Induction of external radiation helps attenuate and/or distort the signal. Unfortunately, this shielding also prevents the normal radiation depicted in Figure 3.8 from escaping! Instead, this radiation reflects back into the copper conductor of the wire and can cause a signal to be self-impeding. This situation is illustrated in Figure 3.9.

FIGURE 3.9.
Shielded electromagnetic radiation.

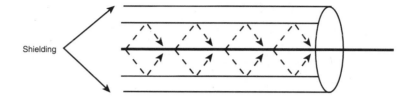

Shielding

Shielding is critical to the successful transmission over straight, single-conductor wiring (like coaxial cable), but it is usually more detrimental than beneficial to twisted pair. Twisted pair wiring uses an error-correction mechanism that is capable of canceling out any inducted noise. Coaxial cabling takes the opposite approach. Rather than cancel out inducted noise, it uses shielding to block its entry to the signal path. The layers of dielectric insulation between its two conductors help minimize the radiation of its own signals. Shielded twisted pair successfully prevents extraneous noise from being inducted. Unfortunately, shielding without dielectric insulation results in the self-impedance of signals.

Unshielded Twisted Pair

Twisted pair wiring also comes in an unshielded variety. Unshielded twisted pair, commonly called "UTP," is available in several different forms, sizes, and grades. As indicated earlier, size describes the number of pairs bundled together. The standard wiring for LANs is four-pair.

Four-pair UTP features eight wires, separated into groups of two. Each pair consists of a positive and negative wire. Each wire is also called a *lead*. Leads are used in pairs. For example, one pair of leads supports only transmissions, another supports reception. The other wires, in most LANs, are not used.

> **NOTE**
>
> LANs that operate at signaling speeds of 100Mbps or higher over UTP typically use all four pairs.

Categories of Performance

Twisted pair wiring is a commodity: regardless of the manufacturer, one can reasonably expect consistent performance. This is due to the degree of standardization that has occurred in the telecommunications industry. If this sounds a bit vague, that's intentional. No single standards body is responsible for the care and maintenance of standards that define twisted pair. Instead, a loose collaboration of ANSI, the FCC, the EIA, and many other organizations provides the standards for cabling and even cable components, like terminators.

If this isn't enough of a radical departure from the normal approach to standards setting, consider this: the existing specifications do not define twisted pair! Although some standards do

3

THE PHYSICAL LAYER

establish guidelines for cabling and/or cable components, twisted pair is defined by Categories of Performance. The categories are defined by their functions, and not by any physical standard. In other words, all a given manufacturer has to do to prove compliance is to demonstrate performance, regardless of how the wire was made, how thick it is, from what it is made, or anything else.

Originally, there were five series of tests to establish benchmark performance categories for twisted pair wiring. These were numbered 1 through 5, and compliant wire was identified as being Category x, or Cat-x, with x being the numeric test series that was achieved. Over time, the market has coalesced into just two viable performance levels: Cat-3 and Cat-5. Categories 1 and 2 were officially obsoleted in 1995, due to inadequate performance vis-a-vis requirements. Cat-4 offers a median level of performance, relative to 3 and 5, but is seldom (if ever) used.

Category 3 UTP offers 16MHz of bandwidth, which translates into signaling speeds up to 10Mbps at 100 meters. Category 4 can support 20MHz, and Category 5 can support up to 100MHz. This range demonstrates why Cat-4 has failed to gain support in the market. It has not been perceived as providing enough of a performance differential to be worth the bother. Anyone needing more bandwidth than Cat-3 can offer simply installs Cat-5. Provided users adhere to the distance limitations of whichever LAN architecture they choose, Cat-5 can provide 100Mbps, 155Mbps, and even 256Mbps. Obviously, as the signaling speed increases, the maximum distance decreases. Nevertheless, the middle ground between Cat-3 and Cat-5 has proven to be uneconomical.

Special Considerations

Twisted pair wiring, regardless of the Category or type, uses separate, physical wires for the positive and negative leads of the transmit and receive functions. For two devices to communicate, they must agree on which device(s) is to transmit and which to receive on which wire leads. Consequently, there is the potential for wiring devices together incorrectly.

Under normal circumstances, devices that are to be wired directly together (a PC and a hub, for example) have complementary interfaces that automatically provide the cross-over function. Terminal equipment, like the NICs in PCs and servers, is considered Data Terminal Equipment (DTE).

Modems, and the ports on a hub, among others, are considered Data Communications Equipment (DCE). The relationship between the lead assignments of DCE and DTE is illustrated in Figure 3.10, using the RJ-45 interface of 10Mbps Ethernet as an example.

These complementary interfaces enable terminal and communications gear to be directly cabled together without causing conflicts between transmits and receives. Under normal operating circumstances, a DCE device always connects to a DTE device, and vice versa, using a four-pair whose leads remain consistent from end to end. Such a cable is called a *straight-through cable*.

FIGURE 3.10.

DCE versus DTE.

DCE		DTE
Receive-Positive (R+)	Lead #1	Transmit-Positive (T+)
Receive-Negative (R-)	Lead #2	Transmit-Negative (T-)
Transmit-Positive (T+)	Lead #3	Receive-Positive (R+)
Not Used	Lead #4	Not Used
Not Used	Lead #5	Not Used
Transmit-Negative (T-)	Lead #6	Receive-Negative(R-)
Not Used	Lead #7	Not Used
Not Used	Lead #8	Not Used

The terms "DTE device" or "DCE device" are used on a per-port basis. Thus, both can apply to any single multiport device. For example, a hub can have both DCE and DTE ports, depending upon the nature of the port. Ports that serve as outbound ports to other hubs are set up as DCE. Ports that are used to connect computing equipment (inbound connections) are DTE. Older hubs had a specific port that was reserved for outbound connections. Some were selectable inbound or outbound.

The current generation of multi-architecture switching hubs has all but obviated the outbound port. High bandwidth, switched backplanes can be used to create extended LANs. Alternatively, a cross-over cable can be used to link two hubs using just inbound ports. The proper uses of straight-through and cross-over cables are illustrated in Figure 3.11.

FIGURE 3.11.

Cross-over Wiring for DTE to DTE communications (RJ-45 10Base-T).

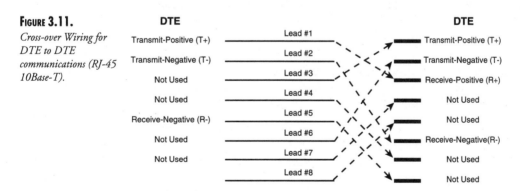

Cross-over cables must maintain the polarity of a physical wire. Positive and negative voltages must be kept separate. The only wires that are crossed over are the positive Transmit (T+) to the positive Receive (R+), and the negative Transmit (T-) to the negative Receive (R-).

Fiber Optic Cable

Fiber optic cables are capable of carrying the higher frequencies of the Electromagnetic Spectrum: light. Fiber optic cables come in a seemingly infinite variety of shapes, sizes, and wavelength ratings. Figure 3.12 demonstrates the side view of a fiber optic cable. Please note, these are of a typical cable and, consequently, may not exactly depict any particular type.

FIGURE 3.12.

Side view of fiber optic cable.

Fiber optic cabling has only three apparent constants:

- The center axis of the cable is occupied by a high-purity optical media that is capable of reliably carrying light patterns over long distances.

- The lack of either an electrical signal or pliable copper conductor means that fiber-based transmissions are relatively secure. Unlike copper wire, fiber optic cabling is virtually impossible to tap into. Remember, when stressed sufficiently, glass shatters. That stops the signal.

- The optical media, called the fiber, is clad with a concentric, protective layer of plastic.

Aside from these basic truisms, there is a world of variety in fiber optics. For starters, the optical media is almost always glass, but can be optical-quality plastic. The diameter varies from 5 microns (millionths of an inch) on up to sizes that are quite a bit easier to see with the naked eye. All types of fiber are usually available in bundles of two or more pairs. Fibers can also come in a variety of frequency ratings; not all are suitable for use in a LAN! The typical LAN-grade fiber optic cable is the 62.5 micron diameter glass variety. It supports multimode communications driven by a Light Emitting Diode (LED).

Fibers are usually described with a pair of numbers. For example, an extremely common LAN-grade fiber is known as 62.5/125 micron glass. The first number is the diameter, in microns, of the fiber. The second number, also in microns, measures the diameter of the cladding that protects the fiber.

Fiber optic cables are used in pairs: one for transmitting and one for receiving. Their uses in a LAN are usually limited to either server connections or hub interconnections. Figure 3.13 illustrates both these uses, as well as the directionality of each fiber.

FIGURE 3.13.
*Uses and directionality
of fiber in a LAN.*

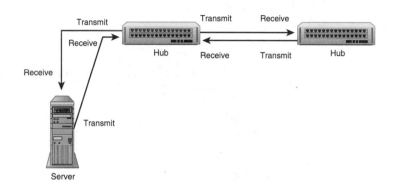

Light can either radiate outward, as in a lantern, or it can be focused directionally, just as a flashlight does. However, even directionally focused light is subject to some measure of dispersion. Anyone who's ever used a flashlight knows that the size of the circle projected by the light's beam increases over distance. This is an important point, as it holds significant ramifications for optical signal transmissions.

Specifically, there are two types of fiber optic transmissions:

- Multimode
- Single mode

There are many differences in the way that communications are driven in each of these fiber optic systems. These differences are centered around the transmission techniques.

Multimode

Multimode transmission is driven by a Light Emitting Diode (LED). An LED that fails, so the old joke goes, becomes a Dark Emitting Diode: DED.

LEDs are not a very concentrated light source; consequently, they require a fairly wide transmission path. They also have a relatively low frequency (for light, that is!), so their bandwidth potential is also fairly limited. The key characteristic of LEDs, however, is their dispersion. LEDs are not capable of tightly concentrating the beam of light. After it is transmitted, the light is subject to dispersion. This rate of dispersion imposes practical maximums on the effective distance of LED-driven fiber optic cabling.

3

THE PHYSICAL LAYER

Figure 3.14 illustrates the normal dispersion of an LED beam within a fiber optic cable.

FIGURE 3.14.

LED dispersion within multimode fiber.

Over enough distance, this dispersion results in some of the LED beam impacting the inside wall of the glass media. When this happens, the impact is at a very shallow angle. Consequently, the light does not escape into the cladding. Rather, it is reflected off the wall at a complementary angle. This reflection puts the dispersed beam(s) onto a collision course with the portion of the beam that remains in an axial transmission path. This is illustrated in Figure 3.15.

FIGURE 3.15.

Reflection causes multiple modes.

It is important to remember that these reflections still bear the same signal as the beam that remains aligned with the center axis of the glass. But, because they are subjected to a series of ricochets off the walls, they travel farther than the axial beam, while the physical media length remains constant. Constant, too, is the speed at which light travels. Remember, 186,000 miles per second is more than just a good idea: it's the law! Thus, the axial transmission arrives before the multiple reflections (that is, *modes*) of the same signal.

A more significant implication of this multimodal dispersion is that even photons can have an impact on other photons. The incessant zig-zagging of beams means that the multiple modes will inevitably cross the center axis and collide with other signal transmissions. In other words, multimode transmissions are prone to attenuation.

Multiple transmission modes can also be prematurely induced by improper terminations on the fiber optic cable, and/or by connectors that are not securely fastened to the hardware interface. Terminations that are not concentric always increase the modal dispersion of the beam. Similarly, terminations that are not secured tightly to the hardware interface also artificially increase multimodal dispersion. Although multimodal dispersion is normal, and may even be relied upon by the hardware, these two factors exaggerate the multimodal dispersion of the signal. Both cause the beam to enter the fiber at an angle to the center axis. This angled entry results in:

- Much steeper angles of reflection than the angles caused by normal radiation of the beam
- Little, if any, of the beam traveling axially

Consequently, little, if any, useable data succeeds in reaching the destination. If the angles of reflection are steep enough, the multimodal paths may be long enough to enable other signals (traveling axially, but transmitted later) to arrive at the destination first! This can confuse the receiving device. If nothing else, it wastes system resources as that recipient tries to decide what to do with these multiple signals.

In short, nothing good can come of these two forms of artificially fostered multimodal dispersion. They should be considered unacceptable.

The myriad performance limitations of multimode fiber optics are balanced against some of their more endearing qualities. Specifically, the cable and the hardware that drives it are both inexpensive compared to single mode systems. The cabling is easier to terminate, because it is several times larger than single-mode fibers.

Single Mode

Single mode fiber uses an Injection LASER Diode (ILD). The word LASER is properly capitalized, as it is an acronym for "Light Amplification by Stimulated Emission of Radiation." LASERS are well known for their highly concentrated beam. This beam still disperses, but almost immeasurably across distances that are practical within the scope of LANs.

In a single mode fiber optic system, a LASER is used to drive the signal through the glass. Its dispersion characteristics are sufficiently mild so that the beam, even at the outer limits of its practical range, does not disperse enough to begin touching the inside walls of the fiber. Consequently, the stream of data that is transmitted remains aligned with the center axis of the glass along the entire path of the media. It reaches its destination in a single mode, in other words, all at once.

Single mode fiber optics are usually between five and ten microns, with a 125-micron cladding. The costs of the fiber and the LASER hardware, in conjunction with the high available bandwidth, make this more of a commercial-grade infrastructure technology than a LAN technology. Consequently, its greatest use is in the commercial telephone networks.

Summary

In the Physical Layer of the OSI Reference Model, frames of data are chipped into streams of 1s and 0s (or ons and offs) for transmission across the network. Although the Physical Layer does not include the transmission media, it must define its expected performance parameters for anything that lies between the two media interfaces of the devices that are communicating. Thus, cabling is an extremely important adjunct to the Physical Layer. Deciding which cable type is best depends entirely on your particular situation. Many factors need to be considered, including the following:

- Physical premise construction
- Capability to add new cabling
- Performance parameters of the various parts of your network
- Embedded base of wire
- Fire codes and regulations
- The Physical Layer specifications that are supported by the network architecture

It is highly likely that the best cabling scheme for you will be a combination of two, maybe more, types of cable. The *de facto* standard in the marketplace appears to be Category 5 Unshielded Twisted Pair for station connectivity, with 62.5/125 micron fiber optics (rated at 850 nm) used to interconnect hubs, as well as to connect hubs to servers.

It is also likely that none of these are well suited to your particular needs. If that's the case, perhaps Chapter 4, "The 'Not-so-Physical' Physical Layer," is for you.

The "Not-so-Physical" Physical Layer

by Mark Sportack

CHAPTER 4

IN THIS CHAPTER

Local Area Networks can also be implemented on an intangible Physical Layer. Such networks, known as wireless LANs, have been around for quite a few years. Only recently, with the adoption of the Institute of Electrical and Electronics Engineers' (IEEE) 802.11 specification, have any standards existed in this area. Consequently, each manufacturer was previously free to develop highly proprietary and non-interoperable products. The functional disparities between these proprietary products centered around their transmission technologies and techniques. The new IEEE 802.11 standard integrates support for many of these previously proprietary technologies and techniques.

This chapter examines the various intangible implementations of the Physical Layer, their transmission techniques and their properties (as dictated by the Electromagnetic Spectrum). This chapter also looks at some of the more salient points of the 802.11 specification.

The Electromagnetic Spectrum

Local Area Networks that use unguided transmissions to transport data and protocols have come to be known as *wireless LANs*. Before exploring the various transmission technologies that are used by wireless LANs, it is necessary to examine the Electromagnetic Spectrum. The Electromagnetic Spectrum defines the physical characteristics of transmissions, according to their frequency.

"Frequency" is one of those funny words that everyone understands, but few can define properly. Frequency is more than just a setting on a radio's dial. It is actually the rate at which an electrical current alternates between positive and negative states. The rate is usually measured in Hertz (Hz). One cycle, or Hertz, represents a 360 degree change. In other words, one cycle begins with the current at the origin, progresses upward to a maximum value, declines back to the origin, passes through it, reaches a minimum value, and returns to the origin.

Wavelengths are also used to describe higher frequency phenomena, like the various forms of light, and both X and gamma rays. A wavelength is the distance from the top of one wave's crest to the top of the next wave's crest.

Figure 4.1 illustrates one Hertz and one wavelength.

> **NOTE**
>
> Hertz, the universal measurement of the frequency of electrical vibrations, or cycles, per second, is named after Heinrick Hertz. Mr. Hertz discovered electromagnetic waves in 1883.

The Electromagnetic Spectrum starts at 0Hz and reaches in excess of 10 to the 20th power! To put this tremendous range of frequencies into perspective, the human ear is capable of detecting electrical vibrations ranging from 20 up to approximately 16,000 to 20,000Hz. This varies greatly by age and by person, however. The human ear is adapted to maximize reception of vocal vibrations, and most voice energy falls between 3,000 and 4,000Hz.

FIGURE 4.1.

One Hertz versus one wavelength.

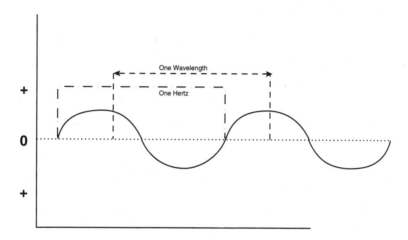

The spectrum continues upward, well beyond the range of human hearing, and encompasses frequencies that are categorized by their physical properties. Beyond audible sound are the radio frequencies (which range from 500 kilo-Hertz—kHz—up to 300 giga-Hertz—GHz—and include microwaves) and the various forms of light, including infrared, the visible spectrum, ultraviolet, X-Rays, and Gamma Rays. The frequencies of light become ridiculously large numbers. Consequently, their wavelengths are used to describe them, instead. Wavelengths, inversely related to frequency, become ridiculously small numbers as one progresses through the various forms of light.

The Electromagnetic Spectrum is illustrated in Figure 4.2, complete with both frequencies and wavelength metrics.

FIGURE 4.2.

The electromagnetic spectrum.

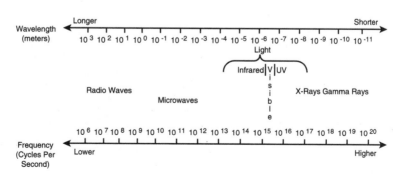

Spectral Characteristics

The characteristics of wave propagation change with the increase of Hertz along the spectrum. The three most pertinent characteristics of the wave, at least as far as wireless LANs are concerned, are the following:

- Frangibility
- Directionality
- Bandwidth

The lower frequencies are remarkably durable. They are capable of penetrating opaque solids, with varying degrees of success. Radio waves, for example, can penetrate all but the densest of materials. Thus, they are not very frangible.

These radio waves also propagate omnidirectionally. That is, they *radiate* (hence, the name *radio*) out uniformly from their transmitter. This is illustrated in Figure 4.3.

FIGURE 4.3.
Omnidirectional radiation of signal.

Radio Transmitter

The higher frequencies behave more like light. In fact, the higher frequencies *are* light. The visible portion of the spectrum is relatively narrow, and is flanked by two other forms of invisible light: infrared and ultraviolet.

Higher frequency signals are very frangible. They become less and less capable of penetrating opaque solids, regardless of their thickness or density, as their frequency increases. They also don't necessarily radiate as illustrated in Figure 4.3. Their propagation can be more directionally oriented. This is illustrated in Figure 4.4.

FIGURE 4.4.

Focused directionality of light-based transmission.

The capability to directionally focus electromagnetic vibrations increases with the Hertz rate. The higher the rate, the better the vibrations can be focused. For example, a lamp can radiate light omnidirectionally. However, a flashlight uses a reflective cone to focus radiating light unidirectionally. The focused light continues to radiate, and forms a conical shape. This phenomenon was depicted in Figure 4.4. Generally speaking, lower frequencies cannot be focused as effectively as higher frequencies.

Bandwidth and the Spectrum

Bandwidth is yet another commonly used term that is poorly understood. It is, literally, the *width* of a communications channel, as measured in Hertz. The prefix, *band*, was the original term used to describe what's commonly known as a *channel*. A channel is a frequency range, designated for a specific communications purpose.

Bandwidth, then, is the difference between the upper and lower frequency boundaries of a communications channel. For example, the 902-928 *Megahertz* (MHz—millions of hertz) band is reserved for unregulated radio communications in support of industrial, scientific, or medical purposes. This portion of the spectrum yields 26MHz of bandwidth.

> **NOTE**
>
> The Federal Communications Commission (FCC) was established in 1934 by the Communications Act of that year. One of the FCC's myriad responsibilities is establishing both the bands and their applications for interstate communications that originate in the United States.

Hertz is typically used only to measure voice or analog communications. Digital communications are more properly measured in *bits per second* (bps). The potential for data rate in fiber-optic systems is usually described in wavelengths, unless a specific fiber-based technology is being described, like FDDI, in which case bps is used.

Hz and bps have a strong, positive correlation, as one bit can be transmitted per cycle. Unfortunately, due to the disparities in the modulation techniques required to support digital versus analog transmissions, the potential digital data rate is always less than the Hz rate. Extending this logic, bandwidth is only a valid metric of frequency; it does not directly measure the data rate of a transmission facility. In the real world, bandwidth has been generalized to mean available bits per second.

Whenever electrical vibrations are used to transport data, analog or digital, the series of vibrations are known as a *signal*. Signals can occur at any frequency, although it is generally acknowledged that anything below 300,000Hz is not practical for use by electrical devices.

What Does This Mean?

The point of this exploration of the physical properties of the various portions of the Electromagnetic Spectrum is to provide the proper context for a meaningful examination of the various approaches to wireless signal transmission in LANs.

Each transmission technology operates in a specific portion of the spectrum. This dictates its physical characteristics. The basic tradeoffs between physical characteristics are presented in Table 4.1.

Table 4.1. Spectrally determined signal characteristics.

Low Frequency	High Frequency
Broad Radiation of Transmitted Signal	Potential for Tightly Focused Transmitted Signal
Persistent Signal	Highly Frangible Signal
Low Bandwidth	High Bandwidth

The physical characteristics of a transmission technology, in turn, dictate the operational characteristics of the wireless LAN. The characteristics of a wireless LAN that are dictated include:

- Maximum effective ranges
- Potential for penetrating sheet rock walls, cubicle partitions, and other physical obstructions
- Maximum transmission rate

NOTE

Spectrum selection has an impact upon the maximum effective distances of a wireless LAN in more than one way. Effective transmission distances, particularly in the more persistent lower frequencies, are also limited by FCC regulations. These regulations impose maximum limits on the power with which transmissions can be made on any given band. Although artificial, and not an innate characteristic of the Electromagnetic Spectrum, these limitations are every bit as real and binding.

The transmission technique used determines the wireless LAN's maximum sustainable data rate. Data rates are always less than transmission rates, due to the overheads of the LAN's protocols, inefficiencies in the way that data is placed on the LAN, and numerous other factors.

The issues identified here form the crux of the functional differences between the various wireless transmission technologies. It is essential to recognize their performance impacts, and the implications of transmission techniques, before selecting a wireless LAN product.

Wireless LANs

The use of either light or radio waves for the unguided transmission of LAN frames and protocols has come to be known as *Wireless Local Area Networking*. This name is misleading. The vast majority of the purported wireless LAN products do not eliminate wire as a Physical Layer component. They merely reduce the amount of wire needed to construct a LAN.

At least four different scenarios demonstrate the versatility of wireless transmission technologies within a LAN.

- Wireless station connectivity
- Wireless peer-to-peer connectivity
- Wireless hub interconnect
- Wireless bridging

Each of these scenarios uses wireless transmission technologies in a different way.

Wireless Station Connectivity

Wireless station connectivity enables a mobile user with a laptop to establish a LAN connection without a dedicated, wired connection to a hub. A wire path is still needed to connect individual workstations to a transmitter/receiver. This is illustrated in Figure 4.5. In this diagram, a laptop computer is connected to a portable radio antenna via its PCMCIA slot.

NOTE

PCMCIA is now widely recognized as the name for a credit card-like device that inserts in a corresponding slot on laptop computers, and provides additional functionality. The abbreviation's expansion, Personal Computer Memory Card International Association, is almost never used.

FIGURE 4.5.
Wireless station connectivity.

Laptop PC

Wireless Hub

The laptop's antenna in Figure 4.5 transmits framed data to, and receives framed data from, the corresponding antenna associated with the so-called wireless LAN hub. For the purposes of illustration it is shown attached, but this antenna is usually a module separate from the hub. This allows the antenna to be mounted much higher than the hub, thereby improving transmission coverage. The two devices must be wired together. The wireless hub is equipped with an uplink wire port that enables it to be physically connected to a more conventional, wire-based LAN backbone. The only thing that's wireless about this example is the connection between the PC and its hub.

This scenario is useful for providing connectivity to a highly mobile work force.

Wireless Peer-to-Peer Connectivity

A simple (but relatively low throughput) wireless LAN can be established between peers. Figure 4.6 shows a wireless peer-to-peer network that can be assembled relatively easily. Each device within the effective transmission range can enjoy resource sharing with peers, provided that they have the appropriate permissions.

FIGURE 4.6.
Wireless peer-to-peer connectivity.

Laptop PC

Laptop PC

The relatively informal nature of peer-to-peer networking directly translates into very low performance parameters for wireless peer-to-peer networks.

Wireless Hub Interconnection

Another approach for building wireless LANs is depicted in Figure 4.7. This approach uses only a single pair of transmit/receive antennas for a cluster of workstations. These workstations are cabled to a conventional hub. The uplink port on this hub is wired to the radio gear. This radio is used to communicate with a corresponding radio that is also hard-wired to the LAN's backbone. The only thing that is wireless about this scenario is the hub-to-hub communications. The benefit of this approach is that it obviates the need for wiring from the telephone closets to the user stations. The user stations can be wired relatively easily using pre-terminated cables.

FIGURE 4.7.
Wireless hub interconnectivity.

The scenario depicted in Figure 4.7 is extremely useful for providing connectivity in buildings that are difficult and/or expensive to rewire. A building may be resistant to wiring if it is historic and, therefore, protected from further modifications. Or, a building may have been constructed in such a way as to make additional wire installation prohibitively expensive. Poured concrete floors without raceways for cabling, for example, greatly increase the cost of running cabling to desktops.

Although the example presented in Figure 4.7 uses radio waves, the example would be just as valid using other portions of the Electromagnetic Spectrum—like LASER or infrared—for its transmission technology.

Wireless Bridges

Wireless technologies can also be applied to other aspects of a LAN. For example, two wire-based LANs can be bridged together using a wireless bridge. This is illustrated in Figure 4.8.

FIGURE 4.8.
Wireless bridging of wire-based LANs.

Wireless bridging enables LANs that are in relatively close proximity, but beyond the maximum network diameter supported by their LAN architecture, to be bridged together. This spares the cost of acquiring two routers, as well as the monthly recurring expense of a leased line that would otherwise be required to interconnect the LANs.

Wireless bridges offer approximately 2Mbps of bandwidth across several miles. This is more bandwidth than a 1.544Mbps T1 leased line can offer, without the monthly recurring expense. The economics of wireless bridging are fairly compelling: for an equivalent start-up cost (radio gear versus routers), the wireless bridge offers "free" connectivity for its entire useful life.

These examples are some of the typical implementations of wireless technologies in a LAN. Other implementations are possible, but they tend to be fairly specific to a single transmission technology, and are presented within the context of that technology.

Transmission Technologies

The four different transmission technologies each utilize a different section of the Electromagnetic Spectrum. These four methods are:

- Spread spectrum radio
- Narrowband or single band radio
- Infrared
- LASER

The first two methods, in keeping with FCC regulations, limit effective transmission ranges by keeping transmission wattage to absolute minimums. The ranges of the last two—LASER and infrared—are naturally limited by their inability to penetrate opaque solids of any thickness or density, as well as by FCC regulations. For example, radio waves are quite capable of penetrating all but the very densest of buildings. Typically, several steel-reinforced concrete walls are needed to noticeably attenuate radio waves. Light, like infrared and LASER beams, is much more fragile. A piece of paper, or even a puff of smoke or fog, is all that it takes to completely attenuate optically based signals.

> **NOTE**
>
> These four transmission technologies presented here are solely for your academic enrichment. They may or may not actually be embodied in generally available wireless LAN technologies.

Spread Spectrum Radio Frequency

The FCC, through Part 15.247 of its regulations, has allocated the 902–928MHz and 2.4–2.4835GHz bands of the Electromagnetic Spectrum for industrial, scientific, and medical (ISM) use. These bands are referred to as the *ISM bands*, and have been allocated for spread spectrum radio transmissions within the ISM arena. Additionally, the FCC recently identified the 5.725–5.850GHz band as also being available for spread spectrum radio transmissions.

The 2.4–2.4835GHz band is frequently expressed in the rounded form: 2.4–2.484GHz.

Use of these bands is unlicensed in that, beyond establishing guidelines for the electrical and electronic devices that use these bands, the FCC does not actively regulate who uses these bands. This is contrary to the model that the FCC applies to other portions of the spectrum. Typically, an individual or entity is given the exclusive license to operate on a specific band within a specified geographic region. Radio stations are a good example. In return for their guarantee to abide by the guidelines established by the FCC, they are given exclusive, regional licenses to specific bands.

Two primary transmission techniques can be used in conjunction with the previously described spread spectrum transmission technologies. These techniques define the manner in which the "not-so-physical" transmission media are used. These techniques are:

- Frequency Hopping
- Direct Sequence

Frequency Hopping

Frequency hopping is a technique that is used only in conjunction with a spread spectrum radio transmission system. Spread spectrum provides an unregulated range of radio frequencies. Frequency hopping can be described as a happy medium between baseband and broadband transmissions. An examination of baseband versus broadband helps to make this description clearer.

Baseband transmissions use the entire available bandwidth as a single channel: the same signal is sent across the entire band. Figure 4.9 illustrates a baseband transmission by presenting a binary stream that completely fills the "pipe" as it transmits. A good example of a baseband transmission mechanism is Ethernet. It uses all available bandwidth, either 10, 100, or more Mbps, as a single transmission vehicle.

FIGURE 4.9.
Baseband transmission.

Broadband transmissions channelize the available bandwidth into multiple, smaller, channels. Each sub-channel is used to support a different signal transmission. This is illustrated in Figure 4.10. An example of a broadband transmission vehicle is cable television. A single coaxial cable provides bandwidth that is channelized. Each channel carries different signals, even though it shares a common transmission vehicle with other channels.

Frequency hopping, like broadband, subdivides the bandwidth into multiple sub-channels. These channels are used one at a time to support signal transmission. Unlike broadband, a signal hops from channel to channel, at a predetermined rate, and according to a predetermined sequence. This is illustrated in Figure 4.11.

FIGURE 4.10.

Broadband transmission.

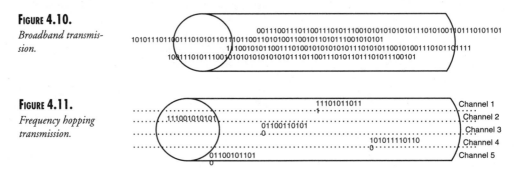

FIGURE 4.11.

Frequency hopping transmission.

Frequency hopping has several benefits. First, it helps minimize the impact of signal interference. Interference, specifically *Radio Frequency Interference* (RFI) and *Electromagnetic Interference* (EMI), can distort a signal in transit. Typically, interference from any given source confines itself to a fairly consistent frequency. Thus, hopping across multiple available frequencies obviates much of the potential harm of RFI and EMI.

Perhaps a more significant benefit of frequency hopping is that it allows multiple access units to be placed within one another's effective transmission zones. Figure 4.12 illustrates the overlap of transmission zones. If the PCs in this figure were using a single frequency, baseband transmission, their two transmitters would conflict with each other. The throughputs of both would deteriorate. Using a frequency hopping, spread spectrum transmission system reduces the potential for collisions. Consequently, the user density serviced with this technology can be increased without compromising LAN performance.

FIGURE 4.12.

Overlapping transmission zones.

The greatest benefit, by far, is the security of a frequency hopping, spread spectrum transmission system. Spread spectrum transmissions are inherently secure. Anyone attempting to eavesdrop on a transmission must do three things:

- Defeat the physical security established around the limited effective transmission range
- Be able to capture signals transmitted on multiple channels
- Understand the seemingly random sequence of transmissions

> **NOTE**
>
> Spread spectrum radio transmission was the brainchild of actress Hedy Lamarr. In 1940, she conceived the idea as a means of securing radio transmission. Two years later, she was granted the patent rights to the concept. Unfortunately, decades would pass before the concept would finally be productized.

Direct Sequence

Direct Sequence, too, is pertinent only to spread spectrum radio frequency transmission systems. Unlike frequency hopping, which hops frequencies in a pseudo-random pattern, Direct Sequence uses the available sub-channels sequentially. Thus, it is easier to defeat the security of a Direct Sequence Spread Spectrum system than that of a frequency hopping system, because the spreading algorithm is much simpler. This concept is illustrated in Figure 4.13.

FIGURE 4.13.

Direct sequence transmission.

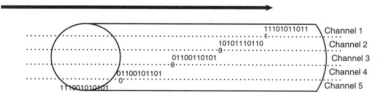

Defeating the security of a direct sequence spread spectrum transmission system still requires the defeat of any physical security that may protect the effective transmission range. Additionally, the perpetrator also needs to be able to trap signals on all the sub-channels simultaneously.

The IEEE has recently standardized wireless LANs through its 802.11 specification. This specification, described in detail in the section of this chapter entitled "IEEE 802.11," incorporates support for both frequency hopping and DSSS transmission systems.

The Pros

Spread spectrum is inherently safe from eavesdropping as it "spreads" transmissions one bit at a time into separate frequencies according to a predetermined frequency hopping algorithm. Defeating the security of this method is almost impossible. It requires gaining physical access to its effective transmission range and knowing the frequency hopping pattern over which the bits are spread.

The recent allocation of the 2.4–2.4835 and 5.725–5.850GHz bands means that spread spectrum technologies need not be low bandwidth. These higher frequencies contain adequate bandwidth to rival the performance of wire-based LANs.

Spread spectrum systems are also relatively inexpensive because the bands are not licensed. As a result, the manufacturers are able to provide the hardware at a cost much lower than that of comparable dedicated frequency products. More importantly, you (the customer and user) do not have to apply to the FCC for the rights to use a specific radio band in a specific location. Thus, you can have a wireless LAN up and running much more quickly and inexpensively than a LAN with a dedicated frequency technology.

The Cons

One of the inherent problems using radio frequency is that radio is not capable of full-duplex communication on a single frequency. Anyone who has used walkie-talkies understands the half-duplex nature of radio communications. Walkie-talkies require a push-to-talk method of transmission. Only one party can talk at a time. All other parties are forced to listen. The radio is either transmitting or receiving, but not both simultaneously.

In Ethernet networks, radio's use of half-duplex mode forces the conversion from the usual *Carrier Sense Multiple Access/Collision Detection* (CSMA/CD) protocol to *Carrier Sense Multiple Access/Collision Avoidance* (CSMA/CA).

These factors, with the overhead incurred by "spreading," reduce effective throughputs in an Ethernet-compatible network to approximately 2Mbps. Maximum effective throughput in a wire-based Ethernet, after subtracting CSMA/CD overheads, is approximately 5–5.5Mbps. This throughput limitation imposes a bottleneck in the current networking environment and prevents the use of any product embracing this methodology in all but the lowest usage applications.

> **NOTE**
>
> One solution that has been found to the problem imposed by radio's half-duplex nature is to utilize two separate frequencies: one for transmit, and one for receive. This enables the LAN to be full-duplex. Consequently, network throughput can be kept on par with wire-based Ethernet LANs.

A second concern regarding the use of spread spectrum radio frequency transmission is the lack of FCC licensing that would guarantee the user clear rights to the frequency within a given transmission zone. Given the transient nature of frequency utilization, limiting transmission wattage serves to reduce the possibility of collision. If throughputs are degraded below the existing 2Mbps level by competition with other spread spectrum devices, consumers have no legal recourse and are forced to accept the lower levels of performance. In a LAN environment, typical transmission zones are between 600 and 800 feet. This concentrated transmission range greatly reduces the opportunity for competition with other radio frequency vehicles.

Wireless bridging components, however, are available that have effective ranges of 3 to 5 miles. Pagers and other devices that use the 902–928MHz band are also direct competitors for this bandwidth. The potential for conflict with other radio frequency vehicles across this range, and the subsequent performance impacts, increases with the relative population densities of the transmission zone.

Single Band Radio Frequency

The opposite of a spread spectrum transmission technique is the single band transmission. Both are confined to the radio wave portion of the Electromagnetic Spectrum, but (as its name suggests) single band uses only a single channel, usually in the microwave band. As was illustrated in Figure 4.2, microwaves are actually high-frequency radio waves. The lowest frequency microwaves behave very much as radio waves do, while the highest-frequency microwaves begin to demonstrate some of the physical properties of light.

The use of a dedicated frequency means that FCC licensing must be obtained before you can legally transmit on that frequency. This technology, as a wireless LAN, was pioneered by Motorola and marketed under the name *Altair* and *Altair II*. Motorola obtained exclusive access to the 18–19GHz band from the FCC for all the major metropolitan markets in the USA.

Motorola acts as agent to the FCC on behalf of any customers wanting to utilize their technology. In this fashion, customers are spared the potential agony of obtaining FCC approval for the use of the frequency.

Implementation is facilitated by the retention of existing premise wire-based LAN backbones, PC NAUs, and software drivers. This implementation is illustrated in Figure 4.14.

FIGURE 4.14.

Typical dedicated channel wireless LAN.

Transmission wattage is approximately 25 milliwatts, which is too low to cause any health concerns that may arise due to the use of microwave transmission in populated areas. This wattage, in combination with the relatively frangible microwave signal, limits the effective range to approximately 140 feet of open air, or 40 feet of obstructed air. Obstructed air assumes three sheet rock walls as interference.

The gross bandwidth is approximately 15Mbps. Subtracting out standard Ethernet overheads plus the wire-to-wireless-to-wire conversion reduces this to an approximately 5.5Mbps data rate, which is the net equivalent throughput of a wire-based shared Ethernet.

Infrared

The next wireless transmission technology—infrared—operates between the visible part of the electromagnetic spectrum and the shortest microwaves. Although infrared is a form of light, it is not limited to line-of-sight vehicles only. This is because infrared is an invisible light. Even though it cannot penetrate opaque solids, it can reflect off them.

Two methodologies have emerged: diffuse and direct. Direct infrared is analogous to a flashlight's beam, while diffuse can best be thought of as a lantern. The flashlight focuses its light in a single direction while the lantern diffuses its light in all directions. A decrease in the intensity of the beam, as in the case of diffusers, results in a commensurate decrease in potential data rates.

Direct infrared technology is used in most, if not all, household consumer electronics with remote control devices. The remote control device must be pointed at the TV, VCR, stereo, and so forth before any commands entered via its keypad can be recognized by the appliance. This same concept applies to a direct infrared LAN.

The diffuse infrared LAN scatters its light omnidirectionally. The intent is to bounce the transmissions off ceilings and walls so that they may contact a transmit/receive device that is not directly in the line of sight.

The Pros

Infrared communications use a non-persistent signal form: light. They are incapable of penetrating even the least dense of opaque solids. As a result, they do not require FCC licensing to use. Rather, the FCC establishes the guidelines and operating parameters for the physical devices that use the Electromagnetic Spectrum. These guidelines are adhered to by the wireless LAN manufacturers, thereby guaranteeing the compliance of the user communities. This spares the users any tedious negotiations or complicated paper chases.

The Cons

Line-of-sight communications pose a severe handicap to forms of light-based transmissions. Many office environments are inherently unsuited, as even a single layer of sheet rock completely attenuates the signal.

Diffuse infrared partially overcomes the limitation of line-of-sight transmission by diffusing, and using reflectivity to radiate outward in ways not possible with line-of-sight direct transmissions. Unfortunately, given the highly frangible nature of an optical signal, much of the signal is attenuated on impact. Consequently, the effective range of a diffuse infrared system is extremely small, that is, less than 100 feet. The sustainable throughputs of this technology are also extremely modest!

LASER

LASER-based transmissions in a wireless LAN environment can be best thought of as a fiber-optic system without the fiber-optic cabling. This isn't a perfect analogy, because most LANs use fiber-optic systems driven by Light Emitted Diodes (LEDs). Nevertheless, the analogy conveys the image remarkably well.

The cost of LASER precludes its use on a station-by-station basis. Consequently, it is better applied in a virtually identical manner to the direct infrared. That is, multiple stations interconnect to an access unit that transmits and receives LASER signals on behalf of a group of stations. Thus, the cost of the LASER is spread across multiple end-points, thereby improving its cost effectiveness.

When LASERs are used in this manner, it is logical to mount the LASER devices near the ceiling, as far away from people as possible. This serves two purposes. First, it all but eliminates the possibility of accidental injury to human eyes. Second, it also reduces the possibility that human actions will disrupt the signal.

Alternatively, LASERs can be used to bridge together wire-based LANs across parking lots or other modest distances. As was explained in the section entitled "Wireless LANs" earlier in this chapter, this application provides more bits per second at less cost than leased lines and routers do.

> **NOTE**
>
> Although the word "laser" has crept into common usage, it is not a word at all. It is an acronym that describes the technique that creates it: Light Amplification by Stimulated Emission of Radiation.

The Pros

LASER light is extremely concentrated, and remains tightly focused. Consequently, it can be used effectively at longer distances than infrared. This enables it to be used as a wireless bridging technology. A LASER-based wireless LAN application works on the same principle as a radio wave application, which was illustrated in Figure 4.8, earlier in this chapter.

The Cons

As both light and infrared are forms of light, they suffer similar deficiencies. Specifically, their signals are frangible. Unguided LASERs and direct infrared are distinguished by two primary differences:

- Unguided LASERs and direct infared use different portions of the spectrum.
- LASERs are actually artificially concentrated light.

These two differences beget other important differences. First, LASERs are much more expensive than a comparable infrared system. They require more power to generate and concentrate the signal. They also give off more heat, though probably not enough to overcome a decent climate control system.

LASERs use the visible spectrum of light. As a result, they are a line-of-sight-only device. Their signal can be attenuated easily by smoke, fog—even raindrops in an outdoor installation.

> **NOTE**
>
> Attenuation is an electrical phenomenon. It is the reduction of a signal's strength caused by traveling through a transmission media. Remember, a signal is an electrical vibration. Energy, in the form of electricity, is expended to propel the signal along its transmission media. The signal is its own energy source, and constantly diminishes itself through travel.
>
> Optical signals are frequently thought of as being "different" from electrical signals. They are pulses of light and darkness rather than the polarity oscillations of an electrical current. Nevertheless, they are an extremely high-frequency vibration on the same Electromagnetic Spectrum. Consequently, optical signals are also subject to attenuation.
>
> Optical attenuation, however, tends to be more of a function of the signal's deterioration via collision with impurities in its transmission media.

A greater concern regarding the use of LASERs is the potential for permanent injury to the retinal sensors and nerves of the human eye. This requires any installation of a LASER transmission system to be carefully planned, especially when it is to be installed in a populated area.

The IEEE 802.11

The IEEE recently completed work on a standard for wireless Local Area Networking (WLAN). Development of this standard lagged behind the market, and was greatly complicated by the need to provide for many of the more common transmission technologies and techniques that were already prevalent in the marketplace.

The finished product specified the Media Access Control (MAC) method and numerous physical layers. As with any layered approach, the functionality of any given layer is insulated from the functionality of neighboring layers. In other words, the MAC Layer functions are not dependent upon data rates or any other characteristics of the Physical Layer specifications. Given the proliferation of Physical Layer technologies, this layering is essential.

This standard includes several sub-functions, including mechanisms to provide access control (both contention based and non-contention based) to several "not-so-physical" media. Each media type, too, is addressed in a separate Physical Layer specification.

Media Access

The media access method of 802.11 is a familiar one to long-time Ethernet aficionados: *Carrier Sense Multiple Access with Collision Avoidance* (CSMA/CA). This media access method was used on Ethernet II or DIX Ethernet.

CSMA/CA strives to avoid collisions by "listening" to the wire before it "talks." In the case of a WLAN, the station that wants to transmit must listen to the channel before transmitting. A clear signal means that it may transmit. If the signal contains framed data, that station must wait.

The CSMA/CA scheme strives to ensure equitable access to the bandwidth while still avoiding collisions. For example, it uses two timing techniques to enforce equitable bandwidth use.

- Minimum time delay
- Random backoff interval

The minimum time delay is used to ensure that a single transmitting station does not monopolize the bandwidth. After each successful frame transmission, the transmitter must wait until a minimum time delay elapses before it can transmit another frame.

The random backoff interval is used in two different scenarios. First, after enduring the minimum time delay following a successful transmission, the transmitting station must then endure a backoff interval before it can listen to the channel. If the channel is clear, it may then transmit its next frame. If, however, the channel is busy, that station must then endure a second backoff interval. This second use of the backoff interval continues repeatedly until the transmitter senses a clear channel. This arbitration method may, at first, sound unfair. In reality, each backoff is of random duration, and each station contains the same mechanisms for enacting a random duration backoff. Consequently, fairness in media access becomes a pseudo-random phenomenon.

Physical Layers

The three Physical Layer technologies that 802.11 supports with this MAC include

- Diffused Infrared (DFIR)
- Direct Sequence Spread Spectrum (DSSS)
- Frequency Hopping Spread Spectrum (FHSS)

Direct Sequence Spread Spectrum

802.11 supports DSSS at 1 or 2Mbps. The different data rates use different modulation techniques. The standard uses a subset of the 2.4–2.4835GHz band, and defines four sub-bands:

- .400–2.425GHz
- 2.414–2.440GHz,
- 2.429–2.455GHz
- 2.443–2.470GHz

Each sub-band is 26MHz wide, and overlaps its neighboring bands by about 11MHz.

Frequency Hopping Spread Spectrum

The 802.11 specification also uses the 2.4–2.4835GHz band, and supports two different modulation techniques and three hopping patterns. The standards-compliant FHSS WLAN can support data rates of either 1 or 2Mbps, depending upon which modulation technique is selected. The hopping patterns are structurally similar, and do not affect the sustainable data rate.

Both techniques comply with a single scheme for sub-banding. The available bandwidth is split into 79 sub-bands of 1MHz each. Each sub-band can support a minimum of 2.5 hops per second (hps) using any of the standardized hopping patterns. The intent of this minimum hps rate is to prevent data frames from being arbitrarily parsed and transmitted on different sub-bands. Frames that are distorted in transit, either partially or completely, need to be completely retransmitted. This scheme guarantees that packets don't arrive distorted.

Summary

The success of the IEEE 802.11 specification should be measured like the other IEEE specifications. If it works as expected, manufacturers will quickly modify their previously proprietary products to provide compliance. This will result in two measurable phenomena:

- WLANs will be able to interoperate across vendor platforms.
- The costs of WLANs will decrease due to the economies of scale that can be achieved by replacing vendor-specific chip sets with a single, standard set.

Wireless Local Area Networking has been an interesting, but somewhat quirky quagmire of non-interoperable products and technologies for the past few years. They failed to gain any broad acceptance, and were limited to market niches. The standardization of a common MAC and Physical Layer by the IEEE promises to overcome many of the previous limitations. The key indicators to watch are interoperability and price per desktop. As interoperability increases, and price per desktop decreases, WLANs may become more mainstream.

It is doubtful, however, that WLANs will ever become a substitute for wire-based LANs. Just as technological developments and standardization have boosted the capabilities of WLANs, their wired cousins have not been stagnating. Recent technological advances and standardization efforts continue to push the performance envelope of wire-based LANs. Thus, just as WLANs start to match the throughputs of wire-based LANs, those LANs increase their clock rates substantially.

Nevertheless, WLANs have some unique attributes that cannot be matched by LANs. Used properly, they can be extremely effective.

The Data Link Layer

by Mark Sportack

IN THIS CHAPTER

The second layer of the OSI Reference Model, as explained in Chapter 1, "A Networking Primer," is the Data Link Layer. This layer provides the interface between hardware and software.

This chapter closely examines the nature, structure, and function of data frames in a LAN by examining specific—and widely used—LAN architectures. These LAN architectures include Ethernet, Token Ring, and FDDI. The frame structures of these LAN protocols is examined, as well as the differences in the ways that each one accesses the physical transmission media. This chapter concludes with a review of the Data Link Layer technology selection and installation considerations.

OSI Layer 2

The second layer of the OSI Reference Model is called the Data Link Layer. It has two sets of responsibilities: transmit and receive.

On the transmit side, it is responsible for packing instructions, data, and so forth, into frames. A *frame* is a structure that contains enough information to make sure that the data can be sent across a network, either LAN or WAN, to its destination. Successful delivery occurs when the data reaches its intended destination intact. Thus, the frame also contains a mechanism to verify the integrity of its contents.

The source node, that is, the transmitter, must receive an acknowledgment that the frame was received intact. Frames that either collide or become corrupted in transit must be retransmitted until they arrive safely. Also, any frames whose receipt was not acknowledged by the intended recipient are also retransmitted.

The Data Link Layer is also responsible for re-assembling any binary streams that are received from the Physical Layer back into frames. Before passing the frame up to the next layer, it performs a mathematical check of the validity of the newly re-assembled frame's contents. This validation is known as a Cyclical Redundancy Check (CRC).

> **NOTE**
>
> Checksums are similar, but less complex, than Cyclical Redundancy Checks (CRCs). Checksum values are created by adding the binary value of each alphanumeric character in a block of data. This value is sent with the data to its destination, in a separate field. The recipient re-computes the checksum and compares its value with the value stored in the checksum field. If the two numbers are different, an error has occurred. If the two numbers are the same, the recipient assumes that no error has occurred. It is feasible that multiple bit errors could have occurred in transmission that yield the same checksum value.
>
> A Cyclical Redundancy Check is a more robust error detection algorithm than a checksum. It is also used to determine whether an error has occurred during transmission. However, the CRC's value is derived in a much more rigorous manner than a checksum. The data is

read as a binary string: this "number" is divided by another predetermined binary number to form the CRC value. In this manner, it becomes much less likely that multiple transmission errors will yield an unchanged CRC value.

Frames that fail the CRC check are discarded, and the machine identified in that frame's source address is told to retransmit. By virtue of implementing this error detection mechanism at Layer 2, Layer 3 protocols can be relieved of the burden of verifying the delivery and integrity of transmitted data. Layer 4 protocols, like TCP and SPX, may contain and rely upon their own error detection and correction mechanisms, regardless of what transpires at Layer 2.

Frames

A frame is a structure used to transport a block of data across a network. The size and structure of the frame are determined by the hardware layer protocol that the network uses, such as Ethernet, Token Ring, and so on. A frame is directly analogous to an envelope: everyone can expect that a #10 envelope is 4 1/8" x 9 1/2". Its payload, however, can vary considerably in size, content, urgency, and so forth.

Knowing the envelope size also does not reveal anything about how it is being shipped to its destination. In a network, the processes used to forward frames are called *protocols*. Protocols also exist at Layer 3 of the OSI Reference Model. These Layer 3 protocols wrap frames in packets and provide for their transport beyond the LAN. These protocols are described in Chapter 12, "Network Protocols."

Typical Frame Components

The typical frame contains only as many fields, or substructures, as is necessary to guarantee safe delivery of the frame to its intended recipient. Commonly encountered fields include

- Start-of-frame delimiter
- Source address
- Destination address
- Data
- A Frame Check Sequence

Frame Definition

Continuing the envelope analogy, after you know the size of the envelopes, you can begin to deploy an infrastructure for processing them in volume. Thus, standardizing the envelope sizes is crucial to ensure that the forwarding infrastructure can accommodate all envelopes, regardless of who manufactured them.

> **NOTE**
>
> Layer 2 data structures that have a regulated, fixed size are called *cells*. An example of a cell-based Layer 2 protocol is ATM. ATM uses 53-octet cells: five octets contain all the header information and the remaining 48 octets carry payload. The payload is always 48 octets, whereas frames can have payloads of differing sizes.

Rather than specifying a single size for all frames, Layer 2 LAN protocols tend to define maximum and minimum sizes for their data frames. Thus, a frame is of variable length. This allows the protocol to maximize the efficiency of any given transmission by optimizing the overhead-to-payload ratio. This ratio measures the efficacy of a protocol by comparing the amount of framing needed with the payload that it can support.

The beginning of each frame is identified by a pre-determined pattern of bits. This is known as a *Start of Frame Delimiter*. The end of each frame is identified either with an *End of Frame Delimiter* or a *Frame Check Sequence*.

Source and Destination Address Pairs

Just as an envelope traditionally bears enough visible information to identify both its originator and its intended recipient, a frame also contains source and destination addresses. The source address contains the machine address code of its originator. The destination address is the machine address code of its intended recipient.

Placing this information at the beginning of the frame spares potential destination machines the trouble of opening up every frame, examining the contents, and then trying to determine whether that frame is, in fact, addressed to it. That process can be both resource- and time-intensive, which results in diminished network performance.

Instead, a frame contains two addresses very close to its beginning: a source and a destination address. Placing these fields as close as possible to the beginning of the frame expedites the frame forwarding process: examining the first 18 octets of a frame can be done *much* faster than examining 1500 octets. The information contained in these fields is used to either forward a frame to its intended recipient, or notify the originator that the frame is undeliverable.

The purpose of the various frame header components is to provide the basic information needed to identify the recipient, the originator, and whether or not the frame needs to retransmitted. The only other field that is common to all frames is the Data field. This is the field that varies in length; all other frame header components are of fixed length, as determined by the protocol's specifications. This field is also the frame's reason for being. If the data doesn't arrive, or if it is damaged before it arrives at its destination, the entire frame is discarded.

Frame Summary

LANs are, essentially, frame forwarding mechanisms. To perform this task efficiently, LANs require that frames be of standardized shape and structure. Standardization ensures that different network components made by different manufacturers can interoperate.

These same standards also provide a common basis for the conversion of frame types between dissimilar network types, as in a translation from Ethernet to Token Ring.

Evolution of Proprietary Frame Structures

The world's first LAN was Xerox's PARC Ethernet. This technology originated as an intra-office, baseband transmission technology to interconnect workstations. It was cobbled together by researchers at Xerox's famed Palo Alto Research Center (PARC) for their own use as an expedient alternative to using floppy disks to share information. Thus, Ethernet was born a fairly crude and simple mechanism, and its simplicity was reflected in its frame structure. This basic technology is the ancestor of today's industry standard frame structures.

Xerox's PARC Ethernet Frame

PARC researchers recognized that its Layer 2 protocol would be transporting higher-level protocols like the Internet Protocol (IP), Xerox's XNS, and others. These client protocols already had their own limitations on data payloads. Thus, rather than put too much effort into defining the hardware layer protocol, it was deemed appropriate to simply provide a 2-octet Type field that identified the type of higher-level protocol that the frame contained. This let the more sophisticated client protocol determine overall frame sizes.

> **NOTE**
>
> An *octet* consists of eight *binary digits* (bits), regardless of what those bits signify. Beware the data communications experts who use the less precise "binary term" or "byte" to describe such structures; they have been spending too much time with programmers. Next, they'll start using even more ambiguous terms like "records" and "files" to describe quantities of transmitted data!

Xerox's home-grown Ethernet lacked sophistication and relied upon client protocols to determine the length of the Data field. As illustrated in Figure 5.1, the PARC Ethernet frame consisted of

- An 8-octet Preamble
- The intended recipient's 6-octet MAC address
- The originator's 6-octet MAC address
- A 2-octet Type field that identified the client protocol embedded in the Data field

FIGURE 5.1.

Xerox's PARC Ethernet frame.

8-Octet Preamble	6-Octet Destination Address	6-Octet Origination Address	2-Octet Type Field	Unspecified Length Data Field

■ A Data field of unspecified and variable length

This protocol broadcasted packets to all devices connected to the LAN. Consequently, all devices had to compete for available packets. A technique known as "Carrier Sense, Multiple Access" (CSMA) was used to facilitate this competition. Each station would listen to the network to see whether it was available for its own use, or whether the network was preoccupied with the transmission of another device's frames. If a device could detect the carrier signal, it could begin transmission. This greatly reduced, but did not eliminate, collisions of frames that were being transmitted by different devices. Recovery of collisions, or other events that resulted in undelivered frames, was left up to the end devices and not handled by the network protocol.

DIX Ethernet Frame

The commercial potential of Xerox's PARC Ethernet was recognized and both its frame and protocol were refined to better suit a broader target market. This second-generation LAN, known as Ethernet II, was widely used. Ethernet II is also referred to as "DIX Ethernet," in acknowledgment of its triumvirate of corporate sponsors: Digital, Intel, and Xerox.

Xerox, the owner of the technology and keeper of its proprietary "standards," assigned a 2-octet Type code to identify client protocols. Xerox's XNS, Novell's IPX, IP, and DECNet are examples. These are higher-level protocols than Ethernet, and have different message size requirements. Unlike its predecessor, Ethernet II couldn't abdicate control over its frame length and still establish the timing needed to support a more sophisticated access method capable of detecting collisions. Thus frame size limits were defined.

As illustrated in Figure 5.2, the DIX (or Ethernet II) frame consisted of

■ An 8-octet Preamble

■ The intended recipient's 6-octet MAC address

■ The originator's 6-octet MAC address

■ A 2-octet Type field that identified the higher-level transport protocol being encapsulated

■ A Data field of at least 50 octets, but not more than 1486 octets total length

It is important to note that despite the definition of a minimum frame length, the DIX standard continued to rely upon PARC Ethernet's 2-octet Type field. This field still identified the client protocol which, in turn, was used to define the frame's length. The client-side transport

(Layer 3) protocols still had their own packet size requirements, but DIX Ethernet used a more sophisticated access method than its predecessor. The new access method, known as "Carrier Sense, Multiple Access with Collision Detection" (CSMA/CD), imposed fairly specific timing requirements.

FIGURE 5.2.

DIX Ethernet frame.

8-Octet Preamble	6-Octet Destination Address	6-Octet Origination Address	2-Octet Type Field	Data Field > 50 < 1486 Octets	Padding

Simply stated, this access method required stations to check the wire to determine whether any other station was already sending data. If the LAN seemed idle, the station was free to transmit. Unfortunately, transmission is not instantaneous over copper transmission facilities. Thus, it was entirely probable that a station would begin to transmit on what appeared to be an idle LAN, only to be hit by an incoming transmission from another station microseconds after initiating its own transmission. This is known as a *collision*.

The addition of Collision Detection to the PARC Ethernet's CSMA enabled the LAN to recover from collisions, rather than rely upon the end devices. Using CSMA/CD, both stations could detect the collision, back off (or cease) transmitting, and begin anew after a brief delay. The duration of the delay is determined by an algorithm known as the Binary Exponential Back-off algorithm (BEB).

The way DIX Ethernet enabled collision detection was by controlling the time required for the worst-case round trip through the LAN. In a 10Mhz Ethernet, this round trip is limited to a maximum of 50 microseconds. Thus, a station has to continue transmitting until after the worst-case round trip time has expired. This is enough time to transmit 500 bits. Dividing by 8 bits per octet means that packets have to be a minimum of 62.5 octets in length for collision detection to work. Xerox rounded this up to 64 octets minimum frame size for DIX Ethernet.

Any frame whose payload (which was still dictated by the higher-level transport protocol) resulted in an overall frame size of less than 64 octets was padded with zeros by Ethernet II until the frame reached this minimum size. This solved the timing problem of collision detection, but forced each protocol to distinguish data from padding. The DIX frame continued to rely upon the Type field to identify the higher-level protocol and, therefore, its Data field length.

Although the Digital, Intel, Xerox version of Ethernet provided additional functionality intended to make Ethernet commercially viable, the only substantive change to the frame was to impose minimum and maximum frame lengths. Xerox, the originator of Ethernet, retained the rights to the technology and, consequently, established and published its standards. This approach to standardization served its purpose: Ethernet became a commercially available product.

Unfortunately, this approach to establishing and maintaining standards for commercial products is not sustainable. A competitive corporation cannot be tasked with maintaining the standards for a commodity product. It will be motivated to act on its own behalf. Thus, for Ethernet to become a truly successful commercial technology, the responsibility for standardization had to be ceded to a neutral entity.

IEEE Project 802

The standards body that has been responsible for many of the extant standards that support today's high performance networks is the Institute of Electrical and Electronics Engineers (IEEE). This standardization work began in February, 1980 (hence, the mnemonic numeric designation of 802), when the IEEE launched its Local and Metropolitan Area Network Standards Committee, also affectionately referred to as Project 802.

This Committee is chartered with the creation, maintenance, and encouragement of the use of IEEE/ANSI as well as the equivalent Joint Technical Committee 1 (JTC 1) standards established by the International Standards Committee (ISO). These JTC 1 series of equivalent standards are known as ISO 8802-nnn. These standards are basically limited to layers 1 and 2 of their Open System Interconnect (OSI) Reference Model. Layer 1 defines the Physical Layer—for example, the media type and the manner in which data is placed on those media. Layer 2 defines the LAN's frame structure and frame forwarding mechanisms.

NOTE

The ISO standards are given 3-digit numerical designations under the heading of 8802. Thus, the *nnn* of ISO 8802-nnn is nothing more than a wildcard attribute that references all the substandards in the 8802 family of standards.

The objective also included establishing the rules that enable all types of LANs to easily pass data between themselves, and to separate the physical media from the LAN protocols. This permits the implementation of the same LAN on different cable plants, without compromising interoperability.

The committee identified the elements required to support its goals and launched task-specific teams to accomplish them. The accomplishments of these teams included the following:

NOTE

MANs are Metropolitan Area Networks. The standards for MANs were also defined by the IEEE's Project 802.

■ 802.1 defined the overview and architecture for interoperability between LANs and MANs. This is the basis for all the 802 initiatives and includes standards for LAN/MAN management and bridging between 802-compliant networks.

■ 802.2 defined the Data Link Layer (Layer 2) standard for telecommunications and information exchange between systems, both LAN- and MAN-based. This specification also provided the backward compatibility required to support a transition from the pre-standard versions of Ethernet to the 802.3 standardized version.

■ 802.3 established the new standard for a LAN that features a Carrier Sense, Multiple Access with Collision Detection (CSMA/CD). This "new" LAN is properly referred to as CSMA/CD, but is popularly known as "Ethernet."

■ 802.4 defines a Physical Layer standard for a bus topology LAN with a token-passing media access method. This LAN is called "Token Bus" and can support 1-, 2-, 5-, or 10Mbps data rates.

■ 802.5 established the standards for Token Ring's access methods and physical signaling techniques.

Though not a complete listing of the Project 802 initiatives, these five items convey the intended benefits of their charter for standardizing Local and Metropolitan Area Networks. Each specification in this family can interoperate through unsophisticated frame conversions because they all have a common foundation. This charter far exceeded the scope of Xerox's standards and, consequently, made DIX Ethernet obsolete.

IEEE 802.2 Logical Link Control (LLC)

The IEEE Project 802 organized its standards around a three-tiered protocol hierarchy that correlated to the OSI Reference Model's bottom-most two layers: the Physical and Data Link Layers. These three tiers are the Physical Layer, Medium Access Control (MAC), and Logical Link Control (LLC). This is valid for all 802-compliant LANs. The MAC Layer addressing specification allows for either 2-octet or 6-octet address. The 6-octet MAC address is the standard. The 2-octet address has been all but relegated to academic discussions.

The IEEE's 802 Reference Model differs from the OSI Reference Model in two significant aspects. First, the 802 Physical Layer is a subset of its OSI counterpart. Second, the OSI's Data Link Layer (Layer 2) is broken into two discrete components: Medium Access Control (MAC) and Logical Link Control (LLC). This correlation is presented in Figure 5.3.

Defining the LLC separately from the media access control enabled interoperability of 802-compliant networks, despite differences in topologies, transmission media, and, more importantly, media access methodologies. The LLC resides above the MAC and Physical Layers of the 802 Model. In this model, media access, transmission media, and topology are highly interdependent. Thus, part of the OSI's Physical Layer was defined as the 802's Media Access Layer.

5

THE DATA LINK LAYER

FIGURE 5.3.

*IEEE 802 correlation
to the OSI Reference
Model.*

OSI Reference Model Layer Description	OSI Layer Number	IEEE Project 802 Reference Model
Application	7	Service Access Points for Higher Layer Protocols
Presentation	6	
Session	5	
Transport	4	#1 #2 #3
Network	3	Logical Link Control
Data Link	2	Media Access Control
Physical	1	Physical

One of the mechanisms that enables LANs of different topologies to interoperate is the LLC sub-frame. This three-field structure is prepended to the Data field of an 802 frame. It is used to identify the destination protocol in multiprotocol machines. This field is necessary due to the limited capability of the 802.3 protocol to identify external protocols. The LLC contains the following structure:

■ A 1-octet Destination Service Address Port (DSAP) field

■ A 1-octet Source Service Address Port (SSAP) field

■ A 1-octet Control field

The LLC sub-frame is illustrated in Figure 5.4.

FIGURE 5.4.

*Logical Link Control
sub-frame structure.*

1-Octet Destination Service Address Point (DSAP) Field	1-Octet Source Service Address Point (SSAP) Field	1-Octet Control Field

The service access points indicate for which upper layer protocol the packet is intended. Protocols are assigned hexadecimal values, which are displayed in the DSAP and SSAP fields of a packet.

The LLC provides addressing and control of the data link. It specifies which mechanisms are to be used for addressing stations over the transmission medium, and which for controlling the data exchanged between the originator and recipient machines. This is done through the use of three LLC services:

- Unacknowledged connectionless service
- Acknowledged connectionless service
- Connection-oriented service

These services are accessed via Service Access Points that are defined between the Network and Data Link Layers.

The first LLC service, unacknowledged connectionless service, is a minimal, but useful, offering. Frequently, Layer 4 protocols like TCP, SPX, and so forth are tasked with providing flow control and other reliability functions. Thus, it makes sense to have a Layer 2 service that does not redundantly provide the same functions, albeit at a lower level. This service cuts down on the communications overheads. Some applications, like the time- and latency-sensitive voice and/or video conferencing, may actually suffer performance degradation by having to establish and maintain connections at this layer.

The next LLC service, acknowledged connectionless service, provides an acknowledgment of receipt, without having any of the overheads of connection management. Fewer overheads directly translate into faster delivery. Adding guaranteed delivery to this quick delivery service creates a useful service whose applications are almost limitless.

The last LLC service, connection-oriented service, provides Data Link Layer mechanisms to establish and maintain connections. This is extremely useful for simple and/or unintelligent devices that may not have Layer 3 or 4 protocols and therefore need to be able to provide these functions at Layer 2. This control function requires the Data Link Layer to maintain a table that tracks active connections.

These services tend to be selected per application, and are transparent to application users. As they are part of the 802.2 foundation specification, they are available to all 802-compliant networks and can be used in internetworking different 802-compliant networks.

IEEE 802.2 Sub-Network Access Protocol (SNAP)

As a means of providing backward compatibility with early, non-standardized versions of LANs, like PARC and DIX Ethernet, a sub-frame structure was developed to provide a mechanism for identifying the upper-layer protocol being transported. The PARC and DIX versions of Ethernet included a Type field in their frame structures. This space was reallocated by the IEEE in its 802.3 standardized version of Ethernet.

The 802.3 Ethernet was a more sophisticated protocol than its predecessors and obviated much of the original need for this field. Some higher-level protocols, however, relied upon this Layer 2 function. The need to provide compatibility with existing Layer 3 and 4 protocols necessitated the development of a sub-frame structure that could identify higher-level protocols. The result was the Sub-Network Access Protocol (SNAP) sub-frame, as illustrated in Figure 5.5.

FIGURE 5.5.

802.2 SNAP sub-frame structure.

1-Octet Destination Service Address Point (DSAP) Field	1-Octet Source Service Address Point (SSAP) Field	1-Octet Control Field	3-Octet Organizationally Unique Identifier (OUI) Field	2-Octet Protocol Identifier Field

The 802.2 specification also provides a SNAP frame structure. This frame builds upon the standard 802.2 frame by adding a 5-octet field that contains a 3-octet Organizationally Unique Identifier (OUI) field, and a 2-octet Protocol Type field. The SNAP sub-framing is an extension of the LLC sub-frame and must be used with it. It can be used with any 802-compliant LAN.

IEEE 802.3 Ethernet Frame

Project 802 defined a standard basis for all Ethernet frame types. The frames are a minimum of 64 octets and a maximum of 1500 octets in length, including payload and headers. The headers are used to identify the sender and recipient of each packet. The only limitations on this identification are that each address must be unique and six octets in length.

The first 12 octets of each frame contain the 6-octet destination address (the intended recipient's address), and a 6-octet source address (the sender's address). These addresses are hardware-level machine address codes, commonly known as MAC addresses. They can be the unique "universally administered address" that is automatically given to each Ethernet network interface card (NIC) at its manufacture. This type of MAC address is represented by six paired hexadecimal numbers, delimited by colons, as in 99:02:11:D1:8F:19. The first two numbers are the manufacturer's ID. Each NIC manufacturer must apply to the IEEE for a unique manufacturer's ID and a range of MAC addresses.

Alternatively, these addresses can be customized upon installation. Customized addresses are known as "locally administered addresses." These addresses can be used to identify the room number, department, owner's voice mail extension, and so on. Using locally administered addresses can provide network administrators with vital information that can expedite trouble resolution. Unfortunately, they can also be extremely difficult and time-consuming to maintain.

802-compliant frames may contain a destination address of a single machine, or refer to a group of workstations with a common, identifying characteristic. Transmission to groups of related machines is known as "multicasting."

Under normal operating circumstances, Ethernet NICs will receive only frames whose destination addresses match their unique MAC addresses or satisfy their multicast criteria. Most NICs, however, can be set for "promiscuous mode." This results in their reception of all frames on the LAN, regardless of addressing. This can pose a security risk for everyone else on the LAN's broadcast bus, and a potential performance problem for the user whose machine is operating in that manner.

Although most of the changes from the previous versions of Ethernet that were made to the 802.3 standard were changes to the protocol itself, there was one other significant change to the 802.3 frame. The 802 committee needed a standard that was complete unto itself and not dependent upon the good behavior of other protocols. Therefore, they replaced the 2-octet Type field of previous Ethernets with a 2-octet Length field.

Having established minimum and maximum field lengths based on a worst-case, round-trip timing window (as previously explained in this chapter in the section titled "DIX Ethernet Frame," minimum and maximum field lengths were necessary for collision detection purposes), it was no longer necessary to defer the determination of frame size to client protocols. Instead, the 802.3 working group redefined this 2-octet field to explicitly define the length of a frame's Data field, and moved protocol identification to the LLC.

The IEEE's 802.3 basic Ethernet frame replaced the traditional Type field with a Length field. The 802.2 sub-frame is used, instead, to identify the type of protocol, if this is necessary. Another change in the 802.3 frame from its predecessors was the requirement for the overall frame size to be between 64 and 1500 octets in length, from the start of the Destination field, through the end of the Frame Check Sequence field.

The preamble is a 7-octet string that precedes each frame, and enables the synchronization of the transmission. This is followed by the Start of Frame Delimiter (SFD). The SFD is fairly self-explanatory: it denotes the start of the frame for all devices in, or on, the LAN. The SFD is "11" followed by the repeating sequence of "1010101010."

The SFD is sometimes considered an integral part of the preamble, and not a part of the frame itself, thus bringing the preamble up to 8 octets in length. This represents another subtle distinction between the PARC and DIX Ethernet variants and the 802.3 standard. PARC and DIX Ethernets used a consistent, repeating "10101010" pattern for the entire 8-octet Preamble. This pattern was used for both synchronization and Start of Frame delimiting.

The next mechanism is the Frame Check Sequence (FCS). A mathematically derived value is stored in this field by the frame's originating computer. The destination computer also knows how to calculate this value and does so to verify the integrity of the frame. Frames may be damaged in transit in a variety of ways. Electro-magnetic Interference (EMI), cross talk, and so forth can all damage a packet without stopping its transmission.

Upon receipt of a frame, the destination computer checks the frame's FCS field for damage through a Cyclical Redundancy Check. The destination computer performs the same calculation as the originating computer did and compares the resulting value to the one stored in the FCS field. If the values are the same, the destination computer knows the data arrived intact. Otherwise, the destination computer requests a retransmission of the frame.

The basic Ethernet frame, illustrated in Figure 5.6, is known as "raw" Ethernet. In reality, raw 802.3 Ethernet is seldom, if ever, used. Instead, it is the basis for extended frames using either the 802.2 LLC sub-frame and/or the SNAP sub-frame.

5

THE DATA LINK LAYER

FIGURE 5.6.

*The IEEE 802.3
Ethernet basic frame.*

7-Octet Preamble	1-Octet Start of Frame Delimiter	6-Octet Destination Address	6-Octet Origination Address	2-Octet Length Field	Variable Length Data Field (> 46 octets < 1482)	4-Octet Frame Check Sequence

Ethernet LLC Frame Structure

The Ethernet LLC frame is a combination of an 802.3 frame and the 802.2 LLC sub-frame. In this implementation, LLC adds three fields to the basic Ethernet frame: Destination Service Access Port (DSAP), Source Service Access Port (SSAP), and Control.

An Ethernet LLC frame has the following structure:

- A 7-octet Preamble that signals the start of a frame
- A 1-octet Start of Frame delimiter that signals the start of the frame's contents
- The intended recipient's 6-octet MAC address
- The originator's 6-octet MAC address
- A 2-octet Length field that identifies the total length of the Data field, including the LLC and SNAP headers
- A 1-octet Destination Service Access Point (DSAP) field that identifies, predictably, the LLC's service access point at the destination machine
- A 1-octet Source Service Access Point (SSAP) field that identifies the originating machine's LLC service access point
- A 1- or 2-octet Control field that indicates the type of LLC frame being carried
- A Data field that contains either 43 to 1497 octets, or 42 to 1496 octets of data, depending upon the length of the preceding Control field
- A 4-octet Frame Check Sequence that is used to check the integrity of the frame

The Ethernet LLC frame structure is illustrated in Figure 5.7.

The Ethernet LLC Frame integrates the 802.2 sub-frame structures, or headers, and permits the identification of the higher-level protocol that is the intended recipient of the frame's contents. Having a mechanism to identify higher-layer protocols provides backwards compatibility with earlier versions of Ethernet whose frames contained discrete mechanisms for protocol identification.

The total length of an Ethernet LLC frame must be at least 64 octets in length (excluding the Preamble and Start of Frame delimiter) to permit proper functioning of the CSMA/CD mechanism. Zeroes are padded to the end of the Data field to ensure this minimum length. The upper limit is 1518 octets, including the Preamble and Start of Frame delimiter.

FIGURE 5.7.
IEEE 802.3 Ethernet frame with 802.2 LLC sub-frame.

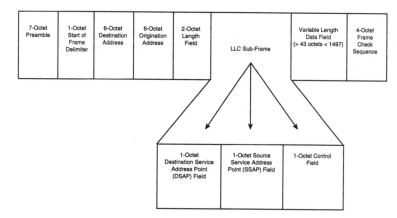

Ethernet SNAP Frame Structure

The Ethernet SNAP frame is a combination of an 802.3 frame and the 802.2 Sub-Network Access Protocol's sub-frame. In this implementation, SNAP adds a 5-octet Protocol Identification field. This field is inserted in the frame after the LLC header. It consists of a 3-octet Organizationally Unique Identifier (OUI) and a 2-octet Type field. These fields identify for which upper-layer protocol the frame is intended.

An Ethernet SNAP frame contains the following fields:

- A 7-octet Preamble that signals the start of a frame
- A 1-octet Start of Frame delimiter that signals the start of the frame's contents
- The intended recipient's 6-octet MAC address
- The originator's 6-octet MAC address
- A 2-octet Length field that identifies the total length of the Data field, including the LLC and SNAP headers
- A 1-octet Destination Service Access Point (DSAP) field that identifies, predictably, the LLC's service access point at the destination machine
- A 1-octet Source Service Access Point (SSAP) field that identifies the originating machine's LLC service access point
- A 1- or 2-octet Control field that indicates the type of LLC frame being carried
- A 5-octet SNAP sub-frame, including a 3-octet Organizationally Unique Identifier field and a 2-octet Protocol Type field that identify the upper-level protocol being carried
- A Data field that contains either 38 to 1492 octets, or 37 to 1491 octets of data, depending upon the length of the preceding Control field
- A 4-octet Frame Check Sequence that is used to check the integrity of the frame

The Ethernet SNAP sub-frame is illustrated in Figure 5.8.

FIGURE 5.8.

IEEE 802.3 Ethernet frame with 802.2 SNAP sub-frame.

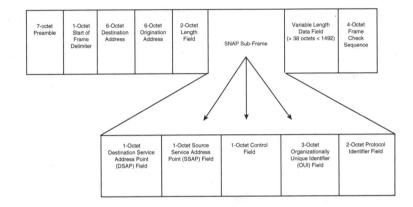

The Ethernet SNAP sub-frame is designed to enhance the capability of the LLC sub-frame to provide backward compatibility with earlier versions of Ethernet.

The total length of an Ethernet SNAP frame must be at least 64 octets in length to permit proper functioning of the CSMA/CD mechanism. The upper limit for an Ethernet SNAP frame's size is 1518 octets, including the Preamble and Start of Frame delimiter.

IEEE 802.5 Token Ring

The IEEE also standardized a message format and protocol for a different, more deterministic LAN known as Token Ring in its 802.5 standard. Token Ring networks had existed since the mid 1970s and were largely an IBM-specific technology. The 802.5 specification is almost identical to IBM's Token Ring. In fact, the term "Token Ring" is used indiscriminately to describe both IBM's pre-standard product and IEEE 802.5-compliant products.

IEEE standardization was pushed by several large companies, including IBM (802.5 Token Ring), and General Motors (802.4 Token Bus). Token Ring offered a more timely and deterministic approach to networking than the 802.3 protocol, albeit at a higher per-port cost. Companies whose applications required timely delivery of data found Token Ring to be the only viable solution for their needs. Although the 802.3 protocol assures only that the packet has been successfully transmitted, it may require multiple transmission attempts. Thus, it can't guarantee a time frame for delivery. The Token Ring topology can, due to its deterministic, ring-shaped topology and orderly access method.

IEEE 802.5 Frame Structure

The 802.5 Token Ring frame structure consists of two parts: the token and the data frame. As previously discussed, the token's frame consists of three 1-octet fields.

The token and data frames are illustrated in Figure 5.9. This figure presents the "raw" Token Ring framing, without the 802.2 LLC or SNAP sub-frames. Like its 802.3 cousin, Token Ring is seldom used in its raw state.

FIGURE 5.9.

The IEEE's 802.5 Token Ring data frame.

1-Octet Starting Delimiter	1-Octet Access Control Field	1-Octet Frame Control Field	6-Octet Destination Address	6-Octet Origination Address	Variable Length Data Field (0 to 4099 octets)	1-Octet Ending Delimiter

The token and data frames have three 1-octet fields in common: the Starting Delimiter, Access Control, and Ending Delimiter fields. The Access Control field is the key to making a Token Ring work. It contains eight bits, one of which must be inverted to de-activate the token and convert it into a Start of Frame sequence.

When the token has been converted to a data frame, it consists of nine different fields and subfields. The first field is the Starting Delimiter, which identifies the beginning of the frame. Next is the Access Control field. This field tells 802.5-compliant devices whether or not they may transmit. This field also contains the bits for Token Ring's priority and reservation system. This is followed by the Frame Control field. This field stores the Type bits that identify the transport protocol. This field is also used to differentiate between data frames and control frames.

The next two fields are the destination and source MAC addresses. Each one is a 6-octet field. These MAC addresses conform to the previously described Project 802 specification, and are identical to those used in Ethernet networks. The Data field for a token-based network varies in size from at least 0 octets up to a maximum of 4099. The last field is the 1-octet Ending Delimiter that identifies the end of the frame.

Although not shown, Token Ring also uses LLC and SNAP sub-frames. This allows them to be bridged with a translating bridge to Ethernet networks without compromising their capability to map received frames to higher-layer destination protocols. The Token Ring LLC and SNAP sub-frames are only pertinent in environments where Token Ring and Ethernet are bridged together.

FDDI

Officially known as *Fiber Distributed Data Interface*, this American National Standards Institute (ANSI) standard LAN architecture is more commonly identified by its acronym: FDDI. Even more frequently, it is pronounced as a word: fiddy. Although it is widely derided as merely a higher speed Token Ring network, FDDI is fundamentally different in its topology, management, and even token and frame structures.

The raw FDDI data-bearing frame is illustrated in Figure 5.10, and has the following structure:

- An 8-octet Preamble that signals the start of the frame
- A 1-octet Start of Frame delimiter that signals the start of the frame's contents
- A 1-octet Frame Control field that signals the type of frame, that is, token, MAC or LLC, priority frame, and so forth

■ The intended recipient's 6-octet MAC address

■ The originator's 6-octet MAC address

■ A variable length Data field that contains up to 4478 octets

■ A 4-octet Frame Check Sequence that is used to check the integrity of the frame

■ A half-octet (four bits) Ending delimiter

■ A 3-octet Frame Status field that contains three 1-octet sub-fields: Error, Address-match, and Copied; each sub-field is set to either "S" for "Set" or "R" for "Reset."

FIGURE 5.10.

The FDDI frame.

8-Octet Preamble	1-Octet Starting Delimiter	1-Octet Frame Control Field	6-Octet Destination Address	6-Octet Source Address	Variable Length Data Field, up to 4478 Octets	4-Octet Frame Check Sequence	1-Octet Ending Delimiter	3-Octet Frame Status

The FDDI frame is a maximum of 4500 octets in length, including data and all frame components. This is the basic FDDI frame. It is usually implemented in one of two sub-formats: LLC or SNAP. Neither one, excluding the Preamble, can be more than 4500 octets in length.

FDDI LLC Frame Structure

FDDI also supports LLC by building upon the IEEE 802.2 LLC layer.

> **NOTE**
>
> The IEEE 802 family of standards have been adopted by the American National Standards Institute (ANSI). Consequently, even though FDDI is not an IEEE standard, it can use IEEE-developed sub-frame mechanisms. This enhances FDDI's capability to function as a high-bandwidth LAN backbone that interconnects Ethernet LANs.

The LLC frame, illustrated in Figure 5.11, is constructed by adding three fields to the FDDI frame. These fields are the DSAP, SSAP, and Control fields.

An FDDI LLC frame has the following structure:

■ An 8-octet Preamble that signals the start of the frame

■ A 1-octet Start of Frame delimiter that signals the start of the frame's contents

■ A 1-octet Frame Control field that signals the type of frame, that is, token, MAC or LLC, priority frame, and so forth

■ The intended recipient's 6-octet MAC address

■ The originator's 6-octet MAC address

■ A variable length Data field that contains up to 4478 octets

- A 4-octet Frame Check Sequence that is used to check the integrity of the frame
- A half-octet (four bits) Ending delimiter
- A 3-octet Frame Status field that contains three 1-octet sub-fields: Error, Address-match, and Copied; each sub-field is set to either "S" for "Set" or "R" for "Reset."

Figure 5.11.
FDDI frame with 802.2 LLC sub-frame.

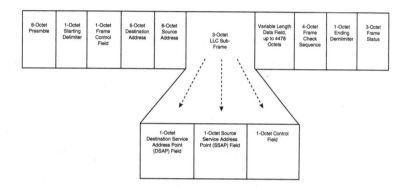

The FDDI frame can be supplemented with the 802.2 LLC sub-frame structures. This sub-frame prepends the DSAP, SSAP, and Control fields to the Data field.

FDDI SNAP Frame Structure

FDDI also supports SNAP by building upon the 802.2 LLC layer of the FDDI 802.2 frame. The SNAP frame adds a 3-octet Protocol Identification field and a 2-octet Type field to the 802.2 LLC sub-frame structure. This frame is illustrated in Figure 5.12.

An FDDI SNAP frame contains the following fields:

- An 8-octet Preamble that signals the start of the frame
- A 1-octet Start of Frame delimiter that signals the start of the frame's contents
- A 1-octet Frame Control field that signals the type of frame, that is, token, MAC or LLC, priority frame, and so forth
- The intended recipient's 6-octet MAC address
- The originator's 6-octet MAC address
- A 5-octet SNAP sub-frame, including a 3-octet Organizationally Unique Identifier field and a 2-octet Protocol Type field that identify the upper-level protocol being carried
- A variable length Data field that contains up to 4473 octets
- A 4-octet Frame Check Sequence that is used to check the integrity of the frame
- A half-octet (four bits) Ending delimiter
- A 3-octet Frame Status field that contains three 1-octet sub-fields: Error, Address-match, and Copied; each sub-field is set to either "S" for "Set" or "R" for "Reset."

5

The Data Link Layer

FIGURE 5.12.
FDDI frame with 802.2 SNAP sub-frame.

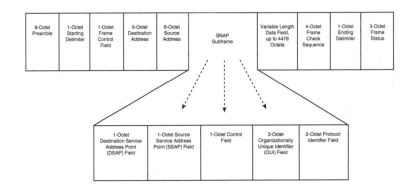

The IEEE's FDDI SNAP frame adds a 3-octet Organizationally Unique Identifier and a 2-octet Type field to the FDDI LLC frame immediately after the LLC header and before the data. These fields are included in the overall length of the Data field.

Concept of Media Access Control

Although putting ones and zeroes onto the physical media is a function of the first layer of the OSI Reference Model, regulating access to that media for transmission is a function of the Data Link Layer. This regulation is known as *Media Access Control* (MAC).

The IEEE 802 specifications recognize three different forms of media access. They are:

- Contention
- Demand priority
- Token passing

In a shared communications network, like CSMA/CD Ethernet, all attached devices share a common MAC layer. The MAC layer provides a Layer 2 broadcast domain, and also forms the universe of devices that share the network's bandwidth.

Contention-Based Media Access

Contention-based media access is embodied in the Carrier Sense, Multiple Access with Collision Detection (CSMA/CD) scheme of 802.3. As its name implies, this access method requires stations to check the wire to determine whether any other station is already sending data. If the station can sense an available carrier signal on the wire, it is free to transmit.

> **NOTE**
>
> Only networks that use a broadband transmission method have a carrier signal. In a baseband system, like any of the 10Base varieties, a series of voltage pulses is substituted for the carrier.

The sensing of a carrier signal does not necessarily guarantee a free transmission media. As indicated earlier in this chapter, in the section titled "DIX Ethernet Frame," transmissions are not instantaneous. Even at wire speeds, an 802.3 frame can take up to 50 microseconds to be propagated across the entire LAN. Thus, it is possible for a station to begin transmitting on what appears to be an idle media, only to have a previously transmitted signal collide with it microseconds later. A collision requires both frames to be retransmitted. The chances of collision increase tremendously with an increase in LAN traffic.

The 802.3 version of CSMA/CD is capable of detecting collisions. This spares higher layers from having to worry about identifying collisions and generating the retransmission. Both stations detect the collision at Layer 2, back off from transmitting for a brief period, and then restart their transmissions.

Demand Priority Media Access

The IEEE 802.12 standard specifies a 100Mbps network that uses the "demand priority" access method, an Ethernet or Token Ring frame format (but not both simultaneously), and a star topology. As a result of its flexible support of frames, the 802.12 LAN has been dubbed "VG-AnyLAN." VG-AnyLAN can operate over four pairs of Category 3 Unshielded Twisted Pair (UTP) copper wiring, Shielded Twisted Pair (STP), Category 5 UTP, and fiber-optic cabling. There can be up to three levels of cascaded repeaters with up to 100 meters between the repeaters and the stations. The network may be up to 4,000 feet in diameter.

This specification provides SNMP compliance by using MIB variables that are similar to Ethernet MIBs and Token Ring MIBs. The 802.12 MIB is actually a superset of both Ethernet and Token Ring MIBs.

The access method is a Demand Priority Access Method (DPAM)—a round-robin arbitration method in which a central repeater regularly polls ports connected to it. This polling is in port order and is done to identify ports that have transmission requests. After the need to transmit is established, the repeater determines whether the priority is high or normal. These priorities are designed to service time-sensitive requests before servicing normal requests for bandwidth. Any ports that are either not transmitting data or have a pending transmission request generate an "idle" signal.

A station's "idle" signal is cleared by the repeater if that station is selected as the next in the priority sequence to transmit. After the idle signal ceases, the station begins to transmit.

When this happens, the repeater alerts the other stations that they may receive an incoming message. The repeater then reads the incoming frame's destination address, looks in its link configuration table, and switches the frame to that destination address as well as any promiscuous ports.

The central, or "root," repeater controls the operation of the priority domain. This root repeater can include up to three levels of cascaded hubs. Cascaded hubs can function as a single large repeater. The central repeater sends all traffic to each lower-level repeater. Each lower-level repeater, in turn, polls its active ports for requests after packet transmission.

5

THE DATA LINK LAYER

No station is permitted to transmit twice in a row if other stations have same-priority requests pending. At the central repeater, a high-priority request is not allowed to interrupt a normal-priority request if that request is already in progress. In a lower-level repeater, the normal-priority request is preempted, so that the high-priority request can be accommodated. To ensure that a request isn't completely ignored, any normal-priority requests that have been waiting longer than 250ms are automatically elevated to high-priority status.

Token-Based Media Access

Project 802's specifications include three different token-based protocols, each with its own media access methodology. These protocols are 802.4 Token Bus, 802.5 Token Ring, and FDDI. Token Bus enjoyed only a limited application base: it was ideal for assembly lines. It has long since fallen into disuse and is now obsolete. Consequently, only the media access methodologies of Token Ring and FDDI are presented in this chapter.

802.5 Token Ring Media Access

In an 802.5-compliant Token Ring network, a special frame (better known as, predictably enough, the "token") is passed from device to device, in sequence along the ring. It can circulate only when the ring is idle. This frame, illustrated in Figure 5.13, is three octets long and contains a special bit pattern. If the token is passed to a device that doesn't need to transmit, it may hold onto the token for 10 milliseconds, or longer if the default value has been changed. If this time expires and the device still doesn't need to transmit, it relinquishes control of the token, which is then sent on to the next device in the ring.

Figure 5.13.

The IEEE 802.5 Token Ring token frame.

1-Octet Starting Delimiter	1-Octet Access Control Field	1-Octet Ending Delimiter

The IEEE's 802.5 Token Ring uses this token to control access to the transmission media. The token contains a Starting Delimiter, Access Control, and Ending Delimiter fields. The Access Control field contains eight bits, one of which must be inverted to de-activate the token and convert it into a Start of Frame sequence.

When this token is passed to a device that does need to transmit, that device seizes the token and inverts a bit value in its frame. This inversion gives that device permission to transmit and is recognized as a Start of Frame (SOF) sequence. The data to be transmitted, as well as other important fields, are appended to this modified token frame and put onto the network. As long as a data-bearing frame is traversing the network, no token is being passed.

It is possible to calculate the maximum time that can expire before a device can transmit. This time can be manipulated either upward or downward by adding or subtracting nodes from the ring. Token Ring networks are ideal for any application that requires predictable delays.

FDDI Media Access

Unlike Token Ring, which uses a priority/reservation access method, FDDI uses a timed token protocol to regulate access to the transmission media. The result is a much more deterministic LAN that obviates the need for an Access Control field in its frame.

FDDI uses the token illustrated in Figure 5.14 to control access to the transmission media. It contains a Preamble, Starting Delimiter, Frame Control, and Ending Delimiter fields.

FIGURE 5.14.

The FDDI token frame.

8-Octet Preamble	1-Octet Starting Delimiter	1-Octet Frame Control Field	1-Octet Ending Delimiter

In practice, and contrary to Token Ring, a FDDI ring can have multiple tokens and/or data frames circulating simultaneously. Any station that seizes the token modifies the token's Frame Control contents. The station then adds its data and puts the token back on the network as a data frame. That station immediately creates a new token and puts it on the ring right behind the data frame. This new token can be seized by any downstream station that needs to transmit.

The data frame is *not* pulled off the network by its recipient. Recipients simply copy the contents of any frames addressed to them as the frames go by. Eventually, the data frame returns to its originator, who then destroys it.

Supporting the simultaneous transmission of multiple data frames enables FDDI to be much more efficient than Token Ring, especially in large or heavily used networks.

Selecting a LAN Technology

Each of the LANs in the IEEE 802 family of standards has its own particular framing structure, media access methodology, and physical transmission media. To select the correct LAN technology, you must understand the benefits and limitations of each frame type, relative to the networking requirements of your users.

The benefits and limitations of each frame type are summarized in this section.

802.3 Ethernet

Ethernet, Fast Ethernet, and Gigabit Ethernet offer 10Mbps, 100Mbps, or up to 1Gbps transmission rate. Specifications in this family use different physical layers with an almost perfectly interchangeable Media Access Layer. Some minor changes were necessary to the media access mechanisms to account for differences in the Physical Layer.

Media access for these three specifications is through a chaotic contention method that does not scale very well. Performance may be boosted significantly by implementing these protocols via a switch. Switches decrease the size of the collision domains without affecting the size of the broadcast domain. In a per-port switched 802.3 LAN, the collision domain is reduced to just two devices: the end device and the hub port to which it connects. This greatly relieves the scaleability issue that plagues shared versions of these specifications.

802.5 Token Ring

Token Ring offers 4- and 16Mbps transmission rates with somewhat predictable delays, due to its deterministic access method. Additionally, the token has priority bits that can be set higher to satisfy the more stringent network performance criteria of critical frames.

FDDI

FDDI offers a 100Mbps transmission rate, and a self-healing dual, counter-rotating ring topology. FDDI can be considered a "Fast Token Ring," as it conducts token-passing in a deterministic fashion. This, and the 802.1 and 802.2 commonalities, are all that these two networks share.

FDDI's clock rate and timed access methodology distinguish it from Token Ring, and position it for different applications within the LAN environment. Its dual counter-rotating rings can automatically and logically wrap together to heal a broken cable. This provides an innate fault tolerance. The drawback to this is a sudden increase in propagation delay in the event of a cable break.

The other major distinction between FDDI and Token Ring is FDDI's loadability. Unlike Token Ring, FDDI can support the transmission of multiple data frames simultaneously. This allows more of its bandwidth to be usable. For more detailed information on FDDI, and all of its features, please see Chapter 10, "FDDI."

802.12 VG-AnyLAN

VG-AnyLAN provides for the accommodation of both Ethernet and Token Ring frame formats. The proposal appears to be highly media independent as it can transmit over four pairs of Category 3 UTP wire, Category 5 UTP or STP, or 62.5 micron fiber-optic cabling.

It also attempts to establish a middle ground between true baseband and true broadband communications by implementing a demand priority media access method. Essentially, it establishes a priority architecture that lets time-sensitive packets get needed bandwidth on demand. It lacks a native mechanism to actually reserve bandwidth, however.

VG-AnyLAN has two other potentially significant limitations. First, it requires four pairs of twisted pair wiring. This may force 10Base-T users to re-wire their stations prior to migration. Thus, even though it was intentionally designed for Category 3 wire, users may still find themselves unable to use existing wire if they do not have four pairs of Category 3 wire at each station. The second limitation is that it does not interoperate easily with "real Ethernet" because it uses a different media-access method.

Summary

The Data Link Layer defines Local Area Networking. Its two primary components are framing and media access control. Each LAN architecture has its own unique combination of supported physical transmission media, framing conventions, and media access control methodologies. When selecting a network architecture, such as Ethernet, Token Ring, FDDI, and so forth, you must give careful consideration to each of these criteria. They must be considered individually and in combination to determine whether or not they are capable of delivering the required LAN performance.

5

THE DATA LINK
LAYER

The Mechanics of Media Access

by Mark Sportack

IN THIS CHAPTER

CHAPTER 6

In Chapter 5, "The Data Link Layer," the various Layer 2 data-bearing constructs—known more formally as frames—are defined and described. In this chapter, the various ways that these frames are actually placed on the transmission media are identified. These ways include token passing, contention, demand-priority, and switched. Each has its own unique combinations of features and functional implications. They are described in more detail in this chapter, and specific examples of LAN architectures that use each one are presented.

Media Access

All networks must have some mechanism for regulating access to the transmission media. This mechanism, known as *media access*, is implemented at Layer 2 of the OSI Reference Model, the Data Link Layer. Although the need for it is universal, there can be quite a bit of variety in the implementation of media access mechanisms. For example, four distinct approaches to regulating access to the transmission media can be found in Local Area Networks:

- Contention
- Token passing
- Demand-priority
- Switched

Each of these media access methodologies is described in detail in this chapter.

Contention-Based Media Access

A LAN that features competition as the basis for arbitrating the right to transmit is more properly described as having a *contention-based media access method*. The sum total of devices that compete with each other for bandwidth is known as a *collision domain*. This method is embraced by the myriad Ethernet variants that have emerged, including the following:

- Ethernet II or DIX Ethernet
- IEEE 802.3 10Mbps Ethernet (CSMA/CD)
- IEEE 802.3 100Mbps Fast Ethernet
- IEEE 802.3z Gigabit Ethernet

Contention-based access is fairly primitive, as it has no centralized regulatory mechanism. Instead, each network-attached device assumes the burden for its own transmissions. Every time a device needs to transmit, it must check the wire to see whether the wire is available or already in use. If it is in use, the would-be transmitter must back down and wait before trying again. Each device is, in effect, competing for available bandwidth based upon the logic and rules established in its Physical Layer. The sum total of the devices that compete with each other for access to the transmission media constitutes the LAN's contention domain.

> **NOTE**
>
> A contention domain is also sometimes referred to as a *collision domain*. This is logical because collisions can occur only among LAN devices that are in contention for the same bandwidth.

Implicit in this description of contention-based media access is that all network-attached devices transmit and receive on the same frequency band. The transmission media can support only a single signal at a time, and that signal occupies the entire band. In other words, the transmission media supports baseband transmission. This is illustrated in Figure 6.1.

FIGURE 6.1.
Baseband transmission.

Baseband transmission technology uses only one channel for all communications. This has two important implications:

- Only one device can transmit at any given time.
- A device can only transmit or receive, but not both simultaneously. This is known as *half-duplex* operation.

Half- Versus Full-Duplex

A half-duplex network permits only one device to transmit at any given time; the others must remain passive and listen for frames that might be addressed to them. This is illustrated in Figure 6.2.

The term "full-duplex network" implies that the available bandwidth is somehow subdivided into discrete channels. Alternatively, physically separate wire paths may be used to create a redundant channel using the same frequency band. The typical full-duplex LAN uses switching technology. In any case, a device may simultaneously transmit and receive. A full-duplex switched connection is illustrated in Figure 6.3.

It is important to note that, in a full-duplex network that uses a contention-based media access methodology, only one device per collision domain may transmit at any given time. The key difference is that implementing a full-duplex network requires the use of a switched port for each device connected. Thus, the number of devices in any given collision domain is just two: the device and the switch port to which it connects.

FIGURE 6.2.

Half-duplex, baseband transmission.

FIGURE 6.3.

Full-duplex, switched transmission.

Timing Is Everything

Regardless of how many devices are in the LAN's various collision domains, or even whether it supports half- or full-duplex transmission modes, some mechanism must exist to regulate the devices' capability to access the transmission medium at any given time. Contention-based media access is one such mechanism. This simple media access methodology became popular with Ethernet II, or DIX Ethernet, as it is sometimes called. It was much more rigorously defined by the IEEE's 802.3 Ethernet specification. Essentially, contention-based media access is a game of timing and mathematics.

> **NOTE**
>
> The IEEE 802.3 specification describes a LAN architecture that uses a Carrier Sense, Multiple Access with Collision Detection (CSMA/CD) media access methodology. CSMA/CD is the proper, albeit unwieldy, name for the variant of Ethernet defined by the IEEE's 802.3.

For timing to be coordinated across all connected devices, there must be a certain consistency to the Layer 2 (Data Link Layer) frames used across the LAN. By their very nature, however, these frames are variable in length. Each one, in theory, can be a different length. Thus, avoiding collisions becomes a more complicated task.

The way that 802.3 CSMA/CD, today's Ethernet, seeks to avoid collisions is by placing upper and lower limits on the size of a frame. Frames must be at least 64 octets, but not more than 1524 octets in length, including payload and headers. At any given transmission rate, these minimum and maximum frame sizes translate directly into minimum and maximum transmission times for standards-compliant frames.

> **NOTE**
>
> CSMA/CD frames that use a 2-octet source and destination addresses, rather than the more familiar 6-octet addresses, can be a maximum of 1516 octets in total length. For more information on Ethernet frames, please refer to Chapter 5, "The Data Link Layer." For more information on the various implementations of Ethernet, please refer to Chapter 7, "Ethernet," and Chapter 8, "Faster Ethernets."

In a contention-based network, the amount of time necessary for each frame to propagate throughout the entire LAN can be used to detect collisions. Remember, contention-based media access assumes that the architecture uses baseband transmission, so the transmitted frame must be successfully propagated over the entire LAN to ensure that any and all recipients receive it.

The frame can be destroyed by collision anywhere on the LAN. Two factors increase the chance of a collision:

■ The number of devices connected to the network

■ The physical size of the network

The more devices there are connected to the network, the more contention there is for available bandwidth. The longer the network, the more time the frame must be on the wire. Both circumstances must be carefully regulated to ensure acceptable levels of network performance.

The number of devices that can be connected to a LAN has, historically, been reduced through the use of such segmentation mechanisms as bridges, routers, and switches. Although they operate in different ways, each effectively reduces the size of a LAN's contention domain. The network's physical size, however, is dictated by the Physical Layer specifications of the various LAN architectures.

Establishing a precise value for the worst-case round trip transmission time was first done in DIX Ethernet. This value was set at 50 microseconds. To ensure that a frame was successfully delivered required the transmitting device to continue transmitting until after this time had expired. This guaranteed that the frame had propagated to the farthest reaches of the network (assuming the LAN was built in compliance with specifications for maximum wire paths and diameters) without colliding. Consequently, operators could be sure that every device on the network could detect the frame on the wire and know not to transmit.

Unfortunately, transmission is not instantaneous over copper transmission facilities. Thus, it is entirely probable that a station can begin to transmit on what appears to be an idle LAN only to collide with an incoming transmission from another station nanoseconds after initiating its own transmission. Both devices detect this collision, back off from transmitting, and begin anew after a brief delay. This is the essence of collision detection. The potential for collisions is illustrated in Figure 6.4. PC number 1 has already started to transmit, but its transmission has not yet reached PC number 2. This second PC thinks that the network is clear, and that it may transmit. Both transmissions will collide, forcing both PCs to back off, endure a pseudo-random waiting period, and then attempt retransmission.

Fifty microseconds, the worst-case round-trip time, is enough time to transmit 500 bits at 10Mbps. Dividing 500 by 8 bits per octet yields 62.5. This means that packets have to be a minimum of 62.5 octets in length for collision detection to work. Xerox rounded this up to 64 octets minimum frame size for its DIX Ethernet. This convention was maintained by the 802.3 specification.

Given that the payload of any given frame was still dictated by the higher level transport protocol, it was quite likely that the occasional frame would be less than 64 octets. Frames that were less than 64 octets long were padded with zeros by Ethernet II until the frame reached this minimum size. Padding solved the timing problem of collision detection, but forced each protocol to distinguish data from padding. The DIX frame continued to rely upon the Type field to identify the higher level protocol and, therefore, its data field length. Although 802.3 doesn't recognize the Type field in this manner, it continues to support the padding of data fields to enforce the 64-octet minimum frame size.

Tangentially related to CSMA/CD's collision detection mechanism is the standard inter-frame gap. The 802.3 variant of Ethernet features a 96-bit gap between frames. All devices know this, and expect it. Contrary to many of the rumors that have been generated to explain the presence of this structure, the inter-frame gap is analogous to a carrier tone in a telephony network. It identifies the transmitter and provides any time that may be needed to continue framing and transmitting data. Thus, in today's Ethernets, a transmitting device sends a frame followed by a 96-bit gap that is interpreted by other network-attached devices as part of the bit stream from the transmitting device. They may not transmit until this gap has passed and the transmitter relinquishes its control over the communications band.

FIGURE 6.4.

A collision in the making.

Collisions

Collisions have a bad reputation among LAN administrators. Even the term, "collision," has a negative connotation. Truth be known, collisions are an error condition. However, collisions are part of the normal operation of a contention-based media access methodology. In networks using this method, collisions do occur. Mechanisms exist to detect, and recover from, collisions. Consequently, do not pay too much attention to the collision rates, and don't panic whenever the yellow collision light on the hub flashes. Trust the network to operate normally. If you've built it properly, including adhering to all Physical Layer constraints like maximum distances for each media type, the LAN automatically recovers from collisions.

If network performance degrades noticeably, the best way to reduce collisions is to reduce the number of devices per collision domain. As mentioned earlier, bridges, routers, and switches can all be used effectively in this capacity.

It is important to note that the chaotic nature of contention-based media access makes the use of such technologies inappropriate for time-sensitive applications. Time-sensitive applications must have a much more predictable and timely means of accessing LAN bandwidth. Contention-based networks are ideally suited for the more traditional forms of networked computing, like terminal emulation, file and print sharing, and so forth.

Token-Based Media Access

The next most popular media access methodology regulates access to the media by passing tokens. Token passing is a phenomenon of LAN architectures that are based on a ring topology. Specific examples are the various implementations of Token Ring and FDDI (Fiber Distributed Data Interface).

A token is a special frame that is passed from device to device, in sequence along the ring. It can circulate only when the ring is idle. This frame is only a few octets in length, and contains a special bit pattern. This bit pattern can be manipulated to convert it into a *Start of Frame* (SOF) delimiting sequence that informs downstream network-attached devices of the arrival of a data-bearing frame. Immediately following the SOF field are the source and destination address pairs, as identified by the transmitting device.

The token is recognized by all devices as being the arbiter of access to the transmission media. If the token is passed to a device that doesn't need to transmit, the device may hold on to the token for 10 milliseconds, or longer if the default value has been changed. This enables a device to finish framing any data that it may be receiving from higher layer protocols that link back up to its applications. A device must have this token to place data frames on the network. If it doesn't have the token, it must wait until it gets the token from its downstream neighbor.

If this time expires and the device still doesn't need to transmit, the device relinquishes control of the token, and sends it to the next device in the ring. The SOF delimiter of a data frame can be reconverted to a token by only the device that owns it. The token eventually returns to its originator as it travels through the ring. The originator then must reconvert the token to a SOF. Typically, this is done after the intended recipient(s) copy the data off the frame and modify a bit pattern to signify their successful receipt of it. This modified data frame continues its travel around the ring until it returns to its originator. The originator acknowledges successful delivery of its contents, and either holds it for the allotted time, or uses it for transporting more data. This token-passing scheme is illustrated in Figure 6.5.

Figure 6.5.

Token passing.

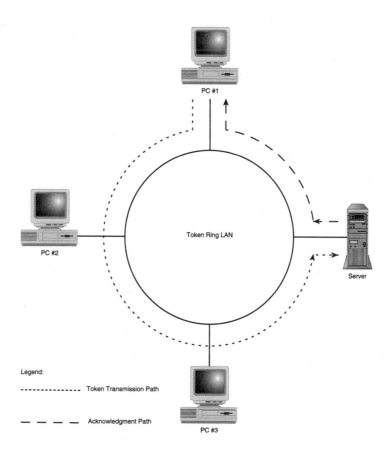

It is possible to calculate the maximum time that can expire before a device is able to transmit. This is done by multiplying the maximum amount of time that any given node can hold a token by the number of devices connected to the ring. To this value should be added the amount of time required for a token to traverse the ring. Although this doesn't include I/O, processing time, spindle and head movement times of disk drives, or any other processor-based source of time delay, it does provide a reasonable estimation of the maximum network time delay that can be experienced.

This aggregate time can be manipulated either upward or downward by adding or subtracting nodes from the ring. Consequently, token-passing networks are ideal for any application that requires predictable delays.

FDDI Token-Based Media Access

FDDI uses a modified form of the token-passing scheme described in the previous section. This modification is subtle, but significant. Rather than keeping all stations idling until the originator receives the acknowledgment of delivery, FDDI uses a quick release mechanism to allow other devices to transmit, even while the original frame is in transit. The quick release mechanism is actually quite simple. Immediately after transmitting a frame (which contains a token modified into a SOF), the transmitter then transmits another token. Thus, downstream stations do not have to wait for the original data frame to return to its originator before they can transmit. Control over the transmission media is relinquished much more quickly in FDDI's version of token-based media access. This is illustrated in Figure 6.6.

Figure 6.6.

Token passing with a quick release.

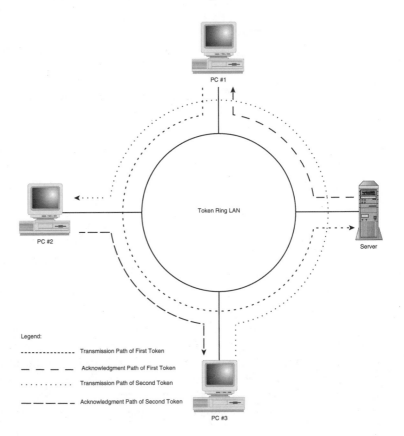

The benefits of a quick release of transmission control are obvious. The next device downstream enjoys the opportunity to transmit much sooner. This device can begin to pull the new token off the ring and convert it to a SOF delimiter even before the first data frame is received by its intended recipient.

The second benefit of this scheme is that it makes the network much more efficient. Consequently, the maximum sustainable throughput of a network equipped with a fast release can approach the theoretical maximum throughput.

6

Demand-Priority Media Access

The *Demand-Priority Access Method* (DPAM) is used by the IEEE 802.12 100Mbps VG-AnyLAN specification. DPAM is a round-robin arbitration method in which a central repeater (the hub) regularly polls ports connected to it. This polling is performed in port order and is conducted to identify ports that have transmission requests. After the need to transmit is established, the repeater determines whether the priority is high or normal. These priorities are designed to service time-sensitive requests before servicing normal priority requests for bandwidth. An idle signal is automatically generated by any port that is not transmitting data. This can include any devices that either are idle or have a pending transmission request.

This idle signal is cleared by the repeater if that station is selected as the next in the priority sequence to transmit. In other words, the repeater identifies the next station in its priority sequence and then instructs it to halt transmission of its idle signal. When the port on that device senses its own "silence" (in other words, the idle signal ceases), it begins to transmit.

When this happens, the repeater alerts the other stations that they may receive an incoming message. The repeater then reads the incoming packet's destination address, looks in its link configuration table, and switches the packet to that destination address as well as to any promiscuous ports.

The central, or *root*, repeater controls the operation of the priority domain. The priority domain can include up to three levels of cascaded hubs. This enables interconnected repeaters to function as a single large repeater. The central repeater sends all traffic to each lower level repeater. Each lower level repeater, in turn, polls its active ports for requests after packet transmission.

No station is permitted to transmit twice in a row if other stations have same-priority requests pending. The central repeater does not allow a high-priority request to interrupt a normal-priority request if that request is already in progress. In a lower-level repeater, the normal-priority request is preempted, so that the high-priority request can be accommodated. To ensure that a request isn't completely ignored, any normal-priority requests that have been waiting longer than 250ms are automatically elevated to high-priority status.

This access method is used only by the IEEE 802.12 specification for a 100Mbps network that uses either an Ethernet or Token Ring frame format (but not both simultaneously), and a star topology. Known as VG-AnyLAN, which stands for *voice grade wiring, any LAN architecture*, it can operate over four pairs of Category 3 UTP, STP, Category 5, and fiber. There can be up to three levels of cascaded repeaters with up to 100 meters between the repeaters and the stations. The network may be up to 4,000 feet in diameter.

VG-AnyLAN has almost completely failed in the marketplace. Although DPAM is technically superior to CSMA/CD as a LAN media access method, it is quickly being relegated to the role of an interesting footnote in the history of Local Area Networking. The higher speed CSMA/CD LANs, like Fast Ethernet and Gigabit Ethernet, offer much simpler migration paths from 10Mbps CSMA/CD Ethernets than VG-AnyLAN does.

Accessing Media in a Switched LAN

In addition to the three basic types of media access, a fourth methodology exists. Though this isn't a clearly defined access methodology, it is being used increasingly in lieu of the other methodologies to bolster the efficiency and performance of LANs. Switching is rewriting the conventional rules about LAN topologies and access methodologies.

As explained in Chapter 2, "LAN Types and Topologies," a switch is a multiport, Data Link Layer (OSI Reference Model Layer 2) device. A switch "learns" MAC addresses and stores them in an internal look-up table. Temporary switched paths are created between the frame's originator and its intended recipient, and the frames are forwarded along that temporary path.

Switching can either be used to interconnect shared hubs, or it can be used to interconnect individual devices. Segmenting shared hubs with a switching hub is known as *segment switching*. This is illustrated in Figure 6.7.

FIGURE 6.7.

Segment switching.

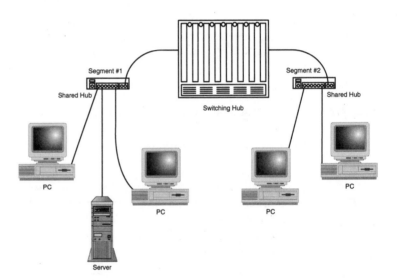

In a port-switched LAN, each port on the switching hub is connected to a single device. The devices can be workstations, servers, or even printers. This is illustrated in Figure 6.8.

Each device connected to a switched port enjoys its own Layer 2 domain, shared only with that switched port. Switching can be used to improve the performance of both contention-based and token-passing LAN architectures.

Switching Contention-Based Networks

In a contention-based protocol, port switching effectively reduces the collision domain to just the switch port and the device that it connects to the network. Depending upon the hardware at both ends, switched CSMA/CD can support either full- or half-duplex connections.

FIGURE 6.8.

Port switching.

A switched full-duplex connection represents the maximum performance that this protocol can support, at any given transmission rate. Each device in the two-device collision domain (device and port) enjoys its own separate network paths, with their own separate bandwidths, for transmit and receive. For example, in a 10Mbps Ethernet that uses twisted pair wiring, one pair of wire supports the transmit function, and another pair supports the receive function for each port-switched device.

> **NOTE**
>
> Although some manufacturers might mislead you into thinking that a full-duplex, switched network connection yields twice the bandwidth, don't be fooled. This technique does, in fact, improve performance, but it does not necessarily double throughputs. Both the transmit and receive functions are serviced by the same Network Interface Card (NIC), and must compete for CPU cycles through a common bus port on the motherboard. Consequently, it is illogical to expect that performance will double. Rather, the performance bottleneck simply moves.

Separating the transmit and receive functions obviates any competition that may have existed. In a full-duplex implementation, the pair of wire used for the switch's transmissions becomes the pair of wire that the connected device uses to receive, and vice versa for the switch's receive wire path. There can be no collisions in this scenario. This was depicted in Figure 6.3, earlier in this chapter.

Switching Token-Passing Networks

Port-switching can improve token-passing LANs in much the same way that it can improve contention-based LANs. The number of devices that pass tokens is reduced to an absolute minimum number of two: the switch port and the device connected to it. The only difference is that these devices pass tokens, rather than compete for available bandwidth.

Unlike a contention-based LAN, a token passing LAN requires the transmitted frame to return to its originator for reconversion to a token before any other devices can communicate. This remains true in a switched environment. Consequently, token-passing networks don't experience the same performance benefit as a contention-based network from full-duplex operations.

Summary

In baseband LANs, arbitrating access to the transmission media is a critical function. Three distinct methods for arbitration have emerged. They are contention, token passing, and demand-priority. In reality, this short-list of options has been reduced to only two practical choices: contention or token passing, as demand-priority is almost completely dead. Curiously, even these two access methodologies are rapidly becoming obsolete with the advent of port-switched LANs.

Each of these media access methods has its own unique combination of benefits and limitations that should be understood before using it as the foundation for an information technology architecture.

Building Local Area Networks

PART

Ethernet

by Mark Sportack

IN THIS CHAPTER

CHAPTER 7

Ethernet, born a quick and dirty mechanism to enhance researchers' capabilities to develop new technologies, has proven itself one of the most valuable and persistent of all information technologies. It has entered its third decade of life, experiencing significant evolution along the way. Some of these evolutionary changes have made it virtually impossible to develop a concise definition of Ethernet.

This chapter examines the various potential meanings of "Ethernet," and identifies the myriad Physical Layer implementations of today's 10Mbps Ethernets. Also included are some of their performance limitations, including both specified and practical limits.

The Various Ethernets

Ethernet originally referred to the proprietary LAN cobbled together by research scientists at Xerox's Palo Alto Research Center. Rather than being a bold new technology developed for its vast market potential, Ethernet (as the researchers called it) was a simple tool that enabled the researchers to share data much more readily as they researched and tried to develop real technologies.

This crude LAN lacked sophistication. It depended upon the better defined Network and Transport Layer protocols for much of its own behavior, including the size of its frames. This original LAN was half-duplex, and used thick, coaxial cabling for interconnecting devices. Its signaling speed was 10Mbps. This original Ethernet is now known as PARC Ethernet, or even Ethernet I (the "I" symbol being the Roman Numeral for the number 1). Obviously, both of these adjectivally-enhanced names were applied after the emergence of other forms of Ethernet. Today, this original form of Ethernet is obsolete and is referenced for only historical and contextual purposes.

Xerox, recognizing the potential value of this technology, recruited partners to bring it to market. The two partners were Intel and the Digital Equipment Corporation (DEC). Together, they instituted a series of improvements to PARC Ethernet and made it a somewhat open standard. This new Ethernet was called Ethernet II.

> **NOTE**
>
> Ethernet II, also known as DIX Ethernet for its triumvirate of creators (Digital, Intel, and Xerox), could not be considered a truly open standard as the standards were controlled by the three primary manufacturers of its components.

One of the first steps was to legitimize Ethernet as a stand-alone networking protocol. This meant it could no longer rely upon Network and Transport Layer protocols to define its frame sizes.

As important as this development was, it paled in comparison to the refinement of Ethernet's media access methodology. The original Ethernet used a very primitive "listen before talking" scheme that was called *Carrier Sense, Multiple Access* (CSMA). In essence, any station that wanted to transmit first had to listen to the wire to see whether it was available. The improvement that was made was the addition of collision detection capabilities. Ethernet II's new media access methodology was called *Carrier Sense, Multiple Access with Collision Detection* (CSMA/CD). For more information on the mechanics of CSMA/CD, please refer to Chapter 6, "The Mechanics of Media Access."

In February of 1980, the Institute of Electrical and Electronic Engineers (IEEE) assumed the responsibility for turning the budding Ethernet into a truly open standard. Truth be told, their goal was not simply to standardize Ethernet. Rather, theirs was a much more ambitious goal of creating standardization and interoperability across multiple networking technologies. They launched their Project 802, with numerous sub-committees and technical working groups to hammer out standards for Local and Metropolitan Area Networks (LANs and MANs).

Project 802 decomposed the typical network into its functional components, and layered them in a logical sequence. Open standards were developed for hardware-level addressing, network management, and network monitoring. These standards formed the basis for numerous local area network architectures such as the following:

- A 10Mbps CSMA/CD form of Ethernet
- Token Ring
- Token Bus
- Other even more obscure architectures

The fact that these architectures enjoyed a common basis for hardware-level addressing, management, and monitoring meant that mixed topology networks could be built without compromising interoperability across otherwise dissimilar network platforms. More importantly, the disparate platforms could be managed and monitored with a common set of standards-compliant tools.

The IEEE's version of Ethernet was formally named 802.3 CSMA/CD. This unwieldy name is almost always forsaken in favor of Ethernet. Call it what you like, this new and improved version of Ethernet built upon the foundation of its predecessors. The CSMA/CD media access methodology was retained, as was the original coaxial-based transmission media and half-duplex transmission mode. Another specification for coaxial cabling was added and, over time, other Physical Layer specifications for twisted pair wiring and fiber optic cabling were also developed.

Today, it is becoming more correct to identify Ethernet with adjectives other than CSMA/CD. Within the past two years, the original 802.3 specification was extended to include a 100Mbps version of Ethernet. This necessitated the development of new Physical Layer specifications, as well as some minor modifications to the media access mechanisms. More importantly, support for full-duplex transmission was added. Full-duplex Ethernet enables a device to communicate over one physical transmission path, ostensibly one pair of twisted-pair wiring in a four-pair bundle, while simultaneously receiving data over another pair. Implemented in a port-switched configuration, full-duplex Ethernet effectively obviates contention-based access to the transmission media. The transmitting device can place frames on the LAN at near wire speeds. Consequently, the use of CSMA/CD to describe the IEEE's 802.3 Ethernet variant is inaccurate.

> **NOTE**
>
> *Wire speed* is the rate at which electrons flow through a copper media. This rate is the theoretical maximum rate that data (which is ultimately converted to a flow of electrons) can travel through the media.

As if this weren't confusing enough, there are even specifications for a broadband, not baseband, 10Mbps Ethernet. One such example is the 10Broad36 specification. Fortunately for you, broadband Ethernets are well out of the mainstream. They aren't covered by any of the Networking Essentials courses, and only superficially resemble the more familiar Ethernets. Consequently, this chapter focuses on just the baseband variants.

To avoid confusion, this book uses the term "Ethernet family of standards" to describe the 802.3 series of standards as a generic, cumulative technology set. The term "Ethernet" is used to describe just the 802.3 series of standards that signal at 10Mbps. The term "Fast Ethernet" is used to describe the 802.3 series of standards that signal at 100Mbps. Similarly, "Gigabit Ethernet" describes the series of emerging standards that signal at 1024Mbps. This book also refers to specific, individual Ethernet technologies by describing the Physical Layer's *Medium Dependent Interface* (MDI) specification (for example, 10BaseT). This specificity is necessary because Ethernet now encompasses quite a vast and diverse array of standards and emerging standards.

Supported Hardware

Before delving too far into the intricacies of Ethernet, it is necessary to first examine the various hardware components that are used to build an Ethernet network. These components are independent of media types, and are referred to throughout the remainder of this chapter, so it is essential to provide the proper context for an examination of their implications in the network.

The hardware that may be used in support of an Ethernet network includes:

- Network Interface Cards (NICs)
- Repeat hubs

- Non-repeating hubs
- Bridges
- Routers

Network Interface Cards

A *Network Interface Card* (NIC) is a printed circuit board that is installed in a vacant slot in a computer's I/O bus. The back of the card contains a physical interface for a specific connector type. Each connector type is designed for a specific transmission media. This card provides the connectivity between a computer's internal system resources and the external resources connected to the network. It embodies the logic of the LAN's Data Link and Physical Layers.

Repeaters

A *repeater* is a relatively simple device that takes an incoming signal, amplifies it without modifying its shape, and puts the signal back on the media. This device operates strictly at Layer 1 of the OSI Reference Model.

The functions of signal amplification and repetition have been bundled into multi-port devices that are used to interconnect multiple devices across the LAN. These devices are commonly known as *hubs*, although they really are just multi-port repeaters.

Non-Repeating Hubs

A *non-repeating hub* is very similar to a repeating hub. The sole difference is that it does not repeat, or amplify, the signals. These hubs do little more than provide a star-topology by aggregating multiple station connections onto a single network device.

Bridges

A *bridge* is a Layer 2 mechanism that enables two segments of a LAN to be linked together. Because bridges operate at Layer 2, they do not recognize the higher layer protocols that are embedded in the frames that they forward. They forward these frames based on a MAC address. For example, the bridge "learns" which MAC addresses are connected to the networks on its various ports. Whenever it receives a frame with a MAC address that does not reside on the LAN segment on which it was generated, the bridge looks up that address in its bridging table (a compilation of MAC addresses, by port number) and forwards it to the correct LAN segment for delivery.

Stringing several bridges together, or even just using them in an environment that is characterized by MAC broadcasts, is a good way to find the limitations of these devices. They have, for the most part, failed to keep up with the increasing demands placed on network devices and have become little more than an obsolete curiosity.

7

ETHERNET

Routers

A *router* is not a Layer 2 Ethernet device. Rather, it is a Layer 3 packet forwarding mechanism. Nevertheless, routers do support interfaces for all standard LAN technologies, and are used in numerous ways. The primary use of a router is to connect the LAN with the networks beyond the LAN's domain. This has three important implications for network design.

First, the Wide Area Network (WAN) is clearly beyond the LAN's domain. Routers remain the technology that must be used to interconnect LANs that are dispersed across large enough geographic regions as to warrant using long haul transmission technologies. Such technologies include dedicated leased lines and switched circuits.

Second, multiple LAN domains may coexist in relatively close proximity. In fact, a single office premise may contain numerous LANs that are dedicated to individual workgroups. Concerns over security may warrant some degree of separation, yet not preclude interconnection. In such cases, bridging the LANs together would be undesirable. Routers provide a little more security, through mechanisms like Access Control Lists, and can effectively internetwork LANs while preserving the integrity of their Layer 2 collision and broadcast domains.

The third implication is borne of performance requirements. Ethernets can become large enough to start collapsing under their own mass. For example, a building may contain an Ethernet that is approaching 1024 devices in size. If the applications supported by this LAN use Layer 2 broadcasts (don't ask why, this is a hypothetical scenario presented for academic value!), it is quite possible that segmenting the LAN with bridges or switches won't improve performance. In effect, the LAN will have had its collision domain segmented, but not its broadcast domain. In this situation, a router may be your only viable option.

Layered Functions

The members of the IEEE began their standardization efforts by separating the necessary functions of local and metropolitan area networking into modules, or layers, based on the sequence of events that occur during a normal communications session. Like many other standards organizations, they created their own protocol stack, rather than adhere strictly to the OSI Reference Model. Figure 7.1 illustrates the IEEE's model, complete with separation of functions into layers, sub-layers, and even different modules within the various layers.

Data Link Layer Functions

The IEEE's 802 specification series breaks the OSI Reference Model's Data Link Layer, Layer 2, into two discrete components. They are named for the functions that they control, as follows:

- Logical Link Control (LLC)
- Media Access Control (MAC)

Their relationship is illustrated in Figure 7.2.

FIGURE 7.1.

Block diagram of the IEEE's 10Mbps Ethernet versus the OSI Reference Model.

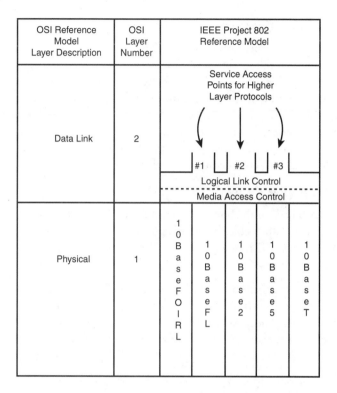

OSI Reference Model Layer Description	OSI Layer Number	IEEE Project 802 Reference Model			
Data Link	2	Service Access Points for Higher Layer Protocols			
		#1 #2 #3			
		Logical Link Control			
		Media Access Control			
Physical	1	10BaseFOIRL	10BaseFL	10Base2	10Base5	10BaseT

FIGURE 7.2.

The IEEE's Data Link Layer components.

OSI Reference Model Layer Description	OSI Layer Number	IEEE Project 802 Reference Model		
Data Link Layer	2	Service Access Points for Higher Layer Protocols		
		#1 #2 #3		
		Logical Link Control		
		Media Access Control		

Together, the LLC and the MAC are the heart of Ethernet. They provide the framing and addressing that encapsulate the data and enable it to be transmitted to its destination. They also contain error detection mechanisms and are responsible for initiating the retransmission of any damaged or lost frames. In short, they control the transmission and reception of data frames, although they do not perform the actual transmission. This is ceded to the Physical Layer.

Logical Link Control

The LLC is the uppermost of the two Data Link Layer components. It insulates the upper layer protocols from the specific access methodology and transmission media. Remember, the 802 series of specifications provides for interoperability between different LAN architectures. The LLC is the mechanism that separates Network and Transport Layer protocols from the vicissitudes of LAN architecture. These higher layer protocols need not know whether they are going to be transported across an Ethernet, Token Ring, or even a Token Bus. Nor do they need to know which Physical Layer specification they will be using. The LLC provides a common interface for all 802-compliant LAN architectures and variants.

Media Access Control

The MAC Layer is the bottom-most of the Data Link Layer's components in the IEEE architecture. It is responsible for interfacing with the Physical Layer and ensuring that successful transmissions and receptions occur. This entails a tandem set of functions: transmit and receive.

The MAC Layer is responsible for encapsulating all data received from the LLC into a frame. This frame contains all the addressing and structure needed to transport the data to its destination(s). The MAC Layer is also responsible for implementing the data integrity test that is used to verify that the contents of a frame were not damaged or altered during transmission.

The MAC Layer also contains the mechanisms that are capable of determining, via the Physical Layer mechanisms, whether or not the communications band is available for transmission. If it is available, the framed data is handed off to the Physical Layer for transmission. Otherwise, the MAC Layer enacts its Binary Exponential Back-Off Algorithm. This awkward name describes an algorithm that generates a pseudo-random waiting period that must be endured before another attempt at retransmission can be made.

The last significant MAC Layer function is monitoring the status of transmitted frames for any signs of a collision. Whenever it detects a collision of one of its own frames, it identifies the data that must be retransmitted, enacts its back-off algorithm, and then re-attempts transmission. It continues to enact its back-off algorithm until the frame is transmitted successfully. This is simultaneously a strength and a weakness of Ethernet. It guarantees higher layer protocols that their data will be delivered. Unfortunately, the chaotic nature of the contention-based media access mechanism can make this an arduous and time-consuming (in the context of computing, that is!) task.

Physical Layer Functions

As with its implementation of the Data Link Layer, the IEEE's implementation of the Physical Layer is broken down into discrete components. The modularity of these components provides flexibility in the adoption of new technologies. If this were not the case, every time a new transmission media needed to be supported, an entire Layer 1 stack would have to be developed. Using the modular approach, only the mechanism that is responsible for interfacing with the new physical transmission media needs be developed: the remainder of the Physical Layer functions can be used, ideally, without alteration. The IEEE's Physical Layer components are illustrated in Figure 7.3 and explained in the remainder of this section.

FIGURE 7.3.
The IEEE's Physical Layer components.

OSI Reference Model Layer Description	OSI Layer Number	IEEE Project 802 Reference Model
Physical	1	Physical Signaling Sublayer
		Attachment Unit Interface
		Physical Medium Attachment
		Medium Dependent Interface

The four components of the Physical Layer include the following:

- Physical Signaling Sublayer (PLS, yes, that's correct, PLS!)
- Attachment Unit Interface (AUI)
- Physical Medium Attachment (PMA)
- Medium Dependent Interface (MDI)

Together, these components provide the entire definition of how transmission occurs between two devices via a network. This includes the cable types (including minimum levels of expected performance), cable connector types, pin assignments of the cable (for twisted pair media only), voltage levels (for electrical signal transmission) or optical wavelength levels (for transmission over fiber optic cables), timing, and even the physical network interface—that is, transceiver—that performs the transmission and reception.

The Physical Signaling Sublayer (PLS) mechanism is indigenous to Data Terminal Equipment (DTE) devices that use 10BaseT. It defines the signaling scheme as well as the interface to the transceiver cable that is used.

The Attachment Unit Interface (AUI) provides the definition of the transmission media specifications. The Physical Medium Attachment (PMA) defines the operational processes and specifications of the transceiver.

The Medium Dependent Interface (MDI) is the most visible aspect of the 802.3 Physical Layer. There are multiple supported MDIs, each one describing the mechanisms needed to support transmission via a different transmission media. The AUI, PMA, and MDI are often embodied in a single device known as a Medium Attachment Unit (MAU). This is the term that the IEEE uses rather than "NIC."

7

ETHERNET

> **NOTE**
>
> The MDI does *not* define the transmission media! Rather, it defines all the mechanisms and processes required to support transmission over a given media type. Its definitions assume a specific, minimum level of performance that is to be provided by the media, as well as the physical connector type that is to be used to connect to that media. This is, however, not a definition of the media itself.

The Physical Layer's Medium Dependent Interfaces

Five distinct MDIs for 10Mbps baseband Ethernet are defined by the IEEE. These MDIs are bundled into modules that define every aspect of the Physical Layer for the different transmission media. Of these five MDIs, two are based on coaxial cable, two on fiber optic cable, and one on twisted copper pairs of wire. Some basic specification limitations apply to all the MDIs.

For example, all media types must comply with a maximum signal path. The maximum allowable signal path is four repeaters. This enables five cable segments to be interconnected, provided that at least two of those segments are Inter-Repeater Links only! This limit is frequently referred to as the 5-4-3 rule, because of the five segments, four repeaters, and maximum of three populated segments.

This numeric limitation can easily be translated into maximum network diameters for each of the physical media by multiplying the number of links by the maximum allowable transmission distance for each media, and then adding all the products together.

Although it would be a bit tougher to come up with a cute, if not mnemonic, moniker for it, 802.3 also imposes a limit of seven bridges for a LAN segment. This applies to all media types.

Another limitation is imposed on the number of devices that a segment may contain. Each segment, regardless of media type, may contain a maximum of 1024 devices. Networks that need to support more than this number must use either a bridge, switch, or router to create multiple segments.

The two coaxial cables allow for some topological variety not supported by the other MDIs, because coaxial cable can be tapped. *Tapping* is a process whereby the two conductors of the cable are pierced, but not broken, with a device known as a *tap*. The tap provides for continuity along the original cable path while simultaneously enabling a new cable path to be branched off of it. This new cable can be used to connect to other network devices, including repeaters, servers, printers, and client machines. 802.3 compliant coaxial cabled Ethernets can support up to 64 devices off each tap. Each tap must be at least 2.5 meters away from any other tap.

Twisted pair and fiber optic cables are point-to-point transmission media and cannot be tapped. Radial expansion of a network using either of these media must be accomplished using a hub.

> **NOTE**
>
> Ethernet cabling has two functional categories: transceiver and bus. These terms date back to Ethernet's early, repeaterless days when it featured a bus topology. Today, transceiver and bus cables are rapidly becoming obsolete, in favor of the terms "station wiring" and "backbone."

10Base2

10Base2, like most of the other Ethernet MDIs, derives its name from the following convention: the signaling speed (in Mbps), plus the transmission method (baseband, in this case), plus the maximum number of meters that the cable can be, rounded to the nearest 100, and then divided by 100.

If this sounds complicated, consider 10Base2. This specification describes a 10Mbps baseband network protocol. It uses a 50ohm coaxial cable that can be a maximum length of 185 meters in length. Rounding 185 yields 200. Dividing 200 by 100 yields 2, the last digit of the MDI's name.

10Base2 networks can be extended beyond 185 meters by using repeaters, bridges, or routers. Using a router to segment an Ethernet actually creates 10Base2 segments that can be tapped up to 30 times, with each tap supporting a maximum of 64 devices.

10Base5

As its name implies, the maximum length for 10Base5 coaxial cable is 500 meters. This MDI uses a much thicker coaxial cable than 10Base2. Transmission efficacy, in copper media, is a function of the conductor's thickness. The greater the conductor's diameter, the more bandwidth can be achieved. Consequently, 10Base5 can be tapped up to 100 times, with a maximum of 64 devices per tap.

Mathematically, one could argue that this means a 10Base5 segment could be built that contained 6,400 devices. Unfortunately, an overarching device number limitation of 1024 is applied to all 802.3 specifications.

10BaseT

If 10BaseT had adhered to the naming conventions applied to the coaxial specifications, its name would have been 10Base1, as it is limited to a 100 meter segment length. For whatever reasons they may have had, the IEEE broke from convention and designated this MDI with a "T" to symbolize its physical media: twisted pair.

7

ETHERNET

10BaseT, contrary to popular belief, does not specify a cable type. Instead, it uses a signaling technique that works on four wires that equal or surpass the Category of Performance #3 for unshielded twisted pair. The four wires are named for their function and polarity. For example, one pair of wires is used to support the positive and negative poles of the transmit circuit. The second pair supports the positive and negative poles of the receive circuit. Hence, the four wires are named as follows:

- T+ for the positive Transmit wire
- T- for the negative Transmit wire
- R+ for the positive Receive wire
- R- for the negative Receive wire

The 10BaseT specification calls for these four wires to be wired to specific pin assignments in the twisted pair cable. 10BaseT repeaters/hubs use pin assignments that enable NIC ports to be cabled to them. For Ethernet repeaters and other Data Communications Equipment (DCE), these assignments are provided in Table 7.1.

Table 7.1. DCE pin numbers and functions.

DCE Pin Assignment	Function
1	R+
2	R-
3	T+
4	not used
5	not used
6	T-
7	not used
8	not used

For Ethernet NICs and other Data Terminal Equipment (DTE), these assignments are listed in Table 7.2.

Table 7.2. DTE pin numbers and functions.

DTE Pin Assignment	Function
1	T+
2	T-
3	R+
4	not used

DTE Pin Assignment	Function
5	not used
6	R-
7	not used
8	not used

Under normal operating circumstances, a DTE device always connects to a DCE device. These complementary interfaces enable terminal and communications gear to be directly cabled together without causing conflicts between transmits and receives. Under normal operating circumstances, a DCE device always connects to a DTE device, using a four-pair whose leads remain consistent from end to end. Such a cable is called a "straight-through cable." There are, however, certain exceptions to this simple DCE to DTE connectivity scheme.

Interconnecting the current generation of hubs results in a DCE to DCE connection. This is the first exception. Hubs used to have separate "out" ports that were configured as DTE. The sole purpose of these out ports was to interconnect with an "in" port of another hub, bridge, and so forth. Many of today's hubs, however, have eschewed this feature in favor of high bandwidth, fully meshed switched backplanes in robust, multi-slot chassis. The manufacturers reason that the backplane can interconnect any LAN hubs that are inserted. Consequently, all ports are configured as "out" ports; that is, they have a DCE pin configuration.

Interconnecting two hubs that have only DCE ports presents a problem. They both transmit on the same pair of wire, and listen on the other pair. The end result is that every packet sent across this link either experiences a collision or is not acknowledged by the recipient. Not a good thing. The answer is to use a cross-over cable that simulates a DCE-to-DTE interface, given a DCE-to-DCE scenario.

The second scenario that can result in something other than a DCE-to-DTE interface is the direct interconnection of two devices equipped with NICS, without having a repeater/hub in between them. This results in a DTE-to-DTE connection, the opposite of the first scenario. Regardless, the net effect remains the same. Communications do not work.

Clearly, this is a highly unusual situation. In fact, outside of testing, there aren't many reasons to interconnect two machines in this manner. This may, however, be changing. The emergence of clustering technologies for low-end computing architectures creates a need for a robust connection to internetwork two devices that are in very close proximity. Given that most early clusters will be limited to two computers, there is little reason to install a repeating hub between them. In fact, the use of a hub in this manner only introduces unnecessary propagation delays. The cluster operates more efficiently without it! The computers' NICs can be cabled directly together using a cross-over cable.

Cross-over cables must maintain the polarity of a physical wire. Positive and negative voltages must be kept separate, because they are directly tied to the signaling scheme used by Ethernet. The only wires that are crossed over are the positive Transmit (T+) to the positive Receive (R+), and the negative Transmit (T-) to the negative Receive (R-).

Differential Signaling

The use of positive and negative leads, or wires, for each function enables the use of a signaling technique known as *differential signaling*. Differential signaling is designed to cancel out the effects of electromagnetic noise on the data. Noise is relatively easily inducted into the wires, and it constitutes one of the graver concerns of transmitting on unshielded twisted pair.

The transmitting device using differential signaling places the opposite forms of the same signal on both transmit leads, T+ and T-. T- receives the inverse of the signal placed on T+. At the other end of the wire, the T- signal is inverted again. T- and T+ should then, theoretically, be equals. Any noise that is inducted is inducted equally across both pairs, at least in theory. Thus, what appears to be a spike on the T+ lead appears as an equal, yet opposite, valley on the T- lead. Adding the two signals together at the terminus of the wire results in the restoration of the original signal. The spike and the valley literally cancel each other out.

This process is illustrated in Figure 7.4. The original signal is placed on T+, an inverse of it is placed on T-. Noise results in a slight spike on the plateau of one Manchester encoded bit on T+. This appears as a slight valley, of equal area, on the corresponding bit on T-. At the terminus, the positive and negative areas of the spike and valley effectively cancel each other out, restoring the original coding.

FIGURE 7.4.

Cancellation of noise using differential signaling.

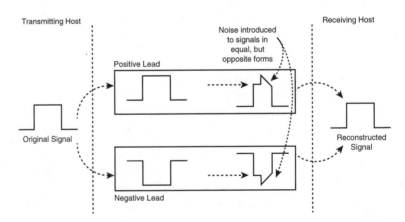

10BaseFL

The 10BaseFL specification provides for the baseband transmission of 10Mbps Ethernet over multi-mode 62.5/125-micron fiber optic cable. The maximum distance for a cable run is 2,000 meters. Like twisted pair, fiber optic cabling cannot be tapped: it is strictly a point-to-point media.

10BaseFL can be used to interconnect repeaters, or even to connect servers to a repeater. Such connections tend to be slightly more expensive than a comparable 10BaseT connection, but it can be extended over much greater distances.

10BaseFOIRL

A relatively recent addition to the 802.3 series is 10BaseFOIRL. Quite a mouthful, for a mnemonic that is intended to facilitate the remembrance of 10Mbps baseband transmission over fiber optic inter-repeater links! Implicit in this definition is that this technology is strictly limited to the interconnection of repeaters. In other words, it is for hub-to-hub connectivity over fiber optic cabling. There can be no other devices attached.

10BaseFOIRL uses an 8.3-micron diameter fiber optic cable that must be driven by an injection laser diode (ILD). This hardware/media combination provides effective transmission of 10Mbps baseband signals for up to 5,000 meters. Unfortunately, both ILDs and single-mode fiber tend to be fairly expensive, which has limited their adoption in the marketplace.

Mixing Media Types

The different Physical Layer specifications and their transmission media should not be considered mutually exclusive. In fact, the very point of having an 802 family of LAN/MAN standards was to facilitate interoperability across different LAN architectures and manufacturers. Thus, it would be rather silly if the specifications did not provide for topologies constructed from a mixture of supported transmission media.

It is quite common for the media type to be matched to the requirements of the LAN's functional areas. Historically, there have been three functional areas:

- Station connectivity
- Server connectivity
- Repeater interconnectivity

As mentioned earlier in this chapter, the emergence of clustering technologies for the low end computing architectures is creating a fourth LAN functional area: cluster interconnect. Unlike the more traditional server-to-repeater connection, decreasing propagation delay while simultaneously increasing bandwidth is absolutely critical to the success of this functional area. Consequently, transmission media that impose the lowest possible propagation delay, with the highest possible bandwidth, should be used for cluster interconnectivity.

Each of the other three functional areas also presents a different set of performance expectations. For example, station connectivity, assuming your work environments have a structured cable plant, are typically very short runs of copper-based wiring. Good choices are either 10Base2 or 10BaseT, although 10BaseT is vastly preferable. Even the relatively thin wiring of 10Base2 can quickly clog cable ducts and raceways.

Server connectivity is much like station connectivity, except that it functions as a traffic aggregation point. Consequently, it is difficult to apply too much bandwidth to this LAN functional area. Good choices are either 10BaseT or, preferably, 10BaseFL.

Repeater interconnectivity is a long-winded way of saying LAN backbone. The links between repeaters can be lengthy. Additionally, LAN backbones are also a natural traffic aggregation point in the network. (That is their primary function!) Consequently, media that can span long distances and still support adequate bandwidth are essential. Logical choices are either of the fiber specifications, although 10BaseT can work (provided, of course, that you adhere to its distance limitations). Also, if you insist on a coaxial cable plant, 10Base5 is well suited to LAN backbones.

IEEE 802.3 Ethernet Frame

Project 802 defined a standard basis for all Ethernet frame types. The frames are a minimum of 64 octets, and a maximum of 1518 octets in length, including payload and all headers except the Preamble and Start of Frame Delimiter. The headers are used to identify the sender and recipient of each packet. The only limitation on this identification is that each address must be unique and 6 octets in length.

The first 12 octets of each frame contain the 6-octet destination address (the intended recipient's address) and a 6-octet source address (the sender's address). These addresses are hardware-level machine address codes, commonly known as *MAC addresses*. They can either be the unique *universally administered address* that is automatically given to each Ethernet network interface card (NIC) at its manufacture, or customized upon installation. Customized addresses are known as *locally administered addresses*. Although potentially valuable, they are extremely difficult to maintain. Consequently, they have fallen into disuse.

The 802.3 Technical Working Group needed a standard that was complete unto itself, not dependent upon the good behavior of other protocols. Therefore, they replaced the 2-octet Type field of previous Ethernets with a 2-octet Length field. This 2-octet field defines the length of the frame's data field. The basic IEEE 802.3 Ethernet frame is depicted in Figure 7.5.

FIGURE 7.5.

The basic, or "raw," IEEE 802.3 Ethernet frame.

7-Octet Preamble	1-Octet Start of Frame Delimiter	6-Octet Destination Address	6-Octet Origination Address	2-Octet Length Field	Variable Length Data Field (> 48 Octets < 1500)	4-Octet Frame Check Sequence

NOTE

The basic IEEE 802.3 frame is often called a *raw Ethernet frame*, as it is seldom actually used in that form. Instead, the basic frame serves as a foundation for supporting sub-headers that facilitate protocol identification for higher layer protocols at the destination machine.

The IEEE's 802.3 basic Ethernet Frame replaced the traditional Type field with a Length field. The 802.2 sub-frame is used, instead of that Type field, to identify the type of protocol, if this is necessary. Another change in the 802.3 frame from its predecessors was the requirement for the overall frame size to be between 64 and 1518 octets in length, from the start of the Destination field, through the end of the Frame Check Sequence field.

Some confusion persists about the exact length of an Ethernet frame. This confusion is caused by three factors:

- The variety of Ethernet frame types
- The flexible-sized payload
- The inconsistency with which the Preamble and Start of Frame Delimiter are referenced

As was demonstrated in Chapter 5, there are five different types of Ethernet frames: PARC Ethernet, DIX Ethernet, Basic 802.3, 802.3 with LLC sub-frame, and 802.3 with SNAP sub-frame. These five varieties represent three different sets of minimum and maximum frame sizes.

Notice the intentional avoidance of specific frame sizes. With flexible payloads, the best you can do is identify the minimum and maximum allowable frame sizes. Understand and expect that actual frames may be any size in between these values.

The last point of confusion involves the preamble and Start of Frame Delimiter (SFD). The preamble is a 7-octet string that precedes each frame and allows the synchronization of the transmission. It is a necessary part of the frame, but it is seldom considered part of the frame itself.

The preamble is immediately followed by the 1-octet Start of Frame Delimiter (SFD). The SFD is sometimes considered an integral part of the preamble, and not a part of the frame itself. Alternatively, one need not look very long or hard to find references that identify the SFD as the official start of the frame.

To avoid confusion, whenever frame sizes are referenced in this chapter, they are specifically identified, and qualified with a description of their starting and ending field names.

Ethernet LLC Frame Structure

The Ethernet LLC frame is a combination of an 802.3 frame and the 802.2 LLC sub-frame. In this implementation, LLC adds three fields to the basic Ethernet frame: Destination Service Access Port, Source Service Access Port, and Control.

Because the 802.3 frame abandoned its predecessors' Type field in favor of a Length field, it was unable to determine which protocol was embedded in the payload. Consequently, a frame received by a computer that supported multiple communications protocols might not be routed to the correct protocol! In other words, the 802.3 frame was adequate to ensure the forwarding of the frame to its destination, but fell short of being able to guarantee delivery to higher layer protocols within that destination machine.

Consequently, the IEEE developed an 802.2 sub-frame structure and standard to rectify this issue. This new sub-frame is referred to as either an 802.2 sub-frame or an LLC frame. When embedded in an 802.3 Ethernet frame, the new frame is illustrated in Figure 7.6, and has the following structure:

- A 7-octet Preamble that signals the start of a frame
- A 1-octet Start of Frame delimiter that signals the start of the frame's contents
- The intended recipient's 6-octet MAC address
- The originator's 6-octet MAC address
- A 2-octet Length field that identifies the total length of the Data field, including the LLC and SNAP headers

■ A 1-octet Destination Service Access Point (DSAP) field that identifies, predictably, the LLC's service access point at the destination machine

■ A 1-octet Source Service Access Point (SSAP) field that identifies the originating machine's LLC service access point

■ A 1- or 2-octet Control field that indicates the type of LLC frame being carried

■ A data field that contains either 42 to 1496, or 43 to 1497 octets of data, depending upon the length of the preceding Control field

■ A 4-octet Frame Check Sequence that is used to check the integrity of the frame

The total length of an Ethernet LLC frame must be at least 64 octets (excluding the Preamble and Start of Frame delimiter) in length to permit proper functioning of the CSMA/CD mechanism. Zeroes are padded to the end of the Data field to ensure this minimum length. The upper limit is 1518 octets, excluding the Preamble and Start of Frame delimiter.

FIGURE 7.6.
The Ethernet LLC frame.

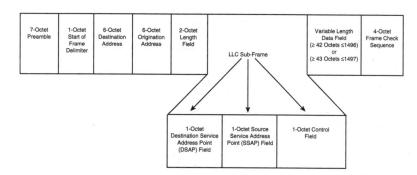

Ethernet SNAP Frame Structure

After developing the LLC sub-frame, concerns arose over the adequacy of that structure. Specifically, it was felt that it could not be used to identify all the higher layer protocols that would eventually need to be identified.

The IEEE went back to work and developed the Sub-network Access Protocol (SNAP) subframe. SNAP adds a 5-octet Protocol Identification Field. This field is inserted in the frame after the LLC header. It consists of a 3-octet Organizationally Unique Identifier (OUI) and a 2-octet Type field. These fields identify for which upper layer protocol the frame is intended on the receiving end.

An Ethernet SNAP frame is illustrated in Figure 7.7. It contains the following fields:

■ A 7-octet Preamble that signals the start of a frame

■ A 1-octet Start of Frame delimiter that signals the start of the frame's contents

■ The intended recipient's 6-octet MAC address

- The originator's 6-octet MAC address
- A 2-octet Length field that identifies the total length of the Data field, including the LLC and SNAP headers
- A 1-octet Destination Service Access Point (DSAP) field that identifies, predictably, the LLC's service access point at the destination machine
- A 1-octet Source Service Access Point (SSAP) field that identifies the originating machine's LLC service access point
- A 1- or 2-octet Control field that indicates the type of LLC frame being carried
- A 5-octet SNAP sub-frame, including a 3-octet Organizationally Unique Identifier field and a 2-octet Protocol Type field that identify the upper level protocol being carried
- A data field that contains either 37 to 1491 octets, or 38 to 1492 octets of data, depending upon the length of the preceding Control field
- A 4-octet Frame Check Sequence that is used to check the integrity of the frame

FIGURE 7.7.

The Ethernet SNAP frame.

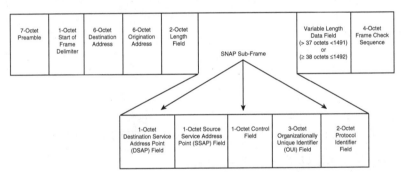

The Ethernet SNAP frame integrates the 802.2 sub-frame structures, or headers, and permits the identification of higher level protocols that are the intended recipients of the frame's contents. This provides backwards compatibility with earlier versions of Ethernet whose frames contained discrete mechanisms for protocol identification.

The total length of an Ethernet SNAP frame must be at least 64 octets to permit proper functioning of the CSMA/CD mechanism. The upper limit for an Ethernet SNAP frame's size is 1518 octets, including the Preamble and Start of Frame delimiter.

For more information on the various Ethernet frame structures, please see Chapter 5.

Delay Budgets

Ethernet's CSMA/CD protocol allows for a maximum of 51.2 microseconds for a round-trip transmission at 10Mbps signaling speed. Each component in the network, including each of the transmission media types and the physical devices, has its own propagation delay characteristics. Consequently, it is a good idea to calculate out the total delay of any given Ethernet *before* you actually build it.

Estimates of Propagation Delays

The following tables provide estimates of the propagation delays that can be expected with each of the listed devices and media. Table 7.3 provides a breakdown of estimated delay, by device type.

Table 7.3. Estimated delay, by device type.

Device	*Estimated Delay (in microseconds)*
Fiber Optic Repeater	1.55
Multi-port Repeater	0.1
Fiber Optic Transceiver	0.20
Twisted Pair Transceiver	0.27

> **NOTE**
>
> The values listed for propagation delay, by device type, are to be considered estimates only! Numerous factors, including temperature, humidity, and even the age and/or manufacturer of an electronic device can all affect its performance. Consequently, it is impossible to provide a precise delay value for any given device type. It is equally impossible to establish a single value that will remain valid for the useful life of the device.

Table 7.4 provides a breakdown of estimated delay, per meter, of the common transmission media types.

Table 7.4. Estimated delay, by media type.

Media Type	*Delay (microseconds, per meter)*
10Base2	0.00514
10Base5	0.00433
Unshielded Twisted Pair (UTP)	0.0057

continues

Table 7.4. continued

Media Type	*Delay (microseconds, per meter)*
Shielded Twisted Pair (STP)	0.0057
Fiber Optic	0.005

Calculating Delay Budgets

Calculating the estimated delay budget of your LAN is a fairly simple process. First, map out the arrangement of network devices, including the length of the links between devices, and the type of media used for each link. Next, count how many of each device type is going to exist in the network, and multiply that number by the delay budgeted for its type. Repeat this process for each of the devices and total up the products of each device type's delay. This is the total hardware delay budget for your network.

This figure must be augmented with the total cable delay budget. Calculating this is equally easy. For each link, multiply the length, in meters, by the number of microseconds delay that can be expected for the media type used. Repeat this process for each of the links and total up the products. This is the total cable delay budget for your network. Adding the total hardware delay budget and total cable delay budget yields the total network delay budget. In order for CSMA/CD to work properly, this value must be less than 51.2 microseconds. If it is greater than, or equal to, this value, you are likely to experience some operational difficulties. If the total network delay budget is close to 51.2, but still less than it, you may experience operational difficulties as your network's infrastructure ages.

> **WARNING**
>
> Avoid the temptation to find the edges of your network's operational abilities. It is a game not worth playing, especially when one considers that the network exists to support users and business processes, and not your heuristic indulgences.

Summary

Ethernet is a rich and diverse collection of technologies. Ethernets can be baseband or broadband, full- or half-duplex, use any one of five different physical media (more, if you are brave enough to venture outside the sanctity of standards!), and support signaling speeds that range from 10Mbps up to 1Gbps.

This chapter provided an overview of the more salient Ethernet specifications. This included the various framing conventions, typical hardware components, media types, limitations of the protocol, how to calculate delay budgets, and even the differential signaling scheme used for transmitting over unshielded twisted pair.

Faster Ethernets

by Mark Sportack

IN THIS CHAPTER

CHAPTER 8

The ubiquitous Ethernet has been so successful at satisfying network requirements that it has been treated to constant refreshes and updates by the IEEE, its caretaker. The two most significant updates involved an increase in its signaling speed.

The first of these faster Ethernets accelerated the original 10Mbps Ethernet to 100Mbps. This necessitated the development of a completely new Physical Layer and modest alterations to the Data Link Layer to accommodate that new Physical Layer. This new standard, dubbed *Fast Ethernet*, appears to have beaten Asynchronous Transfer Mode (ATM) in the high speed LAN market.

The second of these updates is a bit more radical. Most of Ethernet's Layer 2 specifications were grafted on to a completely different Physical Layer—one borrowed from the 1 Gigabit per second (Gbps) Fibre Channel. This change, still being hammered out by the IEEE's 802.3z working committee, will change CSMA/CD Ethernet in many ways. One of the most interesting of the changes posited by 802.3z is the elimination of the familiar CSMA/CD media access method.

This chapter explores the differences between Fast Ethernet and Gigabit Ethernet and the traditional 10Mbps, half-duplex, CSMA/CD Ethernet that spawned these variants.

Fast Ethernet

During the early 1990s, trade publications were filled with glowing reviews of a revolutionary new LAN protocol: Asynchronous Transfer Mode (ATM). Originally a WAN-based protocol intended to service Central Office (CO) to Central Office traffic, ATM was envisioned as a grand unifier. It could integrate LANs and WANs so completely as to make their differences academic. All other LAN technologies, including Ethernet, were doomed to obsolescence by ATM.

> **NOTE**
>
> Central Offices (COs) are the physical premises where the copper telephone wiring from residences and business locations aggregate and terminate in a large telecommunications switch. Each CO is trunked to one, or more, other COs. Together, the overall network forms the commercial switching fabric for telephony.

This grand and glorious vision was derailed by numerous pedestrian factors, not the least of which were the slow pace with which ATM LAN standards (and products) were being developed, and Ethernet's refusal to die. Ethernet, a tired, old, contention-based protocol, waited quietly in the wings until the industry consortium of competitors bogged down under their own mass. An equally daunting challenge facing the ATM Forum was the difficulty of providing robust backward compatibility with existing, but highly dissimilar, LAN infrastructures. Quietly, at first, LAN manufacturers began talking about a 100Mbps Ethernet as a stop-gap alternative to ATM LANs.

A stop-gap solution was necessary because existing LANs were showing their age, relative to the processors and application types that they were supporting. ATM was still viewed as the ultimate solution, but politics within the Forum, as well as the practical limitations of manufacturing sciences, were slowing its progress. Meanwhile, customers were clamoring for a higher performance LAN technology.

While the world was waiting for ATM, Ethernet, it was reasoned, could be given a quick makeover. The Data Link Layer protocols could be retained, and its signaling speed increased by an order of magnitude. The only thing that really needed any work was the Physical Layer: a series of new physical interfaces would have to be developed to accommodate the faster clock rate. It seemed easy enough. The new Ethernet would give LAN managers an option in their migration to ATM.

There were a myriad of proposals, and they came to be known generically as Fast Ethernet. As the concept gained mindshare, the sundry proposals coalesced into two competing proposals. Both were sanctioned by the IEEE under its 802 family of standards. One proposal, which is known today as Fast Ethernet, is literally just the traditional 802.3 CSMA/CD protocol with a signaling speed one order of magnitude faster. Fast Ethernet was standardized as an extension of the existing 802.3 standard.

The other competing proposal became known as VG-AnyLAN, and was standardized under 802.12. This technology, though technically superior with respect to its capability to accommodate isochronous traffic, posed a slightly less gracious migration from 10Mbps Ethernet. For this and many other reasons, including the lack of any must-have isochronous applications, VG-AnyLAN failed to garner any marketshare.

Fast Ethernet's Media Choices

The 100Mbps extensions to 802.3 comprise three different media-dependent interfaces:

- 100BaseTX defines the original 100BaseX specification for Category 5 unshielded twisted pair (UTP) and for Type 1 shielded twisted pair (STP).
- 100BaseFX defines 100Mbps Ethernet over fiber optic cabling.
- 100BaseT4 which describes 100Mbps Ethernet over Categories 3, 4, and 5 UTP.

As evidenced by the naming convention used by these three interfaces, Fast Ethernet has acquired its own form of shorthand notation for its physical interfaces. Unless you know the code, this shorthand can become extremely confusing. Fortunately, the code is relatively simple and somewhat mnemonic. The first numbers, in this case 100, identify the data rate of the specification. Next comes a word; either Base or Broad. Base describes baseband transmission, and Broad describes a broadband transmission technology. The last characters can be alphabetic, numeric, and/or special characters. They are the least mnemonic part of the naming convention, and identify the physical media used by the specification.

The term "100BaseX" is used to refer to both 100BaseTX and 100BaseFX. Similarly, the two twisted pair interfaces, 100BaseTX and 100BaseT4, are sometimes described as "100BaseT." It is important to note that 100BaseX and 100BaseT are *not* physical interfaces! They are generic descriptions of a group of similar interfaces.

Further confusion is caused by the unfortunate naming convention selected by the 802.3 working committee for the two signaling schemes that are used by the Fast Ethernet interfaces. These signaling schemes are 100Base4T+ and 100BaseX. Yes, that's correct: 100BaseX. The same term is used to describe a signaling scheme as well as two physical interfaces.

To avoid confusion, the specific interfaces are referred to by their full names throughout this chapter. The terms "100BaseT" and "100BaseX" are reserved for use only when referring to both physical variants encompassed by those names. Additionally, whenever the term "100BaseX" is used in the context of a signaling scheme, it is identified as such.

100BaseTX

The first classification is called 100BaseTX. This encompasses shielded twisted pair (STP) Category 1 wire and unshielded twisted pair (UTP) Category 5 wire. The second classification, 100BaseFX, is for fiber while the third, 100BaseT4, is for 100Mbps Ethernet over UTP categories 3, 4, and 5. Changes have also been made to the Media Access Controller (MAC) Layer to enable that layer's mechanisms, which had originally been designed for a 10Mbps network, to operate at 100Mbps.

As this standard is an extension to the IEEE 802.3 specification for Ethernet, great pains were taken to ensure that this Fast Ethernet product would bear a very strong resemblance to 10BaseT. For example, 10BaseT can run on two pair of Category 3 (Cat 3) Unshielded Twisted Pair (UTP) wire. Thus, it became important for Fast Ethernet to use two-pair so that migration would not require users to re-wire stations. Indeed, Fast Ethernet can run on just two pair, but those pairs must be Category 5 wire, not Category 3. This tends to obviate the intended benefit of this feature, as not every station wired with Category 3 UTP was given a full four-pair in its original installation. Consequently, many LAN administrators find themselves faced with the need to re-wire, despite the availability of a 100Mbps LAN technology that supports Cat 3 transmissions.

> **NOTE**
>
> It is important to note that although the IEEE's 802.3 specification defines numerous physical interfaces for 10Mbps Ethernet, Fast Ethernet most closely resembles 10BaseT.

100BaseFX

100BaseFX is the fiber optic equivalent of 100BaseTX. They share a common signaling scheme and data encoding technique, but use different physical media. 100BaseFX can support the

100Mbps data rate up to 400 meters over two strands of 62.5/125 micron fiber optic cable. This greatly expands the reach of Fast Ethernet and, as a result, is best used for inter-repeater links.

100BaseT4

100BaseT4 is designed to allow transmission of 100Mbps over four pairs of voice-grade wiring for distances up to 100 meters. Voice-grade wiring is defined to be a minimum of Category 3 UTP. It is also capable of transmission using Categories 4 and 5 UTP.

> **NOTE**
>
> 4T+ does not support 25-pair bundles of Category 3 horizontal wiring. This type of wire was used fairly extensively in the wire distribution systems of many older commercial buildings.

One important functional difference between 100BaseT4 and its siblings is that this specification does not support continuous signaling between frames. This continuous signaling is known as the *interframe gap*. Typically, continuous signaling is used by the transmitting device to maintain its hold on the right to transmit. Other devices interpret the meaningless string of 96 bits as a busy line. If they need to transmit, but see this string, they implement their binary exponential back-off algorithms and wait. Therefore, a specification that does not support this type of signaling has reduced power requirements. This consideration is important for laptop computers and in any other circumstances where power consumption is a critical factor.

Signaling Schemes

Fast Ethernet uses two different signaling schemes for its twisted pair interfaces. These schemes, confusingly named "100BaseX" and "100Base4T+," both support a data rate of 100Mbps. This rate can be supported for a maximum of 100 meters from the hub to the workstation, and a distance of 10 meters from hub to hub, albeit over different physical media. Fiber can be used to transcend the hub-to-hub distance limitation.

> **NOTE**
>
> The term "data rate" should not be confused with signaling speed! Fast Ethernet, widely understood to support 100Mbps, actually signals at 125Mbps. Subtracting the Physical Layer overheads, including the encoding technique, results in a 100Mbps data rate. This is true of 10Mbps Ethernet as well: it signals at 12.5Mbps, but offers a net data rate of 10Mbps.

100Base4T+

The 100Base4T+ signaling scheme enables the 100BaseT physical interfaces to run over most existing Category 3 wiring. The qualification, "most existing Category 3 wiring," is necessary because this signaling scheme requires four pairs. This signaling technique uses three-pair to carry data bi-directionally in a half-duplex mode while the fourth pair is used in a receive-only mode for collision detection.

If this fourth pair detects a signal at the far end of the wire, it informs the Physical Layer protocols that now is not a good time to transmit. The remaining three pairs are used to transmit and receive data, but not both simultaneously.

Each of these pairs can support a data rate of 33.33Mbps. Together, they yield 100Mbps of usable bandwidth. (Let's not hear any complaints from the mathematicians: 3 * 33.33 is close enough to 100 to warrant the claim.)

Three wire paths are necessary because of the 8B6T encoding scheme used in 100Base4T+. In essence, the MAC sublayer passes down octets of binary data to the Physical Layer. The Physical Layer converts each octet, or 8 bits (this is the 8B part of the 8B6T name), to 6 ternary symbols. Each group of 6 ternary symbols is known as a *6T group*. These 6T groups are then split across the three available serial channels—that is, the three pairs of wire available for transmission and reception of data.

> **NOTE**
>
> For readers infatuated with techno-trivia, each ternary symbol (6 are created from each octet of data) takes approximately 40 nanoseconds to transmit at a signaling speed of 125Mbps.

100BaseX

100BaseX was adapted from the full-duplex signaling mechanism of FDDI to work with the Ethernet's CSMA/CD. The FDDI signaling mechanism supports two physical interfaces, Category 5 UTP and 62.5.125 micron multimode fiber optic cabling. Consequently, 100BaseX supports the same cable types and distance limitations as FDDI for these two physical media.

FDDI's interface is called the *Twisted Pair Physical Medium Dependent* (TP-PMD) interface. It uses two pairs of Category 5 UTP to support 100Mbps, full-duplex communications up to 100 meters. If four-pair wiring is used, the remaining two-pair can, theoretically, carry voice-grade communications but not another high-speed LAN.

100BaseX also supports the FDDI Fiber Physical Medium Dependent (F-PMD), which calls for 62.5/125 micron multimode fiber. This interface provides a 100Mbps, full-duplex data rate for up to 400 meters.

The 100BaseX signaling scheme uses a 4B/5B encoding scheme. This scheme accepts *nibbles* (4 bits, or a half octet) of data from the MAC sublayer, and encodes them into 5-bit symbols for transmission. These 5-bit symbols are known as *code-groups*. These code-groups are indigenous to the 100BaseX mechanisms only, and are meaningless outside of that context.

A 5-bit, binary field has 32 possible codes. These codes are used to represent the 16 code-groups of the hexadecimal character set (0 through F). Additionally, 4 code-groups are used as transmission control mechanisms. The remaining 12 possible codes are used as inter-stream filler, or remain undefined.

Maximum Network Diameter

Interoperability at the hub is achieved via a repeater. The specifications for 100BaseT include a universal repeater that supports both physical layers. Up to two universal repeaters, located a maximum of 10 meters apart, can be used in a 100BaseT network.

Segmentation with routers can also increase the network's potential diameter beyond this two-repeater limit.

Fast Ethernet Summary

Fast Ethernet is the extension of the IEEE 802.3 specification to 100Mbps. It, quite literally, is the familiar 10BaseT Ethernet that runs an order of magnitude faster. The increased transmission rate necessitated significant changes to the Media Access Layer of the protocol.

Fast Ethernet has quickly established itself in Local Area Networking. Many manufacturers helped ensure its adoption in the marketplace by offering Network Interface Cards (NICs) that support a dual rate of 10Mbps and 100Mbps. Such cards either can automatically select the optimal speed, given the wiring and distance to the hub, or can be manually set to use either one of the two.

Gigabit Ethernet

A new proposal to increase the signaling speed of Ethernet is called Gigabit Ethernet. The standard for Gigabit Ethernet is being developed by the IEEE under the auspices of the 802.3z task force. It is scheduled for completion, and acceptance as a standard in March 1998. Products that appear before this date are based on working drafts of the specification proposal. How close these pre-standards products are to the accepted standard remains to be seen.

Due to its inclusion within the 802.3 umbrella of specifications, every effort is being made to make Gigabit Ethernet as compatible as possible with its lower-speed siblings. For example, Gigabit Ethernet continues to use the same CSMA/CD protocol, frame format, and frame size as the other Ethernets. These features make backward and forward compatibility with 10 and 100Mbps Ethernets possible.

8

FASTER ETHERNETS

Gigabit Ethernet is initially intended to serve as a backbone that interconnects 10/100BaseT switches. Not far behind are proposals that will make it viable for connecting high-performance servers to the LAN. Gigabit Ethernet is even envisioned as eventually stretching up to 100 meters over Category 5 UTP to desktop processors.

The Physical Interfaces

To jump-start the standards work, the 802.3z team elected to use many elements of the ANSI Fibre Channel's Physical Layer. Fibre Channel, originally developed as a next-generation mainframe channel technology, has been standardized and converted into a LAN technology. To date, there has been little market response to Fibre Channel LANs.

Despite its lack of market success, Fibre Channel offered a proven and viable Physical Layer for the 802.3z team to start from. Given that the intent of the IEEE is to acquire the broadest possible support for their standards, all IEEE standards are presented to ANSI for consideration as a national (versus industrial) standard. Thus, it makes sense to embrace elements of a Physical Layer that has already been ratified by ANSI.

> **NOTE**
>
> Fibre Channel's market woes are more a product of their Data Link Layer and marketing vis-a-vis the installed base of LAN technologies. The Physical Layer specification of this technology offered the IEEE engineers the opportunity to jump-start their efforts to develop a Gigabit Ethernet.

One of the minor problems encountered has been the signaling speed. Fibre Channel signals at 1.063Gbps using an encoding scheme that generates an extra two bits for every octet transmitted. This scheme (known as "8B/10B"), as well as its close relative 4B/5B, results in less than 1Gbps of usable bandwidth. The actual amount is more like 800Mbps. This is still a significant increase over most of the extant LAN technologies, but it lacks the psychological impact of breaking the gigabit barrier. In time, it is expected that the signaling technologies can be bolstered to run at 1.25Gbps. This will yield a net of 1Gbps of bandwidth, assuming the continued use of an 8B/10B encoding scheme.

Gigabit Ethernet will offer the following four choices of transmission media, each with its own physical interface specification:

- Copper coaxial cabling
- Multimode fiber optic cabling
- 8.3/125 micron single-mode fiber optic cabling
- Category 5 Unshielded Twisted Pair (UTP) wiring

> **NOTE**
>
> The multimode fiber optic cabling interface actually supports the use of two different cable types. They are the North American conventional 62.5 micron diameter fiber, and the global convention of 50 micron diameter fibers.

Standardization work, based on these media choices, was facilitated by adapting the Physical Layer signaling technologies of the American National Standards Institute's (ANSI) Fibre Channel standard. Fibre Channel served as the foundation for all but the Category 5 UTP Physical Layer interfaces. These interfaces are described in the next four sections. The maximum link distances specified in each medium-dependent interface were intended to provide adequate performance for most existing cable plants, assuming a worst-case implementation.

1000BaseSX

100BaseSX is the IEEE 802.3z proposed specification for multimode transmission using short wavelength lasers. *Short wavelength lasers* are defined as those lasers that produce light in the 850 nanometer range.

This proposal actually recognizes two different media: 50 micron and 62.5 micron diameter fiber optic cabling. The 50 micron variant can support the full gigabit signaling rate for a maximum of 550 meters. The 62.5 micron diameter variant is limited to a maximum of 260 meters per cable segment.

1000BaseLX

1000BaseLX is the proposed specification for long wavelength laser transmissions. Laser transmissions that are 1300 nanometers in length are considered to have long wavelengths.

This proposal includes three different physical transmission media:

- 62.5 micron multimode fiber optic cabling
- 50 micron multimode fiber optic cabling
- 8.3 micron single mode fiber optic cabling

In its current form, the 62.5 micron multimode fiber can extend to a maximum of 440 meters. The 50 micron multimode fiber can be extended up to 550 meters in length. The 8.3 micron single mode fiber specification, ostensibly the most expensive to manufacture and install, can support gigabit signaling for up to 3 kilometers.

1000BaseCX

1000BaseCX defines the 802.3 proposed specification for transmission over high-quality shielded twisted pair or coaxial cabling. The maximum distance for transmission over either media is limited to just 25 meters.

The very short transmission distance limits this physical interface significantly. One of the proposed uses is to interconnect gigabit switches using a low-cost copper alternative to fiber optics.

Left unspoken by the contributors to the Gigabit Ethernet standards work is that signaling at such a high rate over copper is problematic. Copper transmission facilities can do wonders, provided enough electricity is supplied: the more electrical power is pumped through it, the higher the bandwidth. Unfortunately, copper makes a wonderful electromagnetic radiator. Higher transmission power and frequency result in higher levels of electromagnetic radiation (EMI). EMI emission is carefully regulated by the Federal Communications Commission (FCC), because it uses frequency bands that the FCC regulates.

The net effect is that gigabit signaling can be supported for only very modest distances over copper transmission facilities, using today's signaling schemes.

1000BaseT

The aforementioned Gigabit Ethernet physical interface descriptions are as close to real as any proposal can get. They have reached a final draft form, which means that they have been closed off to any new features. The existing set of features and operating parameters will be subjected to close scrutiny, debate, and (one can hope) ratification by the committee members during March 1998.

1000BaseT, however, is a completely different story. To date, no technology has specified a data rate in excess of 100Mbps over Cat 5 UTP over distances up to 100 meters. Thus, there was no existing physical interface specification that could be used to jump-start this standards work.

A separate task force is working on the standard for 1000BaseT. This team, and their would-be standard, are called "802.3ab." Their goal is to match the performance of Fast Ethernet over four pairs of Category 5 Unshielded Twisted Pair, albeit at a signaling speed of 1024Mbps. This effort was split from the remainder of the 802.3z Gigabit Ethernet work simply because of the amount of work that needs to be done. Remember, the bulk of Gigabit Ethernet was created by mixing and matching the existing Data Link Layer and Physical Layer specifications of different networking technologies. This limited the predominant development efforts to reconciliation of minor disparities.

It is expected that a new, and extremely complex, signaling scheme will have to be developed by the 802.3ab team. Their goal, admittedly aggressive, is to have the standard complete and ratified by the end of 1998.

To date, this team has developed three proposals. Two are very similar, and feature baseband transmission. They will probably be merged into a single proposal. The third one is completely different. It is based on a passband transmission method. Passband is much more complex and technically elegant than baseband transmission. Unfortunately, it also requires more electric power to operate and more logic gates to process in the Network Interface Card (NIC). It also lacks the resistance to noise that differential signaling affords baseband transmissions over UTP. These factors directly translate into less vendor support for this proposal than is enjoyed by either of the two baseband proposals.

> **NOTE**
>
> Passband is a frequency division multiplexing method. Unlike broadband, the number and frequencies of channels are limited to just those that can pass through a given filter without attenuating completely.

The 802.3ab work is viewed as critical if Gigabit Ethernet is to ever prove itself cost-effective as a station-connect technology. The vast majority of installed cable plants utilize twisted pair as the station-connect wiring. Much of this is only Category 3 but, as user groups move, change their station environments, and engage in numerous other activities, the installed base of Cat 3 UTP continues to suffer attrition. Their work presupposes that all new wiring that is installed to support these activities is Cat 5 UTP. As Cat 5 UTP proliferates, the costs of migrating to Gigabit Ethernet (using the 1000BaseT interface) automatically decrease.

The 802.3ab team knows that the challenge it faces is daunting. They are to be commended for taking up the gauntlet. However, the fact remains that they must develop a cost-effective and manufacturable signaling technology that will enable four pair of Cat 5 UTP to support gigabit signaling speeds for up to 100Mbps, without incurring the wrath of the FCC! To date, each pair has been able to support only 100Mbps using conventional signaling techniques. That leaves the 802.3ab team with quite a gap to close.

In anticipation of their inevitable success, the 802.3z team has developed a logical interface that will exist between the MAC and Physical Layers. This interface will decouple the old Fibre Channel encoding scheme from the MAC sub-layer. The intent is to enable other encoding schemes, like the one that will be developed by the 802.3ab team, to be incorporated into the 802.3z standards.

What Else Is New?

A fair question to ask is, "Besides the need for completely new Physical Layer media interfaces, what else is new?" The answer, so far, is not much. Great pains have been taken to preserve as much of the content of the various existing 802.3 specifications as possible. This was done to ensure continued interoperability within the 802 and 802.3 families of specifications. The two areas that have undergone notable change (other than the signaling speed, data rate, and physical interfaces!) are the protocol's interframe gap and the contention-based media access method.

Interframe Gap

The size of the interframe gap is one significant change to the 802.3 protocol that was made necessary by Gigabit Ethernet. As explained in Chapter 7, "Ethernet," the 802.3 CSMA/CD

8

FASTER ETHERNETS

protocol provides for a gap between frames of 96 bits. This gap is actually just a random string of binary characters. Its only purpose (contrary to any rumors that you may encounter on newsgroups!) is to keep the line busy. In other words, it is a stall tactic embedded in the protocol to enable a transmitting station to hold the line while it prepares another data frame for transmission.

With Gigabit Ethernet, 96 bits fly by so quickly that the electronic components on the NIC lose that legitimate stall tactic. More importantly, at the gigabit signaling speed, the minimum frame size of 64 octets is too small to ensure detection of a collision over the network. Remember, the minimum frame size was selected based upon the amount of time that it would take, at 10Mbps, for a frame to reach all stations on the LAN. Adjusting this to gigabit speeds means a significant increase in the minimum frame size. This compromises interoperability with the other, slower, 802.3 Ethernets. This was deemed unacceptable.

The answer to both quandaries was to increase the size of the interframe gap. The gap, in Gigabit Ethernet, is now 512 octets long. One could argue the inefficiencies of using a 512-octet interframe gap for frames that can be as small as 64 octets, but efficiency was not the goal. Interoperability was. To placate the complaint artists, a new feature was incorporated into the 802.3z protocol. This feature, known as Frame Bursting, enables the transmitting station to transmit up to 8192 octets every time it successfully competes for bandwidth.

Contention-Based Media Access

Although not necessarily new—in the sense that it pre-existed the 802.3z initiative—Ethernet's contention-based media access method has been rendered moot. As the IEEE was developing the Fast Ethernet variants described earlier, provisions were made for full-duplex operation.

Full-duplex transmission means that a device can transmit and receive simultaneously, although over separate paths. In essence, the transmitter of one device (for example, the switch port) has a dedicated path to the receiver of another device (for example, a NIC in a computer), and vice versa. This eliminates the competition for the same bandwidth, between transmit and receive functions, that every Ethernet device previously suffered.

In a switched environment, the collision domain is reduced to just two devices: the switch port and the device to which it connects. Implementing full-duplex transmissions over a switched connection literally makes competing for available bandwidth unnecessary. Each device can obtain permission to transmit, and place frames on the media, at near wire speed. CSMA/CD becomes superfluous—a relic of Ethernet's past.

Gigabit Ethernet builds upon this success of Fast Ethernet. In fact, many manufacturers are designing their products to be full-duplex only. This is a testament to the success of full-duplex, switched networking.

Too Good to Be True?

Although technically interesting, and even exciting, Gigabit Ethernet must be viewed without prejudice, and in the context of its intended operational environment. It is targeted by the manufacturing/marketing entities that have created it as a hub-interconnect technology, a server-connect technology, and eventually, even a station-connect technology. Its viability must be assessed in terms of the performance capabilities and requirements of each of those functional areas of a LAN.

Today's desktops and servers are grossly mismatched against the bandwidth offered by Gigabit Ethernet. Even discounting it for its 8B/10B encoding scheme, it still offers 800Mbps of bandwidth. This effectively removes the LAN as the performance limiting factor. Instead, performance is limited by a pair of factors *inside* the computer. First, even SCSI-3 can run at only 40 Megabytes (MB) per second. This translates into a 320 Megabits per second (Mbps) signaling rate. Thus, any activity over a Gigabit Ethernet that requires an I/O call to a SCSI-connected peripheral will be limited by the performance of the SCSI bus.

Functions that can be served without accessing a SCSI peripheral will find themselves limited by the performance limitations of the Peripheral Component Interconnect (PCI) bus. PCI has become the dominant I/O bus architecture in low-end computing. It is used in single-user and multi-user machines alike. In actual practice, most PCI-based computers will not experience much, if any, performance gain when stepping up to a Gigabit Ethernet connection from a 100Mbps Ethernet connection. Their internal components prevent it. Thus, Gigabit Ethernet, relative to today's low-end computing architectures, is superfluous and irrelevant.

Gigabit Ethernet is best reserved for interconnecting more robust mid-range and mainframe computers. These computing architectures are a better match for the bandwidth of Gigabit Ethernet. Alternately, switching hubs that can support a Gigabit Ethernet uplink may find it useful as a LAN backbone.

Summary

Fast Ethernet has proven itself a viable, cost-effective means of upgrading LAN infrastructures. This is essential to keep pace with the ever growing demand for connectivity and bandwidth. The single greatest danger of the Fast Ethernet specification is that it uses completely different signaling schemes for different wire types. Thus, the silicon used for Category 5 UTP is completely different from the technology for Category 3 UTP. Any user group that implements Fast Ethernet using Category 3 wire is actually adding an impediment to future LAN technology migrations by strengthening their investment in voice-grade wiring technologies.

Gigabit Ethernet, although not finished, appears capable of further extending the life of this old protocol. The key difference between these two is that Gigabit Ethernet is more of a niche technology. Its bandwidth is several orders of magnitude beyond the capabilities of most of today's computers. The I/O and system buses used in these machines become the limiting factors that prevent them from fully utilizing Gigabit Ethernet's available bandwidth. In the future, it may grow into more of a general purpose LAN technology, but, for the time being, appears to be of limited usefulness.

For the most up-to-date information about the emerging Gigabit Ethernet, please visit:

`http://www.Gigabit-Ethernet.org`

Token Ring

by Mark Sportack

IN THIS CHAPTER

CHAPTER 9

Token Ring is another IEEE standardized LAN architecture. It shares many common attributes with Ethernet and the other LAN architectures contained within the IEEE 802 family of network standards. As a result, it can interoperate with them through the use of a translating bridge.

Token Ring has also received its fair share of updates since its inception. Originally a 4Mbps technology, it was later updated to 16Mbps. Today, proposals exist that will increase the signaling speed of Token Ring even further, to 100 or even 128Mbps, and eventually 1Gbps.

This chapter provides a description of the mechanics of Token Ring. This includes its myriad frame structures, physical media specifications, its operational mechanics, and a glimpse of its future.

Overview

In its standardized form, Token Ring is a highly deterministic and robust LAN architecture. It owes its name to its round-robin scheme for media access. Unlike Ethernet, with its chaotic and unregulated multiple access methodology, Token Ring permits only a single device to transmit at any time. There can be no collisions.

Media access is arbitrated by passing a token in an orderly fashion. There can be only one token, and it is modified by a transmitting device to form the header of a data frame. Without this token, the data frame's header cannot be constructed, and there can be no transmission. The data in the frame is copied off by the recipient device, with some of the bits in the frame's header inverted to signal receipt. The frame itself is left to continue traversing the ring. When it returns to its originator, that device takes the frame off the network, and strips the addressing and data out. If that device needs to send more data, it may do so. Otherwise, the header is reconverted back into a token and placed on the transmission media, where it travels to the next device downstream.

Passing the token in a round-robin fashion, as illustrated in Figure 9.1, provides each device an opportunity to transmit. To ensure that no single station hogs the bandwidth, a mechanism known as the Token Holding Timer is used to track and regulate the maximum amount of time that any given station can monopolize transmission rights. This timing mechanism is also useful in restoring normal operation of the network in the event that a station holding the token ceases to function. Another beneficial side effect of its token-passing media access technique is that Token Ring networks scale up in size and transmission volumes much more gracefully than do contention-based networks.

FIGURE 9.1.

*Tokens passed
sequentially, in a
round-robin pattern.*

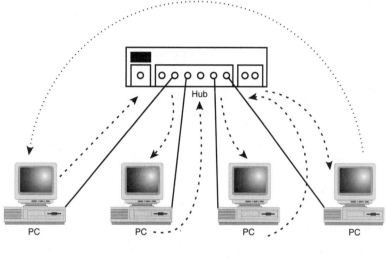

Legend:
——————— Physical Wiring
- - - - - Flow of Tokens and Frames

Standardization of Token Ring

Token Ring, by information technology standards, is ancient. It was originally conceived by IBM as a data center technology for networking mainframe computers. It was first proposed to the IEEE for standardization in 1969. After personal computers (PCs) were developed, it became apparent that Token Ring could serve to interconnect them as well. This was the impetus behind its inclusion in the IEEE's Project 802.

Standardization under the 802 umbrella necessitated making some changes to its Data Link Layer so that it would support hardware-level addressing and bridging with other 802 LAN architectures.

The IEEE designated Token Ring its 802.5 specification. This specification is almost identical to IBM's Token Ring. In addition to the aforementioned hardware-level changes, the IEEE also standardized the message format and Layer 2 protocols. IBM, incidentally, was a major proponent of the IEEE standardization efforts.

Token Ring offered a more robust, timely, and deterministic approach to networking than the 802.3 Ethernet protocol, albeit at a higher per-port cost. Companies whose applications required timely delivery of data found Token Ring to be the only viable solution for their needs. Although the 802.3 protocol assures the packet will be successfully transmitted, it may require multiple transmission attempts. Thus, it can't guarantee a time frame for delivery. The token ring topology can, due to its deterministic, ring-shaped topology and orderly access method.

9

TOKEN RING

Token Ring Frame Structures

By now, it should be fairly clear that Token Ring devices cannot transmit anything without a token. The basic token serves two purposes:

- It is used to arbitrate transmission privileges.
- The basic token frame gets converted to the header of the various specialized frames.

In fact, any function (including data transmission) requires the use of a specific frame structure.

Token Ring supports the following frame types:

- Token Frame
- Data Frame
- LLC Data Frame
- MAC Management Frames
- Abort Frame

The Token Frame

The IEEE's 802.5 Token Ring uses a special bit sequence construct, known as a *token*, to control access to the transmission media. A token contains a Starting Delimiter, Access Control, and Ending Delimiter fields. Each field is one octet (eight bits) in length. The token frame is illustrated in Figure 9.2.

FIGURE 9.2.
*The IEEE 802.5
Token Frame.*

1-Octet Starting Delimiter	1-Octet Access Control Field	1-Octet Ending Delimiter

This frame is passed from device to device, and arbitrates transmission rights amongst the devices on the ring. Given that there is only one token frame, only one station can transmit, or attempt to transmit, at any point in time.

Access Control Field

The Access Control field is the key to the token. Each of its eight bits is significant. As illustrated in Figure 9.3, the Access Control Field of the Token Frame contains the following:

- 3-bit Priority Field
- 1-bit Token Field

■ 1-bit Monitor Field

■ 3-bit Request Priority Field

FIGURE 9.3.
The Access Control field.

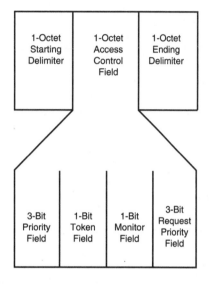

The Priority bit field is used to indicate the priority of the token itself. This value can range from 000 to 111, and is set by the transmitting station. It cannot be modified by other stations. Only stations that have a priority equal to or greater than this field's value may use it.

The Token bit is alluded to earlier in this chapter as the bit that must be manipulated to convert a token into a Start of Frame sequence. Actually, the Token bit is set to 1 to tell other stations that the token is now a part of a frame. That is, it is in use. Tokens, as illustrated previously in Figure 9.2, have this bit set to 0 as they circulate the ring, polling stations.

The Request Priority field permits stations to request higher priority service. Such stations have high priority data and need to transmit as quickly as possible. Stations can communicate their priority needs by setting the Request Priority bits according to the priority of their data (valid ranges are from 000 to 111). This informs the token's issuer of their needs. Ostensibly, the issuer sets its next Priority bit field according to the Request Priority value just received. In this manner, the station with a high priority can secure the next token, regardless of how many stations lie between it and the issuer on the ring.

NOTE

The priority bits range in significance from left to right. The left-most bit is the most significant. That is, it carries a higher priority than the middle or right-most bit. Consequently 010 is a higher priority than 001.

9

TOKEN RING

The Data Frame

The minimum length of a Token Ring data frame is 21 octets. The maximum data frame size is determined by the ring's signaling speed. The time that is required to transmit a frame must be less than the Token Holding Time that has been established. This time is defaulted to 10 milliseconds. In a 4Mbps Token Ring, this works out to a 4500-octet maximum data frame size. In a 16Mbps Token Ring, data frames can be up to 18,000 octets long.

The 802.5 Token Ring data frame structure consists of two parts: the token and the data frame. When a device seizes this token and inverts the Token bit value in its frame, it has taken the first steps towards creating a Data Frame. The next step is to insert and populate the other fields required in the protocol's data frame structure. The complete data frame is depicted in Figure 9.4.

FIGURE 9.4.

The IEEE 802.5 data frame.

1-Octet Starting Delimiter	1-Octet Access Control Field	1-Octet Frame Control Field	6-Octet Destination Address	6-Octet Origination Address	Variable Length Data Field (0 to 4332 octets for 4Mbps LANs, or 0 to 17,832 for 16Mbps LANs)	3-Octet Frame Check Sequence	3-Octet Ending Delimiter	1-Octet Frame Status

As evidenced in Figure 9.4, the three 1-octet fields of the Token Frame are retained in the data frame. To this basic structure six other fields and subfields are added.

The first field is the Starting Delimiter, which identifies the beginning of the frame. Next are the Access Control field (which was described in the section entitled "Access Control Field") and the 8-bit Frame Control field. This field stores the "type" bits that identify the transport protocol. This field is also used to differentiate between data frames and control frames.

The first two bits identify the type of frame: data or MAC management. The next six bits are used to inform the recipient of the priority of the data Protocol Data Unit (PDU) and/or MAC PDU. If this is a MAC frame, this field also identifies which specific MAC management frame type this is. The Frame Control Field is depicted in Figure 9.5.

The next two fields are the destination and source MAC addresses. Each one is a 6-octet field. These MAC ("media access control") addresses conform to the previously described Project 802 specification and are identical to those used in Ethernet networks.

The data field for a token-based network varies in size, based upon the signaling speed of the ring. 4Mbps Token Rings can support data fields that range from at least 0 octets up to a maximum of 4,332. 16Mbps Token Rings can support data fields that are between 0 and 17,832 octets long. These values represent the maximum size of a frame, assuming a 10-millisecond Token Holding Time, minus the 168 octets of the basic frame structure.

FIGURE 9.5.

The Frame Control field.

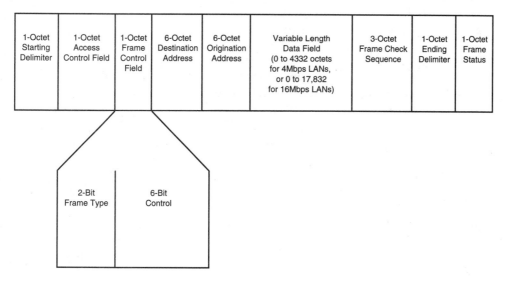

The last three fields in the data frame are the 32-bit Frame Check Sequence (FCS), the 8-bit Ending Delimiter, and the 8-bit Frame Status. The Frame Check Sequence contains a mathematically derived value—a checksum—that is calculated based upon the length and content of the frame. The recipient and transmitter each apply the same algorithm to the frame. If the recipient computes the same checksum value stored in the FCS field (which was calculated by the transmitter), then it can reasonably assume that the contents were not compromised during transmission.

The last two octets, which encompass the Ending Delimiter and the Frame Status Fields, are considered the *End of Frame Sequence.*

This is the basic, or raw, form of the Token Ring Data Frame. In practice, it is used in conjunction with the Logical Link Control mechanisms of the IEEE's 802.2 specification. This specification calls for an additional sub-frame structure to be prepended to the data frame for the purposes of identifying the higher layer protocol for which the frame's contents are intended. This is essential in today's environment of multiprotocol computing and communications. The Token Ring Data Frame with an 802.2 sub-frame is known as a *Token Ring LLC Data Frame.* For more information on the 802.2 sub-frame structure, please refer to Chapter 7, "Ethernet."

9

TOKEN RING

MAC Management Frames

The IEEE 802.5 Token Ring protocol establishes four *Network Management Agents* (NMAs). These agents reside at each Token Ring station device and are used in the normal management operation of the ring. These agents are:

- Active or Standby Monitors (AM or SM)
- Ring Error Monitor (REM)
- Configuration Report Server (CRS)
- Ring Parameter Server (RPS)

Given that the only way to transmit on the ring is to use a token-based frame, it shouldn't be a tremendous surprise that each of these agents can generate several different, highly specialized MAC management frame types. In fact, in an IEEE Token Ring, these four agents have the capability to generate and use 25 different MAC frames! If you feel the need for even more control, the IBM extensions to the IEEE MAC frame structures add another 17 MAC frames, for a total of 42 different MAC frames.

Each MAC frame performs a specific network management function. Some of these functions include:

- Lobe test
- Initialize ring
- Ring purge
- Claim token
- Several Active Monitor functions

The relatively large number of frames makes it pointless to examine them individually. Suffice it to say that these MAC frames are used to collect network performance metrics that can be fed to standards-compliant network management products. Many are described in their operational context throughout the remainder of this chapter.

Abort Frame

The Abort frame consists of just Start and End Frame delimiter fields. Although such a frame structure may seem pointless due to its lack of content and addressing, the Abort frame is used to immediately terminate transmissions.

The structure of the Abort Frame is illustrated in Figure 9.6.

The Fill Sequence

The one transmission vehicle used by Token Ring that is not frame-based is the Fill Sequence. This sequence does not have a starting or ending delimiter. It is comprised of virtually any sequence of 1s and 0s.

FIGURE 9.6.

The IEEE's 802.5 Abort frame.

The Fill Sequence is generated by the transmitting station. Remember, there is only one token, so only one station can transmit at any given time.

The Fill Sequence is used in conjunction with the various frame types in the previous list to avoid quiet time on the ring. *Quiet time* occurs whenever no token or frame is traversing the ring. Quiet time is interpreted by the Active Monitor and each station as a broken ring. Consequently, they initiate their auto-recovery mechanisms to isolate the extent of the break and identify any unreachable stations. This can be counterproductive if the ring hasn't been compromised. For example, if the ring goes quiet because a station has received the token and is holding it while framing data being received from higher layer protocols, the ring is quiet. Other stations can interpret this lack of activity as an error condition.

To combat an erroneous reaction to quiet time, the transmitting station generates a random sequence of 1s and 0s while it is preparing to send a real frame or token. This Fill Sequence is transmitted before and after a frame or token is transmitted. Fill Sequences can also be used by a transmitting station to stall for time. That is, by transmitting a random pattern of bits in lieu of a real frame or token, the transmitting station can stop the clock on its Token Holding Timer. This enables it to hold the token for longer than it would otherwise be entitled.

Understanding Token Ring

The review of Token Ring's various frame structures should demonstrate that it is a fairly complex and very robust LAN architecture. A quick synopsis of its operational mechanics should provide ample context for a more detailed examination of its physical and logical components.

Token Ring uses a token to arbitrate access to the transmission media. Tokens are recognized, and supported, by all stations on the network. There can be only one token, and only the holder of that token may transmit.

This token is passed from station to station, in a sequential manner, and in *one direction only*. Because a ring has no clearly defined beginning or end, the token simply passes around the ring continuously. This is known as a *round-robin* polling technique. Each station that receives the token may convert its bit structure into a Start of Frame (SOF) sequence if it needs to transmit. The token is used to build the data frame. The transmitting station modifies the SOF sequence, adds the necessary data, addresses it, and places it back on the network.

Alternatively, that station may simply put the token back on the network for the next station if it doesn't need to transmit. When the frame arrives at its intended destination, that receiving device does *not* pull the frame off the network. Instead, it simply copies the frame into a buffer for further internal processing. One bit in the original frame's access control field is modified to inform the originating device that the frame has been received. The frame then continues on its journey through the ring until it returns to its originating device. Reception by the originating device constitutes a successful transmission of the frame's contents; the frame's contents are deleted, and the frame is reconverted into a token.

This is the essence of a Token Ring network's mechanics. Of course, it is highly simplified and does not describe any of the details of the various steps and processes. The rules that govern this basic functional behavior of the devices on a Token Ring network are governed by one station on the ring. This station is known as the *Active Monitor* (AM). The AM is reviewed in further detail in this chapter, under the section titled "Active Monitor."

Given this description of the mechanics of token passing, it is obvious that an 802.5-compliant device is inherently half-duplex. That is, it operates in only one of two modes: transmit or listen. A device that is listening simply forwards the token to the next device in the ring. If the token has been converted to an SOF sequence, a listening device checks to see whether it is the destination of that frame. If it is, it buffers the data and passes the still-modified token back to the originator of the frame that it received. The originator then has to acknowledge that the frame was sent successfully, convert the SOF frame back to a token, and put the token on the network.

In transmit mode, as previously described, the device alters the token's bit structure to make the SOF sequence. Once this is done, the device then appends the necessary data and headers. This methodology, contrary to that of Ethernet, runs more efficiently under heavy traffic loads. It does so because transmission permissions are not chaotic (as Ethernet's are) and the frame is not limited to a maximum number of octets.

The Hardware

Token Ring uses a basic set of hardware components that can be used to construct a myriad of topologies in support of token-passing media access. In addition to the requisite Network Interface Cards (NICs), these hardware components include:

- Trunk Cable
- Lobe Cable
- Multi-Station Access Units
- Trunk Coupling Unit

Each component is described in the following sections.

Trunk Cable

The trunk cable is the backbone of the Token Ring network. It is the cable that interconnects each of the hubs ("Multi-station Access Units," in Token Ring-ese).

Trunk cables can be either fiber optic cabling or shielded or unshielded twisted pair. Twisted pair offers an extra benefit when used as trunk cabling: it provides a redundant transmission path. The connection is achieved with a single pair; the other pairs of wires in a two-pair or four-pair UTP cable are not used. If a break occurs (assuming that it affects only one pair of wires), the second pair can be used to wrap the ring back around the damaged section.

Lobe Cable

Lobe cables are used to attach individual stations to a port on the Token Ring hub. As with trunk cables, either fiber optic or shielded or unshielded twisted pair cabling can be used.

It is important to note that, in most twisted pair wire distribution systems installed in commercial facilities, the lobe cable is not a single cable. Rather, it is a series of cables patched together to form a continuous path.

Multi-Station Access Units

A device that serves as both a repeater and point of access for multiple stations (in other words, a hub) is known as a *Multi-Station Access Unit* (MSAU). MSAUs, like many hubs, can be strung together to form larger networks.

As with Ethernet hubs, care must be taken to not interconnect two DCE ports. MSAUs come with ports that are designated as either *Ring In* (RI) or *Ring Out* (RO). It should be obvious that the RI ports are used for inbound connections: they are DCE. The RO ports are used to connect to the RI ports of other hubs: they are DTE. Attempts to interconnect two MSAUs with a pair of either RI or RO ports does not work, unless you use a cross-over cable.

The typical MSAU has between 8 and 24 RI and/or RO ports. These ports are known more formally as *Trunk Coupling Units* (TCUs).

Trunk Coupling Units

Trunk Coupling Units (TCUs) on an MSAU are the physical ports, and the electronics and logic that support those individual ports provide connectivity for stations and other hubs. Inherent in the TCU is the intelligence and electronics to add and remove stations to/from the ring. This TCU capability enables the ring's membership to be dynamically and automatically managed.

> **NOTE**
>
> Stations that are inactive, for whatever reason, aren't really removed from a Token Ring. Instead, the TCU recognizes the station's inactive state and bypasses it electrically when passing tokens and frames around the ring.

9

TOKEN RING

Topology

The physical components just examined are the proverbial building blocks of Token Ring. They can be arranged in a wide variety of shapes, known as *topologies*. The basic topology is a ring: a unidirectional transmission vehicle without a clearly defined beginning or end. In Token Ring, the ring itself can be either physical or logical.

Early implementations of Token Ring were based upon lobe cables tapped into a trunk cable. The entire ring consisted of nothing more than lobe cabling strung between peers. In this topology, illustrated in Figure 9.7, the ring is physical.

FIGURE 9.7.

Physical ring topology.

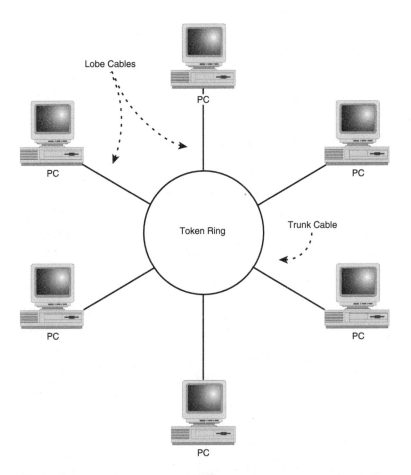

The use of repeaters, also known as hubs or MSAUs, to build a ring results in a physical star topology that serves as the basis for a logical ring. This topology was illustrated earlier in this chapter in Figure 9.1.

In a basic star topology Token Ring, the MSAU serves as the backbone: there is no trunk cabling. Each station connects to the MSAU's TCUs using lobe cables.

This topology can be expanded by adding MSAUs and trunk cabling. Expanding a Token Ring can be a complicated undertaking. Its performance parameters are much more constricting than those of Ethernet. The number of stations per token passing domain is limited to only 260 devices. This and the time that may be required to service that number of devices with a single token may make seemingly easy expansions much more complex.

Dynamic Ring Membership

An important part of a Token Ring network's normal operation is its capability to support dynamic changes in its membership. Membership changes can occur in two ways:

- Normal station insertions and deletions
- Network failures

Understanding the mechanics of this important aspect of Token Ring requires an examination of its membership change processes.

Adding Stations

The simple act of powering a station up does not automatically result in its addition to the ring. It must first pass a series of insertion tests before it is accepted. Insertion tests automatically occur whenever the Token Ring *Network Interface Card* (NIC) is initialized.

The first of the insertion tests is known as the *Lobe Test*. The Lobe Test requires the station to transmit a series of Lobe Media MAC frames. This tests the physical continuity of the transmission media between the station and its MSAU.

If this test is successful, the station must next attempt to physically insert itself into the ring. The station must send a low voltage DC signal, known as a *phantom current*, to the MSAU. This signal is low enough in voltage that it does not have any effect on any data signals that may be traversing the lobe cable. Hence, the source of its name: phantom current.

The MSAU contains relay circuitry that prevents polling of unused ports. Unfortunately, the distinction between an unused port and a used port connected to an inactive device is nonexistent at the Physical Layer. Consequently, the Token Ring uses the phantom current to notify the MSAU that an inactive device is becoming active. The MSAU responds by enabling the station to physically insert itself into the ring's electronics through that previously dormant port. This physical insertion must occur within 5 milliseconds, which is the maximum time that the ring may be broken without generating fault recovery processes.

This physical insertion process enables the joining station to identify the ring's signaling speed and determine whether an Activity Monitor (AM) already exists on the LAN. If no active AM is present, that station becomes the AM upon completing its insertion. The station gleans this

9

TOKEN RING

knowledge through listening for the presence of one of the MAC management frames, specifically:

- The *Active Monitor Present* (AMP) Frame
- The *Purge Ring* (PRG) Frame

If it detects either of these frames, it knows that an AM is alive and well on the ring. If it fails to detect these frames, it transmits a Claim Token and initiates arbitration for AM responsibilities.

The station's next step in joining a ring is to verify that no other stations already have its address active on the ring. This is done via yet another MAC management frame known as the *Duplicate Address Test* (DAT) frame. This simple frame is self-addressed. If the frame returns to the originator as acknowledged by another recipient, that originating station removes itself from the ring by deactivating its network connection and protocols.

If, however, the frame successfully navigates the entire ring and returns to the originating station, it can be assured that no other stations on the ring have its address. But the station is not yet a member of the ring! It must next identify its Nearest Active Upstream Neighbor (NAUN) and Nearest Active Downstream Neighbor (NADN).

These discovery processes help the station define its place within the ring by giving it relatively fixed points of reference. Rather than this being indigenous to the ring insertion process, the mechanism that facilitates neighbor discovery is one of the Active Monitor's ongoing responsibilities. It regularly broadcasts Active Monitor Present MAC management frames. These are sent to its downstream neighbor. This neighboring station accepts the frame, sets the Address Recognized and Frame Copied bits of its header. It also stores the address of the AM, and then sends a Standby Monitor Present (SMP) frame to its downstream neighbor. The downstream neighbor repeats this process. The net effect is that all stations are continuously made aware of any membership changes.

The very last rite of passage that a station must pass before becoming an active station on a ring is the Request Initialization process. In this process, the joining station requests the ring's various operational parameters by transmitting a Request Parameters MAC frame. This frame is addressed to a special server, known as a *Parameter Server*. If no Parameter Server exists, or is available, the joining station uses its default parameters. After this is accomplished, the station has successfully been inserted into the ring.

Deleting Stations

After having endured the arduous series of tasks required to insert a station, rest easy. The de-insertion process is much simpler! If, for any reason, a station is disconnected from the ring, the MSAU's port recognizes the loss of the phantom current and automatically opens its relays for that port. The port, and anything that might be connected to it, are electrically isolated from the ring. This simple process can occur without compromising the functionality of the ring.

Failures

If a station detects a failure in the ring, it responds by beaconing. A *beacon* is a special frame that is transmitted by the station to inform the other stations of the failure. The originating station knows its relative position in the ring and uses the acknowledged beacons to identify the extent of the failure. Stations that fail to respond are assumed to be cut off by the failure. In this manner, the Token Ring protocol allows for some automatic detection and recovery from network-level failures.

The Active Monitor

Token Ring's many rules are enforced by a single station. This station, known as the *Active Monitor* (AM), can be any station in the ring. Usually, it is the first station to become active but, after more stations activate, the responsibility can be contested and passed to another station. The AM monitors all traffic, ensures that the ring's protocol rules are adhered to, and is responsible for initiating any actions that might be necessary to overcome protocol violations or failures.

All the Token Ring station devices have the capability to be the AM, but only one can be the AM at any point in time. The other stations are known as Standby Monitors (SMs).

The AM's duties include the following:

- Initializing the ring by issuing a Ring Purge MAC Frame upon start-up
- Creating tokens
- Providing timing for the network
- Ensuring that tokens and frames do not traverse the ring more than once by inverting the Monitor bit of the Access Control Field of the token/frame

The Active Monitor is also responsible for providing many other ring management functions, including latency buffering. Token Ring's protocol requires the LAN to be large enough to hold an entire token. Some smaller networks might not be large enough to do this, given their transmission speed. *Latency buffering* is the use of a memory buffer to simulate a larger network than actually exists.

A latency buffer equivalent to a minimum of 24 bit times must be provided. A *bit time* is the amount of time that it takes to transmit one bit of information. This AM-provided buffer is known as the Assured Minimum Latency Buffer. This buffer is required by the IEEE 802.5 protocol to guarantee that the LAN's ring is at least big enough to accommodate one token. Given that the token is 24 bits long and the signaling speed is either 4 or 16Mbps, the ring must be large enough to support a round-trip time of either 250 nanoseconds or 62.5 nanoseconds. This shouldn't be a problem, but, as a precaution against unpredictable performance in extremely small rings, the AM is responsible for providing any needed buffering to meet this latency requirement.

9

TOKEN RING

Selecting a New AM

The Monitor Contention Process uses the Claim Token MAC Frame to arbitrate AM responsibilities. This process is initiated by any of the SMs whenever they detect a possible failure of the AM. Numerous possible symptoms can trigger this process. They include:

- The failure of the AM to transmit a good token frame at least once every 2.6 seconds
- The failure of the AM to transmit an Active Monitor Present MAC Frame at least once every 15 seconds
- Unsuccessful ring purge attempts
- Inconsistencies with the clock
- Even the absence of Active Monitor Present or Standby Monitor Present MAC frames after a station insertion. Such frames are normally transmitted within 18 seconds of a successful station insertion.

Other factors, too, can result in the arbitration of a new AM, but these examples should adequately demonstrate the various ways that SMs continuously monitor the AM's performance. Failure to perform its duties can be caused by numerous factors, including the AM losing power, experiencing a hardware or software failure, or simply being physically disconnected from the LAN.

Regardless of the actual cause, if an SM detects a violation of the AM's responsibilities, it immediately generates a Claim Token MAC Frame. After this frame is generated, all stations enter into the contention process.

The AM arbitration process requires each SM to transmit a Claim Token MAC Frame to every other station on the ring. The source addresses of these Claim Tokens are compared numerically to their own MAC addresses to determine which station has the lowest numeric address value. If a station's address is less than the address of a received Claim Token, it repeats the higher value token frame and abandons its own. If, however, its address is greater than the received Claim Token's address, it discards that token and transmits its own. In this fashion, a new AM is selected based upon a consensus of the stations' numeric addresses.

What's Ahead for Token Ring?

Token Ring, overshadowed in recent years by newer and/or faster and better publicized LAN architectures, is beginning to emerge from the doldrums. This rebirth is facilitated by the use of switching technologies to forward frames, as well as numerous attempts to further accelerate Token Ring's signaling speed.

Switching and Dedicated Token Ring

The first major development is the use of port-level switching. A switch is used (instead of a repeating hub) to interconnect the ring's devices. Each port enjoys its own dedicated bandwidth. Competitors for tokens are reduced to just two devices: the station device and the switched hub port to which it connects. Using the correct physical media enables this dedicated connection to support full-duplex transmission. In other words, the station device and the switched port to which it connects can both transmit and receive simultaneously over separate wire paths.

The use of full-duplex port-switching technologies provides the foundation for *Dedicated Token Ring* (DTR). DTR puts the onus on the switch to develop tables that track MAC addresses and correlate them with switched port numbers. Each frame that is received by the switch triggers a table lookup to determine the appropriate path through which to switch it. This is a vast improvement over the traditional half-duplex transmission mode of shared Token Ring.

> **NOTE**
>
> In this context, DTR signifies "Dedicated Token Ring." However, anyone who's ever used a modem and bothered to look at the pretty lights on its face will recognize DTR from its more commonly accepted usage: Data Terminal Ready.

Increasing the Transmission Speed

Several different attempts have been made to accelerate Token Ring's transmission speed from 16Mbps to 100Mbps and even higher. One proposal calls for a new signaling speed of 128Mbps. Others have embraced 100Mbps, with a Physical Layer that could also stretch up to 1Gbps!

The responsibility for hammering out a High Speed Token Ring Standard, ultimately, lies with the IEEE's 802.5 committee. This committee will separate the task into three components, which will be rolled out in stages as they are ready.

100Mbps over Copper

The first component will define the 100Mbps standard for Token Ring over copper transmission media. The plan of action is to leverage existing work in order to bring High Speed Token Ring products to fruition as quickly as possible. Thus, 100Mbps Token Ring will use 100BaseTX as a Physical Layer foundation. The 802.5 Data Link Layer will be grafted onto the 100BaseTX MDI of the 802.3 Physical Layer to create the first High Speed Token Ring.

At first glance, this sort of hybridization may appear heretical, especially to long-time devotees of either Token Ring or Ethernet. Remember, the modularity of the IEEE standards was intentional; there are no interdependencies. Even though 100BaseTX was designed to support an Ethernet Data Link Layer, it was not so tightly coupled as to preclude its use with other Data Link Layer specifications.

As was explained in the review found in Chapter 8, "Faster Ethernets," 100BaseTX can support transmission at a signaling speed of 100Mbps over Category 5 unshielded twisted pair (CAT 5 UTP) for a maximum of 100 meters. An automatic speed negotiation mechanism is included that will control throttling back to a sub-rate if, for any reason, the maximum signaling rate cannot be sustained over any particular connection.

> **NOTE**
>
> The 100BaseTX and 100BaseFX specifications were created during the extension of the 802.3 CSMA/CD to 100Mbps signaling speed. This extension is better known as *Fast Ethernet*. For more information on Fast Ethernet, 100BaseTX, or 100BaseFX, please refer to Chapter 8, "Faster Ethernets."

100Mbps over Glass

The second specification will be a 100Mbps Token Ring that uses fiber optic transmission media. Much like its copper-based sibling, this Token Ring specification will be based on 100BaseFX.

1Gbps

Lastly, the 802.5 committee will be focusing on a 1Gbps version of Token Ring. It is likely that this effort, too, will borrow heavily from work either done or in progress on accelerating Ethernet's signaling speeds. It is expected that a 1Gbps Token Ring will be supported over a fiber optic transmission media, but a copper version won't be far behind.

The 1Gbps version of Token Ring, as with the similar acceleration of Ethernet, promises to be more involved than the leap from 16 to 100Mbps. The extent to which its Data Link Layer will need revision is not yet clear. It does appear unlikely that a 4/16/100/1Gbps auto-sensing Network Interface Card will be a practical reality any time in the near future. The differences in both the Physical Layer and the Media Access Control portion of the Data Link Layer that are necessary to support 1Gbps appear too great to be supported on the same printed circuit board (PCB) as its slower-speed siblings.

Will It Work?

Although the application of switching technologies and faster signaling speeds sounds extremely promising, there remains the nagging question, "Will it work?"

Port-switching, although it is being used to support Dedicated Token Ring, may actually render a High Speed Token Ring moot. The original benefit of a Token Ring network over an Ethernet network was its use of an orderly and deterministic media access methodology. Token Ring could always use more of its available bandwidth than an Ethernet could. As was explained in Chapter 7, the emergence of full-duplex, port-switched Ethernet products changes this. In a full-duplex, port-switched Ethernet connection, there is no competition for bandwidth. The transmitting device is able to put frames on the wire at wire speed. Today, it is possible to drive Ethernets at 98+% of their signaling speed. Consequently, the differences between a 100Mbps Ethernet and a 100Mbps Token Ring become much more subtle and even subjective.

Similarly, the basic strategy of developing a multi-rate product has also been demonstrated with 802.3 products. The intent of manufacturers is to produce 4/16/100Mbps Token Ring products that are capable of automatically negotiating the highest possible signaling speed that any given wire or fiber path can support. The trick will be extending this to 1Gbps.

Many LAN manufacturers are hoping that these efforts will stem the tide of customers that are migrating to Ethernet because of Token Ring's perceived lack of a future. Providing a future at this late stage may do little more than simply reduce the rate of defection to Ethernet.

Other problems, too, threaten High Speed Token Ring's market acceptance. The two most significant are FDDI and port switching. FDDI is already a 100Mbps deterministic ring-based LAN architecture. It will always outperform a 100Mbps Token Ring due to its Fast Release feature. Fast Release, as is explained in Chapter 10, "FDDI," permits the transmitting station to relinquish control over the transmission media by immediately generating a new token after transmitting a data frame. Thus, the very next downstream device can accept the token and begin transmitting its own data, even before the first data frame is off the network.

The bottom line is that, technically, there is little doubt that a High Speed Token Ring will work. Whether or not it will be practical, cost-effective, and (most important of all) accepted by the market is not clear.

Summary

Token Ring has long been regarded as a technically superior and more robust LAN architecture than Ethernet. Recently, however, it has not been treated to the same rate of renovation that its 802.3 sibling has received. Its market share has suffered as a result of this. Recent attempts to shore up this aging architecture appear promising, but only time will tell whether they are too little, too late, to save Token Ring.

Some of Token Ring's endearing qualities remain, albeit somewhat muted by technological advances. It still offers a stronger access prioritization mechanism than Ethernet, better MAC-level error detection and correction, as well as a better ratio of payload-to-frame overhead. Whether or not these mechanisms are enough to validate its continued development and existence can be fodder for highly emotional debate.

Despite these uncertainties about its future, Token Ring does exhibit numerous benefits and limitations in its present form.

Benefits of Token Ring

Shared Token Ring has numerous advantages relative to other LAN architectures. For example, by not using contention as the basis for its access method, shared Token Ring can offer highly deterministic performance. A maximum time can be calculated between the time that a station needs to transmit and when it receives the token that enables it to transmit. This access time can be reduced in predictable increments by decreasing the number of devices on the ring.

This orderly access methodology also imparts other benefits. Unlike shared Ethernet, which can collapse under the weight of its own collisions with as little as 20% utilization, shared Token Ring becomes more efficient under loads. If the load approaches the maximum that can be supported, performance does degrade, but in a predictable and controlled manner that is graceful by comparison to Ethernet.

Token Ring also excels at network performance monitoring. Its Physical Layer specification provides several important mechanisms. These include the Station Management (SMT) agents for data collection and reporting. It also has mechanisms for automatically detecting and advertising hardware failures to other stations on the ring. The Physical Layer also contains some mechanisms for tuning the performance of the ring (if you know how to use them!).

Lastly, Token Ring can support frame sizes up to 18KB. For networks whose applications are characterized by large file transfers, this represents an extremely low overhead-to-payload ratio.

Limitations of Token Ring

Token Ring is not without its disadvantages. As hinted at in the section on its benefits, performance tuning on a Token Ring requires an in-depth understanding of the protocol. Given that its performance tuning capabilities exceed those of other protocols, the limitations of this are somewhat blunted.

A greater disadvantage is the low population density supported by Token Ring. Whereas Ethernet can support up to 1024 devices per segment, Token Ring is limited to only 260.

FDDI

by Mark Sportack

IN THIS CHAPTER

CHAPTER 10

One of the older, and more robust, of the LAN technologies is the *Fiber Distributed Data Interface* (FDDI). FDDI was standardized via the ANSI X3T9.5 specification during the mid-1980s. At that time, high performance UNIX workstations were beginning to appear. These workstations needed a higher performance network than was available. This provided the impetus for ANSI to develop the specification for a suitable LAN.

As Local Area Networking matured, different functional areas began to emerge from what used to be a homogeneous network. Each functional area supported a specific task: server connectivity, desktop connectivity, hub interconnectivity, and so forth. Each of these areas has also experienced an increase in the demand for bandwidth. FDDI, with its high data rate and potential for reliability, became a natural choice for connecting servers, as well as for interconnecting hubs in the LAN's backbone.

This chapter examines FDDI, its physical media and distance limitations, frame structures, its mechanics, and some of its benefits. These provide the context for defining FDDI's role in contemporary and future networking.

FDDI

FDDI is an acronym for "Fiber Distributed Data Interface," but nobody uses that mouthful of a name. In fact, most people don't even spell out F-D-D-I; they slur the letters together and pronounce it "fiddy." FDDI is a robust and reliable LAN technology that dates back to the mid-1980s. FDDI features a 100Mbps data rate and dual counter-rotating rings. These rings can span up to 200 kilometers, using fiber-optic cables. Access to this transmission media is regulated through a token-passing scheme that is similar to Token Ring. The token can pass in only one direction.

In the event of a network failure, the repeaters and/or stations are capable of sensing the loss, determining the extent of the network that has lost connectivity, and automatically (but logically) splicing the two rings together. This is known as *wrap-around*, or *wrapping;* this restores connectivity to as much of the network as possible.

FDDI's self-healing abilities, plus its high data rate, made it the only viable LAN technology for applications with either high bandwidth and/or high reliability requirements. This remained the case for over a decade. Any LAN that needed to support data rates in excess of 16Mbps had to use FDDI. Similarly, any LAN that couldn't afford downtime found FDDI its only viable option. Unfortunately, because it used a fiber-optic transmission media, FDDI was also the most expensive option. This tended to limit its implementation to those highly specialized environments that required either its throughputs or its reliability.

Eventually, other LAN technologies were developed that also reached 100Mbps and beyond. The competition—ATM and Fast Ethernet—were able to meet or exceed FDDI's data rate. This forced FDDI's prices down considerably. Today, FDDI is no longer the elite technology it once was. It remains fairly specialized, but is quite commonly found in mixed topology LANs. Its two primary uses are to connect servers to multi-protocol switching hubs and even interconnect switching hubs into a LAN backbone.

The Functional Components

FDDI is comprised of four distinct functional components. Each component is defined through its own series of specifications. These components are

- Media Access Control (MAC)
- Physical Layer Protocol (PHY)
- Physical Layer Medium (PMD)
- Station Management (SMT)

These components, and their correlation to the OSI Reference Model, are presented in Figure 10.1.

FIGURE 10.1.

The FDDI protocol stack versus the OSI Reference Model.

OSI Reference Model Layer Description	OSI Layer Number	FDDI	
Application	7	No Specifications Defined	
Presentation	6		
Session	5		
Transport	4		
Network	3		
Data Link	2	MAC	S M T
Physical	1	PHY	
		PMD	

Media Access Control

As depicted in Figure 10.1, the top layer of FDDI is Media Access Control (MAC). This layer is equivalent to the Data Link Layer of the OSI Reference Model. The MAC sub-layer is responsible for defining the media access methodology and the myriad frame formats. Additionally, the MAC sub-layer is also responsible for token and frame generation/management, MAC addressing, and even performing error detection and correction upon receipt of data frames.

Physical Layer Protocol

FDDI's Physical Layer Protocol (PHY) correlates to the upper sub-layer functions of the OSI Reference Model's Physical Layer. It is responsible for accepting a data bit stream and converting it to a more suitable format for transmission. This is known as "encoding." The actual encoding scheme used is a 4-bit/5-bit encoding scheme. This scheme accepts 4-bit nibbles (half-octets) from the MAC Layer and encodes each one as a 5-bit symbol. This 5-bit symbol is what

10

FDDI

actually gets transmitted. It is important to note that because the MAC Layer is responsible for generating the frames, and for framing data, every piece of the frame is encoded into 5-bit symbols.

The PHY is also responsible for setting the clocking for the LAN. FDDI actually runs on a 125Mhz transmission clock. The PHY is responsible for generating this transmission clock and synchronizing it across the other stations on the network.

Physical Layer Medium

The *Physical Layer Medium* (PMD, really!) specifies all the attributes that are expected of the transmission medium. These include:

- Medium type
- Transmission signal strength
- Acceptable error rates
- Physical connector types

FDDI, originally, was limited to a single Physical Layer Medium (PMD); 62.5/125-micron diameter multimode fiber-optic cabling. It remained a glass-only technology until the 1990s. Then, the high cost of fiber-optic cable started cutting into its marketshare. The answer seemed obvious: develop a copper-based PMD that could support the FDDI protocols.

In June of 1990, ANSI formed a working committee to build the specification for a *Twisted Pair PMD* (TP-PMD). The TP-PMD was, originally, a proprietary product that grafted the FDDI Layer 2 onto a Category 5 Unshielded Twisted Pair (UTP) Physical Layer. The end result was marketed as CDDI, for Copper Distributed Data Interface. This specification became an ANSI standard in 1994.

A single mode fiber-optic version (SMF-PMD) has also been developed. Based on 8.3-micron diameter fiber-optic cabling and driven by a laser rather than a Light-Emitting Diode (LED), this PMD is more expensive than its multimode counterpart. In its favor is the fact that it can maintain the integrity of the signal for much greater distances: up to 60 kilometers versus the paltry 2 kilometers of the multimode fiber.

> **NOTE**
>
> Although the term "laser" has come into common usage as a noun, it is actually an acronym. It describes the physical process by which the concentrated energy associated with lasers is created. The acronym stands for "Light Amplification through Stimulated Emission of Radiation." Laser is much simpler.

Station Management (SMT)

Station Management (SMT, really!) is a separate module that spans the full stack of FDDI protocols. It communicates directly with the MAC, PHY, and PMD layers to monitor and manage the ongoing operation of the station and the ring. The three areas of SMT functionality, as defined in the ANSI X3T9.5 specification, are

- SMT Frame Services
- Connection Management
- Ring Management

Together, these three functional areas encompass many different services. They are essential to the normal operation of the station and the FDDI ring. Although there are many others, some of the services provided include:

- Station insertion
- Station removal
- Statistics gathering
- Fault identification
- Fault recovery

Although any given station may have multiple instances of the MAC, PHY, and PMD (as is normal with dual-attached stations), there can be only one SMT.

Building FDDI Networks

FDDI has been stereotyped as having a dual, counter-rotating, ring topology. The truth is, there are several different ways to construct a FDDI network. The dual ring is just one of its many forms. To build more effective FDDI networks you must understand the various port types and the ways that stations can attach to the network.

Port Types and Attachment Methods

FDDI recognizes four different port types. They are as follows:

- Port A: Primary In, Secondary Out
- Port B: Primary Out, Secondary In
- Port M: Master Concentrator Port
- Port S: Slave Port for Single-attach devices

These port types can be interconnected in a variety of ways. Before you examine them, however, you should understand the different connection types that are supported. The two basic attachment methods that can be used to connect FDDI devices to the network are

- Dual-attached
- Single-attached

10

FDDI

These attachment methods can be used either with or without repeaters. Attachments can be made between a variety of port configurations. This adds further variety and functionality to the ways that FDDI LANs can be built and used.

Dual-Attached Stations

Dual-attached stations (DASs) feature two sets of media interfaces. This enables a DAS device to have a physical connection to each of FDDI's two rings. Figure 10.2 illustrates the way that a dual-attached station connects to the LAN. Each DAS device has two sets of media interface ports, each containing both A and B ports. Each port contains physical connections for two physical media. Thus, a DAS device actually has four fibers connected to it.

> **NOTE**
>
> A concentrator is a device that aggregates multiple LAN connections onto a common electrical backplane. The most common type of LAN concentrator is known as a *hub*. Concentrators, too, can be dual-attached. Consequently, it would be correct to reference both concentrators and stations with the phrase "dual-attached" (DA) without specifically identifying the devices.

FIGURE 10.2.

Dual-attached station.

As shown in Figure 10.2, the physical device actually becomes an integral part of the two rings, because the Network Interface Card (NIC) provides physical continuity for the two rings between the A and B ports. DAS connections can form a repeaterless, peer-to-peer LAN. This is accomplished by connecting the A port of one device's interface to the B port of another device, and vice versa. The drawback to this is that each DAS device must be powered on and functioning for the rings to be complete. FDDI is capable of wrapping around a break in the ring, but this directly impacts the performance of the entire ring. More significantly, if multiple stations are simultaneously powered down or otherwise out of service, the net result might be two or more smaller ring pairs.

Single-Attached Stations

Single-attached stations (SAS) eliminate the potential performance problems inherent in DAS by eliminating the wrap-around feature. Each SAS device has just a single communications interface, "S," with two media ports. The separate fibers are used to transmit and receive. Both fibers terminate at the concentrator, which provides the connectivity to both rings. A single-attached station and its concentrator are illustrated in Figure 10.3.

FIGURE 10.3.
Single-attached station.

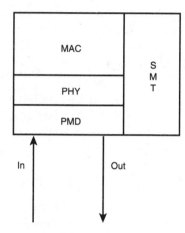

Valid Connections

Given this background on port types and attachment methods, a quick survey of the valid types of port connections should complete your understanding of the various connections that can be made with FDDI. Table 10.1 presents all the valid port connection combinations.

Table 10.1. Valid port combinations.

Port Connection Combination	Use
A and B	Connection of DAS devices in a repeaterless dual ring.
A and M	Connection of DAS device to concentrator in a dual-attached configuration.
B and M	Connection of DAS device to concentrator in a dual-attached configuration.
M and S	Connection of SAS device to concentrator.
S and S	Peer-to-peer connection of SAS devices.

NOTE

The inverse of the port connection combinations presented in Tables 10.1 and 10.2 is synonymous. Thus, B and A is also a valid port connection combination that is functionally indistinguishable from the A and B combination listed in Table 10.1.

Table 10.2 presents those port connection combinations that are deemed *undesirable*. They still function, but are not optimal.

Table 10.2. Undesirable port combinations.

Port Connection Combination	Consequences
A and A	Can establish a peer-to-peer connection, but results in confusing, tangled rings.
B and B	Can establish a peer-to-peer connection, but results in confusing, tangled rings.
A and S	This is a wrapped ring. Can be built manually, but should be left to FDDI's protocols to logically splice together.
B and S	This is a wrapped ring. Can be built manually, but should be left to FDDI's protocols to logically splice together.

NOTE

For more information on wrapped rings, please see the next section, "Topologies and Implementations."

The only port connection combination that is considered illegal and invalid is M to M. This creates a "ring of trees," which is not very useful. This term is explained in the next section, "Topologies and Implementations."

Topologies and Implementations

The previously described port types and attachment methods lend themselves to topological and implementation-level variety. Contrary to the persistent myth, FDDI is not just dual, counter-rotating rings. This is, arguably, its most important topology, but there are many other useful topologies and implementations. Some of the more common variations that FDDI networks can use include:

- Dual ring
- Dual ring with trees
- Single tree
- Dual home
- Wrap-around

Each of the first four topologies offers a different combination of performance features and limitations. The fifth one, wrap-around, is actually seen only during a network failure.

Dual Ring

The basic Dual Ring topology, sometimes referred to as a "Dual Ring without trees," is built from dual-attached stations interconnecting directly with each other. This forms a pair of peer-to-peer rings. This is illustrated in Figure 10.4.

FIGURE 10.4.
Dual Ring.

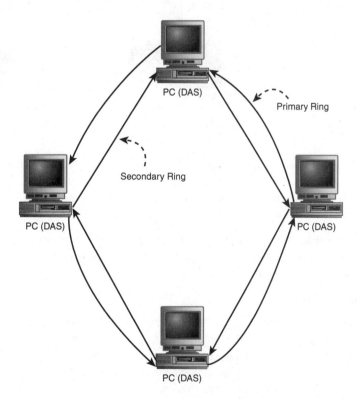

PC (DAS)

Primary Ring

Secondary Ring

PC (DAS)

PC (DAS)

PC (DAS)

The disadvantages of relying on each member in the ring for the entire ring's functionality should be obvious. The rings depend equally upon each of the member devices. If any machine is powered down, or out of service for any reason, the physical rings are compromised. FDDI detects and automatically limits the extent of the damage, but the point is that risks are inherent in this topology. It should be limited to small, highly specialized environments.

10

FDDI

Dual Ring with Trees

The Dual Ring with Trees topology is an enhancement to the Dual Ring topology. This one features tree-like appendages that grow out of FDDI's dual rings. Developing this topology requires the use of dual-attachment concentrators, single-attachment concentrators, and single-attachment stations. Figure 10.5 illustrates a Dual Ring with Trees topology.

FIGURE 10.5.

Dual Ring with Trees.

The key difference between this topology and the basic Dual Ring topology is that devices need not connect directly to the rings. Instead, SAS devices connect to single-attach concentrators. These concentrators, in turn, connect to the DAS concentrators that comprise the backbone of the tandem rings.

This topology combines the reliability of dual rings that automatically wrap around in the event of a failure, with lower cost. SAS components, including concentrators and Network Interface Cards (NICs), are substantially less expensive than their DAS counterparts.

Single Tree

The Single Tree topology, as its name implies, consists of only a single tree-like grouping of devices. There is no dual ring, nor are there any DAS components. Given that FDDI uses a round-robin, token-passing media access methodology, this tree should be regarded as a logical ring. Tokens still pass in a circular pattern across the network, but the topology is based on a concentrator and, thus, is star-shaped.

The obvious drawback to this is that there is no redundant path. This directly reduces the reliability of the network. The benefits, however, are many. First, the cost of building a single tree FDDI network is much lower than that of other topologies due to two main factors:

■ All the devices (concentrators and stations) are the relatively low-cost single-attach variety.

■ The cost of wiring the LAN's backbone is halved due to the use of only two fibers rather than four.

The other main benefit is reliability. Although this may sound contradictory, given the lack of a second ring, the use of only single-attached devices holds an important implication for the overall reliability of the LAN. The impacts of the failure of any given single-attached device are much lower than the failure of an equivalent dual-attached device. If a SAS station fails, the remainder of the network is not affected at all. Similarly, if a SAS concentrator fails, the worst that can happen is that the devices connected to it are isolated from the rest of the network. It doesn't trigger a wrap-around. Wrap-arounds, although touted as a reliability feature, directly impact performance by almost doubling the cable length of the network. Depending upon the specific situation, one could make a credible case that auto-recovery via a wrap-around is less desirable than simply isolating a few workstations in the event of a concentrator failure.

Figure 10.6 shows a Single Tree topology.

FIGURE 10.6.
Single Tree.

■ PC (SAS)　　PC (SAS)

Dual Home

Dual homing is a specialized use of a dual attachment that provides redundant physical paths for critical networked resources. Such resources may include file and/or application servers, bridges, or even your boss's workstation! Please note, dual homing does not necessarily have to include every device on the LAN, thus it is not truly a topology. Instead, it is an optional means of implementing LAN connectivity. It can be used very specifically for individual devices, rather than broadly for all devices.

This implementation can be used only on a Dual Ring with Trees topology. Each device to be dual-homed, by definition, must be DAS-capable. Lastly, it must connect to the network via a dual-attached concentrator. Dual homing enables a critical device to have a primary and a less-desirable (from the FDDI protocol's perspective) alternate connection to the LAN.

The Station Management protocols of the dual-homed device activate the primary connection and leave the alternate connection in a standby mode. *Each connection terminates at a different dual-attached concentrator.* The Station Management protocols can detect this difference in the two connections via their neighbor discovery mechanisms. Station Management then activates the A-port connection as the primary path, and idles the B-port connection. If the A-port connection is lost, for any reason, Station Management attempts to activate the stand-by connection.

Figure 10.7 illustrates a server configured for dual homing within a Dual Ring with Trees Topology.

Figure 10.7.

Dual homing.

Wrap-Around

A wrap-around isn't really a discrete topology that you would build. Rather, it is automatically constructed by FDDI's station management mechanisms in the event of either a station failure or a wire path failure. The failure is isolated by logically splicing the primary and alternate rings immediately upstream and downstream from the failure. Implicit in this definition is the fact that only topologies based on a dual ring can wrap around.

Although the mechanics of recovering from either one are similar, there is one fundamental difference between them. Wire path failures can enable all stations to remain active on the wraparound ring network. A failed station, on the other hand, decreases the population of active devices on the network by one.

In Figure 10.8, a wire failure has afflicted Station 2. Its neighboring stations, 1 and 3, wrap their transmissions around this failure onto the secondary ring to preserve the integrity of the loop. The new ring has a total physical media length almost double the size of the original ring. For this reason, the practical maximum media length in a double ring topology should always be half the maximum supportable length for any given media type.

Although Figure 10.8 depicts a wire failure in the primary path of a station, similar failures can occur in the LAN's backbone. Dual-attached concentrators, too, can use the alternate ring to wrap their transmissions around wire failures.

If Station 2 in Figure 10.8 had failed completely, the wrap-around would have looked slightly different. The ring would no longer extend to that device. Instead, it would be wrapped around at Stations 1 and 3. This is illustrated in Figure 10.9.

Figure 10.8.
*Wrap-around ring
(wire failure).*

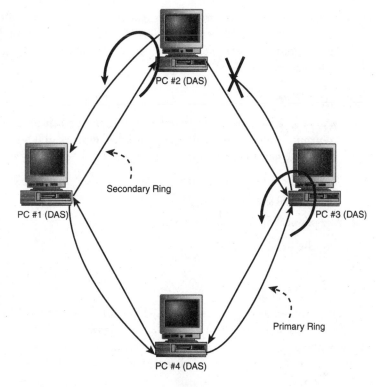

Figure 10.9.
*Wrap-around ring
(station failure).*

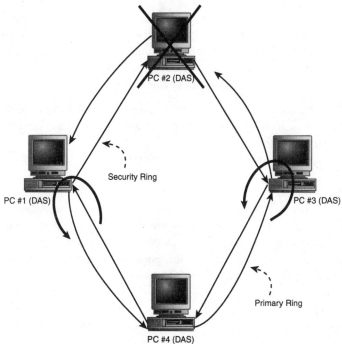

10

FDDI

Devices known as "optical bypass switches" can be used to prevent station failures from forcing a wrap-around. These devices are installed in between the station and the concentrator. In the event of a station failure, these bypass switches maintain the continuity of the wire path without the station.

Network Size

FDDI was designed to be a robust network, capable of supporting high-performance workstations. To maintain high performance for all attached devices, FDDI must impose strict limits on the size of the network. The size of the network can be measured in terms of:

- The number of attached devices
- The physical size of the ring
- The physical distances between devices

All are equally important in developing LANs that can deliver the potential performance of FDDI.

Maximum Devices

The maximum number of devices that any FDDI ring can support is 500. This limitation is actually a function of the maximum allowable propagation delay that FDDI's protocols can endure without compromising its functionality. Each connection adds a measurable amount of propagation delay. The cumulative delays of more than 1000 physical connections exceed FDDI's delay budget.

Though it may seem simple enough to count 500 devices, the challenge lies in being able to precisely identify a "device." In a dual-attached configuration, each device requires two physical connections and, consequently, counts as two connections. Each device in which those connections terminate counts as an additional connection. Thus, a concentrator port and the device to which it connects actually constitute two devices.

A dual-attached backbone concentrator, one that has no station connections, is counted as two connections. Its ports count as a device only when they are used. A dual-attached station, regardless of whether the two attachments home into the same concentrator or two different concentrators, counts as two devices. Single-attached stations count as only one device.

Ring Length

The ANSI X3T9.5 standard does not explicitly state a maximum ring length. Given that the Physical Layer (contrary to popular belief) does not extend to the media itself, this shouldn't be surprising. In keeping with the intent of the Physical Layer, as defined by the OSI Reference Model, the ANSI standard does establish performance parameters that, given any physical media type, impose maximum distances.

In a multi-mode fiber optic ring, the total fiber path must be less than 200 kilometers. Unless your FDDI is to span across a large geographic area, like a metropolitan area network (MAN), this limitation shouldn't be much of a constraining factor in your design. What is important to note, however, is the phrase "total fiber path."

Two important implications lurk in those key words. First, building a large ring that measures 190 kilometers works until a failure forces a wrap-around. Then, the wrapped ring measures something closer to 380 kilometers and the entire network fails. Thus, the maximum ring length must always be cut in half when designing the LAN.

Second, "total fiber path" means just that. All the fiber lengths must be added together to determine the total ring length. This includes the main ring and all the branch cables that connect to stations.

Drive Distance

The *drive distance* is the maximum distance between any two devices. Attenuation is a factor, regardless of which PMD is used. Thus, the distance between devices must be short enough to guarantee the integrity of the signal upon arrival.

For multimode fiber-optic cabling, the maximum drive distance is 2 kilometers. With single mode fiber, this increases to 60 kilometers. However, the copper-based PMDs are much more limited. Shielded Twisted Pair (STP) and Category 5 Unshielded Twisted Pair (UTP) must be kept to less than 100 meters.

FDDI Frames

FDDI is much like Token Ring: all media-based functions must be enveloped in a frame. Consequently, FDDI has numerous frame types that are used in its normal operation and maintenance. These include:

- Basic data frame
- LLC data frame
- LLS SNAP data frame
- Token frame
- An assortment of Station Management frames

Data Frame

The most familiar of the frame types is the raw data frame. This is illustrated in Figure 10.10.

The FDDI frame is a maximum of 9000 symbols in length, including data and all frame components. This is the basic FDDI frame. It is usually implemented in one of two sub-formats: LLC and SNAP. Neither one, excluding the Preamble, can be more than 4500 octets in length.

FIGURE 10.10.

The FDDI data frame.

8-Octet Preamble	1-Octet Starting Delimiter	1-Octet Frame Control Field	6-Octet Destination Address	6-Octet Source Address	Variable Length Data Field, up to 4478 Octets	4-Octet Frame Check Sequence	1-Octet Ending Delimiter	3-Octet Frame Status

NOTE

FDDI's field and frame lengths are frequently cited in references using symbols, octets, or bytes. These terms are not completely interchangeable. Understanding the mechanics of FDDI's encoding scheme can clarify the differences. Unfortunately, precious few care to explore FDDI in this level of detail.

The Physical Layer FDDI protocols encode each data nibble (a half octet) into a five-bit pattern, or symbol, for transmission. Thus, each 8-bit byte (to use the programmer's term) of data passed down from the Application Layer becomes 10 bits, or 1.25 octets. For this reason, the terms bytes and octets are *not* interchangeable!

The frame, and its structural components, can be measured in either octets or symbols. This should not be misconstrued as meaning that octets and symbols are synonymous. For example, the MAC Layer generates frames that are a maximum of 4500 octets long. These octets, both data and framing, are transmitted in 5-bit symbols. At the physical level, these octets are cut into halves, and each half is translated into a 5-bit binary symbol. As transmitted, the frame is a maximum of 9000 5-bit symbols in length. Each maximally-sized MAC frame becomes 5625 octets long when transmitted.

The basic frame contains the following fields:

■ An 8-octet Preamble that signals the start of the frame

■ A 1-octet Start of Frame delimiter that signals the start of the frame's contents

■ A 1-octet Frame Control field that signals the type of frame, such as token, MAC or LLC, priority frame, and so forth

■ The intended recipient's 6-octet MAC address

■ The originator's 6-octet MAC address

■ A variable length data field that contains up to 4478 octets

■ A 4-octet Frame Check Sequence that is used to check the integrity of the frame

■ A half-octet (four bits) Ending Delimiter

■ A 3-octet Frame Status field that contains three 1-octet sub-fields: Error, Address-match, and Copied; each sub-field is set to either "S" for "Set" or "R" for "Reset."

LLC Data Frame

The basic FDDI data frame can also be used to support the functionality specified in the IEEE 802.2 specification for *Logical Link Control* (LLC). The LLC frame, illustrated in Figure 10.11, is constructed by adding a three-field LLC sub-frame to the FDDI frame. These three fields are the *Destination Service Access Point* (DSAP), *Source Service Access Point* (SSAP), and Control fields. They are appended to the beginning of the data field and count as part of its payload.

FIGURE 10.11.

FDDI frame with an 802.2 LLC sub-frame.

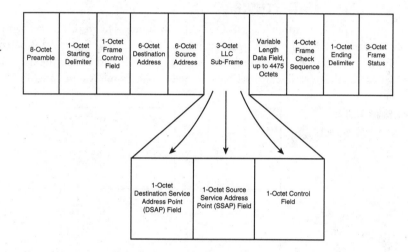

An FDDI LLC data frame has the following structure:

- An 8-octet Preamble that signals the start of the frame
- A 1-octet Start of Frame delimiter that signals the start of the frame's contents
- A 1-octet Frame Control field that signals the type of frame, such as token, MAC or LLC, priority frame, and so forth
- The intended recipient's 6-octet MAC address
- The originator's 6-octet MAC address
- The 3-octet LLC sub-frame, which includes the 1-octet DSAP, SSAP, and Control fields
- A variable length data field that contains up to 4475 octets
- A 4-octet Frame Check Sequence that is used to check the integrity of the frame
- A half-octet (four bits) Ending Delimiter
- A 3-octet Frame Status field that contains three 1-octet sub-fields: Error, Address-match, and Copied; each sub-field is set to either "S" for "Set" or "R" for "Reset."

10

FDDI

The LLC structure was originally intended to augment Ethernet's capability to route received frames to the appropriate protocol/application upon arrival at its destination. This was crucial in multi-protocol machines, because the original Ethernet specification was designed at a time when there were only a few communications protocols. FDDI doesn't, necessarily, suffer from the original Ethernet's limitations. However, by supporting the LLC sub-frame, it can interoperate with Ethernet clients through a MAC-layer translating bridge without compromising end-to-end functionality.

LLC SNAP Data Frame

Similarly, FDDI supports the LLC SNAP sub-frame. The FDDI frame, with the IEEE's SNAP sub-frame, adds a 3-octet Organizationally Unique Identifier and a 2-octet Type field to the FDDI LLC frame immediately after the LLC header and before the data. These fields are included in the overall length of the data field. This frame is illustrated in Figure 10.12.

FIGURE 10.12.
FDDI frame with 802.2 SNAP sub-frame.

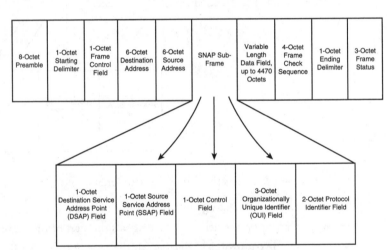

As shown in Figure 10.12, the FDDI SNAP frame contains the following fields:

- An 8-octet Preamble that signals the start of the frame
- A 1-octet Start of Frame delimiter that signals the start of the frame's contents
- A 1-octet Frame Control field that signals the type of frame, such as token, MAC or LLC, priority frame, and so forth
- The intended recipient's 6-octet MAC address
- The originator's 6-octet MAC address
- The 3-octet LLC sub-frame, which includes the 1-octet DSAP, SSAP, and Control fields
- A 5-octet SNAP sub-frame, including a 3-octet Organizationally Unique Identifier field and a 2-octet Protocol Type field that identify the upper level protocol being carried

- A variable length data field that contains up to 4470 octets
- A 4-octet Frame Check Sequence that is used to check the integrity of the frame
- A half-octet (four bits) Ending Delimiter
- A 3-octet Frame Status field that contains three 1-octet sub-fields: Error, Address-match, and Copied. Each sub-field is set to either "S" for "Set" or "R" for "Reset."

FDDI supports the LLC and SNAP subframe structures solely to provide bridging capability with Ethernet. This is necessary only when bridging Ethernet to FDDI, using either Novell's IPX/SPX protocols or AppleTalk. Nevertheless, this functionality reinforces FDDI's capabilities as the backbone in a multi-topology LAN.

The Token Frame

The FDDI Token Frame consists of four fields:

- An 8-octet Preamble that signals the start of the frame
- A 1-octet Start of Frame delimiter that signals the start of the frame's contents
- A 1-octet Frame Control field that signals the type of frame, such as token, MAC or LLC, priority frame, and so forth
- A half-octet (four bits) Ending Delimiter

The FDDI Token Frame is illustrated in Figure 10.13.

FIGURE 10.13.
FDDI token frame.

8-Octet Preamble	1-Octet Starting Delimiter	1-Octet Frame Control Field	1-Octet Ending Delimiter

The token is passed along the ring, in one direction only. The station that has the token may use it to gain access to the transmission media. This is done by inverting a sequence of bits in the Frame Control field to change its state from token to data frame.

Unlike Token Ring, FDDI uses a *quick release* mechanism. Immediately after converting the token to a data frame, and transmitting data, that transmitting device generates a new token. This token is sent to the nearest downstream neighbor. The neighboring device may use it to transmit or simply pass it on. Either way, the original transmitting device quickly relinquishes control over the transmission media. The data frame does not need to return to its originator before another station may transmit.

The quick release mechanism is one of FDDI's better performance-enhancing attributes. It will continue to provide FDDI with an advantage over Token Ring after that framing protocol is given faster signaling and data rates.

10

FDDI

SMT Frames

FDDI, like Token Ring, uses frames to conduct its station management (SMT) functions. The basic SMT functions include:

- Claim Frame (CF) for bidding purposes
- Echo Frames (ECF) for echo testing
- Neighbor Information Frames (NIF) for obtaining neighbor information
- Status Information Frames (SIF) for obtaining status information
- Status Reporting Frames (SRF) for providing status information
- Request Denied Frames (RDF) for denying invalid requests
- Parameter Management Frames (RMF) for providing remote access to other stations

Together, these frames enable the myriad SMT management protocols to support the normal operation of an FDDI network. The actual mechanics of ring operation are explained in the next section of this chapter, "The Mechanics of FDDI."

The Mechanics of FDDI

By now, the frame-passing mechanics of FDDI should be well understood. Like Token Ring, everything is done through the use of frames.

The basic mechanics of FDDI are best understood by examining the protocols by which a station becomes active and is inserted into the ring. Other protocols are adjunct to this, including ring initialization and station de-insertion. These processes demonstrate the role the various FDDI components—SMT, MAC, PMD, and PHY—play in the operation of the network.

Station Initialization

A logical starting point is the processes by which a station initializes itself prior to joining the ring. This initialization is a series of tests that verify the physical integrity of the media link to the ring (or tree), and the readiness of the ring and its attached stations. The station initialization routine is a function of the Physical Connection Management (PCM) protocol. PCM is one of the components of the Station Management (SMT).

The PCM initiates a series of tests that ends with the successful insertion of the station into the ring. These tests begin with the detection of a viable connection to the network. Station Initiation begins with the transmission of Quiet Symbols to the PHY of the nearest downstream station. The recipient station halts any transmissions of its own and enters the *Break State*. This state is so named because, as a station enters it, it must break any existing transmissions and accept the inbound Quiet Symbols.

> **NOTE**
>
> Symbols are the five-bit binary structures that are used to encode data. Given that there are more possible unique structures (32) than there are hexadecimal characters (16), it stands to reason that some symbols cannot be used to encode data. These symbols are reserved for network-level functions. The Quiet Symbol and the Halt Symbol are examples of these reserved symbols.

The Break State is merely a transitional state that lasts only long enough for the recipient to halt its own transmissions. After this is accomplished, that station enters the Quiet Line State. The Quiet Line State is characterized by both the newly active station and its nearest active downstream neighbor simultaneously sending Quiet Symbols to each other. This allows both to know that they are in synchronized states.

After this synchronization occurs, both stations begin repetitively transmitting a different symbol: the Halt Symbol. These symbols are used to synchronize the transmission clocks of the two stations. After the transmission clocks are synchronized, the stations exit the Halt State and enter, curiously enough, the Next State.

During the Next State, the two stations exchange information about each other's ports. Up to this point, each station knows only that the other exists and that both their transmission clocks are synchronized. They do not have any information about what each one looks like. By exchanging port information—such as A, B, M, or S ports—they have a better understanding of each other. This information is also used to identify the port connection combination that is in effect between them. These data are necessary for later station initialization tests.

After these data have been developed, the two stations enter Signal State. A brief transitional state, known as the Idle Line State, separates the Next and Signal States. During this transition, both stations transmit a series of Idle Symbols. These symbols tell both stations that the transmitters are ready to accept incoming signals.

Next comes the Link Confidence Test. This protocol requires each station to see whether the other has a MAC Layer. If so, the two stations engage in MAC frame transmission and token-passing tests. Otherwise, they simply exchange another series of Idle Symbols. If these tests are completed successfully, the stations may progress to the Join State. The Join State's sole purpose is to ensure that both stations activate simultaneously.

After this exchange is successfully completed, both stations' PCMs enter the Active State. This state change completes the Station Initialization process and signals the station's management function that it is ready to join the ring.

10

FDDI

Ring Initialization

After the Station Initialization process is complete, the ring must be initialized. This entails determining which station is to generate the first token and establishing the Operational Token Rotation Time (T_OPR). Stations must bid for the right to issue this token. Bidding is done by assessing each station's default timing requirements. These requirements, stored in a value known as the Token Rotation Timer (TRT), identify how frequently the token must reach that station. The bidding begins with the first active station generating a Claim Frame.

The Claim Frame contains the transmitting station's address and TRT value. This frame is sent downstream, where it is received and compared to the TRT value of the next station. If the recipient's TRT is lower, it discards the received Claim Frame and issues its own. Otherwise, that recipient repeats the original Claim Frame for the next downstream station. This process continues until one of the stations receives its own Claim Frame. It can then be assured that it has the lowest TRT value on the ring and may issue the first token. Its TRT becomes the Operational Token Rotation Time for the entire ring.

This is the essence of the deterministic nature of FDDI: each station has the opportunity to determine the maximum amount of time that may elapse between token visits. The performance of the entire ring may be improved by decreasing the size of the ring (as measured by the number of stations connected to it) or by using the TRT to improve token rotation times.

Summary

For years, FDDI was the only stable, mature, and well-behaved high-speed LAN technology available. Its price, however, tended to limit its implementation to small market niches that demanded high performance. In recent years, FDDI has seen its place in the market challenged by newcomers. Initially, FDDI proponents could confidently assert that theirs was the only stable high-speed LAN. Over time, the competitors became standardized and stable, thereby legitimizing their competitiveness.

Today, FDDI's remaining differentiating points are its reliability and its highly deterministic nature. This combination makes FDDI well suited for use as a LAN backbone and for connecting servers to the LAN.

ATM

by Mark Sportack

IN THIS CHAPTER

Asynchronous Transfer Mode, better known in the data communications world as ATM, was originally conceived as an asynchronous transfer mechanism for Broadband Integrated Services Digital Network (B-ISDN) by the Comite Consultatif Internationale de Telegraphique et Telephonique (CCITT). As such, its use would have been limited to Central Office (CO) to Central Office transmissions. During the early 1990s, its combination of high throughput and low latency was perceived as being ideal for a next-generation local area network. It could, in theory, support the high-bandwidth, low-latency requirements of desktop videoconferencing as easily as it could support traditional interactive applications. Even better, having ATM at the LAN and at the WAN could seamlessly integrate the two.

> **NOTE**
>
> CCITT, loosely translated into English, is the International Consulting Committee for Telephone and Telegraph. The CCITT has since been renamed the *International Telecommunications Union*, or ITU.

This grand vision of network unification launched an unprecedented amount of activity, both marketing and developmental. The ATM Forum emerged as an industry consortium that fed proposed standards to the CCITT. So compelling was the promise of this technology that the ATM Forum's membership soon numbered in the hundreds. The political machinations that inevitably accompany such a large consortium quickly paralyzed the Forum's standards work. It began to seem that ATM was destined to remain that which it was originally conceived to be: a CO-to-CO technology.

Today, after much opportunity has been lost to accelerated and switched versions of Ethernet, FDDI, and Token Ring, the ATM Forum appears to be regaining its lost momentum. It may, once again, become the next-generation LAN. This chapter describes ATM's cell structure, basic services, and operational mechanics, including Local Area Network Emulation (LANE) and switching IP packets over ATM.

The Fundamentals of ATM

ATM inverts the traditional networking paradigm. Traditional networking features connectionless packets that are launched by their transmitting stations with just enough information to identify their origin and intended destination. Thus, the stations can be relatively unsophisticated. The network, however, is given the onerous task of figuring out exactly how to get that packet to its destination.

ATM is the exact opposite of this. The onus is on the end-stations to establish a virtual path between themselves. The switches that comprise that path are given a relatively simple role: relaying cells along a virtual channel through the switched network based on their header information. This is a deceptively simple explanation of an ATM network. To further your command of ATM, it is necessary to understand the nature of its logical connections, as well as some of the more basic aspects of an ATM network, such as its transmission rates and supported media, topology, and interfaces. These topics are examined in this section, and provide the context for a more meaningful exploration of the operational mechanics of ATM that concludes this chapter.

Virtual Connections

Two types of virtual connections can be established across an ATM network:

- A virtual circuit
- A virtual path

A *virtual circuit* is a logical connection between two end devices through a switched network. These devices communicate by passing cells of data back and forth through the logical circuit. A *virtual path* is a logical grouping of these logical circuits. Recognizing such groupings enables ATM switches to perform operations in the aggregate, rather than having to manage each individual virtual circuit.

Each ATM cell contains both Virtual Path Information (VPI) and Virtual Circuit Information (VCI). The ATM switch uses these to relay received cells to the appropriate next device. To do this, the ATM switch must build and maintain switching tables. Much like the old bridge tables, the switch table is nothing more than a list that correlates VPI and VCI information with the physical interfaces of that switch.

If you remember nothing else about ATM, remember that it is connection oriented. It can be used to support connectionless protocols, such as TCP/IP or IPX/SPX, but it does so within the context of a logical connection.

Connection Types

ATM is a connection-oriented protocol that can support two types of connections:

- Point-to-point
- Point-to-multipoint

Point-to-point connections bind two devices together in a virtual connection through ATM's switching fabric. Such connections can be used for uni-directional or bi-directional transfers of data. This type of connection is illustrated in Figure 11.1.

FIGURE 11.1.

Point-to-point ATM connection.

Client PC   Client PC

The second type of connection, point-to-multipoint, is a bit more complicated. This can be used to support only uni-directional transmissions from the single point of origin to the multiple identified recipients. This is illustrated in Figure 11.2.

FIGURE 11.2.

Point-to-multipoint
ATM connection.

Unfortunately, ATM's protocols are not well suited to provide bi-directional point-to-multipoint communications. Nor can they support multipoint-to-multipoint communications of any kind. Both of these forms of communications would be relatively easy to implement in shared media Layer 2 protocols because such protocols would have complex Media Access Control mechanisms that could accommodate multiple simultaneous recipients.

Both point-to-point and point-to-multipoint connections can be established in one of two ways: switched or permanent virtual circuitry. The original focus of the ATM Forum was on Permanent Virtual Circuits (PVCs). In much the same way as in Frame Relay, connections through a (pardon the term) "cloud" of switches can be software defined. These connections always remain active in normal operation, regardless of their traffic volumes.

It remains a bit trickier to develop protocols for Switched Virtual Circuits (SVCs). SVCs are created on demand between two or more endpoints. Cells are then forwarded through this logical channel. After the communications cease, the channel is disassembled and the network can re-use its bandwidth.

Transmission Rates

ATM can operate at many different transmission rates. These rates were, originally, to be based on the Optical Carrier (OC) line specifications. This was consistent with ATM's original mission as B-ISDN's asynchronous transport protocol. Thus, the basic rate of ATM transmission was set to the OC-3 standard of 155.52Mbps. Provisions were made to support the OC-1 rate of 51.84Mbps, as well as to scale upward to the 2.488Gbps of the OC-48 specification. This ensured that ATM would scale well within the well-accepted architecture of the public switched networks.

> **NOTE**
>
> There is even work in progress to scale ATM up to a 10Gbps rate, although this is not intended for use in a LAN.

Adapting ATM to the LAN environment created the need for some variation from its original set of capabilities. Specifically, support needed to be developed for copper-based transmission media that would be consistent with the optically based specifications. Additionally, it was strongly felt that a rate less than the 51.84Mbps of OC-1 would have to be developed for ATM. Two competing proposals were developed: 25.6 and 25.9Mbps. The 25.9Mbps proposal was more logical, because it could be evenly scaled upward into the OC architecture.

The 25.6Mbps specification was cobbled together from IBM's Token Ring chip set. It was believed that such a basis would make 25.6Mbps ATM more reliable than any proposal that lacked a similar, well-engineered heritage. Its heritage, however, resulted in an odd (but relatively functional) data rate. This specification can provide connectivity over Category 3 UTP for up to 100 meters. Ultimately, the 25.6Mbps proposal was adopted by the ATM Forum.

The copper-based variant of OC-1 was designed to provide 51.84Mbps over a maximum of 100 meters of Category 5 UTP. Unfortunately, this specification was based on a new modulation technology known as Carrierless Amplitude Phase Modulation (CAP or CAP-M). Although proven successful in laboratory environments, this technology proved virtually impossible to manufacture on any large scale.

ATM's full rate of 155.52Mbps was also treated to a pair of new physical media interfaces for the LAN environment. The first was Category 5 UTP, which can be up to 100 meters long. The other was 62.5-micron, multimode fiber optic cabling. This media can stretch for up to 2 kilometers.

Topology

Unlike many of today's Layer 2 networking protocols that are being implemented on switches, ATM was designed to be switched. Thus, it features a star topology. Each device connects directly to the ATM switch (it is not a hub or repeater), and enjoys its own dedicated bandwidth to that switch.

This raises an interesting issue: if each station has its own dedicated bandwidth to its switch, does the dedicated bandwidth stop there? Clearly, some multiplexing must be used somewhere in the network, particularly as one exits the LAN and enters the WAN. It is a rare organization that can afford to provide 155.52Mbps' worth of dedicated bandwidth to all its members.

Switches that can support simultaneous, full-rate transmissions to all connected devices are called *non-blocking*. Non-blocking switches require a backplane whose throughput must be at least as great as the aggregate bandwidth it supports to stations. That is, the backplane must operate at a minimum of 155.52 times the number of ports on the switch to qualify as non-blocking. For example, an ATM switch with 8 ports must have a backplane speed of 8 * 155.52, or 1.244Gbps to qualify as non-blocking. Any switches with 8 ports at 155.52Mbps with an available backplane bandwidth of fewer than 1.244Gbps would have to block some of the transmissions if all 8 stations attempted to send simultaneously.

ATM Interfaces

There are many types of highly specialized ATM interfaces. Many are closely related, with only slight and subtle differences made necessary by the arcane legislation that continues to haunt the US telecommunications industry. A closer look at just two of ATM's interfaces should provide the necessary context for understanding ATM's architecture. The two most familiar interfaces are

- User-to-Network Interface (UNI)
- Network-to-Network Interface (NNI)

These names are fairly self explanatory. UNIs are used to connect user equipment to the ATM network, while NNIs are needed to interconnect the ATM switches that comprise the network. These two interfaces are illustrated in Figure 11.3.

FIGURE 11.3.

ATM's user-to-network, and network-to-network interface signaling.

NOTE

Due to its origins as a broadband ISDN technology, ATM's UNI was developed to describe Customer Premise Equipment. Thus, a UNI interface can be used by a privately owned ATM switch that connects to a telecommunications carrier's public ATM network.

The ATM Forum is also nearing completion of a Private Network-to-Network Interface (P-NNI). The protocols in this interface will allow dynamic routing in private ATM networks with multiple switches.

ATM Reference Model

What protocol would be complete without its very own Reference Model? ATM is no exception. The ATM Protocol Reference Model, however, puts an innovative spin on the familiar layered model. It uses *planes*. Planes, unlike layers, are three-dimensional. Without getting hung up on the technicalities of geometry, suffice it to say that each plane represents a separate protocol suite. Together, they comprise the ATM protocol suite. The ATM Protocol Reference Model is illustrated in Figure 11.4, as it compares to the OSI Reference Model.

FIGURE 11.4.
ATM Reference Model versus OSI Reference Model.

NOTE

Although Figure 11.4 depicts the Convergence Sublayer as a fixed part of the ATM Reference Model, it is needed by only a subset of its Adaptation Layers. Consequently, certain classes of service may be provided without using the Convergence Sublayer. This point is further expanded later in this section.

As is evident in Figure 11.4, ATM is limited to Layers 1 and 2 of the OSI Reference Model. Above this would be the traditional transport network protocols and applications. Upper layer mechanisms include provisions for end-to-end data transfer and signaling. These are referred to as the User and Control planes, respectively.

Physical Layer

The ATM's version of the OSI Physical Layer consists of two sublayers:

- Transmission Convergence (TC)
- Physical Medium (PM)

ATM's Physical Layer has twin responsibilities for data transmission and reception. For data transmissions, the Transmission Convergence mechanism accepts cells from the ATM Layer, generates a checksum value that can be used for some limited degree of forward error detection, and then transmits the cell's header and payload one bit at a time over the media.

For data reception, the Physical Medium accepts inbound cells, verifies the checksum value to determine whether the header was damaged in transit, and then forwards the bits up to the ATM Layer for reconstruction into cells.

Transmission Convergence Sublayer

The Transmission Convergence (TC) sublayer is the uppermost of ATM's Physical Layer components. It is responsible for numerous functions including

- Cell delineation
- Generation of the Hardware Error Control (HEC) sequence
- Cell-rate decoupling
- Transmission frame adaptation, generation, and recovery functions

"Cell delineation" is a fancy term for preserving the integrity of cell boundaries upon receipt. This function is critical to the successful extraction of cells from the received bit stream.

Hardware Error Control (HEC) is nothing more than a checksum value. Transmitting stations must generate and check this value, based upon the header contents of the cell. Recipients must recalculate this value to determine the likelihood of the contents having been damaged in transit. Unfortunately, this checksum is computed only on the 5-octet header, and not the entire 53-octet cell. This adds support to the old argument that ATM doesn't really provide forward error detection, despite having a mechanism for it. As is shown later in this chapter, forward error correction is an integral part of many of the Data Link Layer components.

Cell-rate decoupling is a mechanism that is used to match the cell rate of the ATM Layer with the cell rate of the media interface. For example, if the ATM Layer operates at the full rate of 155.52Mbps, but the media interface is limited to 25.6Mbps, the Transmission Convergence sublayer is responsible for throttling back transmissions. Preferably, this is done by suppressing any unassigned cells. Similarly, this sublayer can also insert blank cells to accelerate the ATM Layer's cell stream, if it is slower than the media's cell rate.

The last bundle of functions for which the TC is responsible may seem a bit counter intuitive. These functions involve transmission framing. Transmission frame adaptation is the process by which the TC packages cells into frames that are acceptable to the specific physical media that they are to traverse. Similarly, frame generation and recovery are ancillary functions that create and maintain the appropriate Physical Layer frame structure.

> **NOTE**
>
> The Protocol Data Units (PDUs) created and used by ATM's various Data Link Layer mechanisms are also called *frames*. PDUs are examined in much more detail in the following section, titled "ATM Adaptation Layer."

Physical Medium Sublayer

The Physical Medium sublayer encompasses all the functions that are medium dependent. This includes synchronizing the timing of transmissions across a virtual circuit and transmitting/receiving bits, as needed. It is important to note that, because the Physical Medium sublayer is medium dependent, a separate PM specification exists for each of the supported physical media.

ATM Adaptation Layer

As was presented in Figure 11.4, ATM's version of the OSI's Data Link Layer is comprised of two sublayers: the ATM Layer and the ATM Adaptation Layer (AAL). The AAL is a protocol suite that occupies the upper reaches of ATM's Data Link Layer. Although it is named "the AAL Layer," there are actually three mechanisms contained in this Layer. The AAL is the most obvious, but there is also a CS (Convergence Sublayer) and SAR (Segmentation and Reassembly).

The Convergence Sublayer provides the funnel through which data intended for transmission is received from Layer 3 protocols, and through which any received data is passed back to those protocols. The CS is responsible for properly mapping higher-layer protocol requests for AAL, SAR, and ATM services on both outbound and incoming data. This service is needed only for mapping other protocols such as TCP/IP, IPX/SPX, or even other Layer 2 protocols such as Frame Relay.

The SAR is the mechanism that actually chips data structures received from higher-layer protocols into the 48-octet structures that neatly fill ATM's payload fields. These data structures are passed to the ATM Layer where they become the payloads of cells.

Five different AALs, numbered 1 through 5, were planned. Each one was designed to support one of ATM's four different Classes of Service. These are known as Classes A, B, C, and D. Each class supports transmissions in different ways and, consequently, requires a separate set of protocols at the end stations. Each AAL places the data it receives from the SAR into a pre-cellular structure known as a *Segmentation and Reassembly Protocol Data Unit* (SAR-PDU). SAR-PDUs are passed to the ATM Layer where 5-octet headers are grafted onto them to form the familiar 53-octet ATM cells.

> **NOTE**
>
> Although five AALs were planned, only three remain. AAL 2 was never completed, and 3 and 4 have been combined into a single AAL named "3/4." Thus, the surviving AALs are 1, 3/4, and 5.

Class A Service

Class A service uses the AAL 1. It features Constant Bit Rate (CBR), connection-oriented synchronous traffic. These transmission characteristics are necessary to support isochronous communications such as voice traffic, or even high-quality video transmissions. Additionally, AAL 1 can be used to emulate DS-1 links of T-carrier circuits. It is important to note that data is fed into AAL 1 at a constant bit rate; the AAL cannot make consistency out of chaos! The bit rate constancy must be driven by the application. If the application cannot maintain the data rate at a uniform pace from beginning to end, there is very little that the ATM protocols can do to create a constant bit rate.

> **NOTE**
>
> For more information on DS-1 links and the T-carrier system, please refer to Chapter 14, "Leased Lines."

SAR-PDUs created via AAL 1 have two 4-bit fields prepended to their payload. These fields are the Sequence Number (SN), and the Sequence Number Protection (SNP). The Sequence Number is a 4-bit counter that is reset to 0 for each data unit segmented by the SAR. The SNP is a 4-bit Cyclical Redundancy Check (CRC) number, calculated using only the 4 bits of the Sequence Number. This reduces the payload field of an AAL 1 cell to 47 octets.

An example of an AAL 1 SAR-PDU is illustrated in Figure 11.5.

FIGURE 11.5.
AAL 1 SAR-PDU.

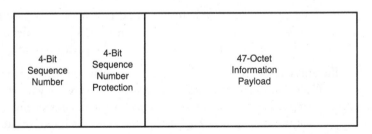

Class B Service

Class B traffic is like Class A traffic. They are both connection-oriented and synchronous. The only difference is that Class B doesn't require a Constant Bit Rate. Instead, it uses a Variable Bit Rate (VBR). In other words, the application has a high time value, and its transmissions must be carefully synchronized, but they come at irregular intervals. This subtle distinction is enough to warrant a separate adaptation layer: AAL 2.

Some video applications, particularly those that feature algorithms that refresh only the changed pixels, are ideal for Class B. Unfortunately, the specification for AAL 2 has never been completed by the ATM Forum. Thus, many information sources identify only AALs 1, 3, 4, and 5, although 3 and 4 are lumped together and designated "3/4." Without a specification defining its structure, any attempt at illustrating an AAL 2 SAR-PDU is purely speculative. Consequently, none is provided.

Class C Service

Class C traffic is connection oriented, and uses a Variable Bit Rate (VBR). More importantly, there are no timing requirements to be satisfied between the end-points; it is asynchronous. Originally, Class C traffic was to be satisfied via AAL 3. Sometime during its development, a decision was made to combine AAL 3 and AAL 4 into a single AAL that could service both Class C and Class D.

> **NOTE**
>
> The combined AAL was rather uncreatively named 3/4, which is pronounced "three-four" rather than expressed as the fractional "three-fourths." In retrospect, given that a subset of Class C traffic was treated to yet another AAL (#5), perhaps the fractional pronunciation is more appropriate!

Many protocols, including Layer 2 protocols such as Frame Relay and X.25 and higher-layer protocol suites like TCP/IP and IPX/SPX, represent Class C traffic. Although these protocols are inherently connectionless, ATM requires that a connection first be established before any cells can be relayed between any two stations. After the virtual connection is established, no restrictions limit what the payloads of those cells may contain. A connection-oriented protocol is capable of encapsulating and relaying packetized data from connectionless protocols.

This creates the need for careful convergence of the higher-layer protocols' functions into the mechanics of the ATM Layer. This is where the Convergence Sublayer is useful. The CS creates a CS-PDU (which, in case you hadn't guessed, stands for "Convergence Sublayer Protocol Data Unit"!) for AAL 3/4. This CS-PDU is illustrated in Figure 11.6.

FIGURE 11.6.
AAL 3/4 CS-PDU.

1-Octet Common Part Indicator	1-Octet Beginning Tag	2-Octet Buffer Allocation Size	Variable Length Information Payload (up to 65,536 octets)	Variable Length Pad	1-Octet Alignment Field	1-Octet End Tag	2-Octet Length Field

As evidenced in Figure 11.6, the AAL 3/4 CS-PDU has the following structure:

- 1-octet Common Part Indicator (CPI)
- 1-octet Beginning Tag (BTag)
- 2-octet Buffer Allocation Size Indicator (BASize)
- Variable length Information Payload (someone wisely avoided using the already widely used acronym "IP" for this field!)
- Variable length padding (PAD)
- 1-octet Alignment field (AL)
- 1-octet End Tag (ETag)
- 2-octet Length field

Each of these fields is significant to the functioning of the AAL. The CPI indicates the usage of the other CS-PDU fields. This usage can vary by operation. The BTag contains a numeric value. The same value is placed in the Ending Tag (ETag). Together, they identify the beginning and end of each CS-PDU. This is necessary because downstream operations are likely to result in each CS-PDU being further segmented into an as-yet-undetermined number of SAR-PDUs.

The Buffer Allocation Size Indicator is used to warn the recipient AAL of the size of buffer it needs to successfully reassemble this incoming CS-PDU. The Information Payload is limited to the maximum size identifiable by the previous field. Given that BASize is a binary structure that is 2 octets long, its maximum value is 2 to the 16th power, which is 65,536. This is the maximum size of the Information Payload. Obviously, this is much larger than the size of an ATM cell's payload, so further segmentation is necessary.

> **NOTE**
>
> The Buffer Allocation Size Indicator is sometimes not used to describe the actual length of the payload. Rather, it is automatically set to a large (if not maximum) value. This is useful in streaming applications where the AAL might not know the exact size of the PDU.

The PAD field is used in those cases where the Information Payload does not equal a multiple of 32. As padding, it is used only to maintain consistent length, and its contents are set to zeroes.

The next field is the Alignment field. This 1-octet field is used solely to increase the CS-PDU's trailer to 4 octets. It is set to zero and functions as structural padding.

The last two fields are the End Tag and the Length. The ETag, as previously explained, mirrors the value in the BTag. The Length field is set to the actual length of the Information Payload field.

The CS-PDU is then passed to the SAR, where it is segmented into as many SAR-PDUs as are needed. This SAR-PDU has the following structure:

- 2-bit Segment Type (ST)
- 4-bit Sequence Number (SN)
- 10-bit Multiplexing Identification (MID)
- 44-octet Information Payload
- 6-bit Length Indicator (LI)
- 10-bit Cyclic Redundancy Check field (CRC)

This SAR-PDU, if you've been counting, is exactly 48 octets in length—the exact length of the ATM cell payload. All that remains is to graft on the appropriate 5-octet header and you have created a cell. This SAR-PDU is illustrated in Figure 11.7.

Figure 11.7.
AAL 3/4 SAR-PDU.

2-Bit Segment Type	4-Bit Sequence Number	10-Bit Multiplexing Identifier	44-Octet Information Payload	6-Bit Length Indicator	10-Bit CRC

Given that many of the fields contained in this SAR-PDU are already familiar, it should suffice to describe the functionality of only the ones not yet presented. The only field not yet discussed is the Multiplexing Identification (MID). This field is used to identify all the cells that are created from any given CS-PDU. These structures can range up to 65,536 octets in length, so they can be chipped into 1,365 cells! This field ensures that the cells are uniquely identifiable as belonging to the same CS-PDU by the recipient. The recipient, in theory, may be receiving multiple streams of cells from different sources simultaneously—hence, the reason for this field's existence.

At the risk of understating the painfully obvious, AAL 3/4 is quite complex and awkward to use. As testimony to this awkwardness, AAL 5 was developed to satisfy a subset of Class C traffic only. AAL 5 is the one adaptation layer that will be used the most. This statement is predicated upon the rather dangerous double assumption that, first, ATM will actually be used, and, second, that the majority of applications supported will continue to rely upon the traditional connectionless communications protocols.

AAL 5 was designed to be a simple and efficient AAL, targeted at the most used portions of AAL 3/4. This AAL also produces a CS-PDU, albeit a much more streamlined one than the one just examined.

The first field in the AAL 5 CS-PDU is the Information Payload. This field can be anywhere from 0 to 65,536 octets long, although a 0-octet payload would be rather pointless. This is followed by a PAD field. Padding is used to ensure that the Payload is a multiple of 48, which facilitates cell creation in the ATM Layer. Next is a 1-octet Control field, which hasn't yet been given any usefulness, and so is defaulted to zeroes. The last two fields are the Length and CRC fields. Again, the Length field is 2 octets long, which yields the maximum value of the Information Payload field. The CRC field is 4 octets long and calculated using the entire contents of the CS-PDU (from the start of the Information Payload to the end of the Length field).

This CS-PDU is illustrated in Figure 11.8.

FIGURE 11.8.
AAL 5 CS-PDU.

Variable Length Information Payload (0 to 65,536 octets)	Variable Length Pad	1-Octet Control Field	2-Octet Length Indicator	4-Octet CRC

The AAL 5 CS-PDU is then passed to the SAR for conversion to a SAR-PDU. The AAL 5 SAR-PDU is a rather unspectacular structure that contains only 48 octets of payload, with no SAR-specific headers or trailers. The simplicity of this AAL makes it relatively inexpensive and easy to implement. The fact that AAL 5 is tailored to what is likely to be the bulk of ATMs traffic also positions AAL 5 as the workhorse of the adaptation layers.

Class D Service

Class D service features a connectionless, asynchronous data transfer. This is useful for relaying LAN or SMDS traffic over an ATM backbone. AAL 3/4 is the combined adaptation layer that services both Class C and D traffic. This almost makes sense when one considers that the only distinction between Classes C and D is that one is connection oriented and the other is connectionless.

The ATM Layer

The ATM Layer and the ATM Adaptation Layers correspond to the Data Link Layer of the OSI Reference Model. Of these, the ATM Layer is the lower and is responsible for establishing virtual connections and for passing cells received from the AAL through those connections. Much of the ATM Layer's functionality depends on whether that layer resides in an end-station or a switching device. Consequently, it makes sense to examine the two alternatives independently.

End-Station

The ATM Layer of an end-station needs to be able to signal other stations that it has data to send them and negotiate the construction of a Switched Virtual Circuit with that station (or stations). Although this may sound simple, entire books can be written about the signaling techniques used to support circuit construction.

The logical circuit must be constructed before the ATM Layer can accept data from the AAL. Data from the AAL is received in the form of a Protocol Data Unit, which must be converted into a cell. This is easily accomplished via the addition, and population, of the header fields.

Switch

The functionality of a switch's ATM Layer is much simpler than its station-based counterpart. Upon receipt of a cell from any of its ports, it is only required to look at the VPI/VCI (Virtual Path Identifier/Virtual Channel Identifier, discussed in the following section) values contained in that cell's header, and compare them to its table of VPI/VCI assignments. This table look-up accomplishes two important tasks. First, it determines what the new VPI/VCI assignments should be. Second, it identifies the port to which that cell must be relayed.

These are the primary functions of a switch's ATM Layer. Additional functions may include setting the Payload Type Indicator (PTI) field (if the network is congested), and implementing any traffic policies that may be in effect. This layer must also provide any buffering and re-ordering of cells made necessary by competition between multiple input ports for the same output port.

> **NOTE**
>
> "Passing a cell out of a port" implies that the ATM Layer hands off the cell to that port's Physical Layer components. The Physical Layer then recomputes the HEC value, and then both creates and transmits the bit stream. In effect, the relayed cell is a very different cell than it was when it was received. Its header has been modified extensively.

The Cell

Once you have seen how the AALs create the basic Protocol Data Units (PDUs), exploring the structure of the actual ATM cells is almost anticlimactic. Nevertheless, the cell is ATM's basic data transport structure. Unlike most other LANs, this Layer 2 structure is of fixed length. ATM's cell is always 53 octets in length. This may sound like an unusual length, especially to anyone who's accustomed to Base 2 and/or Base 16 number systems, and for good reason! The cell length was derived through the time-honored convention of compromise rather than mathematics. The North American contributors to the CCITT's ATM standards body were in favor of a 64-octet payload while the European and Asian representatives felt that a 32-octet payload would be more appropriate. CCITT split the difference and standardized a 48-octet payload with a 5-octet header—hence, the less-than-intuitive length.

There are actually two different cell structures, one for UNI and one for NNI. The differences are all accounted for in the format of the 5-octet header.

UNI Cell Structure

The UNI cell has the following structure:

- 4-bit Generic Flow Control (GFC)
- 8-bit Virtual Path Identifier (VPI)
- 16-bit Virtual Channel Identifier (VCI)
- 3-bit Payload Type Indicator (PTI)
- 1-bit Cell Loss Priority (CLP)
- 8-bit Header Error Check (HEC)
- 48-octet payload

This cell is illustrated in Figure 11.9.

FIGURE 11.9.

The UNI cell structure.

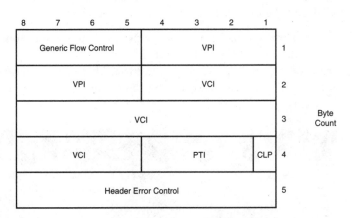

The Generic Flow Control field was envisioned as a mechanism to regulate the flow of data (cells) across UNIs only. Establishing the need for this mechanism and the length of its field were easy tasks. Specifying the actual method and processes by which the flow of data between the two end-stations in a connection could be regulated proved much more daunting. Of all the higher-level services that needed to be defined to extend ATM to the LAN environment, flow control proved to be one of the more divisive and intractable. Today, the GFC is deemed to have local value only. That is, its contents are not carried across an entire virtual circuit.

The VPI field of the UNI cell is 8 bits long. It is used to identify virtual paths, although this is more of an NNI function. Consequently, the UNI VPI field is defaulted to all zeroes, and can be set to other values to facilitate network management functions. As the cell travels into NNI regions of the network, the VPI field may be used by those NNI switches. Remember, switches aren't simple repeaters: they process the cell and rewrite its header before relaying it.

The Virtual Channel Identifier is a 16-bit field that uniquely identifies the virtual connection established during the signaling process. The ATM switch uses the VPI, in conjunction with the VCI, to relay received cells to the appropriate physical port.

The Payload Type Indicator is a 3-bit field, and each bit is significant.

■ The first bit indicates whether the cell's payload originated from within the user or control planes.

■ The second bit indicates whether that cell has encountered congestion in the network.

■ The third bit is used to flag the last of a series of cells that are made from a single AAL 5 PDU.

The Cell Loss Priority field is just 1 bit long. It indicates whether or not the cell should be discarded if it encounters heavy congestion during its passage through the network. Traditional application types require guaranteed integrity upon delivery, and rely upon Layer 4 protocols to reorder any packets delivered out of sequence. It is more important for these packets to arrive intact than it is for them to arrive on time and in order.

This is in stark contrast to the next-generation, latency-sensitive applications like voice and/or video conferencing. These applications require that the data arrive on time. Period. If the packets are late, or damaged in transit, they are simply discarded by the recipient application. Time value is the highest priority. Thus, the Cell Loss Priority bit provides a mechanism for the network to discriminate between high and low time-value cells. High time-value cells that are going to be discarded by their application aren't worth carrying all the way to that application, so the network can simply discard them.

The last field of the UNI Cell is the Header Error Check. This is an 8-bit field that contains the output of a checksum algorithm calculated using the contents of the cell's header fields, excluding the HEC.

NNI Cell Structure

The NNI cell was designed for ATM's original role as a CO-to-CO transport for broadband-ISDN. Its structure reflects that role. The NNI cell contains the following fields:

■ 12-bit Virtual Path Identifier (VPI)

■ 16-bit Virtual Channel Identifier (VCI)

■ 3-bit Payload Type Indicator (PTI)

■ 1-bit Cell Loss Priority (CLP)

■ 8-bit Header Error Check (HEC)

■ 48-octet payload

This cell is illustrated in Figure 11.10.

FIGURE 11.10.
The NNI cell structure.

Given that each of the NNI cell's fields is also included in the UNI cell, it hardly seems worth the effort to revisit these fields. The key differences between the fields in the UNI and NNI cells are the lack of a 4-bit flow control field and the expansion of the VPI to 12 bits. Expanding the VPI field is essential in network backbones. The primary role of a backbone is the aggregation of traffic. Thus, it is possible to have many virtual paths aggregated from the countless virtual circuits that are extended through the network.

Local Area Network Emulation (LANE)

It has long been recognized that one of the greatest barriers to ATM's acceptance as a LAN technology was the tremendous installed base of applications designed for existing LAN technologies. This was particularly true of the IEEE's 802.3 (Ethernet), and 802.5 (Token Ring) specifications. ATM LANs differ in three distinct ways from these IEEE LANs:

- ATM LANs are connection oriented, whereas the other LANs encourage applications to use connectionless messaging.
- Ethernet and Token Ring can perform broadcasting and multicasting readily via their shared media.
- The IEEE MAC addresses are based on manufacturers' serial numbers, not LAN topology.

The ATM Forum met these three challenges to the acceptance of ATM LANs by developing a new ATM service that emulated the IEEE LAN environments. This service is called Local Area Network Emulation (LANE).

> **NOTE**
>
> Networks that are built using the LANE protocol suite are known as Emulated Local Area Networks (ELANs). ELANS can emulate either 802.3 Ethernet or 802.5 Token Ring, but not both simultaneously because no translation bridging mechanism has been defined.

LANE works by enabling end systems—which can be any device connected to the periphery of a network—to connect directly to the ATM LAN. Their software applications still function as though they were directly connected to either an Ethernet or Token Ring LAN. This capability will be critical to any organizations that attempt a graceful, phased-in migration to ATM from either of these other LAN types.

LANE enables ATM LAN clients to access and use existing LAN applications through a software layer added to the emulating devices. This software layer becomes an integral part of that device's ATM protocol stack. The resulting stack is illustrated in Figure 11.11.

Figure 11.11.
The LANE protocol stack.

The emulating device uses a new interface, the LUNI (LANE User to Network Interface). This term is just the tip of the acronym iceberg. For example, the emulated LAN is called an "ELAN." Each client in the ELAN is a LAN Emulation client, or LEC. The individual LECs are addressed via their MAC address.

Each ELAN must have a single LAN Emulation Service (LES). The LES may be contained within a switch or an end-station computer. Regardless, the LES consists of a LAN Emulation Configuration Server (LECS) as well as a Broadcast and Unknown Server (BUS).

As if this weren't enough, there's even a new acronym for the type of logical connection that is established between LECs and the LES in an ELAN: VCC. The VCC is a virtual channel connection, and separate ones are required for ATM's control and user planes.

To visualize this as something other than alphabet soup, please refer to Figure 11.12.

In Figure 11.12, there are two LECs and one LES (resident on a server). The LES server functions as the gateway to the IEEE LAN. The clients may access resources out on that LAN via the LES. This service employs MAC emulation.

FIGURE 11.12.
Typical LANE configuration.

Summary

The original vision of ATM remains compelling: a single technology for both Local and Wide Area Networking that is equally capable of transporting high-bandwidth, low-latency isochronous traffic as well as the more traditional interactive and bulk data communications. The challenges facing ATM and the ATM Forum have remained somewhat constant:

■ Complete the specifications through an open standards process dominated by corporate politics.

■ Develop a cost-effective ATM solution set that will entice customers to migrate from embedded platforms.

For many years, it was difficult to determine which of these was the greatest obstacle. Today, it appears that the ATM Forum has regained its lost momentum and is moving quickly toward completion of the suite of open ATM specifications. That is the good news.

The bad news is that the remainder of ATM's competitive environment has not stagnated. Over the past few years, many other communications technologies have been treated to life-extending refreshes and updates. Thus, they are more formidable competition, in terms of both their technical capabilities and their price/performance ratio, than ever before. Thus, as ATM appears to be overcoming the first of its two obstacles, the second is becoming even more formidable. Only time will tell whether the ATM Forum ever succeeds in achieving its vision for ATM.

Network Protocols

by Mark Sportack

IN THIS CHAPTER

"Network protocols" specifically refer to those protocols that reside at Layer 3 of the OSI Reference Model. These protocols provide addressing that enables data to be delivered across unspecified distances, beyond the domain of the sender's LAN. Typically, Layer 3 protocols use a structure known as *packets* for transporting data.

Although Layer 3 protocols provide the networking mechanisms for forwarding packets, they lack the sophistication to make sure that packets are actually received, and received in the right order. These tasks are left to Layer 4 transport protocols. Transport protocols accept data from higher layers, embed them into segments, and pass the segments to Layer 3.

This chapter describes the functions and interactions of Layers 3 and 4 of protocol stacks before examining the intricacies of some of the more common networking protocols.

Protocol Stacks

A protocol stack is a suite of related communications protocols that offer users the mechanisms and services required to communicate with other network-connected machines. From the user's perspective, the protocol stack is what makes a network usable.

Previous chapters examined the first and second layers of a protocol stack (the Physical and Data Link Layers). These layers are tightly integrated and interrelated. The Physical Layer is dictated by one's selection of a Data Link Layer architecture, such as Ethernet, Token Ring, and so forth.

In this age of open networking and computing, selection of a LAN architecture does not limit the choice of higher-level protocols. Instead, a protocol stack should offer mechanisms that interface with existing, standardized network access vehicles for Data Link Layer protocols.

In much the same way that the first and second layers are interrelated, the third layer of the OSI Reference Model is tightly interrelated with the fourth layer. Layer 3 is the Network Layer and Layer 4 is the Transport Layer. They are illustrated in Figure 12.1. Together, they provide the mechanisms that enable the transfer of information between source and destination machines across a communications network that spans beyond a Layer 2 domain, as well as other functions, such as resequencing packets received out of order, or retransmitting packets not received or received damaged.

Given that these protocols must rely upon a Layer 2 and Layer 1 LAN architecture to actually deliver the data, they must have some means of interfacing with these layers. The technique that they use is *wrapping*. The Layer 4 protocol packages its data, received from higher layer protocols, into segments. These segments are handed off to their Layer 3 counterpart. The Layer 3 protocol promptly wraps a packet structure, complete with source and destination addressing, around the segment and hands it off to the Layer 2 protocol. Layer 2 then wraps a frame and addressing around the Layer 3 data packets. These packets contain addressing that is recognizable by Layer 3 devices like routers and IP switches. Wrapping a Layer 3 (IP) packet in a Layer 2 frame (Ethernet) is illustrated in Figure 12.2. The packet structure counts as part of the frame's data field, even though it isn't really data—just a different layer's structure.

FIGURE 12.1.

*Network and Transport
Layers of the OSI
Reference Model.*

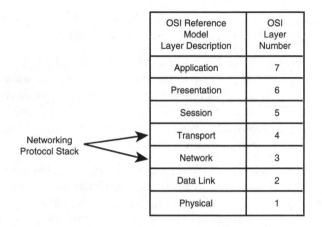

OSI Reference Model Layer Description	OSI Layer Number
Application	7
Presentation	6
Session	5
Transport	4
Network	3
Data Link	2
Physical	1

Networking
Protocol Stack

12

NETWORK
PROTOCOLS

FIGURE 12.2.

*Wrapping an IP packet
with an Ethernet
frame.*

7-Octet Preamble	1-Octet Start of Frame Delimiter	6-Octet Destination Address	6-Octet Origination Address	2-Octet Length Field	20 + Octet IPX Header	20 + Octet TCP Header	Variable length Data Field (>46 octets < 1482)	4-Octet Frame Check Sequence

The frames are used to transport the data and to address the data to the Layer 3 internetworking vehicle at the edge of their Layer 2 domain. This device, typically a router, accepts the framed packet, strips off the frame, and reads the Layer 3 addressing information. It uses this information to determine the next hop in the route to the packet's destination. The packet is then routed to its destination. The last router in the path to the packet's destination must re-wrap the packet in a Layer 2 framing structure that is consistent with the LAN architecture in use at that remote destination.

Layer 3 only provides internetwork data transfers. Layer 4, the Transport Layer, provides the Layer 3 network mechanisms with end-to-end reliability and integrity. The Transport Layer may be required to guarantee error-free delivery of packets and sequencing of delivered packets, as well as to provide quality-of-service guarantees. An example of a Layer 4 is the Transmission Control Protocol (TCP). TCP is almost always referenced in combination with its Layer 3 counterpart, the Internet Protocol (IP), as "TCP/IP."

The use of Layers 3 and 4 by applications to pass data to other computers/applications implies that the source and destination computers are not connected to the same LAN, regardless of how close or distant they are. The two different networks must be internetworked to support the requested transmission. Consequently, the communications mechanisms of Layer 2 are inadequate and must be augmented with Layer 3 addressing.

Although Layers 3 and 4 exist specifically for this purpose, applications can pass data to each other using protocols at these layers, even though they are connected to the same LAN and subnet. For example, if both the source and destination computers are connected to the same LAN, they may communicate satisfactorily using only Layer 2 network frames and protocols. Or, the applications that are passing data might require any of the higher layer protocols' features to support their communications.

There are two types of networking protocols that operate at Layer 3: routed protocols and routing protocols. *Routed protocols* are those that encapsulate user information and data into packets, and are responsible for transporting the packets to their destinations. *Routing protocols* are used between routers to determine available routes, communicate what is known about available routes, and forward routed protocol packets along those routes. Routing protocols are further examined in Chapter 13, "Wide Area Networking." This chapter focuses on the most common routed protocols.

The Internet Protocol, Version 4 (IPv4)

The Internet Protocol (IP) was developed approximately 20 years ago for the Department of Defense (DoD). The DoD needed a way to interconnect the various brands of proprietary computers, and their equally proprietary support networks, across a common internetwork. This was achieved by way of a layered protocol that insulated applications from networking hardware. This protocol uses a model that is slightly different from the OSI Reference Model. It is known as the TCP/IP Model.

Unlike the OSI Reference Model, the TCP/IP model focuses more on delivering interconnectivity than on rigidly adhering to functional layers. It does this by acknowledging the importance of a hierarchical arrangement of functions, but still leaving protocol designers ample flexibility for implementation. Consequently, the OSI Reference Model is significantly better at explaining the mechanics of inter-computer communications, but TCP/IP has become the internetworking protocol of choice in the marketplace.

The flexibility of the TCP/IP Reference Model, in comparison with the OSI Reference Model, is shown in Figure 12.3.

The TCP/IP Reference Model, developed long after the protocol it explains, offers significantly more flexibility than its OSI counterpart because it emphasizes the hierarchical arrangement of functions, rather than strict functional layering.

Dissecting TCP/IP

The TCP/IP protocol stack includes four functional layers: Network Access, Internet, Host-to-Host, and Process/Application. These four loosely correlate to the seven layers of the OSI Reference Model without compromising functionality.

FIGURE 12.3.
*Comparison of OSI
and TCP/IP Reference
Models.*

OSI Reference Model Layer Description	OSI Layer Number	TCP/IP Equivalent Layer Description
Application	7	Process/ Application
Presentation	6	
Session	5	Host-to-Host
Transport	4	
Network	3	Internet
Data Link	2	Network Access
Physical	1	

The Process/Application Layer

The Application Layer provides protocols for remote access and resource sharing. Familiar applications like Telnet, FTP, SMTP, HTTP, and many others all reside and operate in this layer and depend upon the functionality of the underlying layers.

The Host-to-Host Layer

The IP Host-to-Host Layer correlates loosely to the OSI Reference Model's Session and Transport Layers. It consists of two protocol entities: Transmission Control Protocol (TCP) and User Datagram Protocol (UDP). A third entity is being defined to accommodate the increasingly transaction-oriented nature of the Internet. This protocol entity is tentatively called Transaction Transmission Control Protocol (T/TCP).

TCP provides a connection-oriented data transmission between two or more hosts, can support multiple data streams, and provides for flow and error control and even the re-ordering of packets that may have been received out of order.

The TCP protocol header is a minimum of 20 octets and contains the following fields.

■ TCP Source Port: The 16-bit source port field contains the number of the port that initiates the communications session. The source port and source IP address function as the packet's return address.

■ TCP Destination Port: The 16-bit destination port field is the address of the port for which the transmission is destined. This port contains the interface address of the application on the recipient's computer, to which the packet's data is passed.

■ TCP Sequence Number: The 32-bit sequence number is used by the receiving computer to reconstruct the fragmented data back into its original form. In a dynamically routed network, it is quite possible for some of the packets to take different routes and, consequently, arrive out of order. This sequencing field compensates for this inconsistency of delivery.

- TCP Acknowledgment Number: TCP uses a 32-bit acknowledgment (ACK) of the first octet of data contained in the next expected segment. TCP is able to calculate this number by incrementing the number of the last octet received by the number of octets in each TCP segment. The number used to identify each ACK is the sequence number of the packet being acknowledged.

- Data Offset: This 4-bit field contains the size of the TCP header, measured in a 32-bit data structure known as a "word."

- Reserved: This 6-bit field is always set to zero. It is reserved for an as-yet unspecified future use.

- Flags: The 6-bit flag field contains six 1-bit flags that enable the control functions of urgent field, acknowledgment of significant field, push, reset connection, synchronize sequence numbers, and finishing sending data.

- Window Size (16 bits): This field is used by the destination machine to tell the source host how much data it is willing to accept per TCP segment.

- Checksum (16 bits): The TCP header also contains an error checking field known as a "checksum." The source host calculates a mathematical value, based upon the segment's contents. The destination host performs the same calculation. If the contents remained intact, the result of the two calculations is identical, thereby proving the validity of the data.

- Padding: Extra zeros are added to this field to ensure that the TCP header is always a multiple of 32 bits.

The User Datagram Protocol (UDP) is IP's other Host-to-Host Layer protocol (which corresponds to the Transport Layer of the OSI Reference Model). UDP provides basic and low-overhead, data transmissions known as "datagrams." The simplicity of datagrams makes UDP inappropriate for some applications, but perfect for more sophisticated applications that can provide their own connection-oriented functionality.

Alternatively, UDP can be used for exchanges of such data as broadcasted NetBIOS names, system messages, and so forth, because these exchanges do not require flow control, acknowledgments, re-ordering, or any of the functionality that TCP provides.

The UDP protocol header has the following structure:

- UDP Source Port Number: The source port is the connection number on the source computer. The source port and source IP address function as the packet's return address.

- UDP Destination Port Number: The destination port is the connection number on the destination computer. The UDP Destination Port is used to forward the packet to the correct application, after the packet arrives at the intended destination machine.

- UDP Checksum: The checksum is an error-checking field that is calculated based upon the contents of the segment. The destination computer performs the same

mathematical function as the originating host. A discrepancy in the two calculated
values indicates that an error has occurred during the transmission of the packet.

- UDP Message Length: The message length field informs the destination computer of
  the size of the message. This provides another mechanism for the destination computer to use in determining the message's validity.

The major functional difference between TCP and UDP is reliability. TCP is highly reliable
and UDP is a simple, "best effort" datagram delivery mechanism. This fundamental difference
results in vastly different uses of the two Host-to-Host Layer protocols.

The Internet Layer

The Internet Layer of IPv4 consists of all the protocols and procedures necessary to enable data
communications between hosts to traverse multiple networks. The data-bearing packets must
be routable. The Internet Protocol (IP) is responsible for making data packets routable.

The IP header has the following size and structure:

- Version: The first four bits of the IP header identify the operating version of IP, for
  example, version 4.

- Internet Header Length: The next four bits of the header contain the length of the
  header, expressed in multiples of 32.

- Type of Service: The next 8 bits contain 1-bit flags that can be used to specify prece-
  dence, delay, throughput, and reliability parameters for that packet of data.

- Total Length: This 16-bit field contains the total length of the IP datagram measured
  in octets. Valid values can range from 576 to 65,536 octets.

- Identifier: Each IP packet is given a unique 16-bit identifier.

- Flags: The next field contains three 1-bit flags that indicate whether fragmentation of
  the packet is permitted, and whether it is used.

- Fragment Offset: This 8-bit field measures the offset of the fragmented contents
  relative to the beginning of the entire datagram. This value is measured in 64-bit
  increments.

- Time to Live (TTL): The IP packet cannot be permitted to roam the WAN in
  perpetuity. It must be limited to a finite number of hops (see the following note). The
  8-bit TTL field is incremented by one for each hop the packet makes. After reaching
  its maximum limit, the packet is destroyed.

NOTE

IP packets are forwarded across different networks by devices known as *routers*. Each
router that a packet passes through is considered a *hop*. Establishing a maximum hop count
ensures that packets do not loop continuously in a dynamically routed network.

12

**NETWORK
PROTOCOLS**

■ Protocol: This 8-bit field identifies the protocol that follows the IP header, such as VINES, TCP, UDP, and so forth.

■ Checksum: The checksum field is a 16-bit error-checking field. The destination computer, or any gateway nodes in the network, may recompute the mathematical calculation on the packet's contents as the source computer did. If the data survived the trip intact, the results of these two calculations are identical. This field also informs the destination host of the amount of incoming data.

■ Source IP address: The source address is the IP address of the source computer.

■ Destination IP address: The destination address is the IP address of the destination computer.

■ Padding: Extra zeros are added to this field to ensure that the IP header is always a multiple of 32 bits.

These header fields reveal that IPv4's Internet Layer is inherently connectionless: the packet forwarding devices in the network are free to determine the ideal path for each packet to take through the network. It also doesn't provide any of the acknowledgments, flow control, or sequencing functions of higher level protocols such as TCP. It leaves such functions to those higher level protocols.

The Internet Layer must also support other route management functions beyond just IP's packet formatting. It must provide mechanisms for resolving Layer 2 addresses into Layer 3 addresses and vice versa. These route management functions are provided by peer protocols to IP; the routing protocols described in Chapter 1, "A Networking Primer." These protocols include Interior Gateway Protocols (IGP), Exterior Gateway Protocols (EGP), Address Resolution Protocol (ARP), Reverse Address Resolution Protocol (RARP), and Internet Control Message Protocol (ICMP).

Typical IPv4 Operation

The Application Layer places a header onto the data packet, identifying the destination host and port. The Host-to-Host Layer protocol (either TCP or UDP, depending on the application) breaks that block of data into smaller, more manageable pieces. Each piece has a TCP header prepended to it. This structure is known as a "TCP segment."

The segment's header fields are populated appropriately, and the segment is passed to the Internet Layer. The Internet Layer adds the addressing, protocol type (TCP or UDP) and checksum information. If the segment was fragmented, the Internet Layer populates that field as well.

The destination machine performs the reverse of the operation just described. It receives the packets and passes them to its Host-to-Host Layer protocol for reassembly. If necessary, the packets are re-ordered into data segments that are passed up to the appropriate application.

IP Addressing Scheme

IPv4 uses a 32-bit binary addressing scheme to identify networks, network devices, and network-connected machines. These addresses, known as IP addresses, are strictly regulated by the Internet Network Information Center (InterNIC). Although it is entirely possible for a network administrator to arbitrarily select unregistered IP addresses, this practice should not be condoned. Computers having such spurious IP addresses can only function properly within the confines of their domain. Attempts to access the Internet are sure to demonstrate the ramifications of this short-sighted act. Results can be highly variable depending upon a wide variety of factors, but are sure to be unfavorable.

The five classes of IP addresses are each identified by an alphabetic character: Class A, B, C, D, and E. Each address consists of two parts: a network and host address. The five classes represent different compromises between the number of supportable networks and hosts. Although these addresses are binary, they are normally identified with a dotted decimal-style format (for example, 135.65.121.6) to facilitate human usage. The dots are used to separate the address's four octets.

> **NOTE**
>
> "Dotted decimal notation" refers to the conversion of the binary address to the decimal (Base 10) number system. A dot (".") is used to separate the node and network numbers. For example, 100.99 refers to device 99 on network 100.

- Class A IP Address: The first bit of a Class A address is always a "0." The next seven bits identify the network number. The last 24 bits (for example, 3 dotted decimal numbers) of a Class A address represent possible host addresses. The range of possible Class A addresses is from 1.0.0.0 to 126.0.0.0. Each Class A address can support 16,774,214 unique host addresses.

- Class B IP Address: The first two bits of a Class B address are 10. The next 16 bits identify the network number and the last 16 bits identify potential host addresses. The range of possible Class B addresses is from 128.1.0.0 to 191.254.0.0. Each Class B address can support 65,534 unique host addresses.

- Class C IP Address: The first three bits of a Class C address are "110." The next 21 bits identify the network's number. The last octet is used for host addressing. The range of possible Class C addresses is from 192.0.1.0 to 223.255.254.0. Each Class C address can support 254 unique host addresses.

- Class D IP Address: The first four bits of a Class D address are "1110." These addresses are used for multicasting, but have seen only limited usage. A *multicast address* is a unique network address that directs packets with that destination address to predefined groups of IP addresses. Class D addresses are from 224.0.0.0 to 239.255.255.254.

WARNING

The obscurity of the Class D IP address creates a potential disparity between reality and common perception. Although the IETF has defined Classes C and D as separate and distinct in terms of their numeric ranges and their intended functionality, it is not uncommon to find the Class D address range lumped in with the Class C range. This is incorrect, but apparently is being reinforced through certain networking certification curricula.

■ Class E IP Address: A Class E address has been defined but is reserved by the InterNIC for its own research. Thus, no Class E addresses have been released for use in the Internet.

The large gaps between these address classes have wasted a considerable amount of potential addresses. Consider, for example, a medium-sized company that requires 300 IP addresses. A Class C address (254 addresses) is inadequate. Using two Class C addresses provides more than enough addresses, but results in two separate domains within the company. Alternatively, stepping up to a Class B address provides all the needed addresses within a single domain, but wastes 65,234 addresses.

Fortunately, this is no longer the case. A new inter-domain routing protocol known as Classless Interdomain Routing (CIDR) has been developed to enable multiple smaller address classes to function as a single routing domain.

IP addressing requires each machine to have its own unique address. Subnet masks can compensate for the tremendous gaps between address classes by customizing the length of the host and/or network addresses. These two numbers are used to route any given IP datagram to its destination.

Because TCP/IP is capable of supporting multiple sessions from a single host, it must then provide a way of addressing specific communications programs that may operate on each host. TCP/IP does so with port numbers. The IETF has assigned some of the more common applications their own well-known port numbers. These numbers are reliably constant, per application, from host to host. Other applications are simply assigned an available port number.

IPv4 Conclusion

IPv4 is almost twenty years old. Since its inception, the Internet has experienced several significant changes that have diminished IP's effectiveness as a universal interconnectivity protocol. Perhaps the most significant of these changes has been the commercialization of the Internet. This has brought with it an unprecedented growth in the Internet's user population and a shift in its demographics. This, in turn, has created the tandem need for more addresses and Internet Layer support for new types of service. IPv4's limitations have been driving the development of a completely new version of the protocol. This new version is called IP Version 6 (IPv6) but was also commonly referred to as the next generation of Internet Protocol(IPng).

The Internet Protocol, Version 6 (IPv6)

IPv6 is designed to be a simple, forward-compatible upgrade to the existing version of IP. This upgrade is also intended to resolve all the weaknesses that IPv4 is currently manifesting, including the shortage of available IP addresses, the inability to accommodate time-sensitive traffic, and its lack of Network Layer security.

> **NOTE**
>
> IPv6 was originally referred to as IP: The Next Generation, or IPng. The name was probably inspired by science fiction. As the specification was being developed, its name was changed to IP version 6 (IPv6). This name change may or may not be reflected on certification examinations.

In addition to these issues, routing is also driving the development and deployment of the new IP protocol. IPv4 is hampered by its 32-bit address architecture, its two-level addressing hierarchy, and its address classes. This two-level addressing hierarchy (host and domain name) simply does not allow construction of efficient address hierarchies that can be aggregated by routers on the scale that today's global Internet requires.

The next generation of IP, commonly known as IPng but more correctly identified as IPv6, resolves all these issues. It will offer a vastly expanded addressing scheme to support the continued expansion of the Internet, and an improved capability to aggregate routes on a large scale.

IPv6 will also support numerous other features such as real-time audio and/or video transmissions, host mobility, end-to-end security through Internet Layer encryption and authentication, as well as auto-configuration and auto-reconfiguration. It is expected that these services will provide ample incentive for migration as soon as IPv6-capable products become available. Many of these features still require additional standardization. Therefore, it would be premature to expound upon them at any great length.

The one aspect of IPv6 that can, and should, be expounded upon is its addressing. IPv4's 32-bit address length gave the protocol a theoretical capability to address 2 to the 32nd power, or about 4 billion devices. Inefficient sub-net masking techniques, among other wasteful practices, have squandered this resource.

IPv6 uses a 128-bit address and is theoretically capable of 2 to the 96th power times the size of the IPv4 address space. This is 340,282,366,920,938,463,463,374,607,431,768,211,456 mathematically possible addresses. Only about 15% of this potential address space is currently allocated. The remainder is reserved for unspecified future use.

In reality, the assignment and routing of addresses requires the creation of hierarchies. Hierarchies can reduce the number of potential addresses, but increase the efficiency of IPv6-capable routing protocols. One practical implication of the IPv6 address length is that Domain Name

Service (DNS) becomes an absolute necessity, and not the luxury that it had been in the IPv4 network environment.

> **NOTE**
>
> Domain Name Service is the network utility that is responsible for translating mnemonic host names into numeric IP addresses.

As significant as the increased potential address space is, even greater flexibility is afforded with IPv6's new address structures. IPv6 dispenses with the previous class-based addressing. Instead, it recognizes three kinds of unicast address, replaces the former Class D address with a new multicast address format, and introduces a new address type. You *must* understand these new addressing structures prior to undertaking an IPv6 migration.

IPv6 Unicast Address Structures

Unicast addressing provides connectivity from one endpoint to one endpoint. IPv6 supports several forms of unicast addresses. They are described in the following sections.

Internet Service Provider (ISP) Unicast Address

Whereas IPv4 pre-assumed clusters of users requiring connectivity, IPv6 provides a unicast address format designed specifically for use by Internet Service Providers (ISPs) to connect *individual* users to the Internet. These provider-based unicast addresses offer unique addresses for individuals or small groups that access the Internet through a provider. The architecture of the address provides for efficient aggregation of routes in an environment characterized by individual users, as opposed to large concentrations of users.

The ISP unicast address format is as follows:

- A 3-bit ISP unicast address flag that is always set to "010"
- A Registry ID field that is "n" bits in length
- A Provider ID field that is "m" bits in length
- A Subscriber ID field that is "o" bits in length
- A Subnet ID field that is "p" bits in length
- An Interface ID field that is 125 (n+m+o+p) bits in length

The alphabetic characters n, m, o, and p denote variable-length fields. The length of the Interface ID is 125 bits (maximum length of an IPv6 address is 128 bits, minus the 3-bit flag) minus the sum of these variable fields.

An example of this type of address would be 010:0:0:0:0:x, where "x" can be any number. Given that much of the new address space has yet to be allocated, these addresses will contain lots of

0s. Therefore, groups of 0s may be shortened with a double colon (::). This shorthand notation is 010::x.

The other unicast address types are designed for local use. *Local use* addresses can be assigned to networked devices within a standalone intranet or to devices on an intranet that need to have access to the Internet.

Link-Local Use

The Link-Local is for use on a single link for purposes such as auto-address configuration, neighbor discovery, or when no routers are present. Link-Local addresses have the following format:

- A 10-bit Local Use flag that is always set to "1111111011"
- A reserved, unnamed field that is "n" bits in length but defaulted to a value of "0"
- An Interface ID field that is 118 "n" bits in length

The interface ID can be the MAC address of an Ethernet Network Interface Card. MAC addresses, being theoretically unique addresses, can be concatenated with standard IP address prefixes to form unique addresses for mobile or transitory users. An example of a Link-Local Use address with MAC address would be: 1111111011:0:mac_address.

Site-Local Use Unicast Address

Site-Local addresses are designed for use in a single site. They may be used for sites or organizations that are not connected to the global Internet. They do not need to request or "steal" an address prefix from the global Internet address space. IPv6 site-local addresses can be used instead. When the organization connects to the global Internet, it can then form unique global addresses by replacing the site-local prefix with a subscriber prefix that contains a Registry, Provider, and Subscriber Identification.

Site-Local addresses have the following format:

- A 10-bit Local Use flag that is always set to "1111111011"
- A reserved, unnamed field that is "n" bits in length but defaulted to a value of "0"
- A Subnet ID field that is "m" bits in length
- An Interface ID field that is 118 (n+m) bits in length

An example of a Site-Local address is: 1111111011:0:subnet:interface.

IPv6 Transitional Unicast Address Structures

Two special IPv6 unicast addresses have been defined as transition mechanisms to enable hosts and routers to dynamically route IPv6 packets over IPv4 network infrastructure and vice versa.

IPv4-Compatible IPv6 Unicast Address

The first unicast address type is called an "IPv4-compatible IPv6 address." This transitional unicast address can be assigned to IPv6 nodes and contain an IPv4 address in the last 32 bits. These addresses have the following format:

80 bits	16 bits	32 bits
000...0000	00...00	IPv4 address

IPv4-Mapped IPv6 Unicast Address

A second, similar, type of IPv6 address that also contains an IPv4 address in its last 32 bits is known as an "IPv4-mapped IPv6 address." This address is constructed by a dual protocol router and enables IPv4-only nodes to tunnel through IPv6 network infrastructure. The only difference between IPv4-mapped IPv6 addresses and IPv4-compatible IPv6 addresses is that IPv4-mapped addresses are constructs only. They are built automatically by dual protocol routers, and cannot be assigned to any nodes. This address is formatted as follows:

80 bits	16 bits	32 bits
000...0000	FF...FF	IPv4 address

Both the IPv4-mapped and the IPv4-compatible unicast addresses are essential to tunneling. *Tunneling* enables the transport of packets through an otherwise incompatible network region by wrapping those packets in an externally acceptable framework.

IPv6 Anycast Address Structures

The *anycast* address, introduced in IPv6, is a single value assigned to more than one interface. Typically, these interfaces belong to different devices. *A packet sent to an anycast address is routed to only one device.* It is sent to the nearest interface having that address, as defined by the routing protocols' measure of distance. For example, a World Wide Web (WWW) site may be mirrored on several servers. By assigning an anycast address to these servers, requests for connectivity to that WWW site are automatically routed to only one server: the server nearest the user.

> **NOTE**
>
> In a routed environment, the "nearest" interface might not be the one that is closest. Routers use a surprisingly wide array of metrics to calculate routes. Identifying the nearest one depends upon the actual routing protocol used, as well as that protocol's metrics.

Anycast addresses are formed from the unicast address space and may take the form of any unicast address type. Anycast addresses are formed simply by assigning the same unicast address to more than one interface.

IPv6 Multicast Address Structures

Multicasting was supported in IPv4, but required the use of obscure Class D addressing. IPv6 eliminates Class D addresses in favor of a new address format that permits trillions of possible multicast group codes. Each group code identifies two or more packet recipients. The scope of a particular multicast address is flexible. Each address can be confined to a single system, restricted within a specific site, associated with a particular network link, or distributed globally.

It should be noted that IP broadcasts, too, have been eliminated in favor of the new multicasting address format.

IPv6 Conclusion

Despite the potential benefits of IPv6, the migration from IPv4 is not risk free. The extension of the address length from 32 to 128 bits automatically limits interoperability between IPv4 and IPv6. *IPv4-only nodes cannot interoperate with IPv6-only nodes because the address architectures are not forward-compatible.* This business risk, in combination with the ongoing evolution of IPv4, will likely forestall the acceptance of IPv6 in the marketplace.

Novell's IPX/SPX

The Novell protocol suite is named after its two primary protocols: Internet Packet Exchange (IPX) and Sequenced Packet Exchange (SPX). This proprietary protocol stack was based on Xerox's Network Systems (XNS) protocol used with first generation Ethernets. IPX/SPX became prominent during the early 1980s as an integral part of Novell Inc.'s Netware. Netware became the *de facto* standard network operating system (NOS) of first generation LANs. Novell complemented their NOS with a business-oriented application suite and client-side connection utilities.

IPX is much like IP. It is a connectionless datagram protocol that does not require, nor provide, an acknowledgment for each packet transmitted. IPX also relies upon SPX in the same way that IP relies upon TCP for sequencing and other Layer 4 connection-oriented services. The IPX/SPX protocol stack is compared to the OSI Reference Model in Figure 12.4.

Novell's IPX and SPX protocols provide functionality equivalent to the OSI Layers 3 and 4, respectively. The full suite of IPX/SPX protocols provide the functionality of the other OSI layers in four layers.

Dissecting IPX/SPX

The IPX/SPX protocol stack includes four functional layers: Medium Access, Data Link, Internet, and Application. These four loosely correlate to the seven layers of the OSI Reference Model without compromising functionality.

FIGURE 12.4.

Comparison of the OSI Reference Model and IPX/SPX.

OSI Reference Model Layer Description	OSI Layer Number	IPX/SPX Equivalent Layer Description				
Application	7	R I P	S A P	N C P	N L S P	Misc. Protocols
Presentation	6					
Session	5					
Transport	4				SPX	
Network	3	Internet Packet Exchange				
Data Link	2	Open Data Link Interface				
Physical	1	Medium Access				

Application Layer

Novell's Application Layer encompasses the Application, Presentation and Session Layers of the OSI model, although some of its application protocols extend as far down the stack as the OSI Network Layer. The primary Application Layer protocol in this stack is the NetWare Core Protocol (NCP). NCP can interface directly with both SPX and IPX. NCP is used for print, file sharing, e-mail, and directory access.

Other Application Layer protocols include Routing Information Protocol (RIP), a proprietary Service Advertisement Protocol (SAP), and NetWare Link Services Protocol (NLSP), among others.

RIP is the default routing protocol for NetWare. It is a distance-vector routing protocol that uses only two metrics: ticks and hops. A *tick* is a measure of time, and a *hop count*, as explained earlier in this chapter, is the running tally of routers that have handled the routed packet. These two metrics are the basis for IPX routing path decisions. Ticks are the primary metric for determining paths. Hops are only used as a tie breaker in the event of two or more paths having the same tick value.

RIP is a very simple and mature routing protocol. In addition to its limited number of distance-vector metrics, it suffers from a high level of network overhead. This overhead is incurred because RIP routing table updates are broadcast every 60 seconds. This rate of update can have adverse affects on large or very busy networks.

SAP is a unique, proprietary protocol that Novell has successfully used to enhance the client/ server relationship. Servers use SAP to automatically broadcast their available services throughout the network immediately after becoming active on the network. They periodically broadcast SAPs to keep clients and other servers informed of their status and services.

SAP broadcasts generated by a server advertise that server's status and services. These broadcasts include the server's name and type, its operational status, as well as its network, node, and socket numbers. Routers can store information from a SAP broadcast and propagate it to other network segments. Clients can also initiate a *SAP request* when they need a specific service. Their request is broadcast throughout the network segment. Hosts can then respond and provide the client with enough SAP information to determine whether or not the service is available within a reasonable distance.

Unfortunately, SAP is a mature protocol that is becoming increasingly ill-suited to functioning in contemporary networks. As with RIP, service advertisements occur every 60 seconds. On today's large, flat, switched LANs, this degree of broadcasting can be problematic.

The newest Application Layer protocol is Netware Link Services Protocol (NLSP). NLSP is a link-state routing protocol that Novell intends to use as a replacement for the aging RIP and SAP protocols. NLSP only updates routes when changes have been made.

Internet Layer Protocols

The Internet Layer of IPX/SPX correlates loosely to both the Network and Transport Layers of the OSI Reference Model. IPX is predominantly a Layer 3, or Network Layer, protocol although it is capable of directly interfacing with the Application Layer. SPX is distinctly a Layer 4, or Transport Layer, protocol and cannot directly interface with the Data Link Layer's ODI. It must pass data through IPX and let IPX interface with the ODI. IPX and SPX function as sublayer protocols within a common Internet Layer.

SPX is connection-oriented and can be used to transmit data between a client and server, two servers, or even two clients. As with TCP, SPX provides reliability to IPX transmissions by managing the connection and providing flow control, error checking, and packet sequencing.

The SPX header has the following size and structure:

- Connection Control: The first octet (eight bits) of the SPX header provides four 2-bit flags that control the bidirectional flow of data across an SPX connection.
- Datastream Type: The next eight bits of the header define the type of datastream.
- Source Connection Identification: The 16-bit Source Connection Identification field identifies the process responsible for initiating the connection.
- Destination Connection Identification: The 16-bit Destination Connection Identification field is used to identify the process that accepted the inbound SPX connection request.
- Sequence Number: The 16-bit Sequence Number field provides the destination host's SPX protocol with a count of packets transmitted. This sequential numbering can be used to re-order the received packets, should they arrive out of sequence.

- Acknowledgment Number: The Acknowledgment Number field is a 16-bit field that indicates the next expected segment.

- Allocation Number: The Allocation Number field is 16 bits in length and is used to track the number of packets sent, but not acknowledged, by the intended recipient.

- Data: The last field in the SPX header contains the data. Up to 534 octets of data may be transmitted per SPX packet.

Novell's Network Layer protocol is IPX. IPX provides a connectionless, best-effort, datagram delivery service. It prepares SPX (or other protocols') packets for delivery across multiple networks by prepending an IPX header to them. This new structure is called an IPX datagram. This datagram's header contains all the information necessary to route the packets to their destinations, regardless of where that might be.

The IPX header is 11 octets long and has the following structure:

- Checksum Field: The IPX header begins with a 16-bit legacy field that exists solely to provide backward compatibility with its ancestral XNS protocol. XNS used this field for error checking, but IPX defaults this field to "FFFFH" and trusts higher level protocols to detect (and correct) any transmission errors.

- Packet Length Field: This 16-bit field defines the length of the IPX datagram, including the header and data. Packet Length is checked to verify packet integrity.

- Transport Control: This 8-bit field is used by routers during the forwarding of the datagram. IPX sets it to "0" prior to transmission. Each router that receives and forwards the datagram increments this field by one.

- Packet Type: This 8-bit field identifies the type of packet that is embedded in the IPX datagram. This field enables the destination host to pass the contents to the next appropriate protocol layer. Types can include RIP, NCP, SPX, error, and so forth.

- Destination Network Number: This 32-bit field identifies the network number of the destination node.

- Destination Node: This 48-bit field contains the node number of the destination machine.

- Destination Socket Number: Because IPX allows for multiple simultaneous connections to one system, it is essential to identify the socket number of the process or program receiving the packets. This 16-bit field provides this information.

- Source Network Number: This 32-bit field identifies the network number of the source node.

- Source Node Address: This 48-bit field contains the node number of the source machine.

- Source Socket Number: This 16-bit field identifies the socket number of the process or program sending the packets.

Typical IPX/SPX Operation

SPX creates and maintains a connection-oriented bit stream between two networked devices. The protocol accepts large blocks of data from higher-level protocols and breaks them into more manageable pieces that are up to 534 octets long. The SPX header is prepended to the data to create SPX data segments. These segments are passed to the Internet Layer protocol, IPX. IPX stuffs these segments into the data field of its packets and populates all the fields in the IPX header.

These header fields include the network addressing, length, checksum, and other header information before passing the packet on to the Data Link Layer.

Figure 12.5 shows the positioning of the IPX and SPX headers within an 802.3 Ethernet frame. This is the structure used to pass data between the two sublayers of Novell's Internet Layer.

FIGURE 12.5.

Structure of an 802.3 Ethernet frame encapsulating an IPX/SPX payload.

7-Octet Preamble	1-Octet Start of Frame Delimiter	6-Octet Destination Address	6-Octet Origination Address	2-Octet Length Field	30-octet IPX Header	Variable Length IPX Header	Variable Length Data Field (>46 octets < 1482)	4-Octet Frame Check Sequence

The destination machine performs the reverse of the operation just described. It receives the packets and passes them to its SPX protocol for reassembly. If necessary, the packets are re-ordered into data segments that are passed up to the appropriate application.

Data Link and Medium Access Layers

Netware's equivalents of the OSI Physical and Data Link Layers are the Medium Access and Data Link Layers. The Data Link Layer is directly compatible with the Open Data-Link Interface (ODI) standard. Similarly, the Medium Access Layer is directly compatible with all common, standardized media access protocols.

This low-level adherence to open industry standards enables Netware and the IPX/SPX protocol stack to be implemented almost universally.

IPX Addressing

IPX addresses are ten octets (80 bits) long. This is significantly larger than IPv4's 32-bit address, but less than IPv6's 128-bit address. Each address is comprised of two components: a network number up to 32 bits in length and a 48-bit node number. These numbers are expressed in dotted hexadecimal notation. For example, 1a2b.0000.3c4d.5e6d could be a valid IPX address where the "1a2b" represents the network number and "0000.3c4d.5e6d" is the node number.

IPX addresses, too, can be fabricated by a network administrator. However, fabricated numbers run the risk of having address conflicts when they are taken into an internetwork. Invention of network numbers places the burden of maintaining and managing all such fabricated numbers on the network administrator. The better approach is to obtain registered IPX network numbers from Novell.

The universally assigned address (MAC address) on the network interface card (NIC) is usually used as the IPX host number. Given that these addresses are unique, at least in theory and to the extent of the manufacturer's quality assurance, this provides a convenient, unique host numbering.

As with IP, IPX is capable of supporting multiple simultaneous sessions. This creates the need for identifying the specific process or program that is communicating on any given session. This identification is achieved through the use of a 16-bit "socket" number in the IPX header. This socket number is analogous to TCP/IP's port number.

IPX/SPX Conclusion

Novell Inc. has watched the market share of its proprietary IPX/SPX protocol stack plummet under competitive pressure. As open protocol stacks like OSI, IP, and others became available, IPX/SPX suffered. Commercially available office automation software bundles also cut into Novell's sales. Although responsible for their initial success, Novell's proprietary, tightly-coupled series of products has become a liability in a marketplace that values openness and interoperability.

Novell has demonstrated its commitment to regaining its lost prominence by making IPv6 its default protocol for future versions of Netware. To successfully implement this change of strategy, Novell must ensure the compatibility of IPv6 and IPX/SPX. To achieve this goal, Novell has worked closely with the Internet Engineering Task Force (IETF) during the design of IPv6. This has resulted in numerous IPX services becoming integral to IPv6.

Having "set the stage" for its future, Novell now must ensure a seamless migration of its current protocol stack and application suite to this new environment. More importantly, they need to provide value-adding products and services using an open network platform. Novell's vision for the future is to provide Network Directory Services (NDS) and related products for two customer bases: the Internet community and corporate intranet communities.

NDS provides a single, global, logical view of all network services and resources. This enables users to access network services and resources with a single login, regardless of the user's location or the location of the resources.

Apple Corporation's AppleTalk Protocol Suite

As Apple computers increased in popularity, and their users became increasingly sophisticated in their use, the need to network them together became inescapable. It is no surprise that the network Apple developed is as user friendly as their computers. AppleTalk, the name for Apple's networking protocol stack, and its necessary hardware are included with every computer Apple sells.

Connecting to the network can be as simple as plugging in the network connection and powering up the Apple computer. The AppleTalk network is a peer-to-peer network that provides basic functionality such as file and printer sharing. Unlike client/server networks, there are no hardened definitions constraining the functionality of a peer-to-peer network. Each machine can act simultaneously as both a client and a server.

AppleTalk has also been embraced by many other Operating System (OS) manufacturers. It is not uncommon to find support for the AppleTalk protocol stack available on non-Apple computers. This enables customers to use AppleTalk and Apple computers to create or join existing non-Apple client/server networks.

Dissecting AppleTalk

The AppleTalk protocol stack contains five functional layers: Network Access, Datagram Delivery, Network, Zone Information, and Application. Apple's AppleTalk protocol stack closely follows the functionality of the OSI Reference Model on its Network Transport and Session Layers. The Physical and Data Link layers are collapsed into numerous, frame-specific, individual layers. Similarly, AppleTalk integrates the Application and Presentation Layers into a singular Application Layer. Figure 12.6 illustrates this functional relationship.

FIGURE 12.6.

Comparison of the OSI Reference Model and AppleTalk.

OSI Reference Model Layer Description	OSI Layer Number	AppleTalk Equivalent Layer Description
Application	7	Application
Presentation	6	
Session	5	Session
Transport	4	Transport
Network	3	Datagram Delivery
Data Link	2	Network Access
Physical	1	

Apple's AppleTalk protocol stack closely follows the functionality of the OSI Reference Model on its Network, Transport, and Session Layers, but collapses the other four layers into just two.

The AppleTalk Application Layer

AppleTalk combines the functionality of the OSI Reference Model's Application and Presentation layers into a single Application Layer. Because AppleTalk is a fairly simple protocol stack, there is only a single protocol occupying this layer. It is the AppleTalk Filing Protocol (AFP). AFP provides network file services to applications that exist separate from the protocol stack, such as electronic mail, print queuing, and so forth. Any application running on an Apple computer must pass through AFP if it needs to send or receive information across the network.

The AppleTalk Session Layer

AppleTalk's version of the OSI Session Layer contains five primary protocols that provide such services as full-duplex transmission, logical name-to-address resolution, printer access, packet sequencing, and others.

The first Session Layer protocol is the AppleTalk Data Stream Protocol (ADSP). ADSP provides full-duplex connection-oriented services in a highly reliable manner by establishing a logical connection (session) between the two communicating processes on client machines. ADSP also manages this connection by providing flow control services, sequence management, and acknowledgment of transmitted packets. ADSP uses socket addresses to establish this process-to-process logical connection. After the connection is established, the two systems can exchange data.

Another AppleTalk Session Layer protocol is AppleTalk Session Protocol (ASP). This protocol provides reliable data delivery using sequence-oriented session management and the transport services of AppleTalk Transport Protocol (ATP), a Transport Layer protocol.

The AppleTalk Update-Based Routing Protocol (AURP) is used in larger AppleTalk networks. AURP is used primarily for route management and information exchange between routing devices, particularly Exterior Gateway routers.

AppleTalk's session layer also includes a Printer Access Protocol (PAP). Although PAP was originally developed for managing access to networked printers, it can be used for a variety of data exchanges. It provides a bidirectional session between two devices, complete with flow control and sequence management.

The last of the AppleTalk Session Layer protocols is the Zone Information Protocol (ZIP). ZIP provides a mechanism for logically grouping individual networked devices using user-friendly names. These logical groups are called *zones*. In an extended network, computers can span multiple networks, but still be logically grouped into a zone. However, in small, non-extended networks only one zone can be defined.

ZIP uses the Name Binding Protocol (NBP), a Transport Layer protocol, to translate these names to network and node numbers, and the ATP protocol for delivery of zone information updates.

These five Session Layer protocols provide AppleTalk clients with logical connections and data transfers between computers, regardless of how near or far apart they are.

The AppleTalk Transport Layer

The AppleTalk Transport Layer offers transport services to the layers above it. There are four distinct protocols in this layer. The most frequently used protocol in this layer is the AppleTalk Transport Protocol (ATP).

ATP provides a reliable, loss-free mechanism for packet delivery between two computers. ATP uses the sequence and acknowledgment fields in the packet header to ensure packets are not lost en route to their destination.

Another significant AppleTalk Transport Layer protocol is the Name Binding Protocol (NBP). As previously indicated, NBP enables ZIP to translate user-friendly names into actual addresses. NBP performs the actual translation of zone names to network and node addresses. NBP contains four basic functions: registration, lookup, confirmation, and deletion of names.

- Name Registration: Name registration registers a unique logical name in an NBP registry database.

- Name Lookup: Name lookup is provided to a computer that requests another computer's address. This request is made, and resolved, transparently. If the request is made using an object name, NBP converts that name to a numeric address. NBP always attempts to resolve such requests by looking at local node numbers. If no match is found, it broadcasts a request to other internetworked AppleTalk networks. If a match still cannot be found, the request times out and the requestor receives an error message.

- Name Confirmation: Confirmation requests are used to verify object-address relationships.

- Name Deletion: Devices on any network are periodically shut down or removed. When this happens, a name deletion request is sent, and object-name-to-addressing tables are automatically updated.

AppleTalk Echo Protocol (AEP) is another Transport Layer protocol. It is used to determine the accessibility of a system and for computing the Round Trip Transmit time (RTT).

The last Transport Layer protocol is AppleTalk's Routing Table Maintenance Protocol (RTMP). Because AppleTalk uses routed protocols in its Network Layer, it must provide for management of routing tables. RTMP provides routers with content for their routing tables.

AppleTalk's Datagram Delivery Layer

AppleTalk's Datagram Delivery Layer, directly analogous to OSI's Layer 3 (network), provides connectionless, packetized datagram delivery. This is the basis for establishing communications and delivering data over an AppleTalk network. This layer is also responsible for providing the dynamic addressing of networked nodes, as well as MAC address resolution for IEEE 802 networks.

The primary protocol in this layer is the Datagram Delivery Protocol (DDP). DDP provides best-effort data transmission in a connectionless fashion across multiple networks. It adapts its header types, depending upon the intended destination. The basic components remain constant; additional fields are added, as needed.

Datagrams that are to be delivered locally (in other words on the same subnetwork) use the "short header." Datagrams that require routing to other subnetworks use the "extended header" format. The extended format contains network addresses and a hop counter field.

The DDP header contains the following fields.

- Hop Count: This field contains a counter that is incremented by one for each router device the packet travels across. Hop count is only used in the extended header.

- Datagram Length: This field contains the length of the datagram and can be used to determine whether it was damaged in transit.

- DDP Checksum: This is an optional field. When used it provides a more robust form of error detection than simply checking the length of a datagram does. Checksum verification detects whether the contents were changed even slightly, regardless of whether or not the length of the datagram was changed.

- Source Socket Number: This field identifies the communicating process of the machine that initiated the connection.

- Destination Socket Number: This field identifies the communicating process of the machine that responded to the connection request.

- Source Address: This field contains the network and node numbers of the originating computer. This field is only used in the extended header format, and it enables routers to forward datagrams across multiple subnetworks.

- Destination Address: This field contains the network and node numbers of the destination computer. This field is only used in the extended header format and enables routers to forward datagrams across multiple subnetworks.

- DDP Type: This field identifies the upper-layer protocol that is encapsulated in the datagram. It is used by the destination computer's Transport Layer to identify the appropriate protocol to which it should pass the contents.

- Data: The data field contains the data that is being transmitted. It can vary in size from 0 to 586 octets.

The Datagram Delivery Layer also contains a protocol that is used to resolve node addresses into MAC addresses for machines connected to IEEE 802 networks. This protocol is the AppleTalk Address Resolution Protocol (AARP). AARP can also be used to determine the node address for any given station. AARP stores its information in the Address Mapping Table (AMT). Due to the dynamic assignment of node numbers, this table used by AARP is constantly and automatically being updated.

AppleTalk Data Link Layer

AppleTalk's Data Link Layer provides the functionality of the OSI Reference Model's Physical and Data Link Layers. This functionality is integrated into frame-specific sub-layers. For example, "EtherTalk" is a Data Link Layer protocol that provides all the OSI Physical and Data Link Layer functionality into a single sub-layer. This sub-layer enables AppleTalk to be encapsulated in an 802.3-compliant Ethernet framing structure.

There are similar AppleTalk sub-layers for Token Ring (known as "TokenTalk") and for FDDI ("FDDITalk"). These protocols are called "Access Protocols" because of the physical network access services they offer.

EtherTalk uses a line access protocol known as "EtherTalk Link Access Protocol" (ELAP) to package data and place the 802.3-compliant frames onto the physical medium. This line access protocol naming convention and functionality holds true for the remainder of the access protocols. For example, TokenTalk relies upon "TokenTalk Link Access Protocol" (TLAP).

In addition to access protocols that conform to industry standards, Apple offers a proprietary Local Area Network protocol in its Data Link Layer. This protocol is known as "LocalTalk." LocalTalk operates at 230Kbps over twisted pair wiring. It uses, predictably, the LocalTalk Link Access Protocols (LLAP) to assemble frames and place them onto the network. LLAP also includes mechanisms for medium access management, data link level addressing, data encapsulation, and bit representation for frame transmission.

AppleTalk's Addressing Scheme

The AppleTalk addressing scheme consists of two parts: the network number and the node number.

Network numbers are usually 16 bits long, although unary numbering may be used for non-extended or very small extended networks. These numbers must be defined by the network administrator and used by AppleTalk to route packets between the different networks. The network number "0" is reserved by the protocol for use in connecting new network nodes for the first time. The network number must have a value between 00000001 and FFFFFFFF.

Node numbers are 8-bit addresses consisting of four hexadecimal numbers. The valid range of addresses for hosts, printers, routers, and other devices is from 1 to 253. Node numbers 0, 254, and 255, although mathematically possible within an 8-bit binary address, are reserved by AppleTalk for use on extended networks. All node numbering is done dynamically by AppleTalk's Data Link Layer.

AppleTalk addresses are expressed in dotted decimal notation. As explained previously in this chapter, the binary address is converted to the decimal (Base 10) number system, and a dot (.) is used to separate the node and network numbers. For example, 100.99 refers to device 99 on network 100. The leading zeroes are suppressed.

AppleTalk Conclusion

AppleTalk is a proprietary protocol stack designed expressly for networking Apple's Personal Computers (PCs). Its future is directly tied to the fortunes of Apple Corporation and the trajectories of its technologies. As with Novell's proprietary stack, the Physical and Data Link Layers are used to provide compatibility with networking technologies based on established standards. One exception to this is a proprietary LocalTalk Physical Layer that can interconnect Apple computers using twisted pair wiring at up to 230Kbps.

NetBEUI

One last protocol that is worth examining is NetBEUI. This unwieldy name is part abbreviation, and part acronym. It stands for *NetBIOS* (which is an abbreviation for *Network Basic Input/ Output System) Extended User Interface*. NetBEUI was developed by IBM, and introduced to the marketplace in 1985. It is a relatively small, but efficient, LAN communications protocol.

IBM's vision for distributed computing at that time predicted the segmentation of LANs based upon the need to share work. The individual segments would service a community related by their work processes. Any data that needed to be accessed, but was outside this segment, could be retrieved using some type of application gateway. Given this origin, it is not surprising to find that NetBEUI is at its best in small LANs. This vision also explains why NetBEUI is not routable.

This protocol spans Layers 3 and 4 of the OSI Reference Model. Figure 12.7 presents this comparison.

FIGURE 12.7.

Comparison of the OSI Reference Model and NetBEUI.

OSI Reference Model Layer Description	OSI Layer Number	
Application	7	
Presentation	6	
Session	5	
Transport	4	NetBEUI
Network	3	
Data Link	2	
Physical	1	

As evident from Figure 12.7, NetBEUI establishes communications between two computers and provides the mechanisms to ensure reliable delivery and sequencing of data.

Microsoft recently released NetBEUI 3.0. This release is significant for several reasons. First, 3.0 is more tolerant of slower transmission facilities than previous versions. This version is also completely self-tuning. The most significant change made to NetBEUI in release 3.0 is the elimination of NetBEUI.

NetBEUI was replaced with the *NetBIOS Frame* (NBF) protocol in Microsoft's network operating systems. Both NetBEUI and NBF are closely related with NetBIOS. Consequently, NetBEUI 3.0 (NBF) remains completely compatible and interoperable with Microsoft's earlier versions of NetBEUI.

> **WARNING**
>
> NetBEUI, regardless of which version, is integral to Microsoft's network operating systems. If you attempt to run Windows NT 3.x (or higher), Windows for Workgroups 3.11, or even LAN Manager 2.x without NetBEUI installed, your computer cannot communicate.

NetBEUI Conclusion

NetBEUI is a Microsoft-specific LAN Transport protocol only. It is *not* routable. Consequently, its implementations are limited to Layer 2 domains that are homogenously populated with computers that use Microsoft operating systems. Although this is becoming less and less of a handicap, it does effectively limit computing architectures and technology applications.

The advantages of using NetBEUI are

- Computers using Microsoft networking software or operating systems can actually communicate
- NetBEUI is completely self-tuning and runs best in small LAN segments
- NetBEUI enjoys minimal memory requirements
- NetBEUI provides excellent protection against, and recovery from, transmission errors

NetBEUI's limitations are that it cannot be routed and does not perform well over WANs.

Summary

Network protocols reside above the Data Link Layer. When they are properly designed and developed, they are decoupled from LAN architectures (described in Part II, "Building Local Area Networks") and provide end-to-end management of transmissions across LAN domains.

III

PART

IN THIS PART

Building Wide Area Networks

Wide Area Networking

by Mark A. Sportack

IN THIS CHAPTER

Wide area networks (WANs) are comprised of routers, routing protocols, and transmission facilities. Properly constructed, WANs enable LANs to be networked together, regardless of how much geographic distance separates them. The key words here are "properly constructed." Designing, building, and administering WANs requires a very different set of skills than does client/server or LAN administration. This chapter examines the various components that make up a WAN, as well as the relative costs and benefits of each.

Understanding WAN Technologies

Wide area networks (WANs) and their component technologies continue to increase in importance. Not very many years ago, about the only need most companies had for WANs was to internetwork two or more work locations. This is still a valuable and important use of WAN technologies, but other possible uses are rapidly appearing. For example, a company with only a single work location might need a robust connection to the Internet to support marketing, customer care, and many other functions. Alternatively, outsourcing certain operations or functions, as well as collaborative efforts with other companies, can necessitate the internetworking of privately owned LANs.

Unfortunately, WANs are very different from LANs. Most LAN technologies adhere tightly to industry standards. WANs are composite structures built from many different technologies—some standard, and some highly proprietary. Many of the competing technologies also differ radically in features, performance, and cost. The most difficult part of building a WAN is matching the appropriate technologies in such a way as to satisfy the underlying business requirements. This requires a deep understanding of each aspect of every WAN component.

The wide area network's technology base includes:

- Transmission facilities
- Communications hardware, including CSUs/DSUs and the premises edge vehicles (routers and switches)
- Internetwork addressing
- Routing protocols

Each of these technology categories expands into a surprisingly wide array of choices of individual technologies. Within each technology category lies additional variation in terms of manufacturers, models, and configurations. Before selecting vendors and specific products, you should examine each technology for potential performance capabilities relative to your expected WAN traffic load and performance requirements. Although an exhaustive review of each manufacturer's product line is outside the scope of this book, a survey of each technology can provide a solid foundation for your own evaluation of actual products.

Using Transmission Facilities

Transmission facilities used to construct the WAN present the richest array of options for the network planner. These facilities come in a variety of sizes, varieties, and cost. For example, transmission facilities can range in size (bandwidth) from 9.6 Kilobits per second (Kbps) to 44.736 Megabits per second (Mbps), and beyond. These transmission facilities support a digital stream of data at a fixed and predetermined transmission rate. They can be implemented over a variety of physical media, including twisted pair or fiber-optic cabling, and can also support numerous framing formats.

> **NOTE**
>
> The DS-3 specification offers 44.736Mbps of bandwidth. When discussed, this bandwidth is frequently referred to simply as 45Mbps.

These facilities also vary greatly in the manner in which they provide connections. There are two primary types of facilities: *circuit switched* and *packet switched*. These two types encompass all versions of facilities, although technological innovation may be blurring their boundaries somewhat. These technologies are briefly described in this chapter to provide a context for selecting the correct WAN. More detailed information on leased line transmission facilities is available in Chapter 14, "Leased Lines."

Circuit Switched Facilities

Circuit switching is a communications method that creates a switched, dedicated path between two end stations. A good example of a circuit switched network is the telephone system. A telephone is hard-wired to a central office telecommunications switch that is owned and operated by the local exchange carrier (LEC). There are many LECs and even more telecommunications switches in the world, yet any telephone can establish a connection to any other telephone through a series of intermediary central office switches. That connection is a physical circuit and is dedicated to that session for the duration of the communications session. After the telephones terminate their sessions, the physical circuit through the switched telecommunications infrastructure is torn down. The resources are then freed up for the next call.

The creation of a dedicated physical circuit through switches is the essence of circuit switching. Every unit of transmission, regardless of whether it is a cell, a frame, or anything else that may be constructed, takes the same physical path through the network infrastructure. This concept may be applied in several different formats. Three examples of circuit switched transmission facilities include leased lines, ISDN, and Switched 56, all discussed in the sections that follow.

13

WIDE AREA
NETWORKING

Leased Lines

The leased line is the most robust and flexible of the circuit-switched transmission facilities. These circuits are called "leased lines" because they are leased from telecommunications carriers for a monthly fee.

In North America, the dominant system for providing digital leased line service is known as the "T-Carrier system." The T-Carrier enables 1.544Mbps of bandwidth to be channelized into 24 separate transmission facilities over two pairs of wire. Each channel is 64Kbps wide and can be further channelized into even smaller facilities, such as 9.6Kbps. The 1.544Mbps facility is known as the T-1. A higher capacity facility also exists within the T-Carrier system. This is the 44.736Mbps T-3 facility.

> **NOTE**
>
> Leased lines are frequently called "dedicated" or "private" lines because their bandwidth is reserved for only the company that is leasing them.

For more information on leased lines and the T-Carrier system, refer to Chapter 14.

Integrated Services Digital Network (ISDN)

ISDN is a "dial-on-demand" form of digital circuit switched technology that can transport voice and data simultaneously over the same physical connection. ISDN can be ordered in either Basic Rate (BRI) or Primary Rate (PRI) Interfaces.

The BRI offers 144Kbps in a format known as "2B+D." The 2B refers to two 64Kbps B channels that can be bonded together to form one logical connection at 128Kbps. The D channel is a 16Kbps control channel used for call setup, takedown, and other control functions.

The PRI is, typically, delivered over a T-1 facility at a gross transmission rate of 1.544Mbps. This is usually channelized into 23 64Kbps B channels and 1 64Kbps D channel. Higher rate H channels of either 384, 1536, or 1920Kbps can be used instead of, or in combination with, the B and D channels.

> **NOTE**
>
> The 1920Kbps H3 channel is useable only in Europe where the standard transmission rate is 2.048Mbps, rather than the 1.544Mbps rate standard in the U.S., Canada, and Japan. Attempts to use an H3 channel over a 1.544Mbps transmission facility result in unusable channels.

Although ISDN is technically a circuit switched facility, it can support circuit switched, packet switched, and even semi-permanent connections.

Switched 56

Another dial-on-demand circuit switched variant is Switched 56. Switched 56 offers 56Kbps of bandwidth between any two points that subscribe to this service. As with any dial-on-demand service, no circuit exists until a call is placed. Then the circuit is constructed between the origination and requested destination points. The actual path taken through the switched communications infrastructure is invisible, and immaterial, to the end users. This circuit is torn down when the session is terminated.

The non-dedicated nature of Switched 56 makes it an affordable alternative to leased lines. You pay based on usage, rather than for the luxury of having bandwidth reserved for you, regardless of whether it is being used. Balanced against affordability is performance. Switched 56 circuits must set up calls to requested destinations. This takes time. Thus, establishing a communications session can be done much more quickly over a 56Kbps leased line than it can over a Switched 56. After the call is established, performance should be comparable.

Switched 56 is a mature and declining technology. It once offered a combination of lower cost than leased lines, but much higher performance than modems and POTS lines. Today, advances in signaling techniques have enabled modems to close the performance gap. Switched 56 still offers a slight improvement over the so-called 56Kbps modems (despite what their name says, they cannot provide and sustain that transmission rate), but not much. Today, Switched 56 is probably best suited as an emergency contingency to leased lines.

Packet Switched Facilities

Packet switching facilities feature an internal packet format that is used to encapsulate data to be transported. Unlike circuit switched facilities, packet switched facilities do not provide a dedicated connection between two locations. Instead, the premises access facility interconnects with the telecommunications carrier's switched infrastructure. Packets are forwarded in a connectionless manner through this commercial packet switched network (PSN). The lack of a easily defined path between any two locations has led to the overuse of the cloud symbol as the ubiquitous, but amorphous, network. Two examples of packet switched networks are the old but familiar X.25 and its more up-to-date cousin, Frame Relay, both discussed in the following sections.

X.25

X.25 is a very old WAN communications protocol developed by the CCITT (now known as the International Telecommunications Union, or ITU). It was first offered as a commercial service by telecommunications carriers in the early 1970s.

NOTE

The ITU's specifications are sometimes identified with the prefix ITU-T. The *T* suffix identifies the specification as part of the ITU's Telecommunications standards.

13

WIDE AREA
NETWORKING

X.25 supports the use of both switched and permanent virtual circuits. Switched virtual circuits (SVCs) are established as needed, and are dismantled as soon as the communications session ends. Permanent virtual circuits (PVCs) are predefined, logical connections through a switched network between two points. The advantages of SVCs are that they are flexible and can be used to connect any two points within the X.25 network on demand. Their limitation lies in the call setup time that must be endured prior to exchanging information with another device on the network.

PVCs aren't flexible and must be defined in advance. Their primary benefit lies in the elimination of a call setup period. Thus, PVCs are typically used to support communications between devices that need to communicate on a routine and ongoing basis. SVCs are used for ad hoc communications.

X.25 contains a robust suite of error detection and correction mechanisms that enabled it to be a highly reliable protocol having to traverse a noisy electromechanical switching equipment infrastructure. X.25 sacrificed throughput for reliability. Today, in the era of digital and optical communications, the error detection/correction mechanisms of X.25 are unnecessary overhead. These functions are now more appropriately contained at the communicating devices rather than embedded in every network device. Applications that still require the use of the X.25 protocol may find better performance in emulating that protocol over a different transmission facility.

Frame Relay

Frame Relay is a faster version of X.25 packet switching that features smaller packet sizes and fewer error-checking mechanisms. Frame Relay currently supports transfer of packets through only permanent virtual circuits (PVCs) between the network's endpoint routers. Eventually, SVCs will be supported in this protocol, although no timelines for its deployment have been proffered by any of the commercial service providers.

The PVC's endpoints are defined by Data Link Connection Identifiers (DLCIs) and are given a committed information rate (CIR) through the frame relay network. DLCI pairs are also given a minimum available quantity of bandwidth, with the option to temporarily burst beyond that limit under certain circumstances. The use of DLCIs in Frame Relay networks is illustrated in Figure 13.1.

Frame Relay WANs are built by provisioning a point-to-point private line from the work location to the nearest central office that provides this service. At the central office, this private line terminates in a Frame Relay switch that is either fully or partially meshed with the other Frame Relay switches that compose that carrier's Frame Relay commercial infrastructure. Much like the central office voice switches that compose the Public Switched Telephone Network (PSTN), the frame relay switches remain invisible to the user community and its applications.

Frame Relay's primary benefit is that it can reduce the cost of networking locations that are geographically dispersed by minimizing the length of premises access facilities. These circuits are commercially available at 1.544Mbps, with CIRs used to create logical sub-rate connections to multiple locations.

FIGURE 13.1.

Frame Relay's logical pairs of data link connections.

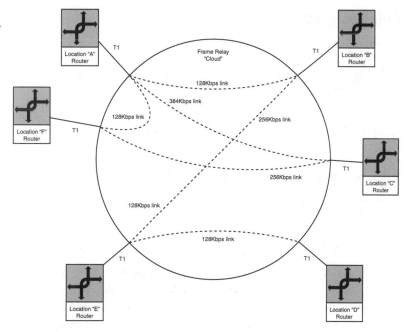

Balanced against this minimization of access facilities cost for point-to-point leased lines is a reduction in performance. Frame Relay introduces a significant amount of overhead in terms of framing and protocol, which is added to the overheads of the point-to-point leased line. The rule of thumb that guides engineering the DLCI and CIRs on a Frame Relay connection is to subscribe a maximum of 1.024Mbps of the 1.544Mbps of available bandwidth. This guarantees that each DLCI receives its committed information rate, and that a margin of extra bandwidth is available for temporarily bursting beyond this rate.

WARNING

Bandwidth subscription is the allocation of bandwidth to channels carved from a larger transmission facility. In Frame Relay, each DLCI must have a rate subscription associated with it. This subscription is the *committed information rate* (CIR).

It is possible to define a series of DLCIs with a cumulative CIR that is greater than the bandwidth available on the transmission facility. Continuing the example of T-1 based Frame Relay, one could configure 2.048Mbps' worth of CIRs over the 1.544Mbps facility. This is known as *oversubscription*. Oversubscription is a bad practice. It assumes that not all the DLCIs will be active and thus not consuming their entire CIR at any given time. This is not an unreasonable assumption, but oversubscription results in the sporadic degradation of service during peak usage periods. If at all possible, avoid using telecommunications carriers that habitually oversubscribe their circuits.

Cell-Switched Facilities

A close relative to packet switching is cell switching. The difference between a packet and a cell is the length of the structure. A packet is a variable-length data structure, whereas a cell is a fixed-length data structure. The most familiar cell switched technology is Asynchronous Transfer Mode (ATM). Although, technically speaking, ATM is currently a circuit-switched technology, it is best categorized independently.

ATM was designed to take advantage of the higher-speed transmission facilities like T-3 and the SONET architectures.

Asynchronous Transfer Mode (ATM)

ATM was originally designed as an asynchronous transport mechanism for broadband ISDN. Its low latency and high bit rate, it was speculated, would make it equally ideal for use in local area networks. The subsequent market hype has almost completely cemented its reputation as a LAN technology, to the exclusion of its capabilities as a WAN technology.

As a cell switched WAN technology, ATM is commercially available at 1.544Mbps (DS-1) or 44.736Mbps (DS-3), although this availability varies geographically. Initially, wide area ATM was available using only permanent virtual circuits, much like the DLCIs of Frame Relay. Ultimately, however, wide area ATM will be a switched technology that is capable of forwarding individual cells without requiring the overheads of establishing a permanent virtual circuit or reserving bandwidth.

Choosing Communications Hardware

The communications hardware needed to build a WAN includes three basic categories: customer-provided telephony equipment (CPE), premises edge vehicles, and data communications equipment (DCE). In this context, DCE refers to the telecommunications carriers' gear. As such, there is very little you can do to actually select DCE, and therefore it is not discussed in this section.

CPE refers to the physical telephony mechanisms that are used to tie premises communications equipment, including routers, LANs, switches, and so forth, to the commercial telephony network of the communications carrier.

Premises edge vehicles are those mechanisms that connect the LAN to the CPE. They generally operate at Layers 2 and 3 of the OSI Reference Model, and are responsible for forwarding and receiving packets, based on internetwork addresses. Edge vehicles are the mechanisms that separate LAN from WAN, in the context of telecommunications. Both CPE and edge vehicles are customer provided.

Telecommunications carriers, of course, deploy a considerable amount of hardware to support the transmission facilities that they provide to customers. Such hardware typically remains invisible to the users and LAN administrators. As such, it remains outside the scope of this book.

> **NOTE**
>
> CPE is also widely interpreted as Customer Premises Equipment. Both interpretations of this acronym are acceptable and convey the same meaning.

Customer-Provided Equipment (CPE)

CPE is the Physical Layer telephony hardware that encodes signals and places them on the transmission facility. This hardware is almost always provided by the customers and is installed in their physical premises, on their sides of the demarcation point. The demarcation point, referred to as the "demarc," is the official boundary between the physical plant of the telecommunications carrier and the customer's physical plant that is connected to the carrier's telephony infrastructure.

The demarc is usually just a modular jack box that is labeled with the circuit identification numbers. The telecommunications carrier owns this box, as well as everything that is hardwired to it. The customer is responsible for all equipment that connects to the modular jack receptacle. This customer-provided equipment is the CPE.

The type of CPE varies by transmission technology. The two most common forms of CPE are the CSU/DSU and the PAD. Both of these are further examined in the following sections.

The Channel Service Unit/Digital Service Unit (CSU/DSU)

The typical WAN is constructed with leased line, circuit-switched transmission facilities. Thus, the typical CPE is known as a CSU/DSU (Channel Service Unit/Digital Service Unit). The CSU/DSU assumes that the transmission facility is a leased line and that no dial-up connections are possible.

CSU/DSUs are data communications equipment that terminates channelized and digital transmission facilities. This termination typically takes the form of a modular jack. The CSU/DSU also features a serial connection to the router at the customer's premises edge, as illustrated in Figure 13.2.

> **NOTE**
>
> It is not uncommon to find people that also categorize routers as Customer Provided Equipment. This miscategorization is based on the compound assumption that the router is an essential part of extending connectivity beyond the local premises and that it must be provided by the customer. These assumptions are generally true, but the router is not considered a telecommunications device. Thus, it is cannot be CPE; it is a premises edge vehicle.

13

WIDE AREA
NETWORKING

FIGURE 13.2.

*The CSU/DSU
interconnecting the
router with the
transmission facility.*

The CSU/DSU provides more functionality than simply transmitting and receiving the physical signals. Depending on the brand and model, CSU/DSUs can also perform line-conditioning and respond to diagnostic queries from the central office. These units are essential in any leased circuit that supports transmission rates of 56Kbps or greater.

Packet Assembler/Disassembler (PAD)

Transmission facilities that use packet switching may require a different device to create and dismantle the packets. This device is known as a PAD. PAD is actually an acronym for "Packet Assembler/Disassembler." A good example of a network technology that uses PADs is the X.25 network. X.25 typically used a 9.6Kbps transmission facility to interconnect a user's premises to the telecommunications carrier's switched network infrastructure. The terminating device on these relatively low-speed facilities was the PAD.

Today's packet switching technologies tend to use circuit-switched transmission facilities. For example, frame relay has clearly evolved from X.25, yet it doesn't use a PAD. Instead, LANs can be interconnected via frame relay using logical subchannels carved out of a T-1 facility. Given that the T-1 provides 1.544Mbps of bandwidth, it must terminate in a CSU/DSU at the customer's premises, regardless of which transmission technology it supports. Thus, a WAN built using Frame Relay features routers and CSU/DSUs at each site. The CSU/DSU at each site connects to a T-1 transmission facility that interconnects them via the Frame Relay network.

Premises Edge Vehicles

A *premises edge vehicle* is the equipment that interconnects a customer's local area network with the CPE. In the typical LAN environment, this is a router. Routers function as the boundary between the LAN and the WAN. As such, their primary responsibility is keeping track of the routes to known internetwork addresses. These addresses are stored in routing tables that correlate the address with the physical interface on the router that must be used to get to said address.

Understanding Internetwork Addressing

Wide area networking invariably creates the need for addressing devices that reside beyond one's local LAN. Internetworking addresses are constructs of Layer 3, the Network Layer of the OSI reference model. These addresses are used to access, and exchange data with, hosts on other subnetworks within the WAN.

The address architecture is determined by the routable protocol that is used within the WAN. Some of the possibilities include IPv4, IPv6, IPX, and AppleTalk. Each has its own unique addressing scheme. Thus, the choice of protocol determines the possible address hierarchies that can be implemented.

Ensuring Unique Addressing

The single most important aspect of internetwork addressing is uniqueness! With the solitary exception of IPv6, any network protocol you select requires that at any given point in time, there is only one endpoint with any given address. Redundant internetwork addresses create routing errors and compromise the consistency of your user's network-based operations.

> **NOTE**
>
> IPv6 contains a new address architecture known as *anycast*. Anycast addresses are easily (even unintentionally) created when the same address is assigned to multiple devices. The network, when receiving packets addressed to an anycast address, simply routes those packets to the nearest device with that address. Thus, anycast devices must be completely interchangeable from both an operational and functional perspective.

Theoretically, if your WAN is not going to be directly interconnected with the Internet, or to any other network, internetwork addresses can be arbitrarily selected. Generally speaking, arbitrarily selecting internetwork addresses is short-sighted and a gross dereliction of duties. That being said, Request for Comment (RFC) #1597 was released in May 1993, and posited a plan to the contrary. Three ranges of addresses that could be used for internal networking purposes only were identified and reserved. These ranges include one each of IPv4's Class A, B, and C addresses. They are as follows:

- 10.0.0.0–10.255.255.255
- 172.16.0.0–172.31.255.255
- 192.168.0.0–192.168.255.255

13

WIDE AREA NETWORKING

These ranges are reserved by the Internet Assigned Numbers Authority (IANA) for use in private networks. One stipulation of RFC #1597 is that these addresses can't be used when directly accessing the Internet. Companies that use these addresses, and subsequently find the need to access the Internet, can use a proxy server with a unique and registered IP address as an intermediary. Alternatively, Network Address Translation (NAT) can be used.

> **NOTE**
>
> If you implement RFC #1597's reserved addresses, you must still guarantee the uniqueness of each device's address within your private network domain. The addresses may not be unique globally, but they must be unique locally.

Internetworking with Different Protocols

Not every WAN has the luxury of using a single routed protocol. Multiprotocol networks present some basic challenges that must be overcome. The problem is providing connectivity across dissimilar protocols. Two approaches can be used: tunnels and gateways.

Tunnels

Tunnels are a relatively simple construct that can be used to pass data through an otherwise incompatible network region. Data packets are encapsulated with framing that is recognized by the network that transports it. The original framing and formatting is retained, but treated as "data."

Upon reaching its destination, the recipient host unwraps the packet and discards the "wrapper." This results in the packet being restored to its original format, complete with its original internetwork addressing. Figure 13.3 illustrates the tunneling of IPv4 packets through an IPv6 network region. Because of the inherent difference in the length of these two protocols' addresses, they are not directly compatible. To overcome this incompatibility, IPv4 packets are wrapped in IPv6 by Router A for transmission through an IPv6 WAN. Router B removes the IPv6 wrapper and presents the restored IPv4 packet to the destination host in a form that it can recognize.

For more information on the Internet addressing of routable protocols, please refer to Chapter 12, "Network Protocols."

Gateways

If your WAN requires the interconnection of subnetworks with dissimilar routed protocols, you need a gateway at the border of the dissimilar regions. A gateway is any device that can translate between the address architectures of the two protocols. Gateways can be routers or hosts. The only criterion is that the device be capable of translating between the two protocols' address architectures.

FIGURE 13.3.

Tunneling IPv4 packets through an IPv6 region.

Routers have two ways of performing such an address translation. First, they can use two different routing protocols. This requires the router to calculate routes, forward route information, and forward packets in both protocols. Routers were designed to operate in multiprotocol environments, so this should not represent any operational difficulties.

Alternatively, a router may have an integrated protocol that is simultaneously capable of routing two different protocols and addresses. Examples of this form of routing protocol are the emerging series of "ng" protocols that are designed to facilitate the migration between IPv4 and IPv6. Specific examples are OSPF*ng* and RI*Png*.

Using Routing Protocols

Dynamic routing protocols are used by routers to perform three basic functions:

- Discover new routes
- Communicate the discovered route information to other routers
- Forward packets using those routes

Dynamic routing protocols fall into three broad categories: distance-vector, link-state, and hybrids, each discussed in the sections that follow. Their primary differences are in the way that they perform the first two of the three aforementioned functions. The only alternative to dynamic routing is static routing, which is described in the section titled "Static Routing."

13

WIDE AREA
NETWORKING

Distance-Vector Routing

Routing can be based on distance-vector algorithms (also sometimes called Bellman-Ford algorithms), which require that routers periodically pass copies of the routing tables to the immediate network neighbors. Each recipient adds a distance vector (its own distance "value") to the table and forwards it to its immediate neighbors. This process occurs omnidirectionally between immediately neighboring routers.

This step-by-step process results in each router's learning about other routers and developing a cumulative perspective of network "distances." For example, an early distance-vector routing protocol is "Routing Information Protocol" or "RIP." RIP uses two distance metrics for determining the best next path to take for any given packet. These distance metrics are time sensitive, as measured by "ticks" and hop count.

> **NOTE**
>
> Routers can use a surprising variety of metrics to determine optimal routes between any given source and destination pair. These metrics are euphemistically referred to as "distances." Distances may actually be time, number of router hops, and so forth, and are not limited to physical distances.

The cumulative table is then used to update each router's routing tables. When completed, each router has learned vague information about the distances to networked resources. It does not learn anything specific about other routers or learn the network's actual topology.

This approach can, under certain circumstances, actually create routing problems for distance vector protocols. For example, a failure in the network requires some time for the routers to converge on a new understanding of the network's topology. During the convergence process, the network may be vulnerable to inconsistent routing, and even infinite loops.

Certain safeguards may mitigate many of these risks, but the fact remains that the network's performance is at risk during the convergence process. Thus, older protocols that are slow to converge may not be appropriate for large, complex WANs.

Link-State Routing

Link-state routing algorithms, known cumulatively as "shortest path first" or SPF protocols, maintain a complex database of the network's topology. Unlike distance-vector protocols, link-state protocols develop and maintain a full understanding of the network's routers, as well as of how they interconnect.

This understanding is achieved via the exchange of Link-State Packets (LSPs) with other directly connected routers. Each router that has exchanged LSPs then constructs a topological database using all received LSPs. A "shortest path first" algorithm is then used to compute reachability to networked destinations. This information is used to update the routing table. This process is capable of discovering changes in the network topology that may have been caused by component failure or network growth. In fact, the LSP exchange is triggered by an event in the network, rather than running periodically.

Link-state routing has two potential areas for concern. First, during the initial discovery process, link-state routing can flood the network's transmission facilities, thereby significantly decreasing the network's capability to transport data. This performance degradation is temporary, but very noticeable.

The second area for concern is that link-state routing is memory- and processor-intensive. Routers configured for link-state routing tend to be more expensive because of this problem.

Hybridized Routing

The last form of the dynamic routing discipline is hybridization. Although "open" balanced hybrid protocols exist, this form is almost exclusively associated with the proprietary creation of a single company, Cisco Systems, Inc. This protocol, Enhanced Interior Gateway Routing Protocol (EIGRP), was designed to combine the best aspects of distance-vector and link-state routing protocols, without incurring any of their performance limitations or penalties.

The balanced hybrid routing protocols use distance-vector metrics, but emphasize more accurate metrics than conventional distance vector protocols. They also converge more rapidly than distance-vector protocols, but avoid the overheads of link-state updates. Balanced hybrids are event driven, rather than periodic, thereby conserving bandwidth for real applications.

Static Routing

A router that is programmed for static routing forwards packets out of predetermined ports. After static routes are configured, routers no longer have any need to attempt route discovery or even communicate information about routes. Their role is reduced to simply forwarding packets.

Static routing is good for only very small networks that have only a single path to any given destination. In such cases, static routing can be the most efficient routing mechanism because it doesn't consume bandwidth trying to discover routes or communicate with other routers.

As networks grow larger and add redundant paths to destinations, static routing becomes a labor-intensive liability. Any changes in the availability of routers or transmission facilities in the WAN must be manually discovered and programmed. WANs that feature more complex topologies that offer multiple potential paths absolutely require dynamic routing. Attempts to use static routing in complex, multi-path WANs defeat the purpose of having that route redundancy.

Selecting a Protocol

Selection of a routing protocol should be done carefully and with an appreciation for the long-term implications of your selection. Your selection of any given protocol directly affects the selection of a router vendor, as well as the operational efficiency of the WAN. The preceding sections on the different classes of routing protocols, as well as the section on static routing, should have amply demonstrated the operational implications of each category of routing protocol. These implications should help you narrow down your options to a single category or class of protocols.

The next step is to determine whether you are going to use one or more router vendors in your WAN. If at all possible, try to select a single manufacturer's products. The reason for this is simple: Open routing protocols enable each manufacturer some latitude for variation. Thus, one manufacturer's version of an open routing protocol is likely to be less than 100% interoperable with another manufacturer's version. Perhaps the best example of this is the well-documented differences between Bay Networks' and Cisco System's versions of the Open Shortest Path First (OSPF) protocol.

If you select a router manufacturer before you select a routing protocol, understand how doing so can limit your selection of protocols. Some routing protocols are proprietary and, consequently, available from only a single vendor.

Understanding WAN Topologies

The topology of a WAN describes the way the transmission facilities are arranged relative to the locations that they interconnect. Numerous topologies are possible, each one offering a different mix of cost, performance, and scalability. More subtly, some functional specialization may be introduced by a topology that has a direct bearing on the transmission facilities. The more common WAN topologies include the following:

- Peer-to-peer WANs
- Ring WANs
- Star WANs
- Full-mesh WANs
- Partial-mesh WANs
- Multi-tiered, including two-tiered and three-tiered WANs
- Hybrids

Although some of these may sound more like LAN topologies than WAN topologies, they are quite applicable in both arenas. Each of these is described and illustrated throughout the rest of this section. Their relative cost, performance, scalability, and technology implications are also examined.

Peer-to-Peer Topology

A peer-to-peer WAN can be developed using leased private lines, or any other transmission facility. This WAN topology is a relatively simple way of interconnecting a small number of sites. WANs that consist of just two locations can be interconnected in this manner only. A small peer-to-peer WAN is depicted in Figure 13.4.

FIGURE 13.4.

A Peer-to-Peer WAN constructed with leased lines.

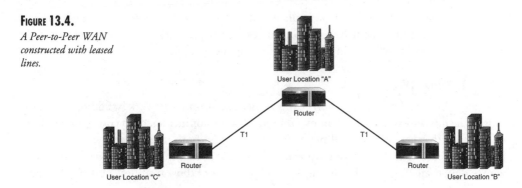

This topology represents the least-cost solution for WANs that contain a small number of internetworked locations. Because each location contains, at most, one or two links to the rest of the network, static routing can be used. Static routing can be time intensive to establish but avoids the network overheads of dynamic routing protocols. Given that there are no redundant routes to be had in this simple topology, the benefits of dynamic routing are limited.

> **NOTE**
>
> In a routed WAN, the number of routers between you and your destination is directly related to the amount of time that a transmitted packet is en route to its destination. Thus, a metric has been developed to track the number of routers in a given network path. This metric is called a *hop count*. Each router counts as one hop.

Unfortunately, peer-to-peer WANs suffer from two basic limitations. First, they do not scale very well. As additional locations are introduced to the WAN, the number of hops between any given pair of locations remains highly inconsistent and has an upward trend. This results in varied levels of performance in communications between any given pair of locations. The actual degree to which performance varies depends greatly upon many factors, including the following:

- Geographic distances between locations
- The type and capacity of transmission facility
- The degree to which the transmission facility is being utilized

13

WIDE AREA NETWORKING

The second limitation of this approach is its inherent vulnerability to component failure. Only a single path exists between any given pair of locations. Consequently, an equipment or facility failure anywhere in a peer-to-peer WAN can split the WAN. Depending upon the actual traffic flows and the type of routing implemented, this can severely disrupt communications in the entire WAN.

Another significant implication of the peer-to-peer topology's lack of route redundancy is that using a dynamic routing protocol to calculate routes and forward packets is a waste of time and CPU cycles. The route calculated between any two points can never change! Thus, statically defining the routes may result in a better performing network.

Ring Topology

A ring topology can be developed fairly easily from a peer-to-peer network by adding one transmission facility and an extra port on two routers. This minor increment in cost provides route redundancy that can afford small networks the opportunity to implement dynamic routing protocols. Given that the cost of most transmission facilities is mileage sensitive, it would be wise to design the ring so as to minimize overall distances of those facilities. This WAN topology is illustrated in Figure 13.5.

FIGURE 13.5.
A ring-shaped WAN.

A ring-shaped WAN constructed with point-to-point transmission facilities can be used to interconnect a small number of sites and provide route redundancy at a potentially minimal incremental cost. The existence of redundant routes through the network means that the use of a dynamic routing protocol affords flexibility not available with static routing. Dynamic routing protocols can automatically detect and recover from adverse changes in the WAN's operating condition by routing around the impacted links.

Rings, too, have some basic limitations. Depending upon the geographic dispersion of the locations, adding an extra transmission facility to complete the ring may be cost-prohibitive. In such cases, Frame Relay may be a viable alternative to dedicated leased lines, provided that its performance limitations are acceptable relative to the projected traffic loads.

A second limitation of rings is that they are not very scalable. Adding new locations to the WAN directly increases the number of hops required to access other locations in the ring. This additive process may also result in having to order new circuits. For example, as shown previously in Figure 13.5, adding a new location, X, that is in geographic proximity to Sites C and D, requires that the circuit from location C to D be terminated. Two new circuits have to be ordered to preserve the integrity of the ring: one running from C to X and the other running from D to X.

The ring topology, given its limitations, is likely to be of value in interconnecting only very small numbers of locations. It is preferable to the peer-to-peer interconnection of locations only because of its capability to provide a redundant path to the locations within the ring.

Star Network Topology

A variant of the peer-to-peer topology is the *star topology*, so named for its shape. A star is constructed by homing all locations into a common location. One could argue that this, in essence, creates a two-tiered topology. The distinction between a star and a two-tiered topology is that the center router in a star topology may also be used to interconnect the LANs installed at that location with each other as well as the WAN.

In a two-tiered topology, as discussed later in this chapter, the second-tier router should be dedicated exclusively to interconnecting the transmission facilities of the other locations. More importantly, a two-tiered topology provides route redundancy by supporting the development of networks with multiple concentration points.

The star topology can be constructed using almost any dedicated transmission facility, including frame relay and point-to-point private lines. The star-shaped WAN is shown in Figure 13.6.

A star topology WAN with point-to-point transmission facilities is much more scalable than a peer-to-peer or ring network. Adding locations to the star does not require the re-engineering of existing transmission facilities. All that is required is to provision a new facility between the concentration router and the router at the new location.

The star topology rectifies the scalability problems of peer-to-peer networks by using a router to interconnect, or *concentrate*, all the other networked routers. This scalability is afforded at a modest increase in the number of routers, router ports, and transmission facilities compared to a comparably sized peer-to-peer topology. Star topologies may actually be developed with *fewer* facilities than ring topologies, as Figures 13.7 and 13.8 demonstrate.

FIGURE 13.6.

A star-shaped WAN.

The scalability of the star topology is limited by the number of ports that the router at the center of the star can support. Expansion beyond its capacity requires either a re-engineering of the topology into a two-tiered topology, or the replacement of the existing router with a much larger unit.

Another benefit of a star topology is improved network performance. Overall network performance in a star topology is, in theory, always better than in either a ring or peer-to-peer network. This is because all network-connected devices are just three hops away from each other. These three hops include the router at the user's location, the concentrator router, and the router at the destination. This degree of consistency is unique to the star topology. The two drawbacks to this approach are the following:

- It creates a single point of failure: The existence of a single point of failure means that all WAN communications can be disrupted if the concentrator router experiences a failure.

- There is no route redundancy: The lack of route redundancy means that if that concentrator router fails, you are out of service until that failure is rectified. Dynamic routing protocols are able to calculate new paths through the network because there are none!

Full Mesh Topology

At the extreme high end of the reliability spectrum is the full mesh topology. This topology features the ultimate reliability and fault tolerance. Every networked node is directly connected to every other networked node. Thus, redundant routes to each location are plentiful. Implicit in this statement is that static routing is utterly impractical. You are virtually forced into selecting one of the dynamic routing protocols to calculate routes and forward packets in this type of network. The fully meshed WAN is illustrated in Figure 13.7.

FIGURE 13.7.

A fully meshed WAN.

This approach minimizes the number of hops between any two network-connected machines. Another benefit is that it can be built with virtually any transmission technology.

Some practical limitations are inherent, however, in a fully meshed topology. For example, these WANs can be fairly expensive to build. Each router has to be large enough to have a port and transmission facility for each other router in the WAN. This tends to make both start-up and monthly recurring operational costs expensive. It also places a finite (although substantial) limit on the scalability of the network. Routers do have a limit on the number of ports that they can support. Thus, full mesh topologies are more of a Utopian ideal with limited practical application.

One application would be to provide interconnectivity for a limited number of routers that require high network availability. Another potential application is to fully mesh just parts of the WAN, such as the backbone of a multitiered WAN or tightly coupled work centers. This option is described in more detail in the section titled "Hybrid Topologies."

13

WIDE AREA
NETWORKING

Partial Mesh Topology

A WAN can also be developed with a "partial" mesh topology. Partial meshes are highly flexible topologies that can take a variety of very different configurations. The best way to describe a partial mesh topology is that the routers are much more tightly coupled than any of the basic topologies, but are not fully interconnected, as would be the case in a fully meshed network. This topology is illustrated in Figure 13.8.

FIGURE 13.8.

A partial mesh topology.

A partially meshed WAN topology is readily identified by the almost complete interconnection of every node with every other node in the network. Partial meshes offer the capability to minimize hops for the bulk of the WAN's users. Unlike fully meshed networks, a partial mesh can reduce the start-up and operational expenses by not interconnecting low traffic segments of the WAN. This enables the partial mesh network to be somewhat more scalable—and thus affordable—than a full mesh topology.

Two-Tiered Topology

A two-tiered topology is a modified version of the basic star topology. Rather than single concentrator routers, two or more routers are used. This rectifies the basic vulnerability of the star topology without compromising its efficiency or scalability.

Figure 13.9 presents a WAN with a typical two-tiered topology. The worst-case hop count does increase by one, as a result of the extra concentrator (the backbone) router. However, unlike the peer-to-peer network presented earlier in Figure 13.4, the hop count is not adversely affected every time a new location is added to the WAN.

FIGURE 13.9.

A two-tiered WAN.

A two-tiered WAN constructed with dedicated facilities offers improved fault tolerance over the simple star topology without compromising scalability. This topology can be implemented in a number of minor variations, primarily by manipulating the number of concentrator routers and the manner with which they are interconnected. Having three or more concentrator routers requires the network designer to select a sub-topology for the concentrator tier. These routers can be either fully or partially meshed, or strung together peer to peer.

Regardless of the sub-topology selected, hierarchical, multi-tiered topologies function best when some basic implementation principles are adhered to, as follows:

■ The concentration layer of routers should be dedicated to their tasks. That is, they are not used to directly connect user communities.

■ The user premises routers should internetwork with only concentrator nodes and not with each other in a peer-to-peer fashion.

■ The interconnection of user premises routers to concentrator routers should not be done randomly. Some logic should be applied in determining their placement. Depending upon the geographic distribution of the users and the transmission facilities used, it may be prudent to place the concentrator nodes so as to minimize the distances from the user premises.

Given that one or more routers are dedicated to route aggregation, this topology can be an expensive undertaking. This tends to limit the use of these topologies to larger companies.

13

WIDE AREA NETWORKING

Three-Tiered Topology

WANs that need to interconnect a very large number of sites, or are built using smaller routers that can support only a few serial connections, may find the two-tiered architecture insufficiently scalable. Thus, adding a third tier may well provide the additional scalability they require. This topology is illustrated in Figure 13.10.

Figure 13.10.

The three-tiered WAN topology.

A three-tiered WAN constructed with dedicated facilities offers even greater fault tolerance and scalability than the two-tiered topology. Three-tiered networks are expensive to build, operate, and maintain. They should be used for interconnecting only very large numbers of locations. Given this, it seems foolish to develop a WAN of this magnitude and not fully mesh the uppermost (or *backbone*) tier of routers.

Hybrid Topologies

Hybridization of multiple topologies is useful in larger, more complex networks. It enables administrators to tailor the WAN to actual traffic patterns, rather than try to force-fit those patterns into a rigid topological model. In other words, the basic topologies presented in this section are little more than academic constructs intended to stimulate creative thought. There are no limits on the topological variety that can be introduced to a WAN. The effectiveness of each topology, and subsequent combination of WAN technologies, depends directly upon your particular situation and performance requirements.

Multitiered networks, in particular, lend themselves to hybridization. As previously discussed, a multitiered WAN can be hybridized by fully or partially meshing the backbone tier of routers. Although there is no right or wrong way to build a hybrid topology, one example of this WAN is illustrated in Figure 13.11. Due to space considerations, the building icons have been omitted from the backbone tier in this illustration.

FIGURE 13.11.
A hybrid topology.

13

WIDE AREA
NETWORKING

An effective hybrid topology may be developed in a multitiered WAN by using a fully meshed topology for the backbone nodes only. This affords a fault tolerance to the network's backbone and can provide some of the hop-minimization of a full mesh network without experiencing all its costs or incurring its limitations on scalability.

Fully meshing the backbone of a multitiered WAN is just one form of hybridized topology. Other hybrids, too, can also be highly effective. The key is to look for topologies, and subtopologies, that can be used in combination to satisfy your particular networking requirements.

Designing Your WAN

Designing a WAN requires the successful integration of all the technical components described in this chapter. Successful integration means that the performance of the finished network meets, or exceeds, performance requirements and user expectations. Thus, it is imperative that you identify and quantify (to the extent that users cooperate) these performance criteria before you begin the design.

WAN Performance Criteria

Many different criteria, or metrics, can be applied to measure the success of a WAN. Many of these are fairly objective and can be automatically extracted from the network monitoring protocols native to virtually every network device. Others are subjective and can be next to impossible to determine in advance. Some of the more common metrics include the following:

- Component up-time
- Traffic volumes
- Delays and latency
- Resource utilization rates

Each of these metrics is discussed in more detail in the following sections.

Component Up-Time

Each physical component of the WAN can be monitored, and measured, for its availability using *up-time*. Up-time is the opposite of downtime: it is the amount of time that the device is functional and in service, relative to the users' requirements for its availability. It is quite common for up-time to be statistically overstated by measuring it on a 7 x 24 basis, even though the users' requirements may be for only 5 x 12. Remember to tailor this, and every other metric, as closely as possible to your users' stated requirements for network performance.

All electronic devices—even the most highly reliable—eventually fail. Most manufacturers provide a Mean Time Between Failure (MTBF) rating for their equipment as a reassurance of how reliable their products are. Typically, MTBF ratings are in the tens of thousands of hours. Conceivably, this could translate into years of trouble-free service. Unfortunately, these ratings are statistically derived. The actual time between failures of any given device depends greatly on a number of factors. These factors include:

- Ambient temperature ranges of its operating environment
- The cleanliness of its commercial electric power
- How well it is handled before, and during, operation

In other words, your actual mileage *will* vary! Monitoring and tracking up-time of individual components enable you to demonstrate to your user community how well you are satisfying their requirements for the network's availability.

Trends in component up-time data can also be followed over time to identify potentially problematic components in your network infrastructure. Such trends can provide information about the general reliability of a given type or brand of hardware, which then can be used to identify individual components that may be at risk of failure.

NOTE

The term *availability* is sometimes used to generically describe aggregate network up-time. It is not, however, a good metric. In theory, network availability provides a quantified synopsis of the network's readiness. In practice, "availability" is so nebulous as to be almost meaningless. To illustrate this point, if a router at a premises location fails, the entire network is unavailable to the users at that location. The network, however, is available to users at every other location. They are not able to access hosts at the impacted location, but are not impeded from accessing every other host in the network. The extent to which the network is available varies greatly by location and by usage requirements. Thus, quantifying network availability can be more onerous than it is valuable.

Traffic Volumes

One of the more important metrics for any WAN is the volume of traffic it is expected to support. Volume is almost always volatile; it varies with time, business cycles, seasons, and so on. In other words, you can count on traffic volumes' being anything but constant. Given this volatility, it is important to measure volumes in two different ways: maximum volumes and average volumes:

- The maximum volume that you expect the network to support is known as the *peak volume*. As its name implies, this is the greatest amount of traffic that you expect the network to have to support.
- *Average volumes* are the minimum traffic loads that you can reasonably expect during the course of a business day from any given work location.

Establishing these two traffic volumes is critical to the sizing of the WAN's transmission facilities, as well as its routers. For example, if you expect any given location to generate a traffic load of 100Kbps during the course of a business day, it is clear that a 56Kbps transmission facility is inadequate.

> **NOTE**
>
> If you use one of the more complex topologies described earlier in this chapter, you need to identify the aggregate traffic patterns and volumes that are going to be placed across your network's backbone routers and transmission facilities.

Delay

Delay is one of the more common metrics that can be used to measure network performance. Delay is the time that elapses between two events. In data communications, these two events are typically the transmission and reception of data. Thus, delay is the total amount of time that is required by the network to transport a packet from its point of origin to its destination. Given this definition, delay is an aggregate phenomenon, with many potential causes. Three of the more common causes include:

■ Propagation delays: This term refers to the cumulative amount of time that is required to transmit, or *propagate*, the data across each transmission facility in the network path that it must take. The size and quantity of each transmission facility in the network path directly contribute to the aggregate forwarding delay of any given transmission. An additional contributor to propagation delay is traffic volume. The more traffic that is flowing across a given facility, the less bandwidth is available for new transmissions. Propagation delays are indigenous to terrestrial circuits, regardless of whether they traverse glass or copper media.

■ Satellite uplink/downlink delays: Some transmission facilities are satellite based. They require the signal to be transmitted up to the satellite and back down from the satellite. Due to the potentially great distances between the terrestrial transmission facilities and the satellite, these delays can be quite noticeable.

■ Forwarding delays: The forwarding delay in a network is the cumulative amount of time that each physical device needs to receive, buffer, process, and forward data. The actual forwarding delay of any given device may vary over time. Individual devices that are operating at or near capacity ordinarily experience a greater forwarding delay than comparable devices that are lightly utilized. Additionally, forwarding delays can be exacerbated by heavy traffic or error conditions in the network. Forwarding delays are frequently identified as *latency* in individual components.

Resource Utilization

The degree to which the various physical resources of the WAN are being used is a good indicator of how well, or how poorly, the WAN is performing relative to the performance requirements. Two main categories of resource utilization rates should be monitored carefully, as follows:

■ Router CPU and memory utilization rates

■ Transmission facility utilization rates

Router Resources

Routers are among the most vital components of any WAN. Unlike the transmission facilities, they are outside the purview of the telecommunications carrier. Thus, they are distinctly the responsibility of the customer. Fortunately, a router is an intelligent device that contains its own CPU and memory. These physical resources are indispensable in the calculation of WAN routes and the forwarding of packets. They can also be used to monitor the performance of the router.

If either CPU or memory utilization rates approach 100%, performance suffers. Numerous conditions can result in either utilization rate temporarily spiking upward, with consequential performance degradation. One example might be a sudden increase in transmissions from the LAN to the WAN. LANs can operate at speeds up to 1Gbps, but usually only at 10, 16, or 100Mbps. Any of these speeds is a gross mismatch with the typical WAN transmission facility, which offers a paltry 1.544Mbps of bandwidth. This mismatch in bandwidth must be buffered by the router's memory. It doesn't take long for a router to become resource constricted, given a sustained period of heavy LAN transmissions.

If such situations are rarely experienced, they should be considered aberrations. Aberrations should be monitored, but they shouldn't drive physical upgrades. However, if these resource constrictions recur, or constitute a trend, something needs to be done. Usually, this requires an upgrade, to either the next larger router or an expansion of memory. If a router is chronically at or near 100% of capacity with its memory, it is time to purchase additional memory.

Responding to chronically high CPU utilization rates might not be as simple as a memory upgrade. There are really only two options for improving high CPU utilization rates:

■ Upgrade to a more powerful router.

■ Investigate the WAN's traffic patterns to see whether the load on the problematic router can be reduced.

Manipulating traffic patterns is really a viable option only in larger WANs with complex topologies that afford route redundancy. Even so, if the router in question is a premises edge vehicle (as opposed to a backbone router), your only option is likely to be the fork-lift upgrade.

Transmission Facility Rates

Transmission facilities, too, can be monitored for utilization. Typically, this utilization rate is expressed in terms of the percentage of consumed bandwidth. For example, if you are using a T-1, a given sample might indicate that 30 percent of its 1.544Mbps of available bandwidth is currently being utilized.

These rates can be tricky to analyze and may be misleading. For example, it is not uncommon for network-management software packages to capture utilization data in time intervals. These can be one hour, five minutes, or just about any other interval. The sampling frequency, if set too coarsely, can miss short-duration fluctuations in bandwidth consumption. If the sampling is too frequent, you could find yourself mired in a meaningless morass of data points. The trick is finding the correct frequency that provides meaningful data about how the network is performing relative to the users' expectations.

Beyond merely selecting the sampling rate lies the issue of *sampling windows*. A sampling window is the timeframe within which samples are to be taken. Establishing a sampling window consists of establishing the frequency and duration of the sampling. The sampling window should be determined by the users' requirements for WAN availability. If the utilization samples are spread over a 24-hour day, and a 7-day week, but the users work only 10 hours per day, 5 days per week, the statistical data will not be indicative of how well the users' requirements are being met.

Utilization rates are a wonderful statistical tool for monitoring and measuring the status of transmission facilities. They are not, however, the only metric for assessing a network's performance. The network is successful only if it satisfies the users' requirements. Thus, a combination of performance metrics that provides a multifaceted, composite perspective is likely to provide a better assessment of the network's successfulness.

Costs of the WAN

Tempering any evaluation of these performance criteria is cost. The costs of owning and operating a WAN include the initial startup costs as well as the monthly, recurring expenses. Not surprisingly, the larger and more powerful network components are much more expensive than smaller, less robust components. Thus, designing a WAN becomes an economic exercise in which a careful balance of performance and cost is achieved.

Achieving this balance can be painful. No one wants to design a WAN that will disappoint the users with its performance, but no one wants to design a WAN that blows the budget, either! Fortunately, several truisms can help guide administrators as they choose the design of a WAN that satisfies existing requirements, provides flexibility for future growth, and doesn't exceed the budget, as follows:

- The capital investments in routers and other network hardware become a fixed part of the network. After they are placed into operation, the logistics of replacing them become quite complicated. Plus, depending upon your depreciation schedule for capital equipment, you might find yourself obligated to use them for five or more years! It might behoove you to purchase a larger but relatively unpopulated router. You can add hardware (memory, CPUs, and interfaces) in the future, as the need for them arises. This makes future expansion possible at modest incremental costs, and little (if any) operational downtime.

■ The transmission facilities are relatively easy to replace with other transmission facilities. They are an expense item, not a capital investment, so there is no depreciation expense to retire. They can be replaced with other facilities as often as your lease agreement with the carrier permits. Thus, you might want to explore your options for meeting performance requirements with the various available transmission facilities and technologies.

Applying the wisdom behind these truisms can help you meet your users' present and future expected requirements—all within the constraints of your budget.

Summary

Wide area networks are complex structures that don't necessarily adhere to any published or open standard. Designing, building, and operating a WAN that consistently satisfies your users' requirements can be a Herculean task. Success lies in understanding the capabilities, limitations, and costs of the various WAN component technologies. This understanding forms the context for their integration. The objective is to build a network in which each component technology is well matched with the performance capabilities of each other component, and balanced against any budgetary constraints.

Chapter 14, "Leased Lines," builds upon your command of wide area networks by examining leased lines in much more detail.

Leased Lines

by Mark A. Sportack

IN THIS CHAPTER

CHAPTER 14

WANs are usually constructed from digital telecommunications facilities that are leased from a telecommunications carrier. These facilities offer customers dedicated bandwidth that can span up to almost 45Mbps. Such transmission facilities are known as *leased lines*. They are an integral part of every WAN, yet remain poorly understood. Their modular connectors hide a vast, complex telecommunications infrastructure, as well as a series of standards.

This telecommunications infrastructure and the standards that support it are given little notice outside of the carriers themselves. Ordinarily, this wouldn't be a problem, but leased lines have evolved into an integral component of today's wide area networks. As such, they should be understood much better than they are today.

This chapter examines the standards that support leased lines in both North America and Europe, as well as some of their fundamental mechanics. It demystifies leased lines and enables you to better design, operate, and troubleshoot WANs.

Overview of Leased Lines

Although leased lines have come to be widely regarded as a digital transmission facility for data networks, they originally were designed as digital voice communications facilities. Conversion of voice signals to digital format offered numerous advantages. These advantages included enhanced regeneration of attenuated signals and more efficient aggregation of multiple streams of data onto a common transmission media. This aggregation is known as *multiplexing*.

Over time, three factors combined to force a radical shift in the way that digital leased lines were used. These three factors are as follows:

- The increased base of digital telecommunications equipment in the carriers' infrastructure
- Development of the support mechanisms for digital telephony
- The emergence of a customer need for high capacity data communications

It was with great reluctance that carriers began leasing these lines to their customers for concentrated voice communications requirements such as call centers or large office buildings with their own private branch exchange (PBX). As distributed networking technologies matured, leased lines began to prove their worth as data transmission facilities. The leap from digitized voice to digitized data was natural; binary digits are binary digits regardless of what they represent. Leased lines have proven so successful as data communications vehicles that their original purpose has been all but lost to historical trivia.

Multiplexing Techniques

Leased lines were originally designed to aggregate multiple voice channels onto a single higher-capacity transmission facility. This function required the development of a mechanism that takes multiple incoming communications streams, regulates their transmission over a common transmission facility, and de-aggregates them back into their individual components for subsequent delivery to their individual destinations. Multiplexing enabled a more efficient intermediary switching of calls. Multiplexing can be done in a couple of ways:

- By dividing the available bandwidth into timed sections (called *time division* multiplexing)
- By dividing the available bandwidth into sub-frequency bands (called *frequency division* multiplexing)

> **NOTE**
>
> Other multiplexing techniques exist, including spectrum division multiplexing, but time- and frequency-based techniques are the most pertinent to this examination of leased lines.

Each of these multiplexing methods is discussed in more detail in the following sections.

Time Division Multiplexing

Time Division Multiplexing (TDM) features the division of the available bandwidth into time slices. A communicating device can monopolize the entire bandwidth for the duration of a time slice. These slices are then shared according to a predetermined algorithm. To give you an appreciation for the complexity of a TDM system, the time slice on a T-1 (a 1.544Mbps leased line) is 125 microseconds.

TDM is inherently efficient because a transmitting station is permitted the use of the entire band. If a station doesn't need to transmit, its time slice is allocated to another station that does. In this manner, the use of the transmission facility's available bandwidth is maximized.

TDM does, however, introduce overhead to maintain synchronization. If synchronization is lost, the transmitted data becomes corrupted. There are two main methods for synchronizing transmission over TDM facilities, as follows:

- Adding bits
- Adding channels

Both methods are valid and deployed in today's leased lines. The European digital signaling standard has implemented the channel-adding technique, whereas North America uses added bits.

Frequency Division Multiplexing

The alternative to TDM is Frequency Division Multiplexing (FDM). FDM is a technique that subdivides the available bandwidth into bands of subfrequencies. Each of these subfrequency bands is dedicated to a specific user or device. Each remains permanently dedicated and, consequently, unavailable for use by other devices even when it is idle! This inherent inefficiency has resulted in the widespread preference for TDM (time division multiplexing) over FDM in telecommunications carriers' systems.

14

LEASED LINES

Benefits and Drawbacks of Leased Lines

One of the more prevalent—but misleading—monikers of leased lines is *point-to-point private line*. From a strictly functional perspective, leased lines offer a dedicated connection between two locations, with minimal communications overheads or framing. However, they do not form a direct connection between two points.

> **NOTE**
>
> At least one telecommunications carrier offered a low-cost alternative to leased lines that was truly a direct, point-to-point connection. This service cost more to engineer and install, but cost much less on a monthly recurring basis than a conventional leased line. The trade-off with the low cost of this facility was the loss of remote trouble analysis capabilities. Each and every trouble call resulted in the dispatch of a technician.

As illustrated in Figure 14.1, this type of dedicated line can take a circuitous path through telecommunications carriers' switching centers. The terrestrial circuit mileage is always greater than the geographic mileage separating the two ends of the circuit because the circuit must traverse the telecommunications carrier's transmission infrastructure.

FIGURE 14.1.

Leased lines are not direct lines.

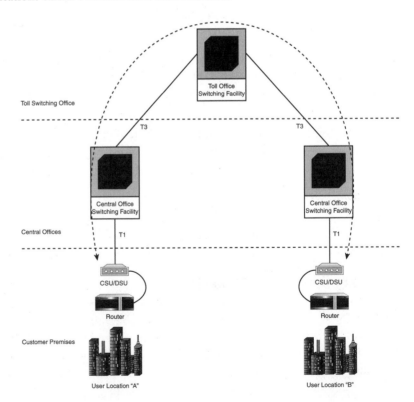

This may seem like a waste of resources. In fact, one could argue that this is much less efficient than running direct connections between pairs of customer locations. The inefficiencies, however, are more than offset by the extensibility of this method of service provisioning. Point-to-point runs of a transmission media become worthless as soon as the two locations at either end of that point-to-point run no longer need to communicate with each other.

As shown previously in Figure 14.1, the switching centers function much as the Main Distribution Frame (MDF) and Intermediate Distribution Frame (IDF) in a building's wire distribution system. The MDF and IDFs provide an aggregation point for the wire that stretches throughout the entire building. This enables virtually every location within a building to share a common set of voice and data communications equipment by providing a flexible, reusable wire distribution system.

Connecting all customer locations back to the telecommunications carrier's nearest switching center results in a re-usable infrastructure. Regardless of changes in communications requirements or aggregate traffic patterns, the connection between the central office and the customer's location remains essential.

An additional benefit of interconnecting locations via central offices is the enabling of remote diagnostics. If a telecommunications carrier were to string cabling directly between two customer locations, it would have to dispatch a technician to perform even rudimentary trouble analysis when the service failed. By having the carriers' switching center(s) in the middle of a leased line, the telecommunications carriers can perform loopback and other diagnostic tests across the entire circuit from the comfort of the switching center. This remote diagnostic capability saves time and money in the isolation of a failure in the network.

To perform remote diagnostics, the telecommunications carrier tries to communicate with the CPE at both ends of the circuit, as illustrated in Figure 14.2.

If the carrier can successfully communicate with both sets of CPE (usually a CSU/DSU), it is relatively safe to assume that the problem does not exist within the leased line. If the carrier cannot communicate with one of the CSU/DSUs, the problem then is isolated to just one segment of the transmission facility. In either case, the time and cost required to troubleshoot are greatly reduced by the remote diagnostics.

Topology of Leased Lines

The actual topology of a leased line can be surprisingly convoluted. Figures 14.1 and 14.2 presented intentionally simplified perspectives of a leased line. In reality, virtually all but the shortest of leased lines requires the building of a circuit through two or more switching centers. The exact shape of the leased line is directly dependent upon both geography and the number of carriers that must be involved. Fortunately, the exact topology of a leased line is seldom of any consequence outside the carriers' domain.

Two necessary prerequisites to understanding the potential topology of a leased line are a familiarity with switching centers and a command of the post-divestiture telephony infrastructure, both covered in the following sections.

FIGURE 14.2.
Leased lines are designed to support remote diagnostics.

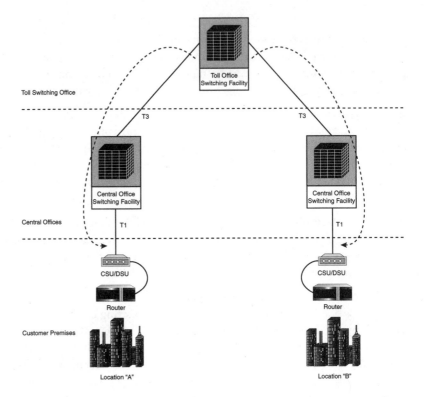

Switching Centers

Many data communications concepts and terms become muddled over time and through mis-use and incomplete understanding. The term *central office* (CO) is no exception. It has become overused and now generically describes telecommunications carriers' switching facilities. In reality, a central office (also known as *end office*) is the bottom layer in a multi-tiered switching topology that constitutes the commercial telephony infrastructure. It is through this bottom layer that the customer premise equipment (CPE) is physically interconnected to the switched telecommunications infrastructure of the carriers.

As such, it is the layer most visible to consumers and data communications personnel employed outside the telecommunications industry. Thus, it is not surprising to find the term "central office" applied generically to all telecommunications switching centers.

The other four layers provide route redundancy in a very large and complex hybrid topology. The five switching layers are as follows:

- Regional switching center
- Sectional switching center
- Primary switching center

- Toll switching center
- Central office

These are numbered according to their class. Before the divestiture of the Bell System on January 1 of 1984, telephone communications were provided by the Class 5 switching centers: the central offices. Such calls were essentially toll-free because the Bell System subsidized the costs of local calls with the revenue generated by long distance calls. Today, this hierarchical model is more of a theoretical target than a rigidly adhered-to service architecture.

The toll switching centers were responsible for interconnecting the central offices that were in close geographic proximity to each other. Thus, local calls could be made despite the origination and destination points being connected to different central offices. The toll switching centers also provided connectivity to the toll-based, or long distance, portion of the telecommunications infrastructure.

The top three layers represented different levels of geographic aggregation for toll calls. The regional switching centers were the backbone of the entire network; there was one in each region of the country, and they were all interconnected. The sectional and primary switching centers were lower levels of geographic aggregation. This complex architecture was designed to provide the most efficient path through the network for any given pair of endpoints. Its size and complexity also provided route redundancy that could mitigate the impacts of congestion or a failure somewhere in the network.

Approximately 20,000 switching centers of all varieties are in the United States. A topologically correct illustration is not practical. It is equally impractical to attempt to illustrate topologically accurate maps of leased lines that are constructed through these switching centers.

These five basic classes of switching centers were designed to satisfy the needs for call aggregation, simplification of billing data, and route redundancy in the pre-divestiture days of telecommunications in North America. Although the architecture proved highly successful in these respects, divestiture forced dramatic changes.

The Post-Divestiture Telephony Infrastructure

Divestiture is the name given to the complex legal processes that broke up the Bell System into fully separate entities. Severe restrictions are now placed on each entity for the sake of stimulating competition and technological innovation. Included in these restrictions are the following:

- Restrictions on the geographic areas in which each entity can operate
- Restrictions on the types of service that each new entity can provide

Together, these two sets of restrictions have effectively compartmentalized the telecommunications infrastructure and created some new terms and concepts. The most obvious compartmentalization is between local and long distance communications. Carriers that provided local connectivity have become known as *Local Exchange Carriers* (LECs). LECs are barred from providing long distance communications. Their domains are known as Local Access and Transport Areas (LATAs).

Carriers such as AT&T that were limited to long distance communications became known as *interexchange carriers* (IXCs). This name is derived from the pre-divestiture term "exchange," which refers to a toll-free area. In the post-divestiture environment, all traffic between exchanges, or LATAs, must be carried by an IXC.

LECs are required, by law, to provide all IXCs with equal access to their customer bases. This concept, known as "equal access," has necessitated the development of *points of presence* (POPs). A POP is some form of IXC presence within an LEC-owned switching center. POPs ensure that all inter-LATA traffic is carried by an IXC. Any communications traffic that is addressed to an endpoint in a different LATA must be routed to an IXC's POP, even if both the origination and destination endpoints reside within LATAs operated by a single LEC. In this manner, the local and long distance communications networks remain completely separated, with POPs serving as the boundary between them.

The POP itself can be as simple as a wire or fiber optic patch panel that connects the LEC's switching facilities to the IXC's switching facilities, or it can be a telecommunications switch.

The net result of divestiture was that the same five classes of switching remain, but are now a patchwork of privately owned networks operated by the various local and interexchange carriers. This patchwork is simultaneously collaborative and competitive in nature. This telephony infrastructure is used to support all types of telephonic connections in the United States, including leased lines.

Digital Signal Standards

Much as any other standard networking technology, leased lines feature standardized transmission schemes. Such schemes define transmission rates and media types, as well as framing formats and multiplexing methodologies.

There are many such schemes and they vary by geography and technology. Some of the more commonly encountered standards include:

- ANSI's Digital Signaling Hierarchy
- ITU's Digital Signaling Hierarchy
- SONET's Optical Carrier System
- SONET's Synchronous Transport Signal system

These are examined in the remainder of this section.

ANSI's Digital Signal Hierarchy

The *American National Standards Institute* (ANSI) set the standards for digital signal transmission during the early 1980s. This family of standards became known as the *Digital Signal*

Hierarchy (DSH). This hierarchy consists of five specifications, numbered DS-0 through DS-4. These specifications, their corresponding bandwidths, and the number of supported voice channels are presented in Table 14.1.

Table 14.1. ANSI's digital signal standards.

Digital Signal Standard	Bandwidth	Number of Voice Channels
DS-0	64Kbps	1
DS-1	1.544Mbps	24
DS-1C	3.152Mbps	48
DS-2	6.312Mbps	96
DS-3	44.736Mbps	672
DS-4	274.176Mbps	4032

NOTE

DS-0 defines the minimum amount of bandwidth required to transport digitized voice. Given that voice communication typically occurs using an 8KHz circuit, and digitizing it requires an eight-fold increase in bandwidth, the DS-0 band was defined at 64Kbps. It is not, however, the basic building block of leased lines. That honor goes to the DS-1 specification. DS-0 describes the voice channels that are carved from the other digital signaling specifications.

ANSI's DS standards have been implemented in a telephony carrier system that is called the *T-carrier system*. There is a direct, one-to-one correlation between T-carrier circuits and their DS namesakes. For example, the DS-1 standard is embodied in the T-1 transmission facility. T-3 is the physical implementation of the DS-3. For more information on the T-carrier system, refer to the section entitled "The T-Carrier System" later in this chapter.

After even a cursory glance through Table 14.1 you can probably recognize at least one of the standards. The T-1 has become so prevalent in networking that almost every network-aware technical person recognizes the 1.544Mbps bandwidth and associates it with that transmission facility. Some people might even recognize the 44.736Mbps of the T-3. The other standards might not be as readily recognized.

The DS-1C, from a functional perspective, is two DS-1s integrated into a common transmission facility. The DS-2 and DS-4 standards have never achieved widespread utilization. This is primarily due to their cost versus performance ratios. DS-3 service is also expensive, but offers a better combination of price and bandwidth than its alternatives.

Today, virtually every situation that requires bandwidth in excess of the DS-3 is satisfied with SONET technology (covered in a following section). Thus, the T-carrier system is used only for T-1, fractional T-1, and T-3 services. The remaining T-*n* specifications have fallen into disuse.

ITU's Digital Signal Hierarchy

The Digital Signal Hierarchy presented in Table 14.1 was standardized by ANSI. ANSI, an American standards body, doesn't necessarily receive worldwide acceptance of its standards work. For example, in Europe, the International Telecommunications Union (ITU—formerly CCITT) created its own family of standards for digital signaling. These standards were named after the committee that recommended them to the ITU; the Conference of European Posts and Telecommunications Administration (CEPT). These CEPT standards are listed in Table 14.2.

Table 14.2. ITU's digital signal standards.

Digital Signal Standard	Bandwidth	Number of Voice Channels
CEPT-1	2.048Mbps	30
CEPT-2	8.448Mbps	120
CEPT-3	34.368Mbps	480
CEPT-4	139.264Mbps	1920
CEPT-5	565.148Mbps	7680

Although the ITU standards use the same basic channel as the 64Kbps DS-0, their aggregations are very different. Thus, the European version of a T-1 is known as the E-1, and it supports 2.048Mbps, compared to the T-1's 1.544Mbps. Internetworking between Europe and North America presents the challenge of mismatched standards, and usually results in unusable channels.

> **NOTE**
>
> If you perform the mathematics, you can see that the CEPT-1 standard (implemented in the European E-1 transmission facility) actually contains enough bandwidth for 32 channels of 64Kbps each. The CEPT-1 and consequently the E-1 circuit can support a maximum of 30 usable channels. The remaining two are reserved for synchronization and signaling. This differs from ANSI's approach in its DS specifications. ANSI imposes framing and timing within each channel, thereby reducing available bandwidth from the stated transmission rate.

SONET's Carrier Systems

SONET is an acronym that stands for Synchronous Optical NETwork. It is basically a series of optically-based transmission systems. It is a highly specialized technology set that was designed expressly for use by telecommunications carriers. It was intended to provide interoperability between switching systems made by different manufacturers, as well as to buffer the disparities in capacity and transmission rates of those myriad systems.

To fulfill this role, physical interfaces, framing conventions, and two families of signaling standards were developed. These two families range from 51.84Mbps to 2.48Gbps.

> **NOTE**
>
> SONET is an ANSI standard that has been embraced, but not wholly adopted, by the ITU. The ITU's version varies subtly, but in significant ways, and is known as the Synchronous Digital Hierarchy (SDH). The basic rate of transmission in SDH is 155.52Mbps, unlike the 51.84Mbps basic rate of SONET.
>
> Another fairly minor difference is that SDH's copper-based transmission standards are known as Synchronous Transport Modules (STMs) instead of Synchronous Transport Signals (STSs).

SONET supports two transmission systems, both discussed in the following sections:

- The Optical Carrier (OC) system
- The Synchronous Transport Signal (STS) system

Optical Carrier System

One last series of standards that warrants examination is the Optical Carrier (OC) system and its copper-based twin, the Synchronous Transport Signal (STS) system. Table 14.3 presents the OC standards, their bandwidth, and the number of DS-0 and DS-1 channels that each supports.

Table 14.3. Optical Carrier Bandwidths.

Optical Carrier Line	Bandwidth	DS0 Channels	DS1 Channels
OC-1	51.84Mbps	672	28
OC-3	155.52Mbps	2016	84
OC-9	466.56Mbps	6048	252
OC-12	622.08Mbps	8064	336
OC-18	933.12Mbps	12096	504

continues

14

LEASED LINES

Table 14.3. continued

Optical Carrier Line	Bandwidth	DS0 Channels	DS1 Channels
OC-24	1.244Gbps	16128	672
OC-36	1.866Gbps	24192	1008
OC-48	2.488Gbps	32256	1344

This table, in theory, can be expanded nearly infinitely by continuing to multiply the basic OC-1. As optical signaling technology continues to improve, it is reasonable to expect greater multiples of the OC-1 rate to become standardized. In fact, the technology exists to transmit at an OC-192 rate! It is also likely that these larger multiples will be retrofitted into the SONET and/or SDH standards.

Synchronous Transport Signal System

SONET's OC rates can also be implemented over an electrical signaling system using copper wiring. These electrical rates are indicated with an STS designation (Synchronous Transport Signal) rather than the familiar OC designation. Aside from this physical difference, there is a one-to-one correlation between the two standards. In other words, STS-1 is directly equivalent to OC-1; STS-3 equals the OC-3 rate of 155.52Mbps; and so forth.

It is important to note that the STS-*n* standards span up to STS-48, which yields 2.488Gbps of bandwidth. Providing this bandwidth to electrical signals over copper presents some significant technical challenges. For that matter, driving a copper wire at rates in excess of 155.52Mbps becomes problematic over distances greater than 100 meters. Consequently, only STS-1 and STS-3 are actually defined and usable. The remainder are little more than theoretical constructs.

The T-Carrier System

The digital signaling standards listed in Table 14.1 are implemented through a physical carrier system. The most prevalent carrier system in North America is the T-carrier system. The leased lines delivered by this carrier system are prefaced with the letter "T." For example, a leased line delivered by T-carrier that conforms to the DS-1 standard is known as a T-1. This important distinction is frequently lost on even the most technical people! Consequently, the terms DS-*n* and T-*n* (where *n* identifies a specific number) are often incorrectly used interchangeably. They are *not* interchangeable. DS-*n* identifies a standard. T-*n* identifies a standards-compliant circuit.

The T-carrier system was originally designed to provide multiplexed voice communications over a single transmission facility. These facilities were used to transport calls between the various switching centers. Twenty-four calls could be carried on a single T-1 circuit. Because the calls were in digital form, they could be amplified and regenerated en route to their destination. Thus, digitized voice signals were inherently more clear than analog voice communications, which couldn't be regenerated.

Digitization of voice signals, however, presented some technical challenges. The T-carrier system implemented several improvements over the earlier carrier systems. These improvements were specifically designed to improve the quality of digitized voice transmission. In effect, these improvements made the T-carrier system a better transport mechanism for digitized transmissions, without biasing towards voice or data. Specific improvements were made in line encoding techniques and framing formats.

T-Carrier Services

As described earlier in this chapter, in the section titled "ANSI's Digital Signal Hierarchy," only two of the DS standards are available as commercial services. These are the T-3 and the T-1. A third service is also available: *Fractional T-1*. Fractional T-1, however, is a subrated variant of the DS-1 specification and not a productized form of the DS-0 specification.

The T-3 transmission facility provides 44.736Mbps of bandwidth. This bandwidth can be channelized into 672 separate channels of 64Kbps each or 28 T-1 equivalent channels. T-3s tend to be very expensive, especially as geographic distances increase. For any networking application that requires more bandwidth than a couple T-1s can provide, a T-3 may actually prove to be the more economical solution.

The T-1 transmission facility is the foundation of the T-carrier system. This basic service provides customers with 1.544Mbps of gross bandwidth. This can be channelized into as many as 24 channels of 64Kbps each, or left whole for high-bandwidth networking applications.

Networks that either can't afford the cost of a full T-1 or don't need its bandwidth may find the Fractional T-1 service more attractive. Fractional T-1 is actually constructed from a T-1 circuit. Bandwidth on that circuit is fractionalized using a device known as a *channel bank*. The subcircuit is usually a 56Kbps circuit, but can be as small as 9.6Kbps. These subrate channels can then be delivered to different customers.

Subrating a T-1 creates the need for maintaining timing across each subchannel. One technique is *bit robbing*. Bit robbing maintains the synchronicity of a channel by appropriating the least significant bit of every eighth frame in the stream for use as a pulse. Robbing these bits, in effect, makes the entire frame that was robbed unusable. Thus, every eighth 8-bit frame is unusable. This effectively reduces the bandwidth available on a 64Kbps DS-0 channel to only 56Kbps. Clear-channel 64Kbps facilities may be ordered from your carrier. These facilities are nothing more than a DS-0 channel from a T-1, without its own timing mechanism.

> **NOTE**
>
> Frames, in this context, differ substantially from the highly developed and feature-rich frames used in LANs. DS frames are minimalist structures. Their functionality is limited to the synchronization of the transmission, and in some instances, error detection and network monitoring. As such, a digital signal frame is usually nothing more than a single bit inserted at fixed intervals in a bit stream.

Line Encoding

Being the first digital system, the T-carrier system needed a completely new line encoding technique. One of the challenges in developing this encoding technique was maintaining the synchronization of the line with an absolute minimum amount of overhead.

Unipolar Binary Encoding

The simplest form of binary encoding is *unipolar*. In other words, the signal is either on (positive electrical charge) or off (no charge). Although it is simple, the fatal disadvantage is that a series of either consecutive ones or consecutive zeroes appears as a flat line. This is illustrated in Figure 14.3.

FIGURE 14.3.
Unipolar encoding of binary data.

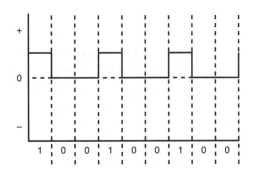

Given the normal attenuation of a signal over distance, it would be relatively easy for the timing, or bit count, to become corrupt. This would adversely affect the data that was encoded. Thus, unipolar encoding was not well suited for long-distance transmissions.

Bipolar Binary Encoding

The alternative to unipolar encoding is bipolar encoding. Bipolar, as its name implies, features the use of both poles of the electric signal. By using both positive and negative polarity, a transition through zero (no voltage) is necessary between digits. This transition, generically speaking, is known as a *return to zero*. It provides an innate boundary between the transmitted bits.

The T-carrier system uses a variety of bipolar encoding called *alternate mark inversion* (AMI). AMI uses both poles to represent a binary "one," and no voltage to represent a "zero." Consecutive ones are represented by alternating poles, and zeroes are always represented by no voltage. The same binary stream illustrated in unipolarity in Figure 14.3 is presented in bipolar encoding in Figure 14.4.

Figure 14.4.

Bipolar encoding of binary data.

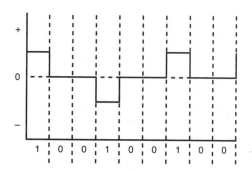

Although this solved the boundary issue between consecutive ones, it left the T-carrier system vulnerable to loss of timing due to a consecutive string of zeroes. To counter this, the T-carrier system implemented a protocol known as the *Ones Density Rule*. This rule limits the number of consecutively transmitted zeroes to fifteen. To enforce this rule, a technique was developed that substituted eight consecutive zeroes with a predetermined pattern. This pattern is called a *word*. This technique was saddled with the rather ungainly name of *Bipolar Eight Zero Substitution*, or *B8ZS*.

Of course, reserving any random string of eight bits for use as a zero substitution string creates the potential for that string to occur randomly as part of the bit stream. That would inadvertently result in the translation of eight legitimate bits of data into zeroes. Thus, to differentiate between the fictional word for the eight zeroes and legitimate strings of data, the bipolar variation of transmitted ones has to be violated. To signal the start of the fictional word for eight zeroes, two positive-voltage ones would be transmitted. This is illustrated in Figure 14.5.

Figure 14.5.

Bipolar consistency signals the start of the fictional word for eight zeroes.

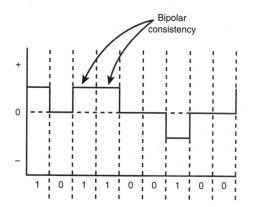

B8ZS is the timing method used on T-1s. It is implemented by the CSU/DSUs at each end of the leased line.

Framing Formats

The T-carrier system recognizes three distinct forms of framing. They are as follows:

- D-4 format
- Extended superframe (ESF) format
- M1-3 format

D-4 Format

The most common frame for T-1 circuits is the D-4, named for the D-4 channel banks that implemented it. This technique places a timing bit before each 24 octets of data. If 24 seems a familiar number, it is because that's the number of 8-bit channels supported by a T-1. Thus, one D-4 frame consists of the following:

- A 12-bit frame alignment signal
- A 1-bit timing signal
- A 192-bit data field

The 192-bit data field is constructed of one octet from each of the T-1's channels. If you do the math, you can see that the D-4 frame adds up to 205 bits. The D-4 frame, however, is universally accepted as being only 193 bits long. The discrepancy arises from the fact that the alignment signal, much like Ethernet's preamble, is not considered a part of the frame.

Extended Superframe Format

AT&T, developer of many of North America's telephony technologies and standards, developed the extended superframe (ESF) in the early 1980s. The ESF was implemented in the D-5 channel banks, successor to the time-honored D-4.

The ESF was designed to further improve the operational efficiency of T-1 transmission facilities. The essence of this technique is a reduction in the number of framing bits used by the D-4 framing method. Whereas D-4 requires 24 timing bits for 24 D-4 frames, the ESF needs only six. Every fourth 193-bit frame has a timing bit. Six of the other bits are used for error correction and the remaining 12 are used for nonintrusive monitoring of the network. This monitoring is nonintrusive in that it does not add any overheads to the bit stream.

M1-3 Format

T-3s use a completely different framing technique called *M1-3 framing*. This naming convention is derived from its functionality: it multiplexes DS-1 channels onto a DS-3. Mathematically, 28 DS-1 channels equal 43.232Mbps of aggregate bandwidth. This fits nicely onto the 44.736Mbps available with DS-3, plus a surplus for use in frame alignment, error detection, and timing.

NOTE

M1-3 is actually just one of a family of three multiplexed interface standards that are known collectively as MX-3. The other two are the MC-3 and the M2-3.

The MC-3 multiplexes 14 DS-1Cs onto one DS-3. The M2-3, as its name also implies, multiplexes seven DS-2s to one DS-3. Given that the DS-1C and the DS-2 are functionally obsolete, their multiplexed interfaces have suffered a similar fate.

M1-3 features a 4,760-bit frame, of which 4,704 bits are dedicated to carrying data. The remaining 56 bits are used for error correction and timing.

Summary

Leased lines are a vital component of today's WANs, but are complex and poorly understood. As with any network technology, they have their own Physical Layer technologies and their own Data Link Layer protocols and framing structures. By understanding these aspects of leased lines and their equally complex topologies, one can become more adept at designing, building, operating, and troubleshooting WANs.

Circuit Switched Transmission Facilities

by Tony Northrup

IN THIS CHAPTER

Almost everyone in the United States works with Circuit Switched Transmission Facilities every day. Yet most people are not aware of their presence. By their very nature, circuit switched networks transmit data reliably and consistently. This high level of reliability has caused the circuit switched network to be used by popular technologies such as Frame Relay and ATM.

The most widely used network in the world, the Public Switched Telephone Network, is based on the idea that conversations across a network should have reserved bandwidth and must follow the same path until the connection is broken. Although this may not be the best method to use for all types of data, it is extremely well suited to the multimedia, real-time requirements of voice, video, and electronic conferencing. As these technologies become more popular in modern networks, so will circuit switched networking.

Switched 56

Switched 56 is generally the least expensive Wide Area Network digital service. It operates at 56Kbps. Switched 56 is provided via standard twisted-pair wiring. Similar to the PSTN (Public Switched Telephone Network), connections are made by specifying a 7-digit telephone number and connecting to another switched 56 circuit or ISDN (Integrated Services Digital Network) line.

A major advantage of switched 56 is that connections are active only when needed and billing is based on usage. In fact, it is common practice for providers to charge the same price for a switched 56 circuit as for a standard voice circuit. Therefore, if local voice calls are free in your service area, switched 56 connections may also be free.

The downside of switched 56 is that it is not easily upgradable; if you need to move to a faster connection, you have to upgrade to a different technology. Another disadvantage of the switched 56 technology is the lack of availability. Today, most parts of the country cannot find a provider for switched 56 service.

Common Uses for Switched 56

Switched 56 is commonly used for low-bandwidth connections that do not need to remain online at all times. Switched 56 is also commonly used as a backup circuit to a leased line, as illustrated in Figure 15.1.

FIGURE 15.1.
Switched 56 as a backup connection to a leased line.

Another common use for switched 56 is *out-of-band* access. This term refers to an organization's connection to a network or server that is completely separate from the primary network interface. Take, for example, the common scenario of a corporate web server. The server typically has a direct connection to the Internet through a leased line, which the general public uses to access information. Administrators may want to access the server without passing authentication information over the public Internet, so they create an out-of-band connection with a switched 56 circuit, as illustrated in Figure 15.2. Using this circuit, they have access to the server on demand and are now entirely separated from any public network. This connection also acts as a backup in the event the primary interface fails.

FIGURE 15.2.

Switched 56 as an inexpensive out-of-band connection.

Public Internet · T1 · Web Server · Switched 56 · Administrator

Switched 56 Technologies

Different technologies are used for switched 56 connections. These technologies are defined in EIA/TIA-596. Only one is really popular.

This technology, named *switched 56 Service Type III*, was developed by Northern Telecom and works on standard telephone wire. This is a great benefit, because those deploying the technology may make use of an existing cable plant, significantly reducing the installation costs.

Data is transmitted across the wire at 64Kbps. This may come as a surprise, because the "56" in the name of the technology refers to the transmission speed. The remaining 8Kbps are used for call setup and signaling.

Frame Relay

Frame relay is a packet switched network commonly used as a WAN link to connect remote offices. Though it is packet switched, it emulates a circuit switched network through the use of Permanent Virtual Circuits (PVCs), which map a path through many switches.

Frame relay exists solely at the lowest two layers of the OSI model. Routers are used at each end of the link to connect the individual networks to the Frame Relay network. Distant offices pay for only a leased line to their provider, and trust the provider to carry the traffic between offices. Redundancy is provided for within the network, further reducing costs and administrative overhead for companies that purchase public Frame Relay services. The companies that purchase Frame Relay carrier services substantially reduce WAN overhead costs. Further, Frame Relay's reliability reduces costs associated with downtime.

Frame relay is commonly used as an upgrade to the outdated X.25. X.25 was designed for a period of networking that was based on analog transmission systems and copper wiring, and was therefore error-prone and unreliable. To combat these problems, X.25 included a great deal of error checking and protocols. Frame relay was designed for a new era of networking, based on digital transmissions and fiber media, sacrificing unnecessary error-checking overhead in favor of speed.

Another advantage of Frame Relay is that it combines many connections, or *virtual circuits*, over a single link such as a leased line.

In recent years, Frame Relay has been used more and more as a transport for legacy traffic, combining several separate leased lines into a single Frame Relay circuit. Even traditionally analog data such as voice is being carried, providing remote offices with a more economical alternative to long-distance charges.

Frame Relay Versus Leased Lines

Frame relay is commonly seen as a competitor of the more traditional leased line. Perhaps the largest factor driving the growth of Frame Relay is its rapid adoption in the place of leased lines from a telephone company.

Frame relay is generally a less expensive alternative to building a Wide Area Network. An organization that chooses leased lines is responsible for the high cost of each connection, one or many of which may span a very large distance. An organization that chooses to implement WAN networking over Frame Relay implements connections across the Frame Relay network, and is responsible for only a leased line from the organization to the cloud itself. This is an especially attractive option to organizations that are connecting over great distances, because Frame Relay does not charge based on the distance between end points. Typically, the breakeven point in leased line vs. Frame Relay pricing happens at between 10 and 20 miles. At less than 10 miles, it is usually less expensive to get a single leased line. At greater than 20 miles, Frame Relay is the more financially attractive option.

By connecting to a Frame Relay cloud, a physical organization can connect to several different partners with a single connection into the cloud, as shown in Figure 15.3. A value-added benefit to this type of architecture is the Internet gateway, a service offered within public Frame Relay clouds that lets customers with existing connections access the Internet, often with the added security of managed firewalls.

Provisioning a leased line from a telephone company to a new partner is an expensive, time-consuming process. Connecting to anyone within a Frame Relay network requires only configuring another SVC or PVC, thereby avoiding the cost and complication of bringing another leased line into a building, configuring a separate router, and maintaining the connection. This gives owners of Frame Relay connections greater flexibility and connectivity than owners of leased lines. The setup process is substantially faster, making companies better able to quickly meet changing business goals.

FIGURE 15.3.

*Comparing Frame
Relay to leased lines*

Leased lines require a separate physical connection for every data connection.

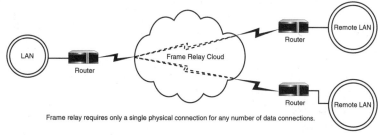

Frame relay requires only a single physical connection for any number of data connections.

Leased lines in themselves have no redundancy; a leased line is simply a single connection between any two points. If a line is damaged by construction, all connectivity through that link may be lost. To make matters worse, telephone companies often make mistakes or have equipment failures that bring circuits down for no good reason. Frame relay does not suffer from this weakness because it is a switched network; if a link between two parts of the network is lost, traffic is simply rerouted with a short delay. If a switch within the cloud stops functioning properly, the other switches detect the problem and begin routing frames through an alternate path. The inherent redundancy of a Frame Relay cloud makes it a more reliable service than leased lines.

Leased lines have guaranteed bandwidth through a process called "time-division multiplexing." Time-division multiplexing offers a slice of a large network link to a particular customer, and this slice is always the same. For example, a T1 circuit always offers 1.54Mbps of carrying capacity. This is an advantage because it simplifies planning, but it is a disadvantage because the bandwidth is always committed, regardless of whether it is used. Further, it does not have the capacity to grow as more bandwidth is required or at times of peak demand. Billing is less than efficient because an organization is charged for the entire bandwidth of the circuit, regardless of how much is used or needed.

Frame relay overcomes these limitations by using statistical multiplexing. Figure 15.4 compares time division multiplexing to statistical multiplexing. Statistical multiplexing enables Frame Relay to not commit all required bandwidth at the beginning of the connection. Although it does offer a CIR (Committed Information Rate) property, guaranteeing companies a particular amount of capacity, it also allows for increased bandwidth at times of higher utilization while not charging for it when it is not in use. Billing is based on traffic, so companies that use less pay less and those that need more have the option to use it.

Figure 15.4.

Time-division multiplexing compared to statistical multiplexing.

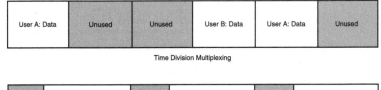

User A: Data	Unused	Unused	User B: Data	User A: Data	Unused

Time Division Multiplexing

Unused	User A: Data	Unused	User B: Data	Unused	User B: Data

Statistical Multiplexing

The differences in how the two offerings provide bandwidth substantially changes the engineering methods involved. Leased lines must be designed around peak traffic needs, which are difficult to anticipate and often change dramatically as a company grows. Frame relay networks, because of CIR and burst capabilities, are designed to meet average traffic needs. These needs are more predictable, and because of the burst capability, less rigid.

Finally, the Frame Relay cloud is more efficient for the provider to offer to customers because it permits shared bandwidth. The provider needs to guarantee that it has enough bandwidth to enable each customer to utilize the full CIR, but bandwidth above that can be shared by many customers. In contrast, leased line providers (generally telephone companies) must have all the bandwidth each customer may ever use provisioned at all times. This gives leased line providers a much lower bandwidth utilization than Frame Relay providers. Figure 15.5 provides an in-depth description of the differences between Frame Relay and leased lines.

Figure 15.5.

A line-by-line comparison of leased lines to Frame Relay.

Leased Lines	Frame Relay
Full mesh architecture requires $n*(n-1)/2$ physical circuits	Full mesh architecture requires $n*(n-1)/2$ PVCs or SVCs, but only n physical circuits.
Difficult and expensive to add and remove.	Additions and removals require only adding a virtual circuit.
Less reliable, no redundancy	More reliable, much redundancy
Low bandwidth utilization	Higher bandwidth utilization

Extended Frame Relay

DLCIs (Data Link Connection Identifiers) only identify a connection between a router and the Frame Relay network; to identify a final destination, these DLCIs must be statically mapped to destinations within the Frame Relay cloud. There is no provision for an address resolution protocol to dynamically map DLCIs to Frame Relay destinations.

LMI (Local Management Interface) extensions make Frame Relay more robust and provide for many advanced features, not the least of which is *global addressing*. Global addressing makes DLCIs unique within a cloud, assigning a specific DLCI to a specific router. This makes the Frame Relay cloud more compatible with common higher-level protocols such as TCP/IP, which assign distinct IDs to each node.

Another useful LMI extension is multicasting. DLCIs in the range 1019 to 1022 are reserved as multicast addresses, known to the cloud as signifying multiple endpoints.

Permanent Virtual Circuits Versus Switched Virtual Circuits

Frame relay provides for two types of virtual circuits: Permanent Virtual Circuits (PVCs) and Switched Virtual Circuits (SVCs). A PVC is statically defined at the time of configuration and ensures the data between two points always follows the same path, making data transfer properties more consistent. SVCs calculate the path each time the connection is established, enabling the circuit to bypass failures within the network. Because a different path is used each time the connection is established, performance characteristics such as jitter and delay may vary. Figure 15.6 details the differences between SVCs and PVCs.

Some implementations of Frame Relay also support multicasting, which enables a server to transmit to many recipients simultaneously. The multicasting is provided for within the Frame Relay cloud; the switches inside the cloud guarantee that all recipients receive the packets to which they have subscribed, while making the most efficient use of bandwidth possible.

Frame relay is flexible, and can be used on links ranging from 56k to T3 (45Mbps) speeds. Further, public Frame Relays clouds generally charge based on traffic, avoiding unnecessary charges for less frequently used links.

The Format of Basic Frame Relay

The term "frame" refers to the groups of data that are switched within the network, because Frame Relay exists at only the first two levels of the OSI model and not at the Network Layer, where groups of data are called "packets."

Packets are passed from individual LANs into the Frame Relay network; Frame Relay, however, makes no distinction between different network layer protocols. Frame Relay handles these protocols transparently by encapsulating them within Frame Relay headers and footers. To be efficient, this encapsulation adds a total of only six bytes.

FIGURE 15.6.

A line-by-line comparison of PVCs and SVCs.

Permanent Virtual Circuits	Switched Virtual Circuits
Connection established only once	Connection established on a call-by-call basis
Frames always follow the same path	Frames may follow a different path for each call
Consistent and reliable	Less consistent and less reliable
Connection is always configured, whether or not it is in use	Connection is released when there is no more information to send
Permanent and guaranteed connections, but poor utilization	Better utilization of frame relay cloud
Difficult to manage	Easier to maintain
Requires a rigid network architecture and more connections for high levels of redundancy	Allows a flexible network architecture requiring fewer connections for highly-meshed networks
Pay a predictable, monthly charge	Pay based on usage: Bandwidth, call length, and number of frames sent.

Ten bits of these two bytes are dedicated to the Data Link Layer address, equivalent to a MAC address on an Ethernet network. This data link address is called the Data Link Connection Identifier, or DLCI for short. Rather than simply identifying a destination, the routers use the DLCI to identify a circuit at each end of the network. It is important to note that either side of a PVC does not necessarily use the same DLCI number; DLCIs are significant only to a particular DTE/DCE (Data Terminal Equipment/Data Communications Equipment) pair. In this way, DLCIs are different from MAC addresses, which are unique universally. DLCIs have too small a range to be universally unique.

Of the remaining six bits in the address, three bits are used for flags that provide for congestion notification: One bit enables frames to be set to a lower priority; the remaining two are reserved for future use.

Realistically, each interface should be limited to between one and four dozen DLCIs.

Designing Frame Relay Networks

One of the advantages of Frame Relay networking is the adjustable, scalable bandwidth. When Frame Relay services are purchased, the provider specifies a Committed Information Rate (CIR). The CIR defines the guaranteed bandwidth between any two locations.

UNI Versus NNI

Two parts of the Frame Relay specification define protocols for User-to-Network Interface (UNI, pronounced "ew-nee") connections and Network-to-Network Interface (NNI, pronounced "nin-ee") connections. UNI was developed by ANSI and the International Telecommunications Union Telecommunication Standardization Sector (ITU-T) and provides specifications for a DTE to speak to a DCE, as illustrated in Figure 15.7. The scope of this standard is similar in function to the X.25 specifications. The UNI specifications are not unlike the United States Postal Service's specifications for addressing a letter: they describe a specific format for the end user to provide, but do not detail how the letter gets there after it is dropped in a mailbox. Instead, the postal service provides certain guarantees as to service, such as delivery time and reliability, and the person mailing the letter is left to trust the postal service to follow through.

FIGURE 15.7.

User-to-network interfaces connect the DTE to the DCE.

Frame relay works the same way: The network and the end-user communicate through UNI standards. The network defines certain quality-of-service guarantees such as Committed Information Rate (CIR), Committed Burst Size (Bc), and Excess Burst Size (Be). Exactly how the network delivers on its promise is up to the provider's discretion.

NNI enables two networks to exchange data without either one having to understand the structure within the individual networks. The NNI specification was developed by the Frame Relay Forum. By using NNIs, Frame Relay providers can expand the usefulness of their networks by providing gateways into other providers' networks, enabling organizations to partner without choosing the same provider. The scope of the NNI standard is shown in Figure 15.8.

FIGURE 15.8.

Network-to-network interfaces connect different providers.

Going Above the CIR

The strength of Frame Relay depends on two parameters called Committed Burst Rate (Bc) and Excess Burst Rate (Be), both of which are specified at the time a PVC is provisioned. Bc is the amount of traffic a Frame Relay carrier can transport above and beyond the CIR. This does not mean the Frame Relay carrier has agreed to carry extra traffic for free; it means that it can accept more than the CIR for a limited amount of time if and only if the traffic pattern averages out to the CIR over a given period of time. The Be is the maximum amount of traffic the provider can accept, but traffic that arrives at a rate between the Bc and the Be is not guaranteed. The relationship between the three properties is shown in Figure 15.9. CIR, Bc, and Be must be specified at the time of provisioning.

FIGURE 15.9.

Be, Bc, and CIR compared.

For example, a remote office has a T1 circuit to its Frame Relay provider and a PVC to the central office with a CIR of 1.0Mbps, a Bc of 1.25Mbps, and a Be of 1.5Mbps. The maximum throughput of the T1 is approximately 1.5Mbps, almost 1 1/2 times the CIR. A user, Teri, uploads an expense report via FTP to the central office across the Frame Relay network. FTP consumes the entire bandwidth of the circuit, and passes 1.25Mbps of data to the Frame Relay cloud.

The burst of data lasts for only one second. During the next second, traffic rate falls below .5Mbps. The average throughput over the two-second period is less than the CIR of 1Mbps, and so the agreement has been kept and all data transfer is guaranteed.

Now consider a slightly different scenario: Teri uploads a 100MB database to the central office. Data transfer is limited by the T1 circuit's maximum throughput of 1.5Mbps. The Frame Relay switch that receives the data calculates the average rate to exceed the CIR and can react in a couple of different ways. The nicest thing it can do is pass all data on to the central office but mark the Discard Eligible (DE) bit in each frame header. The DE bit is used to mark data as low priority: if congestion occurs somewhere else in the network, low priority data may be dropped in favor of higher priority frames.

Another possibility is that the switch may simply drop packets that exceed the CIR. This is normally done in periods of congestion.

NOTE

Switches accept traffic up to the rate of the Be, but not for an extended period of time. Throughput is still required to be below the CIR for a given period of time.

Flow Control in the Frame Relay Network

Two fields in the frame header allow for flow control. These fields are called Forward and Backward Explicit Congestion Notification (FECN and BECN) and they enable switches to ask the end nodes to reduce their bandwidth usage before frames need to be dropped. In this way, the network can slow the rate of traffic from the source instead becoming overcrowded. It is more efficient for a user to spread a file transfer over a longer period of time than it is to have to retransmit frames that the Frame Relay network has dropped.

A Frame Relay switch marks the FECN bit in a frame when it experiences congestion and wants to notify the receiving node. It is then the responsibility of the receiving partner to throttle back the network usage. Alternatively, a switch may mark the BECN bit on traffic returning to the node that is sending too much data. Using the BECN bit is more efficient than using the FECN bit because the host is notified directly.

Only recently has DTE equipment begun to listen and respond to the FECN and BECN bits. If the customer equipment does not act on the requests, these bits are not useful.

Voiceover Frame Relay (VoFR)

A new feature of Frame Relay is the capability to multiplex various kinds of data onto a single physical circuit. Cost factors are driving the adoption of voiceover Frame Relay, enabling remote offices to exchange telephone calls without using the PSTN or leased lines. Organizations that have chosen to use Frame Relay for their data communications and have already made the investment in Frame Relay equipment have an easy migration path to voiceover Frame Relay.

Traditionally, voice is carried over dedicated analog lines or by using digital lines with time-division multiplexing. In this way, bandwidth is guaranteed to each call and the quality never degrades. Generally, a single voice connection requires about 64Kbps of bandwidth.

Voiceover Frame Relay presents an interesting challenge because packet switched networks rely on statistical multiplexing, which works well for data but can degrade real-time applications like voice if congestion occurs. In order to reduce the amount of bandwidth required by each voice circuit and to improve overall utilization of the links, voice streams are compressed by removing pauses and redundant information. Typically, only about 22% of typical voice connection bandwidth is required for high quality service.

To transmit this data over the Frame Relay network, the information is compressed as described above and encapsulated within a data frame. A Frame Relay multiplexer then places these frames onto the same outgoing connection as other network data that may be traveling over the same physical circuit. By combining voice and data onto the same circuits, organizations reduce costs substantially over what they incur in maintaining separate network equipment and links. This process is diagrammed in Figure 15.10.

Figure 15.10.

Voiceover Frame Relay connecting multiple sites.

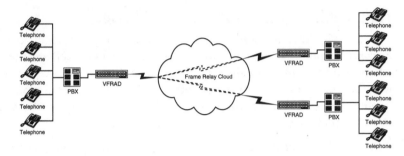

Along with the benefits of compression and multiplexing come several drawbacks. Compression, particularly on congested networks, can be *lossy.* "Lossy" is a term that describes compression in which quality is sacrificed for efficiency. Although a voice conversation may continue despite the lossy compression, the quality is less than that which most people are accustomed to on toll networks like the PSTN. Another disadvantage is the lack of accounting standards for voiceover Frame Relay; existing systems that track and bill for calls may need to be replaced when upgrading to Frame Relay. Packet switched networks like Frame Relay also suffer from delay and jitter, which further degrade quality. ATM was designed specifically to better support real-time applications such as voice, and it is a better, though more costly, alternative.

Private, Public and Hybrid Networks

Frame relay has become such a powerful technology that it has found a strong client base of organizations wishing to utilize it both in privately owned networks and public networks.

Private Frame Relay Networks

Private Frame Relay networks, as shown in Figure 15.11, offer the following benefits:

- Frame relay can make use of the existing network hardware, extending the lifetime and protecting the investment.
- Through shared bandwidth, Frame Relay gives organizations higher utilization over their existing circuits.
- By putting all equipment in the hands of a single organization, that organization can reduce the chances of having network data compromised.
- Frame relay offers greater flexibility and control over the network.

Public Frame Relay Networks

Public Frame Relay networks, as shown in Figure 15.12, offer the following advantages:

- Public Frame Relay networks reduce the cost of ownership because the service provider manages the backbone.

■ Public Frame Relay networks typically have a large geographic availability, enabling many remote sites to connect at low cost and even with dial-in access.

■ Public Frame Relay networks simplify interoperability with third-party organizations.

FIGURE 15.11

An example of a private Frame Relay network.

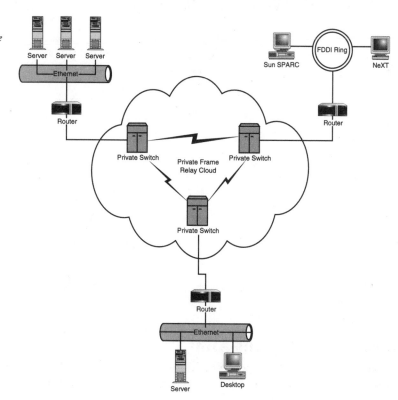

Hybrid Frame Relay Networks

Hybrid Frame Relay networks, as shown in Figure 15.13, offer the following advantages:

■ Hybrid Frame Relay networks reduce cost of ownership by having the service provider manage the backbone.

■ Hybrid Frame Relay networks increase control and security over specific networks.

■ Hybrid Frame Relay networks find the "sweet spot" in the network price-to-performance ratio.

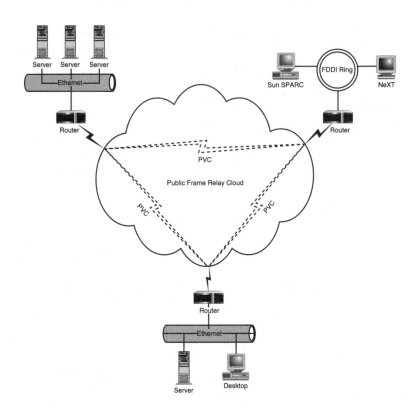

FIGURE 15.12.
A public Frame Relay network.

Internetworking with ATM

Asynchronous Transfer Mode, more commonly known as ATM, is a rapidly emerging technology for many of Frame Relay's current uses. The high speeds, quality of service, and scalability offered by ATM are enticing many companies to move to ATM-based networks. To accommodate this and ease the transition, most public Frame Relay providers are offering or planning to offer transparent internetworking with ATM. Using a gateway such as the one shown in Figure 15.14, an organization can upgrade parts of its Frame Relay network while maintaining full interoperability with remote offices still using existing Frame Relay networks. This also enables a company to migrate to ATM within its own backbone and keep Frame Relay connections with other partners.

Many new networks are still being implemented based on Frame Relay rather than ATM. Internetworking with ATM through a gateway gradually eases a company into the world of high-speed networking and provides experience to network personnel. By choosing to first develop a backbone based on the well-established Frame Relay technology, an organization avoids the high startup costs associated with a complete switch-over to ATM.

FIGURE 15.13.
A hybrid Frame Relay network.

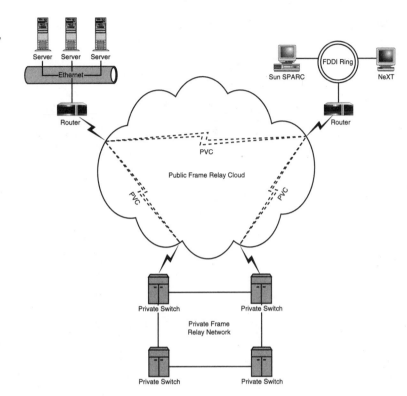

ATM

Also known as Fast Packet Switching, Asynchronous Transfer Mode was developed as a broadband alternative to the ISDN network. Operating at speeds from 1.54Mbps to 622Mbps, ATM is well suited to handle varying types of traffic such as data, voice, and video. One of ATM's primary advantages is that it adapts well to new technologies, offering features such as Quality of Service. A further advantage is that the network may be able to take advantage of higher bandwidths during periods of bursting, utilizing unused time on the wire.

ATM does not switch packets as does a conventional network; it switches *cells*. A cell is different from a packet because a cell has a fixed length, as Figure 15.15 illustrates. In ATM, this length is 53 bytes (48 bytes of data and 5 bytes of header). This fixed length enables the switching hardware to operate at much faster speeds than conventional variable-length switches can handle because only the header needs to be processed. Conventional variable-length packet switches must read and process every bit that comes across the wire to be able to determine the beginning and end of any particular packet.

15

CIRCUIT SWITCHED
TRANSMISSION
FACILITIES

FIGURE 15.14.
A Frame Relay-to-ATM gateway.

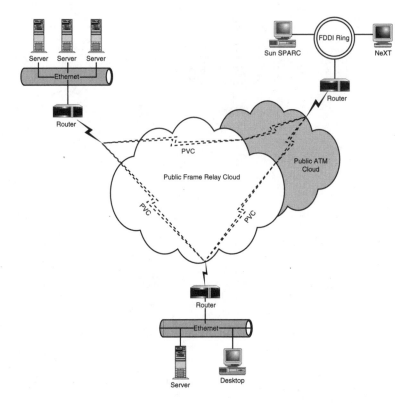

FIGURE 15.15.
Cells compared to packets.

History of ATM

ATM was developed to solve the problems attendant to conventional variable-length packet switches. The primary goal of the IETF ATM forum was to develop a technology that was flexible and scalable.

As long as there have been networks, network managers have wanted to consolidate multiple backbone circuits. Each circuit necessitates additional administration time and adds greater complexity, unreliability, and cost. Traditionally, a backbone link between a corporate office and a remote site consists of a circuit for voice connecting through PBXs and a circuit for network data connecting through routers. As technology such as videoconferencing becomes more commonplace, additional circuits are required.

The developers of ATM, the ITU-T Study Group XVIII, saw this problem and decided not to address any specific technology, but rather designed ATM to work with existing and as yet undeveloped technologies. The ITU is an international organization, and as such its specifications are recognized around the world. This is a dream come true for network engineers and managers: a networking technology that meets their current and future needs.

To support so many different technologies, ATM needs to have extremely low delay and jitter. In essence, the network must be transparent, neither slowing down nor altering traffic in any way. Therefore, ATM must run at high enough speeds so that it does not become the bottleneck in the network that so many WANs do, and it must have almost no packet loss, either as a result of data errors during transmission or packets that are dropped due to overrun buffers.

ATM must also have variable bit rates, providing committed information rates like Frame Relay for real-time applications and allowing for bursty data to better accommodate network traffic patterns. ATM needs to be all things to all people.

Though ATM networks are currently in production use, ATM is still very much under development. Current ATM implementations rely on the vendor to fill in some missing standards. Therefore, vendor interoperability is an issue and every effort should be made to implement new ATM projects on homogenous hardware.

An advantage of ATM is that the switches are *nonblocking*. This term describes a switch that can handle the maximum throughput on each of its interfaces. For example, a switch that has 8 ports at 155Mbps each would require 1.25Gbps aggregate switching capacity.

The Nitty-Gritty of ATM

This section describes the details of how ATM actually works. It does not cover every technical detail there is to know about ATM, but provides a strong foundation for anyone with an interest in the technology.

ATM Layers

To allow for greater flexibility, the ATM specifications are divided into multiple layers. Although not designed to correspond to the OSI model, the primary ATM layers are roughly analogous to the lowest two layers, the Physical and Data Link Layers. The relationship between ATM and the OSI model is shown in Figure 15.16.

FIGURE 15.16.
ATM compared to the OSI model.

Physical Layer

The ATM Physical Layer is directly analogous to the Physical Layer described in the OSI model; it is media dependent and is responsible for actually transmitting the bits. This layer is subdivided into the Physical Medium Sublayer and the Transmission Convergence Sublayer. The lower half, the physical medium sublayer, is responsible for placing bits onto the network medium (usually fiber) and providing timing.

The transmission convergence sublayer is responsible for maintaining cell boundaries, providing for header error control checking, and maintaining the media-dependent frame structure.

ATM Layer and ATM Adaptation Layer (Data Link Layer)

The ATM Layer is responsible for establishing connections across the ATM network.

The ATM Layer maps the Network Layer addresses to Data Link Layer addresses. Four addressing schemes have been developed; the public format is shared by Narrowband ISDN networks.

The ATM Adaptation Layer (AAL) provides the translation functionality between the upper-layer protocols and the actual ATM cells. For example, the AAL splits apart TCP/IP packets into 48-byte segments and encapsulates it in the ATM header.

To support different types of data, different AAL specifications have been provided, as shown in Figure 15.17.

AAL1 was designed to carry analog traffic that would normally be carried by dedicated circuits. It requires a lower-layer media that supports timing control, such as SONET. It provides for guaranteed end-to-end bandwidth.

AAL3/4 is intended to transmit Switched Multimegabit Data Service (SMDS) packets over an ATM network.

Figure 15.17.
A summary of the different AAL types.

	Requires Timing	Data Rate	Connection Mode	Traffic Types
AAL1	Yes	Constant	Connection-Oriented	Voice, video, and other conversation-oriented traffic
AAL3/4	No	Variable	Connection-Oriented	Data
AAL4	No	Variable	Connectionless	Data
AAL5	No	Variable	Connection-Oriented	Data

AAL 5 is the most commonly used ATM Adaptation Layer for connection-oriented network data. It is used for classical IP over ATM and LAN emulation.

ATM Cell Format

The ATM cell is 53 bytes long, with a 5-byte header.

Two distinct header formats are used. The User-Network Interface (UNI) header type is used for all cells sent between end-users and the ATM network. It is very similar to Network-Node Interface (NNI) header type, but with two key differences, as described in Figure 15.18.

Figure 15.18.
UNI and NNI cell formats compared.

	UNI	NNI
VPI field	8 bits	12 bits
Generic Flow Control	4 bits	Non-existent

As Figure 15.19 illustrates, the header is composed of six fields:

- Reserved
- Header Error Control (HEC)
- Generic Flow Control
- Maintenance Payload Type
- Priority Type Identifier (PTI)
- Virtual Path Identifier (VPI)

These fields provide the ATM switches with the information they need to route cells between the source and the destination.

Reserved (1 bit)

The first bit of the ATM cell is set aside for future use. Although a single bit is little to work with, in the future it may be used to change the meaning of the rest of the header.

FIGURE 15.19.
The ATM cell structure.

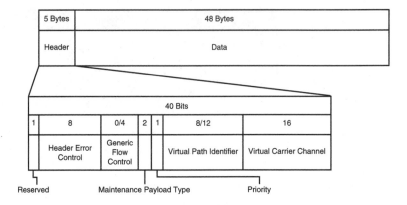

Header Error Control (HEC) (8 bits)

ATM, unlike many other types of WAN circuits, offers no data error control. Instead, ATM depends upon the transmission media to be extremely reliable. This can happen only because ATM usually is transmitted across high-speed fiber-optic networks like FDDI or SONET, and the physical medium is nearly flawless. During the design phase of ATM, it was decided that including error control information within the frame header would require too much space, and that it would make switching slower by requiring each switch to read the entire cell, calculate a checksum, and compare it against a field in the header. All error correction and retransmission must be done by the client and server using protocols like TCP/IP and its associated CRC (Cyclical Redundancy Check) field.

Though ATM relies on the encapsulated protocols for error control, it cannot do so for its own five-byte header. If an error in the header were to occur, the packet could be passed to the wrong switch and cause potential problems. For example, if even a single bit in the header were to be changed in the cell's Virtual Path Identifier/Virtual Channel Identifier, it could result in misrouting.

To detect errors within its own header, ATM includes a single byte of parity called the Header Error Control (HEC). This enables switches to detect whether a single bit has been modified from what was originally sent and to actually correct the error. In this way, single-bit errors are fixed and the packet is forwarded without any interruption in service. If more than one bit is damaged in the header, the entire cell is discarded and no notification is sent to the source. It is the responsibility of the encapsulated network protocol to detect whether information has been lost.

Generic Flow Control (0 or 4 bits)

Intended to be used to establish Switched Virtual Circuits, this functionality has not yet been implemented in the ATM standards. It will enable a user to create a connection to a single endpoint or multiple endpoints.

Maintenance Payload Type (2 bits)

These bits indicate to a switch whether a cell is being used for network maintenance or normal traffic. In this way, cells can be used in the same way that ICMP and NSMP packets are used on a TCP/IP network: to test functionality and measure performance.

Priority Type Identifier (PTI) (1 bit)

This bit is used to enable the ATM network to distinguish between cells with different quality-of-service requirements. The particular meaning of the bit can be defined per cell, channel, or path.

Virtual Path Identifier/Virtual Channel Identifier (VPI/VCI) (8 or 12 bits)

The VPI/VCI field stores the path and channel of the cell destination. This information is unique within an ATM network.

VPIs and VCIs

The Virtual Path Identifier describes an entire route, endpoint to endpoint. The Virtual Circuit Identifier is a connection between two directly connected switches. Each time a switch receives a cell, it may change both values before passing it on to the next switch on the cell's way to the destination. A simple lookup of the VPI and VCI gives the switch the information it needs to know the destination port and the next-hop VPI/VCI.

ATM Connections

ATM provides for two types of connections: Permanent Virtual Connections (PVC) and Switched Virtual Connections (SVC). PVCs are maintained by the ATM service provider and operate in much the same way as Frame Relay connections. A PVC requires careful network design and uses the topologies as leased lines.

When a PVC is provisioned, several properties must be specified to the provider. Each PVC is assigned a Class of Service. The COS specifications include choosing between a variable bit rate and a constant bit-rate type of service. COS is defined each time an SVC is created, allowing for greater flexibility because multiple SVCs can be created between organizations, each with a different COS.

Another property that must be specified is the Peak Cell Rate (PCR). ATM cells are a fixed size; because of that, the Peak Cell Rate specifies the bandwidth allocated to a particular circuit. Furthermore, the PCR can be different for each direction on a circuit, making it asymmetric. PCR is similar to the Committed Information Rate (CIR) defined for Frame Relay circuits.

> **NOTE**
>
> Asymmetric traffic patterns occur for many types of client-server relationships. An excellent example is the common web server: a client issues a simple GET / request to the web server, and the web server responds with a lengthy front page. If this is a typical use for a circuit, the PCR could be much smaller for the client than the server.

SVCs are still very much under development. They will enable end-stations to dynamically create connections and will reduce the need for a rigid, preplanned topology.

Quality of Service

Quality of Service (QOS) is an important concept for ATM networks. QOS describes the traffic properties, such as peak and sustained bandwidth, guaranteed to any given connection. Data that exceeds these specific requirements may or may not be dropped, depending on the configuration of the individual ATM switches.

To avoid losing data, ATM switches use *traffic shaping* to force data into predefined constraints. For example, if an end-node sends a greater amount of data than a given connection can support, the receiving ATM switch queues as much of the data as it can and transmits it evenly within the bandwidth constraints.

An alternative to shaping the data is *traffic policing*. With this policy, incoming data that does not conform to the constraints is dropped or marked as low priority. Cells with a low priority may be dropped farther along in the connection should congestion occur.

Signaling

Virtual connections within a PVC are established on ATM networks using *signaling*. In comparison, connections through TCP/IP are created using SYN and ACK packets, another form of signaling. In order to establish a connection, a router sends a signaling cell that contains special information—such as QOS parameters—to the destination router.

Every switch along the path examines the signaling cell and determines whether or not it has the capacity to support the connection. If it does, the switch passes the cell on to the next hop toward the destination. If it does not, the switch returns a notification message to the source and the connection is refused.

If everything goes well, the signaling request reaches the destination. Assuming the destination can also support the QOS parameters specified, it returns an acceptance message to the requester. On the message's return path, each switch notices the acceptance and makes note of the connection, dedicating whatever resources are necessary. After the message reaches the requester, the VPI and VCI are stored for later uses and the connection is established.

Provisioning ATM Circuits

Purchasing any kind of circuit is never as simple as it should be. Providers may be slow, unresponsive, or may not have the bandwidth to support your requirements. The choices you make during the provisioning process affect the usefulness of your WAN for the entire lifetime of the circuit. Taking time to plan carefully always proves worthwhile in the long run.

Physical Access

For low-cost, low-bandwidth ATM connectivity, routers can utilize a T1 circuit. A multiplexer enables voice, video, and data to be transported over the circuit but is likely to become bandwidth constrained.

ATM access can be integrated into an existing T1 circuit through a technique called "T1 Emulation." This is the process of splitting a T3 into as many as 28 individual channels. Organizations with a T3 infrastructure can integrate ATM into the WAN without using dedicated circuits, thereby protecting their existing investment.

For bandwidth requirements falling between T3 and T1, multiple T1s can be combined for an aggregate bandwidth of 3Mbps or greater. An inverse multiplexer (IMUX) splits information fairly between the individual circuits.

The commonly available but costly T3 leased line provides ATM connectivity at 45Mbps. ATM runs at a full 155Mbps over OC3, but OC3 circuits are not available in every area and are dependent on the availability of SONET.

Although many of the advantages of ATM are lost when interconnecting to Frame Relay, conversion between the two networks is available to organizations that wish to utilize existing network connections and protect an investment in Frame Relay. A gateway between the ATM and Frame Relay network translates frame formats and addresses.

TCP/IP gateways provide ATM users with convenient access to the Internet. TCP/IP packets destined for the gateway are divided and encapsulated within ATM cells. They are then forwarded directly to the TCP/IP gateway, which reassembles the original packets, forwards them to the Internet, and waits for a response. Conversations are stored in the memory of the gateway to enable responses to be forwarded to the proper destinations.

Interoperating with LANE

In Chapter 11, "ATM," you learned about ATM LAN Emulation, or LANE. LANE provides high-speed networking to the local area network by providing functionality that is inherently missing from ATM: broadcasts, name resolution, and more. By combining an ATM backbone with LANE, features such as videoconferencing and high bandwidth—utilizing applications are brought directly to the desktop. Neither the backbone nor the LAN topology becomes a bottleneck, and Quality of Service can be guaranteed end to end.

Migrating to ATM

Although upgrading existing WAN connections to ATM offers many benefits, it is a complicated and expensive task. However, there are many ways to ease the process of migration.

As with any migration, it is good to take it one step at a time. Start by adding an ATM circuit as a backup to an existing WAN circuit between two sites; after the link has remained stable for several weeks, swap the roles of the two circuits so that the ATM link becomes the primary method of communication and the old circuit acts as a tried-and-true backup.

Link by link, circuit by circuit, replace existing WAN connections with ATM. During this period, costs increase because you are paying for twice the connectivity, but these costs are far less than the costs associated with WAN downtime. After the entire network has proved stable and usable with ATM, cancel the old connections to complete the migration.

Summary

Frame relay and ATM provide two of the most common methods of connecting remote networks. By providing interconnectivity with each other, X.25 networks, and the Internet, these networks allow a great deal of flexibility with each physical connection. Both types of networks allow digital and analog traffic, but ATM was designed specifically for real-time applications such as voice and video.

Packet Switched Transmission Facilities

by Tony Northrup

IN THIS CHAPTER

CHAPTER 16

Packet switched transmissions differ from the circuit switched transmissions described in Chapter 15, "Circuit Switched Transmission Facilities." Packet switched networks route each packet through a network individually, rather than through a preset path of switches as with circuit switched networks. This offers the advantage of greater flexibility, because packets can be routed around failed equipment. However, because the route must be computed for each packet, switching in packet switched networks is substantially slower than switching in circuit switched networks.

X.25

X.25 networks are used by customers who contract with a carrier to use its Packet Switched Network (PSN). Billing is generally based on the network usage, and can therefore be variable.

The X.25 protocol itself defines the interface between a network node such as a router (the Data Terminal Equipment or DTE) and a packet switched network (the Data Communications Equipment or DCE). These components are illustrated in Figure 16.1. The network is responsible for carrying the traffic to the remote partner, which has a similar configuration. However, the way the network carries that traffic is not part of the X.25 standard!

FIGURE 16.1.
The components of an X.25 network.

Each provider determines the most efficient method of carrying traffic between customers. So, the term "X.25 Network" is really an oxymoron; a more correct term would be "X.25 Connection." The term was adopted for the entire network because X.25 is the most well-known standard. The scope of the X.25 standard is illustrated in Figure 16.2.

FIGURE 16.2.
The X.25 standard.

The communication begins when one customer of an X.25 packet switched network wants to connect to another. A call is placed, similar to the way calls are placed on standard telephones. If the called system accepts the connection, the two systems begin to transfer data back and forth. After the desired information has been transferred, either party ends the connection, in the same way a party on the telephone hangs up the receiver.

The History of X.25

X.25 was originally designed by telephone companies and other network providers in 1976 as a reliable method of transporting digital data over analog lines. Because it was designed by several different telephone companies, the specification works well regardless of the type of network that carries the traffic. Since then, it has been constantly evolving, with revisions done every four years.

Pros and Cons of X.25

X.25 is an old standard, and that is both its greatest advantage and disadvantage. On the downside, the maximum speed X.25 supports is 56Kbps. This is rarely sufficient to support modern networking, but the high level of compatibility keeps many customers connected into X.25 clouds. It is also the most global standard; most places in the world have a provider offering a connection. In fact, it is administered by an agency of the United Nations, the ITU-T (International Telecommunications Union).

X.25 is far less expensive overall than its most similar peers: Frame Relay or ATM. Perhaps the old axiom is true, "You get what you pay for."

Common Uses

X.25, though considered too old and slow to be useful by many, is still used extensively for applications such as automatic credit card systems, teller machines, loan application processing, medical records databases, and inventory monitoring. Recently, X.25 has become adept at carrying IP traffic, using encapsulation in much the same way as ATM and Frame Relay do.

Originally, the most common node attached to an X.25 cloud was a simple text-based terminal. Terminals attach to the network via a translating service called a Packet Assembler/ Disassembler (PAD). The PAD provides a connection to the network and translates the text to and from the terminal into packets that the X.25 network's DCE can accept. The specific recommendations used by PADs come from the International Consulting Committee for Telephone and Telegraph (CCITT, from the French). They are X.28, X.3, and X.29.

Comparison to OSI Reference Model

The X.25 Protocol corresponds to the lowest three layers of the OSI model, the Physical, Data Link, and Network Layers, as shown in Figure 16.3. Nothing in the standard specifies any higher layers, such as X.25-specific applications.

FIGURE 16.3.
A comparison of X.25 and the OSI model.

			Application
			Presentation
			Session
			Transport
Established SVCs and PVCs, provides for addressing	PLP		Network
Establishing the link between the DTE and DCE	LAP-B		Data Link
Sending and receiving raw bits onto a specific physical medium	X.21, X.21bis/RS232C, RS449/422, V.35		Physical

The Physical Layer

A variety of protocols provide for physical connections between DTEs and DCEs. Some of these protocols are X.21, X.21bis/RS232C, RS449/422 and V.35.

The X.25 Link Layer at OSI's Data Link Layer

A separate protocol describes X.25's corollary to the Data Link Layer, LAPB. LAPB (Link Access Protocol Balanced) is a reliable, error-checking protocol for transferring frames between the DTE and DCE. The LAPB protocol is responsible for initializing the link between the DTE and DCE, and for framing the packets before handing them off to the Physical Layer.

LAPB corresponds well to this layer of the OSI model because it is a version of HDLC, an OSI standard. Those familiar with HDLC with recognize the data structure, as given in Figure 16.4.

FIGURE 16.4.
The X.25 frame structure.

8	8	8	variable	16	8
Flag 01111110	Address	Control	Data	Checksum	Flag 01111110

The LAPB standard includes special fields for synchronizing the beginning and end of frames. These flags contain a special bit sequence, 01111110, or 126 in decimal. The DCEs at each end of the virtual circuit understand that this particular bit sequence never, ever occurs on the incoming line unless it marks the beginning or end of a frame. It is certainly possible that someone might try to transmit this special byte across an X.25 network; when this happens, it is replaced by yet another special character.

The second byte in the frame header is the address, which directs the frame between the DCE and DTE.

The third byte, control, is used to identify the frame format, whether it is an Information, Supervisory, or Unnumbered frame. It also carries the send/receive sequence numbers.

The byte after the frame's data is the Frame Check Sequence (FCS), a CRC checksum. When a host receives a frame, it first verifies that the checksum is consistent with the data carried within the frame. If the frame fails this test, the receiver transmits a Reject (REJ) packet back to the sender to ask that the frame be retransmitted. If the checksum is validated, a Receiver Ready (RR) or Receiver Not Ready (RNR) is sent, indicating whether or not more data can be accepted.

This checksum is key to X.25's reliability and inefficiency. Unlike most protocols, if a packet needs to be retransmitted, it is the responsibility of the *network*. In this way, an X.25 network guarantees 100% reliable transfer of data between end-nodes. This reflects a very different philosophy from most modern protocols, which instead pass the reject notification directly to the host that originally transmitted the data, making the *host* responsible for resending it. This is a substantial commitment because all data that is sent across the network must be cached by the network hardware until receipt has been confirmed.

To clarify this distinction, consider a TCP/IP network. When a user issues a request for a web page, that command is handed down from the browser at the Application Layer to TCP at the Session Layer. As TCP adds header information, it caches the user's data in memory. The data continues its path down through the OSI model to the Physical Layer where it is transmitted to the receiving node. As the destination receives packets, it verifies the data integrity using the CRC field. If an error is found, the receiving node asks the sending node to retransmit the data, which it has conveniently cached. When clean packets are confirmed, notification is sent to the sending node and the packets are cleared from the cache.

In an X.25 network, the DTE has no need to cache anything because the network has an agreement to do whatever is necessary to get everything that is sent across the cloud to the receiving DTE. That overhead puts a burden on the network hardware and limits how much traffic it can carry. Modern networks like ATM and Frame Relay differ sharply in this way; they guarantee only to make a "best effort" to carry the traffic. If an error occurs, the higher layer protocols like TCP/IP must detect the error and handle retransmission.

LAPB has three separate tasks to perform. The first of these tasks is link setup—initiating a connection across a virtual circuit. The second responsibility is information transfer—the actual sending and receiving of information useful to the end-users. After a connection is no longer needed, LAPB performs the disconnection.

The LAPB standard specifies three distinct frame formats, designated by the value in the Control field. Each frame type is useful for carrying a distinct type of data. Information frames carry data that is sequenced and capable of full-duplex transmission. To perform these tasks, it uses a send sequence number and receive sequence number frame. Supervisor frames provide control information, including flow control and acknowledging information frames. Unnumbered frames do not carry sequence information and are used for control purposes, such as starting and stopping a connection.

The Packet Level at OSI's Network Layer (x.25)

The X.25 packet level actually exists only at the Network Layer, but the name is used to refer to the entire suite of protocols. This layer establishes a connection and provides for call establishment, data transfer, flow control, error recovery, and call clearing. Each packet can be a maximum of 128 data bytes long.

The Network Layer is responsible for managing each virtual circuit, and is capable of maintaining as many as 128 simultaneous connections. The fields that make up the Network Layer header are illustrated in Figure 16.5.

FIGURE 16.5.

The X.25 packet structure.

1	1	1	1	4	8	3	1	3	1	Variable
Q	D	0	1	Group	Channel	Rec #	M	Send #	0	Data

The first bit, Q, signals Qualified data and is intended to be used by the encapsulated protocol to separate control packets from data packets. The second bit, D, is used to flag whether the packet is of local significance and traveling between two DCEs (value of 0), or of end-to-end significance, traveling between two DTEs (value of 1). Together, these four bits make up the General Format Identifier (GFI) field.

The next two fields are Logical channel Group Number (LGN) and Logical Channel Number (LCN). Often, these 12 consecutive bits are treated as a single field and referred to as the Logical Channel Identifier (LCI). The LCI identifies a specific connection to the packet switched network. The final byte of the packet header is split into Receive Number and Send Number subfields, which are used for tracking sequence.

One bit of this byte is the M bit, which is used to group blocks of related information that are too large to be placed into a single packet. The M stands for More, specifying that the data is split between multiple packets with a value of 1. This bit takes on a 0 value when the packet is the last of a group. You may recognize this process from other networks; it is very similar to packet fragmentation in IP networks.

CCITT Recommendation X.121 defines the exact format of the Network Layer addresses, or International Data Numbers (IDNs), and is illustrated in Figure 16.6. These addresses identify a unique destination on the X.25 network. The first four digits of the IDN are the Data Network Identification Code (DNIC). The first three digits of the DNIC are country-specific, and the last identifies a specific public-switched network. The rest of the address is used to identify a specific node within the network and is called the National Terminal Number (NTN).

FIGURE 16.6.
The X.121 address structure.

4	4	3	1	10
Called DTE address length	Calling DTE address length	Country Code	P S N	National Terminal Number

After the connection has been established, the X.121 address is no longer necessary. Instead, the Logical Channel Identifier (LCI) is used to identify connection. The LCI is similar to the DLCI in a Frame Relay network because it has only a local significance. X.121 addresses are not needed at all for virtual circuits that have been configured manually; LCIs are used instead to identify a specific circuit.

The Network Layer protocol is responsible for setting up network connections across the X.25 cloud, between remote DTEs. This is in contrast to the link-layer addressing, which connects a DTE to a DCE.

The X.25 Network Layer connects DTEs end-to-end; the link layer connects DTEs to DCEs.

The individual routers use the services of the X.25 protocol to establish a connection to the remote DTE. The connection is initiated by the transmitting DTE sending a call request packet, which contains the destination DTE's X.121 address, to its DCE. The DCE is responsible for transporting that packet across the X.25 cloud. After the packet reaches the destination, the receiving DCE forwards it to the receiving DTE, which verifies that it is the proper destination and decides whether or not to participate in a conversation. Assuming it accepts the call, it responds with a call accept packet and the connection is established.

After the connection is complete, the two participants are ready to send data in either direction. From this point forward, the X.121 address is no longer used. The connection is simply identified to the DCE using the LCN.

Different Types of Networks

In the many years X.25 has been in service, it has been ported to several different network platforms. Each of these different platforms requires a separate Network Layer protocol.

Different networks cannot be mixed on the same physical interface, although many providers support point-to-point connectivity over a Public Data Network.

Public Data Network (PDN)

Defined by RFC 1356, X.25 PDN services provide data connections between customers. These connections are commonly used to transport IP and OSI traffic using protocol encapsulation. In this way, X.25 networks have become useful as WAN links between distant networks rather than just as a simple transport for data terminal traffic.

When a provider carries IP traffic to the Internet, it becomes an Internet Service Provider (ISP). The available bandwidth on this type of network is too low for heavy-duty file transfers to and from the Internet, but it does allow convenient access to those corporations with an existing X.25 link.

Defense Data Network (DDN)

The DDN is a component of the Defense Communications System and is primarily used for switching government data and connecting distant military locations. MILNET, parts of the Internet, and highly-restricted classified government networks make up the collective Defense Data Network. This network is managed by the Defense Information Systems Agency.

Point-to-Point

A point-to-point X.25 connection is essentially a private X.25 network running between two systems. These systems may be connected by anything ranging from a serial cable to a 56k leased line. It may seem odd that someone would choose a packet-switching protocol for a point-to-point connection, but it provides a simple and inexpensive way to expand on existing networks.

X.25 Specifications (RFC 1356)

The actual specifications on which X.25 is based are difficult to read through. To make it even more complicated, the term "X.25," as it is commonly used, is actually a suite of standards. Fortunately, most network managers rarely have to refer to the actual specifications to connect to X.25 networks. Only hardware manufacturers designing network equipment and software developers creating X.25-compatible software need the level of detail these documents provide.

ITU-T (formerly CCITT)

The International Telecommunications Union provided the specifications (or "recommendations," as they call them) for the X.25 protocol suite. They can be found online at http://www.itu.int. Although the full text of recommendations must be purchased, you can still find some useful information. Recommendations of particular interest are Rec.X.25 Version 10/1996 and Rec.X.121 Version 10/1996.

IETF

The Internet Engineering Task Force has released several standards of interest to the X.25 community. Among these are RFC 1356, 877, and 1236. The full texts of RFCs are readily available on the Internet.

RFC 877, Transmission of IP Datagrams over Public Data Network

This is the original specification for encapsulating IP packets over X.25 networks. It also puts restrictions on the X.25 standard to be used when transporting IP.

RFC 1236, IP to X.121 Address Mapping for DDN

This writing specifies a way to translate between class B and class C IP addresses and X.121 addresses.

RFC 1356, Multiprotocol Interconnect on X.25 and ISDN in the Packet Mode

Entirely replacing the original RFC 877, this RFC spells out the methods to be used to send IP packets over X.25 networks. Specific changes from RFC 877 include an increased maximum packet size (to 1600 bytes).

Migrating from X.25

X.25 is an aging standard, and has many significant weaknesses that keep it from being a popular protocol for new configurations. In fact, many organizations that have existing X.25 networks are finding themselves restricted by the bandwidth and are looking to new technologies: Frame Relay and ATM. Both of these technologies provide services similar to X.25, but at higher speeds and without the guaranteed reliability.

The cardinal rule in migrating networks is "divide and conquer." Separate off part of your network and create a redundant link running alongside your existing X.25 connection, as illustrated in Figure 16.7. Transfer the same data, from the same applications, over the new circuit as it is being transferred over the old circuit. Continue using this technique for several months until you are completely confident the new network platform provides identical functionality to the existing configuration and is performing both reliably and consistently.

FIGURE 16.7.
Redundant X.25 and Frame Relay links.

After you reach this state, switch the roles of the two connections so the network you are migrating to becomes the primary and the X.25 becomes the backup. If anything should go wrong, do not hesitate to fall back on the old, reliable connection; that is what it is there for. Again, wait several months with the new connection running production before continuing to migrate the rest of the network. If the new network has a fatal problem, it is better to find out by losing one small part of an enterprise network than by completely losing all connectivity. As each section goes into full production mode, X.25 circuits can be canceled.

This technique provides the obvious benefit of enabling you to test the new equipment for reliability. However, it also gives the support staff a chance to come up to speed on the new technology. Building a strong knowledge base is a key component to any migration; many problems that happen with new technologies are more the fault of insufficient experience than the actual technologies involved.

Many organization may never completely end their reliance on X.25 networking; they may retain connections to continue partnerships with organizations who have yet to migrate or with remote sites for whom it is not feasible. Although X.25 gateways from Frame Relay and ATM networks provide backward-compatibility through the use of gateways, compatibility cannot be guaranteed for every application.

Summary

X.25 is an international standard for low-speed data communications. Although many in the industry consider it an aging, outdated standard, it is still widely used and very popular. X.25 is considered a packet switched network because each packet is routed separately, rather than being routed along with all traffic for a specific virtual circuit through a single path. The X.25 protocol suite maps to the lowest three layers of the OSI model. It provides reliable, sequenced data transmission to anywhere in the world over standard copper wiring.

Modems and Dial-Up Technologies

by James Spann

IN THIS CHAPTER

CHAPTER 17

This chapter examines the capability of other devices, known as "modems," to extend the reach of a network. The cables and topologies examined earlier show how to connect a network together within limited distances. To communicate over longer distances, additional things need to be considered. This chapter examines one of the possible options.

How Modems Work

The word "modem" is a telecommunications term applied to devices that adapt an electronic signal from a business machine into a tone signal that can be transmitted over a communications link. The word itself is a contraction of the words modulator and demodulator. To modulate a signal is to convert it from one state to another. Therefore the modulator/demodulator device, or modem, is a signal converter.

The word "modem" is actually a relatively new word to telecommunications. Originally the devices were known as "data sets." Before 1977, companies that needed to connect a device to a telephone line had to use equipment provided by the then-monopoly phone companies. Following a ruling from the Federal Communications Commission in 1977, individuals and corporations were permitted to provide their own equipment to connect to telephone lines. To this day, all modems must still comply with this FCC ruling known as Part 68.

A computer cannot simply connect to a telephone line and send signals over it because a computer speaks a digital language consisting of electronic signals or states, and a regular telephone line can transmit only analog pulses or sound. The PC itself, being a digital device, talks in a language known as *binary*, which codes information using either an "off" state, represented by a zero, or an "on" state, represented by a one. Digital transmission is always in an exact form of either off or on; there are no in-between states. On the other hand, analog transmission is constantly varying in amplitude (signal strength) and frequency (changes per cycle). See Figure 17.1 for an example of digital and analog signals.

For shorter distances, regular network cables are sufficient. However, when a computer needs to speak to another computer over longer distances, some other form of communication media must be used. The most logical and available choice is the standard telephone line. Unfortunately, as was just pointed out, one cannot take a computer that speaks a digital language and have it communicate with another computer at the other end if the communications media being used supports only analog transmission. For the two machines to communicate over telephone lines, a modem must be placed at both ends of the transmission. The computer sending the transmission must have a modem to convert the digital signals it creates into an analog format to be sent over the telephone line. Additionally, the computer on the receiving end of the transmission must have a modem to receive the analog transmission and convert it back into a digital signal that the computer can comprehend. Figure 17.2 illustrates the transmission between two computers using a telephone line.

FIGURE 17.1.
Digital and analog signals.

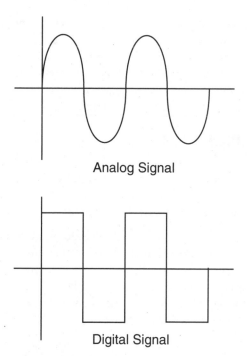

Analog Signal

Digital Signal

FIGURE 17.2.
Communication over a telephone line.

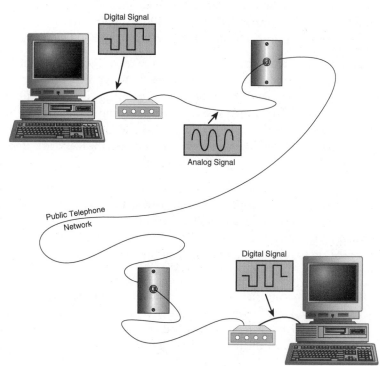

Data communication usually takes place between two devices known as the DCE (data communications equipment) and the DTE (data terminal equipment). A modem is an example of a DCE. It in turn connects to the PC, which is the DTE. The wide variety of equipment available and the diversity of applications on both sides of the DTE/DCE interface dramatize the need for standardizing its mechanical, electrical, and functional characteristics. Some of those standards are examined later in this chapter.

Bits and Bauds

In order for the modem to modulate the digital signal from the computer to one that consists of analog tones to send over the phone line, it has to have some method for varying the amplitude, frequency, and phase of the tones that it sends over the phone line. The number of times that one of these line conditions changes during one second is referred to as the "baud rate."

The term "baud" is used to represent the unique line conditions that can exist. Each unique line condition is also referred to as a "symbol" in most modern documentation. Each of these symbols is capable of representing a specific bit pattern of information. The bit pattern being represented is commonly referred to as a "token." The baud rate itself is actually named after the French inventor Emile Baudot who in 1875 created a 5-bit code to represent the alphabet. Each 5-bit pattern was a token representing a particular letter of the alphabet.

Unfortunately, because the public telephone network was designed for voice signals and not data, it has certain limitations that have to be accommodated. Because the majority of the energy created by the human voice falls between 300 and 3300 Hertz (Hz), communications circuits were designed to carry frequencies between 0 and 4,000Hz, or 4KHz.

In the early days of modem transmission, the terms "bits per second" and "baud rate" were thought by most people to be synonymous. However, that was true only because of the way the signal was being sent. When each baud (or change in line condition) in a message represents one bit of information to be sent, then the baud rate equals the bits per second. For example, imagine a message transmitted at 300 baud (300 line condition changes per second). If each change in line condition represents one bit then the message is transmitted at 300 bits per second (bps).

In order to send more than one bit of information per baud, modulation schemes have been developed that allow for higher bps rates. To send data over the telephone circuit, modem designs typically use a carrier frequency somewhere in the middle of the voice band and superimpose the data on that frequency by modulating it appropriately. The output of the modulation process needs to have a spectrum resembling the truncated portion of the entire voice spectrum that fits within the telephone bandwidth.

For example, imagine that you want to send 2400 symbols per second. To do so you must be able to create 2400 cycles per second (Hz). To use 2400Hz to send the transmission you must select 1800Hz as the carrier frequency and modulate it up or down by 1200Hz to create a range of 2400Hz. This puts the total bandwidth between 600Hz and 3000Hz, which fits inside the range of available bandwidth on a typical phone line (0 - 4000Hz). This range is illustrated in Figure 17.3. Interestingly, this is the form of modulation that is used by the V.32 standard discussed later in this chapter.

FIGURE 17.3.
A 2400Hz bandwidth modulated on a 1200Hz carrier.

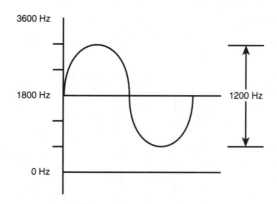

Over time, the quality of the phone network has improved, which has led to more usable bandwidth on a typical phone line. As an additional example, the V.34 standard discussed later in this chapter uses a carrier frequency of 1959Hz and modulates 3429 symbols per second using a total bandwidth from 244Hz to 3674Hz.

For a voice circuit to carry data efficiently, the modulation technique should be designed to tailor the waveform to the characteristics of the channel. This tailoring process gives rise to much ingenuity. The modulation technique must be devised to maximize the quantity of data transmitted and minimize the effects of noise and distortion. A number of internationally recognized methods and transmission rates have established today's data communication standards.

Different modulation schemes enable line conditions to represent different pairings of binary digits. Using a modulation scheme that enables four different frequencies to represent the binary pairings of 00, 01, 10, and 11 actually enables 1200 bits to be delivered per second even though the baud rate is only 600. Faster transmission speeds can be achieved by enabling more line conditions (or "symbols") to represent more bit combinations.

Modem Modulation Types

The process of using a carrier—in this case, the phone line—to carry information between two points is referred to as *modulation*. The analog sound of a human voice constantly varies in frequency and amplitude. If one looks at it on an oscilloscope, a human voice resembles a series of sine waves. Any series of pulses, sounds, waves, or voltages can be represented using a sine wave. The definition of a particular sine wave is characterized by its amplitude, frequency, and phase.

The *amplitude* of a sine wave is its height relative to a value on the y-axis. The *frequency* of a sine wave is the position on the x-axis (time) where the wave begins to repeat. The *phase* of a sine wave is relevant only when comparing it with another sine wave of the same frequency and amplitude. A change in the phase of a sine wave occurs when the wave is time shifted to cross the x-axis at a point that is directly opposed to its normal pattern. Figure 17.4 shows the characteristics of a sine wave.

Figure 17.4.

Characteristics of a sine wave.

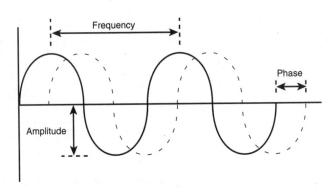

Changing one of the defining characteristics of the sine wave by modulating the carrier is how modems transmit information. Analog modulation can occur in three ways: amplitude modulation, frequency modulation, and phase modulation. Figure 17.5 gives an illustration.

As you can see from Figure 17.5, the first type of analog modulation is amplitude modulation. Amplitude modulation varies the strength of the signal to determine whether a zero or a one bit is being transmitted. In the illustration in Figure 17.5, a signal with a low amplitude represents a zero or "space" and a signal that has a high amplitude represents a one or "mark."

The second type of analog modulation is frequency modulation. Frequency modulation uses a change in the number of times per second the sine wave repeats to indicate a zero or a one. Figure 17.5 shows a sine wave that has a particular frequency being used to represent the zero or "space" and a frequency that is twice the original to represent the one or "mark."

The last type, phase modulation, uses a change in the phase of the wave to indicate a zero or a one. The phase of a sine wave is its position relative to the x-axis. Figure 17.5 shows a sine wave being used to create the zero and a phase shift being used to indicate a one.

Combinations of these three forms of modulation can be used to create more symbol possibilities and, therefore, higher throughput rates. Quadrature Amplitude Modulation (QAM) is just one example of this. In QAM, a combination of phase shifts and amplitude shifts are used to create 16 different states that allow for four bits per baud. If you have a baud rate of 2400, then you could effectively send 9600bps (2400 changes per second × 4 bits per change = 9600bps).

FIGURE 17.5.

The three types of analog modulation techniques.

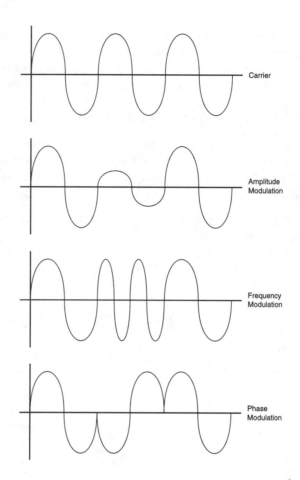

Another form of modulation technique is Pulse Amplitude Modulation (PAM). PAM is the method used in the downstream connection for the new 56K modems that do not have to have an initial Analog to Digital conversion performed on their data streams. These modems still use QAM to send their data back at speeds of up to 33,600bps. For more information on 56K technology, see the standards at the end of this chapter.

Asynchronous and Synchronous

When two devices attempt to communicate with one another they have to have some way to control the flow of data so that they understand where the characters being sent begin and end. The data stream that is actually sent through the modem to the other end of the connection can be sent using one of two forms of coordination. One way to control the timing of the signals being sent and received at either end is by sending the data asynchronously.

Asynchronous communication is the most widespread form used by conventional modems. In asynchronous communication, the information (character, letter, number or symbol) that is sent from one device to the other is represented as a string of bits. Each string of bits is separated from the other bit strings by a start bit and a stop bit. By using a start bit and a stop bit for each character transmitted, each device knows when it is sending or receiving a character and no external timing signals have to be present to control the flow of data.

One of the complaints about asynchronous communication is that approximately 20 to 25 percent of the data being sent is used for control information to "synchronize" the conversation between the devices. The alternative to asynchronous communication is synchronous communication.

In synchronous communication, a timing signal must be present to control the transmission of blocks of characters called "frames." No start and stop bits are used in the transmission. Synchronization characters are used to begin a transmission and to check the accuracy of the transmission. Figure 17.6 offers a comparison of asynchronous and synchronous communication.

Figure 17.6.

Comparing asynchronous and synchronous communication.

Protocols used in synchronous transmissions perform functions that are not performed by asynchronous protocols. Some examples are:

- Checking the information sent for accuracy
- Formatting the data into frames
- Adding control information

Synchronous protocols are used in digital environments. The analog world typically uses asynchronous communications. Most network communications are performed synchronously as well. Some common synchronous protocols are Binary Synchronous Communication Protocol (bisynch), Synchronous Data Link Control (SDLC), and High-Level Data Link Control (HDLC).

Standard Modem Interfaces

Although there are numerous "recommended standards," by far the most important one to the world of modem technology is the RS-232 interface. There are several versions of the RS-232 interface and each one is distinguished by a letter that follows the RS-232 designation. The most common implementation of the RS-232 interface standard is the RS-232C version.

The RS-232 specification is a standard of the EIA (Electronic Industries Association). It is virtually similar to the V.24 standard issued by the ITU-T (International Telecommunication Union—Telecommunications Standardization Sector) formerly known as the CCITT. The RS-232 standard covers four basic areas of information:

- The mechanical characteristics of the interface
- The electrical signals used in the interface
- The function of each signal
- Divisions of the signals for specialized applications

RS-232 and its counterparts provide for serial transmission of data across the interface. In a serial interface, the bits composing the data are transmitted across the interface bit-by-bit, either synchronously or asynchronously.

Even though the DB-25 connector is commonly associated with the RS-232C interface, it was actually not defined as part of revision C. The DB-25 connector was actually defined in the D revision of the RS-232 specifications. Each of the pins in the connector has an assigned responsibility. They are listed below:

- Pin 1: Protective Ground (Frame Ground)
- Pin 2: Transmit Data
- Pin 3: Receive Data
- Pin 4: Request to Send
- Pin 5: Clear to Send
- Pin 6: Data Set Ready
- Pin 7: Signal Ground
- Pin 8: Data Carrier Detect
- Pin 9: Reserved
- Pin 10: Reserved
- Pin 11: Unassigned
- Pin 12: Secondary Data Carrier Detect
- Pin 13: Secondary Clear to Send
- Pin 14: Secondary Transmit Data

17

MODEMS AND
DIAL-UP
TECHNOLOGIES

■ Pin 15: Transmit Clock

■ Pin 16: Secondary Receive Data

■ Pin 17: Receive Clock

■ Pin 18: Unassigned

■ Pin 19: Secondary Request to Send

■ Pin 20: Data Terminal Ready

■ Pin 21: Signal Quality Detector

■ Pin 22: Ring Indicator

■ Pin 23: Data Rate Select

■ Pin 24: External Clock

■ Pin 25: Unassigned

For a transmission of data to take place, the following steps must occur:

■ The communications software in the PC places a voltage on pin 20 (DTR) to indicate that the PC is ready to transmit data. At the same time, the modem places a voltage on pin 6 (DSR) to let the PC know that the modem is ready to receive data or instructions.

■ The PC sends a command to the modem via pin 2 (TD) to let the modem know to go off hook and dial a specified number. The modem responds to the PC with an acknowledgment on pin 3 (RD).

■ After a connection has been established between two modems, the modem sends a signal to the PC on pin 8 (CD) to let the PC know that a communication path exists and that data transfer can begin.

■ When the PC is ready to transmit data, it sends a signal to the modem on pin 4 (RTS), called a "request to send." Unless the modem is busy, it responds to the PC with a signal on pin 5 (CTS) to let the PC know that it may begin transmission of data on pin 2 (TD).

The principal drawback to the RS-232 interface is the distance limitation of 50 feet. This is typically not a problem for a connection between a PC and a modem but can be a concern if the modem has to be placed some distance away from the PC. However, because the normal throughput limitation of an RS-232 interface is considered to be 19,200bps, a shorter cable must be used if you wish to achieve the higher throughput rates available with today's modems. Most modem manufacturers recommend an RS-232 cable of 12 feet or less, and a 6-foot cable is very common.

Although RS-232 is the most commonly used choice for a modem connection, a few others bear mentioning here. They are RS-422, RS-423, RS-449, and RS-530.

RS-422 and its counterpart, X.27 (V.11), cover the electrical characteristics of balanced (or differential) circuits (those in which the positive and negative signal lines are isolated from ground). The balanced circuit is less susceptible to noise and offers higher data rates and longer cable runs.

RS-422 is designed for applications that use twisted-pair wire at distances up to 4,000 feet and data rates to 100,000bps. A data rate of 10,000,000bps is available at a distance of 40 feet or less. These characteristics make it possible to interconnect equipment within a facility without expensive data sets.

RS-423 and its counterpart X.26 (V.10) define unbalanced electrical characteristics similar to those of the RS-232 interface. The new standard, however, permits data rates ranging from 100,000bps over 40 feet to 10,000bps over 200 feet of cable. The present unbalanced standard is roughly limited to 20,000bps and 50 feet.

RS-422 and RS-423 define only the electrical characteristics of the interface; a companion standard, RS-449, defines the functional and mechanical requirements for implementation. Although these new standards were intended to replace RS-232, they have not yet done so.

RS-449 and its companion standards differ significantly from the older RS-232 standard. At the interface control level, 10 new functions provide capabilities for testing, speed selection, and standby operation. Perhaps the most significant new functions are the local and remote loopback signals. These permit, to a degree, the diagnosis of equipment and circuit faults by allowing a loop back to the DTE, to the analog side of the local DCE, or to the digital side of the remote DTE.

RS-530 was introduced as a standard to operate at data rates from 20,000bps to 2,000,000bps using the same 25-pin DB-25 connector that RS-232 uses. The major improvement in RS-530 is that it is not an electrical specification, but rather refers to two other standards, RS-422 and RS-423. These new standards take advantage of the improved performance now possible with integrated circuit technology.

ITU-T (CCITT) Modem Standards

One of the most basic rules about communication is that in order for communication to take place effectively and efficiently, there must be rules that are adhered to so that the communicating devices understand all the components of the communication process. These rules of order are referred to in the data communications world as "protocols" and "standards."

There are many different standards in the modem environment, most of which have been standardized by the ITU-T (International Telecommunication Union—Telecommunications Sector). These standards are commonly known as the "V-Series of Recommendations." Listed below are just a few of the more important V-Series Recommendations.

- ■ V.22: The V.22 standard outlines a 1200bps duplex modem designed for use in the public switched telephone network and on leased-line circuits. It is structurally similar to the Bell System 212A standard but is not backward compatible to the 212A's 300bps speed. Also, the 212A uses Frequency Shift Keyed (FSK) modulation at its lower speed of 300bps and the V.22 uses Phase Shift Keyed (PSK) modulation at its low speed of 600bps.

■ V.22 bis: The V.22 bis (bis means "second") standard describes a duplex modem operating at 2,400bps using a frequency division technique standardized for use on the public switched telephone network. It can also be used on a point-to-point 2-wire leased line circuit.

■ V.26: The V.26 standard specifies a 2400bps modem for use on a leased line circuit. It is a full-duplex 1200 baud modem that uses Dibit Phase Shift Keyed (DSPK) modulation.

■ V.26 bis: The V.26 bis standard specifies either a 2400bps or a 1200bps modem for use on a non-leased facility.

■ V.26 terbo: The V.26 terbo (terbo means "third") standard essentially added an echo cancellation technique to the previous versions of the standard.

■ V.27: The V.27 standard outlines a 4800bps modem that uses differential phase shift keying and can operate in a half-duplex or full-duplex mode. It also has a manual equalizer adjustment. The modulation technique used identifies eight different phases. It is intended for use on dedicated or leased facilities. The terbo version of V.27 allows for a connection to a non-dedicated facility.

■ V.29: The V.29 standard describes a full-duplex, four wire, 9600bps modem used on a leased facility. The carrier frequency for a V.29 modem is 1700Hz and it has a baud rate of 2400.

■ V.32: The V.32 standard outlines a family of two wire duplex modems that operate at speeds of up to 9,600bps. These modems can also be used on the public switched telephone network as well as on leased line circuits. These modems use QAM (Quadrature Amplitude Modulation) and achieve full-duplex operation due to the echo cancellation technique that is used.

■ V.32 bis: The V.32 bis standard is very similar to the V.32 standard mentioned above. The only major difference is in the speed. These modems can communicate at speeds of up to 14,400bps. This is achieved by using six bits per the 2400 baud rate.

■ V.32 terbo: The V.32 terbo specification is actually not a standard but something that was proposed and used by AT&T. It allows communication speeds of up to 19,200bps and works between two modems that support it.

■ V.33: Although the V.33 standard is very similar to the V.32 standard for switched services, V.33 is intended for use on dedicated facilities. The other major difference between V.32 and V.33 is that the V.33 has a multiplexing option that enables it to combine several data sources into a total data stream of 14,400bps.

■ V.34: The V.34 standard was originally written to specify data signaling rates of up to 28,800bps, but it has been modified since the original standard to include data signaling rates of up to 33,600bps. One of the newer characteristics implemented with the V.34 class is the capability of the modem to continuously monitor the communication channel and raise or lower the negotiated data signaling rate as line conditions change. V.34 is also compatible with the V.42 compression standard allowing for faster throughput on the connection. It is also backward compatible with previous modem standards so that it can negotiate a connection with older, slower modems. V.34 is, like the previous standards, capable of working with a public switched network connection as well as a leased line configuration.

■ V.42: The V.42 standard is used to define error detection and correction procedures for DCE devices. It actually defines two types of error detection and correction: LAPB and MNP Class 4. Link Access Protocol Balanced (LAPB) is the method used by the Network Layer (Layer 3 of the OSI model) protocol known as HDLC (High Level Data Link Control). LAPB is the preferred method of error detection and correction under the V.42 standard. MNP Class 4 is actually a secondary method that is available as an alternative.

■ V.42 bis: The V.42 bis standard is an enhancement to the error detection and correction capabilities of the V.42 standard. V.42 bis provides for data compression by the DCE using the error correction procedures outlined in V.42.

■ 56K: Although at the time of this writing there is not a clear definition of the 56K standard, two competing technologies are available that enable the user to obtain a 53,000bps downstream transmission and a 33,600bps upstream transmission. Even though the technology theoretically allows for a speed of up to 56,000bps downstream, the FCC currently limits that transmission to 53Kbps. The idea behind this new technology is that some of the noise involved performing an analog-to-digital conversion (called "quantization noise") can be eliminated in the downstream line if the connection from the upstream modem back to the network is an entirely digital connection. The 56K standard, then, eliminates the need to perform an analog-to-digital conversion downstream, thus eliminating quantization noise and improving the throughput possibility.

Modems and Microsoft Networking

Modems can be used in the Microsoft networking environment to extend a network's reach. In order to use a modem to establish a remote network connection, a user must first set up the modem. In both Windows 95 and Windows NT 4.0, the modem is set up through the Modem applet that is available from the Control Panel. After the modem has been installed and configured appropriately, the remote network connection properties can be set up.

With Windows 95, the user has to use the Dial-Up Networking applet to connect to a remote network or device. Each connection that is set up under Dial-Up Networking can be configured by modifying the connections' properties. Figure 17.7 shows the Server Types properties for a Dial-Up Networking connection. The Dial-Up Networking connection has several properties that configure the way the connection performs. Each connection may have different requirements for each property tab. In Figure 17.7, the properties have been set to establish a connection with an ISP (Internet Service Provider). This particular ISP uses a PPP

(Point-to-Point Protocol) connection and works best if none of the advanced options are chosen. Other ISPs require different advanced options to establish a connection. The lower part of the Server Types tab in Figure 17.7 shows the Allowed network protocols. Most connections use TCP/IP (Transmission Control Protocol/Internet Protocol) as the only protocol used for a connection. Although a connection may be set up to use any or all of the allowed protocols, choosing only the protocol(s) needed simplifies the connection and any troubleshooting, and also allows for improved performance.

FIGURE 17.7.

Properties for a Windows Dial-Up Server networking connection.

With Windows NT 4.0, the user must also configure the Dial-Up Networking applet to connect to a remote system. If the NT system is to be used as a server to which clients connect, then the Remote Access Service must be installed and running. Administration of the Remote Access Service (RAS) is handled by the Remote Access Admin tool that is available as one of the Administrative Tools when RAS is installed. With Windows NT Workstation, only one remote user can connect at a time. However, Windows NT Server supports up to 256 simultaneous remote connections. After a user makes a remote connection, the telephone line becomes transparent and users can access all network resources as though they were connected locally to the network.

The Remote Access Service is installed in Windows NT 4.0 by using the Add button on the Services tab in the Network properties window. To add the Remote Access Service to the list of installed services, you need to have a modem installed and configured and you have to select some setup options such as the protocols you wish to allow dial-in and dial-out callers to use. If you have not run the Windows NT modem installation, the RAS setup prompts you to do that when the service is installed.

Some of the other options available with RAS are the capability to select whether ports (for example: COM1, COM2, and so forth) are available for use as a dial-out port, a dial-in port, or both. In addition, each protocol that is chosen as an allowed dial-in protocol has a configure option that allows other configuration changes. Each protocol has a different list of settings with TCP/IP having the most extensive set of additional options. One other option available with RAS is the capability to require encrypted authentication. If you select to require Microsoft encrypted authentication, you can also use data encryption.

Summary

As modem technology improves, so does the ability to extend the reach of modern networks as well as the speed at which they operate. In the near future, technologies such as cable modems, ADSL (Asymmetric Digital Subscriber Line), and wireless connections will offer new and exciting possibilities for extending networks and connecting with others. To make these new technologies both successful and available it will be important to have newer and better standards and protocols to enforce the regulation of the communication process.

17

MODEMS AND DIAL-UP TECHNOLOGIES

Remote Access Services (RAS)

by Arthur Cooper

IN THIS CHAPTER

CHAPTER 18

What are Remote Access Services (RAS)? Users today expect to be able to use the same applications and services no matter where they are located at any given time. This demand for connectivity has placed a tremendous burden on Information Technology (IT) departments. In order to understand why there is such a need for reliable RAS service, this chapter examines the chain of events leading up to modern RAS. It also explores the remote access solutions used in each era of RAS development. It makes sense to see where we have been in order to see where we are going.

The History of Remote Access Networking

In the late 1950s, it became apparent to most corporations, military organizations, and other agencies using mainframe computer systems that the ability to access data in these systems needed to extend beyond the traditional reaches of the connected terminal equipment. As you may or may not recall, computer data centers in the 1950s were mystical places filled with people in white lab coats. This continued until the IBM mainframe soon arrived, and the modern data center was born.

These data centers made computer services accessible for the masses, but users of these early data centers were forced to deal with many silly rules and requirements put forth by the data center personnel. Many times these rules would place serious constraints on the users. Inconvenient hours, formatting requirements, and any other of a myriad of requirements would make all users feel subservient to the data center. Many times, users would feel belittled when dealing with the data centers. Consequently, managers began looking for ways to gain access to the mainframe systems without having to go through the actual data center.

At this same time, a revolution was happening in the world of computers. The U.S. Government was setting up the Defense Advanced Research Projects Agency (DARPA) to begin testing new ways to connect unlike computer systems together. As management began to move terminal equipment out of the data centers and into their offices, DARPA was experimenting with long-haul connections between data centers. In larger corporations where mainframes were responsible for tracking budgets and inventories, management in these organizations began to realize the importance of decentralizing this information.

If the executives and middle managers were forced to access this data with large, cumbersome weekly printouts, the data they were using was only as good as the last printout. In many cases, a seven-day lag in information was unacceptable. This led to more printouts, and many managers felt that using these reports on a daily or weekly basis was a waste of time. Something had to happen. Access to the data in these mainframes needed to reach the user's level, and it had to happen fast.

Suddenly, something monumental happened. Line drivers and line conditioners became available. These devices allowed the data center to remotely connect terminals to the mainframe computer. The first candidates for these terminals were the managers of the data center themselves. Following that, terminals began to appear all over the workplace. Soon the information that had been available in only one location within the organization was being put into the hands of the people *needing* the information. Imagine that!

The 1970s

In the early days of "number-crunching," it was very rare to find an organization dispersed over a geographical area. For that reason, there was much interest in networking large mainframes together. Corporations, universities, and government agencies were the only major users of mainframe systems, and of the three, the government was the only entity interested in connecting computers that were separated geographically. However, as DARPA (the U.S. Defense Advanced Research Projects Agency) began to perfect the idea of computers communicating with other nonsimilar computers, the private sector began to take notice.

The modem became an extremely important device at this time, and the first modems were really nothing more than acoustic coupling devices that enabled a telephone to interface with a port on a computer system. A user connected to one data center could now gain access to information in other data centers via the network connections that existed between the centers. The modern data network was born.

Computer professionals then began to connect smarter terminal equipment to their mainframe systems. At this same time, terminals started to have built-in memory capabilities. This enabled them to store setup information. That way, when a terminal was used to establish a connection or session with a computer, the common setup commands could be automatically sent between the computer system and the terminal.

This convenience served only to whet the appetite of many mainframe users. The small computer system had arrived on the scene.

Users of data services began to experiment with connecting small computers via modem to their larger cousin—the mainframe. Although the original users of remote access connections were computer scientists and technicians, the concept was proven a sound one. Now it was possible to pass data back and forth between small computers and large mainframe systems.

The 1980s

During the 1980s, mainframes began to lose their importance in the world of computing. The IBM Personal Computer (PC) was introduced in 1981. Several Local Area Network (LAN) operating systems became available, and Novell became the clear leader from a sales standpoint. As small computer LANs became a standard in the workplace, the desire to remotely access these LANs from anywhere via a dial-up connection grew. Modems became cheap and available, and users began to demand quality dial-up connections for their PCs.

Novell, IBM, and Microsoft began to introduce various software packages embedded in their operating systems. These packages were designed to accommodate dial-up service. With emulation programs such as ProComm, PC users could dial into large computer systems or networks that were configured with stand-alone modems or modem pools.

The Advanced Research Projects Agency Network (ARPANET) became the Internet in 1969. Universities and private corporations were soon exploiting it, and in 1984 there were 1,000 mainframe computers connected to each other via the Internet. In the years between 1987 and 1994, the Internet grew from 10,000 connected hosts to two million connected hosts. Users began to demand Internet access from their homes, and Novell and Microsoft were happy to accommodate them. Remote access in the 1990s has been able to closely duplicate and emulate the LAN services that users have come to depend upon.

The Craze of the 90s

Today, it is not uncommon to see the acronym RAS used as frequently as the acronym PC. Users are demanding that RAS networking be able to provide the same power of a LAN connection when dialing in to servers and network systems. Microsoft has built RAS into its NT operating system, and consequently, an entire cottage industry has sprung up in the last few years. Many third-party software packages now exist. RAS has become one of the most important technologies in the world of computing.

For those reasons, any potentially successful IT professional needs a full understanding of RAS. Many corporations are geographically dispersed, and RAS is the best way that employees can maintain constant ties to corporate computing resources. E-mail, work sharing, and many other applications are RAS-capable these days. RAS has earned its rightful place in the IT community. The next sections discuss what RAS does and the features it provides.

Establishing Remote Connections

In order to accommodate a dial-up connection, protocols must be used to standardize the way each end of the connection negotiates the data flowing between the host and the user, as shown in Figure 18.1.

FIGURE 18.1.
User-to-host connection.

> **NOTE**
>
> For the purposes of this chapter, the term *host* refers to the server, computer system, or network that the RAS user uses. The term *user* refers to the small computer or PC that initiates the RAS connection to the host.

In the early days of dial-up connections, the PCs doing the dialing were meant to emulate directly connected terminal equipment. These dial-up connections were used to enable the PC to look and act the same as a terminal directly connected to the host. As a result, the only software needed in the user's PC was dialing software and a program that simulated the same character signals that a terminal produced.

> **NOTE**
>
> ASCII refers to the American Standard Code for Information Interchange, and it is a 7-bit character code. EBCDIC refers to an 8-bit character code invented by IBM, and it means Extended Binary Coded Decimal Interchange Code.

These first dial-up systems were effective, but they were also slow. Modem connect speeds were generally less than 1200bps. Some of the earlier connections were acoustic coupling devices in which the telephone receiver was connected to an acoustic coupler resembling two Mickey Mouse ears.

Developing Protocol Standards

The only protocols that came into play during these early, point-to-point, user-to-host remote connections were the protocols defining the electromechanical standards between the modems and the telephone lines themselves. In the United States, the Bell Telephone Company established standards defining modem-to-modem connections. Early standards were the Bell 103 and Bell 212A standards. Later, these were adopted internationally and the CCITT developed standards V.21 and V.22. These standards define the transmission between two connected modems.

> **NOTE**
>
> The CCITT is an acronym for a French title of the International Telecommunications Consultative Committee. The "V" and "X" standards apply to data communications connections. Typically, the "V" standards are for data connections and modem use over "voice" and dial-up circuits. The "X" standards refer to digital/data standards. These standards are occasionally updated or deleted. The CCITT defines standards that are recommended for use by the entire world. Recently, they reorganized the CCITT, and they are now calling themselves the International Telecommunications Union (ITU)-T.

18

REMOTE ACCESS SERVICES (RAS)

The AT Command Set

Hayes, Inc., came out with the Hayes Smartmodem and standardized the AT (attention) command set for use with PCs and dial-up modems. This AT command set is still used today. Today, the AT command set is incorporated into most terminal emulation software for the PC. It is this AT command set that enables a PC to force a modem off-hook, to dial, and so on. Remember, though, in the early days users had to manually enter AT commands to force the modem to do something.

This connection limited users to performing only those functions the host system could perform. If the direct-connection terminals in the data centers did not have access to network resources, typically the dial-up users didn't have access either.

Perhaps the best example of terminal remote access service is the type of networking that went on in bank computer systems during this period. Banks would network smaller host systems in branch offices with larger mainframe hosts in the parent office. The smaller branch systems were set up to update the larger, central hosts.

Many times, these banks would set up the branch systems to perform an "upward" passage of data from themselves to the central host on a real-time basis. This was done on dedicated telephone lines and modems. However, the "downward" flow of data from the central host to the branch systems was done only once a day. Figure 18.2 shows an example. Branch "A" and branch "B" are indeed connected to the central system. However, they are not connected to each other. Data flowing from the branch systems to the central system is constant, but data flowing from the central system to the branches is on a once-a-day basis. Therefore, the data in the branch systems is always from the previous business day.

FIGURE 18.2.

Central system with branch connections.

Basically, all dial-up access came through a branch office. Dial-up access in those days tried to mimic what the terminals connected to the mainframe by direct wiring were capable of doing. The next section examines the upper-level processes that take place when users initiate remote access sessions with host systems.

RAS Connection Protocols

To examine the upper-level processes of remote connections, you need to explore the two most prevalent connection protocols in use today on remote access connections. As an introduction to the discussion of these protocols, a quick summary of the process that occurs when a user-to-host remote access session is established is in order.

Establishing a Session

To initiate a remote connection, one end or the other (usually the user) dials out to the other end (usually the host). Today, the user's PC running some sort of dialing program accomplishes this. Windows 95 has a built in dial-up networking function. After the modems have negotiated a connection with each other via the telephone line and the carrier is stable between them, digital signals on the output port of the modem pass this information back to the user's PC.

> **NOTE**
>
> Carrier refers to the "pilot" or main analog signal that a modem transmits to another modem over a communications link when a data communications connection is established between the two devices.

Second, the user invokes the software program he or she is using to communicate with the host system. This may be some terminal emulation package such as ProComm, or it may be a built-in dialing program. Again, Windows 95 has built-in negotiation software in its dial-up networking function. Whatever the user needs to do to negotiate upper level processes in the host is done at this time. Perhaps the user invokes some unique program written exclusively for a particular corporation.

TCP/IP Access Protocols

Most people who are involved with remote access connections are connecting to the Internet or the company intranet. For that reason, Transport Control Protocol/Internet Protocol (TCP/IP) is the protocol suite they use to pass data back and forth over the connection. Today, when TCP/IP is being used as the main transport protocol suite, either SLIP or PPP will be used as the main access protocol for dial-up sessions between a PC and a RAS server.

SLIP

The Internet was becoming an extremely important medium in the early 1980s. Perhaps the most important protocol developed in these days started at 3COM Corporation. 3COM developed a technology that would enable TCP/IP packets to be transferred over telephone lines. TCP/IP is still the Internet protocol suite that moves all data from place to place.

The main carrying mechanism that moves data in the TCP/IP world is the IP packet. Without going into a lengthy discussion of IP and IP addressing, IP is the connectionless, Internet protocol that moves TCP and User Datagram Protocol (UDP) packets from one place to another. TCP and UDP packets carry the data the user has sent. In other words, consider IP as the carrier and the TCP or UDP packet as the item being carried.

Any dial-up connection that could carry IP packets needed to be configured to transmit all the characters in the IP packet. 3COM developed a new protocol, and it was called the Serial Line Internet Protocol (SLIP). This protocol was not really a protocol at all; it did, however, act as one. SLIP has never become a standard Internet protocol. All SLIP does is "frame" an IP packet and send it through from one end to the other, as shown in Figure 18.3. This protocol provides no addressing, packet type identification, error control, or compression. However, this lack of capabilities also means SLIP is very easy to implement.

FIGURE 18.3.

SLIP framing of IP packets.

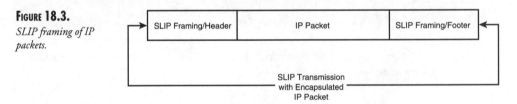

Rick Adams implemented SLIP for Berkeley Unix in 1984, and he released it out into the public domain. Remote access for Internet services became commonplace.

To this day, many PC connection programs designed for Internet connectivity have a SLIP option. The fact that there is no standard SLIP specification means there is no maximum defined packet size. Many forms of SLIP came to be in the late 1980s, but SLIP just provided a frame to carry IP packets over serial lines. Remember, the user's PC still has to communicate with its modem using AT commands. The modem still has to dial out and establish a connection with the host computer's modem. Today, ITU-T standards are responsible for maintaining modem-to-modem connectivity.

SLIP comes into play only after a stable connection has been made between the modems and the user and host system have established connectivity. After this occurs, the SLIP protocol enables the passage of IP packets over this serial user-to-host connection. Remember this: SLIP passes no address information. This means that each computer (host and user) must know the other's address in order for IP to pass back and forth effectively. This is always a function of whatever type of SLIP software/dialer you are using in the user PC and the SLIP software in the host system.

SLIP has many limitations, and users demand error-free connections when dialing into host systems. The fact that SLIP could not perform any compression, addressing, or error checking made users demand a better connection protocol. This gave way to the birth of PPP.

PPP

The point-to-point protocol (PPP) was another design that grew from user demand. This protocol is designed primarily to provide a link between two peers on serial ports. Typically the use of PPP is limited to dial-up user-to-host connections. However, some people use PPP in host-to-host or host-to-router connections. This chapter examines PPP as it is used in remote access, dial-up connections.

PPP was standardized as a true Internet protocol. SLIP never earned that distinction. Many users still swear by SLIP, but the error rate can be astronomical at times. If you want a remote access connection that operates properly when passing IP packets, PPP is the protocol of choice.

PPP also packages the IP packets within its frame as SLIP does, but other things are happening in addition to simply framing the data. PPP also sets up a session of link control between the user and host, and this session is controlled by a Link Control Protocol (LCP). LCP then sets up the link between the user and the host on a PPP session.

This is actually the first thing that happens when a PPP session begins. LCP packets are transmitted between the user and the host. These packets actually configure and test the link that is established. Issues such as link quality and link echo are tested to ensure the link is stable. There are three classes of LCP packets, as follows:

- Link Establishment packets used to establish and configure a link
- Link Termination packets used to terminate a link
- Link Maintenance packets used to manage and debug a link

LCP ensures the link is running and stable and passes this information to the main PPP protocol to declare the link up. After this has happened, PPP then sends out what is called a Network Control Protocol (NCP) packet. The NCP packet is specific for the type of data to be passed over the PPP link.

An NCP packet is sent by the originator of the PPP connection (in most cases, the user who dialed the host). This NCP packet tells the host what type of traffic is to be passed over the PPP link. The name of the PPP Network Control Protocol (NCP) for IP datagrams is called IP Control Protocol (IPCP) and is responsible for configuring, enabling, and disabling IP functionality at both ends of the link. IPCP packets may not be sent until LCP has finished the configuration negotiation phase. After that phase is complete, the IPCP protocol will signal that it is ready to begin forwarding IP packets and datagrams.

After this happens, the user and the host are capable of transmitting and receiving IP datagrams and packets. As discussed previously, IP is the mainstay of the Internet today in terms of the carrying mechanism. For that reason, it makes no sense to discuss other NCPs that PPP may use to transfer data. However, many other NCP protocols are incorporated into some versions of PPP.

Current Trends

SLIP and PPP are definitely the workhorses of remote access sessions these days. It is rare to see users of remote access services using anything other than these two protocols when passing data between themselves and a host system. When setting up RAS Servers in Windows NT, the PPP protocol is used in 99 percent of the implementations of today. However, it is also important to understand the services RAS servers are required to provide once a PPP connection has been established.

> **NOTE**
>
> Do not let the term *services* as used in this chapter confuse you with the term "services" as it relates to setting up a "service" in either Windows 95 or Windows NT Server. These are entirely different terms.

Remote Access Transport Services

In the world of RAS, users are interested in being able to connect to a host system, using that host system for whatever purpose they need, and then disconnecting the RAS connection. It would be impossible in a chapter this size to go into all the different services that a user may use on a remote connection. Instead, this chapter reviews today's most-used services.

How RAS Users Are Currently Connecting

Typically, most corporations fit into one of the following three categories:

- Large corporation: a corporation that has at least twenty-five or more geographic locations minimum. Each of these locations typically has a LAN in place that serves the networking needs of the employees at that location.

- Medium corporation: a corporation that may have more than two or three geographic locations but less than twenty-five. Either there would be a LAN at each location, or there may be a "central" computer system located at the headquarters location. The other locations may connect to the headquarters computer by dial-up connections.

- Small corporation: a corporation that has only one location, and there may or may not be a LAN at that location.

A large organization usually has an established corporate intranet. Users of the corporate intranet are usually using PCs located in their work areas. However, if they are active telecommuters, on-the-road workers, or they are work-at-home types, they may take a laptop PC from place to place.

In order for these people to be productive when using remote access connections, these connections must provide identical services to the user's PC in all locations. Whether he is sitting at the desk in his corporate office using a direct-LAN connection or dialing in from a hotel, what a user sees on the PC screen must be the same at all times. After allowing for exceptions, this should be the goal of any RAS arrangements being implemented on a corporate intranet.

This standard may not apply to users who are in the medium corporations. These users may be used to dialing in to a central headquarters computer on a regular basis. If so, dialing from your home or your place of employment should be the same. Many medium corporations have one central dial-up host that serves the entire corporation. The users in small corporations are many times dialing in to an Internet Service Provider (ISP) and simply using the ISP's e-mail capabilities to pass mail to people in other organizations.

Small corporations, on the other hand, may have better computers, LANs, and connectivity than large ones. This is due to the fact that the costs to improve on a small scale tend to be lower. In addition, some large corporations do not even allow dial-up access into their systems for security or confidentiality reasons. Given any situation, one can make several assumptions about most RAS connections:

- Most RAS connections are established for users to gain access to a LAN, a corporate intranet, or the Internet.
- After the connection is made, most of the time PPP is the protocol used to handle the passage of data through the connection.
- The main data transport service that will be used on this connection is TCP/IP in most cases.

Every rule has exceptions, and these statements can be challenged. But in most cases, these statements hold true. The next section discusses what TCP/IP can do for its remote users.

TCP/IP—The RAS Workhorse

No discussion of RAS would be complete without a discussion of TCP/IP. TCP/IP is one of the most misused terms in the world of computing and telecommunications. TCP/IP is actually two things. First, it is a combination protocol. This combination protocol was formed when the Transport Control Protocol (TCP) was combined with the Internet Protocol (IP). Second, TCP/IP forms the basis of a suite of other protocols that are used on the Internet and in corporate intranets.

Discussion of these other protocols is not within the scope of this chapter. However, the more common ones such as Telnet, File Transfer Protocol (FTP), and Simple Mail Transfer Protocol (SMTP) are all part of this TCP/IP suite. The Internet was the proving ground for these protocols, and long before the Open Systems Interconnect (OSI) Reference Model was put together, TCP/IP was an entirely open system. "Open" simply means that any system claiming to be TCP/IP compliant can communicate with any other system claiming to be fully TCP/IP compliant.

When TCP/IP is fully implemented in RAS user-to-host connections, all the wonderful "toys" users are addicted to on their office LANs can also be used on their remote PCs. Web browsers such as Netscape, e-mail programs such as Eudora, FTP programs such as WS-FTP and others can all be implemented in the remote user's PC.

This is where the world stands now when it comes to using RAS services, and it does not look as if that is going to change for a very long time. TCP/IP has limitations, but it is still the number one protocol used in the world to move data around. The future may change the way an IP packet looks, as the entire networking industry is looking to implement IP Next Generation (IPv6) addressing on all the Internet hosts. This would use a 128-bit versus 32-bit addressing scheme.

> **NOTE**
>
> Currently, an IP address uses 4 octets (32 bits) of information to show an address. An octet is any number between 0 and 255 that is represented by eight bits, hence the term octet. These numbers appear as 00000001, 00000010, 00000011, and so on. However, because humans are not used to looking at numbers in this fashion, dotted decimal notation is used when representing IP addresses. Therefore, an IP address may look like 207.120.10.12. In reality, the address the network sees for 207.120.10.12 on a binary basis is 11001111, 01111000, 00001010, 00001100. IPv6, or IP addressing, version 6, is going to be a 128-bit versus 32-bit scheme.

As far as RAS is concerned, TCP/IP is currently the "number-one workhorse" being implemented in all RAS connections. After the RAS connection has been established, TCP/IP is then implemented and activated by peer processes in the user and host computer systems. For this reason, the user system is assigned an IP address. This IP address is what is used to properly address and control the flow of data from user to host and from host to user.

Assigning IP Addresses

Any corporate LAN or intranet that is using TCP/IP as its means to address systems on the network also assigns IP addresses to RAS users and RAS connections. These IP addresses are either *static*, which means they never change, or they are *dynamic*, which means that the network assigns a different IP address every time the RAS connection is made.

A static IP address is usually used on LANs and intranets that do not have access to the Internet. If they do have access to the Internet, they typically have a gateway and/or firewall system between the LAN or intranet and the Internet. An IP static address is not going to change in a

RAS user's PC. A dynamic IP address is assigned by the host system when the user initiates the RAS connection.

Typically, this is done by the host system using a protocol known as *Dynamic Host Configuration Protocol* (DHCP). This protocol is implemented in a DHCP server (host system), and it assigns and keeps track of the IP addresses that are handed out on RAS connections. DHCP can also be used on LANs to hand out IP addresses when LAN users log on to their PCs.

After the RAS Connection Is Established

To establish a RAS connection, the user's PC (using a modem) dials the host system. The host system answers the call, establishes the connection, and upper processes in the host cooperate with upper processes in the user system to get the transport system running. With TCP/IP, the host either reads the IP address of the user system (if it is static) or it assigns an IP address (dynamic IP is being used). Either one of these actions gets TCP/IP up and running.

Either way, after this has happened (true TCP/IP connectivity is established between the user and the host), the user is now free to start the applications that are to be used over the RAS connection. These applications can now be used to give the user full access to the same services on the office PC.

Most users and hosts initiate TCP/IP as the main transport service on a connection. However, many people out there in the small to medium corporations are still using the NetBEUI protocol. The next section examines that protocol and explains how it operates.

NetBEUI

NetBEUI is not considered a prime transport for data and applications anymore, so a lengthy discussion of how it operates is not extremely beneficial. Before discussing NetBEUI, it is important to describe NetBIOS, because part of the NetBEUI acronym contains NetBIOS. NetBIOS (Network Basic Input/Output System) is a program that enables applications on different computers to communicate within a LAN. It was created by IBM for its early PC Network. NetBIOS was adopted by Microsoft. Since that time, it has become a de facto industry standard.

NetBEUI stands for NetBIOS Extended User Interface and is one of those protocols that lingers on even after outliving its usefulness. Many may argue about the usefulness of NetBEUI, but in all reality, this protocol is not going to remain in use for any amount of time.

NetBEUI came into its own as an important protocol when Microsoft packaged it with its Windows for Workgroups (WFWG) operating system. Previous versions of Windows did not have built-in protocols, and the way they were networked was by invoking network protocols at the DOS level.

NetBEUI is not the protocol of choice for several reasons:

■ NetBEUI is not a routable protocol like TCP/IP.

> **NOTE**
>
> NetBEUI signals have no real means to travel outside the confines of a LAN. In some cases, token ring source routing has been used to route NetBEUI from a token ring LAN, but this method is not efficient or effective. NetBEUI was optimized for the LAN environment only.

■ NetBEUI does not support the routing of messages to other networks, and its interface must be adapted to other protocols such as IPX or TCP/IP. If you feel you *must* use NetBEUI, the best method is to install NetBEUI and TCP/IP in each PC on the LAN. Then you can set the server up to use NetBEUI for communication within the LAN and TCP/IP for communication beyond the LAN. This would be the best way to ensure that NetBEUI causes minimal problems. On a large LAN, TCP/IP is all you need; NetBEUI just slows things down.

■ NetBEUI operates without addressing, on LANs, and it is a very chatty protocol. A lot of information is passed back and forth on computers that use NetBEUI as a data transfer mechanism. This passing information causes NetBEUI to hog a lot of space on the LAN when it is being used. The originating system sends out a broadcast packet to determine where the other computer is. Each computer on the LAN must examine this packet. On a large LAN, this equates to constant packet examination by all the PCs on the LAN.

Some LANs still use NetBEUI. RAS users dialing into these LANs need to use a program in their PCs that is capable of performing NetBEUI connectivity over the dial-up connection. Windows 95 provides this capability in its dial-up networking program. However, the bottom line is that you do not really want to use NetBEUI unless you have to.

IPX/SPX

Novell became a force to be reckoned with in the 1980s. In fact, Novell moved much faster than Microsoft did when it came to providing network support beyond the traditional LAN connection.

Until recently, Microsoft did not feel the Internet was of strategic importance. Networking beyond the confines of a LAN was something the early versions of Windows simply did not do well at all. Novell had more vision in the 1980s. Novell had always adhered to open standards, but in order to facilitate strong sales in the world of networking, Novell opted to invent two proprietary protocols. These protocols are what made Netware the powerhouse that it was in these days. They were:

■ Internetwork Packet Exchange (IPX): IPX is a networking protocol that interconnects networks using Novell's NetWare client/server software. IPX is a packet-oriented protocol. IPX works at the Network Layer of the OSI Reference Model, and it is connectionless. In other words, it doesn't require a connection be set up before packets are sent to a destination. You will recall the Network Layer of the OSI Model is layer 3. Therefore, IPX is considered a Layer 3 Protocol.

■ Sequenced Packet Exchange (SPX): SPX completes the process, because it manages the actual packet acknowledgment between two users on an IPX/SPX connection. SPX does this at the Transport Layer of the OSI Reference Model. Therefore, SPX is considered a Layer 4 Protocol.

One thing makes Novell's IPX/SPX combination a winner: it can be routed. It also performs error checking and allows internetworking of LANs. Because IPX is always dynamically routed and the routing architecture works by learning network addressing automatically, nothing special needs to be done in the setup of an IPX network in order to get routing to function. IPX/SPX networking has several drawbacks, however:

■ It is more limited in terms of how many addresses are available. It consists of a 4-byte network number, a 6-byte node number, and a 2-byte socket number. The node number is the hardware address of the actual user's PC network interface card (NIC). This number must be unique inside the particular IPX network. The network number must be the same for all nodes on a physical network segment. Socket numbers correspond to the particular service being accessed.

■ IPX/SPX connections require the capability to broadcast to other NetWare servers and IPX routers on the network. That is how they can all find one another on Novell networks. Because there is no effective way to broadcast using IP, all the servers and routers on the network need to maintain a list of the IP addresses of the other IPX servers and routers on the network. That can be a limiting factor.

However, as you can see, Novell did take an excellent stab at putting together an internetworking system for its products, but it still is not quite as good as TCP/IP in terms of addressing, flexibility, and capability.

Today, RAS users of Novell LANs and networks are able to utilize certain TCP/IP transport mechanisms by *tunneling* IPX over TCP/IP. Tunneling is done by using UDP, another member of the TCP/IP suite. Novell networks can be set up to take IPX packets and place them inside UDP packets. These UDP packets are then packaged inside an IP packet the very same way TCP packets are packaged in a larger IP packet. After this has occurred, the IPX data is transmitted over the network in these IP packets.

In summation, RAS users are generally on TCP/IP connections when dialing in to the host; however, there may be times when NetBEUI or IPX/SPX can be used. Therefore, it behooves you to know and understand these other two transport protocols.

PPTP

The point-to-point tunneling protocol (PPTP) is gaining a lot of attention lately because it enables RAS users to connect to a host system that may be far away on the other end of a TCP/IP network. In other words, a RAS user can dial into one host system, and this host system can then transfer the RAS user's data to another host system very far away on the same TCP/IP.

Now you are probably wondering why this seems different from a RAS user simply dialing into a host that is connected to the Internet.

After all, after he or she has done this, that connection provides access to all the resources on the Internet. However, when a corporation wants to maintain a private network, and it is not large enough to financially afford the costs of a large intranet, PPTP can help build an intranet-on-the-Internet.

That is the real utility of PPTP. It enables corporations to set up *virtual private networks* (VPN) via the Internet. PPTP comes pre-packaged with Windows NT Server and NT Workstation 4.0, and if you are brave, Microsoft has developed a beta version for the Windows 95 operating system. RAS users can use the PPTP protocol to securely connect to a private network as a remote access client via the Internet. In other words, PPTP enables users to set up and take down on-demand, virtual private networks over the Internet.

PPTP has been successful because a PPTP forum was developed. The companies of the PPTP Forum, which include Microsoft Corporation, Ascend Communications, 3Com/Primary Access, ECI Telematics, and US Robotics, are all working together to ensure that PPTP is developed properly. Figure 18.4 shows how PPTP sets up these VPNs over the Internet.

Figure 18.4.

PPTP and VPN networks.

The process starts when the RAS user connects to a local ISP with a modem. This connection uses the PPP protocol to establish the connection and encrypt data packets. After a connection to the Internet established by the PPP protocol has been established, the PPTP protocol steps in and creates a control connection from the RAS user to the distant PPTP server on the Internet. This is a TCP/IP connection over the Internet, but because it was established by PPTP, it's called the PPTP *tunnel*.

Finally, the PPTP protocol creates IP datagrams containing encrypted PPP packets that are then sent through the PPTP tunnel to the PPTP server. The PPTP server disassembles the IP datagrams and decrypts the PPP packets, and then routes the decrypted packets to the VPN private network. This is typically a LAN on the other side of the PPTP server. In this way PPTP creates a private network connection over the Internet. It is gaining a lot of attention these days, and ISPs are anxious to work with their clients to provide dial-up PPTP for a company's travelling, hotel-bound, or telecommuting workers.

This means that small companies can have an intranet-like private network that runs over the Internet. In this situation, the costs to establish a wide-area network (WAN) using PPTP can be a lot cheaper than having to actually purchase and install dial-up host systems all over the country. The dial-up access is provided by an ISP. When you look at the cost of leased lines to connect hosts together, the amount can be staggering. However, the cheap, flat rate pricing that most ISPs can offer makes it a common sense choice to use PPTP to create a private network. With that in mind, the next section explores the capabilities of the big three networking systems in terms of RAS.

Windows NT RAS Capabilities

Although Microsoft is constantly being told by networking industry professionals that Windows NT is a LAN operating system, and it does not operate well in a WAN, or "enterprise network" situation, it really is not a true statement anymore. If you look at the current situation that Novell is faced with, Microsoft is coming out on top when it comes to corporations choosing a Network Operating System (NOS). After all, Novell is being told by networking industry "watchers" and investors that NT is going to conquer them. This is something they are forced to deal with daily.

Because Windows NT is no doubt the leader of the pack at this time, it is important to examine the two most common implementations of Windows NT RAS:

- As an Internet gateway/router for a LAN
- To provide Internet access for dial-in users

Using RAS as an Internet Gateway/Router for a LAN

Any administrator can tell you that using NT to perform as an Internet router or a gateway is not the thing to do. However, NT RAS is quite capable of doing so, and here is how it happens. In order to act as a router or a gateway, an NT server must have two separate networks connected to it.

An NT server can sit between two separate networks such as a LAN and the Internet. Within the NT server, there are two separate network interfaces. Because the subject of this discussion is RAS, naturally one of these interfaces is a modem. In almost 99 percent of the cases in which NT is configured to do Internet gateway routing via RAS, the other network interface is a standard token ring (TR) or Ethernet network interface card (NIC). Figure 18.5 illustrates this point.

In Figure 18.5, network "A" is an Ethernet LAN connected to the NT server's NIC card, and network "B" is simply a modem for connectivity to the Internet. This arrangement enables the users connected to the LAN to have access to the Internet through the NT RAS server. NT basically routes information between these two separate networks based on the IP address and subnet mask information.

FIGURE 18.5.

*RAS as a gateway/
router for a LAN.*

As an example, assume that the IP address assigned to the Ethernet NIC in Figure 18.5 (network "A") is 234.56.78.90 with a subnet mask of 255.255.255.0. This means the NT server will assume any IP address between 234.56.78.1 and 234.56.78.254 resides on network "A." Any other IP address the NT server encounters is assumed to be out on the Internet (network "B") side of the server.

On the other side of the NT server, a RAS/modem connects to the Internet. This is network "B." The NT server has an account on an ISP, and the ISP assigns the block of IP addresses from 234.56.78.1 through 234.56.78.254 to this NT server.

If a user on the Internet sends something destined for IP address 234.56.78.50, this information is routed to the ISP via the Internet. After the ISP gets the data, it initiates a call by dialing the telephone number of the modem on the NT server. The server's modem answers the ISP's modem and establishes a PPP connection. Now the data destined to the NT server passes through the PPP connection to the NT server. The NT server, in turn, looks at the IP address being sent to it.

Because that address is one of the addresses the server knows is on the Ethernet LAN attached to its NIC card, it sends this data destined for 234.56.78.50 out on the LAN. It flows to a PC assigned this address. That is how Internet data reaches the user on the LAN via the RAS gateway. Now consider the way that information from the LAN destined for the Internet gets through the NT RAS server and out to the Internet.

Whenever users on the LAN send information to each other via TCP/IP, they, of course, use their assigned addresses. Because all the addresses assigned in the example are between 234.56.78.1 and 234.56.78.254, you can have 254 users on the LAN constantly sending information to each other. This includes the NT server, as it is address 234.56.78.90 in this example.

You may be wondering how the NT server knows LAN traffic is passed between users on the LAN and does not need to pass through the server and go out to the Internet. If you recall, the subnet mask listed above and programmed into the NT RAS server for network "A" was 255.255.255.0. This is the magic thing making the gateway function work. Because it has a subnet of 255.255.255.0, the server looks at each IP packet transmitted on network "A," the LAN segment. As long as the first three digits of a packet begin with 234.56.78, the server assumes this data belongs on the LAN and not the Internet. The subnet mask tells the story.

This is how subnet masking works. A mask of 255.255.255.0 is telling the server to review the first three numbers. If the subnet mask were 255.255.0.0, the server would review the first two numbers, and if there were a subnet mask of 255.0.0.0, the server would review the first IP address digit only.

When the appropriate number of subnet digits match the same number of the IP address physically assigned to the server, the server reviews the remaining last digit and ensures it is not 90. If it is 90, the server assumes the data in this IP packet is addressed to itself, and in this example it is. In other words, one of the PCs on network "A" sent data to 234.56.78.90 and the server believes it to be destined for it.

Now, imagine one of the users on the LAN sends out IP packets destined for IP address 236.45.11.2 and the data is destined for the Internet. The NT server looks at the address. Because the first three digits are not 234.56.78, the server knows this data is destined for a system out on the Internet. It passes that data out through the RAS setup, the modem dials the ISP's modem, and this establishes a PPP connection to send the data along its way.

You have just perfected an Internet/LAN gateway in both directions! This is probably the most common RAS setup utilized in NT servers that are hosting small LANs of between 5 and 75 users who want Internet access at an affordable rate. Most ISPs happily assist their users in setting this up, and they assign the IP addresses and subnet mask for your LAN based on your needs, the number of users, and the addresses they have available. It works well.

Using RAS to Provide Internet Access for Dial-In Users

If you want to look at the other side of the RAS coin, you need to understand how RAS implemented on an NT server can provide Internet access for a corporation's employees, as shown in Figure 18.6.

In Figure 18.6, network "A" is a NIC connection, as before. However, in this example the NT RAS server is also tied to the Internet via an Integrated Services Digital Network (ISDN) connection.

Network "B" has the same setup as before. However, now look at this NT RAS server as being a dial-in Internet access point for RAS users as well as an Internet gateway for the LAN users in network "A." The sequence of events that provide Internet access for a LAN user is pretty much the same as it was before, except this time, the RAS setup in the NT server is set up for dial-in only. Because that is the case, any IP packets addressed to an address other than one on the LAN are sent via the ISDN connection to the Internet.

FIGURE 18.6.

Using RAS to provide Internet access.

If a dial-in user wants Internet access, the sequence of events is as follows. First, a user ("Fred" in this example) dials into the modem (network "B"). When a PPP connection is set up between the Fred's PC and the NT RAS server, TCP/IP begins to flow across this PPP connection. Fred then sends out data destined for the Internet.

Assume for the purposes of this discussion that the IP addresses are the same as those used before. If you recall, the NIC in the server was assigned IP address 234.56.78.90 and the subnet mask being used on the LAN segment (network "A") was 255.255.255.0. Assume also that all the remote dial-in RAS users are assigned static IP addresses. Recall that a static IP address is permanently assigned to the user.

In this example, you can use the address 243.65.87.10 to dial up Fred. Now, when Fred gets the TCP/IP flowing between his PC and the NT server, the NT server recognizes that Fred's address does not belong on the LAN. After all, it is not between 234.56.78.1 and 234.56.78.254, and it does not match up with anything else on the server. The server knows 243.65.87.10 is assigned to Fred. Anything Fred sends out not addressed to himself that does not fit between 234.56.78.1 and 234.56.78.254 is sent out to the Internet via the ISDN connection.

As mentioned earlier, the RAS is set up for dial-in only (this is easily accomplished in NT RAS setup options), but this does not mean bidirectional IP traffic does not flow over the PPP link. It simply means the NT server knows incoming requests are to be handled by the RAS modem only, and this also means Internet traffic coming to and from the LAN traverses the Internet ISDN link.

Likewise, after a remote RAS user has dialed into the server and established a TCP/IP connection, any Internet traffic coming to and from the RAS user traverses the Internet ISDN link. If Fred starts transmitting data destined for 166.34.27.128, the NT server knows that address is not on the LAN (network "A"). The server also recognizes it as not being destined for the server's NIC card or for Fred. Consequently, data goes out the ISDN connection to the Internet.

In summation, two major RAS setups are being used today:

- NT RAS can provide routing/gateway service to the Internet for a small, connected LAN.
- NT RAS can provide an excellent gateway to the Internet for dial-in RAS users while still providing the same gateway services for a connected LAN.

Novell NetWare Connect Software's RAS Capabilities

Naturally, any discussion of RAS requires that you look at how Novell is doing things in the world of RAS. Novell is still trying to win the world over to IPX/SPX, so as you can assume, anything new Novell is going to implement in Netware version 5.0 will be based upon this protocol suite. Even if they are implementing TCP/IP, the NetWare servers on the LAN will run IPX/SPX as their main protocol suite. This is the only way Novell can keep everything downward compatible with older Netware systems.

The scenarios that Novell NetWare Connect software uses are identical to the ones Windows NT RAS uses. NetWare Connect setups are used to provide gateway/routing between Novell LANs and either an intranet or the Internet. The only difference is the fact that in most cases NetWare Connect tunnels the IPX/SPX over a TCP/IP connection that resides on an established PPP link. The RAS user implements a connection to the Novell LAN server by dialing the modem connected to the server.

After a PPP link has been established, the host system gets the TCP/IP link up and running between itself and the RAS user's PC. After this link is up, the Novell server begins to pass the IPX/SPX packets used on its network via IP packets. Unfortunately, NetWare Connect has been plagued with problems in almost each revision Novell releases.

The fact is that 80 to 85 percent of new LAN and/or network installations are going in as Windows NT. RAS will no doubt play a small role as far as Novell is concerned, but there is no large established base of RAS users calling into NetWare servers. Furthermore, most of the NetWare servers hosting dial-in RAS services are doing so utilizing one of many third-party software packages that try hard to emulate the Windows RAS software. Microsoft has definitely put Novell way behind in the RAS race.

Banyan Systems' RAS Capabilities

When Banyan Systems introduced the world to its VINES operating system, LAN was not really a household word. The VINES system was very stable, easy to set up, and easy to configure. Banyan made a classical mistake, though. As it developed its products, it did the same thing Sony did with the Betamax Video Cassette Recorder (VCR) system: making it a *closed* system. In most cases, if you wanted to add on to your existing VINES LAN, you had to get the equipment and software from Banyan, at a premium price.

By the time Banyan figured out how to produce some of its products through third-party vendors, it was too late. Now, very few LAN systems are running VINES. Banyan developed a product called StreetTalk, which basically lets you share file and directory resources on a Banyan LAN with other types of file services such as NFS (Unix), Windows NT File System (NTFS), and the old DOS-style File Allocation Table (FAT) systems.

The next part of the puzzle is a product Banyan calls Intranet Connect. This product takes things further by letting RAS users who connect to Banyan servers gain access to all the files, printers, and e-mail resources on the server or on the entire network. It does this by letting you use any Web browser like Netscape or Internet Explorer to access the information. It looks pretty but has not caught on to a great extent. Banyan is not a major player in the RAS game and rounds out the lower end of the big three scale. However, since one out of five existing LAN systems is running Banyan as the operating system, it warrants mentioning.

RAS Security Issues

Security is always a concern on any network, and RAS setups are just as susceptible to security problems. However, the security issues for RAS are really no different than they are for any other network configuration with a few exceptions. On a LAN, security is best managed when the LAN Administrator controls the show. With RAS, there are some precautions administrators should take.

As Windows NT is the main operating system being used for RAS access, here is an NT-specific list of precautions to heed when implementing RAS:

- Ensure that you have installed all Microsoft NT Service Packs. Microsoft puts many security enhancements in these free-downloadable add-ons to NT. These can be found at the Microsoft site: www.microsoft.com.

- Ensure that all of the hard drives on the NT RAS Server are using the NTFS file system mentioned earlier in the chapter. Format any old DOS File Allocation Table (FAT) partitions and make them NTFS partitions. NTFS enables you to place detailed restrictions on files and directories.

- If RAS is acting as a gateway "out" to the Internet for a LAN, you can set it up with your ISP to allow your RAS server to dial outbound calls to the ISP only. Any traffic destined for your LAN can be set up to transfer to the RAS server at predetermined times after a call to the ISP has been established. This prevents hackers from dialing into your RAS server.

- Remove the "GUEST" account from all machines having RAS access. Be sure that the "GUEST" account is removed from the RAS server as well. This is a large problem, as this account is created automatically when NT is installed.

- There is a built-in "EVERYONE" user group. Be sure that this is removed from all local resources on the RAS server. Microsoft's Service Pack 3 for NT has a replacement group called "AUTHENTICATED USERS" that can replace the "EVERYONE" group.

■ Use stringent password policies and be sure that RAS users are changing them at least once every month. Once a week is not unreasonable if the RAS server is placed inside the corporate network firewall.

■ The NT Event Viewer enables you to monitor failed attempts to log in to the system. If you feel you have a hacker problem, use the viewer and observe the actual amount of failed attempts you are experiencing on your RAS connections.

If you implement all of the above and you are diligent at monitoring the traffic levels on your RAS servers at all hours of the day, you can keep the hackers at bay. RAS does allow the use of encryption services. NT 5.0, according to a recent Microsoft press release, will support numerous encryption standards.

No system is ever secure, and as soon as you place a modem on your network, you always open a door to would-be hackers. For example, recall the discussion of banks that used to pass data from their central computers to their branch computers once a day. This practice was an early form of security. Any hacker who could get into a branch computer system could not infiltrate the central computer in terms of adding money to an account. It also eliminated hackers from pulling money down to the branch office.

Three forms of security are used on RAS connections:

■ Password-protection
■ Dialers
■ Callback systems

Passwords

Anyone setting up a RAS system should set up user login IDs and passwords for all the users who connect to the server. In NT, Novell NetWare Connect, Banyan Intranet Connect, and any other remote package, passwords are a standard option.

You must educate users not to use easily detectable words such as their names, Social Security numbers, and so on, as their passwords. These are the first passwords a hacker tries to use. Password use and administration is common sense. Passwords are the first line of defense on most RAS servers.

Dialers

Dialers provide another wall of defense following passwords. Most dialers function by requiring that a secret code number be transmitted to the server by the user of the RAS services. When the user dials into the RAS server, it is configured to ask for a certain code number. This code number may be randomly generated by the dialer or put into the dialer each time the user uses the system to make a RAS connection.

Dialers, code dialers, and code-generating dialers are very popular with large corporations. If a corporation has a large, almost unmanageable amount of people using its RAS services, a dialer can be an excellent way to ensure security is maintained. Weekly code updates can be distributed to valid employees only. In this manner, a former employee or hacker is thwarted when trying to log on to the network.

Callback Systems

These systems date back to the 1960s. In those days, hackers weren't as computer savvy. Therefore, all that was done for security purposes was the adding of a simple callback system. When authorized users entered their login ID and password, the system would hang up, and then dial a pre-determined number to call this user back, thereby ensuring that he was at the appropriate physical station. This worked fairly well until criminals learned how to tap the lines coming out of the computer system. By doing this, they could answer the callback.

Today, callback is used very rarely in private industry, but when used, it is usually combined with some sort of code-generating software. This ensures the person being called back is not a hacker who tapped into the computer system's telephone lines. This type of security is not a standard part of NT's RAS software, and any callback service implemented has to be done with a callback software application. However, if done correctly, callback can be one of the strongest ways to keep hackers out of your system. For that reason, the U.S. Government and many security agencies have implemented personalized callback systems that are virtually "unhackable" in most cases. Many private industry organizations are actually reconsidering the virtues of callback systems, as they can be made almost airtight when combined with code-generation software.

Summary

In this chapter, you read about where remote access service (RAS) came from and where it is most likely going. You read about the way modem connections are made and the SLIP and PPP protocols. These protocols set up the upper-level peer process connection. You read about how TCP/IP rides on top of the SLIP or PPP, and you learned that PPP is used more often than SLIP.

You also looked at the PPTP protocol and how private networks can be "built" upon the Internet with this protocol. You then explored the two main ways RAS is being utilized today: first as a gateway from a LAN to the Internet via RAS-enabled Internet connections, and secondly as an Internet access provider to remote RAS dial-in users.

You also read about the ways security can be implemented on RAS servers and connections. RAS is no doubt here to stay. The developments most apparent in the future are faster modems, better telephone lines, and improved user applications. These three things will combine to make RAS even better than it is today. As long as there are telecommuters, traveling employees, and people who like to work at home, RAS will stay around.

Intranets and Extranets

by Mark Sportack

IN THIS CHAPTER

The maturation of the Internet and the Internet Protocol (IP) has resulted in fundamental changes in the way that companies design and use IP networks. For example, internal IP-based Wide Area Networks are now *intranets*. This is more than just a semantic difference. These intranets are fully functional, miniature replicas of the Internet, complete with company-specific World Wide Web (WWW) content and applications.

Intranets have also sprouted appendages known as *extranets*. Extranets are selective extensions of an intranet into other intranets. This facilitates any mutual business processes between the two or more companies. Examples of an extranet might be a network that supports the *Electronic Data Interexchange* (EDI) between a customer and a supplier, or even the networking established to facilitate outsourcing certain business functions. The result is a semi-private IP WAN: not quite an Internet, but not a private intranet, either. It is an extranet!

An interesting twist on intranets is the use of a tunneling protocol to create a secure virtual private network (VPN) within an otherwise unsecured public network, like the Internet. VPNs enable companies to enjoy the benefits of an intranet, without having to incur the costs of building and operating one.

This chapter examines intranets, extranets, and VPNs. Specific emphasis is placed on their functional distinctions, their operational implications and uses, as well as some of their key component technologies.

Intranets

Initially, intranets weren't really intranets. They were amalgamations of leased lines and routers that companies used to forward packets of data for their users and traditional business application types. The predominant internetworking protocol used in these private leased-line networks was the Internet Protocol (IP). The commercialization of the Internet and the proliferation of hypertext were the impetuses behind the evolution of private IP networks into intranets. Many companies unwittingly began this evolution when they interconnected their private IP Wide Area Networks (WANs) to the Internet. Ostensibly, this was done to provide access to the rich and vast data stores of the Internet, but this was just the first step in a fundamental change in the way that they would use IP WANs in the future.

> **NOTE**
>
> In its early days of commercialization, the Internet still strongly resembled its original academic and scientific origins. Consequently, its signal-to-noise ratio was much more favorable than it is now, and interconnecting with the Internet could, legitimately, provide access to meaningful content. Today, the meaningful content is becoming increasingly obscured by electronic advertisements and mundane content.

After the interconnection with the Internet was established, the evolution from IP WAN to intranet became inevitable. Companies immediately began to look for ways to turn the cost of the interconnection into a source of revenue, rather than strictly an added expense. This meant exploring the technologies needed to build, maintain, and support a presence on the Internet.

Users, too, began exploring the new world. Browsers were free (if you didn't mind download-ing a new evaulation copy every 30 days!), and the net beckoned. These adventurous users quickly tired of surfing. They began experimenting with creating their own individual and/or organi-zational home pages. The net effect was a somewhat ad hoc acceptance of the tools and tech-nologies that would transform internal IP WANs into intranets. The actual transformation would have to wait until companies figured out what they could do (besides play) with these new technologies.

What's So Special About the Web?

The key enabling technology that made the Internet's content available to the masses, both individuals and companies, was the hyperconnectivity of the World Wide Web (WWW or Web). The Web is, arguably, the first successful, *universal* middleware. Its combination of protocols, programming language, and universal client presentation mechanism enables its executable programs, known as "content," to run on almost any physical platform. This is possible because Web programs use a software-based runtime environment: the browser.

> **NOTE**
>
> Middleware is any software that performs a translation, conversion, or other intermediary function. As such, the term can be applied to an incredibly wide variety of software products. The benefit of having an intermediary is that it provides a consistent Application Programming Interface (API), independent of physical platforms.

The *hypertext transfer protocol* (visible as the browser's HTTP command) was developed by CERN, a Swiss particle physics laboratory, to facilitate research on the Internet. This protocol put the Internet's content a mouse-click away. Hiding content location behind a point-and-click graphical user interface (GUI) made obsolete much of the older, more painful means of finding and retrieving Internet files, like the file transfer protocol (FTP) of the IP protocol suite. FTP is still useful, and very much needed; it just isn't used as a primary Internet information retrieval mechanism.

Just as hypertext transfers all but eliminated simple FTP requests, advances in search engine technologies rendered arcane tools like Archie, VERONICA, and JUGHEAD obsolete. They were no longer needed to locate files. More importantly, content was becoming too volatile to be effectively catalogued by such static mechanisms.

> **NOTE**
>
> Cartoon characters and rodents appear to have been the inspirations behind the naming conventions of early Internet search tools. These tools, crude by comparison to today's technologies, were essential to finding and retrieving information from the pre-hypertext Internet. These tools included Gopher, Archie, VERONICA, and JUGHEAD.
>
> Gopher derived from a menu-driven Internet data-retrieval tool. Ostensibly, it could be used to "go for" any of the data items listed in the menus on the user's behalf. The user was relieved of the burden of knowing network addresses and directory structures because the menu system embedded the pertinent information. The name "gopher" is also apparently a clever double entendre as the original gopher software was reportedly developed at the University of Minnesota, home of the Golden Gophers.
>
> Archie is a corruption of the term "archive." It was used throughout the Internet to describe an FTP search engine that functioned as an Internet-level directory, or archive, of files. Archie provided the specific location of those files. Given that FTP was the predominant file-retrieval mechanism, it was imperative to have the exact filename, including the full path of directories and subdirectories, as well as the host's name.
>
> VERONICA is an acronym that expands to *Very Easy Rodent-Oriented Netwide Index to Computerized Archives*. This is a program that enables users to search the Internet's content for specific resources based upon Boolean logic and attributes, rather than just a filename.
>
> JUGHEAD is another acronym that means *Jonzy's Universal Gopher Hierarchy Excavation and Display*. JUGHEAD was a search utility that could be used to search for a keyword across all the links in a Gopher database.

What About Intranets?

The success of the Internet and its World Wide Web accelerated the evolution of IP WANs to intranets. This was facilitated by the continuous development of Web-based software tools that were expressly designed for corporate environments. Software manufacturers realized that the real money to be made in Internet and Web technologies would come from companies, not individual users. Consequently, they targeted this market aggressively, and developed everything from graphical user interface tools for the creation and management of sites and their content to new programming languages specifically designed for private, corporate Web environments.

Database companies, too, provided APIs for their products, as well as middleware that would enable users to extract data from their databases using a browser. The result of these investments in intranet technologies was the rapid success of almost anything Web related. Internal IP WANs became intranets when they embraced the WWW middleware and began using it broadly in support of their business processes. To be sure, early adopters limited their efforts to posting pictures of their family, pets, houses, cars, and so forth, on the Web, but these insipid efforts were a necessary part of learning the capabilities of the new Web technologies.

Today, the browser is well on its way to becoming the universal presentation layer for all interactive applications. Thus, even traditional, interactive applications are poised to become enveloped by intranets. Some of the more obvious examples are the replacement of conversant telephony systems and paper forms with Web-based systems. The possible uses for an intranet are limited only by one's imagination and budget.

The Key Differences Between the Internet and Intranets

Although they may appear similar, technologically and functionally, intranets and the Internet must remain quite separate and distinct. The Internet is intentionally not secured. It is designed to be accessible by the general public, as well as by members of companies, educational facilities, government and/or research organizations, and so forth.

Intranets cannot afford such unrestricted accessibility. Access to networked resources must be parsed out on a need-to-have basis, even within the employees of the company. If such restrictions are essential to maintaining the integrity of the data, then the implications of using IP to interconnect that carefully controlled network environment to the wild and (relatively) unregulated Internet are staggering.

The information assets of private IP WANs that are interconnected to the Internet must be protected from access by the general public. Typically, mechanisms like firewalls, access lists, host and application layer security, and so forth, are used to limit access to the intranet resources from the Internet. Given that the networked computing resources of an intranet are blocked from general access, the intranet (and its content) can't really be considered part of the Internet. Thus, its inward-focused mimicry of the Internet has resulted in its name: "intranet." An intranet is illustrated in Figure 19.1, along with its connection to the Internet.

FIGURE 19.1.

An intranet.

Extranets

As information technology architects have become increasingly familiar with the usage and capabilities of intranets, the need for selectively extending intranets beyond their traditional borders has become apparent. Specifically, any scenarios that feature tightly coupled or interlocking business processes between two or more companies are logical candidates for an extranet. An *extranet* is a selective integration of two or more intranets for the purposes of facilitating specific business processes. Figure 19.2 depicts an extranet that interconnects two private intranets.

FIGURE 19.2.

An extranet.

Developing the extranet requires the interconnection of the participants' networks or intranets. Providing any connectivity at all using IP, or any other open internetworking protocol, results in the exposure of the entire contents of both intranets to accessibility from the other. Any security lapses on one side of the extranet automatically become security lapses for both intranets. The net effect of interconnecting two intranets is the creation of one large but semi-private network. Ostensibly, some measure of trust and mutual dependence or interdependence must first exist on the business level before an extranet can be considered. Similarly, the benefits of an extranet must also be quantifiable and desirable to both parties; otherwise, they would not knowingly undertake such a risky venture.

The key to successful extranetting is to manage the risks down to an acceptable level. This requires understanding the risks inherent in the internetworking technologies.

The Trouble with Open Protocols

Open protocols, by their very nature, are insecure. Their specifications are well known and agreed upon throughout the industry. This shouldn't be misconstrued as advocacy of security through obscurity: it is simply an acknowledgment of the increased risk factors of open protocols. It is a fact that the more well known a protocol is, the more well known its fundamental weaknesses are. These weaknesses can be exploited to gain illicit access to otherwise forbidden networked computing resources.

Open protocols also increase risk by virtue of their enjoying broad support. The more manufacturers support the protocol, the easier it is to develop distributed computing networks with hardware and software from different vendors. Unfortunately, open protocols are not necessarily consistent in their implementation from vendor to vendor. Open standards are developed via a consensual process. The proposed standard is published in a Request for Comments (RFC). The RFC identifies the basic structure, logic, and functionality of the proposal. These are given different levels of priority that include:

- Must have
- Should have
- May have

Over time, and through consensus, the proposal becomes an accepted industry standard. The finished product retains these three levels of priority for its features. Thus, it is sometimes trivially easy to find and exploit potential holes between vendor platforms with an open protocol, based upon the disparities between the various vendors' implementations of it.

The other danger of an open protocol is that the more hosts and devices on a network support it, the more opportunities there are to hack it. The larger a network grows, the more difficult it becomes to keep access privileges and other security mechanisms up to date and synchronized with each other.

> **NOTE**
>
> The term "hack," in this context, means an attack on the defenses of a network, host, or application. This definition might be offensive to application programmers. They regard hacks as generally interesting and amusing programming endeavors (usually in a low-level programming language) that produce little, if any, useful output. Add this to your list of reasons to avoid them!

The Trouble with Connectionless Protocols

A connectionless protocol is one that does not, in and of itself, establish a consistent path for its data transmission. IP is a connectionless Layer 3 protocol. It simply provides enough information in the header fields of its packet structure to identify the originator and the intended recipient. These packets are launched and the network is entrusted to forward them appropriately. It is neither necessary, nor probable, that two sequential packets will travel the same path between source and destination in a very large and busy network. In other words, IP works in a connectionless manner. It does not require that a physical path, or bandwidth, be reserved at the time the communications session is first set up. Each packet is launched independent of the others.

When using a connectionless protocol, it is quite feasible for packets to be received out of sequence. Remember, this is a feature, not a flaw! IP relies upon higher-level protocols like TCP (Layer 4) to make sure that all received packets are resegmented properly before being passed up to higher layer protocols and/or applications.

> **NOTE**
>
> Although IP is inherently connectionless, it can function in a connection-oriented mode through the use of a Layer 4 protocol like TCP. Not all Layer 4 protocols are connection oriented! UDP, for example, is also commonly used with IP, but it is connectionless. Remember this for any certification exams you may take.

The key to the successful operation of a network that uses a connectionless Layer 3 protocol is the routers that comprise the network. More specifically, the key to success is the way the routers are programmed, and how they calculate routes and forward packets.

Routers accept incoming LAN data frames, strip off the framing to reveal the Layer 3 packetized data, and then forward the packet. In doing so, they discard the MAC address pairs. This breaks the audit trail that otherwise would exist between a source and destination machine pair.

This discontinuity at the MAC Layer, though not necessarily significant, demonstrates some of the disconnects that can exist between the protocols that operate at different layers of the stack. This discarding of MAC addresses prevents the use of end-to-end security based upon MAC addresses across a router. This creates an opportunity for unscrupulous netizens.

> **NOTE**
>
> Netizens is slang for network citizens.

Even greater opportunity for security compromise lies in the forwarding of open, connectionless protocols between routers. Remember, a connectionless protocol has no clearly defined path between source and destination. Thus, the routers are trusted to calculate the optimal path between the communicating nodes, and to forward packets accordingly. "Calculating the optimal path" is a euphemistic phrase that masks the complexity of routing connectionless protocols, and the various metrics that routers might use to assess path efficiencies in a dynamic network. It also can be misleading.

In theory, a router is capable of discriminating between multiple possible paths to reach a given destination, and selecting the lowest "cost" path. The cost can be measured in time, distance, and so forth. After the lowest cost path is identified, the packet is forwarded out the port interface that connects to the next hop in that path. The downstream routers perform similar table look-ups and calculations; they are not obligated to deliver the packet along the actual path calculated by any previous routers. Each router is concerned only with forwarding the packet to the next hop. The remainder of the network beyond that port is inconsequential. In other words, the protocol is connectionless. A connection-oriented protocol requires the identification and maintenance of a fixed path through the network of routers. This lack of continuity represents an inherent vulnerability in connectionless protocols.

A more troubling vulnerability is the inability of a router to differentiate between legitimate and fraudulent addresses. They trust that the source and destination address pairs identified in the packet header are both legitimate and correct. Their routing tables correlate the destination address with a port number. They forward the packet out that port's interface. Any security mechanisms based solely on the access rights of the source IP address contained in a packet are easily defeated.

Thus, the stage is set for numerous ways to exploit network-based vulnerabilities. These include hijacking a host address, spoofing a client address, and denial of service.

Hijacking a Host Address

It is quite possible to hijack the IP address of a destination and intercept packets that are intended for it. In a large, complex network, there may well be multiple paths to get to any given destination. Depending upon how the network addressing scheme is defined, a router may actually be fooled into believing that there are two paths to the same host when, in fact, there are really two hosts: one legitimate and one counterfeit.

Obviously, this is an oversimplification that does not get into the minutiae of how to defeat the other layers of security that may exist at either the network or application layer. Defeating them can be a monumental task, if not a logistical impossibility. Nevertheless, this example demonstrates that routers can be duped quite easily. The point in hijacking a host's address is to intercept streams of data, including valid ID and password pairs, that would be routed to it. There are, however, other ways to abuse an ill-gotten IP address.

Spoofing an Address

The other danger with the relative unintelligent forwarding of packets is that it is possible to pretend to be another device, for the purposes of "borrowing" that device's access permissions. Rather than actually steal an address, all that spoofing requires is to somehow manage to generate a stream of packets with the source address of another machine. This is a useful way to defeat simple address filtering mechanisms, like those used in router access lists.

Denial of Service

Breaches of security are not necessarily done to gain anything for the perpetrator. The previous two examples demonstrated such circumstances, but an equally serious threat is known as a "denial of service attack." The perpetrator gains access to a network, host, or application, and proceeds to do anything possible to make that resource unavailable to its legitimate users.

The Trouble with Open Protocols and Extranets

At this point, it should be fairly obvious that building an extranet based on open, connectionless protocols is a risky proposition, even under the best of circumstances. These risks should not be taken lightly. It is already well established that the borders of any IP network must be protected and guarded vigilantly. Failing to do so places all the networked assets at risk. Given this, extending intranets beyond the perimeter of established defenses seems ludicrous. Nevertheless, there are significant potential business benefits that warrant this risk. There are also numerous ways to identify, and minimize, the risks.

Assessing the Risks

Identifying the risks goes far beyond merely identifying the assets that can be jeopardized by the extranet, either directly or indirectly. Remember, you are assessing risks, not compromisable assets. There is a difference!

Assessing the risks of extranetting must begin with identifying the tangible assets that can be compromised through illicit access. These include:

- Data
- Application source code
- Application executables
- Network components
- Network-attached hosts

As important as these items are, they are just the tangible assets. They are the business data, logic, and technical infrastructure that support the business. They are not, however, the business. Including the business functions and processes that rely upon these tangible items rounds out one's estimate of the magnitude of risk inherent in extranetting. As companies become increasingly dependent upon their intranets to support their business processes, the risks must include the integrity of those processes and the capability to perform them. Thus, the capability of a company to function is directly exposed to risk via extranetting.

Clearly, the business risks of unrestricted access over an extranet outweigh any potential business benefits. Consequently, access across an extranet must be carefully controlled and maintained. Access must be limited to just what is absolutely necessary to support the interlocking business processes.

The next issue is how to secure data in transit as it passes across the extranet. Many business managers would have you believe that a properly written partnership agreement affords you all the protection you need. This train of thought is ill-conceived and wrongheaded. All it accomplishes is blame attribution *after* a compromise occurs.

A better approach is to carefully plan every aspect of the extranet's security mechanisms *before* implementation. Equal diligence is due daily to the maintenance of the security mechanisms.

Day-to-day moves, changes, installs, and other rearrangements of the network components can quickly erode the validity of any logic or filters that may be used to enforce security across the extranet. Security technologies, such as authentication and even encryption, are quickly emerging as indigenous extensions of network protocols. Carefully applied, they can almost completely protect the sanctity of data in transit over unsecured transmission facilities.

Rules for Securing an Extranet

Securing an extranet should begin with the identification of a set of rules that describe the desired functionality of the extranet. These rules are the nucleus of the business logic that is to be enforced via router access control lists, firewalls, host and application layer permissions, and any other security mechanisms that might be deemed necessary.

The single most important step is to first identify just those resources that must be made accessible across the extranet. *Access to everything should be explicitly denied throughout the entire intranet!* This should always be your first rule: Deny access to everything automatically, and then explicitly define those permissions that are required.

Permissive rules can be fairly specific. For example, the allowable access of the client with IP address number 128.xx.xxx.x can be limited to the host at 135.xx.xxx.x. Alternately, rules can be more generic and apply to ranges of IP addresses. Just be careful! Security rules are a double-edged sword. The more stringent and effective they are, the more onerous they are to maintain. Do not succumb to the temptation of establishing rules based solely upon their ease of maintenance. If you, or your company, employ a designated data communications/networking service provider, do not let that provider talk you into lax security rules. Providers are motivated to minimize their own administrative burden, rather than maximize the security of your networked resources.

> **NOTE**
>
> The more complex the rule set for a firewall or router becomes, the more CPU cycles are required to apply it. Consequently, the processing delays increase directly with the effectiveness of the security. In circumstances where end-to-end delays must be minimized, it may be necessary to substitute fewer, broader (and draconian) rules, for many individual ones.

19

INTRANETS AND EXTRANETS

Firewalls Are Not Panaceas

If it is deemed necessary to have a firewall installed between the two intranets, it should be acknowledged that firewalls are not panaceas. Firewalls are only as good as their rules. Incomplete sets of rules, rules that were poorly defined, or even rules that are not well maintained can all undermine the effectiveness of a firewall. Firewalls may be a critical component in securing your extranet, but they are only as good as the people that program and maintain them.

Another firewall-related issue is the number needed, and the distribution of administrative responsibilities. Technically, all you really need is one firewall. Properly programmed, it can provide bidirectional protection for both extranet partners. A single firewall solution is illustrated in Figure 19.3.

FIGURE 19.3.

Single firewall solution.

> **NOTE**
>
> The extranets illustrated in Figures 19.3 and 19.4 may appear to be just a single, physical connection between two routers. This is not quite the case. That connection represents the point at which two intranets develop a commonality. This commonality is known as the extranet, and extends to all the network-attached resources that are made accessible across the physical connection between the two intranets.

From many perspectives, the single firewall solution is nearly ideal. It keeps the processing overhead and delays to an absolute minimum. Likewise, costs are also kept to a minimum. Unfortunately, this solution suffers one devastating drawback. Remember, this is the device that separates your intranet from another company's intranet. Do you trust them to administer this firewall? Can you logically expect them to trust you to do it? The answer to both questions is "probably not."

The solution is to have redundant firewalls back to back. This is illustrated in Figure 19.4.

Redundant firewalls double the cost, operational effort, and processing delays. From these perspectives, the use of redundant firewalls is hardly an ideal solution. Despite this, if mutual peace of mind is essential for both extranet partners, this solution may be the only viable one.

FIGURE 19.4.
Redundant firewall solution.

Am I Wasting My Time?

The point of this rather exhaustive exploration of the fundamental traps of extranetting with IP is to elevate your awareness of those traps. This awareness helps you develop more comprehensive and effective security defenses. The point is not to scare you away from extranetting. On the contrary, extranets are likely to increase in their significance in the future.

Over time, extranets will emerge as the preferred interconnectivity vehicle between business partners. In the longer term, the distinctions between the Internet, intranets, and extranets will likely be almost completely erased by technological advances. Improvements in network layer authentication, certification, and (to a lesser extent) encryption will likely afford companies the capability to tear down their firewalls and other physical perimeter defenses of their WANs. In their place will be logically defined intranets and extranets. When this happens, we will have come full circle. The various nets will have reintegrated into a single, ubiquitous Net with logical—not physical—subdivisions. These logical structures are known as *virtual private networks* (VPNs).

Virtual Private Networks

One approach to using the Internet as a secured alternative to an expensive, dedicated, private communications network is known as a *Virtual Private Network* (VPN). VPNs are actually a new twist on an old concept. X.25 packet switched networks, have for decades provided companies with a software-defined, secure network within a larger, public switched network. The public switched network was owned and operated by the telecommunications provider, and access facilities were extended to each of the customers' premises. Each customer could use the network as if it were its own private network, and never see the traffic put on the network by other customers. The X.25 network provided the functionality of a private network, without the cost of building and running a private network.

VPNs are a new implementation of this old X.25 approach to networking. The key differences are that they use more robust transmission facilities and networking protocols. More significantly, they are being used in different ways to support the needs of the business. VPNs are ideal for any situation where it is not cost effective to deploy a privately owned network. Examples are

- A highly mobile work force
- Smaller companies that cannot cost-justify their own private communications network

VPNs can be bought from a telecommunications carrier, much like the old X.25 service. Alternatively, they can be created using existing network infrastructure, such as the Internet or the public switched telephone network, by using tunneling software.

Carrier-Provided VPNs

Carrier-provided Virtual Private Networks are logical, private networks that are constructed within the carrier's public network. The telecommunications industry enjoys tremendous economies of scale. The huge amounts of capital required to build, operate, and maintain public networks must be spread across a very large population of users in order for the service to be affordable. The same concept applies, albeit on a smaller scale, to the private communications networks of companies.

VPNs are a concept, not a product. They have been used extensively for years in both voice and data networks, and continue to enjoy success in both arenas. The reasons for this are simple. Many companies find it cost-prohibitive to build and operate private communications networks. Rather than build such networks, or deny themselves that functionality, they seek a provider than can sell them that service.

The recent interest in VPNs is being generated by the Internet. Many companies, especially the Internet Service Providers (ISPs)and backbone carriers of the Internet, are anxious to increase demand for Internet connectivity and usage. Curious as this may sound, the explosive demand for Internet connectivity has actually leveled off. Consequently, the ISPs find themselves locked in competition for a market that views their service as a commodity.

One of the tactics to increase demand is to find new ways to use the Internet. Remembering that the real money lies within the coffers of corporations (not individual consumers), their quest is to find more ways to drive up corporate demand for Internet connectivity. Using the Internet as a Virtual Private Network is just one solution.

The Internet can be used as a VPN in one of two ways. First, remote workers can access corporate intranet resources by dialing into their local ISP and riding through the Internet to their intranet. This relieves the corporation of having to support dial-in modem pools, but comes at the cost of increased security concerns.

The second approach is to eliminate the intranet almost entirely in favor of a virtual private network within the Internet. This approach, to date, remains more of a theoretical solution than a practical one.

The benefit of either approach is the reduction in the costs of owning, operating, and maintaining communications networks.

Tunneling

Tunneling is a process by which communications occur within the confines of a logical structure established by another communications protocol. This can solve several different network problems that range from the need to secure data in transit to overcoming incompatibilities with either external protocols or addressing schemes. Figure 19.5 illustrates the concept of tunneling through a network.

FIGURE 19.5.

Tunneling through a network.

Regardless of which protocols are used, or what the intent of the tunnel is, the basic technique remains relatively consistent. Typically, one protocol is used to establish connectivity to a remote destination, and another is used to encapsulate data and instructions for transmission through the tunnel.

An example of using a tunnel to overcome incompatibilities in both protocols and addressing is found in the Simple Internet Transition (SIT) suite of tools that accompanies the upcoming release of IPv6. One tool provided by the Internet Engineering Task Force (IETF) to facilitate the migration from version 4 of the Internet Protocol (IPv4) to version 6 (IPv6) is a tunneling technique. These two versions are dissimilar enough as to preclude direct interoperability. Interoperability is simulated by tunneling IPv4 through IPv6, and vice versa.

Tunneling also secures data as it traverses otherwise unsecured domains by providing a protective shell or wrapper. One tunneling protocol that is designed exclusively for this purpose is the Point-to-Point Tunneling Protocol.

Point-to-Point Tunneling Protocol

Microsoft is developing the Point-to-Point Tunneling Protocol (PPTP) to give secure and remote access to intranets via the Internet. This protocol is based on existing open standards for TCP/IP and the old Point-to-Point Protocol (PPP). In fact, PPP remains the communications protocol in a PPTP session.

PPTP creates a tunnel through a network to the destination NT Server, and passes the remote user's PPP packets through it. The server and the workstation enjoy a virtual private network, regardless of how secure, or accessible, the network between them is. Terminating the session at the NT Server, as opposed to some specialized remote access server, enables LAN administrators to accommodate remote users within the context of their existing NT security. The end result is that the user enjoys a virtual private network over a public network, without compromising any functionality. All the services available in the NT domain, including DHCP and WINS, and access to the Network Neighborhood, are readily extended to the remote user.

Although limited to just Windows devices, PPTP offers companies the capability to leverage existing network infrastructures without compromising security (at least, that's the theory!). Thus, a remote worker can connect to the Internet via his friendly, neighborhood, Internet Service Provider (ISP) over either analog dial-up lines or dial-on-demand facilities like ISDN and communicate with an NT Server. The company is spared the expense of building, operating, and maintaining a dial-in modem pool for remote access.

Summary

The success of the Internet has permanently changed the way that businesses build and use IP-based Wide Area Networks. These networks have evolved into intranets, extranets, and even virtual private networks. The significance of these networks transcends their mere name change. They enable business processes to evolve. A company that can manage the successful evolution of its business processes has the potential for substantial improvements in its competitive posture. The key to this success is understanding the abilities and limitations of each technology. This knowledge should provide the context for the application of each network technology. Ideally, the networking technologies can be used to create new opportunities without exposing the company to unnecessary risks.

IV
PART

Operating Networks

Network Operating Systems (NOS)

by Arthur Cooper

IN THIS CHAPTER

CHAPTER 20

The world of networking has gone through many phases in the last 40 years. Starting with the connection of so-called "dumb terminals" to mainframe systems, there has always been a desire to access information and share that information among many users connected to a network. This chapter examines this phenomenon, which came about in the 1980s as a result of the rapid growth and proliferation of Local Area Networks (LAN).

The development and uses of various LAN Network Operating Systems (NOS) consume the bulk of this discussion. Following the introduction of IBM's Personal Computer (PC) in 1981, many users were happy to simply use these devices as IBM had intended: as replacements for dumb terminals. However, many users wanted to connect these intelligent machines together. Various products hit the marketplace, some of which, such as Novell's NetWare, became major players in the world of NOS technology. Now, in the year 1998, clearly it is Microsoft who has become the leader in networking PCs. With this in mind, this chapter takes a short look at the development of general NOS systems before discussing the various systems in the NOS world.

History of Network Operating Systems (NOS)

It was only two short years after IBM's introduction of the PC when Novell came along with its NetWare product. This was the first truly configurable NOS. At the same time, IBM was busy inventing its early PC network capabilities. In order to connect its PCs, IBM invented NetBEUI. Before understanding NetBEUI, you must first understand NetBIOS, because part of the NetBEUI acronym contains NetBIOS.

Novell Dominates the Market

NetBIOS (Network Basic Input/Output System) is a program that enables applications on different computers to communicate within a LAN. "NetBEUI" stands for *NetBIOS Extended User Interface*. IBM's NetBEUI enables PCs to send data to other PCs without requiring more than one return acknowledgment to show the data has reached its destination. Microsoft obtained permission from IBM to use NetBEUI in its Microsoft products, but neither IBM nor Microsoft was able to parlay the use of NetBEUI into anything even closely resembling NetWare.

Novell was on top of the world in those days. At one point in 1986, it was claimed Novell controlled nearly 85 percent of the PC network business, and it may have had closer to 95 percent. Everywhere you looked Novell LANs were chugging away. Microsoft did not see Novell as a threat; it was busy trying to establish a graphical interface for PC users.

The two main protocols invented by Novell that enabled NetWare to be so successful were IPX and SPX. IPX stands for *Internetwork Packet Exchange*. It is a protocol designed to carry data from one place to another. SPX stands for *Sequenced Packet Exchange*. It takes the IPX data and *arranges* it in the correct order when it gets to its destination.

IPX/SPX was, and is, a force to be reckoned with. This combination of two protocols is what gave Novell its competitive edge. Microsoft's LAN Manager product uses the NetBEUI protocol as its main protocol. In order to route data between other networks, LAN Manager must be configured to run Microsoft TCP/IP. Novell dedicated itself to not be responsible for building piecemeal systems similar to what Microsoft was guilty of providing.

New Players Emerge

It was not until Microsoft came out with Windows for Workgroups (WFWG) that any of Microsoft's corporate strides were considered important to the world of NOS development. In the meantime, Novell continued to improve NetWare's capabilities. Novell quietly captured the market. Another player emerged in the 1980s as well. This company created what was considered the best user interface for any NOS in operation at that time. The company was Banyan Systems, Inc., and the product it created was called VINES.

The VINES system was a good NOS, but add-ons and configuration changes were very expensive. Banyan priced itself out of the market when it came to providing user upgrades and add-ons. Some organizations, however, fell in love with VINES. For example, the United States Marine Corps used VINES almost exclusively.

Microsoft started to realize the importance of PC networks, and within the WFWG system mentioned earlier, NetBEUI was built in. This enabled users with very small network needs, perhaps 1 to 100 users, to get a network up and running very quickly. The limitations of NetBEUI and the fact it cannot be routed forced users of very large PC networks to choose Novell. As mentioned previously, Novell invented an entire suite of protocols. These protocols were routable, meaning they could transmit data back and forth between different PC networks.

Microsoft Takes Hold

Microsoft began to see the light in the late 1980s. When users began to believe that a graphical user interface was a great idea, Microsoft reacted with the development of Windows 3.0. This was the first practical graphical user interface that Microsoft developed. Novell designed the system to enable DOS and Windows users to network their PCs quite easily. You would think this was a marriage made in heaven, but apparently, Microsoft felt as though networking services should be incorporated into its Windows system.

Novell had done what it set out to do. It had created a seamless network interface capable of passing data on large interconnected PC networks. Also, because Novell client stations ran DOS, Windows, and other operating systems, users of Novell felt comfortable with using applications with which they were already familiar. Novell simply gave them the capability to share files and other resources such as printers or tape drives.

Microsoft decided to change its strategy at this point. When it became apparent that Microsoft's networking capabilities were far behind those of Novell and Banyan, Microsoft formulated the strategy that it still lives by today. This strategy concerns itself with the built-in functionality of *everything*. Microsoft wanted to incorporate networking services within the Windows operating system. With that in mind, Microsoft developed the Windows NT system.

20

NETWORK OPERATING SYSTEMS (NOS)

What's Happening Now

In today's networking business, software companies are singling out their best applications on an individual basis in order to remain in the minds of corporate purchasers and users now leaning toward Microsoft. It is estimated that by the end of 1998, Microsoft Windows NT sales will have outstripped everyone else in the PC NOS business.

The real irony of the current situation lies in the fact that Microsoft built its Windows NT software around modular components, in a piecemeal fashion. At this point, NT software remains whole, whereas other vendors are forced to segment their products and sell their best applications as separate pieces. Microsoft has no plans to break apart any core NT applications or services.

Some organizations fear Microsoft may become too dominant and prefer to build their own networks from pieces rather than become dependent on a single vendor. By the time Novell sorts things out, it is going to be too late. The so-called "big three" of network systems has now turned into an industry dominated by one company.

Traditional Services of a NOS

Throughout the development of a NOS, users have traditionally required three major services in a NOS, file and resource sharing, configurability and usability, and support after sale.

File and Resource Sharing

There have always been demands for file sharing. This was probably the most fundamental requirement users stressed when demanding network services. Following that, there has always been a marked demand for resource sharing: in other words, sharing printers, tape-drives, and myriad other expensive resources. These are the two basic tenets for a NOS to be considered usable.

Configurability and Usability

The next area of concern is configurability and usability. Novell NetWare administrators all swear by NetWare and Windows NT administrators tell you that not until the graphic environment of NT came along was there ever a good NOS. Still others, such as users of VINES or other lesser-known systems, tell you that their NOS is without a doubt the best. However, there is no doubt that Windows NT provides the easiest interface by far. That ease, however, comes at a price. Although a graphical user interface (GUI) may seem easier to use, many times it does not provide informative explanations as to why something is not working correctly. Microsoft's interface is wonderful as long as everything is working correctly. When something goes wrong, many times a graphic message says something to the effect of, `"Kernal Error 322"`, with an OK button beneath the message. Clicking the button may make the user feel he is accomplishing something, but in reality he is not. Obviously, the error is not *OK*, so unless someone can get to the root of the problem, the interface offers no clues. Microsoft's documentation has historically been less than complete, and many times administrators do not know what they are doing when they simply click on a certain icon or area on their screen. Organizations are therefore forced to expend a great deal to train people to use NT properly.

Novell may not have had a graphical interface in the beginning, but it had something that other NOS vendors did not have. Novell had, without a doubt, the best documentation on the market. Those brightly colored, red NetWare books were absolutely splendid. Novell continues to provide the best documentation of all NOS vendors. Microsoft is getting better, but Novell's documentation made the set-up, configuration, and administration of NetWare an easy task. Banyan's interface was easy to use, and it was quite easy to set up a Banyan network. However, the documentation left much to be desired. It was not nearly as clear as Novell's, and the first-time user of their product was usually quite perplexed as to how to get the network up and running. I will not discuss Microsoft's earlier attempts at networking, as LAN Manager was an absolute debacle as far as set-up was concerned.

When Windows for Workgroups (WFWG) came along, things got slightly easier. Recall that Windows for Workgroups was pre-loaded with NetBEUI only, so if you wanted to use WFWG on a LAN, you needed to load an additional protocol into the system. This was done by the use of the graphical interface, and it generally worked well enough. However, there could be times when Microsoft's interface was cryptic at best when providing status or error messages.

Again, Microsoft had missed the boat as far as ease of use was concerned. Not until Windows NT Server did Microsoft finally come up with an easy interface. As mentioned earlier, this was (and is) a double-edged sword. Further, Microsoft's documentation on earlier versions of NT was worthless.

Support After Sale

If you wanted to get any kind of useful information, it was necessary to seek it out from some-one who had learned how to *do it* on his or her own. I can also remember how disastrous Microsoft's support structure was in those days. Hours on the telephone listening to music were what usually ensued whenever I called Microsoft. Microsoft was so inundated with calls after the release of Windows 3.0, most of which it could not address in a timely manner, that its reputation was nearly ruined. Microsoft's support structure, at this time, was not adequate for the number of calls it was receiving. Many people became very discouraged with the wait-ing associated with each call.

Novell, on the other hand, was always a provider of excellent support and service to its custom-ers. They were prompt, usually courteous, and helpful. Banyan appeared to be a mixed bag. Sometimes it was excellent; other times it was not. Configurability, usability, and support are always important to users of NOS software and systems. Microsoft has apparently figured out how to balance these items, as its NT software is now the undisputed ruler of NOS software and systems.

Banyan Network Systems

Banyan tried to assert itself as a leader in enterprise-wide network solutions with its NOS software called VINES. Banyan has always made claims that its networks are transparent to the user. By making all the resources on a distributed network seem as if they are compiled into one seamless network, VINES claims to be the choice for PC-based network solutions. The following sections review VINES's applications and services.

Services and Applications of VINES

The key to making VINES work over distributed network systems is the Enterprise Network Services (ENS) portion of VINES. ENS includes the following services and applications:

- Directory Services (StreetTalk)
- Network Management Services
- Intelligent Messaging Services
- Security Services

All four of these ENS services work with each other across an entire Wide Area Network (WAN) or distributed network. The next sections review each of these services in brief.

Directory Services (StreetTalk)

Directory and file services are the real "meat" of any NOS, and Banyan has an excellent package to perform these services. The software that enables VINES to provide across-the-board services to all users of the network is called StreetTalk. Banyan developed StreetTalk to standardize file and directory services. This product basically lets you share file and directory resources on a Banyan LAN with other types of file services such as NFS (Unix), Windows NT File System (NTFS), and the old DOS-style File Allocation Table (FAT) systems. The product works well. StreetTalk automatically integrates newly added network locations into the existing network. This makes it very easy to set up and use.

Another feature of StreetTalk is the fact that it exists on each VINES server in the network. When one server running StreetTalk fails, the entire network directory/file sharing capabilities do not fail as you might expect. Each server maintains a part of the "puzzle" and together the StreetTalk information on all the servers combines to form the entire picture. When one server fails, the other servers are still able to locate the users and resources they support.

StreetTalk is fully integrated into every other part of VINES. Mail, print, and file services all use StreetTalk in order to locate a user or resource on the network. StreetTalk enables users to log in from anywhere on the VINES network; interfaces look the same whether users are on the road or in the office. When new devices, users, and resources are added to the network, StreetTalk assigns each of them a name. This is how StreetTalk is able to keep track of everything.

An excellent feature of StreetTalk is its capability to keep users "straight" when they move to a new location on the network. Network changes are a fact of everyday life. StreetTalk enables administrators to leave a user's workstation exactly as it is when the user moves to a new location. StreetTalk determines the new location as soon as the user logs in for the first time. This is a real time saver for network administration personnel.

There is also a service called StreetTalk Directory Assistance (STDA). This service enables users and administrators to look up items, in much the same way that they would view the Yellow Pages. All resources can be listed in alphabetical order using STDA. This makes it very easy to find users, resources, and servers on large VINES networks.

Network Management Services

Banyan uses what it refers to as VINES Network Management Services (NMS). This service has easy-to-use interface screens that provide reliable information to administrators. Items such as user activities, network changes and deletions, security, applications, and performance are all manageable with VINES NMS.

Coupled with this service is the VINES Assistant. This service provides useful utilities designed to maximize network performance and the control of resources for administrators. There are password control utilities, network optimization utilities, and many others. It is a menu-driven system that steps the administrator through each operation.

Intelligent Messaging Services

VINES messaging can set itself up automatically and works well with any third-party e-mail program. It is fully integrated with StreetTalk, so users need to be registered in the StreetTalk database on only one server. Users are then free to "wander" around the network, use their e-mail login to receive mail at any workstation, and view address information pertaining to users on the network no matter where they are located. This is made possible due to the fact that user address information is maintained in StreetTalk only. Therefore, users may choose any e-mail client program they desire to use, and it will correctly communicate with VINES messaging services. Further, these messaging services are tied into the NMS system as well, so administrators can monitor all e-mail if need be.

Security Services

VINES security services are transparent to users of the network, but they are very effective. VINES security services can secure files, printers, gateways, applications, and all other resources. Control of resources is at the source, so even if a hacker was to be physically connected to a server, he is not going to gain access to a resource unless he is in the Access Rights List (ARL) for that server. The ARL keeps track of who is authorized to use what on the network. Using the ARL is a very easy way to manage the security of resources on a VINES network.

VINES-Supported Standards

VINES can support a variety of standards and protocols on its communication links as well as on several client operating systems. The major standards supported by VINES are these:

20

NETWORK OPERATING SYSTEMS (NOS)

- Communications Standards: LAN, dial-up, X.25, SNA, TCP/IP, and IBM 3270 Gateway connections are all supported when interconnecting geographically separated VINES networks into one single system.

- Operating System Clients: DOS, Windows, OS/2, and Macintosh can be used as the client operating system. VINES provides network resources through the native interfaces of these operating systems. Therefore, users do not need to learn a "special" network interface in order to access network resources on their client workstations running one of these operating systems.

Strengths and Weaknesses of VINES

Banyan does not want you to know that VINES has its roots in Unix. In fact, Unix is the underlying operating system that makes VINES operate. Unix is sometimes frowned upon by supporters of current technology. Although Unix has been around for a long time, it is still an excellent operating system. However, the age of Unix tends to scare some people. The real strength of VINES lies in its StreetTalk Directory Service. This hierarchical naming of people and resources for enterprise-wide directory services was actually the first of its kind. It is very reliable and configurable. Another strength of VINES is the fact that it supports multiple platforms via ENS: NetWare, Unix, (AIX, SCO, and Solaris), and NT versions. This enables all these other LAN systems to be included in the StreetTalk directory services.

Despite its compelling strengths, the weaknesses of VINES are many. Hardware device support is extremely limited. Windows NT can detect and set up most hardware devices in seconds. The fact that VINES is built on an old Unix platform means that detection is not viable. Further, VINES can support only a limited number of devices. This fact, coupled with the dismal technical support available for VINES, makes it a poor choice for a new network starting up. My advice is to implement VINES networks only where VINES already exists. Banyan does not have the financial wherewithal to ensure continued research and development of this product. Unfortunately, the future does not look good for Banyan VINES.

Novell NetWare

Novell set the standard when it came to the rapid growth of LANs in the world. Banyan, on the other hand, may have beat Novell to the punch as far as creating directory services. After all, Banyan's StreetTalk was really the first LAN directory service. Before that, Unix Network File System (NFS) services were the only existing file/directory services of note. However, NFS was designed for use on WAN systems that had many different host systems residing on the network. Banyan's StreetTalk was LAN-driven. Novell, however, did not wait too long to play catch-up. In fact, after Novell poised itself to take on networking and LANs, it did so with a mighty force.

There were no other corporations on earth that took networks and LANs as seriously as Novell did in the early 1980s. For that reason, Novell is still the top player in the NOS business. Microsoft, though, is chopping away at that lead. However, according to International Data

Corporation (IDC), in 1996 worldwide shipments of server operating systems totaled 2.4 million units. Of this total, IDC attributed a 41% share to Novell. Between 1996 and 2000, IDC has projected Novell's share of the server operating systems market to grow at a compound rate of eight percent. It remains to be seen who will win. Novell has historically been a better choice when implementing a distributed or enterprise network.

Recall that Novell was the first NOS to support multiple platforms. It was also the first NOS to support multiple and varying topologies and route between these differing topologies. The real boost for Novell was the fact that it was the first NOS to support all DOS-version networks. Novell also gave Apple a fair deal, as NetWare was the first NOS that could provide TCP/IP services to Apple systems. That was a big plus in the heyday of AppleTalk and other Apple systems. The next section discusses the primary features of Novell. These features make Novell NetWare the powerhouse that it is.

Features of NetWare

The main reason that Novell NetWare servers typically outperform other network servers is the fact that NetWare is by itself an operating system. Recall that Banyan has its roots in Unix. Microsoft NT is also an operating system, but it was not designed strictly for network performance and service, as NetWare was. A NetWare server is optimized for network activity. This gives it a great edge over other NOS servers when in operation. The following sections review these main features:

- Novell Directory Services (NDS)
- Security Services
- Database Services
- Messaging Services
- Print Services
- NetWare Loadable Modules (NLMs)

Of these six main services, the NDS offering is what still makes Novell the strong competitor of Windows NT. Following Banyan's creation of StreetTalk, Novell fought back with NDS. The next sections discuss NDS as well as the other five features of NetWare.

Novell Directory Services (NDS)

Novell decided to adhere to the CCITT (the International Consulting Committee for Telephone and Telegraph, abbreviated from the French) X.500 standard when setting up its NDS system. In fact, Novell has been fairly good about following open standards when defining its network products. By adhering to the X.500 hierarchical name space structure, NDS prevents the creation of duplicate objects. Each object must have a Distinguished Name (DN). For example, if you had an employee named BILL in sales, the DN for the user object BILL in the SALES department, which is part of the 2345 organization, would be BILL.SALES.2345. The username BILL (without SALES.2345) is called an RDN, which means Relative Distinguished Name.

In Novell NDS, you must uniquely identify every object in the directory tree. This is accomplished by defining its location. For that reason, you can use the same RDN in more than one container. In Novell NDS, a container is like a repository of information pertaining to a group or cluster of people that exist on certain servers. For example, you can use the RDN of BILL in both the SALES.2345 container and the HR.2345 container. This is a very powerful feature of the NDS system. Following containers, you can break things down to actual components and resources. These are called "leafs" or "leaf objects" by Novell.

To further break things down, NDS intermediate objects, which Novell calls "container objects," are Organization (O), Organizational Unit (OU), Country (C), and [Root]. Usually these leaf objects are users, printers, servers, directory maps, and so on. Novell's use of the term *leaf object* can be confusing, but it makes sense if you think about it. In traditional tree discussions, a leaf is an object at the end of a branch—an object that doesn't contain any objects. Likewise, Novell uses the term to refer to a non-container object—an object that can't contain any objects. Therefore, if something is a "leaf object," it is at the "end" of the directory tree. It is usually a printer or a user, in most cases.

It is possible to create an unlimited number of container and leaf objects in NDS. NDS ships pre-packaged with 37 types of container and leaf objects. These types enable you to manage all your network resources. If new resources are connected to the network, you can define new types of objects and then add them to the NDS name space structure.

Because NDS is displayed in a neat, graphically arranged order, the structure of objects such as users, printers, workstations, and application servers is shown in an organized structure to the system ADMIN user. You can log in as the ADMIN user from any workstation. This enables you to manage the entire directory tree. You can add or remove users, servers, and other network resources. Users need log in only once in order to gain access to all network resources. NDS is probably the best directory service in the business.

Microsoft has tried to rename its NT directory services recently, but they are still not in an object-oriented database structure as Novell's NDS is.

Security Services

Security is another area in which NetWare shines. As the inventors in 1983 of usernames, passwords, and user profiles as far as LANs are concerned, Novell set the standard for security services. The user profile information is all stored on the NetWare network disk in an encrypted format. The wonderful thing about this is the fact that even at a physical server level, users running DOS, Unix, OS/2, or Windows cannot access these network files.

In fact, all password information flows back and forth from the NetWare server to the client workstation in an encrypted format. Even the administrator cannot look at a user's password on the server. The administrator can remove or add user permissions, but it is the users alone who know their passwords. The administrator can define how often a user must change his or her password, but the administrator can never alter a user's password.

Even if users go to the physical NetWare server to log in, they have no greater access to resources than they would have on their own workstations, because NetWare security was built into the NetWare system at the lowest possible level. All attempts to access information or resources on the network go through the NetWare security services system. Novell NDS is closely tied to NetWare security as well. The security service ensures that users can access those services only in the NDS database that their passwords and privileges enable them to access. NetWare security has very few holes; the relatively large number of holes in Windows NT has always been a source of criticism.

Database Services

Novell also made a splash early on by offering LAN database services in a client/server environment. These services make life much easier for those who are developing applications to run on Novell NetWare LANs. Because these database services provide a central repository for information on the server, users had another reason to make Novell the leader in LAN NOS systems for many years. Two major database services are available on NetWare: NetWare Btrieve and NetWare SQL, as follows:

- Btrieve is a database system, indexed with a database *key*, and designed for easy development of vertical applications. Many corporations used the Btrieve system to store records of data on a NetWare server. Users on the client stations are then able to access these records in a speedy fashion.

- In an attempt to adhere to industry standards, Novell developed the NetWare SQL system. SQL stands for *structured query language*, and it was an old mainframe standard used for accessing records stored on a mainframe computer. SQL has many versions, but Novell tried hard to stick with the old SQL standard when developing its LAN version. NetWare SQL takes record management a bit further than Btrieve, as it provides the capability to access Btrieve records from multiple platforms and applications.

Although NetWare uses Btrieve as its underlying record manager, the front-end SQL on NetWare SQL gives many different platforms the capability to access Btrieve records. Consequently, applications developed for either Btrieve or NetWare SQL can share data with each other. Many third-party database applications run on NetWare, but these two are by far the best choice when doing application development on Novell LANs.

Messaging Services

In the past few years, there have been many developments in the area of messaging services. Novell is not alone in the area of messaging services development. At the time of this writing, there was not a great deal of information concerning Novell's soon-to-be-released NetWare version 5.0. No doubt messaging services will receive a revamping with this release, but the basic arrangement Novell has used for years will most likely remain unchanged.

Novell has traditionally called its messaging service NetWare Message Handling Service (MHS). This service provides for ease of message transmission between many front-end applications.

20

NETWORK
OPERATING
SYSTEMS (NOS)

These applications can share data over LANs and Novell WANs. The MHS service can be set up on a stand-alone PC on the network. It can be configured to transmit message data when the user specifies. For that reason, it can take advantage of transmitting when rates on the network are cheaper or traffic volume is lower.

Application developers can get toolkits from Novell to use when developing message-related applications and services. There have been many changes implemented in MHS over the years, but it still provides an effective, cheap method of getting message data from one point to another within a Novell network environment.

Print Services

Print services in NetWare are native to the NetWare operating system environment. The basic services enable users to share up to 16 printers per print server on the network. NetWare networks are capable of having multiple print servers on the network, and the real flexibility of printing in NetWare is the fact that printers need not be attached to the actual print server in order to operate properly.

Indeed, a printer can be attached to the server, but it may also be attached to a user's workstation somewhere on the network. Although the print server still manages the printers not physically attached to the server, it is not necessary to install print server software on workstations that are hosting network printers. All that is needed is a small Terminate and Stay Resident (TSR) program on the workstation that is to host the printer. Therefore, many combinations of printers and print servers may be configured on Novell networks.

NetWare Loadable Modules (NLMs)

NLMs are very important to the functionality of NetWare software. Starting with NetWare version 3.12, NLMs became a mainstay of Novell network operations. These programming interfaces enable client/server applications to run as loadable modules. This provides the power needed to support heavily used network services in the server. NLM applications can have the same access to the NetWare security services, making them safe to control and administer.

The nice thing about NLMs is the fact that you do not need to take the server down in order to load or unload them. Therefore, applications can be loaded when needed and unloaded when no longer needed. Administrators can set up batch files to load and unload NLMs when it is appropriate to do so. Many toolkits are offered by Novell to aid developers when designing applications to run as NLMs.

NetWare-Supported Standards

NetWare can support a variety of standards and protocols on its communication links as well as several client operating systems. The major standards supported by NetWare are these:

■ Communications Standards: LAN, dial-up, X.25, SNA, SDLC, ISDN, T1, TCP/IP, and IBM 3270 Gateway connections are all supported by NetWare. In addition,

Novell has its own product line of NetWare-friendly routers and bridges. The NetWare Link/64 is a device that enables NetWare users to connect geographically separated workstations at speeds between 9.6bps and 64Kbps. The NetWare Link/T1 does the same thing except at speeds up to 2.084Mbps. The NetWare Multiprotocol Router supports IPX, IP, and AppleTalk protocols. It enables users to connect Ethernet, Token Ring, LocalTalk, and ARCnet networks in any desired combination. It also provides for a transparent use of all network resources across each individual network so that users can access all the resources on the connected networks.

- Operating System Clients: DOS, Windows, OS/2, Unix, and Macintosh can all be used as the client operating systems on NetWare client workstations.

Strengths and Weaknesses of NetWare

The major strength of Novell's NetWare product lies in its established history and position as the most used LAN NOS in existence. Although Microsoft has recently taken some of Novell's thunder, these strengths are still worth noting. First, NetWare has the best print and file server software in the business, and it is the sharing of files and printers that makes a network important and useful.

NetWare boasts the best enterprise-wide directory services in the business. The NDS system discussed previously is by far the best of all LAN NOS directory services. When you follow that up with the fact that strong utilities for NetWare are available from hundreds of companies, you can see why NetWare is still a logical choice when you want to establish an enterprise network. Microsoft is very weak on an enterprise level.

However, Novell can use improvement in some areas. First, NetWare lags as an application server. NetWare is an excellent provider of basic file and print sharing. However, when it comes to being a distributed client-server application provider, it falls flat on its face. This is an area in which Microsoft's NT has NetWare beaten hands down.

NetWare is also poor at providing useful data for monitoring network status and overall network management. Although NetWare does have some built-in network management tools, these tools are not very powerful. Many NetWare administrators feel they are unsure as to the status of their networks—whether they are running efficiently or not. Perhaps the next release of NetWare, version 5.0, will address these issues.

Microsoft Windows NT

When the Windows for Workgroups system came along, it was just a stopgap between Windows 3.0 and Windows 95. Windows 95 then had its built-in IPX/SPX and TCP/IP capabilities, which was Microsoft's first impressive attempt at a networking product.

It was perhaps during Windows 95 development that Microsoft realized that in order to be successful, it needed a powerful network and networking capabilities. Soon, a paradox occurred between the importance of network services and the importance of seamless application integration with an operating system. Users decided that applications, graphical interfaces, and the capability to manage and use these applications on a network were more important than simply having a stable network.

Microsoft continued to improve and develop these applications to run on the Windows 95 operating system. Administrators started to believe that if you were going to do any sort of application development, it needed to be done on the Microsoft Windows platform.

Microsoft then developed the NT platform and gave it the same basic graphical interface as Windows 95. Most people were not aware (at least in the beginning) that most applications that would run on DOS would run on Windows 95, but they would not run on Windows NT. When Windows NT Server was released, it was touted as the best NOS to use for networks in which Windows 95 was already installed on the client stations.

After users were used to running certain applications on their Windows 95 workstations, it only made sense that the next versions of these applications should be updated to run on NT as well. In the meantime, most of the old Novell LAN systems were easily upgraded to run Windows for Workgroups on the workstations. This in turn led to an upgrade to Windows 95 on the workstation.

Microsoft's NT Server version 3.51 had myriad problems and anomalies that seemed to present themselves almost daily. Microsoft NT 4.0 was a decent offering. After NT 4.0 was confirmed as a decent, somewhat reliable LAN NOS, Novell began to lose market share quickly. The Microsoft strategy had paid off, and any new LANs being established were moving to the NT NOS in greater numbers. By the time Novell realized what had happened, Microsoft's NT Server 4.0 operating system had become the LAN NOS of choice.

NT's speed was being improved due to the cheapness of the 80486 DX2 series of chips in PCs. Following that, the Pentium chip made PCs run Windows NT very well. Windows won over many of the devoted NetWare-ites due to the integration of applications and network services.

Microsoft had taken pieces of network services, combined them in NT, and had very effectively married these services with the applications running on the clients and servers. The network versions of Microsoft Office and the thousands of other applications that NT is capable of supporting have provided Microsoft an extremely comfortable edge over Novell's NetWare software.

It is now a fact that anyone who wants to make it in the development of applications had better be developing for the Windows NT system. Whether one agrees with it or not, Windows is a dominant force. The next section discusses the main features of NT.

Features of Windows NT

Microsoft NT has so many features that in a chapter of this size, it would be impossible to list them all. For that reason, I would suggest going to Microsoft's support web site:

`http://support.microsoft.com`. There are some white papers there about most of NT's features. However, the following is a list of the major features and a description of what they do:

- NT Interface: The Microsoft Windows 95 operating system user interface has been integrated into NT, making the server interface easier to use and consistent with Windows 95.

- Administrative Wizards: These little helpers place common server tools into a single area and walk you through the steps for each task. Whenever administrators must perform tasks such as adding user accounts, determining file and folder access, and so on, these wizards walk the administrator through the tasks with relative ease.

- Network Monitor: Enables administrators to examine network traffic to and from the server at the packet level. It is also possible to capture traffic for later analysis. This is a nice feature for troubleshooting possible problem areas on your network. This tool shows you where the weak parts of your network are by assessing the flow of traffic on the network. By doing this, it will be able to pinpoint congestion sources, and it will tell you specifically where the problem traffic is being generated.

- Policy Editor and Profiles: Gives administrators the right to manage and maintain the user work environment and actions. This makes it possible for users to have the same interface no matter where they log on.

- Task Manager: Used for monitoring applications and tasks. It provides information on each application and process that is running on the workstation, as well as memory and CPU usage. It can be handy, but to many administrators it is a superfluous function.

- Internet Information Server (IIS): Microsoft has captured a niche with this feature. This service enables an administrator to set up a World Wide Web (WWW) server with great ease. It is tightly integrated with the NT NOS. It gives a LAN administrator an easy way to set up Web services on the LAN server. Basically, any files that exist on a server can be advertised on the Web by using this utility. In the past, setting up Web servers was generally done on older Unix boxes. Microsoft has come up with a graphically driven method to do what used to take hours. Before there were HTML editors, many people were forced to write HTML code using text editors. After their code was written, it would have to be transferred to the Web server either by copying it directly or by using file transfer protocol (FTP) and FTPing it there. This took a lot of time. IIS allows you to do all of these tasks by pointing-and-clicking your way through some setup sequences. This is a strong product, and Microsoft was wise to introduce it when they did.

- Microsoft Index Server: This service automatically indexes the full text and properties of all files on an NT server. This comes in handy when searching for something on an NT system. If you need to find a specific part of a specific file out on the network, this enables you to do so. Also, if you want to, you may search based on keywords within a file. This utility ensures that all of the instances of the use of the word you have searched for are brought to your fingertips.

■ Point-to-Point Tunneling Protocol (PPTP): This protocol provides a way to use the Internet to create a virtual private network (VPN). This VPN can then be used to hook up client PCs with servers. It can support multiple protocols via TCP/IP connections over these VPNs.

■ File and Printer Sharing: Microsoft's Domain Service uses a flat name space structure to define logical network names for users, printers, and other resources in an NT environment. Flat name space structure is acceptable for simple networks in single geographic locations. However, it has significant limitations in environments that are more complex. In fact, all your users and network resources are organized in one list. You can see why organizing users and network resources in one list is time-consuming when you do not use hierarchical file systems. This is why Novell is still considered a better choice in these areas of functionality.

■ Microsoft Cluster Server (MSCS): MSCS provides automatic recovery from server and application failures by providing "clustered" offerings of important applications. MSCS lets administrators perform rolling upgrades on their NT servers. This means that administrators may perform network maintenance without taking important data and applications offline. As long as one of the servers in the cluster is up, the applications remain intact.

■ Microsoft Message Queue Server (MSQS): MSQS provides reliable delivery of messages and data across an NT network. Even if the network and servers are unavailable or unreliable, MSQS uses store-and-forward techniques to ensure that the messages get where they need to go. This works by keeping a copy of the message or data in a file queue until the destination is available for delivery. This is especially useful during times when the network is busy or when a specific destination workstation has failed or is offline.

■ SMP Server: NT allows the use of Server Multi-Processor (SMP) systems. These are very reliable, fast servers in which more than one CPU can be installed in the server. NT scales smoothly from a single CPU all the way up to eight-way SMP servers.

Windows NT–Supported Standards

Windows NT can support a variety of standards and protocols on its communication links as well as several client operating systems. The major standards supported by NT are these:

■ Communications Standards: LAN, dial-up, X.25, SNA, SDLC, ISDN, T1, TCP/IP, and IBM mainframe connectivity are all supported by NT. Microsoft is to be commended for ensuring that any communications link a user can dream up is supported by NT. If you do find something that NT has problems with, there always seems to be a third-party company out there willing to develop a fix for your problem.

■ Operating System Clients: DOS, Windows 3.X/95/NT, OS/2, Unix, and Macintosh can all be used as the operating system on client workstations of an NT network.

Another nice thing about NT is the fact that it can also be run on several different platforms. These platforms include Intel systems, DEC Alpha systems, and other hardware-specific systems.

Windows NT Security

When Windows NT was introduced, it was the first time in Microsoft's history that Microsoft presented an operating system with security. Windows 3.0/3.1/3.11 and Windows for Workgroups provided no password capabilities other than network login security. Any files or directories on PCs using these operating systems could be easily viewed, changed, or deleted. Windows 95 asks for a Windows password, but it seems to do absolutely nothing once you enter it. The Windows NT password is real, it works, and it cannot be breached easily. Security is very serious in NT. From the administrator's point of view, security is highly configurable. Using what Microsoft calls User Manager for Domains, an administrator can assign any level of security to any user for virtually anything. The sharing properties of Windows NT means that files, directories, and entire hard drives can be set up to allow read, read/write, delete, or ownership access to only those users with a legitimate need. Windows NT uses the Windows NT File System (NTFS) when writing its files to a drive partition. NTFS allows the owners of files, directories, and hard drives the ability to totally control what other users on the network may see, use, copy, delete, or write, as far as their files and directories are concerned. This can all be done by users with the proper privileges. This takes a lot of the load off the administrator; he or she will not have to monitor and control the security of all files and directories. As for passwords, the administrator can make a user change the password at fixed intervals. There is a feature to ensure certain users have access to the network only during certain times of the day or night. NT security is excellent.

Strengths and Weaknesses of Windows NT

When looking at the strengths of Windows NT, one must look again at the fact that NT has multiple-platform support that far surpasses the other NOS systems. NT supports Intel, MIPS, PowerPC, and DEC Alpha platforms with ease. This means that anyone starting a new LAN can possibly take advantage of the speed and efficiency of a DEC Alpha server as the LAN's main server. At the same time, the client workstations are cheap, Intel-based 80486 or Pentium systems.

The next area in which Microsoft has won out over Novell is the area of application support. NT is without a doubt the best of the best when it comes to being an application server. The user never sees any differences between stand-alone or network versions of applications running on NT networks. It is seamless and invisible to the client workstations when network resources are used for certain applications.

A third strength of Windows NT lies in the fact that a strong financial base is being applied toward research and development of NT, NT server applications, and NT capabilities. Further, almost 80 percent of the application development taking place in this country is geared to NT development in general. That fact, coupled with the fact Microsoft has pledged "undying" technical support to any of these development efforts means that NT can only get bigger, better, and more reliable as time goes on. What that means for users will no doubt be better graphical interfaces, better applications, easy-to-use Internet tools, and any other myriad possibilities.

Summary

This chapter has examined Network Operating Systems (NOSs) in a general manner, including most important features that any NOS must provide: file sharing and resource sharing, configurability and usability, and support after sale.

Microsoft's NT product is by far the easiest to use of the bunch. Although Banyan's VINES operating system is dying out, it had been the first LAN system to develop network-wide directory services. Novell followed suit with its NDS service that is considered the best in the business to this day.

Although Microsoft has configured its network capabilities in a piecemeal fashion, it has been successful. After all, Novell is now cutting its NOS into pieces to be sold individually, and Microsoft is selling its pieced-together NT as an all-encompassing package. This is due to Microsoft's strategy of application development and support winning out over Novell's strategy of providing the best network platform services. At this point in time, Windows NT Server appears to provide the best package to the network administrator, but you never know what the future holds. Don't count any one company out just yet.

Network
Administration

by Theresa A. Hadden

IN THIS CHAPTER

So far, this book has discussed the basic elements of a network such as cabling, computers, network adapter cards, and so forth. But these elements alone do not enable you to be productive. Good administrative habits are essential. This chapter discusses those elements necessary for administering a network, such as planning, performance monitoring, and troubleshooting.

What Is Network Administration?

Network administration should be proactive rather than reactive. It consists of planning, configuring, and managing all the elements of the network. Some of these elements are local and remote resources, user accounts, and connectivity devices. Its goal is to increase productivity by providing access to necessary resources.

Network administration begins when someone first decides that a network is needed. The first item of business is to define what you want your network to do for you. The answer to this question determines the design and the path to take from now until everyone is using the network.

The most important part of your role as a network administrator is documenting your network's lifecycle, starting with the planning stage and continuing throughout the life of your network. This is also the most commonly neglected component. Think of this as fault tolerance for the network administrator.

The purpose of documentation is to provide for continuation of your network. When creating your documentation, ask yourself what would a new administrator need to know if you were suddenly and completely unavailable. In this vein, administrative passwords should be written down, placed in an envelope, and secured under lock and key. Other key personnel should know where these passwords are located.

The documentation should start with your current configuration, including:

■ What hardware and software are you presently using?
■ Is it adequate for your needs?
■ What do you see in the way of growth over the foreseeable future?

You should include a diagram of all your wiring, including routers, bridges, and so forth, as well as the configuration of each. Be sure to designate a central location for all hardware and software manuals with a tracking system in case materials are loaned out. Last but not least, this missive should include a chronological narrative of each change or addition you make, including hardware and software changes. Keeping a copy of this documentation off site allows for faster recovery in the case of a disaster.

Managing Network Accounts

Before you have your network up and running, you need to decide how to manage access. You want to establish a consistent approach to managing the users' network access. Access includes not only logging on to a particular workstation but also access to resources. Before making this decision you must define both the method you are going to use to assign usernames and your password requirements. There are two main types of network accounts that allow you to manage your users: user accounts and group accounts.

User Accounts

Several global elements may be used to manage user accounts and make administrative tasks easier such as how you name your users and groups. These names should enable you to easily identify the location or job function of the user as well as the purpose of each group. An additional tactic that makes your job easier is the rules you apply to passwords. One of these rules sets forth whether you want accounts to be locked out after unsuccessful logon attempts and, if so, how long should they remain disabled.

> **TIP**
>
> If you suspect that your network has become the object of a break-in attempt, you can verify this by requiring manual reactivation of accounts that are disabled after three unsuccessful logon attempts. In this way, a user must notify you if he is unable to log on. If the user is not the one responsible for the lockout, then you know that an unauthorized individual has been trying to gain access to your network.

One of the most important aspects of network security is passwords. If these passwords are unique and hard to guess, your system is more secure. When planning how to manage passwords, you might want to consider doing some or all of the following:

- Require periodic password changes.
- Keep a password history.
- Have a minimum password length.
- Remind users not to use birth dates, names of spouses, children, or pets, or other personal information that is easy to guess.
- Also, be sure to instruct users not to use dictionary words.

Passwords should be easy to remember so that users do not have to refer to written notes. However, they should be hard to crack. One of the most basic methods of breaking into a system is by using a list of dictionary words and trying each one as the password in an effort to gain access.

> **TIP**
>
> Users often look to the system administrator for assistance in choosing an adequate password. One easy method is for the user to pick two short words, such as *dog* and *walk*, and separate them by a nonalphanumeric character such as %. This results in a password of *dog%walk*, one that cannot be cracked by a dictionary-based password cracking program but is still easy to remember.

Long passwords enhance your network's security by being hard to crack. This is especially true when alphabetic and numeric characters are mixed. Keeping a password history also reduces unauthorized access to your network. A password history prevents users from reusing two or three passwords, only cycling through them when they make changes. Then, if a password should become compromised, it does not become valid every other cycle. In other words, if a disgruntled ex-employee knows Lisa's password, Lisa is not able to reuse that password the next time she has to change it.

The security of your network is further enhanced by requiring that passwords be changed periodically. If a user's password to an account is learned by an outsider, then access is blocked when the password is changed. This limits the time your network is exposed.

Creating/Copying User Accounts

In a peer-to-peer network, anyone who sits down at a computer can access that machine and all its resources. Access to shared resources from other computers may or may not require that you know a password. This model works well in the small network (usually fewer than 10 users) where security is not an issue.

In a larger server-based network, access is given to each user through an individual account. It is through the creation of user accounts and the attributes applied to these accounts that you manage access to resources.

Before creating the first user account (before even installing the network operating system), a naming convention must be established.

> **NOTE**
>
> Although it is perhaps more fun to enable each user to designate an individual, creative name such as Bugsy, HighRoller, and so forth, this leads to administrative difficulties in identifying a particular user. In addition, this method of user identification also causes user confusion when users try to send messages to other users or identify from whom a particular message was sent.

The most workable system for creating usernames is one that enables easy identification of users and complies with NetBIOS naming conventions. A naming system that consists of either the first initial and last name or the first name and last initial are two that are workable and limit user confusion, providing the username is not longer than 15 characters.

NETBIOS NAMING CONVENTIONS

NetBIOS names are used to identify a specific computer or group of computers. These names must be unique and are 16 characters in length. Microsoft, however, reserves the sixteenth character for use as a suffix to define different services or functions on the registered device.

Originally both NetBIOS and TCP/IP utilized a flat name space. This meant that each name had to be unique. As networks became more complex, the available names were exhausted. As a result, a hierarchical naming system was developed. With TCP/IP, this two-part naming convention became *host* and *domain*; with NetBIOS, it consists of NetBIOS name and NetBIOS scope. Windows NT combines the NetBIOS name with the domain name to create the fully qualified domain name (FQDN) for compatibility.

The first implementation of this hierarchical naming scheme relied on flat files for maintenance. These were the HOST file for address resolution using TCP/IP and the LMHOSTS file for NetBIOS name resolution. The implementation of Domain Name Servers and Windows Internet Naming Servers alleviated the need to maintain these flat files.

After a naming convention has been determined, the administrator can begin creating the necessary user accounts. This is usually done through a utility provided by the network operating system. In Windows NT, User Manager or User Manager for Domains is used. The equivalent utility for NetWare is Syscon for Netware, version 3.x, or NWAdmin for version 4.x. Although some UNIX operating systems also provide such a utility, the user accounts are usually created at the user prompt. These user management utilities can be used to designate options such as password requirements and group membership. Figure 21.1 shows the screen for creating a new user account.

FIGURE 21.1.

New User window in User Manager.

A user policy that you may wish to implement is the application of an expiration date for an account. This is a failsafe measure when you are managing users who require only temporary access to your network, such as student employees. You may also designate what hours the user can log on to the network and even limit which workstations the user can use to log on.

Using Templates

Most networking operating systems create both an administrator and a guest account during installation. However, the administrator must then create accounts for all the network's users. Adding a large number of users at one time can be a time-consuming process. Not only does each user account need to be created, but each user's group memberships and access rights need to be assigned.

One way around this is to use a template for the creation of users. First, create a dummy user account with the necessary access rights and group memberships, making sure that the account is disabled. When a new user's account needs to be created, simply copy the template and make necessary changes such as username and password. This method significantly speeds up the process of adding several users at a time.

> **TIP**
>
> In Windows NT, you may add users from the command line by using the cacls.exe utility. This can be used along with a text file containing all the users' information if you must add a large number of users at one time.

Disabling/Deleting

After creating all the user accounts, the administrator can now sit back and think about other things besides user administration. *Wrong*! Users come and go as well as change jobs internally, all of which cause additional work for the administrator. It is important that users who have left the company do not continue to have access to confidential information. It is the administrator's responsibility to ensure that a system is in place to notify the administrator as soon as a user no longer needs an account or that user's access needs have changed. No one is more irate than a user who cannot access the applications and data necessary for performing his job.

> **TIP**
>
> When an employee leaves your company, disable his/her account rather than delete it. Not only does this make your life easier if (s)he returns, but when a new employee is hired to do the same job, you can just rename the account and change the password for the new employee. This way, all the necessary permissions and group memberships are already assigned for that individual to accomplish his/her job. Just be sure to create a reminder to delete that account after an appropriate amount of time has passed.

Group Accounts

Groups are used to organize users into logical collections based on how users need to access your network. Users are granted the necessary resource permissions based upon their group rather than given their rights on an individual basis. Each user who is a member of a group has the same access permissions as the group. Not only does this make your job easier to manage when permissions need to be altered later, but this practice also decreases the possibility of forgetting to give the boss his needed access.

Local Versus Global

Understanding how groups function can be quite confusing at times. A group is part of either the individual machine's security database or the security database for the entire network. As such, they are referred to as either local or global groups. *Local groups* are stored on the individual workstation or server and are used to access resources on that computer. *Global groups* are stored on the PDC (Primary Domain Controller) and are available throughout the domain.

A resource is controlled by a particular computer, either a server or a workstation. The resource may be a file, a folder, a printer, or any other object that might be shared. The local security database controls access to that resource. To grant access to your users, use a group that belongs to the same security database. Therefore, when providing access to a printer, that access should be granted to a local group on the print server. Global group(s) or user(s) may be added to the local group to provide user access.

> **TIP**
>
> One easy way to remember how to use local versus global groups is to think of resources as "living" on a particular computer rather than belonging to the entire network. Therefore, it becomes logical to use a local group to control access to the resource living on that computer.

Global groups are used to organize users at the network level while local groups are used on individual computers. Each user may be a member of several different groups. Groups may be organized by function, administrative division, geographic location, or any other logical sorting you might imagine.

If all users in the Accounting Department need to have access to files in a directory or folder on server S1, a global group can be created, perhaps named *Accounting*, and this group then added to a local group on S1, perhaps named *S1Accounting*. Then on the server S1, permission to access the directory *Accounting Docs* is given to the group named *S1Accounting*.

Another use for global groups is to provide access to resources across trusts. A *trust* is a special relationship created to allow users from one domain to access resources in another domain. They are used to provide for wider access to resources. Local groups cannot cross from one domain to another. By placing users from the trusted domain in a global group, that global group may then be added to a local group on the trusting domain. This enables users from the trusted domain to access needed resources located in the trusting domain.

> **TIP**
>
> When creating a new group using the User Manager in Windows NT, select the users whom you wish to name as members of that group while holding down the control key. After selecting all the users you wish to include, then create the group. The users you have selected are then made members of that group.

Built-In Groups

Network operating systems provide built-in groups with the predefined rights and privileges that are necessary for accomplishing certain routine tasks. These groups are capable of performing certain administrative tasks such as creating accounts or performing backups. This provides a relatively easy format that enables the administrator to delegate certain tasks without granting administrative privileges to others.

See Table 21.1 for Global Groups built in to NT, and Table 21.2 for Local Groups built in to NT. Not all these groups have default members; however, they can be populated to reduce the administrator's workload.

Table 21.1. Built-In Global Groups.

Group	Managed By	Contains
Domain Admins	Administrators	Administrator
Domain Users	Administrators	Administrators
	Account Operators	New Users
Domain Guests	Administrators	Guest
	Account Operators	

Table 21.2. Built-In Local Groups.

Group	Managed By	Auto Contents	Permissions
Administrators	Administrators	Domain Admins	Can do anything except auto access of files on NTFS
		Administrator (user)	

Group	Managed By	Auto Contents	Permissions
Backup Operators	Administrators	None	Backup and restore
			Log in locally
			Shut down system
Server Operators	Administrators	None	Share/unshare resources
			Format server disks
			Backup and restore
			Log in locally
			Shut down servers
Account Operators	Administrators	None	Manage user and group accounts
			Cannot assign user rights or modify local built-in groups
Print Operators	Administrators	None	Manage printers
			Log in locally
			Shut down
Power Users	Administrators	Power Users	Set up user
			Create and modify user accounts
			Add users to users, guests, and power users groups
			Start and stop sharing of local resources
Users	Administrators	Domain Users	Cannot log on locally to DC
	Account Operators		Access resources via only the network
	Administrator (user)		
Guests	Administrators	Domain Guests	Utilize domain resources via the network
	Account Operators		
Replicator	Administrators	None	Manage replication of files

Multiple Logins

It is important for security reasons that users log in at one computer at a time. If a user logs on to one machine and then walks off, the network can be accessed by anyone who walks up to that machine. By preventing multiple simultaneous logons, if the user tries to log on to another machine he is reminded that he is already logged on at another station. This feature may either be implemented through the operating system or via a third-party product.

Managing Resources

A network exists to provide for the efficient use of resources, whether that resource is a database of customer information or the color laser printer. Administering resource access is one of the most time-consuming tasks for any administrator.

Resource management begins with determining a method of naming servers, hosts, printers, and other devices on your network. As when naming user accounts, stick to descriptive names rather than imaginative ones. A good naming plan identifies the location or purpose of each device.

After the resource has been installed, you must provide access to those users who are to be using it. When assigning access to resources such as printers, make your groups as all-inclusive as possible while still taking into consideration each group's unique needs.

Hardware Resources

Hardware resources are the most costly and most visible of network resources. They include printers, scanners, modems, cameras, and slide makers. The administrator has to apply appropriate permissions to give needed access as well as instruct users in how to access the resources.

When one of these resources is not available either through equipment failure or denied access, the administrator faces the user's displeasure. A proactive plan or regular servicing and auditing can help prevent the unexpected loss of use of these resources.

Disk Quota

Throughout the ages, it has been shown that any stored object grows in size until it completely fills its container. The same axiom applies to files whether stored on the server or the user's personal computer. If no policy is implemented that restricts the amount of space a user can use, then the administrator soon finds that all the disk space is completely filled up—often with documents, programs, and other minutiae whose purpose or origin has been forgotten.

NOTE

Certain networking operating systems have the built-in capability to limit the amount of disk space each user can use. The capability to set the point at which the shrinking percentage of free space triggers an alert is also often available. In addition, many third-party vendors offer products to fill this need. This capability does not presently exist in Windows NT.

Files & Directories

Files, and the directories containing them, are generally not thought of as network resources, yet they are accessed by users all day long. All users want to be able to access their own files when desired and know that others cannot see them. Windows NT provides the capability to control access on the directory and file level. These permissions are more efficiently managed by assigning users with like needs to appropriate groups. These groups are then assigned the necessary access permissions.

NOTE

It is possible to assign share-level permissions to directories using either FAT (File Allocation Table) or NTFS (New Technology File System) file systems. These permissions apply only when accessing the directory remotely. NTFS also allows the assignment of permissions applied via interactive or local access on files or directories.

Software Installation/Upgrades

An important consideration when selecting the software packages to be installed is the selection of a virus-checking program. This program should be relatively maintenance-free and provide for scanning of workstations as well as servers. It should also provide the administrator with a method to log significant events and to generate reports.

When planning your network, one of the first questions posed is what you want your network to do for you. Many classifications of software packages, such as groupware applications, may be added to your network to increase productivity. Features that are important include sharing documents, group scheduling, and communication such as e-mail.

After a particular software package is implemented, the administrator must plan how and when software upgrades are to be done. The cost of installation on your client base becomes significant as your user base increases. This makes planning your upgrades very important.

Remote installation can significantly reduce the cost of your network. This may be accomplished either through push technology where the server sends instructions to the workstation to install a program, or pull technology where the workstation asks the server to send the program. Microsoft provides the System Management Server, which has the capability to inventory client machines as well as automate software installation or upgrades.

E-mail Applications

E-mail provides for fast, reliable communication within your organization as well as worldwide. In its most basic form, an e-mail system is a store-and-forward application that consists of a post office where mail is stored and individual mailboxes for each user. The network administrator is responsible for creating and deleting users and groups and managing the e-mail directory. If your local system is attached to another system or the Internet, then the administrator must also oversee the communication with these other systems.

Network Printing

Probably the most common reason for networking, especially in smaller organizations, is to allow for sharing of printers. Sharing printers often justifies the purchase of more expensive printers. When printers do not work, users cannot be productive. As the size of the network grows, the diversity of printers grows.

Each brand of printer and each operating system provides challenges to the administrator. Various tools are available to allow for easier administration. The difficulty with these tools is that they tend to be proprietary and provide information for only that particular type of printer. One of the newest types provides the capability to manage printers via a web browser.

Important administrative tasks include replenishing of printer supplies and attending to regular servicing. The most effective administrative tools are those that encourage proactive administration by providing easy access to data such as the total number of pages printed and levels of remaining supplies such as paper or toner. Another useful feature is the generation of alerts when supplies are low or the time for routine servicing is near.

Many of the newer printers come with installed hardware or software that function as a print server, thereby eliminating the need for the printer to be attached to a computer functioning as a print server. The administrator must then decide whether a single dedicated print server should be used to manage all printers.

When a file and print server is used to provide access to your printers, utilization of computer resources becomes an issue. The computer may experience degradation of its performance if it must manage several printers and support a large number of users. On the other hand, if a dedicated print server is used—even if it is no more than a board installed on the printer itself—it becomes another server that you have to manage.

When printing to a network printer, the job is first sent to the print server by the computer's redirector. The print server then spools the job. The purpose of the spooler is to store print jobs until the print device is available. Spooling is useful when several jobs are sent at the same time or if a slow printer cannot keep up with the rapidity of jobs being sent.

The spooler may reside on the print device, in volatile memory on the print server, or on the hard drive of the print server. After the appropriate print device becomes available, the job is forwarded.

After a printer is attached to the network, access must be granted if users are to be able to print to it. First the virtual printer or queue must be created and named, including loading the correct print driver. Any special printer features must also be configured, such as multiple paper types or duplexing. Once the printer has been created and configured, you need to provide for user access. In Windows NT, the Print Manager is used to accomplish this task. Figure 21.2 shows the printer being set up for sharing.

Each client must then be configured to connect to the printer. The names of the print server and the printer are used to create this connection.

FIGURE 21.2.
Printer Properties.

Management Tools

A wide variety of tools and utilities are available to assist the system administrator in managing the network. The larger the network, the more complex administration becomes and the more vital it is that you have the right tools.

Microsoft Management Tools

Microsoft provides a variety of management tools to help the network administrator in the day-to-day management of the Windows NT network. The most frequently used tools are the User Manager for Domains, the Server Manager, and the Event Viewer.

User Manager

The User Manager for Domains enables you to:

- Select the domain or computer you want to manage
- Manage the auditing policy
- Set the security policies for your domain or computer
- Create, delete, and change user and group accounts

The User Manager is used to create user and group accounts, but it is also used to set global account policies such as password length and expiration, password history, and the number of failed logon attempts that trigger an account lockout. You can also set a policy to forcibly disconnect a user after expiration of the allowed logon hours. Figure 21.3 illustrates the various global account options available to you.

FIGURE 21.3.

*Account policies
available under User
Manager.*

The User Manager is used to grant rights to users and groups. User rights are rules governing what actions a user can perform. These rights are computer-specific and differ from permissions that apply to objects. It is generally a better practice to add users to groups that have the needed rights rather than grant rights to individual users.

User Manager is used to enable auditing. With Windows NT, you can audit both systemwide events and specific actions of a particular user. To track events such as file access or unsuccessful login attempts, you must first enable auditing as shown in Figure 21.4. You may then use the appropriate tool, such as Windows Explorer, to indicate which events you wish to track.

Although auditing provides valuable information for the administrator, it does increase the workload of the computer that is being audited.

FIGURE 21.4.
Enabling auditing.

Server Manager

The Server Manager is used to manage both local and remote computers in your workgroup or domain. When administering a single computer, you may:

- View connected users, disconnect users, or send messages to connected users
- View shared resources and directories
- Manage services and directory replication

Domain-related tasks that are accomplished through the Server Manager include:

- Adding computers to your domain
- Promotion and demotion of Primary Domain Controllers (PDC) and Backup Domain Controllers (BDC)
- Synchronization of the security database from the PDC to the BDC

Figure 21.5 shows the Server Manager.

FIGURE 21.5.
Server Manager.

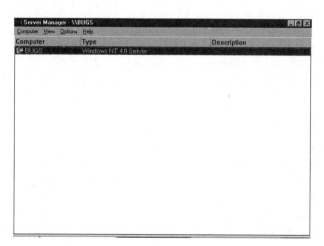

Event Viewer

The Event Viewer is the first place to look if you suspect a problem with your computer. It displays the Security, System, and Application logs. The System log monitors events such as the failure of a driver or service to start. The Security log helps identify any possible breaches to your system's security. And the Application log shows events generated by various applications. You may select to view the logs of the local or remote computers.

Network Client Administrator

The Network Client Administrator enables you to create startup disks that can start a client, connect to installation files on the network, and install the operating system. You can also create client installation disk sets that contain the files needed to install the network client software. The Network Client Administrator also copies the client-based network administration tools to be used on either Windows NT workstation or Windows 95 clients. The last feature of the Network Client Administrator is the capability it gives you to view information on Remoteboot Clients.

Zero Administration

The concept of "zero administration" refers to the effort to simplify administrative tasks. It combines various administrative tools and guidelines to implement centralized management. User access is managed through the use of system policies and user profiles. The goal of zero administration is to reduce the total cost of ownership by reducing helpdesk calls, and still provide user access to needed applications and data.

Microsoft Management Console

Microsoft has introduced the Microsoft Management Console to answer the commonly voiced complaints from system administrators about the plethora of tools that are used to administer the network. Microsoft presently employs separate utilities, each of which provides the capability to accomplish one task. The MMC is not a new management tool, but rather provides a single interface where other tools may be plugged in. This provides a one-stop place where administrators can find the tools used to administer the network rather than having to open and close multiple programs. Not only does this interface make the life of the administrator easier, it also reduces the load placed on the network.

Summary

Network management begins with planning the network from cabling and connectivity to network operating system and software packages. It continues with day-to-day activities of user, group, and resource administration. But just as importantly, it is involved with the long-term planning of the future course of the network. This involves evaluation of how it is presently functioning and what growth is projected. This chapter has discussed some of the tools and techniques that the network administrator can utilize to achieve these goals.

Managing Network Performance

by James Causey

IN THIS CHAPTER

CHAPTER 22

Networks, as you've seen throughout this book, are amazing things, made up of myriad pieces from different vendors and manufacturers that blend together to form a working whole. The fact that you can, with relative ease, put together a network that enables computers to communicate at such amazing speeds, using parts designed and manufactured by so many different sources, is mind-boggling to ponder at times.

It is reasonable to expect something so complex to suffer from problems caused by that complexity, and with networks, that expectation is often well founded. Careful planning, design, and implementation can significantly reduce the amount of time you, as a network administrator, spend troubleshooting network performance issues. No matter how well designed and well laid out your network may be, however, it is essential that you have an understanding of the problems you can run into, and the tools available to help you solve them.

This chapter discusses a number of the most common issues that can impact network performance. In addition, it examines some of the more common tools and techniques used to isolate those issues.

Potential Network Performance Problems

This section looks at some of the issues that can cause problems with your network's performance. Some of these problems are more common than others, but having a knowledge of all of them can help you resolve problems with your network ranging from the simple to the frustrating.

Physical Layer Issues

During the life of a network, the Physical Layer receives most of its attention from network administrators at the very beginning, when the network is first being designed and installed. From that point onward, many administrators forget the Physical Layer, expecting it to cause little or no future problems.

Although the Physical Layer is, indeed, often quite robust and reliable, it can still be the source of many performance problems. These problems include exceeding media limitations, interference, and wear and tear.

Exceeding Media Limitations

All types of physical media, whether twisted pair wiring, fiber optic cabling, or infrared wireless, have performance limitations, based primarily on distance. Exceeding these limits, even by a small amount, can cause performance problems as data degrades to garbage—or simply isn't received at all—by the time it arrives. Problems resulting from exceeded media limitations are difficult to diagnose; problems such as running a cable beyond the recommended length, or stringing repeating devices beyond recommended specifications, or improperly terminating a bus-based media rarely cause a network to simply cease functioning. Instead, intermittent speed and reliability problems plague the network, producing symptoms that can be extremely difficult to track down. The best way to avoid these problems is to familiarize yourself with the recommended limits for length, segment extension, and other such attributes, and take care during design and installation to never exceed those limits.

> **NOTE**
>
> Check Chapters 3 and 4, "The Physical Layer" and "The 'Not-so-Physical' Physical Layer," for information on the limitations that apply to various physical-level media types.

Interference

Most types of network media are susceptible to at least one form of interference. The same electromagnetic wavelengths used to transmit data are often generated by environmental, mechanical, or electronic phenomena, generating noise and interference that can wreak havoc on network communications. Such mistakes as running twisted pair wiring near fluorescent lighting can result in severely degraded network performance from noise. Wireless networks are even more susceptible to interference because they lack even the rudimentary shielding provided by twisted pair wiring. Problems generated by interference can be extremely difficult to isolate. In addition, it can be difficult and expensive to implement fixes to interference problems. As with media limitations, the best strategy for dealing with interference is to avoid problems during the network's installation. Be careful to consider any potential sources of interference, and either carefully deal with them during installation or use a media type that is not susceptible to the interference.

Wear and Tear

Although generally not an issue with wireless networks, wear and tear on network cabling can take its toll on network performance. Whether caused by physical trauma or degradation over time in low-quality components, damaged network media can cause a range of problems, ranging from intermittent connectivity drops in shared media such as coaxial wiring to more elusive performance issues, such as increased vulnerability to interference in a wire with frayed shielding. Wear-and-tear issues are less significant in modern networks; in particular, the replacement of co-ax wiring with twisted pair in many Ethernet networks has nearly eliminated many of the issues revolving around the rather vulnerable, fragile, and exposed wiring and connectors used by that media. The careful planning and installation of wiring in protective conduits, and the use of customized datajacks, can prevent most problems with network wear and tear.

> **TIP**
>
> Are you still using 10Base-2 co-ax wiring? Sick and tired of dropped networks due to broken cable? You can reduce the number of bus breaks caused by simple human error with a simple step at each workstation installation and configuration stop. When (and if) your support staff need to touch a user's workstation, take a minute to show that machine's user(s) how to properly disconnect the workstation from the network and to explain the importance of cable integrity. Although this doesn't eliminate breaks caused by improper cable disconnection, it does sharply reduce their frequency. In addition, you may receive a more subtle payoff when users check the integrity of the wiring in their offices or cubicles before calling the help desk whenever there's a network outage.

> **TIP**
>
> When verifying the physical integrity of your network cabling, don't rely on sight alone, particularly when dealing with bus-based media. Physically check the integrity of each connection. A loose soldering joint or crimp may not be visible at first glance, but can still expose the conductors whenever stress or tension is applied to the cable, increasing the bus's vulnerability to interference and possibly even disconnecting the wire.

Network Traffic Issues

At the same time that networks have transformed the way users do their jobs, the utilization of networks has increased greatly. Whether generated by increased reliance on network services, the use of bandwidth-intensive applications, hardware problems, or sheer numbers of users, network traffic increases are a fact of life on modern networks. Most networks are designed with high levels of traffic in mind; however, as traffic increases, performance can degrade, and often in ways not normally expected. A variety of issues related to network traffic can degrade the performance of networks and are discussed in the following sections.

Network Collisions

Ethernet networking is the most common form of local area network used. As you probably know by now, Ethernet's CSMA/CD method of bus contention generates a jamming signal, known as a *collision*, whenever more than one NIC (network interface card) attempts to send a packet over the network. (For more information on Ethernet and CSMA/CD, see Chapter 7, "Ethernet.")

As more and more workstations attempt to transmit over the network, the number of collisions inevitably rises. Because each collision causes every transmitting workstation to pause briefly, having a huge collision count is definitely a bad thing. In fact, on an Ethernet network, it is possible (though *highly* unlikely) that the collision load may get so high that a workstation may never get a chance to send its packets.

If you're detecting a huge number of network collisions (see the section titled "Tools and Techniques," later in this chapter), your network is probably overloaded. You can try moving to a more efficient media type or one with higher bandwidth; you can also try splitting up your network into multiple *collision domains* (segments on which workstation traffic can collide), either by using more segments or by implementing switching.

> **NOTE**
>
> CSMA/CD networks aren't the only types of networks susceptible to this type of bandwidth clogging. In a Token Ring network, for instance, even though each workstation always gets an opportunity to receive a token and send data over the wire, high levels of traffic can cause extremely long delays between passes of the token.

Inefficient Network Protocols

Different network protocols implement their communication and address resolution processes in different ways, some of which are less efficient than others. Many protocols that provide easier setup and administration via dynamic name resolution, in particular, pay for that ease by hogging the network with name resolution broadcasts. AppleTalk, the peer-to-peer networking protocol used by Macintosh, is notorious for this behavior. NetWare devices using IPX/SPX are also very chatty, sending out SAP (Service Advertisement Protocol) broadcasts on a very frequent basis. NetBIOS browsing, as implemented by LAN Manager and NT-based networks, can also be rather chatty, whether implemented over TCP/IP, IPX/SPX, or NetBEUI.

In a network severely hampered by excessive broadcasts, a number of potential resolution techniques are available, ranging from configuring workstations to eliminate or reduce broadcasts as much as possible, to filtering broadcasts at the router level, to actually switching to a different communication protocol.

Hardware Overload

As network traffic increases, so does the load on the hardware handling that traffic. Intelligent devices such as routers, which must check the headers on a large percentage of packets to determine routing paths, are most affected by traffic. As network traffic increases, the amount of load on these devices increases as well, until the device cannot keep up with the traffic. In some devices, high levels of network traffic can even cause the device to begin generating garbage of its own.

Hardware overload solutions can be dealt with in a number of ways. Using dedicated routing devices rather than multi-homed workstations is a way to increase routing efficiency. In addition, adding routers and splitting your network into smaller networks helps distribute the processing load across multiple devices; however, it also makes the process of routing data more complex.

Poorly Implemented Network Stacks

As networks have become more and more mature, so have the techniques used to develop network stacks and NIC driver software. Many intelligent NICs, for instance, carefully examine each Ethernet broadcast, and interrupt the CPU only if the data being broadcast requires actual system processing time. However, many older NICs and drivers are not so intelligent, and can actually slow down workstations as network traffic increases. Purchasing modern, high-quality NIC devices can help you avoid this problem.

Some network stacks do not properly implement certain types of network services, or do not implement them at all. This problem is seen most often with older TCP/IP stacks, which don't implement more modern services used over TCP/IP, such as multicasting. When a multicast occurs, for instance, some older TCP/IP stacks do not know how to handle the data being sent, and can generate confusing error messages, or even crash, adversely affecting the reliability of the system. These problems can be difficult to detect and diagnose; many times, these problems are assumed to be an "inexplicable crash," and show up only in long-term, detailed logs generated by network analysis software. (See the section titled "Tools and Techniques," later in this chapter, for more information on network analyzers.)

Garbage

Some traffic situations can actually be caused by faulty hardware. It's not uncommon, for example, to see a dying or faulty Ethernet card generate huge numbers of spurious garbage packets, flooding the network with garbage data and collisions.

Garbage can also be generated by electromagnetic interference. In addition, some overloaded hubs, repeaters, routers, and gateways are sometimes observed to generate garbage packets at extreme traffic load levels.

Denial-of-Service Attacks

As the Internet has grown, and more and more enterprises have connected their LANs and WANs to it, attacks against those networks over the Internet have become more and more frequent. One major type of attack is the *denial-of-service attack*, which takes advantage of bugs in TCP/IP implementations or problems inherent in the design of TCP/IP to "flood" a system, causing it to waste huge amounts of processor and network bandwidth responding to false or garbage requests. Some denial-of-service attacks can even cause a system to crash.

Denial-of-service attacks can be countered by keeping up to date on the latest patches and updates to your operating system, and by making careful use of error logging and network analysis.

Address Resolution Problems

Even if a network has low traffic, high bandwidth, and every workstation can send data without apparent limitation, it's all for naught if your network stack can't resolve the address of the destination of your data. Resolution failures, whether caused by the failure of a centralized service (such as Domain Name Service or Windows Internet Name Service) or misconfiguration, can wreak havoc on a working network, and often confuse users and novice support providers.

Address resolution problems can be detected and resolved using some of the techniques listed in the "Tools and Techniques" section of this chapter.

Internetworking Issues

Many of the problems already discussed in this chapter can also affect you remotely, even if you're not experiencing those particular problems on your own network. An overloaded router upstream in your connection to the Internet, for instance, can severely limit or even eliminate your Internet connectivity, as can a misconfigured or downed router or gateway. Major failures on large networks like the Internet can cause a domino effect, as failover traffic (the traffic from the failed links which now has to be carried on redundant links) overloads redundant links, causing connection after connection to drop or slow down. The next section, "Tools and Techniques," describes some methods useful for detecting remote internetworking problems.

Tools and Techniques

Now that many of the potential issues that can affect performance on your network have been introduced, it is time to discuss some of the tools and strategies you can use to isolate and correct those performance problems.

Ping

Ping is probably the first, and most important, diagnostic tool in a network using TCP/IP. Ping is a tool that sends out an "Are you there?" request to a specified host; if that host is alive, it responds with a "Yes, I am" reply to the originator. The Ping software counts the time elapsed between the origination of the ping request and the receipt of the reply, and lists the elapsed time. Thus, Ping not only tells you whether a particular machine is up and responding, but can also show you whether there are long delays in communication between the two; this is invaluable for isolating both outages and performance problems. Figure 22.1 illustrates a typical Ping session.

FIGURE 22.1.
Windows NT Ping utility.

```
Command Prompt

Microsoft(R) Windows NT(TM)
(C) Copyright 1985-1996 Microsoft Corp.

E:\users\default>ping legacy

Pinging legacy.union.indiana.edu [129.79.110.111] with 32 bytes of data:

Reply from 129.79.110.111: bytes=32 time=170ms TTL=125
Reply from 129.79.110.111: bytes=32 time=150ms TTL=125
Reply from 129.79.110.111: bytes=32 time=160ms TTL=125
Reply from 129.79.110.111: bytes=32 time=230ms TTL=125

E:\users\default>
```

This example shows a call to Ping with no command-line switches, and with the name of the host the user wishes to ping passed to it. By default, Ping sends out four sequential ping requests, and lists whether a reply was received and the response time for each ping. Ping has a number of tweaks that can be performed, including changing the number of Ping requests, altering the size of the Ping packets, adjusting the TTL (Time-To-Live) for the Ping packets, and other configuration options. Most of these are not needed for standard diagnostics. For more information on those switches, type **PING /?** at the Command Prompt.

> **NOTE**
>
> Be careful adjusting the size of your Ping packets! Many TCP/IP stacks have recently proved to be vulnerable to denial-of-service attacks using the Ping utility. If, when you run Ping, you specify an extremely large Ping packet (normally around 64KB), rather than rely on the default packet size, the host TCP/IP stack receiving the Ping packet locks up, dropping network connectivity and possibly even crashing the host system. Most affected operating systems have patches available to fix this problem, but not all administrators have applied those patches. Because there's really no good reason to use such a large Ping packet size, you're best off playing it safe and avoiding excessively large Ping packets.

When you're experiencing a network outage or performance problem, use Ping in the following order to help you determine exactly where the problem lies:

1. Ping a host on your TCP/IP subnet by canonical name. If the Ping fails, ping that host by IP address. If the Ping still fails, you know that TCP/IP connectivity is down, at least for your workstation; if it fails on the canonical attempt, but works by IP address, you know that name resolution isn't functioning properly.

2. If the host responded properly when pinged by canonical address, ping the gateway address. If it replies, you know your gateway is alive; if not, you know that you may have any of a number of problems communicating with your gateway device, including incorrect subnet mask and/or gateway address configuration, a polluted arp (address resolution protocol) cache, or a gateway that is simply down.

3. If your gateway responds, ping a host on another local subnet, if available. If that host replies, you know your intranet is functioning; if not, you may have connectivity problems between gateways, or between ports on the same gateway.

4. Ping your intranet's gateway to the Internet. If it responds, your Internet gateway is alive; if not, you have probably isolated your problem.

5. Ping various hosts on the Internet. This enables you to determine how localized your connectivity failure is. (This step assumes, of course, that you're not running a firewall or other security system that prevents you from successfully pinging hosts on the other side of that system.)

If, rather than an outage, you're experiencing slow performance, the same steps can help you determine where the slowdown is taking place—if you pay attention to the response times listed in each Ping request.

TIP

Does your network use other protocols in addition to TCP/IP? TCP/IP diagnostic tools like Ping are useful for more than just testing your IP connectivity; because the same gateway devices are normally used to route both TCP/IP and other protocols, and because most hosts on your network use those same additional protocols, Ping enables you to determine whether those hosts are alive at all. You can also use Ping in combination with other protocols' diagnostic tools (like SLIST on a NetWare network) to determine whether the outage or performance issue applies to only one protocol, or affects all your network connectivity.

Traceroute

As you may have noticed, using Ping to comprehensively diagnose the location of an outage or slowdown can be a rather tedious business. Fortunately, there's a tool that can ease some of that tedium: Traceroute (or TRACERT, as the tool is named under Windows NT).

You initiate a Traceroute by running the program and passing it the name of the destination host. Every TCP/IP connection between yourself and that host is tested to ascertain both network connectivity and response time. The Traceroute utility sends a special Traceroute packet to the first upstream host (normally your TCP/IP gateway), listing the destination of the Traceroute. That first upstream host, if alive, responds to the originator by sending the equivalent of a Ping response, with a confirmation of receipt, and forwards the Traceroute packet on to the next upstream host. This process continues until the destination is reached or Time-to-Live for the Traceroute packet is exceeded. Figure 22.2 shows a typical Traceroute session under Windows NT.

FIGURE 22.2.
Windows NT
TRACERT utility.

Like Ping, the Traceroute utility has a number of configuration options. For more information on options under the TRACERT utility on Windows NT, type **TRACERT /?** at the NT Command Prompt.

Traceroute is extremely useful for isolating the point of a network failure, because it can show which gateway device is not responding, and even reveal whether one port on a gateway device is dead. Traceroute can also show you, with the response time statistic for each response, where network slowdowns are taking place. When used in combination, Traceroute and Ping are, perhaps, the most valuable software tools available to the administrator of a TCP/IP network.

> **NOTE**
>
> Don't like the command-line Ping and Traceroute utilities included with Windows NT? Most third-party TCP/IP utility vendors provide graphical Ping and Traceroute utilities that provide the same level of functionality, but with a more intuitive interface.

Windows NT Performance Monitor

Windows NT includes a powerful tool for diagnosing bottlenecks of various types, including network performance problems: the Windows NT Performance Monitor.

The Performance Monitor (located in the Administrative Tools program folder, under the Start menu) is a flexible, powerful tool for monitoring system and network activity. See Figure 22.3 for a picture of the Performance Monitor in action.

FIGURE 22.3.

Windows NT Performance Monitor charting an RAS session.

The Performance Monitor enables you to watch statistics for various network services, including raw TCP/IP statistics, and statistics for the various network services, such as Server and Workstation. Watching how these statistics adjust under various types of loads enables you to determine whether your performance bottleneck is, in fact, your network bandwidth, or is based on another problem entirely, such as an overloaded disk I/O subsystem, a pegged processor, or some other such issue. The Performance Monitor gives you flexibility in how you gather data, as well: you can interactively watch statistics in the Chart screen, generate logs of performance over time with the Log function, view raw numerical data in the Report screen, or set threshold alerts in the Alert screen. The NT Performance Monitor can be overwhelming at first, but it provides a variety of powerful features for identifying system-specific performance problems.

Network Analyzers

Network analyzers (or "packet sniffers," as they're more commonly known) are designed to watch the flow of data across a network, and enable a network administrator both to watch the type and order of packets sent over a wire and to actually open up packets and see what data is contained in them. Network analyzers, although complex and sometimes difficult to use, provide network administrators the capability to watch how the network interacts with performance problems that are difficult to diagnose or reproduce. If you've set up your network as instructed, but the behavior is not as you'd expect, you can watch how the network behaves on a packet-by-packet basis to best determine how to reconfigure your network. Network analyzers are often useful with problems that aren't easily even seen as network issues; for example, if a series of machines seems to inexplicably freeze at the same time, you can use a network analyzer to capture logs and see exactly what's happening on the wire at the time of the freeze, and determine whether the network itself is the cause.

There are a variety of network analyzers, ranging from expensive, dedicated hardware devices to software utilities. Windows NT Server includes a network analyzer called Network Monitor, which can analyze either the wire to which the server is directly connected or the wire of another NT Server or Workstation on the network (using the Network Monitor Agent service, running remotely on another system). LANalyzer by Novell is another popular network analysis tool, designed to run under DOS and Windows.

> **NOTE**
>
> Network analyzers, with their capability to pull open each and every packet on the network, pose a potential security risk. Because many networks (such as AppleTalk and even Telnet and FTP) use clear-text passwords passed over the wire, anyone with a packet sniffer can determine the passwords people are using. If at all possible, limit the people who have access to packet-sniffing systems to a trusted few. If you cannot do this, make certain that any passwords sent as clear-text over the network are not duplicated by your users on other, more secure machines.

Hardware Troubleshooting

One of the most commonly ignored places to check for network performance problems is at the hardware level. (Ever found yourself spending hours diagnosing a communications outage, only to find that the Ethernet cable wasn't plugged into your NIC?) It's critically important for you to examine the actual hardware your system is using, particularly if you're finding a performance problem that you can't duplicate.

When diagnosing network hardware, it's important to consider the various potential points of failure, and diagnose each one systematically until you discover which is causing the problem. Figure 22.4 illustrates several points of vulnerability, each of which can cause a network outage or performance problem.

FIGURE 22.4.

Potential points of network hardware failure.

In order to detect the hardware problem, trace your way back from the most likely to the least likely cause. Network interface cards, for instance, fail far more often than do expensive leased T1 lines.

To examine this step-by-step technique, consider an example based on a real-life network outage. Sarah, a network administrator for a company on the Left Coast, has a new workstation that doesn't appear to see anything on the network, whether on her corporate intranet or out on the Internet itself. Sarah's first step to determine what's going wrong is to go to another workstation on the same network and check that machine's connectivity. A machine in the office next door is working just fine; this fact lets her eliminate upstream hardware or configuration problems. Depending on how her network is laid out, this revelation might enable her to eliminate differing amounts of hardware; in this case, Sarah's using switched 100Base-T, with in-wall datajacks connected to the actual switch ports, with individual station cables then plugged into those datajacks. Therefore, Sarah has just eliminated the possibility of failure of the switch itself (though one port in the switch may still be dead), or in its connection to the rest of the network and Internet (see Figure 22.5).

Now, Sarah's going to begin by looking at the most likely points of failure: the NIC itself and its connection to the wall jack. First, she checks to see whether any of the card's lights are active. Most Network Interface Cards have at least one light, which flashes to indicate network activity (with Ethernet, normally whenever a collision is detected). Better cards also have another light, to indicate when the card is properly connected to the network, and to indicate whether the cable being used is of the proper polarity.

FIGURE 22.5.
First step of hardware failure point elimination—fewer potential points of failure.

Individual Port on Device

Network Interface Card (NIC)

Station Cable/Shared Bus Cable

Datajack (if applicable)

In-Wall Cable

> **NOTE**
>
> This seems like an appropriate time to get on the soap box about a topic near and dear to my heart: buying high-quality network hardware. There's a wide range of hardware available at different cost levels, each providing different levels of features and reliability. The temptation is often strong to simply buy the cheapest NIC or hub or router available to save some money.
>
> If you're tempted to do this, allow me to plead with you: *Don't do it!* The money you save on cheap, no-name devices with lousy drivers, no diagnostic lights, and difficult hardware configuration options is later spent many times over on the additional time spent supporting it. My mantra on the subject is this: *The little bit of extra money spent on better hardware always pays for itself in reduced support costs.*

In this case, Sarah isn't seeing any lights on the card. This doesn't eliminate any points of failure; at this point, however, many would assume that the Ethernet card is simply dead, particularly if the workstation worked fine before. However, a few more steps are necessary to more precisely isolate the problem. Sarah checks the station cable, looking for damage and making sure that it's plugged firmly into the NIC and into the datajack. Because the cable seems fine, she grabs a cable that she knows is good (possibly from a machine that's working fine), and swaps it with the station cable on the machine she's diagnosing. Still no lights, and no connectivity. She knows she's eliminated another point of failure: the station cable (see Figure 22.6).

Now, Sarah examines the Ethernet card, checking to make sure that it is properly configured and seated in its slot on the workstation's motherboard. All seems to be well, and she needs to try to isolate the problem further. To do so, she connects another workstation and cable that are working fine to the datajack; no connectivity. To double check, she plugs the machine she's diagnosing into another datajack, and suddenly it has connectivity. Now, she's eliminated the workstation's Ethernet card; the problem has to be either a wiring problem between the datajack and the switch, or a dead port on the switch (see Figure 22.7).

FIGURE 22.6.

Second step of hardware failure point elimination—fewer potential points of failure.

Individual Port on Device

Network Interface Card (NIC)

Datajack (if applicable)

In-Wall Cable

FIGURE 22.7.

Third step of hardware failure point elimination—fewer potential points of failure.

Individual Port on Device

Datajack (if applicable)

In-Wall Cable

Sarah now checks the connection at the datajack itself, and determines that the in-wall wiring has a broken connection at the datajack. She quickly repairs the broken connection, and the datajack begins providing connectivity. By systematically isolating potential points of failure, Sarah has avoided stabbing in the dark and has fixed the problem in far less time than would have been the case making rash decisions as to where the failure occurred.

Summary

The process of managing your network's performance can be more complicated than the actual design and installation of the network itself. Understanding the troubleshooting process, the available tools and strategies for diagnosing and repairing your network, and the details of your network's layout is your most powerful weapon as a network administrator. With that knowledge, you can turn the immensely complex task of diagnosing network problems into a far less daunting process.

Data Security

by James Spann

IN THIS CHAPTER

The previous chapters have discussed ways to optimize the network, but no network is truly optimized until it can safely transmit the data. The way to protect the data and make sure it arrives unharmed is through security. Most people tend to think of security as a lock that keeps the bad people out. Although this concept is not wrong, one must actually look at all the components of enforcing the security of data. Not only should one consider the confidentiality of the data but also its accuracy and availability. Although this chapter primarily examines the confidentiality issue, items like uninterruptible power supplies and backup tapes are also important to fully enforce security.

Planning for Network and Data Security

This chapter on security examines one of the most serious threats that any network or user faces: the intentional threat. Although the threat from the outside is viewed by many to be the most ominous one, most studies show that the intentional threat usually comes from the inside of one's organization. In fact, almost 80% of all security breaches that are deemed to be intentional have come from an insider. One word that many people associate with this intentional threat is a person known as a "hacker." For the purposes of this chapter, a *hacker* is actually one of the good guys and the bad guys will be known as *crackers*. Crackers are the persons who use hacking abilities for their own personal gain or some other malicious intent. Hackers do what they do to improve computer security and make programs and applications perform better.

Levels of Security

The first step to implementing security on any system is to develop an understanding of the security settings available for that particular system. With Microsoft Networking, essentially three different types or "levels" of security can apply.

Microsoft Networking uses a concept of sharing to enforce network security. Within Windows 95, the capability to "share" a resource means the capability to make it available for network use. If a resource has not been "shared," then it is not available via the network. Some caveats, of course, apply to this rule, so do not consider it to be a concrete ideal just yet. Although securing network resources through the careful use of sharing is a good start for security, it is also important for users to be able to secure the resources on their own computers. Windows NT users can secure not only network resources but their own local resources as well.

The level of security authorization a user has on a system is determined by the security granted to that user by the system itself. The system's administrator must set up that level of security. The administrator of a particular system has a difficult job in determining what level of security to use both for a particular resource and a particular user. For that reason, it is a wise move to always consider security before any installation or setup takes place. Additionally, the administrator should consider the use of a security policy (discussed later in this chapter) to help enforce security in an even and thorough manner.

The first step in enforcing any type of system security is to authenticate the user. Authentication is typically a process that consists of two steps: identification and verification.

Identification is the process whereby a user identifies who he is to the system. This is typically managed through the use of login names. When a user presents his user name or "login name" to the system, he is stating to the system, "Hello, I am user X." To authenticate the user, the system typically challenges the user's claim by asking for the second part of the authentication process: verification.

Verification is the process the system follows in attempting to validate that the user attempting to log in is actually the person she says she is. It is very easy for someone to walk up to you and say, "Hi, I am John Doe." However, unless he has some form of proof, you really have no way to know whether he is who he says he is. The same thing is true for the computer system.

Anyone can walk up to a computer system and enter "Administrator" as the login name. The computer system must have a way to verify that the user is indeed the administrator of the system. This is typically done by asking the user to provide a password to prove that the user attempting to log in is indeed the administrator.

Therefore, if the user is able to provide both identification (a valid login name) and verification (the correct password for that login name), then she can successfully complete the authentication process. Any user that has been authenticated to the system can then be given certain security clearances to use particular objects on that system. In the case of Windows NT, if a domain controller authenticates that user, then the user has certain security clearances to use particular objects in the domain.

To determine what the security clearances are for a given user, the security policies that are in effect must be examined.

Security Policies

The term *security policies* actually has two different meanings in this chapter. The first meaning, the one discussed here, refers to a standard that is agreed upon by the administrative person or persons to enforce an agreed-upon security level throughout the enterprise. The second meaning refers to an administrative tool that became available with Windows NT version 4.0. That administrative tool is called the *Policy Editor* and is used to set up and enforce a particular environment for users of a system.

A security policy is an effective tool for ensuring that *all* the users in the enterprise conform to the security guidelines set up for the enterprise. An effective security policy has several parts, and each of those parts evolves from the information gathered during the first step in establishing a security policy: the risk assessment.

Performing a Risk Assessment

A risk assessment is the tool that is used to evaluate the enterprise and the risks that it faces. A thorough risk assessment evaluates the following areas:

- Vulnerabilities
- Threats
- Countermeasures

The following sections examine each of these individually.

Vulnerabilities

A good security policy begins with an evaluation of the potential security issues faced by the enterprise. The administrator must start this process off by asking the question, "Where are we vulnerable?" A *vulnerability* is a point at which the system is potentially weak. Some examples of common points of vulnerability are:

- Backup system: If the information is not being backed up to a tape drive or some other form of duplicate storage, then the overall enterprise faces a weakness due to the possibility of data being lost if someone or something harms the data or the media on which the data is being kept. This is true whether the data loss is due to intentional or unintentional causes. See Chapter 24, "Data Integrity," for more information on backups.

- Users: Users can be a vulnerability in two ways. First, if a user is not properly trained on the system or program he is using, he can make mistakes that lead to loss or damage of information. For example, a user that is not trained on the proper use, storage, and creation of passwords could leave the system wide open to an intruder. Or, the untrained user could attempt to save data using the wrong procedure and actually overwrite or delete data accidentally. The second way a user can be a potential security risk is if he desires to intentionally harm the data in some way.

- Physical Security: Although the most common source of intentional harm to an enterprise's data comes from someone on the inside, the common thinking today is to "use a lock to keep the honest people out." In truth, however, if someone wants to get at you or your information badly enough, she can find a way to get to it. The security person's job is to make the security of the system effective enough to keep all but the hardcore crackers and thieves out while still leaving it simple enough for the users to work with. This, obviously, is not a simple task. One way to keep out some of the outside intruders is to enforce physical security. This can be accomplished by putting locks on the doors, putting the servers and other important components in locked areas, and setting up a system of authentication for access to the data as previously discussed.

Threats

In addition to evaluating the potential vulnerabilities that an organization faces, authors of a security policy must consider the possible threats that endanger the enterprise as well. A threat is something that can take advantage of a particular vulnerability. Consider the following examples:

- Cracker: If one of the vulnerabilities is a back door or some other type of hole in the system itself, you can rest assured that a cracker can find it and exploit it. A cracker looks for ways to infiltrate your system and is therefore a considerable threat to it. However, you have to keep in mind that most attacks occur from the inside. This means a cracker may have help on the inside or already be on the inside.

- Viruses: Scanning for viruses is a necessity in every environment. Viruses show up in downloaded programs and files, e-mail messages, and even off-the-shelf software. If one of the risk assessment's vulnerabilities is that no virus scanning is being done on the system, then a virus should be considered a very real threat.

- Environmental: Every regional area of the globe faces different kinds of environmental threats. Volcanoes, hurricanes, earthquakes, tornadoes, floods, and other potential disasters are some of the most difficult threats to protect against. In fact, sometimes the only countermeasure for this type of threat is to make sure that a backup copy exists and that there is some way to restore the backup elsewhere.

Countermeasures

After members of an organization have discussed, identified, and evaluated the potential vulnerabilities and threats they face, they are ready to move on to the next step in the risk assessment and security policy process: countermeasures. A *countermeasure* is something that is done in an attempt to minimize the risk caused by a particular vulnerability or threat. Here are a few examples:

- Backups: Keeping a backup copy of the information contained in the computer systems is one of the best ways to ensure that the organization can get the data back if something happens. This type of countermeasure is very helpful against threats such as equipment failure and natural disasters.

- Physical security: Enforcing a rigid physical security policy is one way to help prevent attacks from outside intruders. Locked doors, electronic access badges, and removable hard drives that are locked in a safe every night are just a few ways to prevent someone from breaking in and gaining access to important information. Just remember that if the physical security gets too cumbersome for the users, they inevitably try to find ways around it and thereby defeat the physical security plan.

- Electronic emissions: Some organizations have to worry about the possibility that the signals that travel through their network cables might be tapped. If this is the case, it might be a good idea to consider using fiber-optic cable to transmit all information, because it is much more difficult to steal a signal from fiber-optic cable than it is from coaxial or some type of twisted pair.

Creating the Security Policy

After the risk assessment has been completed, the information gathered from it should be used to create a security plan that is specifically designed and tailored to the needs of that organization. The security policy should be very thorough and cover such details as:

- Policies: The security plan should state in detail exactly what the policies of the enterprise are regarding security and security-related issues. The policies should be explained to every individual within the organization and each individual should be required to acknowledge their acceptance of, understanding of, and compliance with the policies by signing a statement that indicates that fact. The policies should be very specific and not leave any information out.

- Procedures: Additionally, the security plan should list very detailed procedures that must be followed in order to enforce the security policies. Each individual that is responsible for a particular procedure should be made aware of the responsibility and the consequences of performing the procedure inadequately. It is a good idea to also have each responsible party sign the procedure(s) for which he or she is responsible to indicate approval and understanding of the tasks proscribed.

- Updates: A good security plan is only as good as the information contained within it. If that information becomes outdated, then the security plan does also. It is a good idea to continually re-evaluate the organization's vulnerabilities, the potential threats, and the available countermeasures, and to keep the security plan updated on a consistent basis.

Workgroups, Domains, and Trusts

One of the things that can affect the security policy of your enterprise is the implementation and configuration of your network. With Microsoft networking, a network may be implemented in essentially two ways. One method is called *workgroup networking* and the other is called *domain networking*.

Workgroup networking enables users to find resources easily by categorizing them by location. Locations include both the devices on which resources are located and the workgroups in which they reside. The workgroup does not assist the security of the network directly, but it does make the network easier for users to use and therefore a little less prone to errors. See Figure 23.1 for an example of a Windows 95 Network Neighborhood browser window.

The only thing that determines to which workgroup a particular device belongs is how the device was configured. Users are not confined to browsing their workgroup; they can browse any workgroup they can see on their network. If the computers being used to form the workgroup are running Windows NT, then some additional security measures can be taken. Users can be authenticated by their usernames and passwords before they access a particular resource on the network. However, with Windows 95 or Windows for Workgroups, users can be verified only by means of a password because a valid username is not required.

FIGURE 23.1.

*A Windows 95
Network Neighborhood
browser window.*

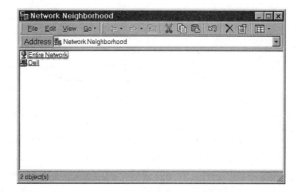

The only problem with using Windows NT systems in a workgroup to provide security is that to enforce rigid security, each user must have a valid username and password on every system he or she wants to access. This can lead to an administrative nightmare. With Windows NT, an administrator must ensure that every time a user wants to change a password, the change is made on all the systems on the network the user needs to access. If the user has a different password on each system, then it is the user who has an ominous task to face. The user must then remember several different passwords, generally by writing them down or creating easily guessed passwords, which should be a violation of the security policy.

Microsoft's answer to this dilemma was to create an administrative tool called a *domain*. A domain is a collection of all the devices, users, and resources into one cohesive administrative unit. When a user needs to have access to the domain, she simply logs in to the domain. After a user is authenticated, she automatically has access to all the domain resources that her security privileges give her access to without having to log in to each one separately. See Figure 23.2 for an example of a domain and its resources.

FIGURE 23.2.

*An example of a
domain.*

A domain enables the administrator to effectively manage several users, resources, and devices while keeping the administrative tasks relatively simple. Having several thousand users or several thousand network resources can lead to administrative difficulties because there are more items to administer. If this happens, the first reaction of the administrative team is to start dividing up the tasks into different administrative groupings, which typically leads to the creation of multiple domains. If an enterprise makes the decision to create multiple domains, then it is back to the original problem. Having multiple domains causes the users to need multiple login names and passwords or, if the login names and passwords are the same, then the administrative team must keep all the domains up to date.

To solve this dilemma, Microsoft created another administrative tool called a *trust*. A trust relationship is used to enable users to log in only once to their primary domain but then give them the access (where security permits) to other resources in other domains. If the trust relationships are set up properly, a user can log in once and still use all the network resources he is authorized to use. When a trust relationship is created, the accounts domain (the domain with the user accounts in it) becomes the *trusted* domain and the resource (the domain with the resources to which the user needs access) becomes the *trusting* domain. See Figure 23.3 for an example of a trust relationship.

Figure 23.3.

An example of a trust relationship.

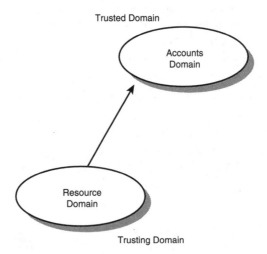

The Four Domain Models

Microsoft has created four different domain models that can be set up depending upon the configuration of the organization. Figure 23.4 shows the Microsoft chart that helps an organization determine which domain model might be the best choice.

The first domain model, the *single domain*, is relatively straightforward. The single domain model does not require any trust relationships and, as you can see from the chart in Figure 23.4, a single domain works for up to 40,000 users in an environment that has a centralized MIS department and centralized resources and users. Refer to Figure 23.2, earlier in this chapter, for an example of a single domain.

FIGURE 23.4.

Choosing a domain model.

Domain Attribute	Single Domain	Master Domain	Multiple Master Domain	Complete Trust
Fewer than 40,000 users per domain	●	●		
More than 40,000 users per domain			●	
Centralized account management	●	●	●	
Centralized resource management	●			
Decentralized account management			●	●
Decentralized resource management		●	●	●
Central MIS	●	●	●	
No central MIS				●

The second domain model is called the *master domain model.* A master domain consists of two or more domains with one of the domains being the master domain. The master domain is also referred to as the *accounts domain* because the user accounts are typically set up only in the master domain. The master domain model works well for organizations with a centralized MIS department and centralized user management. The subordinate domain(s) are normally set up around the resources they provide and are referred to as the *resource domains.*

In order for a true master domain model to exist, a one-way trust relationship must be set up between the resource domain(s) and the master domain. Figure 23.5 shows an example of a master domain with two resource domains. Notice how the arrows are drawn in Figure 23.5. The arrow always points to the trusted domain. The reasoning for this is that the master domain is providing the authentication for all the users. The resource domains are saying to the master domains, "I trust you to provide login authentication for all the users." That way, the users have to log in to the network only once.

FIGURE 23.5.

The master domain model.

Master Domain

23

DATA SECURITY

The third type of domain model is the *multiple master domain model*. In the multiple master model, at least two master domains have user accounts in them. There are normally two or more resource domains as well. Each resource domain must have a one-way trust relationship with each master domain. The master domains normally have a two-way trust relationship between themselves.

Figure 23.6 shows an example of the multiple master domain model with two master (accounts) domains and three subordinate (resource) domains. Multiple master models work best for organizations with more than 40,000 users that have centralized account management for different sites or regions. An example might be an enterprise that has corporate offices in the United States and Europe. There could be a master domain for each region and then several subordinate domains as necessary.

FIGURE 23.6.

The multiple master domain model.

The last type of domain setup is the *complete trust model*. In the complete trust model, each of the domains forms a two-way trust relationship with each of the other domains. Although this involves plenty of trust relationships to manage, it can sometimes be the best method for an organization to employ. The complete trust model works for any number of users and is pictured in Figure 23.7.

FIGURE 23.7.

The complete trust model.

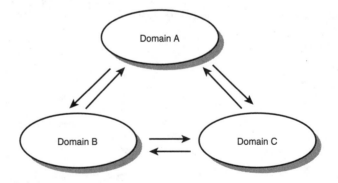

Setting Up Security in Windows 95

Before beginning any discussion on security within Windows 95, it is important to note that Windows 95 offers only basic security for those who need to protect their systems against a casual browsing user, not against the individual who is a diehard cracker. The login procedure of Windows 95 can be defeated without a lot of effort by someone with the know-how and desire. If you need more security than that, you should use Windows NT Workstation as your desktop operating system.

You can also enforce security with Windows 95 by enabling network users to browse shared resources on individual machines. Setting up shared resources on a Windows 95 machine enables the user or administrator to configure the resource with a password if desired. Windows 95 offers the following three levels of access:

- Read: Read access enables the user to look at, run, open, or copy a file to some other location. A user with Read access cannot change the existing file, delete the file, or add new files.

- Full: Users with full access can manipulate files and directories as they want.

- None: The only way to truly keep other users out of a network resource that has been shared on a Windows 95 machine is to require users to give a password to gain access to the share. Anyone who does not know the password cannot access the resource from the network. With Windows 95, you can grant different passwords for Read access and Full access.

Password-Protected Shares

To set up a shared resource with Windows 95, you must first have the proper Microsoft Networking components installed, which include File and Printer Sharing. The easiest way to share a directory (*folder* in Windows 95 terminology) is to browse for that directory using Windows Explorer or My Computer. After you find the folder that contains the files or folders you want to share, simply use the secondary mouse button to click once and bring up the context menu for that folder. See Figure 23.8 for an example.

Select Sharing to get to the Share Properties box for that folder. After you have opened the Share Properties box for that folder, you must decide what to name this shared resource. See Figure 23.9 for an example.

Some things to consider about the name of this shared resource are:

- Who needs to access it? If you expect to have users on DOS-based machines trying to find the share, it is best to use eight-character names with no spaces or illegal characters so that the DOS users can gain access to the share more easily.

- What name to use for the share? Obviously, a name like WORDDOCS is a good way to describe a shared resource such as Word documents. But a share name of DOCS might work just as well. You can give a more descriptive comment about the share in the box below the share name, so you don't need to get too complicated with the share name. Just remember that the more logical the share name, the easier it is for users to find and use it.

After you have created a name for the share, the next box provides a place for a comment that describes the share to other users browsing for resources. The next step is to decide:

■ What type of access to assign to the share? Remember that three types of access can be assigned. Users can have *read* permissions, *full* access to the folder and its contents, or *no access* at all.

Selecting the OK button when all the fields are filled in establishes the share and the associated settings for it.

Figure 23.8.

Right-clicking to set up a share in Windows 95.

Figure 23.9.

The Sharing Properties box.

Setting Up Security in Windows NT

Windows NT gives users the same capability to share resources that Windows 95 does. The only difference between the share properties for a Windows 95 system and a Windows NT system is that additional types of access can be assigned. Windows NT also has the additional capability to assign access on a user-by-user basis. Figure 23.10 shows an example of a Windows NT Share Properties dialog box. To assign security in the Windows NT environment, select the Permissions button in the Share Properties dialog box.

FIGURE 23.10.

Windows NT Share
Properties dialog box.

Figure 23.11 gives an example of how to set up different types of access for different users and groups. You can see from the example shown that actually four types of access can be assigned to a Windows NT share.

FIGURE 23.11.

An example of four
types of share
permissions in
Windows NT.

■ No Access: The No Access permission is not used for every user to block his or her access to a share. The No Access permission is a special revoking privilege that is used to take away rights from a user that might acquire rights indirectly from somewhere else. Users do not have rights to a share in Windows NT unless they have been given those rights. No Access is used when a user or group has access it does not need, but the administrator finds it easier to use the No Access capability to remove that user or group's permissions to this one share rather than completely rearrange the users and the groups to which it belongs. As an example, consider a user, Bob, who is a member of a group, Students. The Students group is set up with different types of access to several different shares. Students have Read privileges to a share called Files and the administrator does not want to give those Read privileges to Bob. It would be easier to assign No Access to Bob for this share than to go through and set up a whole new set of rules or another group just for Bob.

■ Read: Read permissions are essentially the same in Windows 95 and Windows NT. Individuals with Read permissions can look at a list of files, open files, read the contents, and copy the files.

■ Change: Change permissions enable the users to do all the things that users with Read permissions can do. In addition, users with Change permissions can change and delete the contents of existing files and directories.

■ Full Control: Users with Full Control permissions are not limited to what they can do with the shared directory or files.

Windows NT also has the capability to protect local files in addition to the ones that are shared. To accomplish this, the files or directories must be located on a partition that has been formatted with NTFS (New Technology Filing System). NTFS has the capability to offer security for the files and directories stored on the partition.

To assign local permissions, you must access the Properties box for the directory or file and select the Security tab. The Permissions button on the Security tab enables the user or administrator to configure security settings for the files or directories even if the user is accessing them from the system on which they are located rather than from across the network. NTFS permissions apply even if no share is set up for the directory.

NTFS provides for very specific capabilities to be assigned to the users. In addition to providing additional settings, NTFS enables the user or administrator to set up Special access and choose a unique configuration. The settings (other than Special Access configurations) under NTFS are:

■ No Access: Just like Windows NT Share permissions, No Access is not a rights assignment but rather a revoking capability.

■ List: Gives the capability to see the files in the directory.

■ Read: Basically the same as with Windows NT Share permissions.

■ Add: Enables users to add files (write) to a directory but not to a file.

■ Add & Read: Just as it sounds, gives users the read capability and the add capability.

■ Change: Once again, very similar to the Windows NT Share permissions. The only thing users do not get with Change permission is the capability to take ownership of objects and change the permissions for the objects.

■ Full Control: Exactly as it implies, users have full control of any objects for which they have this permission.

Figure 23.12 shows a few examples of NTFS permissions being assigned.

FIGURE 23.12.

Permissions assigned to a folder on an NTFS Partition.

The letters in parentheses after the type of permission assigned relate to the actual physical capabilities being assigned to the user. The list of possible choices includes:

■ R: Read

■ W: Write

■ X: Execute

■ D: Delete

■ O: Take Ownership

■ P: Change Permissions

Many more relevant issues surround the methods used to establish permissions for users. To be very effective, one must absolutely understand all pertinent issues related to how permissions are assigned and how the share permissions and local permissions interact with each other. Also, an administrator must consider how to assign the rights most effectively so that users have the appropriate rights to carry out their tasks while making sure that no one user has any rights he does not need to have.

It is important to note that the network permissions a user gets from various assignments of rights are cumulative. The local permissions a user gets from various rights assignments are also cumulative. However, the relationship between local permissions and network permissions is not a cumulative one but relies on the most restrictive permission gained from the accumulation of network permissions and local permissions. Because that is rather confusing as a description, an example is helpful.

In this example, a user, John, is a member of the Student group. He is attempting to use a resource on the network. The resource, referred to here as FILES, is a directory of files. Because this resource is a network resource, John must connect to the resource machine through a share that has been set up to enable users to get to FILES. This network share has two permission assignments allocated to it. The first assignment gives Read permission specifically to John. The second assignment gives the Student group the permission of Change. Because John is a member of the Student group, John also gets the CHANGE permission.

As stated previously, the network permissions acquired are cumulative. That means that John has both the Change permission and the Read permission. They add together to form the level of access that John gets to this network share. The highest level of access John can have to this network share is currently Change. Remember that Change permission includes everything that READ provides so it can simply be said that John has Change permission to the FILES resource.

Now imagine that the FILES resource is actually located on a disk that has been formatted with NTFS. That enables the system administrator to assign local permissions to the resource in addition to the network permissions that have already been assigned. For the purposes of this example, the FILES resource has a local permission assignment of Read for the user John. We will also include a local permission assignment of Full Control for the group Student.

Because local permissions are cumulative, John has Full Control as his effective local permission assignment. Again, remember that Full Control includes the capability of Read. The caveat to remember here is that John is accessing this information from the network where the highest level of permission he has is Change. Therefore, when John tries to access the FILES resource from the network, he has Change permissions. The easiest way to remember this is that when comparing the total of all of the network permissions assigned with the total of all of the local permissions assigned to a user, the most restrictive total applies.

Because of this confusion, it is not uncommon to see most administrators set up all the network permissions for resources that lie on NTFS partitions as a share with Full Control permissions for Everyone. The administrator then goes back and gives specific permissions to users by implementing the local NTFS permissions. Remember, because the most restrictive permission applies when the local and network permissions are compared, the effective permission in this case is always the local or NTFS permission.

C2 Compliance

One of the biggest issues surrounding the acceptance of Windows NT by several major government agencies and larger companies was its capability to meet the specifications of the Trusted Computer System Evaluation Criteria (TCSEC). TCSEC is more commonly known as The Orange Book. The Orange Book defines a set of criteria that enables systems to be compared and ranked as to the type and adequacy of the security they provide. The rankings range from A to D with D being the least secure and A being the most secure. Within each lettered ranking are different classes, the best-known of those being the C2 classification.

Meeting the C2 requirements requires adhering to all the specifications of that classification in the Orange Book. One of the most popular misconceptions is that Windows NT meets the C2 specifications. To clarify, Windows NT version 3.5 Service Pack 3 was evaluated against the C2 requirements in the summer of 1995. It met those requirements and actually met most of the B2-level requirements as well. However, because it was submitted for evaluation at only the C2 level, that is the only level at which it was approved. This means that although it seems logical to assume Windows NT version 4.0 is C2 secure, it has never actually been awarded that designation.

It is also important to note that both the Windows NT Workstation and Windows NT Server platforms were evaluated but that no networking components were installed. This means that if you hook a Windows NT system up to a network and use it on a network, it does not meet the specifications of the C2 platform that was evaluated by the NSA (National Security Agency). To meet the requirements for secure networking, a system should be evaluated against another book in The Rainbow Series called The Red Book. The Red Book defines criteria to evaluate networks for security.

Auditing

One of the most powerful security features of the Windows NT platform is its capability to provide the administrator with a detailed tracking of almost any event that occurs while the system is running. An audit log can be a very useful tool for proving who or what did something to the NT system and when it occurred.

Although auditing seems like a tool that every system should have running at all times, administrators and users need to consider an important performance issue. The easiest way to explain the performance issue is to examine it with an analogy. Pouring yourself a glass of water seems like a easy task that should take only a few moments to complete. However, think about how long it would take for you to complete that same task if you had to do the task and write down a detailed description of every step you took to complete the task. That would certainly take a lot longer. This is essentially the same issue faced when the auditing capabilities are turned on in most network operating systems.

For this reason, most administrators and users typically elect to use the auditing features on only the systems that require it most. They also tend to be rather selective about which items they want to audit. It should be noted that a newer and faster system, which has been properly configured and is not overloaded with other tasks, should be able to handle most, if not all, of the tasks required of it with very little performance degradation.

To use the auditing capabilities of Windows NT, open the User Manager or the User Manager for Domains applet and select Policy from the menu bar. From the drop-down Policy menu, select Auditing. Figure 23.13 shows the Audit Properties dialog box. To turn the auditing capabilities on, select the Audit These Events radio button and then select the appropriate success or failure items to monitor. After auditing has been turned on, the administrator can select additional auditing settings for any files and directories on the system that are stored on an NTFS partition.

FIGURE 23.13.

The Audit Policy dialog box.

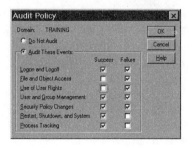

Diskless Workstations

One way to prevent users from copying information off the network systems and putting it on floppy disks or their local hard drives is to make sure they do not have a local hard drive or floppy disk drive. If the computer system does not have a hard drive or some other method of booting up from that workstation, then the system can be a diskless workstation on the network.

Diskless workstations typically use a special network interface card that has a boot PROM (programmable read-only memory) chip on it. The PROM chip is used to load the network software into the machine's memory and enable it to attach to and boot up from operating system files that are stored on the network.

Encryption

As was stated earlier in this chapter, anyone who wants to get to your information badly enough can find a way to get to it. The last line of defense that administrators and users have is the capability to encrypt their data so that if someone does get to the information, he will still have a lot of work to do before he can read it or use it.

Encrypted data is transformed or "locked" into some other form that is not easily guessed or read, but that can be retransformed or unlocked when necessary through the use of a key. The encryption process is basically the same as "locking" the data so that no unauthorized parties have access to it. The unlocking process is actually referred to as *decryption*. Essentially, only two methods are used to encrypt data: transposition and substitution.

With transposition, the order of the bits being sent is rearranged. For example, imagine that you want to send a message of "Hello" to another user. You and the other user agree that the key to your transposing is to move the first letter of each word to the back of the word, so you send "Elloh" as the message. If you use substitution as the method of encryption, then you must find some other pattern or value to substitute for the message you are sending. If the key to your substitution is to use numerical values for the letters of the alphabet, then the message becomes "8 5 12 12 15."

If you choose only one transposition or one type of substitution, then someone can figure out the message without too much trouble. For that reason, most popular encryption methods in use today use a series of transpositions and substitutions. A mathematical formula is used to determine the key, which is used to encrypt and decrypt the message. When both parties know the same key used to encrypt or decrypt the message, the encryption technique is known as *symmetric cryptography.*

However, at times encryption must be used between parties that do not share the same key. To do this, *asymmetric cryptography* must be used. Asymmetric cryptography requires each party to have both a public key and a private key. The public and private keys are related to each other using a mathematical function so that they become a set of keys used for encryption. The public key is made available to anyone who wants to send a message. The message is encrypted using the public key and can then be decrypted only by using the private key. Because the user to whom the message is being sent always retains the private key, she is the only one who can read the message sent to her.

Two of the most popular encryption schemes are DES (Data Encryption Standard), which is the official standard of the U.S. Government, and RSA, which is named for the people who created it.

Virus Shields

No discussion of network security would be complete without mentioning viruses, Trojan horses, logic bombs, and other sorts of wildlife. A virus is a program that runs when an infected program is executed. It stands to reason then that only executable files with extensions like .EXE, .BAT, .COM, and .SYS can become infected. As with a biological virus, computer viruses live to replicate and copy themselves to other systems and to other files.

Some viruses do nothing more than replicate and occupy space, but others can cause massive damage and even self-destruct when they are run. If anything harms the data or constricts the access to it, then a security violation has occurred. Viruses are most definitely a concern for all systems. Viruses can be acquired from the network, from downloaded files, from shareware and freeware programs, and even off-the-shelf software. To prevent these monsters from rearing their ugly heads and affecting your systems, you need to have some form of countermeasure.

Virus scanners and virus shields are two types of devices that can protect your systems. Each one provides a different type of protection. Virus scanners can be run any time a virus is suspected or on a scheduled basis. They do a thorough job of inspecting whatever files are selected and they attempt to find and remove any viruses that are detected. Virus-scanning programs typically use a database of sample virus code strings against which the files are compared. These database files are usually referred to as *virus definition files.* If a virus scanner locates a particular string of code, then it has found a virus. Most virus scanners can also remove the viruses they find. To keep your system thoroughly protected, the virus definition files should be updated regularly.

A virus shield is a type of program that runs when the system boots and keeps running in memory the entire time the system is on. The virus shield constantly monitors all processing while attempting to locate a virus. The idea is for the virus to be caught before it gets on the system. A virus shield examines programs before they execute to attempt to catch the virus before it replicates or does any other type of damage. After they are caught, viruses can normally be removed before causing any harm, and normal execution of the program can continue.

Summary

Protecting network integrity and securing data are tiresome tasks with many threats and vulnerabilities to watch out for. However, with time, patience, knowledge, and the correct hardware and software tools, data can be secured. Whether the threat is from the outside or the inside of the organization, the correct security policy protects the entire enterprise.

Data Integrity

by James Causey

IN THIS CHAPTER

CHAPTER 24

What, exactly, is the meaning of the term "data integrity"? Throughout this book, various types of data integrity have been discussed, from ways that various network protocols and implementations assure that your data arrives as it was sent, to security measures designed to prevent unauthorized individuals from viewing or modifying data that they shouldn't.

This chapter, however, gets more specific: it describes the thoughtful, practical steps you, as a network administrator, can take to reduce the chance of major system failure and to reduce your vulnerability to such failure as much as possible. A number of different methods and techniques can prevent, to the greatest degree possible, the loss of your users' critical data and the placement of your head on the chopping block.

> **NOTE**
>
> In reading this section, you may hear Chicken Little's voice nagging you to watch out for a falling sky. Try to look past that; the point of this section is not to make everything into a catastrophe, but to illustrate from experience the reasons why computer systems are vulnerable and why data integrity measures are critical.

It's easy to overlook data integrity concerns, particularly in the modern age of highly reliable hardware and advanced network operating systems. However, a number of ugly—but important—facts still apply to every network server, and they eventually come around to bite you if you don't pay attention to them:

- Every disk drive *will* fail.

  Disk drives are highly complex mechanical devices, built to exacting tolerances. The reliability and lifespan of disk drives has increased significantly over the past decade, but disk drives still can and will fail; it's just a matter of when. The situation is dicier still when you consider that every manufacturer occasionally makes a bad drive, which fails long before the average for that model. In addition, drives are highly sensitive to their environment; many large, high-speed drives can be induced to fail if relatively strict temperature tolerances are exceeded (for example, if the air conditioning fails). Trusting your data to the reliability of a magnetic disk drive is a bold but incautious act.

- Mechanical devices have a limited lifespan.

  This is an extended version of the first fact: every mechanical or electrical device will someday fail, whether you're talking about cooling fans, power supplies, or motherboards.

- Electricity is fickle.

  The power provided to most residences and businesses and used by most computer systems is filthy, subject to unpredictable brownouts and surges and spikes, which can fry your system or simply destroy the power supply. In addition, an act of God or bad weather can cause a power failure at any time. Perhaps you're one of those lucky people who has a machine room with filtered power. Even so, is there anything to stop a fellow administrator from accidentally kicking your power cord out of its jack?

■ Murphy wasn't kidding.

Whatever can go wrong, *will* go wrong. For instance, most CPUs last far longer than their useful lifespan; that does not, however, mean that you should rely on your CPUs to never fail. Does your integrity plan include contingency plans for tragic circumstances, such as a fire or a structural failure in your building? Could your business recover from a major environmental or natural disaster?

This chapter discusses the various strategies and techniques you can implement to protect yourself and your customers from system failure. Some techniques may be unnecessary for many enterprises, or outside their means; many strategies in this chapter, however, apply to every site, no matter how big or small. Although many details focus on Windows NT Server, most techniques in this chapter can be applied to any network operating system.

The first section in this chapter describes the various measures you can implement to protect your installation of Windows NT Server from failure. The next looks at strategies for maintaining and protecting actual user and business data, as well as the server hardware itself. Finally, the summary lists the topics discussed and evaluates which strategies to implement in your installation.

Protecting the Operating System

Windows NT is a modern network operating system, with many powerful features that make it quite flexible in its role both as a personal workstation and as a network server. Windows NT is also a remarkably reliable operating system. I've had a well-cared-for NT Server go for over a year without crashing or being rebooted, except for software installation. However, as previously discussed, bad things can and do happen, and eventually your NT Server may crash and may damage essential files in the process, thus preventing itself from rebooting. As anyone who has experienced this can tell you, the process of repairing a dead NT Server (or any network server, for that matter) can be a nerve-wracking experience, particularly because many of the techniques involved are anti-intuitive to some.

However, you can greatly reduce your vulnerability by planning ahead and taking a number of simple steps that can make those painful hours spent after a major system failure far less stressful, and that can significantly reduce your chances of losing data.

This section begins by describing some planning and installation strategies that can make your server more reliable and easier to fix in an emergency. It then describes maintenance tasks to help you best prepare for a future disaster and to reduce potential downtime to a minimum.

Installation Procedures

You can use a number of different strategies during installation to greatly reduce the chance of having to struggle to bring your server back online in the event of an emergency, as well as reduce your chance of losing data after a crash.

Using File Systems Wisely

Windows NT Server can use a number of different file systems; most people simply use NTFS (NT File System) for their entire server, which, at first glance, appears to be the obvious choice. NTFS was specifically redesigned for the high-performance network operating system environment in which NT was designed to exist, and in the process, the designers of NT improved upon FAT (the File Allocation Table file system used for MS-DOS), eliminating many of its flaws. For example, FAT, being originally designed for small hard drives, could originally access only very small partitions; in order to provide support for larger partitions while still maintaining backwards compatibility, future versions of FAT used highly inefficient clustering schemes on larger drives, thus wasting large amounts of disk space for small files. NTFS uses much more intelligent clustering, greatly reducing the amount of wasted disk space. NTFS also provides support for features that FAT simply cannot, such as file- and directory-level security, customizable streams for serving different file system types to other operating systems, and transaction logging, which enables NT to easily recover from file system corruption caused by inadvertent system halts. All these excellent features make NTFS a shoo-in for the file system used on most NT Servers, as well they should; for the actual data on your server, NTFS is normally the best, and in fact only, choice. But you may want to consider maintaining a small FAT partition on your server's boot disk.

After reading all the advantages of NTFS over FAT, it may seem patently insane to suggest maintaining a FAT partition on your boot drive. Isn't FAT less secure? Isn't FAT less fault tolerant? Isn't FAT wasteful?

All these things are true; however, the value of having a small FAT partition on your boot disk can often outweigh the potential drawbacks. FAT can be accessed by nearly any operating system, including (obviously) MS-DOS. If your server should crash, you can easily boot to a copy of MS-DOS on the FAT partition (or even boot from a DOS floppy), and attempt to repair the essential system files, run the Repair process from the Windows NT installation program, or even reinstall Windows NT from that partition. On my servers, I always keep a healthy FAT partition (at 300-500MB) on the boot disk, with a copy of the NT Server installation files, as well as backup copies of the machine's essential startup files (NTLDR, NTDETECT.COM, BOOT.INI), copies of the system boot sector and master boot record (made with DISKSAVE.EXE, from the NT 4.0 Server Resource Kit), a full bootable copy of MS-DOS, and enough free disk space to accommodate the temporary space needs of the NT Server installation program, in case I should need to run it. This provides me a number of advantages: first, I can install NT from the hard drive rather than from CD, which makes the install run much faster. Second, if the server crashes, I can always reboot into MS-DOS and begin my repair efforts from there. Should I need to simply replace an essential startup file, I can do it quickly and easily. Should I need to use my Emergency Repair Disk, I can start the repair process directly from the hard drive, rather than my NT floppies and CD. (The Emergency Repair Disk is discussed later on in this chapter.) I can also run basic DOS diagnostic tools on my system's hardware to determine its functionality, and I can use a simple DOS network stack to grab needed files from other servers during the repair process. All in all, having a bootable FAT partition on my boot disk has saved me many hours of frustration. The primary downside to this strategy is security; someone who can boot the machine into MS-DOS can also wreak havoc on the server. However, no security plan is valid without formidable physical security measures. Even an NTFS machine can be booted with a DOS floppy, and the hard drive wiped or NTFS files modified (using the freeware NTFSDOS utility) if someone can gain access to the console. On the other hand, if unauthorized individuals can't reach my server, I never have to worry about them booting it into DOS and damaging it, either from the hard drive or from floppy.

> **NOTE**
>
> Still concerned about the security repercussions of maintaining a FAT partition on your boot disk? Keep in mind that users of NT for ARC-compliant RISC systems have had to deal with these issues for years because the firmware on those systems requires that you use a small FAT partition for the boot files. Again, as I stated above, *no security measures suffice if your server is not physically secure.*

Keep Backup Copies of Your OS Directory

Another technique I find useful for server installations is to make a backup copy of the default operating system installation directory (which, for NT 4.0, is \WINNT). It's simple: after you've completed the installation of the operating system and things seem to be running well, copy the directory to another directory (for example, \WINNTBKP). Then modify your BOOT.INI to give you the option to boot into that second directory. Should later changes or problems cause the system to be unable to load, you can always boot into your backup copy and retain the same hardware and driver settings and the same SAM database. It gives you an instant "rollback" capability—you can return to a functional operating system immediately, rather than stay down until you can repair the damage just done.

> **TIP**
>
> If you use this technique, it's important to remember to update your backup copy whenever you are confident you've reached a new, stable point in the server's life, or just before you're about to make a major change to the server. For example, it's wise to make a fresh backup copy immediately before installing a new Service Pack.

24

DATA INTEGRITY

Domain Redundancy Features

Planning on using an NT Domain? Is there any question in your mind as to whether or not you should maintain Backup Domain Controllers? Purge your doubt and be free; *you should always have at least one Backup Domain Controller in a production environment, if at all feasible.* If you're strapped for resources, use a lower-end machine for your BDC; the only capability it needs is to receive updates to the Domain SAM database. If, for whatever reason, your Primary Domain Controller goes down, it's nice to be able to maintain standard production login and logout services until your PDC can come back online. If worst comes to worst and your PDC must be reinstalled, you still have a copy of your critical Domain SAM. Making certain that you cannot lose your Domain SAM is invaluable, particularly in large multi-departmental production environments, with the complex structure of user rights and trust relationships that can come crashing to a halt, requiring a great deal of reconfiguration should you be forced to re-create your Domain.

> **TIP**
>
> Do you work in a multi-location, Wide Area Network (WAN) environment? If so, consider keeping one of your BDCs offsite; that way, if something catastrophic happens to your normal worksite, you're all the more able to maintain production services.

Maintenance Techniques

Now that you've reduced your vulnerability to data loss as much as possible during the installation process, it's time to focus on the preventative maintenance measures you can take over the lifetime of the server to minimize your downtime.

The Three Boot Disks

The three boot disks are the first three diskettes of the Windows NT installation diskset. These three disks enable you to boot your system and initiate the Repair process or begin reinstallation, even if you're running NTFS and/or using SCSI controllers. *Keep these three disks handy!*

> **NOTE**
>
> Keeping the three boot disks handy is somewhat less necessary if you're keeping a copy of the NT installation files locally on your bootable FAT partition; however, I still like to have these disks nearby.

Lost your first three floppies? Never had them in the first place? Well, you can make them from the NT installation CD. Just pop in the CD (or find your copy of the installation media on disk or over the network), switch to the appropriate directory for your hardware (for example, \I386 for Intel platforms), and run the following command from a DOS prompt:

```
WINNT /OX
```

or from Windows 95 or Windows NT:

```
WINNT32 /OX
```

You need three floppy diskettes. Any information already on them is destroyed.

NT Boot Floppy

Old DOS wizards are used to being able to boot their machines from a floppy diskette, in case of emergency, to access the data on the hard drive. Unfortunately, there's no obvious way to do this under Windows NT; it can, however, be done.

First, format a floppy disk under Windows NT. *For this disk to function as an NT boot disk, you must format it under Windows NT.* Formatting this disk under Windows NT ensures that the boot sector of the diskette attempts to execute the NT Boot Loader (or NTLDR). If, for example, you attempt to boot your system with this floppy in the A: drive, you receive the following message:

```
Cannot load NTLDR
```

Obviously, then, the process is not quite done.

To complete the process, copy the following files to the floppy disk:

```
NTLDR
NTDETECT.COM
BOOT.INI
```

This disk enables your system to begin the boot process, perform essential hardware detection, and locate the NT system files on your hard drive. This is no guarantee that you can then boot the system; if the kernel is corrupted, for instance, or the registry cannot initialize, the boot process still fails. However, if your problem is simply a corrupt or missing boot file, this disk enables you to restart the server and replace the damaged files.

> **TIP**
>
> Make sure you create an updated version of this disk after a successful Service Pack installation, in case any changes have been made to these files.

Using Emergency Repair Disks

One of the most neglected, yet most handy, techniques to keep yourself and your data out of trouble is to religiously maintain and update your Emergency Repair Disk. The Emergency Repair Disk contains a number of different files and Registry hives that are critical to the startup and functionality of an NT system. Should your system become corrupt or unstartable, you can run a repair process to replace your damaged files and/or Registry hives with the hives from the Emergency Repair Disk, or, alternatively, from a repair directory on your hard disk.

24

DATA INTEGRITY

Most people create an Emergency Repair Disk during the initial system installation process, when prompted by the installation program. However, those same people often do not update this disk at all after this point. Let me emphasize, from painful experience: *an out-of-date Emergency Repair Disk can be as bad as not having an Emergency Repair Disk at all*. If you've significantly modified your hardware settings, applied Service Packs, or added large numbers of users and groups since the last time you generated an Emergency Repair Disk, an unpleasant surprise awaits you when you use it to "repair" your system, as your NT machine suddenly regresses in time to an older, less functional version of itself, losing any new users, groups, and hardware or software customizations. The machine may not even be able to start at all.

How, then, do you update your Emergency Repair Disk? With the Repair Disk Utility, or RDISK.

To start the Repair Disk Utility, run the program RDISK.EXE from a Command Prompt or from the Start Menu.

> **TIP**
>
> If you intend to update your Emergency Repair Disk frequently, as well you should, you may find it handy to place a shortcut to RDISK.EXE on your desktop, or in your ...\Start Menu\Programs folder.

The Repair Disk Utility is simple and easy to use; see Figure 24.1 for an illustration.

FIGURE 24.1.

The Repair Disk Utility in Windows NT 4.0.

As you can see, you have only two options (other than to pull up the Help utility or to quit the application): Update Repair Info and Create Repair Disk. The first option makes a copy of the latest versions of all the pertinent files into the %SYSTEMROOT%\REPAIR directory on your hard disk; when the copying process is over, you are asked whether you wish to make an Emergency Repair Disk with those new files (you need a blank diskette if you wish to make the disk). The second option creates an Emergency Repair Disk with the files already in %SYSTEMROOT%\REPAIR. See Figures 24.2, 24.3, and 24.4 for illustrations of this process.

FIGURE 24.2.

Updating repair information with RDISK.EXE.

FIGURE 24.3.

RDISK.EXE *prompting to ask whether you wish to make an Emergency Repair Disk.*

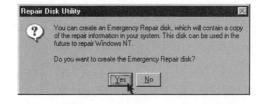

FIGURE 24.4.

Creating an Emergency Repair Disk with RDISK.EXE.

The Emergency Repair Disk (and the %SYSTEMROOT%\REPAIR directory) contains the following files, by default:

- AUTOEXEC.NT and CONFIG.NT

  These files are used by the 16-bit MS-DOS subsystem to initialize environmental settings for MS-DOS and Windows 3.x applications running under NT.

- DEFAULT._

  This file contains a copy of the Registry hive HKEY_USERS\.Default, which contains system environmental settings for all users.

- SAM._

  This file contains the default SAM (Security Account Manager) database created during initial operating system installation; this SAM contains only the default groups included with NT, and the administrator username and password you selected during installation.

- SECURITY._

  This file contains the default security information for the SAM database created during initial operating system installation; see the preceding discussion on SAM._ for more details.

- **SETUP.LOG**

  This file contains the locations of essential system and application files to be replaced during the installation process, as well as cyclical redundancy check (CRC) information used to verify the repair files themselves.

- **software._**

  This file contains a copy of the Registry hive HKEY_LOCAL_MACHINE\SOFTWARE, which contains initialization and customization information for the software installed on the NT system. This key contains much of the information traditionally stored in .INI files in 16-bit Windows.

- **system._**

  This file contains a copy of the Registry hive HKEY_LOCAL_MACHINE\SYSTEM, which contains operating system, driver, and hardware settings.

How do you use the Emergency Repair Disk? Initiate the repair process by starting the Windows NT installation program (using either the NT CD in a bootable CD-ROM drive, the first three floppies of the NT setup disk set, or the copy of Windows NT's installation media you've stashed on your FAT partition—see how handy that's become?), and then select R for "Repair a previous installation." You can select which areas you want Setup to examine for possible repair. Your options are

- Inspect Registry Files
- Inspect Startup Environment
- Verify Windows NT System Files
- Inspect Boot Sector

Eventually, you are asked for your Emergency Repair Disk; if you don't have it, Setup attempts to read the necessary information from the %SYSTEMROOT%\REPAIR directory, if it can find it.

You are asked whether you wish to restore Registry files; you can select which ones, if any, to restore from the copies on your Emergency Repair Disk. Your options are

- SYSTEM (from system._)
- SOFTWARE (from software._)
- DEFAULT (from default._)
- SECURITY and SAM (from security._ and sam._)

> **NOTE**
>
> Any changes to the system made since this Emergency Repair Disk was last updated are lost. For this reason, it is *crucial* that you update your repair information every time you successfully complete any significant system updates or changes.

> **TIP**
>
> If you choose to replace the SECURITY and SAM data, your current list of users, groups, and security policies is replaced with the default ones created when Windows NT was first installed. On many systems, particularly Domain Controllers, this is a Bad Thing.
>
> You can, however, use the latest version of your SAM database and security policies in your repair information, in place of the original data. You do this by specifying a command line switch to the RDISK command.
>
> You can use two different switches. The first, /s, skips the dialog box and immediately begins updating the repair information in %SYSTEMROOT\REPAIR. You are then asked whether you wish to save that information to a new Emergency Repair Disk.
>
> The second switch, /s-, behaves like /s, but it does not prompt you to create an Emergency Repair Disk; it simply exits immediately after updating your repair information.
>
> It's important to note that your SAM and SECURITY files can grow to exceed the size of one floppy disk, depending on how many users and groups you have in your database; this can cause the Repair Disk generated to be flawed and can corrupt the repair data on your hard drive. For this reason, it's always wise to make a backup copy of %SYSTEMROOT%\REPAIR before attempting to use either of these command-line switches, to ensure that you can still make an Emergency Repair Disk if the process fails.

As the repair process continues, Setup prompts you when it finds a version problem with a file. You can choose not to repair the file (in case you have manually installed drivers or updated files since the system was installed), to go ahead and repair the file, or to repair all problem files automatically. It's probably best to let Setup prompt you for each file, so you can verify that it's not replacing drivers or other files that you've manually installed.

> **NOTE**
>
> It's important to update your Emergency Repair Disk whenever you update your system with a new Service Pack, so that a repair process won't roll you back to a pre-Service Pack state or break any of your software that requires a certain Service Pack level. Check the README file included with your most recent Service Pack for more detailed information on keeping your Emergency Repair Disks current to that Service Pack level.

When the repair process is complete, you are prompted to remove the disk from your floppy drive and restart. If all goes well, your system then boots and functions normally.

Keep in mind that the Emergency Repair Disk is no substitute for a sound backup strategy; you still need to perform regular system backups to keep complete backups of the Registry, as well as non-system data, on the machine.

24

DATA INTEGRITY

Also it's probably a good idea to keep multiple copies of your Emergency Repair Disk. Label each one with the date, time, and status of your system at generation time, set the write-protect tab on the disk, make a backup copy of it (with a program such as DISKCOPY, included with Windows NT, or the shareware package WINIMAGE), and store it somewhere safe. Don't keep updating the same floppy, in case you ever have to fall back to a previous configuration.

Disk Administrator Configuration Disk

There's another disk that is just as important to maintain as your Emergency Repair Disk, but even fewer administrators use it (or even know that it exists, for that matter). This disk, which can be generated by the Disk Administrator application (located in the Administrative Tools common program folder), contains the following information:

- Disk partition configuration
- Drive letter assignments
- Fault-tolerant sets (such as RAID arrays and volume sets)

It is *critical* to maintain a reliable Disk Administrator configuration backup disk, particularly if you're using any type of fault-tolerant disk set; if you don't, repairing or reinstalling your operating system could result in permanent data loss, which can really ruin your day. You should create a new configuration backup disk whenever you update disk partition or fault-tolerant set information.

To create a backup diskette, you need a formatted floppy disk. Start up Disk Administrator (located in the Administrative Tools program folder), go to the Partition menu, select Configuration ->, and then select the Save... option from the submenu. You are prompted to insert a formatted floppy diskette; do so and hit OK.

To restore your configuration from that diskette, run Disk Administrator, then select Restore... from the Configuration -> submenu, in the Partition menu. You are asked whether you're sure you want to restore your configuration information; click Yes to continue.

Just as with an Emergency Repair Disk, it's a good idea to keep all your Disk Administrator backup diskettes and to keep a backup copy of each one.

Using NT Service Packs and Hotfixes

Another important part of keeping your NT server as reliable as possible is keeping up-to-date on the latest Service Packs available from Microsoft. Service Packs contain regression-tested updates to the operating system that fix known bugs and security problems, ranging from minor annoyances to severe reliability concerns. Running the latest Service Pack level on your system helps you make sure your system is as reliable and secure as possible. Service Packs are cumulative releases; you need apply only the latest Service Pack to receive all fixes and updates made available with previous Packs.

Occasionally, a problem with NT crops up that is too severe to allow Microsoft to wait for the next Service Pack to provide a fix to its customers. For this reason, Microsoft has recently begun the process of making "hotfixes" available. Hotfixes contain emergency patches to security or reliability problems. Hotfixes generally require that you be running a certain Service Pack level in order to use them. Keep in mind that Microsoft does not regression-test hotfixes before releasing them and that they can cause problems in certain environments; for this reason, Microsoft recommends that you apply hotfixes only if you're experiencing trouble with the specific problem that hotfix addresses. However, in a real world environment, administrators often find themselves applying hotfixes as soon as they come out, as a preventative measure, particularly with the rash of TCP/IP security hotfixes recently made available.

> **NOTE**
>
> The installation of a Service Pack or hotfix replaces NT default installation files and drivers with modified versions that contain updated code. When you change hardware settings or add drivers, NT often copies default system installation files during the configuration process; these default files overwrite the Service Pack or hotfix files, thus eliminating the benefits of that patch. For this reason, you should try to avoid using Service Packs or hotfixes until your system's configuration is as static as possible; if you make changes, you must reapply the latest Service Pack and any hotfixes you're using.

Before applying a Service Pack or hotfix, make sure you have all the following:

- A recent, reliable backup of your system
- A fresh Emergency Repair Disk
- A fresh Disk Administrator backup disk
- Copies of all custom hardware drivers on disk
- An NT boot disk

More recent Service Packs give you the option to keep an Uninstall directory so you can roll back to a pre-Service Pack state in case of problems; hotfixes, however, do not provide this option. In both cases, it's wise to have all the resources necessary to enable you to fall back to your previous configuration, in case the Service Pack or hotfix breaks your system in any way. (Sadly, this has been known to happen.)

After you test your system following the update, create a new Emergency Repair Disk and back up your system again. Check the README included with your update for any specific procedures for making sure your backup contains the updated system files.

24

DATA INTEGRITY

Keeping Your Data Secure

Another important part of any data integrity strategy is making certain that your system is secure. If someone can successfully execute a denial-of-service attack on your system, or worse yet, break in and manipulate data or damage your operating system, you lose data just as effectively as if your server had crashed.

Windows NT is a highly secure operating system; however, as it matures, security holes and problems are constantly being found, much as with UNIX. For this reason, it's critically important to stay abreast of the latest patches and advisories made available by Microsoft, both in the form of Service Packs and hotfixes, as well as recommendations for security procedures.

The Windows NT Resource Kit includes a great deal of information on keeping your NT system secure, as well as a utility called C2Config that can assist you in setting your system to meet the C2 security specifications, in preparation for certification. (C2 is a level of federal computer security certification.)

Protecting Your Hardware

So far, this chapter has introduced ways to keep your operating system as reliable as possible and to quickly repair it if disaster should fall. However, even the most reliable, best-cared-for operating system is only as good as the hardware on which it runs; if your hardware continually suffers failures—whether from reliability issues or outside influences—you are bound to suffer downtime. Luckily, such hardware-related downtime can be reduced or even prevented in a number of ways.

Uninterruptible Power Supplies

Computer systems, of course, use electricity. The electricity is used for a variety of tasks, ranging from powering the raw muscle of mechanical devices like hard drive motors and fans, to coursing through the microscopic circuitry of the CPU. The sheer complexity and compact size of the electronics in your system make them quite sensitive to problems with power. In an ideal world, the electricity used by your system would always operate at the same frequency, with no fluctuations or terminations in service. Unfortunately, in the real world, electricity is delivered to you across a vast grid of conductors, where it's also being tapped by thousands of other devices. The electrical grids in use today were never originally designed for the exacting tolerances of computing devices (and probably couldn't truly accommodate them, anyway, for fiscal reasons); thus, problems ranging from constant fluctuations in the power to complete power failures are ubiquitous.

Everyone has, at one time or another, lost work due to a power failure; it's the ironclad lesson on the importance of saving work often. Fortunately, such occurrences normally affect only one user's work. Ponder for a moment, however, the detrimental affect a power-induced downtime can have on a network server used by many, many people. In addition, power problems can cause data loss; if a system crashes or loses power in the midst of a critical operation, data can be rendered useless, operating systems can be prevented from booting, or the actual hardware itself can even be damaged.

Four major power-induced problems need to be addressed:

- **Power Failures:** This first problem is the most obvious. If you lose power, your computer shuts down immediately, often in the midst of a critical operation, causing untold damage.

- **Electrical Noise:** Electromagnetic radiation caused by improperly shielded electronic devices, or even environmental phenomena, can pollute the power supply with electrical noise that can wreak havoc on sensitive electronic devices.

- **Power Surges:** Ever had a TV or telephone destroyed by a lightning strike? That was a dramatic (and rare) version of a power surge, in which the power supply suddenly delivers electricity which spikes to a level far higher than needed—high enough to actually destroy the equipment drawing that current. Most power surges aren't nearly that dramatic; unfortunately, small surges are far more common, and even a slight surge can damage some equipment.

- **Brownouts:** Brownouts are the evil sibling to power surges; they occur when the electrical supply is strained beyond its capacity to deliver the needed current, so the supply delivers less power instead. Lights suddenly dim, and electronic devices may flicker on and off from the lack of power, or even be damaged.

The most common power protection device used by computer owners is the surge suppresser; this device is designed to provide protection against sudden spikes in the electrical supply by clamping down on the current, preventing the excess power from leaking through. Many of these devices also provide filtration for excess noise. Unfortunately, the vast majority of these devices on the market aren't capable of protecting against truly massive surges, and their protection may also be weakened or eliminated by a surge. In addition, they provide no protection against voltage sags or complete power failures.

However, there is a better solution: the Uninterruptible Power Supply, or UPS, for short. UPSs were designed originally for one purpose, as implied by their name: to give a reliable power supply to computers. Every UPS uses a battery, which charges during power service; if power fails, the device switches over to battery power, giving users enough runtime to save their work and gracefully shut down their system, or, on some very large units, to continue with their work. As UPSs have evolved, even more services have been added to some. These services include

- Surge suppression and power filtration
- Remote shutdown capabilities

Many UPSs are equipped with advanced circuitry, designed to enable them to communicate with the operating system on the machine they're protecting. The UPS can log data such as system temperature, humidity, and power quality on the host system. In addition, when power fails, the UPS can log the event and track the remaining runtime on its battery; should power not be restored within a certain period of time, these UPSs can even gracefully shut down the system they're protecting, and power off!

Modern UPSs equipped with such services are ideal for a modern networking environment; a properly-configured UPS can protect a system without any human intervention, and some models can even page an administrator in case of an emergency.

How, then, can someone pick the UPS that's best for their needs? It is important to consider a number of factors when searching for a UPS:

- UPS Type: There are two different types of UPS—offline and online.

  An offline UPS is the simplest and the least costly. An offline UPS uses the AC (alternating current) power delivered by the mains both to provide electricity to its loads and to charge its battery. When a power failure is detected, the UPS rapidly switches its loads over to the battery. When mains power is restored, the UPS then switches back to that current.

  Although they are cheaper to produce, offline UPSs have a number of problems. First, the amount of time necessary to switch from grid power to battery power, although tiny, can cause some systems to crash. Second, many offline UPSs convert the DC (direct current) power from the battery to square wave AC, rather than the natural sine wave AC delivered by the power grid. This square wave power can cause many systems to freeze and damages any sensitive electronics over a sustained period of time. More advanced offline UPS devices attempt to deliver a "simulated sine wave" using many smaller square waves. These simulated sine waves reduce the potential for damage, but they don't totally eliminate the problem. See Figure 24.5 for an illustration of different types of AC.

  Third, any power filtration or surge/brownout protection provided by an offline UPS must be of the traditional type; most are no better at these tasks than a traditional, high-quality standalone surge protector.

  The second type of UPS is the online UPS. An online UPS delivers all power to its loads from the battery and continuously keeps the battery charged with the AC power. See Figure 24.6 for an illustration.

  Because the power being delivered to the loads comes from the battery, rather than directly from the AC line, power delivery is constant, even if the AC mains power flickers on and off. The power delivered by the battery is clean, with no surges or brownouts. Online UPS devices are more expensive, are harder on batteries, and are more sensitive to environmental extremes of heat and humidity. Unless cost is the most important factor, however, online UPS devices are superior to offline devices.

Figure 24.5.
AC waveform types.

Normal AC Sine Wave

AC Square Wave Generated By
Most Offline UPS Devices

Simulated AC Sine Wave
Generated By Some Offline UPS Devices

> **NOTE**
>
> Is cost a factor preventing you from purchasing an online UPS? Consider the cost of any potential damage or downtime caused by the limitations of an offline device, and you may find that the online UPS is a far cheaper option in the long run.

Figure 24.6.
An online UPS.

24

DATA INTEGRITY

- Load Capacity: UPS devices are rated to deliver a certain maximum load in watts. Exceeding this load severely reduces battery life and can destroy the UPS. Make certain that you purchase a device with enough capacity to not only maintain all the devices attached to your system, but to also maintain enough additional capacity to give plenty of time for your system to gracefully shut down.

- Signaling Capability: Most UPS devices have the capability to signal your system in order to log events, send alerts, and shut the system down. High quality UPSs include their own custom software for monitoring UPS status and controlling your system; less expensive devices rely on the software included with your operating system (such as Windows NT's built-in UPS service). The custom software included with a higher-quality UPS is generally worth the extra money; it normally includes the necessary signaling cable and provides features that outstrip the operating system's own UPS software.

- Battery Replacement: The battery in a UPS is generally a large, heavy, highly toxic item, requiring factory servicing to replace it at the end of its useful life. Some more modern UPS devices, however, have field-replaceable batteries, making your life less complex and reducing system downtime.

- Additional Features: More expensive devices include even more features, such as the capability to monitor temperature both inside and outside the UPS, humidity monitoring, network configuration and management, and other such features.

Due to their great expense, UPS devices were once a luxury; now, however, even superb devices with high-quality software are reasonable, and the protection they provide to your hardware is absolutely invaluable in a production environment.

Environmental Factors

Computing devices are also sensitive to the environment around them; extremes in humidity and temperature can be extremely detrimental to their functionality and can cause hardware freezes and device failure.

Modern hardware is, thankfully, far more resilient and less sensitive to environmental factors than it used to be; gone are the days when entire buildings could be heated with the excess heat generated by a company's computing devices. It's still important to keep temperature and humidity within acceptable limits, however.

In many offices, the standard climate control systems designed to keep humans comfortable are sufficient. However, those climate control systems are not always completely reliable (humans don't normally stop functioning under occasional temperature or humidity extremes!), and conditions that humans may find comfortable or even tolerable can be excessive for hardware. For this reason, many enterprises develop machine rooms for their mission-critical hardware.

Using a machine room gives you control over a number of factors. First, you can keep the room at a set temperature and humidity level. Second, you can keep your sensitive hardware and data more secure by restricting access to the room. Third, you can provide reliable power services by giving filtration and battery backup to the entire room, rather than relying on individual UPS devices. Fourth, you can centralize many of the major hardware administration tasks for your entire enterprise.

Machine rooms require a huge initial capital investment; however, for many enterprises, the protection provided is more than worth the cost.

Physical Security

The best data integrity measures are meaningless if anyone can access your hardware and manipulate data at the console, or more bluntly, damage your hardware, disconnect power or network connections, or steal data.

The best measure for providing physical security for your system is to lock it away in a secure room, preferably a machine room. However, this may not be an option for everyone. You can provide some protective measures, however, even in an insecure location. Most systems, for example, enable you to set power-on passwords in the system's CMOS memory; this prevents people from restarting your machine and gaining access using a boot floppy or via other OSs installed on the system. In addition, many server-class systems enable you to prevent the system from being booted from floppy (via a jumper setting on the hardware), and also enable you to lock the system's case to prevent someone from accessing internal devices or changing jumper settings. Investing in even these basic security measures can provide you with a great deal of return in enhanced data integrity; however, nothing other than locked, secure access to your systems can prevent someone from executing a physical denial-of-service attack by disconnecting power or destroying your hardware.

Hardware Redundancy

As computers have evolved, they've become more and more reliable each year; hardware failure is no longer nearly as common as it used to be. However, it can still happen; hard drives fail, CPUs overheat and die, fans stop functioning, network cards blow up. For most tasks, this risk is acceptable; if worst comes to worst and some piece of hardware dies, it and its lost data is replaced and the machine is restarted. However, some businesses have systems that cannot *ever* suffer downtime; for this reason, many server manufacturers have developed hardware with built-in redundancy features.

Some systems give you the capability to install multiply redundant hardware devices with automated fail-over switching to a working device should one cease functioning. Such redundancy can apply to cooling fans, power supplies, network cards—even hard disks and CPUs! (Redundant disk systems are discussed later in this chapter.) Although these systems are often quite expensive, many enterprises are willing to pay the price to ensure that downtime caused by hardware failure cannot happen.

Protecting User Data

Failure of some sort is destined to happen; whether caused by hardware giving up the ghost, a malicious attack, or simple bugs in the operating system resulting in a system crash, it's not only possible but likely that your system will eventually go down. In the process, you may lose the data your users store and manipulate on your systems. However, you can protect yourself from even these ugly facts of life with two different measures: sound backup strategies and redundant disk storage.

Backing Up Your Data

The concept behind data backup is simple: keep a copy of critical data in case you suffer disk failure. You can back up your data to a number of different types of devices.

- Online Backup: The term "online," when used with respect to data storage, refers to a storage medium that's constantly, and instantly, available to the system. The disk storage normally used by your computer is *online storage. Online backup*, therefore, refers to simple, easy-to-implement backup measures, such as keeping a mirror copy of your disks (see "Redundant Disk Storage," later in this chapter, for more on disk mirroring). Online backup, although quick and easy, is also quite costly and rather inefficient; you're really getting effective use of only half your online storage media, because half of your disk space is used specifically to maintain an exact copy of your production data.

- Nearline Backup: "Nearline" refers to storage media that are not always kept online, but can be made available quickly and easily. Nearline backup is traditionally implemented on removable media (ranging from floppy diskette, for very small files, to large removable optical disks) or on large, custom jukebox devices using arrays of optical disks or tapes. Nearline storage is a powerful backup mechanism, providing not only rapid, reliable, and easily-accessible backup, but the capability to store huge amounts of data that is not commonly used in a way that can still be accessed easily. Nearline storage, however, can be expensive, and normally consumes large amounts of physical space, either with media storage or with large, bulky custom devices.

- Offline Backup: Offline backup strategies are the type most commonly implemented. Offline backup involves copying data onto small, convenient, removable media, often using compression techniques. The most commonly used offline backup media is magnetic tape. Offline storage is relatively cost-effective and simple to implement; however, it tends to be rather slow, and magnetic tape is notoriously unreliable, requiring careful handling and storage. The small size and reasonable cost of offline backup media makes offline backup the most commonly used strategy by far; for this reason, the remainder of this section focuses on offline backup media.

Offline Backup Devices

You can find a number of different offline backup devices, each with its own advantages and disadvantages. These devices include:

- ■ Proprietary Tape Cartridges: Proprietary tape backup devices, such as systems based on 3M's TRAVAN cartridge system, are most commonly found on personally-owned workstations; they tend to be quite slow, with highly limited storage capacity. However, the low cost and ease of setup makes them ideal for individual PCs not located on a local area network.

- ■ Digital Audio Tape (DAT) Cartridges: DAT is the most commonly found backup mechanism on small-to-medium-sized servers. DAT drives are data-only versions of consumer digital audio tape decks, and use the same helical-scan mechanism (similar to the strategy used by VCRs) to store vast amounts of digital data on small tape cartridges. (See Figure 24.7 for an illustration of helical-scan storage.)

FIGURE 24.7.

*Helical-scan magnetic
tape storage.*

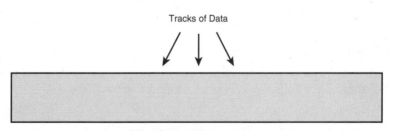

Direction of Storage ⟶

| Individual Track of Data |
| Individual Track of Data |
| Individual Track of Data |

Standard Magnetic-Tape Storage (Audio Cassette)

Tracks of Data

Helical Magnetic-Tape Storage (VCR and DAT)

There are a number of standards for data storage on DAT tape. Most modern standards support only 4mm cassettes, although both 8mm and 4mm DAT drives were available originally. DAT tape capacities vary, depending on storage protocol and the compressibility of data. DDS-2, the most popular current standard, can store up to 4GB of raw data on a 120m-long 4mm DAT cartridge, with the potential of storing up to 8GB of compressed data. Most DDS-2 drives can back up data at rates approaching 20-30MB per minute, depending on server and SCSI controller load. Real-world rates tend to be much slower. Some newer DDS-2 drives can back up data

24

DATA INTEGRITY

much more quickly. DDS-3 drives improve on DDS-2, both in capacity (12GB native, 24GB potential compressed) and speed (potentially 50-60MB per minute). Jukeboxes are available to automatically swap DAT tapes for large backups, increased backup speed through data striping, or offline storage.

DAT drives are quite common and are well-supported by various operating systems. The media is relatively cheap and widely available. However, their backup rates are relatively slow, and DAT drives are notoriously quirky, requiring frequent cleaning and meticulous verification of each backup to ensure data integrity. Due to the constantly dropping cost and industry proliferation, however, DAT drives will continue to be a good solution for some time.

- Digital Linear Tape (DLT): Digital Linear Tape (DLT) is a newer standard, using larger tapes than DAT. However, DLT tapes are much faster (potential speeds approaching 100MB per minute) and can store much more data (capacities of up to 40GB per tape). DLT drives are quite expensive, as is DLT media; for large backups or time-critical backups, however, DLT is a superior solution. DLT backup solutions also tend to be more robust than DAT.

- Advanced Intelligent Tape (AIT): AIT is a very recent backup solution and has little driver support in most operating systems. It is, however, a very attractive backup solution; AIT drives boast the capability to back up up to 50GB of data on a single 8mm cartridge, at rates of up to 300MB per minute! Each cartridge includes onboard controller electronics to manage compression, storage, and cataloging, thus increasing throughput and reliability. The drives and media are quite expensive at the moment, however, and as mentioned above, system support is likely to be sparse for some time.

Backup Software

Now that you've selected a backup device, you're ready to start backing up your data, right? Wrong. You still need to choose a backup software solution.

Many operating systems, such as Windows NT, include some form of backup software; most of these packages are rudimentary, however, providing only limited management, cataloging, and timing options. Reliability is also somewhat of a factor with these built-in solutions. (The old adage, "You get what you pay for" comes to mind.)

A number of third-party software solutions for all major operating systems expand on the capabilities of those limited backup packages. Such software, such as Arcserve by Cheyenne and Backup Exec by Arcada, include advanced scheduling, management, tape cataloging, and verification features, as well as higher reliability and robustness. When choosing backup software, it's important to ensure that the software supports your backup device, and it's also wise to ask around (on Usenet, for example) for opinions on usability and reliability.

Backup Types and Strategies

Now that you have both hardware and software, you're ready to enter the world of backup bliss. All you need is a manageable strategy for comprehensively backing up all your data.

First, it's important to understand the various types of backup most software can perform.

The first type is a *full backup*. A full backup backs up all the selected data to tape, and sets the archive bit for each backed-up file to mark that the file has been backed up. A variation of the full backup is the *copy backup*, in which all data is backed up to tape but the status of the archive bit is not touched. Full backups capture all data to tape, but they can be time-consuming.

The second type is the *differential backup*. Differential backups back up only those files whose archive bits are not set (that is, those files that have been modified since the last backup was run). The differential backup leaves the archive bit alone, however; subsequent differential backups include all changes made since the last reset of the archive bit, including the files backed up on the current differential backup. Differential backups are useful to provide additional coverage between periodic full backups; a strategy using full and differential backups requires only two tapes (the most recent full backup and the most recent differential) to restore all backed up data. However, you pay for this convenience in media inefficiency (the same data is backed up multiple times) and in backup lengths that increase over the interval between full backups.

The third type of backup is the *incremental backup*. An incremental backup copies only those files whose archive bits are not set, just as a differential backup does. However, the incremental then resets the archive bits, as does a full backup. Subsequent incremental backups copy only the files that have changed since the most recent incremental. This makes faster, more efficient backups in between full backups. Restoring data becomes more complex, however, because it needs both the most recent full backup and each subsequent incremental tape to restore all backed-up data.

The fourth backup type, daily backups, copies files based on most recent modification date; if a file has been modified on the day the backup is being performed, it is copied to the backup media.

In choosing a backup strategy, weigh the convenience of restoration against the time required for each backup cycle. Most backup strategies combine periodic full backups with daily backups, either differential or incremental. In some production environments, the benefit of being able to rapidly and easily recover from a system failure outweighs the inconvenience of the time needed for each backup; in other environments, there's little or no time in which you can lock out users to perform a backup, so the fastest, most efficient strategy is most important. In such an environment, you may even have to first copy data to a second drive or server that can be locked down, then perform the backup to tape.

24

DATA INTEGRITY

> **NOTE**
>
> One factor not yet discussed is the capability to back up your workstations to tape. Many backup solutions have the capability to back up remote workstations to a server's backup drive. These solutions are extremely convenient, enabling administrators to centralize backup facilities; however, they can be complex to set up, often requiring client agent software on each workstation. Such strategies often also use tremendous amounts of network bandwidth.

It's also important to consider tape rotation schedules. The type of tape rotation schedule best for you depends on a few factors:

- Backup strategy
- Length of time for which to maintain archived data

If it's important to you to keep every backup archived safely away, your rotation schedule becomes simple: use a new tape for each backup. The cataloging, storage, and fiscal investment in such a strategy can be prohibitive, however.

One common strategy is to have five daily tapes, which are reused, and one weekly tape, which is archived and replaced with a new tape each week. This enables you to keep weekly full backups stored safely away, but economize on the use of smaller, daily backups.

Another strategy is to simply use twelve tapes over a two-week period: one tape per week for each week's full backup (a total of two tapes), and 10 tapes for the dailies. By rotating through these twelve tapes, you keep tape costs to a minimum. However, these tapes receive more wear and tear, and you have only two weeks' worth of data to fall back on.

Consider your long-term archival needs, as well as your needs for backup speed, convenience, and reliability, when developing a backup scheme.

> **NOTE**
>
> All these strategies and rotation schemes assume your data can all fit snugly on one tape; the same principles apply to multi-tape backups, but the complexity involved is greater.

Backup Scheduling

Another important factor to consider in your backup strategy is when to run the backups. Most businesses can safely run a backup overnight; in many 24-hour operations, however, this window of inactivity is not available. Open files are generally ignored (and therefore not backed up) by most backup software. In order to get the most reliable backup, you need to find some way to ensure that the files you need to back up are closed (often by forcing logoff and file closure before the backup runs). On many systems, however, some files are kept open perpetually by software. In these situations, creative schemes (such as redundant disk storage, or data replication across multiple servers) are required to ensure maximum data integrity.

Backup Reliability

Ever tried to restore a backup, only to find that the tape was bad, or the data was corrupt? Make certain you monitor all verification logs to ensure that your backups are being made safely and consistently.

Backup Storage

Backups are intended to provide data integrity in case of disaster, including destruction of the backed up system; if that same disaster can take out your backups, you haven't gained anything. For this reason, many enterprises rely on secure off-site storage. Many firms exist to provide this service, and they often include couriers to pick up your backups, cataloging services, and refreshing services (copying older tapes to newer tapes). Off-site storage can be expensive, but it may be worth it to a 24-hour, mission-critical system.

Backup Security

One thing many administrators don't consider is the security of the data on their tapes. Your server may be extremely secure to unauthorized access, but if someone can read your backup tapes, you're still vulnerable. This is a particular concern when using off-site backup; for this reason, use backup software that lets you encrypt or password-protect your backups.

Redundant Disk Storage

Data backup cannot address a few major data integrity concerns. First, there's the issue of backup scheduling itself: any data modified since the most recent backup is lost in a catastrophic failure. Second, there's the issue of open files: it's generally impossible to back up open files, and many systems keep a number of files open as a matter of course. Third, recovery time is a problem: the several hours often necessary to recover from tape can be a major problem for some real-time work environments.

These problems can be addressed, however, by the use of RAID (Redundant Array of Inexpensive Disk) storage. The RAID concept is simple: use multiple disks to provide disk hardware redundancy, thus greatly reducing the risk of data loss due to disk failure. The RAID concept has been expanded, as well, to provide for enhanced disk subsystem throughput through the use of multiple drives.

There are a number of different RAID levels; each provides different features, and each has its pros and cons.

The first, RAID 0, simply provides enhanced performance: RAID 0 stripes data across multiple disk drives (see Figure 24.8). This system increases throughput by increasing the likelihood that the disk subsystem will be able to fetch different portions of the same file from multiple

24

DATA INTEGRITY

spindles at the same time. RAID 0 provides no additional fault-tolerance benefits; in fact, a RAID 0 system is more vulnerable to failure because it has more than one disk, any one of which can fail and ruin the volume.

FIGURE 24.8.

Illustration of RAID 0 (striping).

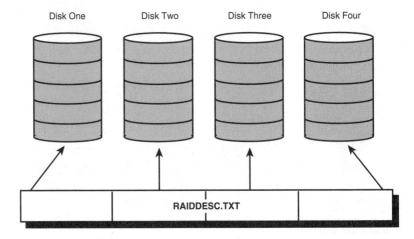

RAID 1 consists of either disk mirroring (maintaining the same data on multiple disks) and/or disk duplexing (maintaining mirrors on separate disk controllers, to eliminate the risk of controller failure). RAID 1 provides both fault-tolerance and, in advanced systems, greater performance because the same data can be read from multiple disks and/or controllers.

RAID 2, which is extremely uncommon, stripes data at a bit-by-bit level across disks.

RAID 3 stripes data at the byte level across all disks and uses an additional drive to store checksum parity data. Should one drive fail, the parity data can be used to rebuild the RAID set on a fresh replacement disk with no data loss. RAID 3 sets often perform quite well, due to the striping of data, and also provide high fault tolerance. Fault tolerance can be improved by mirroring the parity drive so that there is no one single point of disk failure.

RAID 4 stripes at the block level and uses a parity drive like RAID 3. RAID 4 can potentially be more efficient than RAID 3, because data is fetched and stored in single read-write passes.

RAID 5 stripes at the block level, like RAID 4, but unlike RAID 3 and 4, it also stripes the parity data across all disks. This eliminates the performance bottleneck of maintaining parity data on one disk, enabling the system to perform write operations more quickly, but can make RAID set rebuilding slower.

RAID can be implemented either in software (such as the RAID solutions included with Windows NT, which can support RAID 0, RAID 1, or RAID 5) or in hardware, with special operating system-transparent RAID controllers. Hardware solutions generally perform far better but often cost a great deal. Hardware solutions, however, provide the additional capability to hot-swap drives: should a disk in a RAID set fail in a hot-swap set, you can simply replace the bad drive with a new one, thus eliminating system downtime. Some hot-swap systems even allow for the installation of a fail-over disk, which is instantly merged into the set in the event of a disk failure. You can then simply replace the bad disk with a fresh one, which then becomes the new fail-over disk.

Implementing Your Data Integrity Plan

This chapter has presented you with a vast array of options and techniques to make your data more secure. Most sites find it inappropriate or resource-prohibitive to implement all the strategies here. All are valuable, however, so which strategies should you use?

In developing your data integrity plan, evaluate the following factors:

- Importance of Data: How important is my data? Is it critical that I lose none of it, or is simply keeping my server as reliable as possible sufficient because I can easily replace it? Is using backup enough or should I also use RAID? Can I afford a few hours of downtime, or do I lose money during each second that the system is unavailable?

- Practicality: Is administration of these systems my sole task, or do I have other responsibilities that limit the amount of time I can spend on data integrity? Do I have a staff of operators that can focus on these techniques? Can my company afford a machine room, or should we just use a UPS and keep an eye on the temperature and humidity?

- Risk: How at risk am I? Do I live in a major urban area or out in the boonies? Am I likely to suffer security attacks? How vulnerable am I to natural disaster or acts of God?

A Brief Missive on Data Integrity

One of the most common mistakes I see among beginning systems administrators is a lack of consideration of data integrity techniques. The high reliability rates of modern hardware, combined with the stability and advanced data protection techniques used by modern operating systems, make it easy for network administrators—experienced and inexperienced alike—to ignore important data integrity concerns. Among more conscientious administrators even, data integrity is often pushed aside in the face of day-to-day firefighting tasks, being left to be done "as soon as I have time." In this section, I intend to play a little dirty and frighten you with many of the possible threats to your system's integrity that you probably haven't thought of, each of which can cost you lost data, lost time, or a job, if not considered and planned for.

Let me give you a real-world example of the costs of ignoring data integrity, pulled from a mixture of both my own experience and that of people I've dealt with. Ralph Doe, a network administrator at Refined Widgets, is severely overworked. He's in charge of implementing and supporting the network infrastructure for a rapidly growing company and can just barely make heads or tails of his workload. A huge amount of the time he should be spending on maintaining his network and his servers is used up by politically powerful (read: impatient) users with simple, but frustrating, usage concerns on their personal workstations, who aren't willing to deal with the front-line support staff. Ralph recognizes the importance of a serious data integrity strategy, but he can't take the risk of offending the powerful users constantly placing demands on his time. As a result, he often has to rush through other tasks that more directly fit his job description.

Ralph has been instructed to bring up a new file and print server for the Accounting department, which has been moved into its own branch office. Ralph relies on his years of experience and purchases a high-quality, extremely reliable server, with plenty of RAM and hard drive space, and installs Windows NT Server. Ralph makes an Emergency Repair Disk and backs up the server's disk partition scheme in Disk Administrator. Then, he creates a large Volume Set using multiple drives, but as he's preparing to back up the new disk partition scheme, he gets interrupted to go show the Vice President for Marketing how to install a new screen saver. When he returns, it's well after five o' clock, and Ralph needs to pick up his kids. He rushes through installing the system's Uninterruptible Power Supply and doesn't get a chance to set up the server's DAT drive before he has to run. He begins the migration of data from the old server to this new one, and leaves for the evening.

The next day, Ralph barely has a chance to touch the new server. After the copy of the department's data from its old server was completed, the administrator for that site removed the data from its disk. Ralph has just enough time, between diagnosing a router failure and helping the Vice President's secretary install a new e-mail client, to check and make sure that all the data for the Accounting department got copied over correctly. He attends a staff meeting in the afternoon, and leaves for the evening.

That night, a powerful thunderstorm blows through Ralph's town, dropping lines and severely damaging the local substation. Ralph's office loses power for nearly an hour. The UPS on Ralph's server switches to battery properly, and when its battery capacity reaches the designated point, it attempts to gracefully shut down the server. However, in the process of rushing through the UPS installation, Ralph didn't grab the correct cable for the UPS; instead, he just has a standard 9-pin serial cable. When the UPS sends the signal to shut down to the server, it's never received; the server continues to run as the battery drains. Eventually, the UPS battery fails, and the server is powered off during the middle of a page fault.

When Ralph arrives in the morning, he sees a boot failure message on the server. Confused, he checks the UPS, and notices that he used the wrong cable. Cursing himself, he begins the process of restoring the server's boot files. After an hour of twiddling, the server boots up once again, but it cannot access any of the data on Ralph's volume set; he forgot to back up the partition data after spanning the volume set, and the server no longer knows how to access that data. Ralph curses himself yet again, and prepares to restore the data from tape, but suddenly realizes that he never had time to set up the DAT drive, and he doesn't have a reliable backup of the server's data. At this point, Ralph panics; he's lost the Accounting department's data, and they'll be coming in to work at any minute.

Ralph's situation is one many network administrators could find themselves in very easily; the constant demands on their time and pressures to perform many tasks make it easy to put off something like thoroughly planning and implementing a data integrity plan. However, when things go wrong, explaining that you didn't have time to properly implement data integrity probably won't save you from being canned for losing critical data.

> **NOTE**
>
> Are you trying to implement a sound, practical data integrity plan, but your management isn't willing to invest the resources? Make a business plan. List the costs and resources needed for your data integrity plan; weigh them against the costs of losing important data or suffering downtime. If the payback for your plan isn't enough to justify the expense, scale it back; if it is, a business plan helps convince management to back you up.

Summary

Data integrity is always recognized as a good idea; however, it's rarely implemented properly, due either to insufficient resources (in capital, time, or equipment) or lack of knowledge about all vulnerabilities, or both. This chapter has given you the tools necessary to design and implement your own data integrity plan, not only to keep your users happy and productive, but also to keep your head on your shoulders when disaster strikes. Remember the curse of the network administrator: when things are working well, no one notices your existence (or they may assume you're not doing very much work); when things go wrong, however, you are instantly at fault for everything. Do your best to make sure it's difficult for things to go wrong, and that you can quickly and easily recover if they do; it makes your life and your customers' lives easier.

Preventing Problems

by David Welk

IN THIS CHAPTER

The complex networks of today require a proactive, forward-thinking management system, which takes into account all aspects of the computing environment. The difficult task of ongoing maintenance often takes up all the available time of the network staff. Obviously, it can be very hard for an organization to break from the reactive mode and begin to plan and analyze the day-to-day issues.

Network Control Operations and Disaster Operations are two essential processes that must be considered, analyzed, and planned for in order to keep a network running optimally. This chapter discusses specific applications of these operations throughout several environments. Two of these applications of network control operations—baselining and monitoring—are proactive operations that are not getting done within most of today's networks.

An additional proactive strategy that, unfortunately, too few organizations deploy, is a disaster recovery strategy. The final portion of this chapter discusses methods for implementing and testing a disaster recovery strategy and plan. Strategies for testing and refining the network disaster operations are discussed at the end of the chapter.

Proactive Network Control Operations

The discussion surrounding proactive network control operations takes on a different, more serious connotation when linked to overall network problem prevention. It is common to hear other employees talking about the sensitivity of certain functions and their criticality to the daily operations of an organization. The discussion centers on the failure of the organization to closely monitor these operations or to provide adequate maintenance. This lack of action almost always causes extra problems for these operations as time passes.

These functions are the "easy to talk about" and "hard to implement" operations that almost always receive a level of priority lower than they should. This section of the chapter talks about the importance of standardization, documentation, and network management, and their significance in maintaining the health of the network.

Most operational groups tend to be satisfied with less-than-perfect solutions just because they work. Most organizations, when utilizing the best software and hardware solutions that are available today, should realize extremely desirable benefits and features that work very well. What keeps this from happening? Quite simply, it's the lack of time, the shortage of staff, or the difficulty of the specific operation that causes proactive tools to get lower priority and attention. Determining standards and proactive procedures can be an exhausting, never-ending process. Documenting these standards as well as documenting the network information is extremely time-consuming. However, this investment of time is well spent! All pertinent user information as well as the inventory and configurations of network hardware should be recorded and stored. Inventory information for both desktop hardware and software is essential to managing system upgrades and ongoing maintenance.

Of course, there is a whole array of less glamorous functions, too. Necessary evils such as tape backup routines and rotations, uninterruptible power systems and battery maintenance, and software licensing have to be implemented and completed. Day-to-day upkeep of databases for mail lists and server maintenance forces information systems personnel to keep moving all the time. The luxury of proactive network control operations loses a lot of luster during the day while routine business fires are being extinguished.

From a technical perspective, network management devices are among the most under-used tools available to network managers today. These management devices include such functions as, for example, the setting of threshold levels on critical hardware components. Monitoring these settings, adjusting them to be more useful, and paying attention to their details all pay excellent dividends during times of crisis.

A discussion concerning proactive network control operations would not be complete without some linkage to the Internet and all the business-based intranets springing up throughout the world. The key concept in proactive network control and management within these environments is security. A recent study has shown that network managers consider security to be the single most important factor concerning them within their own networks today. The multitudes of anti-virus software and organizations bringing security products to market also point to the increase in awareness of these security requirements.

> **NOTE**
>
> The recent study refers to a marketing presentation report published by 3Com Corporation, which ranked the concerns of network management personnel. In this presentation, which was developed to market the features of a new class of switching product, security was cited as the number one concern for network managers today.

There is little doubt that Internet access has increased significantly over the last few years. Not too long ago, most organizations had very few requirements for Internet access and therefore didn't offer it to their employees. Lately, no organization can keep their employees from spending some time on the Internet every day of the week. The arguments occur daily as to whether this is a good or bad thing for corporate America. There is no doubt in my mind that Internet access is a good thing. The downside to this very high level of external access is that it provides a greater number of openings for the unscrupulous people in networking to attempt to gain illegal access.

What makes a network secure? The answer is not as difficult as one may guess. Strong security policies that are rigidly enforced are the foundation for a secure network. Complete knowledge of the user community—including those using dial-up access and all after-hours activities—gives administrators an awareness of significant details that may indicate attempted intrusions, as well as the tools to create an accurate and secure authentication database. Strict requirements for desktop modems, which are sometimes the openings hackers use to gain network access, and password privacy alleviate most of the means of gaining illegal entry. Some of the articles about network intrusions state that the great majority of break-ins are from internal employees. Stressing the importance of prudent computer usage and alerting all users to potential openings into the network go a long way toward tightening the deadbolts on the network.

Gifted programmers and unauthorized hackers can wreak immense havoc with great ease in many of today's networks. This is not only through the access they may gain to critical information, but also through the development and circulation of virus software. These viruses can destroy months and years of work. Policies that address the manual passing of software between computers as well as governing downloads of software from the Internet are necessary to screen as much harm as possible from the network.

Many virus-scanning software packages are available today. From high-end server-based packages to low-end down-and-dirty shareware, this software can be very important to protecting the health of a network. The extent to which these applications are run is important to determine, but more important is the actual execution of the software and maintenance of the virus database. Generally, these databases are updated monthly. Of course, the whole argument about who is benefiting from these virus alerts can create another book, so for the purposes of this discussion just consider it wise to seek out and run the most appropriate software for your situation.

Applications for Proactive Network Control Operations

Although proactive network control operations are talked about more often than actually deployed, a certain amount of work really should be done to ensure highly reliable network access to both the local user community and the remote user community. The first section of this discussion addresses these critical operations and many others as they pertain more specifically to the larger, enterprise-wide networks.

The following section talks about certain other operations that have a better fit within the small- to medium-sized organizations. The funding and staffing is generally much smaller and less skilled at this level. That fact points to a need for a better utilization of the available resources. Many times the network administrator happens to be simply the person who understood computers the best. These people mean well but just don't have the overall understanding of how computers and systems work. The frailty of computer systems, if not properly understood, eventually brings everything down.

The point at which networks outgrow the "small to medium" classification is when they are required to support more than one thousand users. These networks typically are the ones that are accustomed to remaining somewhat stable and unchanged for long periods of time. The sheer number of users and the potential for 24-hour uptime requirements force network mangers to put off standard maintenance and upgrades. This network stability is normally good except that the deployed technology tends to become outdated and the network upgrade becomes a big project. Avoiding these big projects is another by-product of systematic and timely maintenance and upkeep.

The final section under this topic discusses the needs of the smaller, remote user community. The needs of this environment are certainly not as great as those of the previously discussed environments. The health of the remote users, though, can be just as critical to the overall health of the corporate network, if analyzed as a whole, when a high number of similarly-sized environments exist. Often central site talent supports these remote networks over some wide area connection. This factor obviously makes it more difficult to quickly troubleshoot and solve problems within the remote environment and can also lead to an unhealthy corporate network.

The Enterprise Environment

The high-end complexities of networking equipment, which are essential to supporting the enterprise-wide requirements of the largest organizations, can be both exciting and frustrating for the people who are charged with keeping the network running well. The best hardware and software solutions can often be implemented with the appropriate training required to keep this equipment maintained correctly parceled out to the staff. This keeps network personnel skills at sharp levels and provides fields for individuals to specialize in and add value for themselves to their organizations. On the other hand, many sleepless nights and ruined weekends occur because the networks can't be changed or upgraded during operational hours.

Many large organizations also have detailed change management operations, which allow for discussion and anticipation of network changes and outages. This proactive tool often finds the shortcomings in back-out plans and provides other departments with advanced notice of network outages. Because there are times when off-hours work has to be accomplished—such as by the accounting department during tax season—open discussion of planned outages avoids missing deadlines imposed by the government. Certainly, an outage during this time would be a costly mistake and might end up costing some employee her current job.

There are also the other departments in Information Systems, such as the mainframe group or mini-computer operators, that are linked to the network and to specific servers. Typically, these environments host users from the wide area side of the network and may have to support different time zones and availability requirements. The types of proactive functions and routines that have been run for years in mainframe systems have been finely tuned to provide better than 99% up times. Certainly, the client-server world is not at that level yet, but it is fast approaching it. The hardware is improving tremendously as the software keeps gradually getting smarter. This combination will enable failures to be avoided and bypassed quickly. The perception that the network is always there and performing well is a hard ideal to live up to, but it can be done!

E-mail, voice mail, and other network communications are further areas that routinely require and usually get the amount of proactive maintenance required to perform effectively for long periods of time. The main reason organizations have been successful at proactive management with these systems is that they have staffed sufficient numbers of people and trained them adequately to do their jobs. These very expensive systems are important to the daily functioning of the entire organization. In many cases, a high-ranking executive may get immediately on the phone to IS if he has a problem with his electronic or voice mail.

How can these different environments be supported proactively in an enterprise-wide network? The answer is relatively straightforward here. Personnel and procedures, correctly trained and applied, are the keys to a reliable network.

An often overlooked but effective proactive function is membership by staff personnel in user groups and attendance at trade shows. The large corporations that finance these networks usually have the capability to fund fault-tolerant, redundant infrastructures that can withstand many types of minor outages. These funds should further be spent on education of staff technical people to properly configure and maintain the network components.

Because the environment spreads out over a wide area, it is usually difficult to get to some portions of it. This is another good reason for strong and accurate documentation. As sites are installed and upgraded, records should be updated also. These records, if accurate, go a long way toward helping central site people solve remote problems. Of course, if the environment is very large, these tasks become more difficult. That reason alone is why regular upkeep of documentation is important. Never letting the tasks get too far out of hand helps ensure that they will get done. When a job gets to the point that it requires a week of dedicated time to update some records, the job simply does not get done. The result is inaccurate and therefore worthless documentation.

Another very useful function is known as *standardization*. With standardization, after the most appropriate hardware and software solution is chosen for the job, this same solution is implemented throughout the environment so as to establish a level of consistency. This consistency is the key to effective proactive management. Standardizing makes ongoing maintenance and support easier. Having personnel proficient in many software packages is nearly impossible. Having a strong person in one application is very common, though. This is a direct result of standardization and training.

The Small-to-Medium Environment

The largest percentage of business organizations probably resides within the loose boundaries of this classification. Groups of more than ten and less than a thousand users can be considered small-to-medium. Typically, users' needs and skills are varied and create extra confusion for network support staffs. Some users have strong computer skills and have the ability to find wonderful pieces of software throughout the Internet. These users can very easily download virus-infected code and spread it within the corporation instantly.

To satisfy a need for certain location presence, some organizations must deal with a shortage or complete lack of good support people. These companies very often cannot afford strong talent and may even try to educate internal people. If internal education works, the newly trained employee is likely to take his skills on to the open market and improve his spot in the pecking order of life. What does this shortage of adequate staff do to hurt the network and its components? History suggests that in situations with minimal staff, personnel tend to avoid most of the tedious operations. Proactive maintenance such as tape backups are not being routinely done and maintained. Little fault tolerance and power backup capabilities are usually incorporated into these environments. Financing these "luxuries" is difficult, and often organizations have to make a conscious tradeoff: susceptibility to business downtime for reduced overhead expenses.

What proactive functions are so important that they just have to get done in the small and medium environments? Again the answer here is documentation and standardization. These tools maximize the efficiency of the limited resources. Regular tape backup procedures can scarcely be considered a luxury in any environment anymore, so having someone take responsibility for backups and their proper storage is crucial. Making sure tapes are rotated and stored correctly is important to ensure that when data is needed off a backup tape, it can be found easily and restored.

The typical obstacles to protecting information within a network can become even greater in the smaller network environments. Small-to-medium organizations tend to have a higher proliferation of modems and modem access and therefore a higher vulnerability to penetration from hackers. Employee turnover also tends to be a little higher, making it easier to loosen password security. Procedures that address these types of vulnerabilities must be deployed correctly to help in securing the overall network for the organization.

The Remote User Environment

Unfortunately, the remote user environment provides almost insurmountable complications for proactive management. Remote users rarely have local access to adequately trained people for any kind of computer hardware or software maintenance. In fact, knowing how to use a word processing application is often enough to make someone the computer guru for the office! Historically, central site support staff have found these users hard to work with. Although they have a level of knowledge that makes them *think* they know what's going on, they don't have a view of the overall network and how their piece interacts with it. This is why small acts—such as reconfiguring a server to broadcast extra data or a router to filter something—can affect the wider enterprise network.

What are some of the basic requirements for proactive control in these environments? The answer is to have some set standard for the types of devices that are deployed at these locations. In order for remote managers to correctly diagnose problems through their understanding of the correct operation of these devices, some standard set of procedures must also be followed.

It can be very costly to deploy network hardware that is capable of remote management and that can also act as an intermediary system for larger, more powerful systems in an overall network management solution. The simpler solution that usually gets deployed involves less intelligent equipment and the keeping of spare parts at the central location. Again, proactive maintenance and reliability is exchanged for cost savings.

Network Testing, Baselining, and Monitoring

The purpose of this section is to demonstrate the importance of network testing, baselining, and monitoring, and tie them together through an overall proactive strategy—a strategy that acknowledges the importance of proactive management. A by-product of all this proactive network control is accurate documentation. The strategic importance of accurate documentation can be summed up easily: the managers of the network know what is supposed to be going on. The relevance of this fact is that they should also know when the network is *not* performing correctly or when it is even a little out of whack.

A very popular term in the networking industry is "baselining." There are many variations on what the term actually means, but in general, it defines the performance level of the network at some point in time. Compare this to what a doctor does for her patients by performing physical examinations over a period of time. The doctor knows how things have been and can note the changes. These changes are indicative of something good or bad and it is the responsibility of the doctor to figure out what those changes mean. When you apply this same idea to the network, it is easy to see how accurate knowledge of performance, high usage times, and other utilization statistics provides excellent insight into the efficient operation and management of the network.

How is baselining accomplished? Typically, an organization with a larger network already owns the types of tools necessary to do the baselining service themselves. Protocol analyzers and servers with big hard drives help to capture current utilization statistics and store them for future manipulation. Smaller organizations often rent this type of equipment or hire a consulting firm to do this work. The by-product of performing this function again is good, accurate documentation. From this documentation, managers can assess areas of weakness and begin to provide for improvements. This improvement process might mean setting up a larger budget or evaluating redeploying existing equipment. The good news here is that the network's condition is being evaluated before a crisis occurs.

What does network testing provide for proactive network management? In large organizations that can provide a non-production lab environment, testing enables administrators to evaluate the results of implementing new software and hardware without interfering with normal information flows. This luxury may not be available in medium groups, or may not be the best option for some large groups, so off-hours testing of upgrades and changes has to be done. Many times the complete impact of a change is not witnessed until the network load of the whole organization is brought to bear on the change. This is the reason for well-thought back-out plans. These plans describe the steps required to restore the network to the previously functioning state.

Other functions require regular testing also. Regular tests need to be performed on backup tapes using features such as searching and selective restore. Weekends are often a great time to kill the power and evaluate the effectiveness of the UPS systems. The larger companies may even have diesel-generated power. Successful startup of the backup generator, after losing total power to a facility, can keep a company in business through some rough times. Whether this function will deploy as expected can be determined only through a scheduled and implemented proactive testing process.

One area discussed throughout this chapter is security. It is important to focus on two aspects of security: monitoring the licensing of software, and periodic and random security checks. These types of functions are rarely done in any environment outside of the larger enterprise network. *Proactive monitoring of software licensing* can keep an organization from being fined for software piracy. These fines are generally very large and can be just as damaging to an organization as a security breach. *Random security checks* can verify system security integrity and also identify improper usage of software licenses. Although security is often not a major concern in smaller organizations, they are just as vulnerable to security breaches. Corporate spying goes on in today's world. Attacking the supplier of piece parts to a large organization can often yield valuable information. This might be as effective in meeting a spy's goals as breaking into the large organization's network and host systems.

Refining Existing Network Control Operations

Although the level of hardware redundancy and network management skills declines as the size of the network shrinks, it is still very possible to develop a solid workable proactive network control plan with reduced resources. Many of the barest necessities—such as backup routines—can be automated now. The level of computer literacy is advancing quickly and even the smallest groups usually have at least one person who can change a tape from a backup drive.

If organizations establish and stick to a clear-cut strategy, they are in a position to resolve problems or overcome failures quickly and easily. Monitoring and testing enable administrators to develop improvement schedules and plans, which are essential to constantly improve the capabilities of the environment. This is similar to the process of continual improvement being deployed in the manufacturing sector today.

Fault-tolerant hardware platforms such as mainframes, mini-computers, and desktop computers all come with a certain high price tag. It may seem easy to choose less-expensive items early in the decision process. This may not always be the best decision, though, if the cost of ongoing operations becomes high. Expensive equipment with a high level of fault tolerance is often deployed within high-end organizations at the central locations. This same high cost, however, often keeps redundancy options from being implemented in the networks of smaller and remote groups.

Additionally, strategies that encompass routine tape backup procedures, use of uninterrupted power supply equipment, and proper backup and rotation of all software media prove to be the most effective at providing enduring up-time and network stability. Legal usage of licensed software and policing of the end-user community are also recommended policies that tend to get overlooked at many organizations. Clear-cut processes that are well documented make all these rigorous duties much easier. Taking the time to perform these functions correctly is very important in avoiding time and money losses down the road. It is always less expensive to pay the price required to do the job correctly in the first place than it is to repair the resulting problems later.

The last piece of a solid overall proactive strategy, and often the most overlooked portion, is the personnel on staff and the brainpower they bring to the team. Participation in User Group activities provides outstanding education and an additional reference for staff members to develop proactive network control strategies. Early exposure to hardware and software bugs via group membership and documents can prevent users from having to personally experience faults in their own networks. Additionally, exposure to good resources can help them troubleshoot and resolve problems quickly. Timeliness is the key to effective management and for strengthening the perception of a highly reliable, stable, networking environment.

Proactive Network Disaster Operations

This section of the chapter discusses the set of operations known collectively as "disaster recovery." These are the proactive operations used to define and test the plan for restoration and recovery of the network following a serious disaster. It is interesting to note that these operations are less likely to be implemented in any network that isn't enterprise-wide and supporting large amounts of mission-critical data. The loss of data can be just as damaging to a smaller organization as a large one, but the willingness to take the risk is much higher. Many times "willingness" is nothing more than a reaction to the fact that the necessary dollars are simply not available.

So what are proactive network disaster operations? It would seem that they are the operations that most network managers never want to have to implement. No matter how hard you try to build in the tolerance to fault and disaster, it is not possible to account for everything. In environments where money is not a major issue, practically all possible disaster scenarios can be accounted for. Most organizations, though, have limited finances available and must evaluate and prioritize resources.

Prioritizing the resources necessary to salvage the operations of the business has to come first in the planning of network recoveries. This plan must include plans for staff members to relocate or do whatever is necessary to complete their regular jobs despite the network problem.

Fortunately, several major organizations today specialize in customizing disaster recovery strategies for other organizations. They often have locations with hardware and software available to back up most types of data centers. Of course, the types of hardware and software systems that need to be recovered are defined during contract negotiation and it becomes the responsibility of the service provider to have your company's functional areas ready to go, on a moment's notice.

The major "disaster recovery" service firms provide a good answer for very large companies, but after the largest thousand or so organizations, the overall sizes of the companies start to get smaller. How do these less-than-major organizations support their networks and business requirements during times of crisis? They—just as every other organization—must think about their business needs and determine solutions in advance. That proactive thought process is the focus of this chapter. Spending the time necessary to figure out what could go wrong and what can be done to make that as painless as possible to the organization is very important.

As the chapter discusses the small-to-medium networks that exist in the majority of business environments, it focuses on the little things that can be done to help avoid big problems during troubled times. Persistent application of difficult processes enables a company to be ready to resolve a crisis. Paying attention to the needs of the business in disaster plans is important, also. Trying instead to only guess what the priorities of business are can be a career-ending decision. Leaving out a piece of the business that is less well-known can easily spell trouble for some senior IS manager.

Finally, the chapter talks about the small workgroup environments and the small businesses. These organizations can least afford the types of outages that may keep them out of business for a week or two at a time. Luckily, services are available that can keep up a small business by leasing space and computer hardware. Here again, proper use of backup and restore functions can lead to a surprisingly easy network restoration.

Applications for Proactive Network Disaster Operations

There are several alternative applications for proactive network disaster operations. The large, enterprise-wide networks encompassing many cities and individual locations are the first networks analyzed. Because these are the glamorous, mainframe-based networks on which all large companies run their businesses, it makes sense to give them top billing here. These enterprise-wide networks also contain bits and pieces of all the smaller environments. Many of these larger network environments also have some mini-computer functionality to support along with buildings full of desktop computers.

The small-to-medium organizations with less than a thousand users are analyzed second. Many assumptions are made about the subtle differences between medium organizations and large ones. For the purpose of this chapter, a medium organization probably has less extensive network requirements and a limited geographic area of exposure.

Finally, the small remote workgroup encompassing only handfuls of users is discussed. This prototypical environment is part of each of the previous two environments but is discussed alone because so many workgroups such as these don't have the corporate big brother to lend them a hand. The importance of good network management techniques and philosophy is stressed, because good network management provides a higher level of safety when network downtime is directly connected to lost revenue.

The Enterprise-Wide Disaster Recovery

The term "enterprise" is used often today to describe most large networks. Although it is true that enterprise networks are large, it is possible for a large network to not be enterprise-wide. For this chapter, the term "enterprise-wide" describes a network of networks. These individual sub-networks generally fall under the ownership of one organization. Fortune 1000 companies build these types of networks and support mainframe-based computing, mini-computer–based computing, and micro-computer networks. Although the means of communication and levels of technology differ greatly, all these environments require specialized talents and skills. Only the very large organizations can afford to support all these functions.

Because network disaster operations also require dedicated and expensive personnel, it is often an area that is allowed to kind of "run in place." Typically, these staffs are charged with operating regular network monitoring and security procedures, also. These are some of the reasons that medium-sized organizations don't build enterprise networks.

How do these big companies plan for and execute their disaster recovery operations? For the most part, staffs assigned within their information systems groups take year-round responsibility for these tasks. These groups plan the tests that occur two to four times a year. They schedule the meetings and produce the reports. The business units typically choose their own level of cooperation. Senior management usually provides some prodding to be on board with the testing and have plans for support in times of trouble.

As was mentioned earlier in this chapter, there are third-party organizations that handle the disaster recovery operations for many large companies. Typically, they offer some large computing center that has a high level of communications capabilities. These capabilities are taxed as each new customer brings its own unique network design to the center for failure security. The wide area communication that is a big part of enterprise-wide computing has to be transferred to these disaster facilities. This is where special arrangements with the long distance carriers come in. Most of the bigger nationwide carriers have capabilities to "swing" a network from one point of focus to another. As expected, the cost of these services is enormous and is something companies avoid using if at all possible.

These enormous computing centers can also do the same magic in support of mid-size computing networks. One of the innate benefits of the mini-computer technology is its capability to spread or distribute information across several locations. This feature lends itself very nicely to workable disaster recovery scenarios. Because only one center is typically knocked out at any time, that center can easily be relocated to another location within the local organization. Organizations never like to lose business, but comparing the productivity loss of only a single location to that of an entire organization is something to consider during planning.

The Small-to-Medium Network and Disaster Recovery

For the purposes of this chapter, small-to-medium networks are considered to be those built around mini- and micro-computers. These constructs have many plusses and minuses. The advantage of this environment is its distributed capabilities. This keeps failures at any single point from being disruptive to the entire organization. These environments usually allow for some delay between the processing of information and the usage of the printed reports. This less than real-time functionality enables services such as the regular mail and some overnight delivery services to act as workable substitutes during many types of computing outages.

Where do disaster recovery operations fit within these networks? They exist as part of many people's everyday routine. The analysts within several departments are expected to meet two times a year and establish some functional plan for resolving things in the event of some disaster. Ideally, at least one time each year an actual test is executed. The list of areas to fix is usually very large and after the test is done, the planning receives less than the necessary attention. This is the downside for organizations that already have stretched budgets and staffs.

The benefit of having several locations within a limited geographical area is apparent when it comes to personnel relocation. This physical relocation alone can keep a business running during extended outages. In the case of micro-computers, the equipment can be moved around fairly easily, also. In addition, people tend to pull together during a disaster. The group's synergy provides for significant productivity improvements. These improvements can make up for the loss of routines and normal resources.

Turning more specifically to micro-computer networks or LANs, much of the necessary functionality can be easily moved or redeployed. Users may be forced to give up some performance and ease of use but should still be able to accomplish their jobs. A good maintenance plan includes regular server backups with rotated storage of the tapes. This plan ensures easy restoration of servers and functionality in remote locations. The ease of dial-up functions in today's network environments enables users to have quick and somewhat easy connectivity to distant locations. This connection should be adequate to accomplish many business functions.

The Remote User and Disaster Recovery

Believe it or not, remote users are usually accommodated fairly well in normal disaster recovery scenarios. Because most enterprise-wide networks contain these remote user communities, it makes sense for them to be supported during disaster outages as well. The ease of changing the direction of dial-up facilities, such as analog telephone and ISDN, enables these small groups of users to adjust quickly to the network changes.

The unfortunate side for these smaller workgroups is that they usually lose the regular support and the level of resource access to which they have been accustomed. It is during these times that the field users appreciate the corporate teams. The rest of the year the corporate folks are under-appreciated and referred to by many loving nicknames.

Testing Disaster Recovery Operations and Strategies

In some very large corporations, network disaster operations and disaster recovery tests are a regular part of the corporate culture. As many as four times a year, a disaster is simulated and the recovery plan is allowed to unfold. All the problems created during the drill are usually recorded, analyzed, and fixed for the next test. Whole departments may be instituted to monitor and analyze the ongoing performance of the network. These same groups may also be tasked with designing and analyzing disaster recovery tests.

Over the course of several years, a very sound and stable plan emerges. This plan encompasses support for all the major computing platforms and identifies areas of risk as they exist today. The plan discusses the deployment of resources and facilities for changing communication requirements. Experience suggests that these plans are very wide in scope but often get deployed during times of disaster in some smaller scenario. The techniques and lessons learned are the same. The fortunate organizations that proactively planned and tested and made the necessary changes are ready to adapt. Having the capability to react is a distinct advantage in the business community and the cost/benefit analysis of its price tag should be seriously considered during planning sessions by senior managers.

Refining Existing Network Disaster Operations

Executing disaster drills over the course of a year enables the forward-thinking organization to discuss the strengths and weaknesses of its disaster recovery strategy. These organizations usually have internal workgroups and departments that schedule and manage these disaster recovery operations.

These "disaster recovery" or "network planning" groups always get the attention of the individual business units because they typically can help out a recovery analysis project with financing. These groups also get a high level of attention from the information systems people because IS staffs are required to participate and make the disaster recovery tests successful.

Generally speaking, these tests are very expensive with high travel costs. Using the relevant information and learning from these tests enables the company to fix weak areas in its recovery plan and maybe even retest the revised plan in a future scenario.

It is hard to make the follow-up sessions successful. The company has experienced a rather stressful disaster test and is beginning to settle back into normal routines. The meetings and reports required to do a thorough follow-up just require more time. It is important, however, to follow these exercises with prompt attention. As in any good project, there must be closure. The closure from a good disaster test is discussion of benefits and weaknesses. These discussions lead to good ideas for the next round of testing, and a new project can unfold as the old one is put to rest.

Summary

Problem prevention has been the focus of this chapter, and trying to identify and eliminate problems before they get out of control is the important concept here.

This chapter also focused on environments of several different sizes, and discussed the tradeoffs involved with each within network disaster operational functions. The first half of this chapter presented information on many of the different proactive operations that can be carried out within a network management organization. This discussion recognized that these operations become low-priority responsibilities for all members of the network team and many pieces fall through the cracks.

The second half of this chapter provided insight into effective network disaster operations. Although it seems that only the high-end organizations can afford to implement these procedures, all organizations can use some level of planning and deployment. Many ideas were presented to help all sizes of organizations develop some plan for improvement.

CHAPTER 26

Troubleshooting Problems

by Richard L. Peete

IN THIS CHAPTER

The dreaded phone call, or the visit by a distraught user, informing you "The network is down!" can turn your relatively calm day into a mass of confusion and concern. No matter how well your network planning and implementation has gone, you will eventually be faced with solving a network-related problem. These problems can occur for a variety of reasons. Unfortunately for the Network Administrator, they are often highly visible events, which need to be resolved as quickly as possible to keep your organization functioning at its peak.

If you have followed the advice and directions earlier in this book, you have already documented your network's architecture and its systems configuration, and established an operational performance baseline. This information can be a great help in the diagnosis and resolution of network difficulties, because it provides a reference "checkpoint" from which deviations that may have caused the problem can be identified more easily.

The key to resolving network problems is to develop a logical, structured analysis approach toward problem identification and correction.

Logical Fault Isolation

If you are reading this book, you are probably either in charge of a network or at work in an Information Systems department supporting a network environment. This means that you probably have already had some experience, good or bad, diagnosing computer problems.

Structured Analysis has been used in many disciplines as a way to define a step-by-step, logical, and repeatable process toward an end. In this case, the desired end is the accurate identification of both a network problem and its cause, leading to the selection of the appropriate resolution.

Using this technique to isolate the specific problem, or *fault*, is called *Logical Fault Isolation* and is the most effective means for finding the correct solution, the first time. The tactic of applying solutions randomly is potentially dangerous, often introduces additional problems into the mix, and results in the expenditure of large amounts of time and resources. And time and resources mean money—money better spent on more worthwhile projects.

The isolation process has six steps, which eventually lead to the proper resolution of a network problem. Used together, these steps can be easily remembered as the "ADJUST" method.

- Assess the priority.
- Discover pertinent information.
- Justify probable cause(s).
- Unit test and isolate.
- Study and evaluate results.
- Transcribe results and process.

Following these six steps provides a consistent approach toward problem determination, even in the most difficult of situations. The following sections examine each of these steps in greater detail to give you a better understanding of their purposes and benefits.

Assess the Priority

Some might suggest that this is the most important step in the ADJUST methodology. The user community places constant demands upon people in any network support position—demands that require the efficient allocation of available resources. Being able to quickly assess the impact of a reported problem is a key competency for those tasked with keeping an organization's network infrastructure afloat.

Every user thinks that his problem is the most important. The reality is that everything cannot be resolved at once. In fact, attempting to do so can lead to further complications if changes to the network architecture are not done in a coordinated fashion.

Not every problem is a true emergency. It is essential that reported problems be classified into a priority queue that shows each problem in its order of necessity. Network support staff should address the most immediate problems on the list, even if they are not the most appealing.

Fight the temptation to "knock out the easy ones first." The time spent on those problems is better spent focused on the critical concerns. Responding to a user request for access to the new color laser printer may be easier than solving a routing problem on your network, but the impact of that routing problem is more deserving of your attention.

Discover Pertinent Information

Information discovery is the first step in the process of resolving any network problem. The initial communication you receive notifying you of a network problem is not likely to contain all the pertinent information. As you work through the process of problem identification, information is power and can make it easier for you to arrive at an accurate determination.

Your two major sources of information are your users and the reports generated by network monitoring tools and utilities. Collect as much information regarding symptoms, operating environment, software, hardware, error messages, and other results as you can. Try not to filter out information at this stage.

Interview Your Users

Most network problems have an impact upon your user community. Don't ignore this large source of information. Besides, users are always willing to offer any information that might help you solve their problems.

Many technicians are reluctant to do this because of the impression that users do not have sufficient technical expertise to provide useful analysis. In reality, users often have very helpful input to offer but are not being questioned correctly. As with all things, "garbage in, garbage out."

You need to understand your users' terminology and technical skill levels. Ask them for their observations, not their assessment. Find out what they *expected* to happen, and what *actually* happened.

Some questions to ask your users are:

- Can you describe the problem you experienced?
- Which software application(s) were you using at the time?
- Has anyone else experienced this problem?
- Did you experience any slowness in the network at the time?
- Were you using a network resource like a hard disk or printer?
- Are you still connected to the network?
- Did you have to restart your workstation after the problem occurred?

Interviews of this kind can offer insights into network and application behavior. These insights can, in turn, lead you in the correct direction and help narrow the list of potential problem areas.

Analyze Network Activity

The other information resource is the reports generated by the various network monitoring utilities available for the Windows NT Server network operating system. The information in these reports should be compared against your baseline configuration and performance characteristics. Deviations between your baseline information and the current network reports should be investigated. They may indicate where possible causes may lie.

Check the history of changes made to either the network, the affected workstation(s), or software applications involved. A quick review of this log may show whether this problem has occurred before and what was done to resolve it.

Implementing *System Change Control*—the process of tracking the history of changes made to the network's infrastructure (devices, workstations, servers, printers, system configuration, software, and so forth)—can be a real plus. System Change Control is a process that was originally defined by the Project Management Institute of Carnegie-Mellon. It is a process by which organizations can track problems and solutions for historical reference and documentation. It helps you track any configuration and software changes made to network devices. Knowing how, when, and why a network modification was made can often provide the key to solving an unexpected side effect of that change.

> **TIP**
>
> For medium-to-large network installations it is highly recommended that a network management system be implemented to inventory all network devices and workstations attached to the network. Microsoft's System Management Server v1.2 can integrate this functionality into a Windows NT Server network solution.

Create a checklist of questions that your interview process should cover before moving on to the Problem Determination phase. This document should be a "living document," changing as you gain more experience in network troubleshooting and learn more about the unique combination of software and hardware in your specific network environment.

Basic questions on this form might include:

- How many users were affected by the problem?
- Were they all on the same network segment?
- Was the entire network affected?
- Can the problem be reproduced?
- Is the problem application related or network related?
- Has any equipment been moved, modified, or replaced recently?
- What other software was involved (include version numbers)?
- Has anyone else attempted to fix this problem in the past?
- Was a new application recently installed on this workstation?

After you have collected all the available feedback related to the problem at hand, you are ready to begin the process of determining what caused it.

Justify Probable Causes

The next step is to analyze all the information gathered in the discovery process and begin to develop a list of possible causes of the problem.

Ask yourself:

- Does the data suggest that a particular segment or component of the network is involved?
- Does the problem seem to be localized to just one workstation?
- Are common components involved (network adapters, vendors, software drivers, software versions)?

In the previous step ("Discover Pertinent Information"), you were advised to not eliminate any piece of information provided by your various sources. Now is the time to examine all the information you've accumulated and evaluate it based upon your experience, the technical reference materials at your disposal, and the results of your baseline comparisons. Look for common patterns in the symptoms or results. As you come up with your list of possible causes for the network problem, questions like those above can help you narrow your list down to the most likely culprits and give you justification for making your selections.

Try to rank the list, showing the most likely candidates first. The more experience you acquire, the easier it is to assess where the problem lies.

Unit Test and Isolate

This is the moment of truth. You have taken the time to gather the pertinent information. You have taken the time to organize and analyze that information into a set of potential causes. You have ranked those possible scenarios from most likely to least likely. Now it is time to come up with *solutions*!

After your list is complete, an iterative process of "Test, Evaluate, and Isolate" is used to narrow the list of potential causes down until you find the real problem.

Starting with the most likely candidate from your list, determine the solution that you expect to best rectify the situation.

> **TIP**
>
> Many resources can help with the identification process. For Windows NT Server networks, two highly regarded resources are available.
>
> The first resource is Microsoft's Hardware and Software Compatibility Lists. These two lists show all the hardware devices and software packages that are proven to be compatible with the Hardware Abstraction Layer (HAL) of NT's Network Operating System. The other resource is the Microsoft Technical Information Network (TechNet) CD-ROM and its online subset, the Microsoft Knowledgebase.

For example, if the problem involves the inability of a workstation to recognize a file server, you might come up with the following set of causes:

- Bad physical connection (cable, connectors, hub, terminators)
- Incorrect or obsolete network client or protocol(s)
- Bad or incorrectly configured Network Interface Card (NIC)

Always apply solutions one at a time. This makes it easier to undo each solution and reduces the possibility of one change impacting the success of another. By applying each solution individually, you are utilizing an isolation technique that increases the probability of a successful result. Applying multiple changes in hopes of solving a problem often results in unexpected side-effects that may only exacerbate the situation.

Test the solution to determine whether it resolved the problem. If it did not, back out the changes you made and determine a solution for the next probable cause on your list.

> **TIP**
>
> If you can back up the files and/or configuration information for the components on which you are working before beginning this "test, evaluate, and isolate" process, do it. Always have a fallback position in case things get too complicated to roll back.

It is very important to remember (that means "document") the changes you make so that you can record them for later archival or undo them if those changes are ineffective (or make things worse). You never know whether a change you make may cause the problem to worsen rather than improve. Failure to document has come back to haunt many administrators, when a supposed solution has unexpected consequences and the administrator is unable to undo the changes.

Study and Evaluate Results

If your test solves the network problem, you have succeeded! If the problem persists, continue with the next possible cause on your list. If you exhaust all the items on your list, then you need to start the ADJUST process again, back at the Discovery step—there is obviously a piece of information that your gathering process has failed to produce.

If you find yourself at this point, do not be afraid to ask for help from more senior people. They may be other individuals in your organization. They may be from the firm that installed your backbone. They may be professional contacts you have made outside the organization.

Find them. Engineers are often reluctant to do this because they take so much pride in solving problems on their own. However, this can sometimes be counterproductive. It pays to take advantage of all available sources of knowledge.

There are many newsgroups and mailing lists on the Internet that respond to inquiries from engineers looking for solutions to problems. The best network analysts develop a network of professionals to whom they can go for ideas and feedback. Aspire to be that kind of network analyst.

Transcribe Results and Process

After ensuring that the problem has been successfully resolved (ask your users—they can tell you), it is time to document the problem: its symptoms, the cause, the resolution that was applied, and how you figured everything out. It may also be necessary to update your network architecture, infrastructure, and system configuration parameter information if your resolution required changes in those areas.

Following System Change Control methodologies ensures that you continually update and publish the adjusted baseline each time it is modified. This history can then become a useful tool the next time a problem has to be researched.

This information should be stored in a problem resolution database, which becomes your best resource for future problem solving. It also becomes an important training resource for new staff and provides the organization with a knowledgebase customized to its networking environment.

This structured method for problem resolution can take time when you are faced with a complex networking anomaly. But keep in mind that if you do it correctly, you need go through this process only once. And with the gradual development of your own knowledgebase, the process becomes more and more streamlined.

Common Networking Problems

This section lists some of the more common networking problems that administrators face on a day-to-day basis. Although every network has its own unique configuration and characteristics, many of the issues here are certain to have some relevancy to your environment.

Physical Media

The physical media of a network (the cables, connectors, hubs, network adapter cards) are the most vulnerable to breakage and should be the first things checked when a network connectivity problem occurs. A short or break in a cable can cause one workstation, or an entire network segment, to fail to connect to a server or recognize other network devices.

Administrators need to develop a method for determining whether a connectivity problem is located within the affected workstation(s) or the physical media connecting them. This should be the first step before taking more invasive actions (reconfiguring computers, swapping adapter cards, removing/updating drivers) on a workstation.

If you have a spare machine with a working network interface card, it can be used to test the cable. If the spare machine connects to the network resource in question, then the problem is in the workstation rather than the cable.

Some likely areas to investigate are the following:

- Make sure the cable is firmly connected to the workstation and that connectors are not frayed or weakly attached. This is especially true with coaxial cable plants.
- Make sure you have not exceeded the recommended cable lengths for the type of cabling being used. Each cable type has very detailed specifications for length, number of extents, and impedance.
- Use a Time-Domain Reflectometer to determine whether you have a short or break in the cabling. This is a must when tracking down problems in cable runs inside walls and cabinets.

26

■ Make sure you are using the same type of cable throughout the network. Special equipment is necessary to support multiple cable types in a network (routers, bridges, and so forth). Make sure they are operating correctly.

■ Check your terminators to make sure the network is not experiencing infinite resistance problems.

Cabling Specifications.

Cable Type	Maximum Length
Thinnet Coaxial	185 meters
Thicknet Coaxial	500 meters
Unshielded Twisted Pair (UTP)	100 meters
Shielded Twisted Pair (STP)	100 meters
Fiber Optic	2 kilometers

Network Interface Cards (NIC)

Another frequent culprit causing networking woes is the infamous network interface card, or network adapter. The successful operation of this card requires that two things be done correctly:

■ The adapter card must be firmly seated in a slot on the workstation's motherboard.

■ The proper drivers must be installed and configured to match the network architecture.

Sometimes network cards just stop functioning, due to age, environmental agents, quality, or amount of continuous use. Often, however, a network adapter fails to work because of configuration errors or compatibility problems with the workstation or its operating system.

Some likely areas to investigate are the following:

■ Are there lights on at the back of the card? There should normally be one or two LEDs on the back end of a network card. One is a "link light," which shows that the card has established connectivity with the network at the Data Link level of the OSI model. The second light is a "transmission light," which blinks as the card receives/sends information across the network. (No lights means no connection.)

■ Have any new network-aware applications been installed on the workstation recently? Some applications install their own drivers, which may not be compatible on your network or the OS version on that workstation.

■ Check the date of the existing network drivers installed from the Network Control Panel. (Perhaps the vendor has newer drivers that would resolve the problem.)

NIC Configuration Parameters

Every network card has its own configuration parameters, but the primary areas that cause headaches are *Interrupt Request (IRQ)* settings, the *Base I/O Port Address*, and the *Base Memory Address* for the adapter. If any of these is incorrect or in conflict with another device in the workstation, the NIC does not operate consistently, if at all.

An Intel machine has 16 IRQ values (0-15). These are assigned to various devices and serve to alert the processor when the device needs attention.

Table 26.1. Interrupt Request Numbers.

IRQ	Device
0	System Timer
1	Keyboard
2	Programmable Interrupt Controller
3	Communications Port 2 or 4
4	Communications Port 1 or 3
5	Printer Port 2 (LPT2) or "open"
6	Floppy Disk Controller
7	Printer Port 1 (LPT1)
8	Real Time Clock
9	Redirect from IRQ2 or "open"
10	open
11	open
12	PS/2 Mouse Port or "open"
13	Math Coprocessor
14	IDE Hard Drive Controller
15	IDE Hard Drive Controller or "open"

The Base I/O Port Address serves as the "doorway" through which all communication between the processor and the device is channeled.

The Base Memory Address is a memory location where a buffer is kept for data being transmitted to and from the network. This address is often hexadecimal D8000.

Some likely areas to investigate are the following:

- Has the workstation's network configuration been changed recently? If so, find out why and what the previous settings were.

- Does the configuration process attempt an "auto-configuration" mode? Sometimes these do not work. Try setting the card manually.

- Are any of the three primary parameters in use by another device? If so, reconfigure the adapter to ones that are open. If there are no available values, or if the adapter does not offer a wide-enough selection, you may need to reconfigure or remove existing devices.

Network Protocol Mismatch

For a workstation to communicate across the network, its network adapter card must share a common set of protocols with the network devices the workstation needs to access. The configuration for each protocol is different.

In many cases, several network protocols must be transmitted across a single network adapter card. This process of "binding" several protocols to one network adapter is accomplished by using either the Network Device Interface Specification (NDIS) or Open Data-link Interface (ODI) protocol stacks.

If all other network adapter checklists show no configuration or mechanical problems, protocol mismatch is the next thing to check. A workstation configured for IPX/SPX (NwLink) Protocol can never successfully communicate with a file server configured for TCP/IP.

This problem is common in networking environments that have multiple server platforms (UNIX, NetWare, Windows NT Server).

Some likely areas to investigate are the following:

- Has this workstation accessed the server in the past and lost that capability, or has it never successfully connected?

- Check the Network Control Panel and see which protocols have been installed on the workstation. Are they all correctly bound to the network adapter?

- For each protocol installed, are all its configuration parameters correctly filled in? For example, the TCP/IP protocol suite requires an IP Address, Subnet Mask, and a Default Gateway Address. Are they filled in properly?

- If this is a TCP/IP network, is the workstation getting its IP dynamically (via DHCP or BOOTP)? Is that assignment process working?

- If this is a TCP/IP network, is the DNS IP Address entered correctly for this segment?

- If this is an IPX/SPX network, is the correct frame type being used?

Network Congestion

The primary symptom of congestion is poor network performance within a segment of your network or across the whole network. This may occur only occasionally, during times of high usage. In other cases, this can build up slowly over a period of weeks or months until the level of performance degradation is intolerable.

The causes for this can be varied. You need a network monitor to determine the level of bandwidth being used across the network, the times of peak usage, and the types of packets being transmitted. A protocol analyzer can give you more information regarding the segments having the highest amount of traffic and any bottlenecks across the network.

Some likely areas to investigate are the following:

- Is this a recent problem or is it commonplace? Congestion may be an indication of poor network design and can be resolved only by revamping the network backbone.
- Check for high numbers of packets from one IP address. A malfunctioning network adapter card could be "chattering" and sending lots of unnecessary packets.
- Check to see whether any new applications have been installed on the network. Perhaps a client/server application is generating lots of packet traffic.
- Has the user community increased significantly? Perhaps the network needs to be augmented to handle the natural growth of your organization.
- Which protocols are being transmitted across the network? How many protocols are being used in your network? To keep traffic to a minimum, the fewer the number of protocols the better.
- Is NetBeui running across the network? NetBeui is a broadcast-intensive protocol. Try utilizing WINS servers to reduce NetBeui broadcasts, or tunnel NetBios through TCP/IP or IPX and eliminate NetBeui entirely.

Broadcast Storms

A *broadcast storm* describes a scenario in which a network's bandwidth is literally filled to capacity due to an excessive number of broadcast packets. When this occurs, network performance slows to a crawl.

Broadcast storms often result from malfunctioning network adapter cards and hubs. They can also be caused by excessive broadcasts across NetBeui-based networks.

To diagnose a malfunctioning device, you need the help of a protocol analyzer to help isolate that device so you can replace it. If you use internal routers and routable protocols, you might be able to lessen the impact of a broadcast storm because routers do not route broadcast traffic.

Power Problems

When the power in a building goes out, even for just a few seconds, it can have an unpredictable (and often negative) impact on network and other electronic components. Power coming back on can also cause problems due to the initial "surge." Machines need to be protected against the sudden outage of power and the sudden surge of returning power.

An Uninterruptible Power Supplies (UPS) unit can provide sufficient power to servers and other computer equipment to give them time to execute their normal shutdown procedures. In fact, some UPS units can interface with servers to initiate a system shutdown in the event of a power outage. This is a very useful feature given that no one may be in the office when the outage occurs.

Look for UPS units that also provide line conditioning. This feature keeps the current flowing to the servers constant and even. This eliminates or lessens the normal dips and spikes in power. Those power fluctuations can eventually cause premature failures in power supplies, hard drives, and motherboards.

Although most organizations are wise enough to protect their servers with a UPS, other components (printers, hubs, routers, firewalls, user workstations, and so forth) may not be so equipped.

Server Problems

The biggest server-based problems that impact a network are the following:

- Lack of sufficient processing power
- Lack of sufficient memory capacity
- Loss of information due to hard-drive crashes

The more services, user sessions, authentication, and I/O requests a server has to handle, the larger the need for raw CPU processing power. Network performance can suffer when network usage increases beyond the capacity of the servers that run the network. A Performance Monitor can monitor the drain on CPU resources and identify when a server may need to be upgraded to multiple processors or have its workload distributed among other machines.

Another resource that is closely related to the overall throughput of a network is the amount of memory (RAM) to which the operating system, services, and applications have access. Memory is especially important for database servers and servers that process system authentication and security requests. When in doubt, add more memory.

A server disk crash can be a catastrophic event to an organization if certain safeguards have not been put in place. Solutions such as implementing RAID Level 5 (disk striping with parity) fault tolerance can reduce the impact of an individual drive going bad. But a larger plan needs to be implemented to handle larger failure scenarios. Many organizations have mirrored drive and server farms in place so that if one server goes down, sufficient redundancy is available for immediate, or engineer-assisted, transition to a backup solution.

This is less of a troubleshooting concern than it is a consideration during the initial planning of your network design. Realizing the value of your organization's data, a comparable data backup and recovery plan, including an offsite data-storage rotation, should be a part of any network implementation.

Tools for Gathering Information

A variety of tools is available, at both the hardware and software level, to help you gather real-time information from the network. This information in turn helps you diagnose network problems and provides clues that can point you toward resolutions.

The previous section mentioned several of these tools, which are explained in more detail in the following sections.

Digital Volt Meters

A Digital Volt Meter, commonly referred to as a DVM, is a basic electronic measuring device, which in simple terms measures the amount of voltage passing through a resistance. Many of us know it as a device to measure the voltage of batteries or electrical outlets.

In a networking environment, its primary use is for continuity testing. In nontechnical terms, it is used to determine whether current from one end of a cable reaches the other end. If there is no *resistance*, then current is flowing through the cable unimpeded. If there is resistance, there may be a break in the cable.

A DVM can also test for a "short" in a length of cable by placing one lead on the inside "core" of the cable, and the other lead on the shielding layer. If any current registers, the shielding and the core are touching somewhere in the cable, causing a short.

Time-Domain Reflectometers

A Time-Domain Reflectometer, or TDR, sends pulses along the cable at regular intervals. This device looks for breaks or other imperfections in the cable that might prevent it from carrying a signal across the network. The difference between this device and a DVM is that a TDR provides an estimated distance to the break.

The TDR analyzes the pulse readings and displays a result indicating where along the cable the break might be. A good TDR should be able to locate a break in a cable within a few feet. It does this by measuring the amount of time it takes for a pulse to reach the break (or short) and bounce back to the device.

TDRs can be used for both electrical and fiber-based cabling.

Oscilloscopes

An oscilloscope is an electronic device that measures the amount of signal voltage per unit of time. It has a display to show the results of its readings. When used in conjunction with a TDR, it can display shorts, bends and crimps in cable, breaks, and attenuation.

Advanced Cable Testers

These testers go beyond just looking for cable break and imperfections. They can display information about resistance, impedance, and attenuation (loss of signal strength).

These devices can provide real-time information on:

- Error frame counts
- Message frame counts
- Beaconing
- Congestion errors
- Excess collisions
- Late collisions

Advanced testers can monitor network traffic and can even be focused to follow the traffic between two specific computers or devices. They can provide information about a particular cable or network adapter card that you suspect may be causing problems.

Protocol Analyzers

A protocol analyzer, like an advanced cable tester, performs a number of functions during real-time analysis of network traffic. But it goes even further. It can actually transmit, capture, and decode packets. It also can provide statistics based upon real-time network traffic.

This is probably the most popular analytical tool of network engineers because it covers the whole gamut of testing needs. With the capabilities of a protocol analyzer, you can detect:

- Network bottlenecks
- Failing network adapter cards
- Connection errors
- Faulty network components (hubs, repeaters, and so forth)
- Protocol problems
- Broadcast storms

A hardware protocol analyzer usually contains a built-in TDR so it can locate cable breaks. But its strength is to take that analysis all the way up the OSI Reference Model. This means that it can analyze traffic at all levels of the OSI Model.

A hardware protocol analyzer can therefore be used to evaluate the effectiveness of a segment and measure the traffic to and from a computer on that segment. It can be used to track the protocols moving along Wide Area Networks and the Internet.

Network Monitors

Microsoft Windows NT Server comes with a *network monitor*, which is a software implementation of a protocol analyzer. This software enables a workstation to capture and monitor network traffic going to and from the machine on which it is being executed.

When the monitor is executed from a promiscuous modem, traffic can be monitored even if it is not directed to the monitoring machine. (A standard modem does not provide access to packets not destined for the machine in which it is located.)

Monitors can capture, decode, analyze, and provide statistics about packet types, errors, and traffic to and from any computer on the network. Microsoft's Network Monitor can generate charts of network traffic at various intervals and can be run to get "snapshots" throughout the day (with information being saved to disk for later review).

It is very important to use network monitors to determine baseline performance statistics. These statistics can then be used in the troubleshooting process to identify abnormal traffic/activity.

Performance Monitors

The Windows NT Performance Monitor is a general-purpose software tool that can monitor all activities taking place within a file server. It can monitor the activities of all services and devices in the server. Network traffic that is processed by the server can also be tracked. This tool can give a good profile of a server's workload over a period of time—information that can be very helpful when assessing deviations from normal activity.

Helpful Resources

Many sources of technical and advisory information are available to help you make the best decisions regarding network maintenance and to help you troubleshoot network difficulties. Some resources are available in the public domain; others require a subscription or other fee.

Some of these resources are described in the following sections.

Vendor Technical Support

The most obvious resources available to network engineers are the companies from which they purchased their network hardware, software, and connectivity. If these companies offer technical support, take advantage of it—even if it's for only one year. You are sure to find it to be worth the money when you are installing and maintaining a complex network environment.

In addition, many of these companies have users' groups around the country made up of real people, working in real network shops, and encountering the same pitfalls and challenges that you are. Find a users' group in your area; these people often end up being your best peer consultants and they can give you "real world" answers to your problems.

Internet Newsgroups and Mailing Lists

The Internet can be a treasure chest of technical information. Several NT and networking mailing lists and newsgroups provide a forum where questions and scenarios of all kinds can be posted. People seem more than willing to show others that they are knowledgeable.

Obviously, you have to test out these suggestions for validity, but I have found people to be genuinely motivated to help out a fellow engineer.

Download Sites

Vendors post bug fixes, software patches, updated device drivers, maintenance utilities, and other tools on their company sites to help facilitate the successful implementation of their products. Most of these vendors provide file servers, running the File Transfer Protocol (FTP), for access via the Internet. Others provide a Bulletin Board Service (BBS) for their customers to access.

Magazines and Technical Journals

There are literally hundreds of magazines, newspapers, and technical journals, both printed and online. These publications are full of technical tips, hints, and reviews of software and hardware products and services. These can often be solid resources of troubleshooting information.

Technology changes so rapidly now that you need to keep yourself current on upcoming trends and technologies. Books are a wonderful resource but they can quickly become outdated given the pace at which this industry is moving.

Subscribe to magazines like *LAN Magazine*, *NT Magazine*, *Data Communications*, and *Communications Week*. Consider subscribing to online news services like NEWS.COM on the Internet, which sends an email each day with technology headlines. There are even online newspapers that you can configure to present only the topical subjects in which you are interested.

Microsoft Windows NT Hardware/Software Compatibility Lists

Microsoft maintains a list of vendors who have gone through a certification process to have their products "certified" to operate under the Windows NT Server/Workstation environments. Many network problems have been traced to a network adapter or hard drive controller card that was not certified to be compatible with NT Server.

The Hardware Compatibility List (HCL) and the Software Compatibility List (SCL) can be found on the World Wide Web at Microsoft's web site `http://www.microsoft.com/ntserver/info`.

Microsoft Technical Information Network

TechNet is a CD-ROM of technical information, software drivers, patches, service packs, and tools that focus on aspects of networking across all of Microsoft's product offerings. This is a subscription service that distributes two CD-ROMs on a monthly basis. Contact Microsoft at 800-344-2121 for more information.

The Microsoft Online Knowledgebase

The Microsoft Knowledgebase is a searchable index of technical reports. It can be found on the World Wide Web at Microsoft's web site at `http://www.microsoft.com/ntserversupport`.

Windows NT Server Resource Kit

This is a wonderful collection of utilities, documentation, and other resources for NT network administrators. This CD-ROM includes resources for both NT Server and NT Workstation. Consider this a "must have" for NT-based networks.

Summary

Successful troubleshooting techniques don't just happen. They are developed through a structured, repeatable, documented process that improves with use. It involves collecting information, analyzing that information, and pursuing a course of action based upon that analysis.

Taking a methodical approach helps take the "art" of troubleshooting and turn it into a science. Following a step-by-step process of elimination, you reduce the potential for key information to get lost in the chaos of the "knee jerk reaction."

Take the time to develop a plan for tackling problems. Plan fault tolerance into the design of your network and the security of its information. Take advantage of the many tools and diagnostic databases available to improve your research and problem-identification skills. Build and maintain your own database of solutions that are unique and customized to your particular network environment.

Purchase the diagnostic hardware necessary to make efficient and accurate assessments. Remember, the cost of these tools is minimal in comparison to the impact a prolonged network outage has on your organization's operational effectiveness and productivity. Establish a network of professionals to whom you can turn when you encounter particularly difficult problems.

Remember that most networking problems are related to physical media concerns: cabling, connectors, hubs, and network adapter cards. Next in line are the client software, device drivers, and protocol/hardware configuration settings. Work the OSI Reference Model from the bottom up as you work to resolve connectivity problems.

Lastly, keep cool. No matter how bad things may be, keeping a cool head and working through your troubleshooting process always results in a faster resolution than the chaotic "shotgun" approach.

V PART

Appendix

Technical Glossary

GLOSSARY

AAL (ATM Adaptation Layer)   ATM contains an adaptation layer that is responsible for creating the 48-octet datagrams that become the payloads of ATM cells. There were five different AALs, numbered 1 through 5, originally planned. Each one is designed to support one of ATM's four different Classes of Service. These are known as Classes A, B, C, and D. Each class supports transmissions in different ways and, consequently, requires a separate set of protocols at the end stations.

Active Directory Service (ADS)   ADS is an advanced directory service native to Microsoft's Windows NT release 5.0 that is designed to facilitate the scaling of intranets. All networked resources are catalogued as "objects" into a central directory. This centralization makes all networked resources much easier to manage and access. The user is relieved of the burden of finding resources: they are all in the Active Directory of ADS.

Active Monitor (AM)   Token Ring's many rules are enforced by a single station. This station, known as the Active Monitor, can be any of the stations in the ring. Usually, the AM is the first station to become active. Ownership of AM responsibilities can be contested and passed to other stations, after more stations activate. The AM monitors all traffic, ensures that the ring's protocol rules are adhered to, and is responsible for initiating any actions that might be necessary to overcome protocol violations or failures.

ANSI (American National Standards Institute)   ANSI is a private, non-profit organization. Its charter is to facilitate the development, coordination, and publication of voluntary national standards.

API (Application Programming Interface)   An Application Programming Interface is a standardized software interface that an application program uses to access lower-level services.

Application Layer   The top layer in the seven-layer OSI Reference Model is the Application Layer. Despite its name, this layer does not include user applications. Rather, it provides the interface between those applications and the network's services.

attenuation   Attenuation is a decrease in the strength of a transmitted signal.

ATM (Asynchronous Transfer Mode)   ATM is an evolving switched network technology known for scaleability and consistency. ATM technologies can be used in both the Wide and Local Area Networks.

backbone   A LAN's "backbone" is the portion of its facilities used to interconnect all the hubs.

BGP (Border Gateway Protocol)   A modern routing protocol used between systems.

bps   The bandwidth of a data communications frequency, and the physical media that supports its transmission, is measured using the number of *bits per second* (bps).

Categories of Performance   Performance ratings of unshielded twisted pair is rated by a series of performance thresholds defined by the EIA. Categories 3 and 5 remain the only two commonly-encountered performance levels.

Category 3 UTP   Category 3 (Cat 3) UTP offers 16MHz of bandwidth, which translates into signaling speeds of up to 10Mbps at 100 meters.

Category 5 UTP   Category 5 UTP can support transmission of up to 100MHz for up to 100 meters.

CCITT (International Consulting Committee for Telephone and Telegraph)   The CCITT was the organization responsible for setting many of Europe's telecommunications standards. It has reorganized itself, and changed its name to the International Telecommunications Union (ITU).

checksum   A forward error correction mechanism used in the data transmission. Checksum values are created by adding together the binary value of each alphanumeric character in a block of data.

CIR (Committed Information Rate)   A term used for Frame Relay to describe the guaranteed minimum amount of bandwidth available at any given time.

circuit   The electrical or optical connection that forms the physical connection between any two points in a Wide Area Network.

circuit switched network   A network that features packetized data that travels through the same series of switches to reach its final destination.

CISC (Complex Instruction Set Computing)   Refers to a microprocessor architecture that features a robust instruction set that attempts to perform as much work as possible with each instruction, as opposed to emphasizing the speed with which individual instructions can be executed. CISC instructions do not execute as quickly as instructions in a RISC architecture, but each instruction accomplishes more work than a RISC instruction.

client   Any computer that accesses resources stored on servers, via the LAN.

cluster   A loosely coupled set of computers that function as a single computer. Clusters can take a seemingly infinite variety of topologies, each tailored to extract a different combination of benefits from the distributed redundancy of the cluster's resources.

coaxial cable   Coaxial cable, almost always referred to as *co-ax*, has two concentric conductors. It is, quite literally, coaxial in that both conductors share a common axis. The most common version of this cable type consists of a single conducting copper wire that is insulated by a dielectric material. This dielectric material is then wrapped in another cylindrical conductor. This cylindrical conductor can be either a solid or braided wire. The conductor is then wrapped in another layer of insulation and the whole assembly is covered with a protective outer jacket of either polyvinyl chloride (PVC) or Teflon.

CPE (Customer Premises Equipment)   Hardware used to connect to a WAN circuit that is physically located at the customer's site.

A

TECHNICAL
GLOSSARY

CRC (Cyclical Redundancy Check)   CRC is a more robust error detection algorithm than checksum. It is also used to determine whether an error has occurred during transmission. However, the CRC character's value is derived in a much more rigorous manner than is a checksum. The data is read as a binary string: this "number" is divided by another predetermined binary number to form the CRC value.

CSMA (Carrier Sense, Multiple Access)   CSMA was the primitive contention-based media access arbitration mechanism used by Ethernet I.

CSMA/CD (Carrier Sense, Multiple Access with Collision Detection)   CSMA/CD is an improvement over the CSMA media access arbitration method. It, too, is contention-based, but it provides mechanisms to prevent, detect, and automatically recover from collisions that would, inevitably, occur. CSMA/CD first appeared in Ethernet II, and was retained by the IEEE's 802.3 version of Ethernet.

CSU/DSU (Channel Service Unit/Data Service Unit)   The device that connects a network node to a WAN link.

DAS (Dual-Attached Stations)   FDDI provides for dual-attached stations. Such stations feature two sets of media interfaces: one for each of FDDI's two rings.

Data Link Layer   The second layer of the OSI Reference Model is called the Data Link Layer. Like all the layers, it has two sets of responsibilities: transmit and receive. It is responsible for providing end-to-end validity of the data being transmitted. On the transmit side, the Data Link Layer is responsible for packing instructions, data, and so forth, into frames. A *frame* is a structure indigenous to the Data Link Layer that contains enough information to make sure that the data can be successfully sent across a LAN to its destination. The Data Link Layer is responsible for detecting and correcting any and all errors. The Data Link Layer is also responsible for re-assembling any binary streams that are received from the Physical Layer back into frames. Given that both the structure and content of a frame are transmitted, the Data Link Layer isn't really re-building a frame. Rather, it is buffering the incoming bits until it has a complete frame.

DCE (Data Communications Equipment)   DCE is a defined interface for multi-conductor copper cabling. This interface provides a pairing of transmit and receive conductors that is complementary to the Data Terminal Equipment (DTE) interface. A DCE interface can only be cabled to a DTE interface, otherwise communications fail.

demarcation   The point from which the customer takes responsibility from the phone company for a WAN connection.

demultiplexing   Separating multiple types of data from a single link into their original components. See *multiplexing*.

distortion   The unwanted modification of signals in transit. Distortion may be caused by either electromagnetic interference (EMI) or radio-frequency interference (RFI).

DIX Ethernet   See *Ethernet I.*

DLCI (Data Link Control Interface)   In a Frame Relay network, the address used to identify a particular PVC.

DLM (Distributed Lock Manager)   DLM is an essential technique for controlling the modification of data in databases that are shared across multiple CPUs.

DPAM (Demand-Priority Access Method)   A round-robin arbitration method in which a central repeater (also known as a "hub") regularly polls ports connected to it. This polling is performed in port order and is conducted to identify ports that have transmission requests. After the need to transmit is established, the repeater determines whether the priority is high or normal. These priorities are designed to service time-sensitive requests before servicing "normal" requests for bandwidth.

DTE (Data Terminal Equipment)   DTE is a defined interface for multi-conductor copper cabling. This interface provides a pairing of transmit and receive conductors that is complementary to the Data Communications Equipment (DCE) interface. A DCE interface can only be cabled to a DTE interface, otherwise communications fail.

EGP (Exterior Gateway Protocol)   An aging routing protocol used between autonomous systems.

ELAN (Emulated Local Area Network)   The *emulated LAN* in a LANE environment is called an ELAN.

EMI (Electromagnetic Interface)   A low-frequency induction that can distort transmitted data.

encapsulation   A method of carrying packetized data from one protocol across a link in the data portion of another protocol's packet.

Ethernet   Ethernet describes the many forms of a LAN protocol that features Carrier Sense, Multiple Access, with Collision Detection. This protocol was standardized by the IEEE in their 802.3 specification.

Ethernet I   The world's first LAN was Xerox's PARC Ethernet. This technology originated as an intra-office, baseband transmission technology for interconnecting work stations. It was cobbled together by researchers at Xerox's famed Palo Alto Research Center (PARC) for their own use as a superior alternative to floppy disks for sharing information. Later, after the more self-contained and well-behaved version (known as Ethernet II) was created, PARC Ethernet became known as Ethernet I.

Ethernet II   The PARC Ethernet technology was updated and standardized. This standardized, second-generation LAN is known as Ethernet II. Ethernet II is also referred to as "DIX Ethernet," in acknowledgment of its triumvirate of corporate sponsors: Digital, Intel, and Xerox.

FDDI (Fiber Distributed Data Interface)   FDDI is a 100Mbps token-passing LAN that was standardized via ANSI's X3T9.5 specification.

fiber optic cable   Fiber optic cables are capable of carrying the higher frequencies of the Electromagnetic Spectrum: light. Fiber Optic cables come in a wide variety of shapes, sizes, and wavelength ratings.

frame   A structure that contains enough information to make sure that the data can be sent across a network, either LAN or WAN, to its destination.

Frame Relay   A type of switched WAN transmission facility. Frame Relay enables the definition of multiple, logical permanent virtual circuits, each with their own minimum amount of bandwidth over a single transmission facility.

frequency   The electromagnetic wave continuously oscillates in a somewhat symmetrical pattern, from positive to negative, as it travels. The rate at which this oscillation occurs is called *frequency*. Frequency is measured in *Hertz* (Hz).

Gbps   The abbreviation for billions of bits per second.

GHz   The abbreviation for billions of Hertz per second.

GUI (Graphical User Interface)   Operating systems, such as Microsoft's Windows family of products, utilize a visually-oriented environment that enables the user to access resources with a pointing device. This visually-oriented environment is known as a Graphical User Interface.

Hertz   See *Hz*.

Hz (Hertz)   The number of oscillations in the electromagnetic wave, per second. One cycle, or Hertz, represents a 360° change in one second.

IAB (Internet Architecture Board)   The IAB, formerly known as the Internet Activities Board, governs the technical development of the Internet. It contains two working committees, the *Internet Engineering Task Force* (IETF), and the *Internet Research Task Force* (IRTF).

IEC (International Electrotechnical Commission)   Founded in 1909, the IEC is headquartered in Geneva, Switzerland, and sets international standards for anything electrical and electronic.

IEEE (Institute of Electrical and Electronic Engineers)   The IEEE is responsible for defining and publishing telecommunications and data communications standards. Their most significant effort has been the definition of the standards for local and metropolitan area networks (LANs and MANs). These standards, embodied in a large and complex series of technical standards, is generically referred to as "Project 802," or the "802 series of standards."

IEEE 802.1   802.1 defined the overview and architecture for interoperability between LANs and MANs. This is the basis for all the 802 initiatives and includes standards for LAN/MAN management and bridging between 802-compliant networks.

IEEE 802.2   802.2 defined the Data Link Layer (Layer 2) standard for telecommunications and information exchange between systems, both LAN- and MAN-based. This specification provided the backward compatibility required to support a transition from the pre-standard versions of Ethernet to the 802.3 standardized version.

IEEE 802.3   802.3 established the new standard for a LAN that features a Carrier Sense, Multiple Access with Collision Detection (CSMA/CD). This "new" LAN is properly referred to as CSMA/CD, but is popularly known as "Ethernet."

IEEE 802.4   802.4 defines a Physical Layer standard for a bus topology LAN with a token passing media access method. This LAN is called "Token Bus" and can support 1, 2, 5, or 10Mbps data rates.

IEEE 802.5   802.5 established the standards for Token Ring's access methods and physical signaling techniques.

IETF (Internet Engineering Task Force)   The IETF is responsible for setting the technical standards for the Internet, as well as the defining new standards for Internet technologies.

IGRP (Interior Gateway Routing Protocol)   A widely used link-state routing protocol developed by Cisco Systems. IGRP is proprietary, and only supported on Cisco routers.

IP (Internet Protocol)   IP was originally designed for a military wide area network. It has risen to prominence as the Network Layer protocol for the Internet and for intranets.

IPX (Internet Packet Exchange)   Novell's proprietary Network Layer protocol suite is IPX. It is almost always referenced in conjunction with Novell's proprietary Transport Layer protocol, Sequenced Packet Exchange (SPX). The combined protocol suite is called IPX/SPX.

IRTF (Internet Research Task Force)   The IRTF researches new technologies that may be of value to, or have any impact upon, the Internet. Technologies deemed to be of potential value are referred to the Internet Engineering Task Force for further investigation.

IS-IS (Intermediate System to Intermediate System)   An OSI-based protocol.

ISO (International Organization for Standardization)   The ISO was founded in 1946, and is headquartered in Geneva, Switzerland. It is a voluntary, non-treaty organization that is chartered by the United Nations to define international standards. Its charter includes literally all fields, except for anything electrical or electronic. One of the more significant (for networking) standards produced by the ISO was the OSI Reference Model. ISO is actually a mnemonic designed to facilitate the organization's recognition in multiple languages. ISO is derived from the Greek word *isos*, meaning equal or standard. ISO is not an acronym for the name.

ITU (International Telecommunications Union)   Formerly the CCITT, the organization responsible for setting many of Europe's telecommunications standards.

Kbps   The abbreviation for thousands of bits per second.

kHz   The abbreviation for thousands of Hertz per second.

LAN   See *local area network*.

LANE (Local Area Network Emulation)   LANE enables ATM LAN clients to access and use existing LAN applications through a software layer added to the emulating devices. This software layer becomes an integral part of that device's ATM protocol stack.

laser   "LASER" has come into common usage as a noun but it is actually an acronym. This acronym describes the physical process by which the concentrated energy associated with lasers is created. The acronym stands for: Light Amplification through Stimulated Emission of Radiation.

LEC (LANE Emulation Client)   Each client in a LANE ELAN is known as a "LAN Emulation client." The individual LECs are addressed via their MAC address.

LES (LANE Emulation Server)   Each ELAN must have a single LAN Emulation Service (LES). The LES may be contained within a switch, a client computer, or a server.

LGN, LCN (Logical Group Number, Logical Channel Number)   These numbers are used to uniquely identify a virtual circuit in X.25 networks.

LLC (Logical Link Control)   The LLC provides addressing and control of the data link. It specifies which mechanisms are to be used for addressing stations over the transmission medium and for controlling the data exchanged between the originator and recipient machines.

local area network (LAN)   LANs are used to interconnect devices that are in relatively close proximity. The basis for LANs was defined in the IEEE's Project 802 family of specifications.

local loop   The last section of a circuit that spans from a telephony carrier's central office to the customer's premises. Often referred to as "the last mile."

LUNI (LANE User to Network Interface)   ATM's LANE necessitated the development of a new interface, the LUNI. This interface is used by LANE clients to access the LANE server, where the actual emulation occurs.

MAC (Media Access Control)   Although putting ones and zeroes onto the physical media is a function of the first layer of the OSI Reference Model, regulating access to that media for transmission is a function of the Data Link Layer. As standardized by the IEEE, this regulation is known as "Media Access Control" (MAC). The IEEE recognizes three methods for regulating media access: contention, demand priority, and token passing.

MAN   See *metropolitan area network*.

Mbps (megabits per second)   The abbreviation for millions of bits per second is Mbps. The lowercase *b* denotes bits per second, not bytes. Mbps is used to measure throughput.

MBps (megabytes per second)   This is a metric of throughput, expressed in millions of bytes per second. The capitalization of the letter B designates bytes, as opposed to bits.

metropolitan area network (MAN)   Metropolitan Area Networks were defined through the IEEE's Project 802, the same initiative that standardized LANs. MANs are more closely related to WANs than LANs, because they are used to interconnect limited geographic areas. They remain relatively obscure and seldom used.

MHz   The abbreviation for Millions of Hertz per second.

MPPP (Multi-Link Point to Point Protocol)   This protocol enables a dial-up connection to utilize multiple links.

multiplexing   Combining multiple types of data onto a single link.

Network Layer   The Network Layer, Layer 3 of the OSI Reference Model, is responsible for establishing the route to be used between the originating and destination computers. This layer lacks any native transmission error detection/correction mechanisms and, consequently, is forced to rely upon the end-to-end reliable transmission service of the Data Link Layer. This layer is used to establish communications with computer systems that lie beyond the local LAN segment.

NIC (Network Interface Card)   A Network Interface Card is a printed circuit board that is installed in a vacant slot in a computer's I/O bus. The back of the card contains a physical interface for a specific connector type, which is designed for a specific transmission media. This card provides the connectivity between a computer's internal system resources and the external resources connected to the network. It embodies the logic of the LAN's Data Link and Physical Layers.

NNI (Network to Network Interface)   A connection between networks.

OSI Reference Model   The *Open Systems Interconnection* (OSI) Reference Model was developed to facilitate the open interconnection of computer systems. The OSI model categorizes the various processes that are needed in a communications session into seven distinct functional layers. The layers are organized based upon the natural sequence of events that occur during a communications session.

OSPF (Open Shortest Path First)   OSPF is an open-standard, link-state routing protocol.

packet switched network   A network that features packetized traffic, forwarded through a series of switches to its destination.

peer-to-peer networks   A peer-to-peer network supports unstructured access to network-attached resources. Each device in a peer-to-peer network can be simultaneously a client and a server. All devices are capable of directly accessing data, software, and other network resources. In other words, each networked computer is a *peer* of every other networked computer; there is no hierarchy.

permanent virtual circuit   A software-defined connection across a circuit switched or packet switched network. After they are defined, PVCs are always online.

Physical Layer   The bottom layer of the OSI Reference Model is called the "Physical Layer." This layer is responsible for the transmission of the bit stream. It accepts frames of data from Layer 2, the Data Link Layer, and transmits their structure and content serially, one bit at a time. It is also responsible for the reception of incoming streams of data, one bit at a time. These streams are then passed on to the Data Link Layer for re-framing.

POTS (Plain Old Telephone Service)   The abbreviation for plain old telephone service. This jocular expression describes the voice-grade services of the Public Switched Telephone Network.

PPP (Point-to-Point Protocol)   PPP is the newest packet-framing protocol that provides self-configuring, full-duplex, bi-directional peer-to-peer connections to a wide range of hosts.

PPP Multilink Protocol   A feature of PPP that makes possible the combination of several data pipelines into one large pipe for faster transmission speeds.

PPTP (Point-to-Point Tunneling Protocol)   The creation of a virtual client-server link that is tunneled through an IP network. Tunneling enables clients to use a WAN as their virtual network.

PPTP Control Connection   The Control Connection is responsible for the creation, management, and termination of its corresponding PPTP tunnel.

Presentation Layer   The Presentation Layer is Layer 6 of the OSI Reference Model. It is responsible for managing the way that data is encoded. Not every computer system uses the same data encoding scheme, and the Presentation Layer is responsible for providing the translation between otherwise incompatible data encoding schemes.

PSTN (Public Switched Telephone Network)   The abbreviation for the technical description of the global, voice-grade telephony infrastructure. The service provided across this infrastructure is often described as POTS.

quality of service (QoS)   Any means of identifying the time value and/or priority of a given packet as it traverses a network.

RAID (Redundant Array of Inexpensive Disks)   RAID started out as a simple idea for developing auto-recovering, fault-tolerant, large logical disk drives from small, inexpensive drives. The multiple drives are housed in a common chassis. Data is written redundantly to multiple drives, thereby providing protection from the loss of a disk drive. When a drive is lost, and then replaced, the surviving RAID devices automatically detect the broken file system and reconstruct. The rapidity with which this recovery is effected depends upon the level of protection implemented. RAID support now has seven separate levels: RAID-0 through RAID-6. The first five were originally defined RAID 1 through RAID 5 at the University of Berkeley. These levels represent different combinations of cost and protection from failure. RAID-0 and RAID-6 are products of the marketplace. It is important to note that RAID is not a formal standard. Consequently, there is tremendous disparity between the levels of support provided at any given RAID level across vendor products. Many vendors recognize only the original five Berkeley RAID specifications, numbered 1 through 5.

■ **RAID-0** (Redundant Array of Inexpensive Disks, Level 0)   Data is striped across multiple disks, without any error correction or redundancy.

■ **RAID-1** (Redundant Array of Inexpensive Disks, Level 1)   Data is mirrored. One drive serves as the operational drive, with "live" contents. The second drive is an online backup of the first drive that is automatically updated: every write operation performed on the first disk is automatically duplicated on the second.

■ **RAID-2** (Redundant Array of Inexpensive Disks, Level 2)   RAID-2 is a more robust implementation of RAID-0 that includes error checking and correcting codes (ECC). Data is striped across multiple disks. This facilitates recovery from damaged data.

■ **RAID-3** (Redundant Array of Inexpensive Disks, Level 3)   RAID-3 stripes data, in bytes, across multiple disks. One disk is used exclusively to record parity data.

■ **RAID-4** (Redundant Array of Inexpensive Disks, Level 4)   Stripes data, in blocks, not bytes, across multiple disks. One disk is exclusively reserved for the recording of parity data.

■ **RAID-5** (Redundant Array of Inexpensive Disks, Level 5)   This level of support is the most commonly used of the seven variants. Like RAID-4, it stripes data, in blocks, across multiple disks. The difference is that RAID-5 writes its parity data across multiple disks.

■ **RAID-6** (Redundant Array of Inexpensive Disks, Level 6)   This variant provides all the functions of RAID-5, but also implements redundant disk controllers, cabinet fans, and buses.

A

TECHNICAL GLOSSARY

RAS (Remote Access Server)   Microsoft's software module for the Windows environment that manages remote access to LAN-attached resources.

repeater   A device that accepts transmitted signals, amplifies them, and puts them back on the network. In a LAN, a repeater—more popularly referred to as a *hub*—enables multiple devices to be networked together by providing multiple ingress points to the network.

RIP (Routing Information Protocol)   A older distance-vector routing protocol.

RISC (Reduced Instruction Set Computer)   A microprocessor architecture that features a relatively small set of simple instructions that execute more quickly, but perform less work, than a CISC instruction. Historically, RISC computers have been reserved for computationally-intensive applications.

RFI (Radio Frequency Interference)   A high-frequency induction that can distort transmitted data.

RMON (Remote Network Monitoring Specification)   An updated version of SNMP. RMON is designed to provide interoperability between network monitoring and management devices from different vendors.

routed protocol   A network protocol, such as TCP/IP or IPX/SPX, that can pass data through different network segments to reach a destination.

routing protocol   Routing protocols are used by routers to communicate with other routers. The purpose of such communications is to develop and maintain tabular information about potential paths through the routed network to any given destination.

SAR (Segmentation and Reassembly)   ATM contains a protocol suite that segments outbound data into a protocol data unit. These units are used to create cells. Inbound data must be re-assembled before it can be passed up to the next higher-level protocol.

SAR-PDU (Segmentation and Reassembly Protocol Data Unit)   Each AAL places the data it receives from the SAR into a pre-cellular structure known as a *Segmentation and Reassembly Protocol Data Unit* (SAR-PDU). SAR-PDUs are passed to the ATM Layer where they have 5-octet headers grafted onto them to form the familiar 53-octet ATM cells.

SAS (Single-Attached Stations)   FDDI provides for single-attached stations. Such stations feature one set of media interfaces that can be used to connect to a ring-with-trees topology.

SCSI (Small Computer Systems Interface)   SCSI (pronounced "scuzzy"), is a hardware interface that is used to interconnect hosts and peripheral devices. SCSI has been extended into multiple specifications. These specifications can support anywhere from 7 peripherals up to 15, and data rates from 5 to 40MBps.

- **SCSI-1**   The original small computer systems interface, this was more of a concept than a product, and was quickly superseded by SCSI-2.

- **SCSI-2**   The first standardized form of SCSI, this specification features an 8-bit bus that supports a total of 8 devices (including the adapter card), and has a data rate of 5MBps. Single-ended cabling is limited to 19.7 feet. Differential cabling can extend to 25 meters.

- **Fast SCSI-2**   Fast SCSI-2 increased the data rate to 10MBps. Maximum supported single-ended cable length decreased to 9.8 feet.

- **Fast Wide SCSI-2**   Fast Wide SCSI-2 was a further improvement in the SCSI-2 specification. It features a 16-bit bus. This enables 16 devices (including the adapter card) to be interconnected, with a data rate that can range from 10MBps to 20MBps.

- **8-bit Ultra SCSI-3**   The 8-bit Ultra SCSI-3 specification was, as the name implies, a new variant based on an 8-bit bus. The improvement came in a 20MBps data rate for the 8 devices. Maximum length of single-ended cables depended upon the number of devices. 9.8 feet could be used for 4 or fewer devices, otherwise the cable had to be no greater than 4.9 feet.

- **16-bit Ultra SCSI-3**   The 16-bit version of the SCSI-3 specification features a 16-bit bus, with commensurate number of devices, and a 20 to 40MBps data rate. The same cable length limitations for the 8-bit version apply.

server   Any LAN-attached computer that hosts resources that are shared by other LAN-attached devices.

server-based networks   Server-based networks introduce a hierarchy that is designed to improve the manageability of a network's various supported functions as the size of the network scales upward. Often, server-based networks are referred to as *client/server networks*.

Session Layer   The fifth layer of the OSI Model is the Session Layer. This layer is relatively disused: many protocols bundle this layer's functionality into their transport layers. The function of the OSI Session Layer is to manage the flow of communications during a connection between two computer systems. It determines whether communications can be mono- or bidirectional. It also ensures that one request is completed before a new one is accepted.

shielded twisted pair (STP)   Twisted pair wiring with a layer of either foil or braided metallic wire that envelops the twisted pairs. This shielding lies directly below the surface of the jacketing. Its purpose, ostensibly, was to enable the twisted pairs to operate in environments that were prone to *Electromagnetic Interference* (EMI) and/or *Radio Frequency Interference* (RFI). In practice, it actually impedes with the normal functioning of the twisted pairs.

SLIP (Serial-Line-Interface-Protocol)   A packet framing protocol that uses serial lines to transmit data. It was never standardized and did not support many of the advanced functions needed in this type of connection. This was the forerunner of PPP.

SNMP (Simple Network Management Protocol)   A protocol that gathers information from networking hardware to monitor its performance.

SPAP (Shiva Proprietary Authentication Protocol)   A proprietary version of PAP made by Shiva, Inc. to support its remote access product.

SPX (Sequenced Packet Exchange)   Novell's proprietary Transport Layer protocol suite.

statistical multiplexing   Dividing a single circuit into multiple connections based on a bandwidth-sharing scheme.

STP   See *Shielded Twisted Pair*.

Striping   A technique that simultaneously writes redundantly to multiple disks with a single write instruction. This technique makes it possible for any given file to be read faster, because multiple devices are simultaneously retrieving it.

Switched Virtual Circuit   A connection across a packet switched network that forwards packets individually, rather than via a predetermined path.

TCP (Transmission Control Protocol)   TCP is a Transport Layer protocol that is frequently used in conjunction with IP. These two protocols are frequently mistook for a single protocol because they are almost always referenced together as *TCP/IP*.

TDM (Time-Division Multiplexing)   Dividing a single circuit into multiple connections based on a time-sharing scheme.

transmission facilities   The media used to transport a network's signals to their destination. Media types can include coaxial cables, twisted pair, and even fiber optic cabling.

Transport Layer   The Transport Layer is the fourth layer of the OSI Reference Model. It provides a similar service to the Data Link Layer, in that it is responsible for the end-to-end integrity of transmissions. Unlike the Data Link Layer, the Transport Layer is capable of providing this function beyond the local LAN segment. It can detect packets that are discarded by routers, and automatically generate a retransmit request. Another significant function of the Transport Layer is the resequencing of packets that may have arrived out of order.

twisted pair wire   Twisted pair wiring, used to support voice communications, has become the de facto standard wiring technology for LANs. A twisted pair consists of two relatively thin wires, 18 to 24 American Wire Gauge (AWG), or 0.016 to 0.035 inches in diameter. These wires are coated with a thin layer of polyvinylchloride (PVC), and spiraled around each other. This twist is highly functional: it helps cancel out any EMI that would otherwise be inducted into the copper by providing a balanced radiation of energy between the two wires.

UDP (User Datagram Protocol)   UDP is another Transport Layer protocol that is used in conjunction with IP.

UNI (User-to-Network Interface)   A connection between an end-node and a network switch.

VCC (Virtual Channel Connection)   The proper term that describes the type of logical connection that is established between the LECs and the LES in an ATM ELAN. The VCC is a virtual channel connection, and separate connections are required for ATM's control and user planes.

virtual private networks (VPN)   A private network that is connected across a public network through the use of tunneling and/or encryption.

WAN   See *wide area network*.

wavelength   A metric used to measure the intensity of electromagnetic energy. A wavelength is the distance from the top of one wave's crest to the top of the next wave's crest. This metric is reserved for the higher-frequency phenomena, such as light, X-rays, and gamma rays.

wide area network (WAN)   WANs are used to interconnect LANs across geographic distances.

X.121   The protocol that X.25 relies upon for its network addressing.

X.25   An aging network specification for transporting packets across a public switched network.

Index

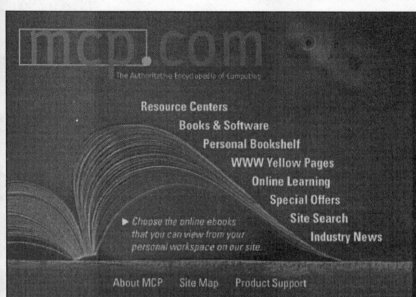